THE COLLECTED WORKS OF JOHN BRANDANE:
THE NOVELS

THE COLLECTED WORKS OF JOHN BRANDANE

Rory Aforesaid and other One-Act Plays
Glenforsa (1921) *with Alec Wilson Yuill*
The Change-House (1921)
Rory Aforesaid (1928)
The Happy War (1928)
The Spanish Galleon (1932) *with Alec Wilson Yuill*
Man of Uz (1932)

The Treasure Ship and other Full-Length Plays
The Glen is Mine (1923)
The Treasure Ship (1924)
The Lifting (1925)
The Inn of Adventure (1932)
Heather Gentry (1932)

Three Novels
My Lady of Aros (1910)
The Captain More (1923)
Strawfeet (1930)

THE COLLECTED WORKS OF JOHN BRANDANE
VOLUME 3

My Lady of Aros
and other Novels
The Captain More (1923)
Strawfeet (1930)

John Brandane

Kennedy & Boyd

Kennedy & Boyd
an imprint of
Zeticula Ltd
Unit 13,
196 Rose Street,
Edinburgh,
EH2 4AT

http://www.kennedyandboyd.co.uk
admin@kennedyandboyd.co.uk

First published:
My Lady of Aros (1910) by Sir Isaac Pitman & Sons, Ltd
The Captain More (1923) by Jonathan Cape
Strawfoot (1932) by Constable

Introduction copyright © Ronald Renton 2022
Cover photograph copyright © Ronald Renton 2022
This edition copyright © Zeticula Ltd 2022

First published in this edition 2022

ISBN 978-1-84921-157-4

All rights reserved. No part of this publication may be reproduced, stored in a retrieval system, or transmitted in any form or by any means, electronic, mechanical, photocopying, recording or otherwise, without the prior permission of the publishers.

Contents

Introduction	vii
Glossary of Gaelic Words	ix
Glossary of Scots Words	xi
My Lady of Aros (1910)	1
The Captain More (1923)	183
Strawfeet (1930)	367

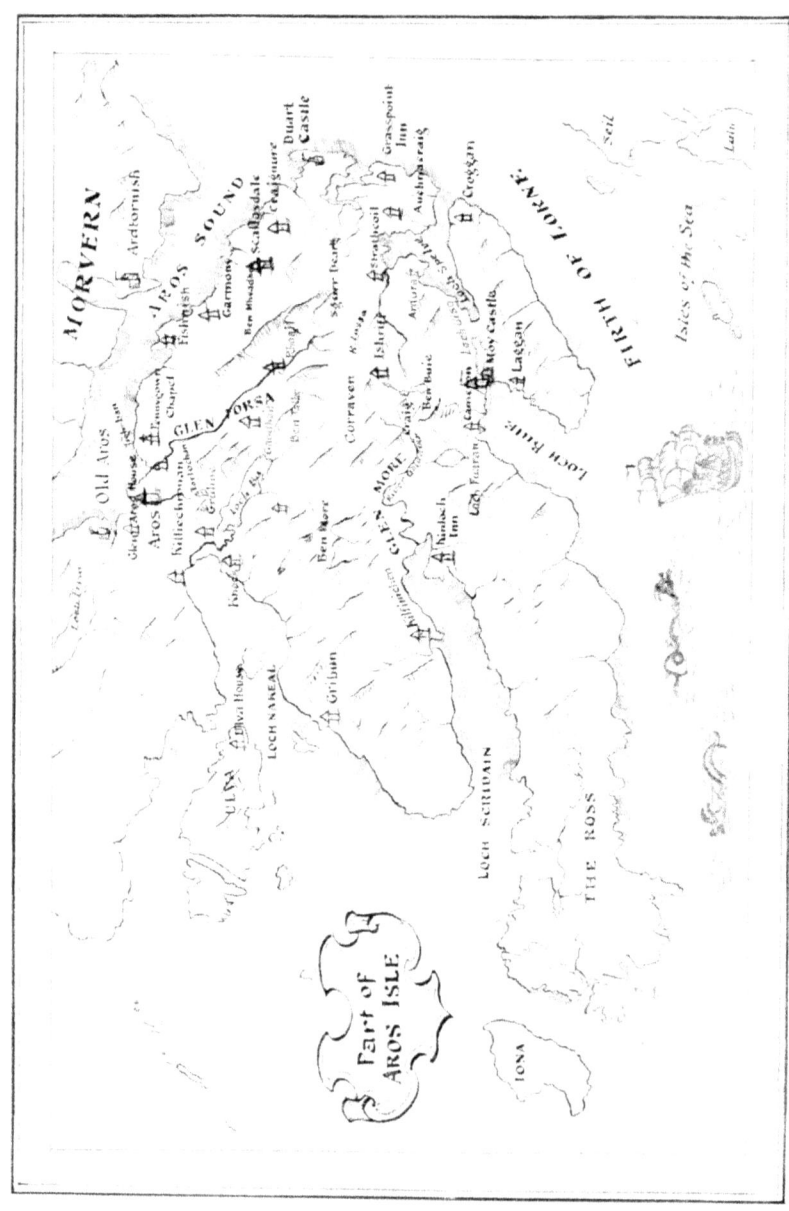

Map used by Ian Fraser in his Journeyings in the Isle of Aros, A.D. 1759

Introduction

John Brandane (1869-1947) –
dramatist and novelist

John Brandane (the pen name for Dr John MacIntyre) was arguably Scotland's best known resident dramatist in the 1920s before the emergence of that other great doctor/dramatist James Bridie (OH Mavor).

He was born in Rothesay on the Isle of Bute on 14th August, 1869. His family moved to the Bridgeton area of Glasgow and as a boy he worked in a Glasgow cotton mill and between the ages of 15-27 was employed as a clerk in a warehouse. During his latter years in the warehouse he took up the study of medicine at Glasgow University. In 1901 he graduated and while specialising in surgery at Glasgow Royal Infirmary he met and became a friend of Bridie. Since he had not taken a holiday for six years, for the sake of his health he obtained his first medical post in a rural practice on the Island of Mull and remained there until 1908.

His first known venture into literature is a long short story called "In Aros Isle" which he wrote in 1905. With advice on its plot and characterisation and praise for its "zest" from Neil Munro this developed into the novel *My Lady of Aros* which was published in 1910. Its setting is the location for almost all of Brandane's later work — Eilean Aros or Aros Isle, a thinly disguised Island of Mull. Like Neil Munro's *Shoes of Fortune*, it deals with the abortive Jacobite Rising of 1759 and treachery — in this case the treachery of the heroine's double dealing spy brother Norman.

From 1908 until 1912 Brandane moved to England and was a general practitioner in a rural area in the Thames Valley. While there he paid occasional visits to London where performances by the Abbey Theatre Players from Dublin turned his mind towards writing drama. In 1912 he returned to Glasgow and remained in general practice in the Hyndland area until 1935. During WW1 he served as surgeon in a hospital in the French sector of the Western Front at Arc-en-Barrois near Verdun.

When he returned to live in Glasgow he was to become deeply involved in the city's theatrical life. He renewed his acquaintance with A W Yuill and together they pushed the cause for a native Scottish drama and began writing for the Scottish National Players. His first one act play (with Yuill) *Glenforsa* (1921) portrays a spirited and drunken quarrel between two friends, Glenforsa and Oskamull, the gambling away of Glenforsa's Mull properties and the romantic entanglement of the two men with two sisters. This was followed by another one act play *The Change House.* In 1922, when he was 53 years old, he became a founder member of the Scottish National Players and in effect their in-house dramatist since almost all of his plays were performed by them.

1923 saw the performance of what is probably his most important full length play *The Glen is Mine*. This work has good characterisation and a strong theme, the future of the Highlands: are industry and progress preferable to the destruction of the old Highland way of life? The ending, however, shies away from a bold resolution and opts for a safer, more sentimental conclusion. In 1923 he also published the novel *The Captain More,* a re-working and extension of the ideas of his play *Glenforsa.*

1924 saw the performance of the full length romantic comedy *The Treasure Ship* with its background of the salvaging of treasure from a Spanish galleon supposedly sunk in Tobermory Bay. In 1925 *The Lifting* (a development of the one act *The Change House*) a full length play full of irony and coincidence set in the south of Mull near Lochbuie goes back to the period of 1745 Jacobite Rising. It demonstrates the honour and decency of the hero Iain in sacrificing his life to protect the friend whom he had inadvertently implicated in the killing of an "enemy" before the beginning of the play.

In 1926 Tyrone Guthrie directed Brandane's one act comedy masterpiece *Rory Aforesaid* with its wily elderly protagonist. This was followed by the grim and ironic one act *The Happy War* (1928) set in war-torn France, the full length comedy *Heather Gentry* (1932), the historical one act *The Spanish Galleon* (1932) (again co-authored with Yuill) which deals with the sinking of the galleon in Tobermory Bay and *The Inn of Adventure* (1932), a stage adaptation of the novel *The Captain More*. His final play, *The Man of Uz* (1938), is his dramatic representation of the suffering of Job.

Perhaps, outside his plays, the most interesting achievement of his later literary work is his third and final novel *Strawfeet* (1930). This deals with the First World War and is set partly on Mull and partly in France on the Western Front. Like *My Lady of Aros* it deals again with espionage and betrayal but this time in contemporary life. Brandane is one of the few Scots to have written a novel dealing with the First World War. And he dedicated it to Neil Munro, "Master of those who know the Gael".

In 1935 he found the demands of medical practice in the city and authorship too heavy. He returned to the Highlands to rural practice in Lochgoilhead in Argyll. He died there on 17th October, 1947.

Glossary of Gaelic Words

Aghmhor	happy
Albainn	Scotland
Amadan	fool
An Gillie Dubh	The Dark-haired lad
Beannachd leat (singular)	Blessing on you, goodbye
Beannachd leibh (plural))	
Beag	little
Bodach	old man
Caileag bheag	little girl
Cailleach	old woman
Cailleachean	old women
Canach	wild cotton
Canntaireachd	chaunt
Cas-chrom	plough
Cibeir	shepherd
Ceilidh	story-telling, gossip, folk tales
Clachan	a group of cottages
Cladh Phobuill	The Burying Place of the People (or Tribe)
Clarsach	Highland harp
Cnoc-na-croiche	Gallows-Hill
Co tha sin?	Who is there?
Cogadh no Sith	War or Peace
Creach	spoil, plunder
Crodh Chailein	Colin's cattle
Crotnag	shepherd's crook
Cuach	cup, wooden bowl
Cuarain	foot-covering of the raw hide
Dhia!	God!
Direach sin!	Just so!
Drammach	meal and water
Dugh	dark

Duin'-uasal	gentleman
Eilean	isle
Eilean Dhia	isle of God
Feasgar math!	Good evening!
Fin McCoul	Legendary Gaelic hero
Fleurisch	Flint and steel
Garron	Highland pony
Ghaol mo chridhe!	White love of my heart
Gillie	a lad, a Highland commoner
ille!	lad
Iorraman	boat-songs
Laochain	my hero
Maam	a round, steep hill
Mainnir nam Fiadh	The Playground of the Deer (a hill)
Marbh phaisg ort!	Death-wrapping be on thee!
M'eudail!	My treasure!
Mallachd ort!	Curse on you!
Mo chridhe!	My dear!
Mo thruaigh!	My sorrow!
Mogain	footless stockings
Och, ille, ille	Oh, lad, lad!
Och, ochan!	Alas, alas!
Och, ubh, ubh!	Oh, dear, dear!
Oidche mhath!	Good night!
Ruapais	The Careless One, the Rigmarole
Sassenach	Southerner
Seanachaidhean	story-tellers, bards
seilisders	sedges
Sgalag	ploughman
Sgian dubh	black knife
Slainte mhath!	Good health!
Slainte mhor mhath!	Great health!
Slan lea!	Farewell!
Suas e ... suas e	up with it ... up with it
Taghairm	invocation (of spirits)
Tearlach	Charles
Tearlach Og	Prince Charlie
Thoir an aire!	Look out!
Tir-nan-Oig	Land of the Ever-Young
Tonnag	a small shawl

Glossary of Scots Words

Airt	direction
Bannock	scone
Bawbee	halfpenny
Body	person
Bouman	cowman, or crofter
Breaking	bankruptcy
Brock	beast
Causey •.	causeway
Cogie	wooden bowl
Craig	throat
Cruisie •.	metal lamp
Deave	deafen
Doer	agent
Ettled	intended
Fleeching.	scolding
Girning	complaining peevishly
Gowff	gust
Greetin'	bewailing
Hamesucken	Assaulting a person with violence in his own house.
Haud	hold
Haud till't!	Hold on!
Howe and corrie	hollow and height
instrument o' sasine	An attestation by a Notary Public certifying the bargain.
Jalouse	surmise
Jo	lover
Lave	remainder
Loon	fellow
Maun	must
Mirk	dark
Oxter	armpit

Scunner	disgust
Scrape, the	the 'Forty-five Rising
Shaw	thicket, plantations
Skirling	shrieking
Smeddum	spirit
Snood	a ribbon for the hair
Soumings	allotments
Spate	flood
Spier	enquire
Spring	lively tune
Stravaging	wandering
Tacks of land	portions of land
Tacksman	a lessee of land who sublets to crofters
Thrapple	windpipe
Tinchel	hunt
Tocher	marriage portion
Trusty	secret agent
Tyke	dog
Wadset	a pawning of land
Warlock	wizard

My Lady of Aros

To my Friends in the Isle of Mull

I wrote this tale when I dwelt amongst you in the darling Isle. Will you accept the dedication of it, with my love? And will you pardon the liberties taken with the strict letter of geography and of history? I think the chief of these is that I have set the House of Aros somewhere about the beginning of the Gruline Road, just where it debouches from Salen. And, to speak the white truth—always a difficulty with the Romancer—I should not wonder, indeed, if in my fancy the Laird's Study stood where now Black Watch Cottage shelters so cosily.

J. B.
January, 1910

"*An-t-Eilean Muileach, an-t-eilean aghmhor,*
An-l-eilean grianach mu'n iath an saile,
Eilean buadhmhor nam fuar-bheann arda,
Nan coilltean uaine, 's nan cluaintean fàsail."
DUGALD MACPHAIL.

'O the Island of Mull is an isle of delight,
With the wind on the shore and the sun on the height.
With the breeze on the hills, and the blast on the Bens,
And the old green woods and the old grassy glens."
Translation of *An-t-Eilean Muileach* by JOHN STUART BLACKIE.

Contents

1:	The *Theseus* anchors in a mist	5
2:	Squalid Story	9
3:	A maker of maps	13
4:	The flight from Tiree	16
5:	The spy	19
6:	The laird's study	24
7:	Under Aros roof-tree	30
8:	Morag	37
9:	Fraser's tale	44
10:	Garden secrets	49
11:	The Fairies' Castle	53
12:	The Tiree men	60
13:	Plague	64
14:	Norman	71
15:	The repeated phrase	78
16:	The postscript	82
17:	The pedlar from the Ross	85
18:	A message from France	94
19:	The tacksman	99
20:	The cave at Cameron	103
21:	The dance at Moy	108
22:	Night in the woods	115
23:	The Rivals	117
24:	The quarrel	120
25:	Besieged	124
26:	A lady in a blue riding-habit	131

27:	Red rowans	136
28:	Norman plays high	140
29:	MacQuarie's cards	145
30:	The letter	150
31:	Perplexity	153
32:	Deaf Alan	156
33:	The Clachaig pass	160
34:	The woman answers	168
35:	Drumfin goes fishing	172
36:	"Beannachd leibh!"	179

1: The *Theseus* anchors in a mist

It is many and many a year ago, yet you still may hear in Isle Tiree of the stormy October day when the guns of a great battleship of the Second George called for aid along its misty shores. It is not, however, by reason of this wildest of tempests, which nigh drove the *Theseus* to her doom, that the generations of islesmen keep fresh the memory of that morning; it is because there began then the old-time tale which is here set down.

For half the preceding night the storm had muttered and threatened all along the fringes of the Hebrides. Then, with the first raw grey of dawn, these feints at onset gave way to reality, and the eager gales poured across Atlantic leagues to whip the scant coast herbage thinner yet. The gaunt cliffs of Mull and Skye thrilled to the swing and shock of waves, mighty and untiring. But green Tiree is cliffless, and her sunken reefs and sandy bars—doubly treacherous as the mists came on— gave neither roar of breakers nor vision of leaping spray such as her sister-isles had afforded for warning to unlucky mariners. The surges never broke fully on her hidden shoals; and if they broke lightly, they seemed on the instant to call *hush!* as if to screen their error from the enfolding and conspiring mists.

It is still a riddle how the *Theseus* came there; but come there she did, and in a bad hour. All the way from the Virginias she had safely voyaged, and here in the homeland seas she was like to have ended her days. Ransome, her captain, was beside himself, and no wonder he bit his finger-nails as the fog thickened despite the rising wind. It was the lead that told him first of all how far astray he was; and at last he anchored. But his anchors dragged once or twice, and—to add to his miseries— a gun had broken loose, disabling several seamen before it was tripped and lashed securely. And now he paced his quarter-deck, listening for an answer to his last gun-fire. A soaking mist was around, so that in front he could barely see the ship's waist; above him the mainyard was invisible, and the squalls that at intervals tore the curtains of vapour apart showed nothing but fresh banks of fog sweeping down on him from every side. Below him he heard the churning of the yeasty sea; above, the wind whistling in the cordage as it slatted against bare poles. From the foc'sle there came at intervals the bos'n's whistle and faint calls in response; and then the ship rocked to the recoil of the next gun-fire. Ransome paced the quarter impatiently back and forth, his foul-weather clothes dripping, his clean-cut features sodden and glistening, his shoulders, by reason of this burden of anxiety, drooping overmuch for a man of fifty years.

But a new piping from the bos'n's whistle straightened his back of a sudden; there were shouts from the ship's waist, and from somewhere on the face of the angry waters voices were to be heard replying. For the moment Ransome looked for another craft too close to be safe, and involuntarily glanced aloft to see if the fog had thinned sufficiently to show her yards. Then a blast from the nor'west tore open a lane in the mist, and he saw what looked like a cutter drift past, her sails stowed, her men at the oars. But an alert seaman had flung a line, and now ran along the bulwarks, crossing quarter and poop, and coming down with a slide on the captain's walk behind the state-room. He called out that he held the cutter safely, and several of the crew coming aft, Ransome took up his post under the great stern-lanthorn, and saw to the lowering of a rope-ladder.

"Pilot, sir," cried the bos'n in Ransome's ear. "Says he can take us out into open water, fog or no fog."

"Let him come aboard, then," said the captain. "We'll give him his price, whatever it be. Haul in."

There were shouts and counter-shouts, and the delay had almost proved fatal, for what with the sagging of the frigate and the cutter on the rise and fall of the waves, it looked as if the line must be cut, if the little craft were not to be capsized or its timbers torn asunder. And yet—it seemed the most foolhardy of things—the bos'n at the end of the ladder was bargaining with the pilot—an oddly dressed fellow in a habit that savoured more of the parson than of the mariner.

"Phoebus! Will you never ha' done?" cried Ransome to the bos'n. "What's money at a time like this? Give him what he asks, and let him come aboard."

The bos'n scrambled back to the rail of the stern gallery and whispered in the captain's ear.

"Heard you ever such folly?" cried Ransome passionately. "Seize the fat rascal, Adams. Press-gang him—kidnap him, sir!"

Adams scratched his head. "We'd lose time, sir," said he, "an' we'd lose boats and men, too, in a sea like that. An' even if we didn't, he'd slip us in the fog belike."

"Damn you, Adams, do as I say ... Or, no—Mr. Beckles!" he called to the first officer who, with several others was looking down on him from the poop.—" Mr. Beckles, man the whaler. But, no," he added, "send for the surgeon.—Or Fraser? —Are you there, Mr. Fraser?"

A tall young man came to the rail of the poop, and passing a long leg over, dropped easily into the stern-walk and saluted.

"Mr. Fraser, kindly go aboard the cutter which you see below. It comes from the Isle of Tiree, which, I'm led to understand, is close at hand. These savages refuse us the services of a pilot, it seems, unless we lend them a surgeon to aid a sick man on the island: so the bos'n tells me. In a case like ours—in a sea like this, we cannot force them. Kindly go ashore with them, sir. You can pick us up in the Clyde, I make no doubt—that is, if we ever get out of this cursed fog. Please go first. Their pilot refuses to leave until you enter their cutter."

There was no time to lose. Fraser swung over the rail and went down the ladder, passing the bos'n, who avoided him with the monkey-like agility of the practised sailor. The surgeon dropped into the boat, and on the instant a dark figure scrambled from the stern over the bowed shoulders of the rowers, and crawled past him. Fraser saw a pale face, fat and bearded, a coat of many capes encircling a heavy body, and a pair of splay shoes with silver buckles. The man went nimbly up the ladder.

"That a pilot?" said Fraser to himself, "a queer one, then. Lucky I'm out of the *Theseus*, if his are the hands that steer."

He looked up to wave a farewell to the ship's company, but the frigate was gone from sight. The painter had been cut, and the walls of fog had closed down on them. Yet still the ship's neighbourhood was evident from the pungent odours of the last gun-fire, from the sounds of the gale shrilling eerily in her tops, and from the distant piping of the bos'n's whistle, calling the men to the anchor capstan. And fainter and fainter yet came the sailors' chanty in response, as the Tiree men's oars stroked easily over the surge, making as if by instinct for an invisible shore.

It was all so uncanny and sudden, that Fraser found himself laughing nervously before he could overcome his surprise at this rapid transference of duties. But a few moments ago he had inhabited a floating city, alive with a goodly company, knit together by discipline of the sternest. And here was a wrench that for the instant left him with a feeling of helplessness, and a desire to lean on a commander or a subordinate: it mattered little which, as long as he might turn to him with a sense of common duty—a sense of common danger. It was but momentarily, however, that this mood lasted, and soon the young surgeon turned his thoughts to the work in hand, and set to questioning the oarsman nearest him as to the sick man on shore.

"Oh, he'll be a MacDougall, and married on a second cousin of Deaf Alan," said the man in bad English.

"Deaf Alan?" queried Fraser.

"Yes, yes. Just Deaf Alan—he'll be piloting the big ship now," said the old man, pointing into the mist.

"Oh, the fat fellow? He looked more like a clergyman than a sailor to my eye."

"That's just what he is, sir—a minister, and a good sailor forbye. Whether it's at bridal or burial, at tiller or nets, with his book or his gun, it's just he that's the pretty man." There was a hint of enthusiasm in the ancient's voice.

"And what now is the matter with this second cousin's sick husband, whom he sets such store by?" pursued Fraser.

"A knife, sir."

"A knife?"

"Ay, just a knife between the shoulder-blades, sir."

Fraser entered into this spirit of grim conciseness at once.

"Who put it there?" he asked.

"Ah!" said the greybeard, with a wary look at his interrogator, "but it's now that you are asking me the question." He shipped his oar. "Here is the landing, sir," said he.

2: A Squalid Story

Fraser stepped on dry land with a sigh of relief. Albeit the storm was as high as ever, and the clinging mist as all-encompassing, still the fickle sea had been left behind. And now his elbow was gripped by his friend from the cutter.

"Your patient's at the change-house," said he; and they went forward into the fog. All Fraser could discern was that for a time they traversed a stretch of sand, and then for a space a stretch of grass and heath. At length an indistinct bulk of building seemed to advance on them suddenly, and through the vapours a point of light showed, marking a low doorway. But even as they came up to this place some dark figures issued from its portal, staggering under a heavy burden borne on an osier hurdle. One glance at the stark outline of its covering told Fraser and his companion that they had come too late; and they stood for a moment with uncovered heads until the little group had moved off into the mist.

"They're for Sunivaig," said the old man. "His wife's people belong to that side ... But come your ways in, sir, and rest. This is the Inns, as you'd say in the South, and so I'll bring you to the landlady."

The surgeon followed him through the dark of a passage into a long, low-ceilinged room, poorly lit by one deep-set window, and scantily furnished with several chairs and a bare table. In a deep roomy fireplace a cosy fire of peats glowed warmly, and standing facing it and looking away from Fraser were a man and a woman.

"The doctor from the big ship, Mrs. MacNeill," said the surgeon's guide.

The couple before the fire wheeled round. Fraser noted that the landlady was of the customary buxom and garrulous type, but her companion gave him pause: he had an air of breeding, his clothes fine, his white hair in a roll, his bronzed oval of a face delicately featured. Instinctively, even as the landlady curtseyed, the surgeon addressed the man.

"I am too late, I see," said he.

"'Tis what I have been saying of myself to Flora here," said the stranger ... "Oh, no," he added in answer to Fraser's quick glance of enquiry. "I'm no surgeon, but in a wandering life I've picked up a few trifles of leechcraft, and some of these good people, finding I was in the Isle, unearthed me."

Sir," said Fraser, bowing, "had we been in time I should have been glad to have worked with you. I am but a surgeon's mate."

The old gentleman laughed. "And I not even an apprentice," said he.

"But you'll have to be going, sir," interposed the landlady, a trifle uneasily, her hand on the stranger's arm. It seemed to Fraser that her anxiety was too plain lest there should be further conversation with himself; and he stood aside stiffly as the other passed him.

"I am honoured in this meeting, sir," said the man, bowing. "Good-bye."

Fraser returned his salute in silence, and Mrs. MacNeill showed her companion down the passage. It was at this juncture that the surgeon for the first time noted that his old sailor friend had disappeared, and he turned to the doorway to look for him. As he did so a hurried whispering from the lobby came to his ear, and a name was several times repeated that took his fancy strangely: "Drumfin— Drumfin" was the word. Then a door closed, and the landlady bustled cheerfully ben to turn the peats and bewail the weather.

"Such sleet as this fog has now turned to! You came indoors in time, sir," she cried. "But it's soaking you are all the same. You must change, sir."

Fraser threw aside his sea-cloak and protested himself as comfortable as he could desire.

"It's your death you're courting, sir, if you'll no do as I bid you ... Yet surely now you'll take my commands in the matter of cordials, then; and it's the good French aquavity I'll be bringing you ... Mr. Fraser? Is that the name, sir? ... Maybe you'll have the Gaelic, sir?"

"The Gaelic?" said Fraser, smiling. "No; but my father had it before me, if there's any virtue in that."

"Do you tell me?" cried the good dame, and her face flushed with pleasure, as she busied herself with stoup and glasses.

And now Fraser saw that her Highland pride was aroused. He saw, too, not without anxiety, that her next enquiries would involve a trying climb on his part into the heights of his genealogical tree, and in sheer defence he led off the subject at once.

"Is the old gentleman a laird in the Isle?" he asked, choosing the first suggestion of memory.

On the instant the woman dropped a glass, and thereby hid a sudden change of countenance, as she stooped to pick it up. It was a keen glance she flashed at the surgeon before she answered.

"Not what you'd call a laird, sir; maybe a laird's doer, or factor, might be nearer it, maybe. He's a fine man, but it's just his name is the thing I'm aye forgetting ... But, eh, sir, isn't it a woeful business this killing of the Chisholm man. And in my house of a' houses, sir! What's to come of it? What's to come of it?"

It was clear that she had but followed Fraser's example in leading off from the subject proposed. It suited his mood, however, and he coaxed and coaxed her into the details of the tragedy, until finally she rehearsed the tale connectedly. How much of her volubility depended on her interest in the story—how much on her desire to take her hearer off the track of her late visitor, were questions that came often uppermost in Fraser's mind in after years. At present the narrative itself absorbed his attention.

"This is the way of it, sir," said she, "and little enough does my decent change-house deserve to be mixed up in it. The like never happened to me when my dear man had life and was with me... out this is the way of it...

"There's one Angus MacLean lives here—only a tacksman in Craigmore, 'tis true, but still a second cousin to the MacLean over in Isle Aros yonder. And now he's an old man, this Angus MacLean, but twenty years ago he was young and gay; and it was then he married a wife, just before the time of Tearlach Og, you ken. The wife—well, as for her, there was another she loved—a Chisholm man from Strathglass on the mainland he was. But he had jilted her, had the Chisholm man—jilted her sorely. And so what does my lady do, but up in a fit of rage, and marries this MacLean I speak of to spite the man she loved.—Such creatures are women, sir.—*Mo thruaigh, mo thruaigh!* Do you follow me, sir?"

Fraser nodded.

"She rued, and she rued, and she better rued; and the drink did the rest. And all her days these twenty years gone has she mourned, old wife as she is, for her early love—the sorrow of it! And still the drink and the drink; and the goodman nigh demented at the sight of her and the thocht of her... But I'll be just bothering you, and you so wet and weary—?"

"Never the bother," said Fraser. "It's the good tale you're giving me. Go on."

"Oh, my sorrow! but worse to come! The first lover came back, sir—oh, he came back—an old man, a mariner-man, a man of dreadful ongoings, they tell me, among the Paris Highlanders after the Scrape—an old man, I say, he that had given the lass no word but the waiting one in the days gone by— a story he had told to many a girl, if all tales be true. He comes back, this old runt of a sailor, and he is drinking heavy in this very change-house every day; and aye stirring at the old thoughts about the Prince."

"The Prince?" said Fraser. "You mean?"

The woman's face flushed. "Let it bide at that, sir—we'll name no names... But about this sailor-man—everyday he's drinking, I say. And one day in his cups he says something he better never have said; and some hearing it and being friends to Angus MacLean, carried it to him. A lie it was, but the rumour of it got about till it was ever in the ears of Angus MacLean—this lie from the lips of his wife's old jo, as gallant with the tongue as ever... And, oh, sir,—ah, if you but had the Gaelic, sir, till I could put it to you in the good language— he came down to the Inn, did Angus MacLean, the jilted woman's husband, and he found his enemy sitting over this very fire, sir, his punch steaming in the eyes of him. They say that the others tried to soothe them, but there were high words between the old fools, and before you could turn a bannock, the Chisholm was knifed almost to the heart. And then Angus MacLean, with blood on his fingers, walked home to his own hearth, its peats white in the ash, and a drunk woman skirling upstairs. And there he sat him down as still as a stone. That was yesterday, yet there they say he still sits over a dead fire, never stirring nor speaking. But Lord send he stirs before Deaf Alan returns, or there will be blood on more than one man's fingers."

"Deaf Alan?" asked Fraser, "the pilot to the big ship—the man who exchanged for me?"

"The same, sir; and kinsman by way of marriage to this man that's dead ... Oh, Deaf Alan's just Deaf Alan, sir; until you ken him, there's no description of him will serve. And when all's said and done, Mr. Fraser, he's better unkenned."

"And that's the true word, Flora," said a boyish voice from the doorway of the chamber.

Looking round, Fraser beheld a slight figure, clad in a dripping cloak, surmounted by a pale face with aquiline features, a wisp of straw-coloured hair falling over the low brow.

3: A maker of maps

"Mr. Cattanach!" cried the landlady. "And in such a storm! You'll have done little map-making the day, I'm thinking."

The youth laughed lightly, and coming forward, tossed off his sodden wrap-rascal, and bowed to Fraser.

"This is the surgeon from the big ship," said Mrs. MacNeill, "Mr. Fraser by name, sir."

"Sir," said the young man, saluting again, "a glass of wine with you, if you'll honour me. My name is Cattanach. I have heard of your merciful errand, and of how you have lost touch with your ship. Lord! how I wish my task in life had been somewhat after your pattern."

Fraser bowed in reply, and accepted the invitation to wine.

"In chirurgery now," went on the youth, seating himself glass in hand, to steam his legs at the peat-fire, "—in chirurgery there might be something of newness day by day—a limb to mend, a life to save. But in cartography—at least in cartography of these parts, look you, all one can do is to say amen to the markings of old Timothy Pont's wonderful maps."

"I've heard them praised before now," said Fraser.

"Sir," said the youth, "they're the very devil."

The surgeon studied the young man as he blustered thus. There was something of effeminacy in his face, yet had he airs of decision that were not unmanly; and, as the night wore on, his conversation was engaging to a degree. And so it came to pass that after the first bottle of claret, when Fraser discovered that the new-comer was to lodge there that night, an arrangement was made that they should forthwith sup together. With the first of the viands the talk came back to Deaf Alan.

"What is this I heard at Scarinish, Flora?" cried Cattanach to the landlady, who waited on him as he carved the capon. "Deaf Alan has been blaming me, they say, for hounding on those two old fellows to a quarrel? Is it so?"

The good lady blanched a little. "That was the tale, sir," she said.

"I'll not deny I told old Angus of the scandal this Chisholm was talking," said Cattanach. "And I did rightly, I think. For I'm far from saying I disapprove of spirit in an old man, when it's such a virtue in youth—eh, Flora? ... Even if it goes the length of killing" —he lunged with his carving-knife at the breast of the fowl. "But, keep me, madam! Never a word to Deaf Alan as to what I did then or what I say now. You see," he added to Fraser, "he's kin to the dead man, and fell handy with his oxter-knife."

"You've the true word there," said the landlady under breath.

"This Deaf Alan," said Fraser, "is a minister, is he not? And yet I hear oftener of his knife than of his Bible. Read me the riddle, Mr. Cattanach."

"Minister?" said the other. "Aye, but an unfrocked one—unfrocked for some dirty casuistry in a pamphlet some years ago, published—where do you think?—in no less a place than London, sir... Tiree and London—what do you think? ... Stap me, he's a wonder, is Deaf Alan... And his Bible, say you? I think the old Highland customs are his Bible, sir: they come first with him everywhere, I'm told. And I doubt not but that if he returns, he'll order things so that Norman Cattanach makes acquaintance with some Highland customs little to Norman's liking... But enough of Alan, Mr. Fraser. For the present, sir, our skins are whole; so come, let us talk of these wonderful Americas you have but left."

And thus they sat far on into the night, talking of the Canadian campaign, Fraser rehearsing the rumours of it as he heard them in Virginian waters, and Cattanach supplementing these with a wealth of details from some obscure French sources to which he seemed to have the fullest access. This youth's mind the surgeon discovered to be as acute as any he had ever encountered; yet was there something a-wanting in the fellow—something that caused Fraser to bridle his tongue at times when his utterance was frankest. Already he noted that he had been drawn by Cattanach into an avowal of partial sympathy with the American colonists in their troubles with the home government. He remembered, too, with a start, that he was still a King's officer, and that it behoved him to be circumspect. Do what he would, however, the talk drifted on to a discussion in high politics.

"Heard you never a whisper in Virginia now," said Cattanach, "that with all this pother in Canada and in India—with our Americas restless and France hostile, a new Stuart rising would be an easy matter?" The map-maker spoke in a low tone, his glance on the chamber's door to see that they were private.

"Heavens, man, no? Never a renewal of that old madness, surely?" said Fraser.

"But yes, none other, sir."

"Ah, no. There was a time, let us allow, when that cause may have been worth red blood in streams. But nowadays—well, the thing's a bubble —a breaking bubble that deceives no one, Mr. Cattanach."

"Of that I am not so sure, sir. But deceive or not, do not you see, Mr. Fraser—let the bubble break, or let the bubble soar, at least it would distract England by either performance, and so serve England's enemies—France especially."

The surgeon smiled a negative with the wise air of a man a few years older than his companion.

"Mr. Fraser," said Cattanach earnestly, in reply to this smile, "how long have you been away from home waters?"

"Two years."

"Three months are enough for a scheme of the kind I speak of, sir."

Something in the youth's air startled Fraser, and he eyed him questioningly. The other returned his glance and nodded as if in answer.

"What would you give, Mr. Fraser, to avert such a disaster as a renewal of this old Stuart folly?" said Cattanach, suddenly rising, as if with a determined air; and crossing to the fireplace, he faced suddenly on the surgeon, his eyelids narrowed, his wisps of blond hair falling over them. "What would you say, if I told you that the work of planning another Stuart rising is on foot now, and in this very isle, sir?"

"What madness—what utter madness!" said Fraser slowly.

"If I read you aright, sir," went on the other, with something of missionary zeal, "you are a man with ideals—one who would serve his country's good, be the cost little, be the cost much. I, too, have my visions, sir. Here is our opportunity, and here let us seize it. I am but a travelling student, you a surgeon, and neither of us seems trained for the work of a spy. And here we are, set as by Providence in the midst of a coil of conspiracy. For the agent of the Prince himself is here in hiding, fast weaving the nets for his master to draw—taking these poor islesmen's silver for a cause already lost."

"Who is this?" asked Fraser.

"MacLean of Drumfin—straight from St. Germains but a week ago, if you please."

"Drumfin?" said the surgeon, recalling the name he had heard whispered so persistently in the passage that afternoon, "Drumfin?—a tall old man, white-haired, with a long oval of a face, sun-tanned?"

"The man to a button," said Cattanach excitedly. "And fine brown eyes, a trifle sad—eyes that would make a beggar's fortune. Where did you hear of him?"

"Hear of him? He stood but four hours gone where now you stand, his back to the cruisie there."

Cattanach's face wore a sphinx-like smile now.

"Who but he would have dared it?" said he half to himself. Then, holding out his hand to Fraser, he added: "Look you now; is it a compact? Will you help me track this man? Let us thwart him at every turn. If need be let us place him where English law will have its say. Is it a bond?" His long fingers were outstretched suddenly.

The surgeon clasped them. "A bond be it," said he.

4: The flight from Tiree

On the morrow after the compact the hunt was up, and Fraser and his new friend set out on the trail of the Jacobite agitator. But their quarry had played the game of outlaw too often and too long to make the hunters' task an easy one. Dreary journeys over moss and heather, frequent soakings in heavy rains, tedious hidings on the hill or in caves, did something to chill the surgeon's initial enthusiasm; but what finally crushed it out of life was a discovery he made after some three weeks of these adventures.

They stood one evening at fault in their tracking on a wide stretch of fog-ridden moorland, and queried the way of one another.

"Your map then?" said Fraser.

"None of mine," said the youth, "if it please you. Here is old Pont's drawing: it's vastly before aught else."

He produced a print and held it out to the other.

"Excellent," said Fraser, glancing at it. "And your compass?"

Cattanach stared blankly. "My compass—? ... You mean—?"

In a flash it dawned on the surgeon that he had been fooled. Why was this man puzzled as to the uses of the very tools of his trade?

"Your magnetic compass, sir," said Fraser icily; "surely as necessary a part of the outfit of a map-maker as of a mariner, if either is what he seems."

Cattanach laughed. "Eh, bien, you have unscreened me at last," said he coolly. "I am indeed no cartographer. To speak quite plainly, sir, I am in his Britannic Majesty's secret service. And I am greatly in your debt for the assistance you have given me in this matter of the tracking of Drumfin. But, pray now, do not let us quarrel over a little harmless dissembling."

For answer Fraser only regarded him steadily, his fists clenching ever so little.

"If you are tired of this business, so am I," went on Cattanach blandly. "Drumfin is too much for me; and, if the fog lifts, I am for the mainland to-night. I've a cutter trysted for moonrise at Craigmore Bay. Will you voyage with me?"

The oily tones of the fellow made Fraser grue. Yet sick at heart though he was at the thought of further commerce with a paid spy, the proffer of an early chance of rejoining his ship and returning home overcame his scruples.

"Agreed," he said curtly, and turned on his heel.

The fog was now lifting in patches, and after some ventures they at last struck the path and by nightfall were on the braeside above Craigmore. Here they lay in the heather until the moon rose and showed them the great sea-stretches blown clear of mist as a nor'west wind strengthened into a gale. There was half an hour more of waiting, and then round a sandy spit came a cutter handled with great skill by a single occupant. It tacked easily, and ran in to the side of a finger of rock that pointed seawards and served as a pier; and Fraser and Cattanach stealing down, embarked at once. As the vessel was poled off there came from the shadows of the dunes on the shore a hoarse voice: "*Beannachd leibh!*"

"*Beannachd leibh!*" called softly the steersman in return, and the cutter headed for the open sea.

Cattanach and the man at the tiller held a whispered converse in Gaelic for a little, while Fraser, going forward to the bows, snuggled himself in his cloak and set to brooding on his prospects of picking up his frigate in the Clyde. It had been a tiring day; the solace of the swing and splash of the little craft was wonderfully soothing, and soon he fell into a gentle doze.

When he awoke the moon was setting, and he saw that hours must have passed; for, though there was plenty of scud in the sky, his sailor's eye could make out enough of the stars to show him that the cutter's course had been altered. And with reason, too, for her head was now to a tearing blast, and with sail well-reefed she was thrashing right heartily out to sea, and into the stormy night.

"Too much for her. Had to go round," said Cattanach when Fraser staggered aft to the midthwart, and sat down beside him there.

As they were placed both were facing the steersman, and now for the first time Fraser caught full sight of his face as the moonbeams fell ghostily on it.

"My God, Cattanach," he whispered. "It's MacLean—it's Chisholm's murderer!"

Cattanach in reply smiled dreamily with half-shut eyes. "Yes, it's Angus," said he. "A little more of my dissembling, Mr. Fraser. To tell truth, he is flying Tiree because our friend Deaf Alan returned there yesterday. For since his return Alan has been making kind enquiry as to the health of Angus and myself... The good, kind Alan—eh? ... Therefore it is that Angus and I make our little voyage together." He laughed lightly as he saw the perplexity deepen on Fraser's dark face. "And," he went on, "—and you are with us, my friend, because, in an open boat, and in stormy waters such as these—well—three are better company than two, Mr. Fraser... Not so, eh?"

Throughout that night of storm the little cutter battled for her life, and there was good reason before daybreak to appreciate the value of a third hand in her crew. By turns each took the tiller, and by turns they rested as much as they dared. At dawn the Tiree man and Fraser were almost spent, but Cattanach seemed tireless. His badinage never ceased; his delicate airs were never abated through it all; and after hauling on a stay, he would re-arrange his cloak and hat as daintily as if he were in a London street, and wait the next onset of the gale with equanimity. Fraser, indeed, could not help but admire the man's coolness, though all his banter and fine airs seemed so much blasphemy in the face of that awful sea and sky.

With sunrise the storm abated; by ten in the morning they were able to put about and run towards the mainland again, and noon found them weltering through the first sleet of winter at the mouth of Aros Sound.

5: The spy

THE wind was still nor'west and full in the track of Kyle Aros. There were variations from the on-pouring of the gale, however; gusts came from the cliffs walling the Sound on the west; and then a hiss of mingled spray and rain urged Fraser, now at the tiller, to a wariness that was absent as long as the timbers' strain and joggle told him of a wind already reckoned with. Yet, even when danger menaced, his work was done with a lassitude plainly not of the flesh alone. Storms of the black tropics at Panama, the bitterness of a winter on the Labrador—these had made no harmony with his spirit at any time; but here in the seas of home, the grey sky and the stormy waters were attuned to his mood as never before.

Cattanach in a cloak and tricorne crouched at the steersman's feet on the weather side, and smiled up as engagingly as ever at the set face above him.

"Mr. Fraser," said he, "I've been regretting —"

Fraser looked down. "Yes?" he answered, breaking silence for the first time in many hours.

"I've been regretting the three hundred crowns you've lost through Drumfin's evasion of us."

"I would not have touched a penny," said the surgeon quietly, his eye on the sail.

"Ah! the disinterested lover of his country?" said Cattanach, and putting a chilled hand on his heart, he assumed a smile that was half a sneer.

"What you will, sir, what you will," returned Fraser. "But at least, I confess, I could not stand idle and see those poor peasants suffering further impoverishment through paying a double-rent to the rebels. And so I played the hound to the hare of the man who misled them. But as for the price set on him, it might have gone hang, had I but laid hands on the fellow."

"Ah!" said the other derisively. "You played the spy in honour's service?"

"Spy?" retorted the surgeon. "It was an act, not a habit, sir. And at least it could not be called my trade."

"No?" said Cattanach, and now, for the first time, he bit his lip. "No, the enthusiasm—or shall we say, the patriotism?—necessary for the work is not quite common, I fear."

"That there are refinements in the matter of patriotism," said Fraser coldly, "I doubt not." He appeared to be studying the set of the mainsail. "But it passes my comprehension this particular tint of the virtue patriotic which I find in a Highlander who is in outward appearance an agent of the Paris Jacobites, but in reality a Hanoverian secret service man."

"Poor Norman!" sighs Cattanach, playfully affecting remorse. "And that's me in all my blackness! Poor Norman!"

"You see my difficulty?" asked Fraser, unheeding his antics. "Such a man would be a blending of the lover of his country, and the traitor to his clan, would he not?" A wave-top, thrashing and jubilant, fell on the other just then; but unruffled, he shook his drenched sea-cloak daintily and replied:

"It is truth you say; and difficult is the word. Pink me, sir! I have trouble enough to understand myself at times, let alone other people trying. Yet look at your own case, my friend."

The steersman only nodded in reply.

"Are not the difficulties there as numerous, the contradictions as irreconcilable. Here you were, a surgeon of the King's Navy, dropped as from the clouds on Tiree—your errand your noblest one of healing. You claimed to love the islesmen, their simple talk, their homely ways. Your own father, you told me, was Gaelic. And yet, when Drumfin came to them, worshipped as he was, and almost a king uncrowned, it is to him you played the bloodhound, as you put it. Is there, indeed, no obscurity in the action, sir? Will you still tell me the reward did not tempt?"

"I tell you it did not," said Fraser, a little roused at last. "As to Drumfin—? For him to sow the thoughts he sowed; to take the crofters' silver and leave in return—what? Unrest, suspicion, hatred unslumbering to the Reigning House! Pah! Let him at once get over the water again to his backstairs work in French convents and Spanish palaces."

"Stap me!" cried the spy. "What a flurry for a non-combatant. You do not fear—" And he broke off suddenly, as his gaze turned landwards.

Aros!" he said to himself aloud. "Aros, the darling spot!"

It was a familiar eye he bent on the misty shores of a bay opening up on the west, where, distant and grey, a mansion sat cosily under a huddle of pines.

"You know these parts, sir?" queried Fraser.

"Know them, know them?" repeated the other absently, his glance ranging every howe and corrie. "Yes, yes, I know them. And by the same token," he went on, rousing suddenly from his reverie, "if you don't jibe her at once, you'll have us on the skerry."

Squalls were too frequent to allow of jibing; so the steersman put about instantly, and, as he did so, sent a cry of warning to MacLean, asleep under a spare sail in the cutter's bow, who, wakening, protruded his head, and showed the bird-like nose and eyes of his face hidden for the most part in a clout tying up the jaws.

"*Mo thruaigh!*" he cried. "What now, lad, what now? My poor head!" and in Gaelic he cursed a toothache heartily, and rolled to windward as the boat fell off on a new tack. But while he wound himself anew in his wraps, he happened to glance over the gunwale at the misty hills and the pine-encircled house set beneath them on the shore of the bay they were nearing.

"*Och, ochan!* and there is Aros itself," he said, turning round with a look of meaning at Cattanach, who made as if to avoid it by resuming his conversation with Fraser.

"Know these parts?" went on the spy. "Ay, and well, too; and so also, as you can see, does Angus MacLean there—indeed, the laird of Aros lands is no less than second cousin to him, and speaking by the map, as one might say, his nearest relative. As to the why and wherefore of my own acquaintance with the landscape, my surgeon, never mind. But had it not existed you'd have sent us on the reef. And then—? Why then, we'd all have gone to join poor Chisholm in the shades."

At the last words he lowered his voice and fixed his eyes on the figure in the bows, now stolen under his canvas once more.

"Poor Chisholm, indeed!" said Fraser.

"Now, there's patriotism," chuckled Cattanach. "There's love for one's country; there's your spy who is in earnest—the man who dies at his task."

"Chisholm? The dead man?" cried Fraser in a loud whisper. Hitherto he had treated his companion cavalierly, but now his interest was awake, and in the surprise the words had aroused, he let the boat yaw, and some water was shipped. "Chisholm, a Government trusty? Was he, too, with you?" he exclaimed.

"*La! la! mon mêdecin!*" protested the other, "a little less of Aros Sound down my stock, if it please you." He pushed a fringe of wet hair from off his forehead, and, smiling, resumed in low tones: "Chisholm, hey? You never smoked him? Fie, fie, my dear Fraser!" He wagged a reproving finger.

"But—but—?" said the surgeon. "But it was personal only—the quarrel he died in, was it not?" A sudden suspicion had possessed him, and he bent forward threateningly to Cattanach, his features sterner than ever, his fingers clenching on the sheet. "Where were the causes politic for his death?" he whispered hoarsely.

"You are so kind as to ask, Mr. Fraser," was the enigmatic reply. "Like yourself, you see, Chisholm desired a close and speedy acquaintance with Drumfin."

"Yes, yes. But the quarrel—the quarrel with Angus was personal, was it not?" asked the steersman quickly and in low tones, his eye on the bows where MacLean lay snoring.

"Personal? Oh, yes, my good surgeon," and the pale wet face smiled evilly.

Fraser had glanced momentarily at the scud and the waters; but his whole countenance was changed in that instant, and when he turned it on Cattanach again, it was contorted from its grimness as if sick with disgust. Here was a fight on the past—here was a key to many a dark door of memory.

"You devil!" he whispered.

"Ah!" said Cattanach in assumed delight. "You perceive? How good of you, lud!"

"And this unfortunate," said Fraser, looking down on the wet canvas moulded in relief over the slumbering islesman, "this poor clod is branded murderer in your stead?"

"In my stead?" said the youth softly. "But no, monsieur; your pardon. 'tis now an affair for all three of us."

"Oh, blind that I did not see!" said the surgeon bitterly. "In the hunt for Drumfin you found poor Chisholm your rival...? And so you rid yourself of him by means of the jealousy of MacLean?—for 'twas none but you that set him the length of killing."

"Lud, what insight!" sneered the other. But his smile was feeble now.

"And then came my turn?" said Fraser, watching narrowly the effect of his guessing. "'Twas I was the next tool? ... Oh, monstrous! oh, unclean!"

As Cattanach beheld the surgeon's passion, his smile grew feebler still, until it faded wholly on white lips. There came a furtive glance to his prominent blue eyes; and his pallid features bore a look of mingled vanity and distress; vanity in the shrewdness which had pressed these men into his plotting's service; distress that this weakness had made him so glib of tongue. But his discomfiture was only momentary, for he shuddered daintily at his rude surroundings, and gathering his knees in a hug at once affectionate and forgiving, was soon at ease with himself again—with the old, gay, insouciant self.

Fraser turned his glance from the plotter to the plotter's dupe, and the hard lines of the face softened in pity as he looked down on the prone figure in the bows. The contrast of the two appalled. There were grey hairs and a story of passion; here was youth itself, and yet how old in serpent wisdom. He flushed angrily. Flame and blackness of the pit had been around his last days in green Tiree and the flight thence; yet these, the chief actors in the tragedy, seemed dead to the terror and pity of it all. Oh, fool!—he said inwardly—fool! to have tied himself to creatures of such spirit! He had hoped to touch the heroic among the primitives of the isles; but now came disillusion complete, and already he wished himself back on the cobbles of Cheapside, where his father had both home and business-house ... Home ... the old folks and the little sister! ... the little sister a-dance on the stairs between the ancient parlour and the quarters where the clerks sat quill-scratching among bales of taffeta and paduasoy...

Cattanach's voice broke rudely in on his thoughts.

"A-dream, monsieur? You'll have us on the rocks once more. Let me have the helm, sir."

They had, indeed, again run close to Aros shore; and Fraser saw that with this wind and tide they could not make the mainland of Lorne ere evening fell. Should they anchor for the night or hold on? Even as he hesitated Cattanach's hand, reaching for the tiller, came in contact with his, and he shuddered and drew off as though a leper had touched him.

The movement said more than many words, for wrath suppressed turned the spy's cheek, pale though it was, to the death-white. Then the surgeon spoke, staring the while at the light of hate newly sprung to life in the basilisk eyes, and his utterance seconded his action.

"Ugh!" he said. "Keep off!"

The words were scarcely said, the movement hardly made, when Cattanach in a passion of rage threw himself towards the helm. But Fraser, with outstretched arm met the attack so suddenly as to fling him off to leeward, so that he fell back into the well of the cutter, where for a space he lay helpless, looking dazedly at the unmoved steersman swinging with the swell high above him. For a space only, though, for a quick launching of his foot towards the tiller, did what his hand had failed of doing, and wrenched the bar from the other's grasp. It jammed among smashed timbers in the cutter's side. The boat jibed at once. On the very instant a squall from Glenaros burst on them, and a faulty grommet gave way; then, the boom swinging free, cracked in two over the lee-runners, while the sea hissed white with repeated gusts. MacLean, suddenly awake, scrambled to the throat-halyards; Cattanach took the peak-lines; the surgeon tore the tiller free and threw his craft up in the wind. But before the others could loosen and lower, another gowff of icy air fell on them. The boat heeled in broken fashion: some of the lines ran suddenly, so that the gaff's throat jammed; and the boom swaying errantly, struck all save the helmsman to leaping waters.

Fraser stooped to throw an oar to them, and then, as he recovered himself, beheld the flood lipping the gunwale, and very sure and insistent, pour slowly in upon him.

He sprang clear of the sail, and was gripped by ice-cold water that now held nothing of the craft that might sustain him. Yonder, something like a seal's head bobbed obscurely as the sleet-shower parted for a moment; one of his fellow-voyagers he surmised. Then the salt spray passed his lips; and his breast came nigh to bursting—he was sinking, sinking, unplumbed tides thundering in his ears. But he rose again, and struck out for the vague mountain-mass in front. And so swimming, the sound of rushing waters gave place to a music, faint and delicate, and gracious airs of summer played around him; and he seemed to fall peacefully asleep.

6: The laird's study

THE house of Aros was an oblong block of building, which with some tiny offices and a walled garden flanking it, stared north-west up the Sound from a multitude of little windows in a harled façade that was bare and grey despite the porch's massed ivy. On all sides save seawards the pines stood close, tossing tops black and roaring in the sleet from the Kyle; while between the mansion and the straggle of township set near the shore, a river drummed in spate.

The laird's study was on the ground-floor, and a gap had been cut in the hedge opposite its windows, so that one saw over the stream and the hamlet roofs to the Sound dipt in by the Morvern and Ardnamurchan hills.

There were three people in this chamber, who looked out with varied emotions on the tempest; and so absorbed did all seem in the world external, that it might be thought there was some fascination for them in the beauty of the drifted showers that were like smoke for fineness, or in the white wonder of the spindrift whirling most arbitrarily around a single brown sail thrashing down on Aros. But each was busy with other thoughts than those that came with the wind and rain.

The man with the silver hair who turned from the far casement, and crossed the great room to sit in the ingle-neuk, one elbow on the knee-flap of his muddy riding-boot, beheld in the fire's red heart naught but a woman's face, so like to that of the girl in the window-seat yonder. "Her mother's eyes; her mother's smile," his sad heart said unceasingly.

Close by the lady stood a youth in kilt and plaid, who looked out into the winter gloaming, and saw nothing there but a great radiance and in the midst a happy bridal; for him, in truth, the wind's shrill pibroch was only a wedding-rant. Out from the mist and the gathering dusk, O miracle! beamed the face of the girl by his side.

And she—? Neither joy nor sadness possessed her quite, rather a rush of angry thoughts: her brother and his Prince in hiding in strange lands, even such hiding as this poor exile by the fire— her father's muddled estate-books—the last soumings of the tacksmen—the improved prices of black cattle—the continued emigrations of her countrymen to the Americas: a medley of poetry and prose all this, but never a thought for the suitor by her side. So forgetful, indeed, of his presence had she become, that when he spoke she started visibly.

"And what keeps Aros, cousin Morag?" he asked in tones so low as to leave himself unheard by the man in the distant ingle.

"His journey was to Corrie to-day, but he should be back ere this," she answered. "He went to reason with the bouman there, who speaks of a flitting to Georgia, no less." She folded her arms tightly as she spoke, tugging back her tartan screen from her shoulders in a movement of irritation.

"No less, you may well say," said the young man in surprise. "It will not be hereabouts, surely, that the rents are rising?"

"And how should they rise, cousin, when we have not a tacksman but is Highland, and among them never a Campbell?" said the girl bitterly. She flashed out a smile the next instant, however, and after knocking absently on the pane with her fingers for a little, turned an arch look on him and said: "It's a Lochaber lass who is going away with her people, and the Corrie bouman must be following her, amadan that he is."

"Lochaber, of course," said the chieftain. "And it's all one story there since the Red Fox was killed, though it's years ago: indeed, what can the poor folk do but leave? And as for following his heart, Morag MacLean, it is not me that will be blaming him, let me tell you." He glowed virtuously as he spoke, and the girl tossed her fair side-curls and smiled again.

But presently she fell moody, and picked up a month-old copy of a *Scots Magazine*.

"Read that," she said, pointing to a page. "There's a text for a sermon, cousin Kenneth."

He took the journal, and scanned the passage underbreath, the girl's foot tapping emphasis to his slow and lifeless rendering of the passage.

"Fort-William, Sept. 4th," it ran. "Yesterday sailed the 'Jupiter' from Dunstaffnage Bay, with about 200 emigrants on board for North Carolina, from Appin in North Argyleshire. Though formerly among the first to take up arms against the Reigning House, they now declare their readiness to support government, in case they find it necessary, on their arrival in America. They allege, in justification of their emigrating in these troublesome times, that it is better to confront an enemy in the wildest desert in that country, than to live to be beggars in their native land; that the oppressions of their landlords are such, that none but the timid will bear with them, while an asylum can be had in these wild, but happy regions of America, for those who have a spirit to seek for it. Many of them are among the best in circumstances in this neighbourhood; one of them went away with his seven sons. In short, the uncharitable exactions of the proprietors of lands will soon banish the old inhabitants, and depopulate this poor, but once happy country, which, as Ulysses says of Ithaca, is ' A barren clime, but breeds a generous race.'"

"Yes," said Morag, her colour high, her eyes on the storm-swept Kyle: "a generous race. But ... a barren clime? Ah! Eilean Aros, Eilean Aros, is it so they would miscall you: bens and glens and green silent places that my heart knows best? Never a blue shining sea-loch, never a dark lake of it all, Pennyfuaran, never a swirl of Lussa or Forsa, but the fish will leap to give it the he. Your birds thick in the waving birches, your deer throng on the misty corrie; it is not you they will be meaning, *mo chridhe*. And your happy folk, Eilean Aros; is it that they can leave you, *eilean aghmhor, eilean Dhia*?"

"Now here is one would leave to-morrow," said the young man warmly, "if the girl were a lass he kens, no Lochaber about her, but just plain Aros Isle."

"La, what happiness for the lass, sir, if she but cared for the man," said Morag, and again there came a rogue's smile to her lips.

"And there is just the trouble, cousin—"

"Listen," she interrupted—" Listen, and I'll tell you what I'd wish, if I were the maid from Benderloch." Her eyes sparkled; her colour came and went a little; but she had surely missed the serious airs of the chieftain, or ever she lightlied him as she did. "I had rather an old man with white hairs—a man who had seen Gledsmuir and Culloden, and a weary sight of days in caves and heather; I had rather it was Drumfin there that sighed his heart out on the quay at our sailing than the handsomest youth in all Keith's Highlanders. And for why, Mr. Hanover—for why—? Ah! but that's what I'll never tell to mortal, as long as white roses are as little worn as at present they seem to be, sir."

"Your returned exile then would have the advantage of his grey hairs, cousin," said Pennyfuaran; "I was but aged ten in the 'Forty-five, and could have ill told a dirk from a cruisie. But I'm thinking for some of us younger folk, Warburg Fight and Fellinghausen were just as namely as the fields you mention."

"Oh, Frederick, my Hanover!" hummed Morag, improvising for the moment.

"Fellinghausen," said the chieftain, unheeding the taunt. "'Twas there I was at my blackest and lowest, wounded and stricken, stark on my back in the dark and the rain, and only one thought to keep me alive, Morag." His face, handsome, though lacking something of manliness, was sun-browned, save for a patch on his forehead that lay fair and white, where the cock of his bonnet had protected it from exposure; and in this quarter-circle of clear skin there now came and went a tide of flushings. "Only one thought to keep me alive, I am saying, Morag—a picture, a memory of a day when you wore the tartan of the MacKinnon, and said a word I have not forgotten, for it brought me back from the dead."

"A schoolgirl's ploy, that tartan, and I take back the word," she rapped out with smiling lips, that were solemn the next moment, when in a flash she beheld the man in deadly earnest. "Oh, Pennyfuaran!" she said brokenly at the revelation his face now made.

He cast a glance down the room at the old man by the fire, stepped deeper into the window's embrasure, and took her hand. She did not withdraw it, yet her face, he saw, had fallen from brightness to wanness and her lips were trembling with fear. Like some chill air of the night a presage of defeat fell on him, and he dreaded the words he had to speak.

"Oh, cousin Kenneth," she said faintly.

"You shall not answer me now," he said; "I'll say no further to-day."

"Kenneth, Kenneth, it is but the one answer to-day, or to-morrow, or in time to come; and it must be—No."

He turned blank eyes on her, and put out a hand to the heavy curtain, as if to steady himself.

"God forgive me!" said Morag. "I feel as if I had done murder."

He only stared dully.

"Oh, be kind," she whispered: "we cannot part like this. And, indeed, and indeed, it is grieved for you I am, Kenneth dear. I feel like one who has taken a life."

"Taken a life," he said wearily. "And why not? Why not take it back? Did I not say it was life you gave me at Fellinghausen yonder, in the dark and the rain—the dark and the rain?"

He walked slowly away to the far window, and looking out, saw no longer the mist opening up visions golden—saw nothing now, indeed, but the riot of the hungry waves. The girl left tearful in the window-seat turned listlessly the faded pages of the journal in her lap. By the fire the old Jacobite still sat pondering.

Constraint was too weak a word for the atmosphere of the room, when the door opened suddenly, and there entered a tall, stout gentleman, unwigged, his bald pate a-glisten.

"Aros at last," cried the old man by the ingle. "Me the day! A woeful meeting!" And he rose to grip the laird's hands.

"Gillian? Aros to me from you? And why not Alasdair as of old?" asked the new-comer, looking down at him affectionately, and patting the long brown fingers.

"Ten years, Alasdair, ten years; and a-many things in this old noddle," said Drumfin, searching the lines of Aros' face lovingly, "make me forget even the language of the heart."

"The Gaelic, Gillian? Never?"

"Ay, the Gaelic, Alasdair. For Paris, Florence, Avignon, and where not else—a Babel of unchancy tongues, man—play the devil with the Gaelic as with much more. But, ah, my dear, it is worth all their palaces a thousand times to be at peace in Aros, even with a memory that fails."

"And, father," broke in Morag, "he is come straight from the cave on Beinn-nan-Uaimh, where he has lain for days, it seems. And he sat dripping wet for hours—where do you think—? in the kitchen, no less."

"It's an old trick, Alasdair," said Drumfin, smiling, "and it serves hereabouts as well as in the Hollands, I find. You are always safe for a warning at the back-door, you see; at the front entry, you are never sure. And in the kitchen you'll hear what the old campaigner has aye a fondness for—the news of the countryside."

"And 'tis only the littlest bite and sup he took, sir," went on Morag. "And he would not hear of his room being fired, until he had seen yourself, fearing danger to you. It's the red chamber I'll get ready, father?"

"Ay, the red room, Morag. Tuts! Gillian, you'll stay, you'll stay—Fawkener's men have left Duart for the mainland again, and we'll take our chance, man."

Morag gave a smile and a nod to Drumfin that said, "I told you so," as she went off to her housekeeping duties. But at the door she halted with never a smile, and her backward glance at her cousin was solemn and pitiful.

When she had gone, her father turned eagerly to the exile. "And—?" he said, and paused: for not till then had he noticed Pennyfuaran's presence. At the entrance of Aros, but a moment before, the young chieftain had turned, and despite his bitterness of soul, could not but devour with admiring regard the picture the two old comrades made as they stood clasped there, smiling, fraternal. But now he caught the glance old MacLean gave him as he halted in his speech, saw its import in a flash, and his face flamed scarlet. Here was added gall to a cup already full.

"You might have spared me that, Aros," he said, not without a touch of dignity, as he made for the door. "My people were as fairly Charlie's men as yours, and did as little, more's the pity! But we may not be so far back, next rising," he added, darkly.

Drumfin stayed him with a hand on his shoulder. "Stir not for me, sir," he said, "for I've nothing to hide from you. Aros was a bit flustered at the sight of your kilt, and he meant his look for discretion only. You ken whose name was on his tongue?"

"Sit you down, Kenneth," said Aros. "I ettled no harm. 'Twas but the glint of your uniform that put me out for the moment."

"As for another rising—" said the exile. He shook a dubious head. "Expresses I have in plenty —from the Gasks, from Dr. King, from Elcho, from d'Aiguillon—and all anent that same. 'Sound here,' and 'sound there'…'Spier this man,' and 'Spier that,' they say … Oh, and happy I'd be to spier, if aught might come of it!"

"My God!" said Aros. "Does he not know how things stand … himself?" He gave the last word in a whisper.

"Himself," said Drumfin sadly, his face lit with a pale radiance. "Ah, yes, he knows. In his heart he knows it futile, and that's his hell."

Pennyfuaran took a deep breath; Aros gulped noisily; Drumfin hung his head. There was silence as of an oratory in the dim room for a space.

"He knows," went on the old Jacobite. "And yet they deave with their questionings. They deave me, although 'twas weel-kenned of most when I last left France, for what I came over-seas— nought but a double-rent, and the indulging of an old man's fancy for the desire of his eyes—a sight of his native glens."

The talk drifted on; old times, old friends, the changing world, the coming days. So, over a punch which Aros brewed, the two ancients renewed their earlier years; and as the elders waxed arduous in reminiscence Pennyfuaran was left out in the cold. Again he turned to the window-seat, brooding afresh on his new-born pain, and absently watching the clouds forming from the void and breaking in rack and flight to the zenith—noting the play of the stormy waters around the little sail thrashing down the Sound.

The next instant he cried aloud and stood with face close-pressed to the window-pane, for a line of flying spray was scouring white across the Kyle, and the sail was gone. The others crossed the room quickly to the casement, and he explained rapidly. But gloaming was fast thickening, and with the squall had arrived an added mirk, so that nothing could be clearly seen.

Drumfin was the first to speak.

"Quick, Alasdair," he cried to Aros, who still stood at gaze. "Lights! Lights and men!"

Strangely enough the laird answered him in Latin:

"*Ruunt et terras turbine perflant*," he quoted. "You're the ready one as ever, Gillian. Lights and men! Lights and men! And now, as in 'Forty-five, all I'm good for is a phrase from Virgil."

His feet shuffled undecidedly; and it was not until Drumfin put a hand on his elbow and hurried him into the transe, that he was himself again.

Pennyfuaran was cloaked and ready, when they reached the hall; and just then Morag ran downstairs with a lit cruisie shaded by pink finger-tips.

At sight of her so circumstanced, an old-time memory of her mother came to Drumfin, and all unthinking, he saluted her with a scrape and a bow of the fashion of thirty years before. Then, recovering himself confusedly, he joined the others. The next instant they were out in the gloom and the rain, among the group of fishers and crofters already on the trot for Aros Point, where, with this wind and tide, the foundering seas were wont to bear their spoil.

7: Under Aros roof-tree

THE wind flowed gustily all night long across the three miles of the island's waist that divided the Sound from waters Atlantic. Aros lay at the east of this rift in the hills, and the spruce and larch sheltering the great house soughed stormily to the ear of the servitor in an upper room, keeping vigil by a castaway from the wrecked cutter.

Always was there heard the swish of the branches, the singing and drumming of the river swirling seawards in the blackness outbye. But at times a sudden access of fury took the gale. Far away the hint of some new trouble brewing would be audible above the more constant sounds of storm, and, swiftly gaining strength, this rumour became a tumult of a sudden. Momentarily and furiously the blast possessed the house, until it trembled; then, as it swept over whipped waters to Morvern, what seemed, by contrast, the very soul of quiet succeeded, and after a space, the ear was again aware of nought but the sough of the firs and the noise of the river girning at the bridge. But even in the tempest an islesman will find lullaby, and soon the watcher dozed at his post.

In dreams, Ian Fraser swam upwards through racing tides to a star burning solitary in the night above a woman's face; a star, golden, celestial in its calm shining; a woman's face—so sweetly kind, so beautiful, the grey eyes lit with some marvel of a great desire. Yet he awoke only to the guttering of a smoky candle set before the grotesque features of a goblin.

He rubbed heavy eyelids with his left hand, for a sound of pain warned him of some injury to his right, and rubbing once more, observed that the goblin nodded and snored in sleep. Despite his general sense of *malaise*, he smiled at the odd face with the peaked eyebrows and tufted beard set above the tiny body. He smiled, and yet he sighed, for the reality gave too great a contrast to the vision. Again he recalled his lady of dream —that lovely face transparent in its purity, its longing for some grand miracle of the goodly life; and he fashioned in fancy once more the very accidents of her dress, the velvet snood, the fair side-curls, the tartan screen. If this were dream, was never dream so real, and still so fair.

And so, incredulous, he gazed at the slumbering servant, and sighed again. Then he stole gently from bed, and as he reached the floor, discovered with a groan that his injuries included a sprained ankle.

"Hand and foot," he said, "yet alive. But where—?"

He found his garments dry and warm beside a fire of peats, and dressing in part, he limped silently around the shadowed room, nursing his arm the while. There were some chairs, a table, a chest, and a second tester-bed, which was tenantless. The door unbarred easily, as did also the two windows. From each casement, open in turn, he tried to interpret the outer world, but the obstinate dark still held, and little was to be seen save a forest of tossing branches, black against a fainter blackness. It was as he turned away from the second window that his eye fell for the first time on the candlestick that supported the tallow's pungent flame. He was in a mood to suspect every danger, but this observe gave his suspicions pause for the moment. Come! He was in luck; this was no mere inn, it would appear, for the piece was of silver and massive.

So much content came with this reasoning, that he halted to debate the wisdom of awakening the attendant, when there fell a lull in the noises of the storm. And just then, the imperfectly closed window nearest him opening slowly inwards with the wind, a chink of glasses came from below, and, faintly and afar, a musical chuckle, bird or human, he could hardly say.

Instantly he leant outwards from the sill of the window. The rain had gone, and from the rack and scud an occasional star peered out at the only light in this strange house, the candle beside the nodding goblin yonder. But was it the only light? He pressed still further outwards, and saw a luminous line fall thin and clear on grasses swaying ghost-like in the night-wind.

Coming back to the door he listened, but unavailingly, for the wind cooed and groaned anew through every stick and stone of the place. The very sound of it boded danger, and urged him to further search and caution; and so he loosed the bar and stole out to where the well of the stair opened, a cavern for blackness. A plain balustrade of wood met his hand; gropingly he followed this to the wall, and then, returning, found the rail shaking a trifle on the curve of the steps. He moved cautiously downwards, but slipping, caught at the baluster with his injured arm, withdrew it in an agony of torture, and fell with a rattle to the foot of the stair. His head entangled in a fold of curtain, he found himself with his nose at a strip of light coming from below a door, and his injured limb doubled under him at such a disadvantageous angle, that the pain accompanying his attempts at rising brought him nigh to sickness and fainting. He could hear no sounds of alarm from behind the door; the voices there were in quiet talk, and he felt sure the hurricane's outcry had hidden the noise of his disaster.

But now he saw himself faced by a compulsory eavesdropping, and this, even if peril menaced, his spirit could not brook, so at the next savage onset of storm he tried again to rise. Again he failed, and sank back, covered with sweat, and half-swooning. Perforce he had to hear the words from behind the curtained door.

"I spoke of it in Rome to Sir Hector many a year ago, just the month before his death, indeed, and that was in 'Fifty," said a calm voice. 'As you ken, he knew the clans and the countrysides as well as most, and even then, when the occasion was the more fitting, he was never of that way of thinking."

"And Elcho? What does Elcho say?" was asked in youthful tones.

"Elcho?" said yet another voice, and there came a musical chuckle. "I'll warrant his standing is only this:—' *Redde argentum!*' It will be nothing with him, but, 'Try again, or turn again, my Prince: go or stay. But pay me back my loan of fifteen hundred.'"

"Yes," said the first speaker—and something of passion was now in his voice. "That's Elcho— poor Elcho! And more than he have the same tune, I fear. Then there are Forbes and the Oliphants asking the Prince for an outspoken word on the Church. Lord!—how can the man have ought clear on divinity, when in the humanity he sees about him there is so little to put faith in ... Too many Elchos, I tell you ... Would to God he had but a dozen true hearts patterned on Lochiel that's dead and awa'—I tell you they'd save him yet—some few that would bring him back the best of his own lost youth—that or nothing."

The sounds of the tempest drowned all for a little, and then in a lull came the low even tones again:

"And, as you ken, the lave in Scotland just lost what little heart they had, when Archie Cameron went to his death."

What more the listener heard was ravelled, less from any indistinctness of the words than from the increasing faintness caused by the pain of his injured arm. But his senses were still so far his own as to show him that here was a household of Jacobite conspiracy, as flagrant as that of the isle-men in Tiree; and here was he, a Government servant, still striking blindfold into the midst of these coils of treachery to his masters. What to do? What to do?

In another overwhelming of the place in the noises of the outer night, he stumbled with a great effort to his knees. But his arm doubled, and he fell with half his weight upon the door, so that it gave lightly. His eyes were dazzled of a sudden, by the light that filled the room he had so unceremoniously entered; there was a clatter of glasses, a smell of wine that spilled and sprayed in his face momently as it fell; whilst an old gentleman with a bald pate, half-entangled in a tablecloth, slid to the floor, and throttled him in fumbling fashion.

"Death without priest to you!" spluttered his assailant in Gaelic. "Listening? Scum of the pit! Take your knife to him, Pennyfuaran, and give him a better end than he deserves."

Above the bald pate Fraser saw another face, white with passion—that of a young man in Highland army costume. He saw his hand, too, and it held the black knife ready. But he was also aware of a thin sword-blade sweeping over all three, and in one fiery, gliding movement, threatening each equally. For if its point menaced his heart, its edge came close to the hairless scalp of the elderly warrior, and was not far from the knife-arm of the younger. He beheld the wielder of the weapon in a stately old gentleman, whose bronzed oval of a face framed in silver hair, smiled down on him reassuringly. There was something strangely familiar to Fraser in the new-comer's aspect.

"Keep clear, Drumfin," cried the youth in the kilt and plaid. "I have him—spy that he is!"

"And if you but scratch him, Pennyfuaran, I have you. Lord! what wild cats we have become! Even the meditative Aros, who thinks himself good only for Latinity, has turned to war again. Come out, Alasdair. Come out, Pennyfuaran."

They obeyed, crouching from underneath his sword-arm, and leaving the other erect with his hanger's point still at Fraser's breast.

"You are our guest from the sea?" asked the swordsman.

The surgeon was too dazed to reply. One word sang in his brain: one word only had meaning— "Drumfin." It was by this name the young Highlander had addressed the man who stood over him —the man who but now had saved his life by his ready sword. Here again was this courtly old gentleman, with all the airs of a *maitre-d'armes*, —the Jacobite agitator—the fugitive he had tracked through half Tiree. Of a truth, the tables were turned with a vengeance.

"Will you explain your presence here, sir?" asked Drumfin, releasing his guard so that Fraser could prop himself on his left side.

In a word or two the surgeon depicted his amazement and sense of danger on awaking in a strange house; his cautious reconnaissance; his accident; his weakness that hardly left him now the wit to frame his thoughts.

"I see—I see—" said the swordsman encouragingly.

"Let me ask him a little more pressingly, sir," interposed the sceptical Pennyfuaran; and he crossed the black knife to his left oxter. Before any could speak or move, all the barbarian in the youth flashed out, and he flung himself under the swordsman's steel, making for the throat of the fainting man.

The hanger gave a little twist, and nicked across the knuckles of the chieftain's right hand, so that the knife fell even before the blood showed.

"You are hasty," said Drumfin. "The man is really fainting, I believe, and it's me that this concerns more than any of you. Aside, man, aside, —spy or no spy, he's my concern, I say."

Bestriding Fraser in a single movement, he thrust his thigh forward suddenly and taking the shoulder of Pennyfuaran as if by accident, sent him sideways.

The sick man saw and heard no more just then, for the long-drawn agony of his doubled arm suddenly swept him into unconsciousness.

When he came to himself, he found that he was in his bedchamber again. The candle still flickered smokily, but through the lozens of the window he saw the dawnlight trembling in a sky of quiet grey clouds, and he noted that the crying of the winds was gone. The old gentleman with the shining pate bent over him, a bowl of posset in his hand, and at the first quiver of Fraser's eyelids he showed discoloured teeth in a musical chuckle. With alacrity the young man made as if to sit up in bed, but sank back with a cry of pain as his weight fell once more on the hurt arm; and solicitous and fearing the worst, the laird set the dish aside, and shuifled ineffective on the floor, stuttering the while. The sea-waif quickly recovered, however, and raising himself with his left hand, stretched it in turn for the vessel and took a long draught.

"More wine than milk, I fear," said the laird. "I mixed it hurriedly."

Fraser thanked him with a smile, set the bowl down, and forthwith stripping his right forearm, patted the swollen muscles, turning the wrist gingerly and grimacing all the time. So preoccupied with his examination indeed did he become, that he forgot the old man, gravely observant, with airs as respectful as if some rite of the Church were being performed, and when he looked up, he flushed with annoyance at having allowed himself anything but a demonstration in private.

"Is it broken it is?" asked the laird.

"Faith! how should I know?" said Fraser, fencing the question.

"It's a leech's skill you have in the moving of it anyway," said the other.

"Then God help the leech's patients, if his skill be not more than mine. But 'tis a sling it wants, I should say."

"Will a scarf serve?" said Aros, giving him a silken square from the table. "There's a surgeon-man in the isle—a MacNab. But there's many a hill to hunt for him, aye travelling as he is."

"The isle," cried Fraser, for it came on him with a horror that he might in some strange fashion have been carried back to Tiree. "What isle, sir?"

"Eilean Aros," said the laird.

"Ah!" sighed the youth in a sudden relief, as he knotted the silk in a triangle and adeptly slipped head and arm to place in it—" Ah! And you took me from the sea, sir?"

"From the tangle and the black rocks of it, rather—a much easier task."

"You got the others?"

"None."

"They were swept off before we foundered," explained Fraser. "We were three in all."

"Peace to their souls," said Aros softly. And then as softly, but with shifting eyes and shuffling feet he asked: "A long voyage?"

Fraser caught a glint of the other's suspicious glance, and parried.

"Far and far enough," he said. "From Uist all the way, and a sorry day it was we ever left Lochboisdale." The half-truth stuck in his throat, and he reddened. Then, in order to avoid further questioning, he said, stammering the while, "But you must tell me to whose kindness I owe my life. My own name is Fraser, and I went south on business of the King's Navy."

"A good Scotch name," said the laird, his eye still sidelong. "You'll ken the Lovat country, I'll warrant?"

"I know what you mean," said the young man. "But no; I am London-born: and till a little ago I never saw the Highlands save from shipboard."

Aros' brow cleared quickly. "But you were asking my name," he said. "And it's just Alasdair MacLean of Aros: a poor man and a poor country."

He turned to trim candle and fire, and so missed the dropping of the jaw and the general air of discomfiture which Fraser now presented.

"So, that's it," murmured the youth, settling down in bed so as to bring his face into shadow. "It only needed this to give the final turn to the comedy."

It was not enough, he bitterly told himself, that he should owe his life to the sword of the man whom he had hounded through Tiree only a fortnight before, but now, when he would fain show his gratitude, his very proximity threatened the safe hiding of the Jacobite. For, outside Tiree, he remembered, the nearest friend of the unhappy man he had aided in his flight thence, was the laird of Aros, and it was here that Chisholm's avengers—the Sunivaig MacLeans, would ferret first. In their view, he doubted not, he was art and part in the manslaughter, and he did not overlook his own danger. But what concerned him was the eye of publicity that his night's lodging would turn on Drumfin's place of hiding, and at any moment some of the garrison of soldiery in the island might hear of the exile's stay in Aros. His teeth clenched at the thought that his mere presence should so imperil the safety of this man he had so misunderstood. And straightway he determined that, lamed though he was in hand and foot, he would be packing ere night came.

"A bonnie pickle, as my father would say," he muttered underbreath—" A bonnie pickle. And Aros Point and the black rocks of it, and me wet in the sea-tangle, would be a prettier story, I'm thinking."

Soon the laird, hearing deep suspirations that warned him further talk would keep his guest from needed sleep, stole from the room. But the eyes turned to the wall were for long unclosed. Later, the sea-waif slept, and again he dreamt of the star and the woman's face, alike in their unearthly beauty, and dreaming still, awoke to a sound of a clear high singing.

The winter sunshine filled the room, and across the notes of the song, came the trill of a robin in the pine branch that swept the opened casement. Fraser robed as quickly as his hurts would allow, and stole to the window. Past the corner of the building ran a gravelled path, edged with box and ending in a clump of yews—the entrance to some kind of garden, he surmised; and behind the trees he caught glimpses of something light like a woman's dress. Thence came the singing, sweetly wild, and with plaintive minor notes—a farewell—a lament—a strain to bring the ardent tear, if one but knew the tongue of this strange land. "Return, return," the melody seem to say; and it brimmed with regret, with longing, with sorrow, it charmed him to oblivion of his wounds. And then the singer came into view and moved towards him slowly.

She was a young woman clad in a dress of some kind of sprigged calico over which she wore a little grey cloak and hood; and she carried a garden basket filled with white roses. The hood had fallen back, so that the surgeon saw her fair side-curls and the black velvet band retaining them. Her face—? her face —? It was his lady of dream! She still sang, her brown eyes musing and passionate, her voice breaking in the very ecstasy of art—oh, surely the face of an angel rapt above all earthly things.

But as the girl caught sight of the youth at the casement her song ended abruptly, and for a moment she halted, the great eyes upturned, the least hint of confusion in her air. Then an arch look stole to the earnest face, a queer little line of humour twitched the solemn lips, and a high colour crept to her cheek.

"Flowers, sir? Will you buy?" she cried, holding up the white roses towards his window, and smiling outright. Then came a little laugh, and she glided from view around the angle of the house.

Fraser stood as if petrified.

"No dream, but the truth in very deed," he said. "And not too elysian for a laugh and a taunt, the rogue! So she thinks I do not know the meaning of white roses? Does she, too, hold me for a Hanoverian spy, I wonder?"

He paced the bare chamber, debating the situation anew, for already a score of reasons presented themselves against too precipitate a departure from Aros. It was in vain he told himself that he was there to no purpose; that his paths were laid elsewhere; that he but endangered Drumfin by his presence. Another voice argued that he must stay since he owed the exile some requital, and on a point of peril to the old man, he might be of some service. Again, by remaining he might the readier clear himself of suspicion before these worthy folk of Aros. And so on, and so on.

But through all the mist of his imaginings a fair face shone, shaking sunny side-curls roguishly, and whispering:

"White roses! White roses! Flowers, sir? Will you buy?"

8: Morag

STRAIGHT and tall as a spear, despite his limp, was this young man that went about Aros township after three days more of his bed. The gossip ran that MacNab, the island surgeon, was expected soon, and that the stranger awaited his skill: otherwise his business had instantly taken him south. But some of the older folk, who had recognised Drumfin, and in whose remembrance Culloden day burned clear and bright as the fire of the torturer, were none so sure of the tale, and, with nodding heads, looked uncanny things.

He had a kindly face, if a plain one, this shipwrecked man; yet clean-shaven as he was, you saw his features for strong and resolute. As often as not he walked abroad bareheaded, a shovel hat of MacLean's under his arm, his own dark hair tied in a bag-ribbon. What took the *cailleachean* more than anything, setting them to vigorous scoldings of the distrustful among their men-folk—was his essay at the Gaelic: a phrase or two picked up from his father, and these in a voice, manly, with notes of rare tenderness. This voice was his grand asset against suspicion; but it is also true that he had a way with little children that went to the heart. Tiny maids smiled fearlessly to him, as they had never smiled to a grown-up all their days; and when he carved a ship for Callum Beag's little son, whittling it with his left hand from a billet of wood held between his knees, the child and his mates crowded silently around and hailed him with frank looks as a comrade who understood the freemasonry of boyhood.

But at times the sense of intimacy failed; the stranger seemed alien, restless, and impatient; and this cottar and that had repeated enquiries from him as to the coming of the surgeon from the Ross. Even the laird, abstracted as he was in his schemes of adjusting his properties' management to the changing times-—bored daily now, as Martinmas term drew near, by tacksman and crofter regarding wadsets and services—even the worried laird saw through Fraser's courteous attempts at dissimulation of his uneasiness. Vaguely he now thought of the young man as a naval officer on some Government survey or the like, for Drumfin had not discovered Fraser's identity to him. Spy he could not hold him, let Pennyfuaran rage as he would. Was it not plain he but awaited the coming of Doctor MacNab to mend his arm? And yet there was a gravity in the demeanour of his guest, a suddenness in the way he roused himself from fits of meditation, that bespoke something more than this only. "God help him! it's maybe my own case," said Aros half-humorously, half-bitterly, and holding his tobacco pipe aloft to chuckle more at ease. "God help him! He may be even in the south there as I am here — setting tacks of good land far below market value to keep old friends from breaking."

A week had passed since the injury to the arm, and it had become increasingly painful; the sprained foot, however, though weak, was now a bagatelle. But it was abundantly plainer every day now that the stranger fretted over the island surgeon's delay, and Aros was apologetic on Doctor MacNab's behalf.

"A little old body, skilly enough," he said, "but just ganging where it likes him best, when his calls are many. He'll but leave the house of his last patient when he's by with him — kill or cure. And there's many a clachan to hunt or we find him."

Fraser acquiesced moodily and pondered the more. He noted that Aros' household had suddenly reduced itself since he had been able to leave his room. Pennyfuaran, he heard, had gone to the south of the isle, where his home lay. Drumfin he had not seen since his midnight rencounter with him; yet the surgeon had an uneasy feeling that he still haunted the house or its environs, and that his own presence there was the cause of the exile's secrecy. Remained Aros and Morag, the girl with the white roses — his lady of dream. She perplexed and fascinated by turns, for something of the smiling disdain in her offer of the roses had never quite left her attitude towards him; and this was a challenge to clear himself of suspicion, not because she had made it so, but because Fraser was Fraser.

He saw little of her except at meal times, and then, save for a flash, of merriment that at intervals transformed her face, she seemed as abstracted and watchful as her father in the presence of her guest. But she could be just, the surgeon argued; the lift of that fine brow, the candour of those eyes, meant something her rogue's smile could not gainsay — those eyes, what colour were they now, grey or blue? Light-hearted, full of the joy of life if you will, yet a word or two of hers at dinner last night had shown him her sympathy for her poor cottars, her understanding of the tragedy of a hard lot without remedy. Sincerity, courage? Yes, she had these, he said.

It was after a mid-day meal, passed for the most part in attempts of all three to make the infrequent breaks in the accompanying silence less boring than the silence itself, that Fraser, coming down to the lawn paced there for a little, deep in thought. For the hundredth time he asked himself, why should he stay on in Aros? Why should he longer risk delay in the matter of his arm? The whereabouts of Drumfin were now unknown to him, and without his confidence, he was scarcely in a position to do him a service, should occasion arise. As to the girl and her father — why should his peace of mind be perturbed because they misunderstood a chance comer across their paths such as he? To many, he knew, the affair would appear so trivial as to cost not a single heartburning. For a moment he assumed the true spirit of the Pharisee, and told himself how differently any of his recent shipmates would have met the situation: a word or two of blustering protest, a quarrel, and straightway a departure for the dockyards of the south, where a tale of Jacobite conspiracy, in a lonely Hebridean isle, would be magnified into a French invasion. He smiled grimly as he drew the picture, and more grimly still as he beheld himself embarked on a different course—a course that would take him, he knew, far from a speedy return to the orlop-deck of the *Theseus*. Yet this smile ironical was one of recognition also, since he saw himself about to indulge a familiar passion, that of burning his boats behind him: for it was thus he was wont to secure himself against retreat from his ideals. In the end, however, he had a moment of insight and self criticism.

"Duty be damned, sir: it's sheer vanity," he told himself, as his contemplated course of action came clearly into view.

Yet the truthfulness of this conclusion was easily outweighed by its unpalatableness, and he soon took a more charitable view of the case. His plans must have matured rapidly, for he suddenly halted in his slow pacing, wheeled right about, and went off swiftly to the cottage of Callum Beag. Here he found the tiny one with the ruddy curls, and, selecting his billet with care, he set to work whittling untiredly. Golden-head asked what queer ships were these he made; and Callum himself cast not a few wondering glances at the flat slips of wood the young man fashioned. Little Neil was assured that a big and proper ship would be built tomorrow, but it needed many kisses from Fraser to chase the tears away, when the brown eyes saw the result of the day's toil stowed away in the big playfellow's coat-skirts.

The wooden slips were still in the pockets of the surgeon when early in the forenoon of the following day he made his way to the garden that lay by the side of Aros House. It was an old pleasure-ground, cinctured by high walls hid in a green cloak of ivy and tiny fern, and without this again by a screen of oaks. So sheltered was it that October airs had left roses and hollyhocks in wild profusion and full bloom. Less favoured flowers were gone a month past, but these held out gallantly, and backed by hedges of dark laurel and copper beech, made a brave splash of colour in a place with more than a hint in it of the dour and sombre. The gravelled walks between box borders converged to a mounded sundial, about whose base harts tongue and royal grew lush and large, and set facing this, on a crescent of turf, was a bench of rough-hewn stone, mossy and weather-beaten.

Fraser seated himself on the worn flags. It was the ninth day of his sojourn in Aros, and a grey day it was, the clouds too much for the sun, a wind from the sea volleying through the glens, but absent from this nook of perfume and rich hues. Of a morning, he had observed that Miss Morag came here for flowers, presumably for house decoration, and so he awaited her approach, the volume in which he meant to appear absorbed, dangling at the length of his long left arm.

At a click of the gate he rose, and bareheaded as he was, lifted his hand to his forehead in salute to the girl as she entered. Morag flushed a little at sight of him and gave him good-morning. She had indeed seen very little of the mysterious stranger save at meal-times, and although she joined in the general conspiracy of suspicion regarding him, at heart she was frankly curious as to the real nature of events, and not unprepared to find herself mistaken.

"Does the arm progress to health again, Mr. Fraser?" she interrogated a trifle nervously.

"Indeed, and that is what I ask myself for several days now, madam," he said. "But what is an arm broken, when the question is one of the breath of one's lips?"

"And that is truth," she replied. "Yet I could wish all the same that Doctor MacNab were come." An awkward pause and then: "Are not the flowers wonderful?" She smiled archly, and fingered a white rose with meaning. "Even with winter coming over the hill, see how they bloom. The whole isle is green all the year round almost, and this corner keeps so storm-sheltered. As for snow— it never lies in these parts over three days at a time save every fourth year or so. Oh, it's we are the lucky folk, Mr. Fraser! For look even at this matter of the snow, sir: how different on the mainland now?"

How queenly and guileless she looked as she bent her steady gaze on him, and yet—and yet, how furious-fast her heart was beating for a space, lest he should guess the presence there of the imp inquisitive that prompted the question. Would he talk of the south and himself? she wondered. . "Why, yes," he said, "it is indeed vastly different in the south. The post-runners or the mail-drivers on the Borders could tell you a tale of turnpikes in February or March. 'tis days or weeks at times that the snow lies breast high there. And as for Christmas weather—"

He broke off abruptly as two figures appeared on a side-path. One was a tall gentleman with silver hair, his costume, save for his fall and ruffles of white lace, wholly of black. The other was a rough packman fellow with a box of red wood on his shoulders, and a *cromag* in his hand; he was speaking in a soft Irish brogue, but ceased abruptly at sight of the girl and Fraser. The first-comer bowed to Morag, and then with his uncouth companion passed hurriedly out of sight behind some yews.

"Ah, Drumfin!" said the surgeon, half to himself, yet half-aloud, somewhat startled at the apparition.

He recovered instantly from his surprise, but what was his confusion to behold Morag breathing fast, her cheeks white and red by turns, her eyes fires that scorched. It was as if she had dealt him a blow, and instinctively he put up his hand to ward himself, and fell back a step.

"You spoke, Mr. Fraser, did you not?" she asked chilly.

"Madam?" he stammered.

"You will explain, sir, will you not?"

"Madam—how?"

"How you come to know this gentleman's name, sir?"

Fraser saw himself trapped. It was plain the girl had heard nothing of his meeting with Drumfin on his first night in Aros, and he looked round reddening at the thought that he must give her a story that her father had thought it wise to withhold. How to justify, how to disentangle his actions from appearances dubious in their very essence? He spread hands deprecating, but her foot tapped angrily on the russet leaves.

"An answer," she said, unmoved, unbending.

"Listen, then," said he. "Conceive my situation on my first awakening in Aros, when my last memories were of rocks and breakers. Gratitude and gratitude only, was in all my thoughts."

Her foot still tapped; her eyes still burned.

"Gratitude, yes. But could I tell you what dangers came before the storm and my casting— away, dangers not to the body alone, madam, but to the very element you deem me lacking in, a little thing called honour—if I could show you this, you would understand how to gratitude succeeded alarm."

Briefly he recounted the happenings on his first night under her father's roof. He flushed a little as he told of his discovery at the study door; he flushed more darkly still as he observed a little threatening movement of her brow and lips that cried "Eavesdropper" louder than any words, and he paused as the meaning of the look came on him suddenly.

"Ah," he said simply, "you will not understand."

"And little wonder!" she cried cruelly. "It was not among court trustys I was bred."

"Trusty?" he said, wincing, white to the lips. "I am not that. I have told you the cold truth. But I am no spy."

"At least you're in the Hanoverian's service," she said, with a fine inconsequence. "And you're Hanover in politics also, I'll wager."

"That's as maybe, madam. Yet till this moment I have never heard it charged as the equivalent of the informer's meanness."

"You'll be telling me next, you're Jacobite," she said.

"And I shall think it no crime, Miss MacLean, to confess I am not."

"Tush! then it's plain you're Hanover."

"Madam, if you'll have it so." He bowed in irony. "But are we not twenty years back, if we make the distinction?"

"Are we indeed so far afield?" she asked, her uplifted eyebrows eloquent. "Then why does a poor gentleman from Paris so disquiet you?"

"The Prince—" he began and paused. "Surely you cannot think that cause anything but hopeless?"

"Ah, there shows the advocate at last!" she cried. "Hopeless? And why, sir? Do you think the Highlands are of yesterday, that even our Prince's failings can make us forget the tales of the years, or the hopes they stir? Give us again the old ways and the old life. Is it not worth wounds and cold hearths to bring them back? Give us the chief—the kindly chief, and his people— the kindly people. And let the Prince—." She halted.

"Let the Prince take his own gate?" said Fraser, smiling.

A little dimness came to the girl's fine eyes. "Ah, no," she said softly. "It's in a green quiet glen of old Albainn I'd make his home—one whence he'd see the sky stretched over the sea, and the sun going down in it— where he'd be having the dear memories of the days of the heroes. And, oh, it's kindness, kindness, and nothing of reproach I'd be for giving him!"

"And would he reign, your fairy Prince?" asked the man smiling.

She turned on him, elate of a sudden, quivering with emotion, her ideal on her brow. "And even if he has failed us, Mr. Fraser—even if he has failed us? Look you, there's never a clear night in Aros, sir, but I can find a new star in the sky." A prophetess—a sybil—beautiful and young, yet with the wisdom of years on her lips—it was thus he saw her as he stood at gaze, and her passion of conviction was so infective that he sighed.

"Ah," he said, "if I could only believe. But I am, I fear, a Laodicean for either faction. ' A plague on both your houses,' say I."

"Even Hanover?" she asked with the eagerness of the proselytiser who sees a hint of response to her efforts.

"Even Hanover," he said, "since I've seen the Americas, where in his own colonies your Hanoverian oppresses to the death."

There was silence for a little now, and Fraser made an effort to leave this ground already so torn with the conflict as to render further fencing unsafe.

"But all this is foreign to your question regarding winter in the south, Miss Morag," he said abruptly.

The girl reddened, remembering her ruse to bring this man to speak of himself. Her head dropped suddenly to watch a foot tossing dead leaves to and fro, and so brought her fair side-curls from out her hood of pink sarcenet to hide cheeks flaming. In her present mood of missionary of her ideals, she was wildly angry with herself for the prying meanness of her earlier attitude, as she reckoned it; and she did not answer.

"And yet, madam, if you will but allow, I had rather turn to something of more moment than any of our recent topics. Will you overlook what must seem a monstrous impertinence in me, if I speak of a matter personal, and on so brief acquaintance?"

But the girl was still wroth with herself, and therefore distrustful of a further passage of arms.

"You must make me no confidences, sir," she said fierily. "I forbid it."

"I beg of you—" he protested.

"Nay, then, you send me away," and she made as if to leave him.

"I must risk the offence, madam," he said. "You desert a sinking ship, I fear."

The metaphor caught her, and she halted on the going.

"It was of set purpose I came here this morning," he went on. "It is all so sudden, so strange, so abrupt, I know; but I came to ask a service of you. There is none here in whom I can so safely confide."

Startled anew, Morag looked up at his grave face, but composed herself with an effort.

"Then in that case," she said, "it were best that we walked up and down while I gather a rose or two for my basket. "For," she added, innocently enough imputing herself, "I must avow that curiosity is not a new trait in some folks hereabout."

9: Fraser's tale

THEY paced slowly under the ivy-covered walls, and round the roses odorous; and here, as in a cloistral stillness, they heard the sea-wind calling in the outer world of shore and hill, while not a dead leaf stirred to it at their feet.

"Yes," said Fraser, "I have thought of everyone: yourself remains. And first of all it is some part of my own story you must hear, for it may help you to a better opinion of me than of a spy."

"Mr. Fraser!" she cried, protesting.

"Your pardon, then. But here is the tale," he said ... "I have been for three years surgeon in the Navy of this Hanoverian you detest, and—to be exact—I was surgeon's mate five weeks ago on board the *Theseus*, 84 guns. It was late July when we left Louisburg, and early August when we came down to the Virginias, and so home."

"The Virginias?" cried Morag, "Why 'tis there that Cousin Elspeth lives. Pray, tell me, is there further trouble with the Governor?"

"Still trouble, madam. And to my mind the Assembly has the right of it."

"Yes, yes," she answered. "But do not let me interrupt, I beg of you.—The *Theseus*, you said?"

"The *Theseus*, yes. Our orders were sealed. But when we were nearing Scotland, it was plain our business lay there, for no sooner did we lift the Lewis than we set to cruising about it in the strangest of fashions."

"Ah!" said Morag, her grey eyes flickering swiftly with sudden fire.

"And if it was not the Long Isle, it was Skye, and in rough weather, too. It was common talk that the French desired a diversion from the attentions of King George on the St. Lawrence; and, indeed, to speak plainly it was hinted your friend, the Young Chevalier, was about to aid them by repeating his Scottish visit of fourteen years ago."

He stopped, laughing gently but outright in his scepticism.

The fire in the grey eyes flamed high. "It seems you think it no likely tale, sir," she said coldly. "But pray, go on. I remember the storms of August."

"The storms, yes, and fogs also, Madam. We had to anchor three days in Lochboisdale, no pilot to be had, and the mist like curtains of parchment.

When we came out it was clearer a little, though still dirty weather, and we drove south and south, until at the end we lost our reckoning 'twixt Coll and Tiree."

"I remember the fogs," said Morag impassively.

"We flew signals, we fired guns, and at last a smack came off from the Tiree shore, with a pilot on board. He, however, would come with us on one condition only; and since we could not press-gang him in the middle of squalls and mist, we had to accept his terms. His kinsman was at death's door, and if he came aboard us, then we must send a surgeon ashore to him: he would not leave his cutter, he said, until a doctor was put over the ship's side. And so it was that I was sent, while the frigate went off in a driving sleet."

"Nay, sir, now I remember. The *Theseus*? Did she not sail safely into the Bay of Tobermory one day a full month ago, coming down the Sound a week later? A great tall ship she was, too," said Morag, forgetting her politics for the moment, while her fine eyes danced at the romance of the bargain. "And the pilot's kinsman?"

"Ah, poor body! He died before I reached his bedside."

"Ah, he died? Poor pilot! Does he know yet, I wonder? Poor pilot!" said the girl pensively. "But," she went on, her voice changing quickly—"but if you are a surgeon in the Navy of this man you call King, why do you await the coming of a simple country physician to mend your arm?"

"Because I wish no one to know I am a surgeon —the surgeon from the *Theseus*, who landed in Tiree some five weeks ago. For by all tokens, that is a man who'll have cold comfort from some folks in the Isles if he is discovered. And, meanwhile, here is this arm of mine that will be healing in a pretty crook before your Doctor MacNab arrives, if there be none to help me with it."

He looked enquiringly at the girl, and even the light falling on her cheek from her hood of pink silk, could not hide her sudden pallor.

"Oh, what do you wish? I'll do it at the telling," she said in a strained voice.

"Hush! It is but a little thing, if a needful, Miss Morag. We shall want some handfuls of wool and some strips of linen rag."

"I'll carry them under the roses in my basket," she suggested, a faint smile dawning on her trembling lips, "—under the white roses, sir."

"You will have your jest, madam," he said. "I fear I put you to a vast annoyance."

She murmured indistinctly in reply and went off at once towards the house, whilst Fraser stalked over the fallen leaves, his little volume to his nose, but an impatient eye on the garden gate. He sighed in relief, when she returned, the least trifle breathless.

"Will it please you—will it please you to sit beside me here on the bench, whilst I unwrap this arm of mine?" said he.

They seated themselves, the girl on his left and more breathless now.

"'tis work more fitting for a man, Miss Morag, but, as I say, I have no choice in the matter."

He lifted the sling, and throwing back the shoulder of his sleeveless coat, showed the swollen limb. Then he produced two flat pieces of wood from the skirts of the garment.

"All I ask from you is a pull with your right hand on mine: a hearty handshake as it were," he said.

The girl bit her lip savagely, and her hand went to her heart. But Fraser looking up in alarm at the sudden movement, her fingers strayed from the flowered calico over a breast that heaved to the lace of her pelerine, and, adjusting the knot there, she said, with a tremulous assumption of calm;

"Do you mean setting the bone, Mr. Surgeon?"

He smiled assurance in reply. "Bones," he said. "There are two, I believe, if Doctor Douglas and my memory are right." He nodded to the part of the seat where his little text-book of anatomy lay, its leathern covers still salt-encrusted. "But the break is simple, and the work is nothing if you are brave. See ... I sit so . . ." He sat upright on the rustic seat. "I brace this arm with my left ... so ... while you stand in front and stoop to stretch the limb evenly. Then here are the boards, and the wool makes pads for them; and these strips of linen are ties, you see ... so one this side ... one that ... Tie so ... again —"

He repeated the manoeuvre, while she watched steadily with bright eyes.

"You have your lesson now," he said. "It is cruel to ask this of you, but what can I do else? Come, your hand —"

There were two white faces when the work was done, and the man's brow dripped sweat on the knot of the last tie.

"Oh, is it rightly done?" asked Morag anxiously. "As well and truly as if the Royal College themselves had been your instructors," he answered, smiling feebly. "And now, we'll hide it in the sling, and forget all about it, for you want more roses, don't you? Shall I finish this story of mine, whilst you go on with your flower-gathering?"

"Why, yes," she answered. "Am not I the mindless one, not to ask you? 'Twas this horrible arm that made me forget."

"And it's but in explanation of my secrecy regarding its setting, that I offer to trouble you further," he said.

And so they followed the maze of the garden walks, the girl gathering her roses, and Fraser telling his tale.

"I stayed with the Tiree folks longer than I had need to," he said. "But the truth is their ways of life were something new for a sailor, and, London-born though I am, my fathers before me had lived the lives of these same people. For there I was, if not in my own calf-country, at least in that of my forebears."

"You tell me?" said Morag.

"Yes, even my father, who is a City merchant, had the Gaelic, you must know, and had dealings with the Highlanders all his days, in the Scrape, as he called it, and before and after that."

"You tell me?" said Morag again, and smiling. "No wonder you're only half-Hanover."

"In any case," said Fraser, "I suppose it's something in the blood that no amount of trading in silks can wean us of; but there I was, and my heart in my mouth at the first word I had of leaving the place. For the storm came to an end, and a smack was to sail for the mainland. Ah! Miss Morag, I don't know how you feel, but the little burns and a bush or two in a glen there, seemed harder to part from after a week's acquaintance than anything I'd known for years, East or West."

"It's me that kens," said the girl, her rapt eyes on Ben Shiante, seen mistily through the oaks.

"Well, that's the grip of my heart that yon place took," said Fraser. "And so, as I said, there was the packet for sailing when the storm had passed, but go I could not. And afterwards —well, there were other storms — But oftener it was my inclination—my sentiment—call it what you will, that kept me back... Kept me back until the thing happened that now keeps me in hiding here... Kept me back until I had tied myself to one fleeing from what was only rough justice, for he had killed a fellow-creature. Who he was matters little now, for he died off Aros Point nine days ago. And then—why then, though no sheriff's writ runs in these outer isles of the sea, as you know, there's the clan—or, despite the late acts, the spirit of the clan—not yet dead. So, because of the clan this man fled; and because of the clan Ian Fraser hides his skill of surgery, and asks a woman to do ungentle tasks."

"Oh, sir, how I am grieved for you," was all she said, and by the least movement of her head her fair side-curls were again let droop, this time to hide her eyes.

Fraser gulped a little. It was the one heartily friendly word he had heard for a weary time, and it came from one who seemed to understand. So far, it had done him good to relieve his soul, but he was now dangerously near to elaborating a melancholy that was not unpleasant. Did the girl intuitively recognise the way he went downwards? or was it really a return of suspicion on her part that made her say:

"And so I did you an injustice, Mr. Fraser, in thinking your chief concern was for your Government's danger from us poor Jacobites. Yet all the while it was but your anxiety to keep your own skin whole?"

The shaft stung, not by reason of its keenness, but because he felt the blow unfair, and, flushing, he decided on an immediate retiral. Yet thinking he saw the rogue in her eye, he forgave the stroke instantly, and, smiling, said:

"You see too deeply into motives for me to risk a longer stay, so permit my withdrawal before you rend every mask of fair appearance from me. My thanks for your aid in surgery, madam; and I leave you to your roses."

She looked down at her foot tapping the fallen leaves, and framed a reply of speech more gracious; she smiled her kindliest. But the wicket clicked, and he was gone.

10: Garden secrets

THE girl walked back to the seat of mossy stone, and found there the little weather-beaten text-book of anatomy.

"Why, 'tis Mr. Fraser's," she said, sitting down and laying it aside. "This comes of his haste. Well, then, let him return for it as quickly." And she tossed her head.

Then, sunk in a day-dream, her lips half-parted, the least tinge of damask in her cheek, she switched the leaves at her feet to and fro with a twig of hazel. Her eye followed the swift cloud-carry, which the gales of the outer world were chasing, followed the dark cloud-shadows, as swift, passing and passing continually over the bronze and fawn of the hills, over the flicker and gleam of the watercourses. In Glenaros woods the winds piped joyously, and the pungent odours of the shore were wafted to her. All the wilds cried holiday, and called on her, their child, to come to them. But a little frown had gathered on her brow, and she sighed softly: her mood and Nature's, it seemed, were for the present at variance.

Of a sudden she started and looked up. A slight, delicate youth had approached noiselessly over the carpet of sodden leaves, and now stood before her, smiling, and with something of a pose in his figure, wrapped as it was in a long cloak bearing many mud-stains.

"Norman," she cried, and was in his arms.

"Hush, little sister, hush! ... Who was this that left you but a little ago?"

She crimsoned fully now, as if he had read every mood of her reverie.

"A Mr. Fraser," she said: "a shipwrecked man. But, oh, Norman, how travel-stained and weary you are!"

He smiled approval of her attentions, and yet looked down on her as if she had been some backward schoolgirl not yet lesson-perfect.

"Always the little sister, eh?" he said. "Let us finish Mr. Fraser first, my dear. Does he know me, I wonder? Do I know him?"

"How should he know you, Norman? His being here at all is the merest accident."

Again he shook his head reprovingly, and smiled down at her from his prominent blue eyes.

"Still, 'tis but the question we must always be asking, if we are to be prepared. Has he not by any means heard that the little sister has a wicked brother, a ruffler, a Jacobite agent, a gambler, eh? one who cannot come to his father's front door by daylight?" He gave a crafty side-long look at the girl, and, his arm encircling, he patted her shoulder.

"Nothing," she said. "He knows nothing, I tell you. Come indoors instantly to fire and wine, sir. What a life of dread poor Norman leads! Poor Norman!"

"Indoors? Not yet. I dare not." He shook his head doubtfully, his eye still on the garden gate, through which the surgeon had passed but a little ago. "Come," he said, "we are unsheltered from any chance-comer's eye at the wicket there; let us take the path behind the yews, ill-omened as they are, for I've much to tell to the little sister."

They left the seat for a path that ran some twenty paces behind it, a clump of yews and hollies intervening; and they had but reached the further end of the track, when Fraser, unnoticed, returned for his forgotten volume. He had just found it, when there came from behind the thick wall of trees the sound of voices—a girl's and a man's. The girl's he recognised instantly for Morag's. But the man's—? It seemed as if his every fibre became rigid at the well-known sound. It was the voice of Cattanach.

As if impelled by some power not himself he stole close to the dark foliage, and peered through. The tousle of blonde silken hair, the full blue eye, the cursed simper: Cattanach it was, without a doubt, and his arm encircled Morag. Fraser choked at the sight, and his temple pulses hammered; his vision failed, and he clung to a branch unsteadily. Then, as he heard them address each other as brother and sister, a profuse sweat broke over him, and he slid weakly to his knees among the rank grass. The contradiction was too unnatural, too terrible: this man, base to the depths of all cunning—this man, brother to that creature of fire and spirit and high ideals, habiting a world of beauty he knew nothing of!

A word or two of their talk came to him; his horror increased a hundredfold, and he stumbled unsteadily, yet stealthily to his feet and sought the wicket unperceived.

Behind the yews the young man with the prominent blue eyes was smiling down on Morag.

"Yes; in affairs at last, dearie," he said. "In affairs, at last, I tell you." He pranced a step of dancing and gaily dangled his cloak from side to side.

"You take the affairs lightly enough then, sir," she smiled. "You mean—?"

"I mean that I have the news from Glengarry, and that there is no surer hand, Morag."

"The Prince, Norman?"

"Yes, the Prince, madam. He is coming again and soon."

There were instantly tears of quiet happiness in the girl's eyes.

"Ah!" she sighed contentedly, and that was all. Then, after a space, doubt returned. "But can it be really true?" she asked.

"As certain as the sunrise to-morrow morn," he answered. "Murray and Clancarty have arranged it all. Choiseul and Belle-Isle have promised. Prussia will help, if need be. The British fleet is busy in the Canadas, and we have two of the best admirals that ever sailed blue water—Conflans and Thurot."

"La! there are fine names in plenty, sir. Is there never a Highland one besides the Murray?"

"The little sister, the little sister!" He patted her shoulder with the air of the well-pleased tutor. "Of course, of course: for there's never a clan on Lochgarry's old list but that we'll have it out in better numbers than ever. And what do you think? Besides the raid on the Highlands there's London to be attacked. Oh! I'll warrant you, we'll show them war."

"War!" said Morag fiercely, her eyes ablaze.

"War!" he cried. "And who think you is his Highness' *chargé d'affaires* in the Isles?"

"Oh, Norman, who but yourself?"

The young man seemed startled for a moment at the thought.

"But, no—blessing on you!—what are you thinking of, girl? It's scarcely so far forward I am. No, no. It's an old friend and a staunch— Drumfin, if you please; and he is in Tiree, I hear."

"Drumfin?" cried the girl, "but no; he is in Aros Isle, sir; and with no thought but that of renewing acquaintance with friends and haunts of his youth—the exile's eternal weakness. So I fear your story's miscarried, Norman. 'tis not Drumfin."

As she spoke, she missed the flash of secret satisfaction in the blue eye of her companion. He snapped finger and thumb and hopped as in sheer delight.

"The story is true enough, I tell you," he said, halting before her, his hands on her shoulders. "But 'tis as you say about Drumfin. When he came to Scotland he knew nothing of all this; 'twas part of Clancarty's plan, you see. Timely on the spot, Drumfin would know nothing if arrested before the affair was ripe. But when the hour struck, and his Highness' commission came, who more active and trusty than Drumfin, will you tell me? 'Twas part of the plan, I say, to use him. And, indeed, things could not have fallen out better than they have done."

"Why," said Morag in a solemn surprise, "we're in the very heart of it, dear brother, it would seem."

Norman evidently saw less of the high seriousness of the case in which they stood, for he skipped delightedly again.

"In the very heart of it!" he cried. "Think of it, *mo chridhe!* What happiness!"

She blushed, and smiled gladly back to him.

"Why," she said. "'tis but half an hour since Drumfin passed this very spot."

"Lord!" cried the youth, paling through his ivory skin. "You do not tell me he is even in my father's house?"

"It's just the same I'm telling you," said Morag.

He glanced around slowly and furtively, his face grave, as if he feared meeting Drumfin's quiet eye at any point.

"Never?" he said. "Alone?"

"Yes, alone—. But no, not now. For such a queer man came to him this morning—an Irish pedlar, by his looks. Indeed, it was but a little ago, as I say, that they went down this alley together."

Norman bit his lip savagely. "Ay," he said, quite chapfallen at this last piece of news. "And he'd have a red box—this pedlar—a red box on his shoulders, Morag?"

"The very man, Norman."

"Just as Glengarry wrote me," said he musingly. "By the Lord, he's got the route already then."

"The route?" asked Morag.

"The Prince's route, Morag; his armament, dates of sailing, and his landing-place. He'll have full details of Conflans and Thurot, I'll warrant. Ah! it's glad I'd be to have his post, little sister!"

"But come in to him, and hold council," said the girl.

He smiled. "Still so innocent?" he asked. "That is not our manner of working, little one. No, no: he must not see me, and I must not see him, and we can then take oaths to that effect. You perceive, dearie? Even now I must be off for the high road."

A curlew called just then from the distant shore, and he took the proferred advantage.

"Listen," he said.

Again the sea-bird called.

"A signal?" she queried.

"A signal," he lied glibly in return. "And good-bye is what it means for us, little one. But, first, listen. If you hear of aught that you think I should know at any time, you must send to Clachaig in the hills behind here. Cattanach at Clachaig, that will find me. For it's there I'll be waiting and waiting to help towards what you and I still sigh for, lass. A kiss, little sister."

Their lips met. Then he struck a pose half-ludicrous to make her smile through her tears, pointing one toe, whilst his head was thrown back like a harlequin's. He laughed aloud as he climbed the wall and seated himself on the coping.

"Good-bye," he cried, mocking the sad looks his departure had called up. "Good-bye. Am not I the dolorous one? Hear me weep."

His wild laughter rang out eerily through the stillness of the place. It came in a faint shrill peal over the yew tops to where Fraser paced uneasily at the mansion's gable end, and he shuddered as he heard it.

11: The Fairies' Castle

THAT night Fraser awoke to a grip on his injured arm. Past the undrawn curtains of his chamber-window there poured the glory of moonlight, its spectral beams whorled on the bare wooden floor by the bull's-eyes in the lozened panes, and in the faint radiance he beheld the face of Belle, the Aros House servant, scared almost to the ridiculous.

"Sir, oh, sir," she whispered; "rise, or you will be killed," and vanished.

He guessed her meaning instantly, and, too good a seaman to overdo the hurrying, clad himself quietly and effectively against the hint of cold in the air. Then, as he opened the door a crack and peered out, his left arm was suddenly seized, and he flung back so fiercely from the grasp that the door clattered to the shaking wall. His sound hand went to his hanger, but he withdrew it when he saw the pencils of moonlight strike on a woman's figure clad in a cloak, whose hood encircled the pale face of Morag MacLean.

She beckoned him silently, and he followed her downstairs, where again she took his hand. Thence they glided, rustling and tip-toe, along a narrow wood-lined corridor to a final flight of steps that left them on a floor of flags. A door opened from this cold room on a bit of rough lawn above the river; and across the open ground, swept by frosty airs and moonlight, they ran noiselessly, save for the jingle of a chain-catch on Fraser's cloak. They reached the shelter of the leafless birches fringing the stream, found the great stepping-stones uncovered, the water racing swift and black under tinkling plaques of new-born ice, and, crossing to the further side, the open was taken again on a slight ascent. Then, the track running beneath some oak and hazel, the few squares of orange light that marked the House of Aros were lost to view. It was here Morag turned eagerly to her companion.

"'tis the Tiree MacLeans, Mr. Fraser: they have come sooner than you thought, you see. Did you not know that the man who did this thing was cousin to my father in the second degree? Did you not guess the dead man's friends would come knocking at my father's gates in their search for the slayer?"

"I knew him for your father's cousin," said Fraser wearily.

"Then you should also have known that you risked your life doubly in Aros; for even if these Sunivaig men should discover that cousin Angus is dead, they would still hold you guilty, in that you aided his escape. And they are indeed savage, these folk: pit and gallows at Duart used to know them well in the olden days, when they were roving in the isle. The dark ones! their curses as black as the knives they fingered!"

"Knives?" asked Fraser, halting and looking back.

She interpreted the glance at once, and said coldly:

"My father? Oh, he is safe enough; or is it here his daughter would be? Drumfin is returned, and with him."

"Did they indeed threaten with knives?" asked Fraser gloomily, as they resumed the path.

"Why, yes. Their hands were busy enough, though they never drew steel. There were seven, and Deaf Alan to head them, if you please."

"Deaf Alan?"

"You do not know him, sir? He who wrote the wicked book for the London printer, and was unfrocked for it."

"Lord," said Fraser, "books and printers are many in London town and both are wicked, madam. I've no traffic with them, you may be sure, or I'd never be the saint I am, Miss Morag."

"Jest as you will, 'twas a grave enough matter for us three an hour ago, when these wild men broke in on us. My father and Drumfin were discussing some lines of Virgil; and I was busy at bits of estate-work, when there came a knocking, and forthwith these islesmen entered without a by-your-leave. Then before the parley was well begun the dear father saw it all—he that is for ordinary so excitable—and what does he do, but, cool as a court-lawyer, take up my tally-book and scribble your name across the figures."

"I see," said Fraser.

"I understood him at once, and in order to send Belle to you, slipped off as naturally and as soon as my fears would allow."

"I see," said Fraser. "Did they appear to suspect my presence in Aros?"

"Why no: how should they?"

"Then what danger to me does your father fear?"

"Oh, you don't know these wild isles of the sea, the clans of them!" cried Morag. "News goes fast, and they'll not be long in Aros without hearing of you. There's Deaf Alan—the smooth one—little will pass him. Oh, had you but seen him stroking his dirk-sheath before my father's face—the bold one! He's mad for the old ways—"

"A little weakness of your own, is it not, Miss Morag?" interjected Fraser, smiling.

"Tush!" and she halted to stamp her foot— "Will you still jest on occasion so serious, sir? 'tis for the old ways he is mad, I say; but 'tis for the worst as well as the best. And with him the clan's very teeth must be paid for. Let me tell you, sir, that if he is in the isle to-morrow, and routing for news of his quarry, there will be no safety for you in Aros township. Thus we take time by the forelock to-night; but it's in rough fashion you must pass the dark hours at the Fairies' Castle, I fear. Do you know it?"

"Not I," said Fraser blankly, with a shrug of his shoulders; and as if careless of whatever chance befel him, he stared upwards at the stars dusted over the clear blue sky above.

"I pray you," chid the girl, "not so hopeless, if it please you."

Indeed," he said, smiling, "it is not as you surmise. My thought is rather that we magnify the danger unduly."

Oh!" she cried, and crimsoned darkly, and he saw his error instantly.

"Your pardon," he said. "I—"

"And can you believe me so fond of midnight adventures with a stranger, sir, as to seize the least pretext for them? Do you imagine Highland usage as less delicate than that of the South?"

Fraser inwardly cursed his blundering, and sought for a word of excuse, but she spoke again before he found it.

"The man you helped was kinsman to my father, let me remind you: and so it is that I am here. Please you, follow me."

Imperative, she took the woodland way at a rapid pace, leaving the man no choice but obedience, and he pursued her lithe steps in laggard fashion, with something like sulking in his air, until he beheld her turn with a gesture of impatience, and await him. Instantly, fearing a second outpouring of her wrath, he capitulated.

"I crave pardon," he said. "I am a selfish boor, I confess. I shall do as you wish, madam."

Her eyes flashed, and she made no reply. But she pushed on, as if to hide the tumult of her thoughts. Oh, soon, soon, she told herself, he would learn to think of the Gael in truer fashion. Soon he would see what chivalry was—what loyal hearts could dare; and he and his breed would no longer sneer every generous impulse out of life. Her Prince—her Prince was coming—was coming again! ... How she would humble this man! But—failure? Ah, should the Prince fail—what then? ... Oh, then would she show him how his great spirit bore its sorrow—how ten thousand hearts were broken in the breaking of her Prince's heart!

And there also should this Southerner find humiliation — in the thought that he had helped in victory so shameful —

Suddenly it came on her with a glow of her whole being that she was unusually preoccupied with plans for the discipline of this stranger's spirit. Was it because a hint of a reason for all this dawned on her, that she began to make endeavours after a return to matter-of-fact by urging him to a faster pace?

"A little quicker, I pray you," she said. "You do not know whom we flee, sir, or your steps were lighter."

They went on over the mossy track that now left the wood and took them by a rampart of rock to a steeper ascent of the hill. The winds of the day had fallen, and far beneath, they saw the Sound, quiet in unwonted fashion, the moon's path fair and unrippled from Innimore to Aros. A croaking heron flapped shorewards from the wood they had left; a stoat, already in winter-white, flashed and halted, and flashed again across their path; for the rest, the hare and the blackcock were the only living things that stirred. Higher still they climbed, their breathing a little faster now, and the fragrance of bog-myrtle around them. They passed between the twin-peaks of a little hill, and the girl looked round, shivering in a faint breeze that was now felt on the western side of the height.

"Oh, I trust I have not misled," she said feebly, looking out over the great fields of mountains spread fair and far beneath the moonlight's witchery. "I can see two waters only, but as yet not our mark—the loch in the west there. Further still, sir. Come."

They descended into a little plain with many little pools of peaty water in it, and not without difficulty advanced towards a great mound in front, where soon the outline of massed stones on its summit rose black against the azure of the sky.

"Ah," said Morag, "the Castle."

The escalade of the steep little hill on which the ruin stood was stiff work. Twice the girl, exhausted, slipped on the wet turf; and, at last assenting to Fraser's appeal, she seated herself on a boulder on the eastern face of the ascent in order to await his return.

When at last Fraser had climbed the hundred feet or so of rock-strewn hill-side, he found himself on a little plateau with a rude wall, massive though dry-built, surrounding its almost circular outline. The ruin must indeed be ancient, he pondered; testimony of its age lay even in the meagreness of the remnant left, for although the wall was some ten feet in thickness, its height measured only half this at most. Here and there were hollows, marking where chambers or stairs had opened, and he noted how these might offer hiding from an enemy, or shelter in stress of weather. For the rest the hill was an ideal place of refuge, and commanded the isle as from an eyrie. Yonder were two of the signs for which the girl had asked: Loch Frisa to the north, the Sound to the east. And now a shimmer of moonlit tides gave the third of the marks, for here Loch-na-Keal, an arm from the Atlantic, was thrust inwards to the island's mountain-roots. At sight of these surrounding waters, the sailor in Fraser came dominant, and unconsciously he fell to admiring the strategy of these builders of earlier years, who—plainly sailors as well as warriors—had so wisely chosen this vantage-ground in the waist of the isle. He dreamed on the past and saw again their beaked galleys float darkly on the wave—a Viking argosy. His imaginings, indeed, took him so completely from himself, that for the moment he had quite forgotten the matter he had in hand and the meaning of his errand among these moonlit hills, when a faint cry came to him, a woman's wail, and he suddenly recalled his plight, his waiting companion, and all the ordeal of the present hour.

He scrambled down the eastern face of the hill, and looked for the girl's figure, but the westering moon made shadow here—shadow as of ebony, and he stumbled as he went, seeing no sign of her. "Miss Morag," he called; yet the only reply was the eastward-flowing wind calling hush among the grasses. An echo from the twin-peaked hill startled him as he called again, and then in a flash, this lone high moorland with its tussocks of creamy moss, and its peaty pools through which he plashed desperate—this harmony of gloom and fair lights as of mother-o'-pearl, became a horror to his soul.

He plodded distracted around the base of the Castle hill, and ever his call in the dark brought wilder fears as it echoed fainter and fainter in the high gullies above Aros. Oh, worse than fool, he thought, that he should do this thing! Was it to save a poltroon such as he from a scuffle with some islesmen that this high-spirited lass had risked so much? Oh, fool; oh, fool! Again and again he called her name, beside himself with apprehension.

He had made the circuit of the great mound unrewarded, and now, the mosswater at his ankles, he stood at bay and looked around. Then his eye found a spot of whiteness in the gloom, and he strained upwards to it instantly. It was Morag's face. The girl lay pale and breathing faintly: and she smiled wanly, but spiritedly to him before she closed her eyes in a spasm of pain.

"You are hurt?" he cried, kneeling beside her.

"A sprain only, I think," she answered, and again the wan smile. "And of all places the fashionable one, if I may judge from your sling, sir surgeon—the right arm."

It seemed that after she had rested a little, she had attempted to follow him up the hill. Then a foot slipped, the wrist doubled under her, and the pain had been so great as to cause her fainting.

"Look at it, surgeon," she said. "Would not a fracture there be more *á la mode*?"

Fraser examined the wrist, and was able to assure her that a sprain was the worst that had happened. Her kerchief, dipped in a stream, served as a temporary dressing, and the surgeon halved his sling of silk to share it with her. Then they turned homewards.

"And so you come back to Aros with me to see me safe? I protest 'tis a Highland convoy this," said Morag gaily.

"And how?" asked Fraser.

"Oh, one sees a friend home to his lodging, and then the friend returns the favour. And so they may go on for a round of the clock."

"Ah," said Fraser absently, "how I regret that sprain!"

"Oh, la! as if I had not done well enough by guiding you once, sir?" she said archly.

It was now the surgeon's turn to show a high colour.

"Oh, 'twas not of the Scotch convoy I was thinking," he said rather awkwardly.

For reply, she tossed her fair side-curls.

"I mean—I should be vastly pleased—" he stammered.

"Because of the sprain?" asked the rogue. "How strangely you mingle pleasure and regret, sir!"

Thereupon Fraser assumed a moody silence, finding himself so poor a match in this wordy warfare; a hundred sharp retorts rose in his mind, indeed, yet an opening never came for any of the weapons he fashioned so finely. But now, as they regained the mossy plain, and the uneven ground made progress more difficult, not a little satisfaction mingled with his solicitude, as he saw her bite her nether lip when a false step in the gloom jarred her injured arm. The agony of the wrist was in truth at one time so great that she swayed a little as if about to faint again.

"You are still pained," said he, coming close to her. "Will you take my arm?"

"La! indeed, sir; and which?"

She laughed gleefully, if feebly, and her old self was in her voice, as she demonstrated the difficulty of the problem.

"You cannot come to my left side, sir, for 'twould then be your maimed right arm I'd sacrifice. And if you take the other side, what of my poor hand?"

She laughed again, but despite her gaiety, swayed in a sudden pallor, and there was nothing for it but his left arm round her waist.

"'Tis a trifle awkward, I confess," said she faintly, when the first shock of surprise at his daring had passed. "Yet if we can but keep step we'll do none so badly. What monstrously frail creatures we be, that a little pain should so unsteady us! Let us give thanks, Mr. Fraser, that it was no worse. An ankle now! La! how horrible!"

Half-way back to Aros she suggested that she felt better and might do without his aid, and so Fraser relinquished his grasp reluctantly and by stages.

They approached the township cautiously lest the Tiree men should be abroad, but at last they halted without mishap at the stepping-stones on the Preacher's River.

"There now is one part of a debt discharged," sighed the girl. "And Angus MacLean's kinswoman will sleep the sounder to-night because of it. I've shown you the best hiding in all the countryside, sir, so back to it as fast as you can, if you are wise; for though Aros is safety for me, 'tis danger still for you. To-morrow I'll send you food and news by the trustiest I can find. *Slan leat.*"

"And what is that, Miss Morag?"

"Why 'tis the good word of farewell I'm giving you."

They shook hands left-handed, but like good comrades, and she went down the bank to the first of the stepping-stones. Fraser stood dark in the moonlight, watching her as she balanced unfairly on it, a crust of thin ice crackling under her feet; and he saw how her hurt hand, entangled in the folds of her cloak was suddenly disengaged to check her unsteadiness, as she slipped and retreated to the hither side again; so, tossing off his sling, he was beside her in an instant.

"Your permission," he said.

And all in a dream she felt herself lifted and borne over the boulders in the bed of the stream. Momently he paused when he reached the birches on the other side, before he set her down, but in that second he had turned her face from his own shadow, so that the moonlight fell on her broad forehead and quiet eyes. There was something in her look that was eloquent of understanding, something of pity for his lot, and something also, that, despite her recent merriment, mingled all these with a hint of the old sorrow of the world, and the tragedy of life itself. Passion in that instant came to birth and death in his face, and he placed her gently on earth again, yet not without a grimace of pain at a movement of the splint on his broken arm. Then he held the birch-twigs cavalierly aside, and bent to kiss her fingers.

"*Slan leat,*" he said, and resuming the stony path across the river, he was soon high on the moonlit heath once more.

12: The Tiree men

FRASER waked where he couched in a niche of the Castle wall, to the crowing of cocks, distant and multitudinous in Aros township. Stiff, despite the heaped bracken over and under him, he shivered in the frosty air and looked eastwards for the dawn. But no dawn was there; and he noted that the moon floated only an hour's space lower in the heavens than when he settled to rest, yet what a pother all the fowls in Aros were making. For sure there was something astir down there.

He moved out from his shelter and advanced to that portion of the broken bastion looking towards the village. And then ere he had barely distinguished the shadows of boscage around the mansion, he fell back again within the circle of the ruin, and stole cautiously to his hiding. Two figures were climbing the Castle-mound about a dozen yards beneath him, and indistinctly he was aware of several other forms on the mossy flat below. He called to mind desperately that the moon was setting behind his chosen chamber of hiding, and that the shadows of the broken wall would aid. And then, hardly had he pushed the bracken over the opening of his little nook—hardly was his hanger laid ready to his left hand, and his injured limb comfortably disposed, ere the new-comers appeared, sprawling over the broad wall of the fort.

He noted the bonnets of thrum, the leg bare between short breeks and stockings, the feet-coverings of hairy hide, as peculiarities of dress unusual in Aros, and he guessed the men accordingly as out-dwellers. Yet their attire did not suggest Tiree men as he knew them. Who could they be? There were six in all at first, and they stood in a group, gabbling uncouthly, until a squat figure swung over the wall and joined them, signalling to a corner of the enclosure not ten paces from where Fraser lay. Here they crouched around a bundle of twigs that was soon alight, and the watcher breathed easily, for it seemed that a bivouac and not a search was imminent. A brew of some kind was set in a pannikin hung from three cross-sticks, and as the blaze grew stronger, Fraser discovered the last arrival more clearly. In his huge cloak of many capes, which flapped like evil wings with every motion of the man, his tricorne with a plain cock, his stockings and buckled shoon, he passed for a person of quality compared with his company. These, however, made little ado regarding him, but chatted among themselves, whilst he cowered dully alone. But at a turn of the wind he changed positions with one of the men at a sign, and although no word was spoken, there was deference enough shown by the coarser-clad fellow as he gave up his sheltered seat.

This veering of the wind brought with it a stench well-nigh unbearable even to one familiar with the sick-bay of the *Theseus*; for now it whiffed across the encampment, and Fraser viewed with horror the hairy coverings of the clouted feet of these wild fellows. Yet he soon forgot the odour of the cuarain of the strangers, in the revelation of the face and figure of their leader now fairly seen in his new post, curiously lit as he was by mingled lights from moon and fire. The flabby pale cheeks above a not unhandsome beard, the pouched eyelids—these combined with a splay-footed gait and a something of a paunch to suggest the man of the desk rather than of the camp. And then the final touch in the way of identity was the presence of woollen plugs in the ears.

"Deaf Alan and his Sunivaig men," said Fraser. "But they seek eye for eye in easy fashion surely?"

He tried to argue from their demeanour to the purpose of their presence there. They feared no attack, for no watch was set, and their fire was unscreened. No search was made, so they could not suspect him near. What was it then? Cattle-lifting in prospect or but a partial secrecy before their next move in the blood-hunt? It was only as they grew more voluble with the circling of spirit-horn and snuff-mull that the small Gaelic of which he was master served him finally to perceive that they had news of a deadly sickness in Aros and elsewhere in the countryside; that they now fled the plague; and that for the present at least their quest was forsaken. Said one in Gaelic:

"It's an old word, 'When the herring are in the North, Red Murdo is in the South,' but, please God, we'll get our fingers on their thrapples yet."

"Keep the fire lower, Neil, or we'll make a beacon for all the glens," said another, kicking out a root the first speaker had just placed on the blaze.

The gnarled mass of wood slid outwards, rolled against a stone supporting Neil's spirit-horn, laid temporarily atilt against it, and at once the vessel was prone, the greedy earth taking the draught. The cup's owner, little and brindled, was instantly at the throat of the other, but the assailed had gained his knees, and his black knife was ready. Sideways they fell, locked and struggling like fighting cats; the burnt earth had them one minute, the hot ashes the next, and at last the gipsy-pot and sticks went headlong over. Then the flabby-cheeked parson stood erect suddenly, his many wings of black cloak flapping; and if his hat was in the embers, yet he held a gillie, torn from each other, in either hand. He kept them apart for some seconds, spoke with something of clerical unction a low soothering word to either, and let them go. Then all sat down to the spirit-horn again. But once more ere dawn broke clear, the quarrellers were at each other's necks, and again the deaf minister plucked them apart as readily as if he but snapped a merrythought.

With the first scad of light in the east the encampment broke up; a rough stirabout of meal was partaken of, and the islesmen departed, clattering down the stone-strewn slopes of the hill's western side. The watcher among the bracken saw them cross the knolls and hollows lying between them and the drove-track leading to the lochs of the west; saw them reach the level and break into a trot, a dot of a figure in a many-winged cloak, hirpling in the rear.

"Here then is my safety," said he. "For this plague has sent them back to Tiree on the run."

And the next instant he cursed himself for the most selfish of knaves, for a vision of danger from the pest to those in Aros flashed sudden on him. Drumfin? Morag? As if frozen he stood, and in reverie beheld the girl, tall and with a head of a queen, her eyes pity and love, her voice tender to beguiling, her arch smile that seemed the heaven-liest thing on earth—beheld her become stricken and wan and sorrowful, her queenly head so lowly. Indeed, he was groaning aloud as he roused himself, and descended the mound on the Aros side.

More than half the distance to the township had been traversed in the grey daybreak, when he stopped at a little pool in a stream near the oak-wood's margin, and, reddening hastily at some passing thought, made a hasty toilet. It was awkward enough attempting the bathing his head and shoulders with one hand, yet even if his face had received attention from both, his frame of mind was such as to leave him dissatisfied with the outer man, and he recognised with another uneasy flush a new-born fastidiousness as to matters of personal appearance—a trait none too common among those accustomed to the rough life of the ship-surgeon.

He finished dressing, and as daylight came fuller, he knelt beside the pool, and looked at the plain features gazing up at him from its mirror of smooth water. Again he dreamt of that fair face so close to his in the moonlight only some hours gone, and instantly he saw clearly the meaning of his new solicitude for externals. Then hopelessness descended like a pall, and melancholy brought forgetfulness of his task in Aros. Poor, friendless, unhandsome and fugitive: what had he to give?

His work ambition boundless? Oh, yes, a hunger for his work, fierce as his ambition's appetite, to know surely and to help with certainty in this one thing in a dark world—the suffering of man. Soul and spirit, passion and sin, he would leave to other masters, but give him in this regard the hope of succour to his fellows. To live no idle moment; to concentrate almost savagely his every power toward this end; to hold in vigilant curb the sudden accesses of emotion, of sentiment, that on occasion surprised him out of himself, and left his ideal of unceasing toil at his art, fading and powerless—these were the thoughts he found rising in his mind. He brooded thus for a little and then returned to earth. Abstractedly he smoothed back his wet hair, and attempted to tie his bag-ribbon with one hand, but failing, he left it undone, and turning to take a last look at the pool's mirror, was astonished to see reflected above his face the face of Morag MacLean.

"And, indeed, la! I thought you daft, sir," she said. "Nay, nay, do not rise. Give me the ribbon."

With many little tweaks and tugs unnecessarily vicious she bunched the chevelure, and tied the knot.

"There! I hope you'll not again attempt that task unaided. I'll warrant I'll hurt you more next time," she said. "See," she went on, holding up the basket she carried. "Soups and cordials for you. Why have you left your hiding, sir?"

He recounted the night's adventure.

"And there are the Sunivaig MacLeans for you!" she cried scornfully. "Is it so our branch of the clan would defer a judgment, do you think? To run from a sickness!"

Then she laughed high till her voice seemed part of the music of the waters spilling over rocky steps from the pool at their feet.

"But, indeed, I forget that they do you a service in going, Mr. Fraser. And if I blame them for lack of smeddum, let me thank them for an unwitting kindness to a friend. Shall we return to Aros, sir?"

He took her basket and they came back to the Preacher's River. At the stepping-stones, she said:

"Last night's alarm and your flight have made known who you are in some fashion to all our household, and I fear the Tiree men will soon get word of you. Yet not from Aros folk, for I think you may trust them as fairly as you did Morag MacLean, and you may be thankful you have someone else to lean on besides that broken reed. 'tis the MacPhails at Tigh-ban who are down with this pestilence newly come amongst us. Will it please you to see my father about it? But am not I the mindless one, and you foodless all this weary time. I'll call Belle."

She bade him good-bye in the hall, and ran lightly upstairs. He was at gaze moodily after her, his thoughts busy with the medley her brother's return must now make, when she wheeled swiftly and tripped down to him again, saying with the least hint of the rogue in her eye:

"And then, when your weightier affairs have been seen to, here's a wrist of mine and a bandage."

It was a man full of wrath at himself she left, for not till then had the careful draping of her camelot mantle recalled her injury to his mind.

13: Plague

FRASER found that the laird's attitude to his cousin's death held less of fuss and fever than he anticipated.

"Poor Angus," said Aros gravely, as they sat together in the study, whither he had taken the surgeon in order to thank him for his aid to his relative —" Poor Angus! And so it was he that was with you when the boat went down? A death in the cold Sound! Poor Angus! It was but a bare life for him, in any case. Only a second cousin, Mr. Fraser, but still our kin, you see — our kin. And a tacksman only, sir, but nearer Lachlan Mor in blood than ourselves who count near enough to be a little proud of it. Sir, a glass of wine with you, and again my thanks!"

Over the claret he melted into a mood of half-confidences.

"There's a certain Mr. MacLean of Drumfin staying with us at present," he said. "You may remember meeting him, though somewhat at a disadvantage, on your first night in Aros." He chuckled melodiously. "It might be as well to say nothing to anyone of his being here, Mr. Fraser. You'll understand; it's a matter of a little fondness for a cockade devoid of colour."

Fraser bowed, and the laird returned to ruminating on his second cousin once more.

"Poor Angus, poor Angus! And then these Sunivaig folk," he said. "Heard you ever the like? 'tis a pretty pass when neither Kirk here nor Sheriff in Inneraora can hold them from routing and roving. There's only the plague to stop them, it seems. Sir, with this way of it in the Highlands, you'll have little love for your father's calf-country, I'm thinking."

Fraser protested himself as not unpleased with his adventures so far: last night's lack of sleep was the worst of it, he vowed.

"As regards your safety now," said Aros. "I have gone over things with Drumfin: and he agrees with me that your best chance of the mainland is to keep clear of the beaten tracks — Grasspoint and the like."

"You think so?" said Fraser absently.

"And as for time — well, you're safe as long as this plague holds, for if I know the breed of these Sunivaig men, they'll never show face again till it lifts."

"Ah!" said Fraser brightening, "then in that case, sir, let me help fight the pest until your surgeon arrives."

Aros nodded; and the young man went on with a flushed cheek:

"Not that it's pity only for these sick folk that moves me, you'll understand. There's all that: but beyond it, there's a consideration of more selfish cast; for here as elsewhere I find myself full of hopes of a useful life, no idle moment in it; and here as elsewhere, little or no performance to justify the hopes, sir—nothing but wafts of sentiment, Heaven knows." He paused, halting for a word, and still reddening.

"Ay, ay," said Aros chuckling and blinking, "are you, too, hit? Man, I thought myself the only one in these parts in such a quandary. Ay, here am I, and at sixty years I'm just as I was at your age, Mr. Fraser; for 'tis my all I'd give—little enough—but 'tis my all I'd give to fill the shoes of a man of active life. And yet when it comes to the bit, it's a pipe and a verse of Horace I'm hankering after. Oh, man, if a body could but be one thing fairly!"

Fraser felt uncomfortable so to have stirred the old fellow with a tale that was but a decoy. For in his mind's eye just then there was not a vision of sick men with himself arduous in their service; it held nothing, indeed, but the picture of a girl's face framed in a hood of pink sarcenet, and set against a background of dark yew; so he offered instant solace to a pricking conscience by proposing to set out for the afflicted township without delay.

"Do you so, sir," said Aros. "Do you so —God!" he added regretfully, "but I envy you. Why didna my father make me a leech, I wonder?"

They parted then, and instantly Fraser's anxiety to depart for the plague-spot was supplanted by a desire for surgical attendance on Morag's injured wrist. Therefore it was that he hung about the grounds of the house, awaiting the opportunity of an unobserved approach to the girl, when he might acquit himself of an apology he had been conning half the morning. But after two hours of patient pacing, he learnt his vigil useless, for the servant informed him that the lady had gone off on ponyback just after her return from her morning walk. A letter of some kind, the serving-man said, had occasioned this hurried departure.

A little later in the day Fraser set off to his appointed task at the stricken clachan. It was now the hour of the mid-day meal in the township, and the cottars, home from their patches of rough ground, came to the doorways to look after him. The arrival of the pestilence was exactly timed to the coming of this stranger; already the story from Tiree was gone abroad and his identity half-guessed, and, for all his soft voice and winning ways, the old wives now held him for a Jonah.

But he swung on, unheeding their unfriendly looks, and at last reached a group of little houses set near the shore, two miles east of Aros. Here was Tigh-ban, where the sick men lay. The infected folk were chiefly fishers, touching, by reason of their work, at many mainland ports, and in this way carrying fever to their homes. Fraser halted at the first of the huts—a miserable rickle of pebbled walls and turfen roof, and rattled at the osier hurdle that served for door. It was an old man, grizzled and bent, half-doited and half-deaf, who opened to his knocking, and to him the surgeon explained in his scant Gaelic that he was the doctor.

"The doctor?" whispered old Niall Ban. "The doctor, the doctor? But 'tis Murdo's hour; 'tis his hour, poor Murdo! 'tis the good son he was to me; but there's been something following him for years."

He slithered indoors, and Fraser followed. He passed the cow and its follower, which had their home in the forepart of the chamber, and reached the untidy bed of the patient. The peat-smoke from the fire set midmost of this part of the room obscured all things, but the light from the small window and the chimney-opening was enough to show the nature of the illness at a glance. The open eyes steadily fixed in unconsciousness, the fingers plucking at the counterpane, the dusky mottling of the skin seen on the bared and twitching forearm: here was an ancient foe as common as it was deadly, known to him of old in Sicilian lazarettos, and in not a few of His Britannic Majesty's frigates over half the world. It was jail-fever, the grisliest of the dragons his profession had to fight; and not without reason had the Sunivaig MacLeans shown heels to this enemy. It needed even some screwing-up of his own courage before he came close enough to do his work. But it was an instant's wavering only. He felt the sick man's pulse, and sat motionless for a little, estimating its strength; then, producing lint and scalpel, he proceeded to a phlebotomy without more ado.

He found seven men ill in the little clachan. In regard to air and light supply, the houses were as hopeless as any hospital on the orlop-deck. Hopeless, too, in the matter of attendance, for three cottages with a patient in each had but one woman for nurse amongst them all; in other four cases, it was father or son who waited on father or son, and all without heart or spirit. The rest of the little community had vanished; it was said that they had gone to the sheilings of last summer to await the passing of the plague.

"It's away they are," whispered old Niall Ban. "They left Murdo. It's running they went. But their hour is following them."

His head splitting with an ache the foul air of the dwellings intensified, Fraser stole out from the group of huts. He would seek a fresh breeze on the ben above Callachly, he thought, before returning to Aros, and accordingly he struck across the bog to the hill-foot. As he ascended the heathery slope he looked back on the sweep of the grey Sound on whose waves the declining sun sent broad shafts of light from a watery-looking sky. In the little patches of fields there was none at work; no shepherd's whistle on the hill; no drovers with their ruddy cattle dotting the roads;

not a man at the spade, nor a woman at the creel in the peat-cutting; only in the village-street an occasional figure, solitary, strange. And but two days ago what a hive by contrast! All was eloquent of the terror of the plague.

Glowing with his exertions, and consciously taking deep draughts of the clean air, he was mounting still higher, when his eye caught sight of something moving down the hollow of the great glen that ran south from Callachly. The townships— Kilbeg, Rhoail and Gaodhail—smoked faintly from the grassy hollows where they lay hid in the floor of the glen, giving a sense of companionship in this trough among hills lonely and awesome. Indeed, but for these spirals of thin reek, he would have felt some concern at the thought of a journey in these wilds achieved by a lady who, mounted on a little garron, now approached along the river's bank. The pony picked its way by the side of the Forsa, which wound in eerie curves through the green basin of the strath, and unexpectedly heaped shingle banks here and there above the flat. On a far corrie of Ben Creagach some hinds and a stag raised their heads to look at the horsewoman; and these, with himself and the approaching traveller, seemed for the moment the only living things in all this wilderness.

He had already guessed the lady as Morag, so, descending, and finding on a nearer view that his surmise was correct, he hastened to meet her. The road ran here between a high gravel heap and the river's edge, and he halted at the beginning of the passage, since it was somewhat narrowed by the crumbling away of the bank of the stream. The girl had not observed him yet, and he noted that he had never seen her face so pale; pensive and brooding she came, her eyes downcast, her figure statue-like: it was a strange Morag. Her garron ambled along contentedly, but at last shied violently at sight of Fraser, and the lady looking up with a start, alighted instantly. Instantly also she swung her mount across the track, effectually blocking the way, while she grasped her riding-crop aggressively.

"You?" she cried.

"I intrude, it seems?" said Fraser.

"Do you go far, sir?" she said with something of a sneer. "Only an evening ramble I doubt not?"

"Yes, an evening ramble," he said coldly; "but since I offend—" He made as if to pass her.

"No, no," she cried in alarm, and by an adroit movement of her shaggy mount she blocked the narrow track even more securely. "Your escort to Aros, I beg of you!"

She paused awkwardly enough, but did not move from her position of defending the road, while Fraser gazed at her in pained amazement. Then she flung back her head as in defiance and returned his look. But her face was very white, her lips quivering, and the next moment her eyes were tear-suffused, and her cheeks glowed hotly. She laid an appealing hand on his arm.

"Oh, be kind, sir, if only for my sake. Come back with me, come back with me!"

With eyes that brimmed and burned she searched his face, as who should say: What do you know? whilst he stood erect and pale, confounded by this passion of her prayer, these changes of her mood.

"Your servant, madam," he said, and turned with her.

Again her whole nature took a rainbow change, her face shone, while she smiled on him from misty eyes. And now they went on in an ominous silence, the surgeon leading the garron with his uninjured hand. But if he had been astonished at this quick alternation of smiles and tears, he was to be yet further mystified by her sudden return to matters of fact when next she spoke.

"You have a little sister, Mr. Fraser?" she asked.

"In London, yes."

"Muriel, I think, you said?"

"Muriel, yes," he answered, charmed for the moment from his present cares, for in fancy he heard the childish voice at a ballad.

Morag smiled in reply to his brightening countenance.

"How old is the little sister now?"

"Why—eleven—no—twelve. Muriel... Muriel ... "He doated on the memories the name recalled. "'tis two years since I saw her."

"Two years—a long time. But you will soon see her?"

He gave a quick glance at the fair face that seemed so ingenuous. "Ah, yes," he said; "soon. But first there is this plague to be quit of."

"Yet Doctor MacNab comes and the little sister waits. Fie, fie, what a lazy brother!" Where were her tears now? She laughed with a merriment that he told himself was divine.

"I fear the little sister would scarce approve if I left these poor sick folks because another comes to help in their healing," said he.

"Then you do not go even when Doctor MacNab comes?" she queried, suddenly halting, and there was something harsh and metallic in her voice.

He turned to find her changed again, the laughter had gone from her lips, and her eyes were once more a mingled dew and fire. And yet, even then, amidst all her bewilderment, one thought and one thought only was sweeping in on his heart and brain in fuller and fuller tides, possessing him wholly: a secret terror—a secret gladness—it caused him to shun her gaze. She saw his glance quaver and fail, and forthwith misinterpreted.

"I knew, I knew," she cried, and flung an arm aloft, as if to denounce him for the spy she thought him. "'tis not the plague alone that holds you here; 'tis not alone your charity that binds you to the Isle?"

This was again a different Morag—different, indeed, from her of the moonlit heath of twenty hours ago. What had happened to poison so her every thought of him? asked Fraser of himself. There she stood, and on her features so fair, so tragic, loathing mingled with the triumph of her discovery.

"It is not these alone?" she repeated, pale and breathlessly eager.

"Not these alone, madam," he said simply. "There is another bond, but it is not what you deem. I am no spy—Must I repeat it?—I am no spy."

Impatient in her unbelief, she stamped her foot.

"Is the bond that holds you aught that will bear the light of day?" she said.

Even as they were uttered he forgave the words. All his being cried out to him to enfold her in his arms and hush this shrill wrath in the murmur of protesting love. "So dear, so dear," he told himself. "So dear, so dear." And yet he held his peace. But the longing he suppressed from speech stole to his eyes at last, and as he raised them, calm and reverent to her face, she read the message he had not spoken and quailed before its intensity of appeal.

It was just at that moment that a noise of padding hoofs fell on their ears, and a little man wearing goggles and a broad-brimmed beaver, and mounted on such another shaggy pony as Morag's, appeared round the end of a grassy mound. On his saddle in front of him he carried a wig with bob-curls, but at sight of the lady this was hastily donned, and, dismounting, he bowed as if in a minuet.

"Dear Doctor MacNab," cried Morag briskly, another change of manner appalling Fraser by its swift appearance, "and but newly from the Ross? We are much beholden to you for your haste, sir. What with broken bones and deadly plagues, are we not in a sad way, Mr. Fraser?" She indicated her companion's arm in the sling. "Mr. Fraser, a surgeon of the Navy. Doctor MacNab of Aros Isle." There was an attempt at gaiety in her tone, but she was none the less distrait as she turned aside to an outcropping rock and mounted her garron.

The old surgeon bowed to the introduction, his whimsical little red nose in the air, whilst he turned droll eyes on Morag, saying:

"And it's myself I should be healing, physician as I am. Never a visit to Aros House, but a new wound, madam." He put a hand to his breast and sighed. "Plague? A broken arm? What are these to a fractured heart, Mr. Fraser?"

Morag's laughter in reply was a trifle strained, and she showed a hint of red in either cheek as she went ahead of the men, and left them to follow discussing the pestilence.

In the midst of a harangue on the fever, the old surgeon broke off all at once. "What was it?" he said suddenly. "Now I remember! ... Miss Morag!" he called.

She waited till they came up.

"Oh, I but wanted to say that had I not known your brother was in Paris, I could have sworn it was he who passed me at Rhoail there, not an hour gone. A remarkable likeness, madam. Now who can it be?"

Morag's cheeks were now chalky-white again: but she was so far herself as to give a warning glance in Fraser's direction, and the old babbler held his peace instantly.

"Who, indeed, could it be?" she said. "Norman, as you know, cannot leave Paris with safety... But I keep you from your plague and its humours, I fear. I see Mr. Fraser still eager to discuss his treatment." And so she rode on, leaving Fraser more thoughtful than ever.

Dr. MacNab returned to the point at which he had broken off—a matter of a rabbit-soup. To the old fellow the rabbit was anathema.

"A little nosing brat of a beast living in the bowels of the earth, sir! Phew! And indeed, Mr. Fraser, a possible cause of the pest, sir; yes, sir!"

Regarding the need for a continuance of Fraser's attendance on the sick men the old surgeon was equally emphatic.

"Miss Morag questions the necessity of this," said Fraser.

"Then Miss Morag is kindlier in her thoughts of my ability than I am myself. You must stay, Mr. Fraser, till we finish one way or another. You hear us, Miss Morag," he called to the girl who was entering the porch of Aros House, just as he dismounted.

"I hear you, sir," she replied without turning her head. But Fraser saw the fair neck flush rosy as she spoke.

14: Norman

A YOUNG man with pale face and smiling blue eyes breasted the hill above Torlochan, singing as he came. The mountain winds raced to meet him, and he laughed boyishly as they tossed his heavy yellow locks this way and that; he sang the louder for all their bufferings. At times he leapt runnels that he might have stepped across with ease; and once he halted on an outcropping rock to turn in a pirouette upon it—surely a high good-humour this. But at last he broke into a soliloquy—always a sign of earnest with him, whatever his playtime mood might seem.

"'Tis worth wetting one's feet for, Norman, my dear," said he. "This will be no paltry two hundred pounds, and a crown a day for life. 'What is it now?' old Grandpa Vaughan will ask. 'The Prince's route in the new rising,' say I. And 'Gad, you're the match of us all,' he'll say. 'Pickle himself can't compare with you, sir.' Tis you are the king of the fishers, la!'"

And so Norman MacLean came singing over the hills to Aros. Word had come from Ben Talla to Rhoail-—where he had made his new hiding—of a strange vessel at anchor in the Witches' Bay, and he had instantly set out to reconnoitre. It might mean that the Fort-William garrison had got wind of Drumfin; or it might be a move of some brother-spy —Bruce or Pickle himself—who would gladly forestall him of his prey and its price; so, smiling and singing, he came through morning mists on Torlochan Hill, and thence through Glenaros wood to Glenaros shore. He took post finally on a rocky point over against which the ruin of the older Castle Aros could be faintly glimpsed through the curtains of fog as a ghostly tower suspended in mid-air. In the shallow waters inshore where Aros River chased the outgoing tide, a shadowy schooner swung at anchor, and when the mist had cleared from the coast, she showed as a peaceful-looking bark with a hull of black and salmon-colour.

But if the fog-bank thinned landwards, it was a different story on the Sound. Dense and belted, the white vapours lay motionless in the curve of the Kyle, and it seemed plain that it was this impenetrable pall that had sent the vessel inshore for safety.

No sign of life was to be seen on her. But it was not the first adventure of the kind in which the youth on the beach had taken part, and he deemed a close approach inadvisable. He could wait. His eye caught a patch of grass encircled by the black rocks, and he smiled approval of its proximity as if this had been his due, as if it had been spread by some elfin valet for him and him alone. Still humming an old-time air—it was "Macintosh's Lament," but he hummed it happily, no import of its profounds of sadness seeming to touch him—he tossed his dark cloak over the green spot, stretched himself prone and lay *perdu*, raising his head now and again for a glance at the schooner.

But after a little he tired of his task, and, finally, for lack of better sport took to tossing from hand to hand some trinkets from the pockets of his skirted coat; for all his pale cheek and clever eye, a child amid his toys.

Among the mass of rings and pendants and snuffboxes with portraits on their lids, were a few tiny miniatures; and latterly he discarded all the trumpery except these ivories, which he rattled like dice, or shuffled as they had been cards. There were three in all, and all were representations of women's faces—delicate ethereal limnings, where the tints of the cheeks and the eyelashes' faint shadows seemed those of life itself, or rather of some distant fairy life, silent, smiling, and a-dream. The simper no longer dwelt on his hps, however, for although he still soothed the old lament softly, something of the dark and ancient lore of his race returned to his memory, as he beheld the persistent luck with which one of the miniatures ever turned uppermost. It held a woman's portrait, a face encircled with dark hair, a face, mignonne, alert, lips pouting, the wide eyes watchful.

"'Toinette," he said, addressing it—" ah, 'Toinette, if only you were here to share the honours of the game. But could I trust you, Tony? Would you play fair, my dear?"

He ceased for an instant in order to gaze quizzingly at the schooner; anon he toyed with the miniatures again, and deigned a glance at the other faces.

"The far too sensible Marguerite!" he said. "And Marie! Marie—my little saint of the forests of Angers! Ah, Marie! all too good for poor Norman! What a world! what a world!"

He laughed softly and kicked light heels in air.

"And 'Toinette—the false 'Toinette? To think that of all three it is only she who comes back to me in midnight dreams. There's the irony—there's the smart, Norman, my dear."

A faint sound of voices, a foot knocking on the stones of the beach, roused him from his reverie, and he swept a handful of trinkets into either pocket of his coat, and lay still as the rocks around, for he saw two men approaching the very point where he lay.

"Drumfin," he chuckled—"Drumfin—on his guard against the schooner. What luck, Norman!"

He scanned the other and recognised him also.

"Pennyfuaran returned?" he said. "Bravo, Morag! It seems your singed moth does not dread the fire."

The exile and his companion were almost over the youth before he stirred and looked up smiling. Drumfin frowned at sight of the pale sinister face gazing up from amid the rock and seaweed, like some gnome from the earth's depths pushing out to the glad day. His hand was even on his hanger, when Pennyfuaran signed to him to desist, and hailed the apparition.

"Why, if it be not Norman himself!" he cried.

"And who is here but Pennyfuaran," said Norman smiling again. He did not rise.

Drumfin's face cleared in part, but his brows were still a trifle drawn, as he gazed down on the delicate, mobile face, while Pennyfuaran spoke a word of introduction.

"You will pardon me if I do not rise, gentlemen," said Norman. "Indeed, you were well advised if you also seated yourselves here, so will you be less easily observed from the ship. I take it your errand is the same as mine, sir," he went on, addressing Drumfin. "You watch her movements?"

"Why, yes," said the exile, sighing. "There's little else to do."

Pennyfuaran seated himself, but Drumfin still remained standing, an abstracted eye on Norman.

"I must have known you as a boy," he said at last. "But it is some other set of recollections that your face now stirs. Why, yes ... at Avignon ... Was there not a lady ...?"

"The Prince's friend?" queried Norman.

"Why, yes ... but—"

"Could it be de Talmond now?" hesitated the youth, a wary eye on the other.

Drumfin caught the look and grew suddenly wroth. It was plain he suspected this young man of an attempt to mislead.

"No," he broke out passionately, and there and then the mere sign of his anger seemed an incongruity with the man himself. Was it the memory of his Prince's follies that stirred him so strangely, or something in the smiling countenance of the youth at his feet?" No," he said. "Not Talmond, sir, nor Montbazon, nor Guéméné. 'Twas la Baronne—la Baronne—?"

"De Bas-Ondulé," said Norman, his face a trifle haggard now.

"Why, yes, sir, the same."

"The cat! Have not I heard of her? But why should features so commonplace as mine recall hers so beautiful? I never beheld the lady, and, traitress to my Prince as she proved, had never a desire to see her."

"No?" said Drumfin. "And you never saw her? 'tis strange your face recalls hers then, for since her fall ten years ago, I have never spared her a thought."

"Strange, indeed," said Norman— "woundily strange! Yet though I was in Avignon at the season of her discovery, I knew nothing of her. I jalouse that it would be my face brought the time and place to mind, and so her ladyship of fond remembrance?"

"It may be," said the exile.

"I trust the accident is not prejudicial to your good opinion of the son of my father, sir? Drumfin and Aros were aye friends and on the right side."

The old Jacobite bowed again.

"And indeed," went on Norman, "though it's myself that's saying it, still and on its truly nothing but mixing black and white to name that woman and myself in a breath, for my instincts are as loyal as my father's; and, young as I am—though it's myself that's speaking—I have done work for . the cause." His voice lowered as in modesty while he concluded. "Indeed, sir, to tell you frankly, and in despite of Pennyfuaran's presence, I have Clancarty's confidence in the immediate business in hand."

Drumfin winced as if in pain. "And," went on Norman, noting the start, "it's for no other reason I'm watching the schooner here. I trust, sir, this new-comer bodes no evil to us."

The old man shook his head. "I cannot tell," he answered. Yet he did not turn to look at this ship that threatened danger, for it seemed even as if he saw the greater peril close at hand, and he kept his steady eye on the youth couched on the rock at his feet.

"She shows no bustle anyway," said Pennyfuaran. "'tis the fog-bank on the Sound has sent her in, I suppose."

"Agreed," said Norman. "A sailor's terror this same fog. And yet it is nought to what I saw in Tiree but the other day—a mist of weeks, and thick enough for a knife to cut."

"In Tiree?" said Pennyfuaran. "Were you there? Then you'd know of cousin Angus and his trouble?"

"Why, yes," answered Norman. "You have it already, it seems. But, of course, I had forgotten," he said, addressing Drumfin. "You were there at the time, sir, did I not hear?"

"Not quite," said Drumfin. "I happened to be away the day the man was stabbed."

"Poor Chisholm!" said Norman. "A decent body! Misguided though—misguided!"

"'Twas a Mr. Fraser who told us of it," said Pennyfuaran.

"Fraser!" cried Norman in affected surprise. "The trusty?"

"A spy, you mean? No," said the chieftain.

"He is a surgeon from a ship of the King's Navy."

"The same—the same! Spy and surgeon, both! It was he who pushed on poor Angus in a quarrel personal—the hound!—so that he might rid himself of a rival in his traitor's trade, for Chisholm was also a trusty, it seems."

"Spy?" said Pennyfuaran. "Fraser?"

Norman chuckled. "Spy and surgeon," he said. "He has a travelling wardrobe, has Fraser. But tell me this, Pennyfuaran: Is he in the Isle, this Fraser? For if he is, good-bye from me to Aros, let me tell you."

Pennyfuaran's cheeks flushed, and a hint of moisture came to his eyes. "He's still in Aros," he said quietly, as if restraining himself, "and in your father's house, Norman. He has a broken arm, you must know; and then he has some plague-stricken folk in hand. It's these that keep him waiting on, I believe."

"Cousin," said Norman gravely. "I am glad you've told me this. For neither you with your half-and-half ways, nor I, nor any white cockade, is safe with him here. That schooner, believe me, is less dangerous, were she as full of Hanoverians as the horse of wood outside the walls of Troy was of Greeks. Man, he'll stop at nothing, will Fraser."

Excited by the harangue, Pennyfuaran got to his feet, and Norman rising with him, stooped to take up his cloak. As he raised the heavy mantle, something fell from its folds, tinkled on the rocks, and then lay on a little pad of bladder-wrack, looking up appealingly at all of them—a miniature of a lady with dark hair unpowdered, with pouting lips, with steady, watchful eyes.

Drumfin gazed at it fixedly, while Norman, pale and dry-lipped, picked it up. For a moment he looked at it critically, head to one side, and then with a little forced laugh and a bright eye, handed it to the old Jacobite.

"A fair face—something magical in its attractiveness, I opine. I found it in an old curiosity shop of the Latin Quarter in Paris, I remember. I wondered then if it could be from life—I wonder yet. But from any view, a fair face and something magical in it, I say."

It was a keen eye the old man turned on the speaker, but the youth did not redden: the actor in Norman had the upper hand now, and it was a strong hand. Not merely fear of discovery held him true to his art: it was vanity also of his proficiency therein, and delight in the encounter, unsought as it had been. He was quite collected, and, despite his desperate pass, an old-time air was humming all the while through his clear shallow brain—the lament he had trolled in the morning as he came over Torlochan.

"A fair face and something magical," said Drumfin contemplatively, turning the miniature this way and that; "yet it were best never to have seen it in the flesh. Wondrous and beautiful, and yet she flung wide and far the ashes of death. It is the Baronne de Bas-Ondulé, Mr. Norman, whom you say you have never seen."

His eyes were piercing now, but the youth was still smiling bravely back to them, when suddenly Pennyfuaran, to whom all this was a trifle bewildering, broke in:

"Leave Bas-Ondulé for a moment, gentlemen, and look at the Witches' Bay, I beg of you. Yonder is your horse of Troy, Norman."

Down the side of the black and salmon-coloured hull, little figures in red and white were slowly dropping into boats—the Hanoverian soldiery; and instantly the three men on the rocks ran for the shelter of Glenaros woods. Once they were under the cover of the trees Drumfin spoke to the others.

"Get back to Aros with all speed," he said. "I go north."

They parted in the wet thicket straightway, and the young men left him standing deep in thought, as they crashed through the undergrowth and disappeared. Then, once Norman McLean was out of sight, the exile bestirred himself: yet it was not to the north he set his face. He turned southwards from Aros, and, passing it far to the west, journeyed by the devious ways of the old and half-forgotten tracks that led to Moy, twenty miles away.

Norman and Pennyfuaran, intent on their own safety, beheld nothing of all this change of front, and pushing clear at last of the birches and dwarf oaks on the lower slopes of the hill, laid themselves, prone and panting, on the wet heather, and looked down through the soft rain on Aros.

"See," said Norman. "Yonder they go, the Sidier Roy, thick as swarming bees. Lord, it's your King's men have the best of it, Kenneth MacKinnon. A roof over one's head most nights in the year is aye something."

"Roof or no roof," said the chieftain, "it's me would be glad to change places with you, cousin. Since I met you to-day, I've done naught but groan at my own lot and envy yours."

The other glanced sharply at him.

"Is it Morag?" he said.

"As usual, Norman, you've guessed the bigger half of the trouble. It is Morag, and it's—we'll say—my blood and name as well ... Oh, King's man? Me?"

"Ay, you're only half-Hanover, Kenneth, I can see that. But what puzzles me is, that wholehearted Hanover seems a likelier winner of the race, if all reports be true?"

"You mean just what, Norman?"

"I mean Fraser, cousin. Oh, I ken, I ken! for I hear tales as good as a news-letter. I mean Fraser, man: courteous and attentive, he's ever about her, is he not? And you ken it, too, cousin mine."

Pennyfuaran flushed. "It's me has the heavy heart," he said weakly.

"He? A suitor to sister of mine?" cried Norman in a white heat of scorn. "Were it not for the highest of all interests at stake, I'd be at him with a knife this very hour, I say. I tell you, Kenneth, he's spy and worse than spy."

"God!" cried Pennyfuaran. "But for his broken arm, I'd challenge him."

"So?" said Norman. "Yet is it fair to leave the girl unwarned? For myself, I've but hinted it to her as yet. The task is delicate, you see: and one fears to hurt the little sister. But all the same it is cowardly not to tell; and it's clear to me now I should have been more open with her."

There fell a silence for a httle between them then, but at last Pennyfuaran rose to his feet, and extended his hand.

"I'll be going down now," he said. Then, as if repeating a lesson, he continued, "Yes, I'll be going down now."

Norman scanned his face narrowly, and nodded approval of the results of his scrutiny.

"Good luck!" he said, and standing high on a little rocky bluff, he watched in sober silence as the chieftain's kilted figure descended the hillside.

But when Pennyfuaran had passed out of sight within the screen of birch, Norman laughed softly, and made a pirouette on the rock, his mantle floating wide as he revolved to the accompaniment of snapping fingers. Then he ceased and set off for Rhoail. Sunset found him recrossing Torlochan Hill, leaping the water-courses lightly and with laughter, and ever and anon humming, well-pleased, the sad old lament he had trolled through the mists of the morning.

15: The repeated phrase

Little and lonely and sad, a ruined chapel of pre-Reformation times looked out on the grey Sound from a tiny headland at Pennygown. Below the cliff stood the chapel's successor—a thatched barn-like structure called the preaching-house; and here the Gualachaolish minister held sermon to the Aros folks, but only on every sixth Sunday, however, for his district was wide, his stations were many, and his horses few and elderly.

A fortnight after the advent of the Sidier Roy there was a preaching, and though the plague was known to be still present in Tigh-ban, yet the red coats of the soldier-lads proved too much for the fears of the lasses of the glen, and they came to the service in flocks. What with the grenadiers' scarlet tunics and the tartan tonnags of the maids, the little place was gay with colour. The Aros household were present, and just at the opening psalm, Pennyfuaran joined them.

Morag met his startled eye, as it rested on her face for an instant. All through the service she wondered at the strangeness of his glance; and when the preacher's soft Gaelic, droning and sibilant, had ceased in the closing benediction, and the rustle that preceded the departure of the worshippers was heard, she again caught his look, strained and angry, bent on her. Instinctively she fell behind as the common people departed, and leaving her own party, sought distraction in a word or two with the old clergyman.

Pennyfuaran saw the evasion, and came out of doors alone. The soldiers and the glen lasses were dotting the road to Aros, yet there were a few luckless girls unattended by cavaliers, and these had seated themselves on the broad stairs that mounted the wall surrounding the graveyard and the ruined chapel. They were busy removing shoes and mogain preparatory to their return to the wilds of the strath, when they caught sight of the chieftain and scurried off; and he sat down on the steps they had vacated. Aros passed with a kinswoman from Calgary on his arm; but Morag still accompanied the fagged minister, even to the saddling of his garron in the cave that served for stable.

At last the old clerk mounting wearily, rode off, and the girl came back and up the path to where Pennyfuaran sat waiting.

"A penny for your thoughts, cousin Kenneth," she said, with a gaiety assumed.

"They are of you, and it's a King's ransom rather than a penny's their price," said he.

She laughed and tried to fathom him at a glance. Had he forgiven her already that he spoke so lightly? Were bygones to be bygones, despite his face so grim?

"They are of you and of the first day I saw you. 'Twas in this very place, cousin," he continued.

She shuddered in mockery. "A place of graves?" she said.

"It was one day long ago when I was but a boy. You were lost from home, and a tired little lass tending an injured lamb was what we found."

"I remember," she cried. "Silver, my collie, brought you in a pack, and I was fearful of the dog lest he should be jealous of the lambkin."

The chieftain's brow cleared, and he laughed boyishly. "Let us go into the chapel, cousin, and picture it again," he said.

They mounted the steps to the wall-top and, descending the interior flight, passed through the cemetery, and came within the ancient chapel. Morag looked round at the lichens on the great stones, madder and orange and crotal-grey; at the grasses topping the outline of the ruin, their thin spears and pennons clear-cut against the sky.

"Years and years, and it does not change," she said. "Here is the broken cross where you found the lamb and me, and both asleep."

In front of the eastern wall was the upright shaft of a Celtic cross, the terminals gone, and on its westward face, a rude figure of the Mother and Child.

"And the Holy Ones were watching over you," said Pennyfuaran softly. "May they ever watch, Morag."

His tone startled her; she found his eye hard and earnest on her again.

"What do you mean? You are strange to-day, Pennyfuaran. Is there danger?"

He turned abruptly from her and paced nervously over the slaty tombstones that floored the place; his face was twitching.

"What do you mean?" she asked again.

"I cannot tell you," he said. "And yet I cannot hold my peace."

He paced the flags anew, and his footfalls were dully reverberant in that lonely place.

"Oh," he cried suddenly, and there were tears in his eyes. "I cannot forget. I can never forget. Indeed and indeed, Morag, I can never forget." He seized her hand and kissed it passionately.

She strove to withdraw her fingers and was silent, looking away from him through a window-slit to where, across the grey waters, the towers of Fiunary sat bowered even at winter's opening in boscage of the greenest.

"I can never forget," was all he could reiterate with pale lips. "Morag, Morag!" he cried, and releasing her hand, he remained with arms outstretched. But she did not move from her gazing across to Fiunary; and so he stood, the handsomest of figures in the bright tartan of his clan, the red tide of flushings coming and going in the quarter-circle of clear skin on the fine brow.

At last she turned, and he saw a little wrinkling of her forehead he had never seen before. That was all, but in a flash it changed the fine gentleman so play-actorlike, to the barbarian, and tossing his plaid on his shoulder, he brought his clenched hands together in a sudden convulsive movement.

"Then it's with this Hanoverian I've to deal," he said, his mouth hard. "And let me tell you, Morag MacLean —"

He stopped at sight of her. She had been moving towards the doorway, but now she halted, her eyes close-shut as if trying to blot out some ugly vision, and when she opened them anew, he could not face her.

"Let us get into the open, sir," she said, as if oppressed by lack of air; and they went out of the ruin and towards the steps in the churchyard wall. "You mean Mr. Fraser, the surgeon?" she continued.

"Surgeon? Surgeon and spy, and worse than that," he said hotly.

"Let the spying rest for proof, cousin. But you call him Hanoverian. Whose service do you own yourself? Are you not of the King's army, sir? And as for Hanoverian and Jacobite, Pennyfuaran — do we not go twenty years back if we make the distinction?"

In her heat the phrase had escaped her before she recognised its purport fully or its origin.

"Ah," said the chieftain. "And is this Morag MacLean? Why, the very words are Fraser's words, his stock argument, indeed!' Twenty years back if we make the distinction? ' His very words! Can this in truth be Morag MacLean?"

It was indeed but a fortnight gone since Fraser had himself used this reasoning to her opposing, and she reddened at the discovery. Where were her ideals now, and her thoughts of her brother's work for the cause? She felt ashamed of her disloyalty, and yet through all her confusion a secret thought made music in her heart. It was just then that Pennyfuaran caught a hint of wavering in her mien, and pressed on with his task.

"And is this Morag MacLean?" he repeated. "Is this the lady who snuffed me out like a farthing taper, because I thought more of my father's lands than of the House of Stuart; because I thought forfeiture a worse evil than George the Second for King? I say it plainly, I say it again—this man has bewitched you—spy as he is, and worse than murderer."

"And that's a lie, Pennyfuaran," she answered, mounting the steps and halting to look down on him.

"It's the white truth," he cried angrily. "And but for the Sidier Roy so close, your brother himself would be here to prove it."

"A lie," she muttered with pale lips, and would have fallen, but he ran up the flight and helped her in safety to the ground.

Fainting though she was, his passion was such that he could not restrain himself. "The truth, I say, Morag, and it was Norman himself sent me to tell it you."

She made never a word of reply, and after a space the two-mile walk back to Aros was resumed moodily and in silence. Passing Tigh-ban, they looked across the fields to the cottages where the plague still held, and saw the distant figure of a tall man with a slung arm, who appeared on the sky-line and waved a hand to them. Pennyfuaran smiled grimly, as he walked on without any signal of response, but Morag paused for a moment to look at the form outlined against the heavy clouds ribbed grey on grey.

"It cannot be," she said with a fall in her voice. "Yet Norman —?"

The moorland stretched seawards, so cold and cheerless and shadowed in the evening light that all perspective seemed lost. It was even as if all the waste and silent places of the earth had suddenly-interposed, evoking the darkness to aid in the separation of these two. The stillness weighed on the girl's heart like lead, and she moved on, unreplying to the gesture of the dim figure on the dark ridges above Tigh-ban.

16: The postscript

ONE evening a fortnight later there were acrid fumes and strange odours around the plague-spot, for it was the night of the fever's quittance, and the surgeons were busy with a disinfection as the Navy understood it. A bucket of Archangel tar had been carried from hut to hut, and red-hot irons having been thrust into this, vapours were produced that well-nigh made short work of the little strength the survivors retained. Yet the resultant coughing and sneezing made no impress on the professional conscience of Dr. McNab, for he declined desisting until a second fiery ordeal had been performed by means of a light applied to some gunpowder steeped in vinegar. Happily these smoky torments were short-lived, and at last the assiduous medicine-men rested from their labours.

Ever since the fever's outbreak the surgeons had quarantined themselves, sleeping of nights in a little hut of turf set on a strip of pastureland between Tigh-ban and the sea; and now, as darkness fell, Fraser lay awake on the low bank of bracken-covered sods which served for bed, listening to the deep breathing of his companion, and summoning up again and again memories of his lady. Something that alienated was between them, he felt; for even if the fever's presence held them apart, yet the remembrance of several unreturned salutes was bitter yet. What could be amiss?

Through breaks in the rude wall chill airs blew, and a splutter of rain came frequent, while mysterious drippings in the dark told of leaks innumerable. Cold comfort it was to think of his task finished, if his absence from Aros House had cost him an estrangement so momentous. He tossed uneasily, and envied the sound sleep of the old man on the turfen bank opposite; even the rattle of the hailstones that succeeded the soft smirring rain did not disturb this ancient's slumbers.

A slit in the angle of the hut caught his eye. Elusive and faint was the light that showed there; he fancied it a belated glimmer of the sunset reflected from the wave-crests of the Sound, as the north wind sent them shorewards to end in the swish and trample of the surf. And now he could think of one thing and one thing only—that magic blush of Morag's half-turned face, when she heard he was to stay on in Aros. Ah, Morag, Morag, what were the thoughts that had issues so lovely? As he dreamed, there came a sudden illumination of the whole field of the army of billows, and lightning ripped the sky jaggedly from horizon to zenith. Afar faint thunder crackled and purred. The wind rose, and soon again came the onpour of hail and sleet, incessant, fierce. Shivering in the searching currents that detached themselves from the whinnying blast outside, he lay listening for the next onset of storm, then sprang suddenly from his couch and ran to the few boards that served to bar the entry to the hut. His left hand was on his hanger, for above the rumour of the coming tempest he heard the sound of running feet. He pushed the door wide open and aside, and peered out; and the next instant another lightning-flash split the heavens and revealed to him across the slant of the hail Charlie Ruapais, the Aros serving-man. The little wizened-faced fellow was out of breath.

"Oh, sir, sir," he cried, "that ever I should come near this pest—that ever I should see the day; but 'tis a message from Miss Morag." He fumbled in his breast. "Shield me, God!" he cried. "Have I lost it?"

"Here, quick—into the hut," said Fraser.

"But—the plague, sir —" cried Charlie.

"In, man, in," said the surgeon.

Doctor MacNab roused slowly to the sparking of flint and steel inside the little room, and was soon kneeling with the others around the horn-lamp set on the floor of pine-needles. The Ruapais discovered the packet just as the lanthorn was lit. There was a map of Aros Isle by Blaeu of Amsterdam, and a triangle of paper containing a few hastily-scribbled lines, signed with Morag's initials.

"Will you pardon Haste to be Forward in writing you," it ran; "but I have it from a Sure Hand that the Sunivaig MacLeans mean to revisit Aros this Night, and if you are to be Safe you must instantly take to the Hill. What a Countryside it is! Charlie is only free to Guide you clear of our Lands, for he must return to go with me on my Journey to Moy to-morrow. My Father sends me there because of the State of the Isle, so disturbed is it not only by Sunivaig men, but by the Military. You will heed my warning, will you not? I trust your arm is better. How Fortunate your work with the Plague is over. Farewell." MM.

"P.S.—I shall be at Craig about Noon. But you must not Think of joining us there unless you can do so safely.'"

Fraser flushed as he read the last words, and he went slowly over them again.

"In the name of Heaven," broke in MacNab, "how do these Tiree folk learn so expeditiously of everything? The fever on its last day, and already they are here!"

"Oh, sir, sir, will it please you to come?" gabbled Charlie, moving uneasily in his sodden clothes, and blinking into either face appealingly.

Fraser scanned the postscript anew, then placed the map and the note in his breast, picked up his sea-cloak, and extended his hand to MacNab.

"Good-bye," said the old surgeon in reply, "and for your aid many thanks, sir. And, man, get you off those splints in a week, if you wouldna have your arm as stiff as a cromag."

His counsel was still in the air, when the young man departed into sleet and darkness.

"Hill or river, sir?" asked Charlie of Fraser.

"Hill. And at the trot. We want to be well away before the next flash."

Fully a mile of bog and thicket had to be traversed before rising ground was won. But the thunderstorm had passed far to the south now; the infrequent lightnings were but flickerings, and as they left the level the hail ceased, a soft rain blurred all things once more, and the wind fell. In order to avoid any chance comer from Gaodhail or Rhoail, they took the shoulder of Beinn-nan-Uaimh, and by the time it was climbed the showers had gone, the sky was partially clear of clouds, and in the faint starlight the fugitive could dimly discern the landmarks Charlie gave him. Here they were to say good-bye, and they paused to look around. All was still and holy, peaceful and kindly, in the dark of the hills and the vast of the blue above, so different from the storm-encircled shore they had left, where even now were all the fury and passion of the Sunivaig clansmen's chase.

"And you hold Ben Talla to the west; and you leave the Forsa at its beginnings; and on and on till Glenmore comes to you. Then west it will be again until you reach Inshriff; and so on by the drove-track till you see Craig. And that's far and far enough for a winter's night, but you'll get it by the paper Miss Morag sent. You follow me, sir?"

"Surely, Charlie, surely. And with all that, and your good wishes, I'll come safe to Craig ere morning breaks. Good-night. *Oidhche mhath.*"

"*Oidhche mhath*" said Charlie, and went down the hill.

When he was out of sight Fraser took out his letter once more, and tried to read its wonderful postscript, but the starlight was too faint for this; so with a happy sigh he returned the papers to his breast, and stepped out cheerily for the head of the glen.

17: The pedlar from the Ross

DURING all his later life, Fraser never forgot that night. The track ran by the river, and he was always eerily near to this liquid thing, brawling or whispering in the dark on his left. On his right the bog was everywhere to unfamiliar eyes, and often he sprang back bemired, but in time. Unnoticed, he passed through the sleeping townships. It was a nightmare of a journey, and as luck would have it, he made better speed than Charlie had allowed, and so overreached his mark before the dawn, which found him two miles past Craig, wandering on the slopes of Corraven.

The coming of day had been a streak and a glint behind the mountaintops. Soon it was a glow, and now the sky was flooding with a radiance which seemed to the weary traveller to become more and more intense with every step he took down the hillside. Never had there been such a day of brightness since the world began, he thought; and again he conned the postscript of last night's letter, humming snatches of sailor-song the while.

When the hill fell away more steeply and he saw something else than sky and moor—the great strath stretching east and west, with the droves track and the river winding side by side down it-middle, the sight took him by rapid avenues of thought to the world of ships and cities and men.

On the other side of the valley was a wilderness of mountains upheaved jaggedly in masses of mauve and sable; and surely by contrast there was something restful in the blue coils of smoke here and there above the dark dots of little houses in the scraggy fields by the riverside. His heart leapt, for one of these little dots was Craig, his trysting-place with Morag at noon.

Coming at last to level ground, he struck the road close by an empty sheep-fank, under whose wall he sat down to rest and consult his map. Craig lay to the east, he saw, a backthrow of a mile or two, and he was still hunting for the mark of Moy on the old print, when a clear sound of singing fell on his ear. Then, on the road and past the angle of the fank-wall, came heavily a great hill-cow with shaggy rust-coloured hide, and behind it keeping time to the canntaireachd she lilted, danced a slim Highland lass of sixteen or so. A leaf-tipped hazel-wand whisked her charge this side and that while she swung gracefully across the path and over again as in the start of the reel. But a movement of Fraser's made known his presence, and at the consciousness of a spectator she stopped suddenly, wide-eyed and blushing to the braid between forehead and hair.

The man resting by the wall looked on her smilingly and did not move, but before he could speak, she had dashed like a fawn past her great beast, and was over the rise of the road and out of sight. The cow turned a mild eye of enquiry on the intruder, and then resumed its dull padding onwards. Looking down at his garb, Fraser quizzed himself as to his appearance. He had taken off his cloak, it is true, yet there was nothing alarming in the apparel its removal disclosed. Hose a trifle muddy, rims of rust on coat-buttons and shoe-buckles, a rude string of canvas attaching his tricorne to his coat-collar, his linen travel-stained, and the rest of his costume in keeping with these enormities—he enumerated all, and smiling grimly, hastened to add to these the offence of two days' lack of shaving. But in any case one thing was sure—he had a tryst at Craig at noon, and, however *déshabillé* he might be, he would keep it. To one so uplifted the vagaries of this shy little herd-lass were nothing, and so he unconcernedly took the track again. Over the rise of the road he saw a cot half a mile away, and leaving this, still in full flight, was the Highland maid. A woman came to the entry of the hut, and, her hand shading her eyes, she looked hard and long at him, then entered and closed the door.

Whether it was hunger or curiosity that impelled, Fraser could not have told, but he made straightway for the little dwelling, and knocked. Thrice he rapped, and then peering into the rude window, saw something move in the interior's gloom. To further knocking, however, there was no response, and he resumed the highway. Another half mile off lay two huts close together beside a burn that clattered to meet the river, and he saw that peat-stacks hid the doorways as he approached, so that he could not make out if they kept open house for him or not. But a reduplicated sound of drawn bolts told a plain tale; on rounding the peats, closed doors again met his eye. And the only answer to the appeal of his knuckles was a sound of many whisperings within.

"A most hospitable side of the country," he said as he turned away. "Give me Tigh-ban itself, if it comes to an exile here."

Craig, he assured himself, could not be far off now, and, with Morag awaiting him, he would soon have a better greeting than this of the snecked gate. The map gave the house as south of the river, and from another rise in the road he saw the heaped winter fuel that betokened cottages near. The bent-thatched huts lying close to the stream did not take the eye readily, but at last he made them out, three or four in all, the little buildings of rude stone, grey and unmortared, leaning in shauchly fashion against each other.

But when he crossed to them over the stream of the Goladoir by means of the usual stepping-stones, he came again to shut doors, and shut they kept, too, despite his knocking. Then a dog howled in one of the huts, and instantly from the others there came a chorus of barkings. Irate, Fraser consulted his map afresh, and finding this was Craig and none other, he hammered incontinently at the door nearest him. At the last he called all his poor Gaelic to command, and cried out in it to the inmates, and a man's voice rephed in English from the interior of the cottage:

"Who are you? What do you want? Where are you from?" asked the voice.

"l am a friend of MacLean of Aros."

"Are you a pedlar?"

"No."

"What do you wish?"

"Direction to the party of Miss MacLean of Aros. She was to have come this way before noon to-day."

"We know nothing of her party ... You are no pedlar?"

"No, I tell you."

"Where are you from?"

"Aros, by Glenforsa."

The door opened and a young man came out, scratching a head covered with fair curls, fine and tiny. He eyed Fraser dubiously. His cheek had never felt steel, and the same fine crisp hair covered it: he was muscular withal.

"Have you seen a pedlar carrying a red box?" he asked.

"No pedlar have I seen, and none do I wish to see," said Fraser testily. "What ails you at the pedlars? My business is with none of them, but with Miss MacLean, whom I was to have met here in order to a further journey to Moy."

"Then will it please you to come in, sir," said the man, still glunching and glooming. "We see few strangers this gate, and we'll aye need to be careful."

The traveller followed him into one of the huts, and in the dark of the interior, a group of folk pushed behind the door by which he entered, and, whispering noisily in Gaelic, took refuge in another apartment that reeked of cattle. It was a bare earthen-floored kitchen he entered, a bed in one corner, a fire in another, with an attempt at a clay chimney projecting over the peats; while in a third corner was a great rude table with bannocks and bowls of broth on three sides of it. Fraser had evidently interrupted a meal, and he began with apologies, which were quickly silenced by protestations of equal civility from a sonsy young woman of great physical beauty, the red and brown of her cheeks being health itself. In several journeys she carried the rough fare ben the house, then laid a fresh white cloth; and whereas the meal had hitherto been brose and bannocks, she now made him a dish of tea.

"Miss Morag's friends are ever ours, sir," said she. "And if it's your will, I'll give you tea—dear as it is—thick enough for the spoon to stand on end in. Your arm will be hurt, sir," she added after a pause.

"Nothing of moment," said the surgeon, making acquaintance eagerly with some broiled troutling that accompanied the brew.

The woman proved to be the wife of Alasdair Ban, the youth who had opened the door to him, and since it was now half an hour after noon, the traveller began to question her about the road to Moy, and the probable cause of Morag's delay. No person had come from the Inshriff, or east side of the glen, but in the early morning twenty or more of the MacAllisters, a gipsy tribe, had passed from the west side—from the Ross probably—the men, women and children on foot, their tents on two led asses. To this story of his wife Alasdair Ban added the information that the gipsies had brought word of a death from plague on Lochlay-side; and such a horror was in the man's look and tone as he spoke that Fraser judged it well to say nothing of the sickness in Aros.

"Would it not be the wise thing for me to go on to Inshriff, and ask for Miss Morag there?" said Fraser at last.

"You might well be doing that same," said Alasdair.

"Will you guide me there?"

"'tis the straight road without a guide, sir."

"But, man, I'll pay."

"Pay, or no," said the man slowly and looking meaningly at his wife. "Pay or no, I maun wait here the day."

"It's the rude folk you'll be thinking us, sir," broke in the handsome wife, her red cheeks flaming redder, "but, you see, there are only old men and weans here beside himself—and there's the pedlar coming."

"Oh, damn the pedlar!" said Fraser. "What has he to do with it?"

There fell a silence. The Highlander poked the peats vigorously, and his wife, her back to the traveller, busied herself with some dishes. Then Alasdair turned, the cleek in his hand, and said:

"It's this way, sir; it's what I am going to say is this. Here was this Irish pedlar at Lochlay-side —he and his brother—when a woman died of the pest. It was he and his brother coffined her; it was he and his brother buried her. Paid and well-paid, too—oh, yes, it was well-paid they were. But it has gone abroad that they are full of the pest themselves. Before the story got about, the younger went off in a smack to the mainland, and by all accounts he's clear. But by the word we have of the other, he's making for Torosay. Nor bite nor sup did he get in the Ross, and so he has been driven far on the road this way. It's a God's pity for the man, but he's bringing seven deaths in his hand, and under my roof he'll not come. It's a God's pity! And still and on I'll stay here till he pass, if he be not dead ere this."

Fraser looked wonderingly at the man as he stood there, the peat-cleek grasped nervously in his hand, his whole frame shaking with the passion of his fear.

"Yonder is a cogie of milk, yonder are bannocks," cried the Highlander. "As he comes by, he'll see us leave them for him by the roadside. Aught else he may whistle for."

The man's panic had caught his wife, and over her task of rinsing dishes, she was sobbing gently with averted face. The ragged mob of bairns and ancients ben the house were mumbling and hustling against the door, their terror at the high words manifest in the confused noises they made.

Fraser pondered his next move. It was a clear hour past noon, and Morag had not yet come. He decided to go on to Inshriff, and accordingly took farewell of the cottar and his wife. As he departed he heard the old folk and the children flocking back from the cold outer room to the warmth of the kitchen peats. Already the sun was low, the air chilly, and he stamped numb toes on the hard of the road, his huge shadow on the heather making giant antics as he did so.

The glen now wound north, and the great walls of hills came crowding closer on the track which grew rapidly steeper, but at the end of this ascent the heights fell away again on either side, and quite a broad valley came into view. To the south a chain of lakes ran, interlacing with mountain-spurs, like the spaces between half-plaited fingers. Close by the roadside was a little grey tumble of buildings set on a flat of vivid green: Inshriff for a surety.

A rocky track went down to the sweep of field around the farm, then came a cobbled court, with a barn and stable facing each other, the back of the dwelling-house forming the third side of the square. From the path's direction it was evident that the back entrance to the dwelling was oftener used than the front, and Fraser was soon tirling at the little mean door of white wood. It was twilight now, and the man who answered the knocking held a lit cruisie in his hand. Grey-whiskered, and with the eyes of a ferret, he bowed and fawned and snuffled to Fraser with all the graces of a Frenchman, rubbing his knuckles in the air all the while, until the surgeon sickened to look at him.

"Well, well," he said in answer to Fraser's question, "and it's Miss Morag and her servants you're looking for? No, she's not come this way yet, sir; not yet. Well, well! and you'll be from the Ross, sir? Well, well!"

Fraser answered that he was not from the Ross, but from the east side of the Isle. He spoke sharply, for the fellow's obsequiousness disconcerted him, and he felt the little ferret eyes search all over his person and rest on his splinted arm.

"Well, well! And you are from Aros, sir? Well done, sir! And you came by the Maam?"

Fraser replied that he had come by Glenforsa. The fellow's manner perplexed him; it was servility itself, yet his questions were those of an equal, and he stood blocking the door without invitation to enter, his politeness expending itself on barren courtesies of tone and bearing. Thinking he would try another issue, the traveller asked suddenly: "The pedlar, has he passed?"

"What pedlar, sir? No pedlar, sir. Is it a packman, sir?"

Again the mechanical smile, the rubbed hands, and the keen glance, then a slack mouth, and an air of innocent curiosity. The transition was too rapid for good acting, and Fraser's jaw tightened as he eyed the man.

"I see," he said drily.

The little eyes shifted and fell; then an easy facile smile folded itself on the mask of a face once more. Fraser looked at him for a moment without a word further, and turning on his heel, strode off in haste, for even the fingers of his injured limb tingled to beat the treacherous jaws of the fellow. As he reached the roadside he stumbled on a little bowl of milk half-empty and he saw that some crumbs of bread lay scattered on the surrounding grass.

"So," he said to himself, "the pedlar has passed Craig after all, and without Alasdair Ban setting eye on him. He must have taken a byway there."

No sooner had the traveller entered the fringe of trees on the crest of the brae than the man in the yard of Inshriff ran across to the stable, and saddling a dun pony rapidly, he led it to the house-door. "Murdo," he called. A voice within returned the hail. "Here's the piper to pay," cried the man with the ferret eyes. "There's a young bird here with a broken wing, asking for Miss Morag of Aros and I've sent him chasing the cuckoo. Pennyfuaran's at Kinloch, and he should have kent of yon ere this: and here is the night and it's a bonnie road for an old man like me. Canny, lad, till I come again in the morning."

Next moment he was mounted and trotting back by the road the surgeon had come.

Fraser, all unconscious of the excitement he had caused in Inshriff, was industrious with his map, and heard nothing of the splutter the rider made a mile away. From the rude print he saw that Glenforsa debouched on Glenmore about two miles further on, and, stepping out, he soon reached this opening in the northern wall of the valley. It was by this way he had himself passed, through the dark of the preceding night; it was by this very route Morag should have come. Had something detained her? Or had she chosen another road for Moy? But evening was fast advancing; the pedlar's story was still in his mind—in fact, if the breadcrumbs spoke truly, the poor man could not be far ahead. It was just possible the sick packman had crossed Morag's route in his wanderings, and Fraser pushed on in the hope of overtaking him.

Half an hour later his shoes were sounding on the pebbly bit of road which ran through the hazel-wood of Benadd. It was mirk enough here, but none so black as to prevent him beholding dimly, when half-way through the copse, the figure of a man rising from his hands and knees by the roadside, stumbling on for a step or two, and so to his knees again. Just as he reached him, the weakling went down once more and this time prone, the wooden box slung on his shoulder clattering where he fell.

Here was the pedlar at last. Fraser raised the flabby length of him, legs trailing, to a mossy bank near by, and endeavoured to set him against a tree-bole, but the man responded too limply and fell sideways like one drunken. A thick sweat was on his hot hands; his tongue lolloped big and horrible from his mouth; a wisp of long hair hung over one eye, and, moving his limbs uncertainly, he whimpered like a snared animal. The surgeon sought for a forgotten flask of spirits, and repeatedly wetting his finger-tip in the liquid, he touched the tongue of the sick man with it. But the patient was now stertorous and whining by turns; and so for a full hour of the chill night, Fraser squatted in the dank undergrowth, moistening the swollen tongue, until at length there came a drowse that stilled the wailing and the hands' tremulous movements. It was a slumber of over an hour's space, and when the waif wakened, the surgeon ran down to the Lussa for some water, his hat serving for pitcher, from which his hollowed hand helped the poor black tongue to a lapping. Then to sleep once more.

By this time a thin fall of snow was come, dusting finely through the spare branches above; beyond the edges of the wood, Fraser saw, the rock and heather were turning white. Then a wind sighed among the birch and hazel, the water ran less quarrelsome, while the snow-flakes fell faster and bigger. The surgeon grew anxious as he watched the weather change, for the sick man's chest was rising and falling in the shallowest of fashions. But the wind did not rise, and as the snow flitted down in heavier and more insistent lines, the chill air passed. Worn as he was with the previous night's adventure, Fraser never wavered in his tendence; sometimes water, sometimes brandy, he held to the cracked lips, so that frequent short naps followed, and by daylight the pedlar could speak.

"'Sowl!" he said, "but 'tis lovely this is."

Very gently Fraser coaxed his story from him, and with intervals of delirium his tale was soon told. It was what the surgeon had expected. The sick man had taken byways and quiet paths off the beaten track, it seemed, seeking, when occasion demanded, shelter from wind and rain and darkness. But the word had gone before that he was plague-stricken, and the shut door awaited him everywhere. Sometimes he found food set by the way-side; sometimes none; and all the while there hung over him the terror of his loneliness and his illness, of the winter night and the wild hills. The last two days were nearly all blackness; up till then he could clearly recount the weary record of his staggerings and stumblings by corrie and glen.

Once he paused in his story, taking in the air hungrily with short breaths, and the surgeon sighed as he felt the pulse and found it fluttering.

"Will I manage, sir?" asked the sick man.

Fraser turned away his face, for the beat at the wrist was weakening rapidly. The dawn was breaking now, and the tracery of snow-laden twigs above lent a shadow that made the features of the pedlar more ghastly still, as he read his answer in the other's silence.

" 'Mother av Hivin!' Tis a pore counthry will lave a man die on the roadside. 'Twas not so in the ould days when the holy wans were in yon place beyond the Ross."

Fraser looked at the dark west where the dying man's gaze lingered. Behind the glens and the hills, and set in the sea at the end of the road-which this poor man had trod, lay the holy place of Scotland. For centuries, and by this very track it might be, the preachers of the cross had come from Iona, and so to wider lands beyond. And this was the fruit of the travail of their souls—this stricken man dying by the wayside at the end of his awful pilgrimage? This—? Was this all?

But his reverie took another flight: a dream of the little sister in London-town came to him, and he saw himself -and the child under the trees at Richmond. It was a sunny day and warm and the flecks of light streaming through the sycamores in full leaf, fell golden on Muriel's hair as she danced everywhere on the sward, making chaplets and posies of daisies. And here was this black thing, Life, waiting for her so fragile. Oh, if he could but gather her and all things tender and fair in arms compassionate to shield them from this nightmare of a world!. . . Then, beside the little sister's face came another, aureoled also in hair of gold. Morag! Morag! What of defeat or disaster could the future hold for her that he would not withstand to the uttermost, if she but gave him the right! ...

Of a sudden, his musing was broken in upon by the croaking voice of the pedlar—

"There's something still to say—something I forgot, sir. 'tis these black fits that send me all astray ... Look in the box, your honour ... It was early yesterday before the faintness came on my spirit that the dark thing happened. Just above Inshriff it was that I saw it—a chase and a fight and a lady cruelly done by.—Water, sir.— Just above Inshriff it was, and me spent and helpless on a rock on the hill. There were six or seven wild fellows crying and shouting, her pony running free, and her maid wailing. And 'twas the devil himself in a long cloak with wings that called them on like so many hounds—-a fat beast of a priest he was. And the lady, God love her, the poor creature — But in the box, sir ..."

"What else, man, what else?" said Fraser, nipping the wrist savagely, and testing the pulse again.

But the dying man smiled vacantly and silently, and slid down in collapse, and the surgeon saw the end was coming. He sprang to the red box, and opened it by its strap and buckle. On the top of a heap of ribbons and trinkets lay a long fold of grey muslin, and Fraser, with a face as white as the pedlar's, recognised the tissue of the pelerine with whose breast-knot Morag's hand had toyed so daintily many a time. He had but marked it for hers, when the man astraddle the bank beside him suddenly gave a quavering heave of the chest. The surgeon glanced quickly at his face and waited, listening. There came a second gasp and a third and then the pedlar had gone on a longer journey than any he had yet known.

And so Fraser scraped the snow from the turf under the birch and hazel shaw, and made a shallow grave, and built a little cairn.

18: A message from France

Six miles west of Craig, and thirteen from the grave of the dead pedlar, stood Kinloch Inn on the shore of Loch Scridain, and facing Ben More. As night fell the snow and the winds possessed the little hostelry. No matter if the depths of the glen were quiet, winds there were ever at Kinloch, for the great bulk of the Ben caught every ocean blast and sent it swirling back on this little two-storey building, all narrow gables and high chimneys.

Kinloch was busy at seasons, for the drovers from the Ross made much use of the Inn on their way to Grasspoint Ferry. But to-night there was no stir about the place, no smell of cattle in the air, and where often the whole six windows blazed cheery and heartsome only two were alight. Into the upper room a giant of a landlord came and went, the handsomest of figures had he worn the philabeg, yet handsome enough in trews, his features a trifle heavy, but a good-humoured mouth behind the great beard. He had placed candles on the sideboard as an additional grace to a room already well-lit by a roaring log-fire, and by dripping cruisies hung on the mantel. Pennyfuaran and Drumfin sat on either hand the great open chimney-place; between them the landlord pushed a little table set with heavy coloured glasses, and then retired at the sound of a knocking below. He reappeared with a steaming punch-jug and a small envelope of leather.

"'Twill be for you, sir," he said, handing the packet to Drumfin, and the exile unfastened the button, and took out a parchment superscribed: "To Mr. Oliver.

"With all Haste."

"Yes, it's for me," he said. "Send the man up."

"'Twas a woman left it, sir, and she's gone."

"Was there not a pedlar with her?"

"No pedlar, sir; but I was to say that he was ill, and would have delivered yesterday, had he but been able."

"Ill, poor devil. Where, I wonder?"

"The woman is gone, sir, and in a great hurry, too. I do not even know her."

"Queer," said Drumfin. "But I wish she had but left the pedlar's direction. Ill, poor devil! ... You may leave us, MacKay."

"Your pleasure, sir," said the landlord, and slipping a little dish of silver on the cloth, he withdrew.

As the door closed, the exile looked at the letter, and then at Pennyfuaran. "It's Cousin Peggy again," he said.

"It's you are the happy man," sighed the chieftain. "Read on, man, read on. Ne'er fash about a poor trimmer like me."

Drumfin broke the seal, and found a letter in a cipher he knew well. He translated it slowly. As he did so his face hardened, and when he had finished, he sat gazing for long into the red of the fire. But of a sudden his eyes grew moist, and his lean brown hands went up to his face. It was only for a second, however, and then he was himself again; yet the sight of an emotion so unusual in his friend, unmanned Pennyfuaran.

"God! What's wrong, Drumfin?"

"All," said the other. "Read that—or rather, listen, while I translate. Here it is: 'Destroy all lists and papers. Thurot useless now. Conflans beaten, his ship, the "Soleil Royal," and the "Heros," stranded at Croisic. Seven ships are come in. Ten are flying at sea. C.P.'"

"What does it mean?" asked Pennyfuaran.

"A new rising and a new failure. This is the chief of the two fleets that were to have aided, and it is scattered to the four winds."

"As black as that!"

"May it be no blacker before the affair finishes," said the exile. "You will keep secret regarding this, lad. For the note is but ten days old, and it will be another ten days before the news is public."

"You may trust me, sir," said Pennyfuaran fiercely. "King's man or no, you may trust me."

"Delay means the safety of many, you'll understand," said Drumfin, abstractedly taking up the tiny chalice of silver which the landlord had laid beside the punch.

"What's that?" asked the chieftain.

The dish of metal had a bowl no larger or deeper than the hollowed palm of a man's hand, and from either side of it a little flat handle projected. There was a scroll of oak leaves running around the margin, and when the exile saw this, he bent his head and kissed the cup reverently.

"It's the Lochalsh stirrup-cup," he said. "It seems MacKay has recognised me."

"You tell me?" cried the young man, and springing to his feet in ecstasy, he spilled some punch into the silver and, gasping and coughing, tossed off the draught. "Pity me! The man's no backward for an innkeeper," he went on. "I'll speak him fair about guarding his tongue."

"Pennyfuaran, man, let him be," said Drumfin. "You go the very way to injure him deeply. If he is an innkeeper, still and on he is Highland, and of the right side, else how does he come by this cup? Besides, he is a

Lochalsh man, you see. I'm safe, man, safe, and I'd be quiet and resting, if you'd but let me." He turned to his favourite occupation of watching the fire's red heart.

Unheeding the rebuff the young man sat down, and filled himself some punch, calling on the other to join.

"And the Prince quaffed you, you limmer," he said, toying with the cup of silver. "The darling Prince! And what though he fails a hundred times, he's still my darling!. . . A toast, Drumfin!' The days that are by wi't.'"

The Jacobite replied with a nod only.

"You're scarcely companionable," protested the youth. "Take your glass, man."

"It's the memories I'm having, Pennyfuaran," said the exile. "Let me be, lad, for the little time I'll have in the glens of remembrance. It's sore thinking I am of the old days—the days when everyone but the King's man wore the tartan." He glanced meaningly at the other's dress.

Pennyfuaran reddened, and reached for a fresh supply of punch.

"The kilt and the plaid?" he said, swinging his haunch and looking down at the dress. "And thanks to Mr. Pitt for them. But King's man or no, Drumfin; Charlie's man or no, try me; there's none will do better by your exile than Kenneth MacKinnon of Pennyfuaran. Haud till't, and I'll play you a spring that'll send the black sorrow flying."

He went to the door, and called loudly in Gaelic, and some distant sounds replying, he said:

"Lend me your pipes, MacKay."

"There's a new reed, sir," answered the landlord.

"New reed or no, bring them to me, you sinful man."

MacKay brought the pipes, and the chieftain taking them, swung the bag to his oxter. The room was big, but all too small for the tuning of the drones that followed; blaring and roaring they sounded, a storm for fury and discord. Then at last the melody came, and away went MacKinnon with a swing and a hit in his step, the streamers of his pipes and the fringe of his plaid sweeping the wood-lined walls, as he turned in the far corner. High and clear and piercing, the air held the big landlord on the stairs, the apple of his throat gulping. High and clear and tremulous now, and still the silent man on the hearth sat gazing into the midmost red of the fire. Lost faiths and passions of old time; the wind in the firs and the roar of many waters; love and death and battle; the march of the clans; the holiness of morning and the tenderness of the afterglow; the salute to the victorious, the lament for the fallen; the hopelessness of the exile, and the cry for the far land of home—the land of soft mists and sea-born hills, of the green straths where the deer came in the dawning: it was these the wild magic of the pipes recalled to life in the chambers of imagery. In reverie the man by the fire saw again Lochshiel on the day of his Prince's splendour; and again he beheld the heights above Glenfinnan alive with the waving tartan. But the vision faded—it flashed and faded; and high on the pass where the clansmen had thronged, empty now and silent, there rose to the pines and the stars a single note of beauty, despairing yet exultant, mingled of sadness and joy, prophetic of fulfilment, aspiring. Drumfin saw and heard it all; then the close came in discord and wail, and the player laid the pipes tenderly aside.

"You're a King's man, Pennyfuaran; and you can do yon?" said the exile. It was an eye of fire he turned on the youth.

"Be damned to the King," said the other, busy at the punch again. "I'm for Pennyfuaran on either side, and no forfeiture." But he reddened, and added after a pause: "Yet it's well you ken, Drumfin, where my folk would have been in my father's time, if it werena for Duart's arrest. And we'd have made as good Jacobites as some, I wot."

The flush passed from Drumfin's face, and the kindling from his eye, and he turned again to his gazing at the flames of clear orange in mid-fire, murmuring to himself: "Like his father before him, the play-actor aye uppermost."

Young MacKinnon sat moodily silent now, for the emotion bred of his playing had passed, and in the patch of white on his forehead the red flushings were coming and going, for it was always thus with Pennyfuaran when he had had a spell of the piping and drinking. After a little he retired to a shady corner of the ingle, and screwing his practice chanter together, he tootled and buzzed and squeaked at grace-notes and little runs of airs for a while. There was only the hint of a melody now and again, dismissed as soon as caught, and a new one sought for, and this he would elaborate with an artist's ease, to be forgotten in a moment in the next elusive air he fashioned.

"Is it Moy again for you to-morrow?" he asked Drumfin in a pause of the practice.

"Moy? Yes," said the exile. "Had I foreseen this snow, I'd never have left it."

"I thought as much, I was for Moy myself."

A little gentle smile flickered on Drumfin's tanned features. The chieftain saw it.

"You smile, Drumfin," he said, "and I ken what makes you. You jalouse I was but going there for hints of how the wind would blow from London or Paris. You think I speak truth when I call myself a trimmer?"

Drumfin did not answer.

"You think I keep in touch with you but for the sake of being on the side of the dog that's uppermost, sir? And the damnable thing is that you're right."

"I guessed as much, laddie. And you ken now, without a journey to Moy, which dog is uppermost."

"I ken, I ken, God pity me! ... And Drumfin, man, you're sorry for me, are you not? Say you're sorry for me, sir."

"Yes, I'm sorry."

"And, by God!it's me that's sorry for myself ... You'll believe me, Drumfin, when I say that?"

"Yes, I believe you, Kenneth."

The insistent Highlander was somewhat appeased by these admissions, and set to his tootling and squeaking once more, a little film of moisture in his eyes. All his airs were now more melancholy and piercing than ever, and each broke abruptly and was replaced by something yet more poignant and appealing. But in the midst of his practice he suddenly ceased, for there came the sound of a loud and masterful knocking below, and the landlord's voice was heard in converse.

19: The tacksman

"It's busy we are to-night, Drumfin," said MacKinnon drily, as he rose and went to the door. "Is it bad luck I've brought with my chanter? I trust it's no red-coats, for King's man or no, I'm with you. Have your hanger ready."

Opening the door, he listened at the top of the stair.

"It's Callum from Inshriff, the fox!" he said. "I must see what brings him this gate." And he went downstairs.

Callum it certainly was, rubbing his hands in air, and cringing on the kitchen's sanded floor.

"It's me you'll be wanting, MacQuarie?" said Pennyfuaran.

"Your honour, yes. Will it please you to come outside and look at my horse?"

It was past midnight now, and round all the four walls of the house the Ben More squalls were sweeping. Yet the two men went out into the dark and flurry of the storm, and passing unnoticed the pony at the nose-ring, walked shorewards.

"Well, well, sir," said MacQuarie, halting at last. "You'll be wondering at me bothering you?"

"I make no doubt but you've good cause," said Pennyfuaran, and his tone was that of conciliation —of submission even, for somehow he felt that it was this the man's attitude demanded.

"Good cause—good cause? Well, Pennyfuaran, it's you'll be the judge. You'll ken Miss MacLean of; Aros, sir?" —

The chieftain started at the question, but a hand on his elbow gave an intimate shake, at once waggish and impertinent, and signified that the tacksman knew his innermost thoughts in the matter.

"Well, well, sir, is it so? ... I just thought as much." —

Pennyfuaran could not see the little ferret eyes, but he knew they were trying to read his emotions, even in the dark, and trying, too, with some measure of success. It was as if he had made full confession of all his passion to this fellow by his side, cringing and masterful at once.—

"Ay, ay, sir, I thought as much—and, you see, thinking as I did, Pennyfuaran, I guessed that if I could put it in your way to do the lady a service of some importance, you'd stand in better favour than you do. You see, I'm speaking freely, sir."

"Yes," said Pennyfuaran, breathing quickly. "Damn you."

"Well, well, sir, you'll no be angry now?" The chieftain could imagine the smile apologetic in the dark. "It's only poor old Callum."

"Go on, man, go on."

"And Murdoch and I—we said: ' We'll do it; we'll help the chieftain; and then when the lady is won—well, maybe Pennyfuaran will let Inshriff go rent-free to Callum. And, indeed, he might be doing something for Murdo, too.' ... You see, sir?" Again the shake of the elbow.

"Go on, man; go on."

"But you see, sir, that's just what Murdo and I were thinking—we were just thinking it, sir."

"It's more than Inshriff I'd give for that same winning, Callum MacQuarie," said Pennyfuaran through his teeth. "But I ken you'll part with nothing till you have my promise; and I give it."

"Well done, sir—and something for Murdo, Pennyfuaran, something for Murdo: Torness now, or Benadd, sir?"

"Either, man, either, he'll have either, I tell you, if I have success in the affair."

"Then here's the way of it ... It was Murdo was taking the hill this morning—home from Glencannel he was coming, when he saw Deaf Alan and some of his wild Tiree men hiding in the wood at Benadd, and he watched them for a bit. You'll ken Alan's errand as well as me, sir, I'll warrant— a hunt for Angus MacLean, tacksman in Tiree, and second cousin to Aros. And it seems that neither plague nor soldiermen has put him off his purpose."

"Yes, yes. But Miss Morag, Callum?"

"Well, well, you're quick at taking a point, sir. She was with them."

"With them, MacQuarie?" cried Pennyfuaran in an excited whisper. "Is it kidnapping?"

"'Tis just that—the fools! I believe she was on the road for Moy, coming down from Aros by Glenforsa. But they are fools, sir, fools or mad! They must have some wild notion of holding her for a hostage until Aros gives up cousin Angus. And yet the Sidier Roy are everywhere! Well, well!"

"The fools?" said Pennyfuaran. "The devils, you mean!"

"Well, well, sir, both," said MacQuarie. But where's the ill wind that blows nobody good? The snow had come by the time Murdo gave me the tale, and so I followed their tracks ... You take me, sir? The lady is in danger, and who but Pennyfuaran to the rescue? And it's Callum MacQuarie that kens her prison."

"My Callum!" cried the chieftain delightedly. "The best of rogues!" And he shook the tacksman affectionately one hand on either shoulder. "Now tell me—where?—where?"

"You'll mind Inshriff, Pennyfuaran?" "Rent-free, yes. And a swatch of Torness for Murdo ... Where is she?"

"Well, well, sir, but it's you that's hasty. She's in Cameron Cave."

"That's nothing, then—a night's journey at most."

"And yet, sir, my story is not ended. For here but three hours gone this very night, there comes to Inshriff a man asking for Miss Morag. All the airs of a *duin'-uasal* he had, and a broken arm forby."

"Hell!" said Pennyfuaran. "It's Fraser."

"Well, well, sir! And is Fraser his name? ... But Miss Morag is safe, sir, where this Fraser will never find her. And the safer, too, that Belle is with her. Belle? Well-named, say I, deaving even Alan with her ongoings. Did I not hear her, as they lay in Cruach Ardura waiting for the dark? Such a tongue, sir!"

"Yes, yes," said the other, "but it's of the man with the airs of breeding and the broken arm, I'm thinking."

"Fraser, sir, I doubt not. To judge by his bearing he was at ease in these parts. What's to be done, sir?"

"To be done—to be done?" repeated MacKinnon abstractedly. "It's myself must manage it. No outside help, if I am to stand well in the affair. Now, if Drumfin were not here —"

"Drumfin!" cried MacQuarie, his ferret eyes beads of piercing brightness as he came suddenly into the slant of rays from the inn-window.

"Drumfin? Yes, you toad!" cried the chieftain, his hands on Callum's throat, and there was no question now as to who was master. "What have I said? Have I let it slip my foolish tongue? ... But if you breathe it, if you even breathe it, I'll —" A hand went to the knife in his stocking.

"Canny, Pennyfuaran, canny," gasped the tacksman, escaping his hold. "Well, well—well, well! What business is it of mine? If Drumfin cares to leave France, if he cares to risk his neck, let him. He'll be none the worse of me, sir."

The young man still glowered at him, his hand on his *sgian dubh*. "Remember," he said.

"What's your will, then, sir," said the other crossly, adjusting his coat-collar. "What's to do in your own affair?"

"Belle is with her, you say? Have you a watch on the cave in case they move?" "I have set Rob the Tinker, sir."

"Then back to Inshriff with you, until I get quietly clear of the inn here. I'll come on to you there some time to-night, late or early, as I find it safest ... And Callum, see ..." He put a finger to shut lips, and tapped his black knife meaningly.

"Well, well, sir," said MacQuarie, expostulation in his accents. And Pennyfuaran went indoors.

A moment later the landlord came out and found the man with the ferret eyes doubled up in a fit of silent laughter beside the horse's head. At sight of the innkeeper, however, he started erect, and asked for a cup of ale. Then he swung on to his pony, and went off cautiously through snow and wind and darkness, and so into the mouth of Glenmore. But so obsessed by one idea was he, that the fury of the elements troubled him but little, and he laughed low as he rode. "Drumfin," he repeated to himself, and chuckled softly.

20: The cave at Cameron

It was daylight full and fair when Fraser came to the cross-roads at Strathcoil, two miles west of his last night's resting-place. At the cottage here the old folks were kindly and asked no quizzes about a pedlar, but gave the wanderer a meal beside a log-fire, and straightway packed him to bed. For this old man and his spouse one thing only was evident: here was a traveller spent and famishing, and the remedy was clear. Who he was mattered little; and they pottered around him with slow feet and bent backs, their courtesy ungrudging and delicate.

When at length the surgeon slept it was deeply, and evening shades were fast thickening ere he wakened to the sound of a well-known voice in the next room. Springing out of bed, he dressed hastily, and came ben to find Charlie Ruapais crouched over the peats, a bowl of broth on his knee.

"*Dhia!*" cried Charlie at sight of him, and laying down the vessel hastily, he caught Fraser's uninjured hand and burst into a fit of the most passionate weeping. Concernedly the old folks looked on, lifting their hands in air, shaking their heads, and whispering in Gaelic.

"Oh, sir," cried Charlie. "The black day, the black day!"

The surgeon tried to soothe the little man by patting and hushing, but to no purpose.

"Have you a horse, sir?" sobbed the wizard-face. "Oh, sir, have you by any chance a horse?"

"Never a horse, Charlie. Why do you ask?"

"She is at Cameron, sir—Miss Morag, I mean ... I've caught my pony afresh, and were you but mounted, we'd be at her side within the hour."

In the light of the pedlar's story, Fraser saw the little man's meaning, and so, turning to his frail host, he explained, in what Gaelic he could command, his instant need of a horse. So impressed had the old man been by the tears of the Ruapais and the grave bearing of Fraser that he doubted little but that a matter of importance was in hand, and forthwith he took the surgeon to a shed where a little garron stood. The saddle was of coarse grass, the stirrups naught but looped ropes of woven bent, but Fraser was in no cavilling mood and mounted at once. One of his few guineas went to the old fellow; Charlie trotted out his pony, and they were off with all speed on the road to Cameron.

They dismounted five minutes after setting out, however, for here the track lay over Ardura Brae; and as they led their panting beasts up the steep, Charlie breathlessly told his story.

About noon on the previous day, Miss Morag, with Belle for maid and himself for gillie, had set out from Aros for Moy. They had come by way of Glenforsa to Inshriff without mishap, save for some bogging of Belle's pony. But just at the entry to Glenmore some six or seven rough fellows had started from the heather, one attempting to seize the bridle of Morag's garron. Whipping the fellow's face, she freed herself, but mired her beast at the river-side, and so was carried off. Belle was also seized, despite resistance with nails and tongue. As for himself a leg-grip had unhorsed him, yet he was left behind in the chase of the others, and his bolted pony having returned, he captured it and sought to flee homewards. From the manner of the spreading of the assailants over the country, however, he had no choice but to head away from Aros, and take the Strathcoil road, full drive. Then, just as he out-distanced pursuit, his pony in turn got bemired, and there was nothing for it but to take to his heels, leaving the beast to struggle free as best it could. He sought refuge in the wood to which Fraser and the pedlar came some few hours later, and as he hid here close and still, the kidnappers passed on the march for Ardura—Miss Morag and Belle on their garrons, and riding beside them a stout man who wore a coat of many capes and showed wool-plugged ears.

At that time the snow was too light to help his tracking the troop, and so he had to skulk far in the rear, following thus for miles. At last, the falling dark and his ignorance of the strange countryside forced him to give up his tracing of the enemy; but he knew enough of the larger features of the district to hazard a guess as to their goal. Surely the oncoming night would drive them to shelter, if only for the lady's sake; and what more likely than Cameron Cave? And so he found. From the wet sands he had watched the guarded glimmer of their camp-fire in this cavern throughout the night; and, bitter of heart, had lain among weeds and shingle the long forenoon. But no movement had been made; so thinking his quarry safe to lie quiet in the day-time, he had harked back, impatient and hot-foot, making for Craig and looking for Fraser, and just as he reached Strathcoil, had encountered his pony wandering on the brae-face of Ardura.

"And the trouble is, sir," concluded poor Charlie, plaintively, "that a smack may land them all in Lorne before we can whistle. The black day, sir, the black day!"

Ian Fraser's heart beat fast and angrily. Was this indeed King George's own kingdom, that a man should be hunted like a beast of the chase, and a woman of gentle birth kidnapped as if she were a Carolina slave-girl? His wrath was such that when he had mounted his little steed at the head of the steep rise, he unwittingly dug his heels with savage force into its sides, and the garron went off at full gallop down the woody track, Charlie's voice squealing terror far behind. Such a way was on the beast that Fraser could not hold him, and so they thundered over full burns, and round sharp angles of the road, and always under a tunnel of trees, till sweeping clear of the fringes of oak and hazel, they emerged in sight of hill and sky once more, on a gentle fall of country with a sheet of water in its midst.

Twilight had fallen, and a wan and fading gleam lay on the waters of Loch Spelve. A wild country this and a desolate. The track stole furtively along the shore between the still waters and the upsweep of the hills, and keeping by it, they came, as the night closed, to the cliffs and pines of Loch Uisg. A mile or so farther on they tethered their mounts in a thick wood of spruce, for Cameron lay only three miles off, and they must now approach with greater caution.

It was here that Fraser first removed sling and splints from his arm to find that five weeks' rest had knit the bones fairly, if not strongly, but had stiffened the joints; and now he set about suppling these, as further advance was made towards Moy.

Save for the sound of breakers on Cameron Sands, thunderous in onpour, musical in backwash, the night had fallen marvellously still. Behind them lay Moy township, a dozen dots of light plainly to be seen, around the base of Ben Buie's mass, but from where they lay, the intervening woods hid the Castle tapers from view. Overhead the stars seemed farther off than was their wont, small and uncertain in a violet haze; yet a clear scad of light showed far on the horizon, between the twin headlands of the bay, and by its aid the searchers went on towards the cliffs that rose in front, knobbed, scarred, fantastic, every second mass a giant's face grimacing.

At last a flickering gleam, faint and rosy, indicated the cave and its bivouac, and having looked to their weapons, Fraser and his companion began their troublesome crawl through the whins. The task was not quite noiseless, for the ground was stony to a degree, but the murmur of the surf was constant, masking the sound of knocking pebbles, and they soon lay breathing quietly before the cavern's mouth. A stone dyke, dry-built, had been made across the opening of the hiding-place for three-fourths of its length, forming a partial outer wall. This was but a foot across, and only some four feet high, so, removing his tricorne, the surgeon got to the angle where rock and wall met, and peered over.

The rich dim light from a peat-fire, all aglow and almost smokeless, fell on Morag's face. She sat on a heap of bracken, a screen of tartan drawn around her, her hands clasped over her knees, her gaze on the fire's red embers. At once the strategist in Fraser gave way to the lover, and for a little he failed to note the disposition of the enemy, for he had eyes only for the light flashing and falling on the girl's cheek and brow—on the clear profile of a face as untroubled as ever it had been in Aros, and as lovely in this place of peril as in the home garden amongst the October roses.

Wrapped in a plaid, Belle lay slumbering beside her mistress, and in the obscurity of the cavern's rear, two old crones were hunched. Three rough-looking fellows sat with their backs to the loosely-built wall, passing a snuff-mull at intervals to one another, and Fraser recognised in one the cuarain and other oddities of garb that had characterised the Tiree men he had seen at the Fairies' Castle. All were silent, and an air of constraint sat on the men. The flame flickered, and with each of its leaps the white roof of the cavern seemed to close down suddenly on the prisoner, and eerie, threatening shadows to fall on her from the crossed sticks over the fire.

The surgeon retired to crouch in the furze and hold counsel with Charlie. Then, upstanding side by side, they started to race across the intervening ground, and came with all their bodies' weight on the piled stones of the wall. With a clatter it gave inwards on the heads of the men sitting below, and what further rubble they could seize, the attackers pushed over the fellows sprawling beneath the ruck of this downfall. Fraser, grappling with one of the men, was clouted on the head by a further toppling of stones brought about by the over-zealous gillie, and Charlie himself was impeded for a little by unexpected falls of stone. Morag had now started to her feet in alarm, while in the far corner Belle and the *cailleachean* were whimpering.

But the fortunes of the fight were soon evident. One of the kidnappers had been stunned by the tumble and now breathed deep and snoring as in an apoplexy; another had been knifed by the Ruapais with a venom scarcely to be expected of one so puny, and now lay in a daze of terror that rendered him powerless. As for Fraser's man, the surgeon's left hand had already well-nigh throttled him. Indeed, the task was easy beyond imagining — easy to the verge of ridicule, when one remembered the expense of spirit that had gone to the undertaking; and kneeling with his hand still on the neck of his opponent, Fraser was able to look up at Morag and see her face lit by another glow than that of the firelight, for she had recognised him.

"Quick, Belle! Quick, Charlie!" cried the surgeon. "Quick! To the sands, and make for Moy! I'll follow."

They hurried from the cave, and he was left with the old dames mumbling excitedly, and the only life-like man of the three fast growing weaker under his cramped fingers. He waited until his enemy's twitchings passed into stupor, and then released his grasp. But scarcely had he risen to his feet when he was overborne by the rush of a fresh assailant, who suddenly entered the cave. From the first Fraser fell that the new-comer's grip was that of a trained wrestler: the clutch of the left arm, and the passage of a hand under it to lever the neck downwards told him that this was not an encounter of so easy disposal as the last. He flung himself flat on the earth, therefore, and rising again instantly, disengaged his head. But his left arm was still held powerfully, and at an attempt to grip his opponent's left, his weak right hand held so feebly that when he essayed haunching his man, he missed. He gripped anew and haunched anew, when he had freed his sound arm, however, and getting the fellow back to back, he threw him with a supreme effort, clear over his shoulders. The man fell heavily; Fraser was kneeling on him next moment, and, pouring with sweat and breathing in short gasps like beasts of the forest that war to the death, they now lay close to the fire, its faint glow revealing their faces to one another.

"MacAllister!" cried the surgeon. "What takes you this gate?"

"Mr. Fraser? And it's you," replied the gipsy in surprise.

It was indeed one of the plague-stricken men, whom the surgeon had nursed back to life at Tigh-ban some weeks before.

"And it's you, sir?" said the fellow, sitting up as Fraser relinquished his hold. "*Och, ochan!* To save my life and then to break my bones, sir!"

"You wrestle well after such an illness, Rob. But why are you here?"

"Och, I'm just anywhere, sir, at times."

"Why, Rob, why?"

"Well, sir—Och, yes, I'll aye mind yon at Tigh-ban —Och, yes, I'll just tell you why."

"Tell me, then."

"Och, yes. It was for the big tacksman I watched the cave—MacQuarie, sir. I ken the lass and I like her—Miss Morag, that is. And Inshriff was to bring help, you see, to get her away. But you werena counted on: and not kenning you, sir, I couldna help a fling at you—and asking your pardon."

"MacQuarie of Inshriff?" said Fraser. "An old man with grey hairs and a ferret look in the eyes?"

"The same, sir. Man, you have him—a ferret, you said—a ferret."

"So MacQuarie knew," said Fraser, musing. "Well, Rob, tell him when he comes that the lady is safe in Moy."

"Och, I'll never face him now, sir. It's mad he'll be ... Moy? ... Och, is it there you go, sir? Then take poor Rob. It's Moy Dance, and oh, but it's grand. Take poor Rob—take poor Rob."

"Moy Dance?" said Fraser, caressing his stiff arm.

"Ay, sir, ay. Och, take poor Rob. For it's to-night you'll see gentrice, I tell you—enough to fill half Edinburgh. A' airts they've come, sir— Kinlochaline, Lorne, Ardgour, and Drimnin. And there's a deer-tinchel the morn, and you'll think a town was set hereabouts instead of caves and fisher-lads."

"Come then, Rob," said Fraser. "It's quite a raree-show we'll have."

The foolish fellow squealed in delight at the invitation, and went off in front over the sands, whistling and making little goat-like skips this way and that, while Fraser followed slowly through the whins, and at last saw the high and distant tower of Moy show litten windows against the violet sky.

21: The dance at Moy

TILL he was won back to London town, Fraser never thought to see so many candles alight as he beheld some hours later, when he entered the assembly-room at Moy. He understood now the mock pageant he had beheld as he came from the cave—a group of barefoot half-clad children dancing under the spruce trees on the fringe of the Castle grounds, and carrying burning strips of fir: poor cold little revellers of the night, mimicking the radiance here. Radiance there assuredly was in the longhouse, as the dancing pavilion was named; but above the lights were high glooms also, where, still and darkling, the portraits of three old-time warriors looked out on the brilliance and movement below. Gloom and shadow deeper still were on the old music-gallery at the far end of the hall; and out of this dusk, and over the oak of the gallery-screen, swung midwise a little silken banner with the Moy device, the seals supporting, and the scroll: Vincere vel Mori. But the armorials of the other MacLeans were not wanting, for between the sconces set around the hall albeit flapping dangerously near the tapers, were embroideries with variants of the arms of the clan—Coll, Ardgour, Dochgarroch, Brolass, Scallasdale, and Treshnish, they ran.

Fraser stood at gaze. Outside were the night and the hills; and here was something so different from the wild life of wood and shore he had been leading of late. The shout of the dancers and the beat of their feet in the time of the reel sang in his ear, the sight of the strutting player skirling away as he swung his pipes on a little platform under the music gallery—these were like strong wine to a famished man. It was figure of eight in the reel now, and double time, too, fingers snapping, heels light, thirty couples if there were one, and fingering impatiently at the lame arm, again in a sling, though unsplinted, he looked eagerly about him for Morag. But for his injured limb, he thought, she would scarce recognise him: bathed and shaven, his hair knotted afresh in a broad black ribbon, he felt as if he had but newly come to himself from a land of nightmare. The younger Moy had provided him with a costume of his own that fitted perfectly, and clad in a court-suit of murrey-coloured cloth with stockings of thread to match, he looked not unhandsome, despite his plain features. For the first time in months, also, he wore a solitaire and ruffles of lace, and not unconscious of the grandeur of his raiment he stood in the doorway and looked round, his heel tapping the floor in rhythm with the music.

Close by him were gillies—among them Rob MacAllister, perspiring and gleeful—cottars, crofters, tacksmen, and their women-folk, vigorous in the swift motions of the dance. Yonder, under the little banner of Moy, the more graceful and restrained movements betokened the gentry; and yonder, too, an occasional kilt and plaid among them told of the presence of an officer from Stirling or Inveraray, an ensign of the Black Watch, or a lieutenant of Keith's Highlanders.

A portly figure in Highland dress descended from a seat at one side of the daïs where the piper stood straining mightily—Moy himself, and treading daintily between the dancer's heels and the candle-drippings, he came down the hall to Fraser. The surgeon, remarking his approach, saw him to be a man of over fifty, light of foot for all his weight of body; a humorous grey eye, a shaven cheek, ruddy and smiling; his manner that of the courtier, and his bow graciousness itself.

"Mr. Fraser, I believe? A King's man, I hear, and of the Navy? Nay, nay, you look at my kilt, and now you think me of the Army. But no, 'tis only a little liberty I take with the law."

"Surely, sir, there's some talk of the Act's repeal?" said Fraser.

"I've heard as much, sir. But no matter for your politics—no matter for your service of the Hanoverian, sir, I claim your better acquaintance for your timely aid to my niece of Aros, and it's my thanks I give you. There's a vast many of the MacLeans would have gladly been in your shoes. And some MacKinnons, too, I wouldna wonder," he added as he broke off chuckling.

"MacKinnons, sir?" asked the surgeon.

"MacKinnons, yes, For you must know that MacKinnon of Pennyfuaran, the girl's own cousin, came to the rescue an hour after you had left the cave: and it's a disappointed man he is, I can tell you."

"Pennyfuaran?" said Fraser. "Why, I know him. Is he here? Indeed, 'twas but luck that sent me so soon, and you must credit him with a share of your thanks."

Moy smiled mysteriously. "It's more than he'd do for you, Mr. Fraser—more than he'd do for you .... But look at the lassie's pluck now! To see her here, fresh and happy as a bird at dawn, after stravaging the country with these wild fellows for two days and a night! Wonderful, I call it, wonderful!"

He asked as to whether young Moy had seen him comfortably disposed, and Fraser answered that he was monstrously obliged by all their kindness.

"After three nights of the heather," he said, my present content is sufficient recompense for any little service I may have rendered your kinswoman."

"Three nights?" cried Moy. "Then you'd be overtired for the next foursome even if your arm allowed, I fear. But let me at least present you to my company, for this reel is about to finish."

They engaged themselves between the swinging dancers and the greasy strip of floor under the candle-sconces, and arrived safely at the platform under the music-gallery. Here Morag was seated on a low couch, and beside her stood Pennyfuaran in kilt and plaid of bright tartan. The lady was in white, with a bunch of rowans in her breast, and she looked down shyly for an instant as Fraser came forward.

"An if I be weary," she said to her cousin, "what tiredness must be Mr. Fraser's lot, after his journeyings of the past week? Let alone injured arms. I fear both of us are too far travelled to set foot to reels this night." Her little slipper, scarlet as the rowans she wore, twinkled from the muslin folds and vanished. "But you remember each other surely? Cousin, here is Mr. Fraser; Mr. Fraser, Pennyfuaran."

The surgeon bowed to the handsome Highlander, who replied, his face, despite its bronzing, flushing and paling unusually as he gave a clammy hand; and just as the eyes of both men met, the piping ended abruptly on the linked couples swinging for the last time in the reel of the moment. A confusion of voices ensued, and the numerous and hasty presentations in which Fraser now took part, drifted him away from MacKinnon. But once again, across the bobbing heads and puffs and laces, their eyes challenged.

It was not until some time later that Fraser found himself at Morag's side.

"You must have thought me ungrateful, Mr. Fraser," said she, "that thanks were not my first words to you. But, indeed, with so many folks around, it was too hard a task. And now I thank you, sir."

The thanks came in a glance; and to the surgeon the room seemed to sway around him, the piping to die away, and the grey eyes to shine and glow ineffably.

"Did you come straight from Craig to the cave?" she asked.

As briefly as he could he told her his history for the last two days.

"And to think I was warning you of the Sunivaig folk, when it was myself that needed the caution," she cried.

He agreed: and so they smiled and chatted for a space, recounting their adventures again and again, and like happy children, ever finding something more wonderful to wonder at. At last Morag rose.

"But what foolishness for you and me to be story-telling here," she said "when we should be in the land of Nod, Mr. Fraser! Weary you have been and weary you will be at this rate of working. Shall I ask Pennyfuaran if you may retire becomingly at this hour? I see him moving this way?"

"Pennyfuaran? No!" said Fraser, glowering at that chieftain advancing from afar. "Is he the master of the ceremonies here, or only your trusted adviser in these affairs?"

There was in his tones the hint of a bitterness he could not conceal, for though the matter was but a little one it irked him strangely that she should so defer to Pennyfuaran. For reply Morag turned on him steady eyes, something burning deep in them, and said:

"That is a question, sir."

"I put it down for as much," said Fraser dourly, wondering at her heat, and, guard as he would, he had already caught some of her fire.

"I think it is a question with a taste for gossip behind it," went on the lady, reddening a little.

And Fraser, gulping down wrath at himself and all the universe, was already in deep waters. He began stammeringly:

"I fear you misunderstand—" She silenced him with a look of flame, and he bowed and turned away slowly. Joining Moy just then he did not see the fire of the grey eyes die beneath a soft dew of tears; or her fan artfully plying to hide them. The chief of MacLean was fuming when Fraser came up with him, for a message newly received had perturbed him greatly.

"My people have failed to trace either Tiree men or gipsy-folk," he said. "It was not so in my father's time, Mr. Fraser: we could always lay hands on them then, and they kept pit and gallows busy, I can tell you. Cnoc-na-Croiche was at Gualachaolish yonder, and you'd often see something hanging on the cross-tree clear on the sky-line—and that's ten miles away from this end Loch Uisg. Lord of Regality my father was, but not even Argyle himself can claim that in these sad days, and when I clap hands on these fellows, it's to a body they call a sheriff in Inneraora they maun go.—A bonnie countryside this is becoming!—But every craig of them will yet wear a hempen collar, I tell you.— A bonnie countryside!—That's what Aros will think it, I swear, when his own daughter is not free to travel it unharmed." And on and on he puffed and threatened.

A little later, as a country dance closed, Fraser felt his arm tugged, and looking round in the crush beside the piper's platform, he saw Pennyfuaran beckoning him. He followed, and the young chieftain slipped quietly on to the stage, making his way to the twilight that held its rear. Here he swung some tapestry aside, and they passed through a doorway.

"By your favour, a word with you in a retired place," whispered Pennyfuaran in the dark of the passage. "We should be observed if we left the hall by the main door, but this stair leads to the gallery, seldom used and quite secluded, I believe."

They went cautiously up some steep steps of wood and emerged in a place of shadows close to a smoky roof of cracked plaster. Indistinct forms in the darkness showed where, from other days, the musicians' seats still stood, and bulking largely above all was a clarsach in its woollen shroud. Outside this black nook the light of the dancing-hall seemed trebly brilliant; below them the appearance of the dancers flitting through, their figures had some touch of the unreal and fairy-like.

"We are private here," said Pennyfuaran, "but none the less we may moderate our voices with advantage, I think. I but wanted to say that Miss MacLean's friends are beholden to you for your kindness to her in the matter of this kidnapping. I am her cousin, and speak for her friends, you understand?"

"I understand," said Fraser curtly. "But I also wanted to say to you that Miss MacLean's friends know well how things stood in Tiree when Chisholm, the spy, went to his death."

"You mean—what?" asked the surgeon.

"I mean that we know it was his brother-spy who pressed on Angus MacLean to the killing of Chisholm," said the other through close teeth.

"Heavens!" cried Fraser in a whisper, rapid and tense. "I trust neither Miss Morag nor her father know of this?"

"And for why, Mr. Fraser?"

The surgeon looked at him in amazement.

"Come, sir, for why?" pursued Pennyfuaran. "Shall we not tell the lass that you are a manslayer and a spy simply because she has a liking for you?"

Fraser's hand leapt from its sling and sought the place where his hanger was wont to be.

"I take your meaning," he said, recovering himself. "You think it was I who betrayed Chisholm, and trapped MacLean into the killing of him?"

"Think, be damned," said Pennyfuaran. "I ken it, man."

"And I ken it false," said Fraser quietly. "But you're convinced you have the truth of it, I see: and as for myself, I've no desire to probe to the start of the lie. In a dirty business of a defamation such as this, there's always the risk of tarred fingers."

"Tar on your fingers," sneered the other in low cold tones, "would maybe more to your mind than blood on your sword."

"Sir, if the blood were yours, 'twould be six and half a dozen," said the surgeon. "And though my arm is weak, I daresay 'twill serve me for an occasion such as you seem to desire."

"By now, we should have a moon," said the Highlander coolly, "and we can risk an absence at this late hour. Will it please you to move out of doors?"

"Assuredly," said the surgeon.

They turned with wary feet to the door giving exit to the gallery, but a quiet voice from behind the draped harp made them halt suddenly.

"Come back," it said.

"*Dhia!* "said the Highlander, his knees giving, and grasping a curtain, he stood, frozen with fear, but Fraser moving in the direction of the voice, he at last followed him. Behind the clarsach they saw a cloaked figure of a man seated in the shadows, and looking out on the throng of dancers in the blaze of light below. The rant of the pipes seemed to leave him unmoved, and it was not the whirling of the reel he followed with his sad eyes, yet there he sat watching. It was, indeed, only momentarily that he turned his glance on the quarrellers; the next instant his gaze was turned on the hall below.

"Drumfin!" exclaimed Pennyfuaran in an excited whisper. "Still here, and after such a message as yon? The glamour's on you yet, man. What a sorrow you are; for here are incomers enough to-night and a fair peppering of Hanoverians among them."

"Have you got the news yet?" asked the old man, turning his deep-set eyes on the chieftain.

"Never a breath, Drumfin. You still have time to be clear of us all, I'm sure."

"Oh, leave Drumfin to Drumfin then," said the exile: "and consider your own affair—your business with this gentleman here: for it seems to me more pressing than any matter of mine."

"You heard us, sir?"

"Yes, unwilling I heard: but willing enough I intrude. And first, let me tell why I'm here," said the Jacobite. "I came because it's twenty years—God pity me!—twenty years since I last saw an assembly at Moy. Old memories were stirring, and so the chief himself set me here before the dance began. And as he did so, he told me of a service done to a lady we all know and admire." He bowed to the surgeon. "You see your quarrel is not Greek to me, Mr. Fraser, though the ground of it is a trifle obscure to Pennyfuaran and yourself. It has something to do with a Tiree story that came first from an acquaintance of my own, I believe."

"Give me his name," said Fraser hotly.

"No, I'll not do that, sir. But I'll also say this: that he was an acquaintance of another acquaintance of mine—a lady—la Baronne de Bas-Ondulé. You'll have heard of her, I doubt not?" said Drumfin to the surgeon, but looking meaningly at Pennyfuaran.

"Not I," said Fraser.

"No? And you'll not have a miniature of her next your heart?" said the old man, smiling, his eye still on Pennyfuaran.

"Indeed, no, sir. You mystify me."

"I expected I would, Mr. Fraser; and I am glad I did. And to speak quietly: of two tales on any matter, I'd prefer the one from the man who had no miniature of Bas-Ondulé in his breast-pocket, to the one from the man who had. You take me, Pennyfuaran?"

"I do, sir," said the chieftain.

"Then let your quarrel stand, man."

"There is no occasion, sir," said Fraser in a hot whisper. "I think we both know of other grounds for a mutual distaste. If Mr. MacKinnon has difficulty in finding them, I have none."

"So!" said Drumfin. "So! But Pennyfuaran in his heat has forgotten the sad case of mind and body in which you find yourself, or surely he'd have set his challenge for a fitter time."

"I thank you," said Fraser. "But your scruples are as needless as they are generous, sir. I hope I am not so exhausted as to be unprepared for anything he asks of me."

"Pennyfuaran, man, will you let him?" appealed Drumfin.

"Indeed, Mr. Fraser," protested Pennyfuaran with sudden warmth. "I dealt unfairly with you in my haste: and that's the truth. You are but hanging on your legs, I ken; and I'd as lief kill a whole man as half a one."

The surgeon smiled. "So I may be fit at the earliest then, I make haste to retire," he said.

He bowed awkwardly enough and with stumbling in the darkness, and crept cautiously to the little doorway. Reaching the assembly room, he made brief adieux to Morag, to Moy and some others, and withdrew.

Meanwhile, in the dim gallery above, Drumfin sat and watched.

"You could not make her out from this point," said Pennyfuaran in answer to a question. "She did not dance because of tiredness consequent on her late adventures, and she is now seated on a couch under this gallery. But since we disperse before long, you should see her cross the floor."

He took his leave of the exile, and quietly joined the throng in the hall.

Half an hour later, Morag stood for a little in the centre of the dance-room, Pennyfuaran by her side, attentive, docile, discreet. She was saying good-bye to her acquaintance right and left, with many laughing apologies for her absence from the reels. Wearied, yet beautiful in her langour, she turned eyes, sad beneath the merriment they assumed, to the old music-gallery, and looked curiously at a corner of it where something seemed to draw her gaze. But nothing was visible there save the high glooms and shadows. And yet among these sat a man with silver hair, who bent his head on his hands as he beheld her, and groaned in inward agony:

"The red rowans and the little red shoes and the dress of muslin white ... And her mother's face, God pity me!"

22: Night in the woods

FRASER left the longhouse in order to return to his room in the Castle, but, crossing the intervening strip of greensward he halted to look round at the half-moon surging through white billows of cloud to the east of Ben Buie's peak. The enfolding woods murmured; the voice of distant inland streams was heard; the cool night called him, wearied one, to its heart, and he turned off through the laurels to the tall pines' witchery of shine and shade.

Fatigue oppressed him, and yet the wheels of his mind raced in fevered haste. Again and again his high words with Morag and his quarrel with Pennyfuaran were re-enacted in his hot brain, and ever that fiery look of the girl's burned through all his fancies. Unhappy, he passed from the screen of pines and came through oak and sycamore to a little track that led down to a stream of full volume flowing quietly through level ground. It was crossed by a rough bridge of wood, and here he stood for a little to watch the eddies swirling like smoke-wreaths from under the bleached grasses at the water's edge. But, restless still, he returned to the pinewood, and paced noiselessly over its carpet of brown needles. From far he heard the beat of the dancers' feet and the faint note of the pipes. Then the music fell still for a space longer than the usual interval, and a sound of distant voices took the air: the assembly was breaking up. The succeeding silence oppressed, and he halted as if to hear some whisper across its vastness, for it was even as if the cold beauty of this world of night were articulate, and yet, because of his distraction, he could not hear.

He came back aimlessly in the direction of the stream, and was about to emerge from the shade of the oaks when Morag's voice fell on his ear: earnest, imploring, entreaty most passionate, these were her accents; and next moment he beheld her coming towards him. By her side a cavalier, cloaked and muffled, stalked on, irresponsive. He saw them pause at the bridge, their talk serious, their voices low; he saw Morag's Nithsdale hood fall back, and the man replace the covering deftly and with a familiar air, and at the sight his teeth gritted, his temple pulses throbbed. Then he turned off in rapid silent flight.

Barely half an hour later, Pennyfuaran, whom the quarrel had no less excited, swung hastily down the path to the rustic bridge, and saw two figures start apart at his approach. As he passed, Morag's grey eye came liquid into the moonbeams for an instant, and in quick surprise the chieftain lifted his cap and paused momentarily. The full significance of the discovery seemed to reveal itself to him just then, and, gnawing savagely at his underlip, he strode on again, making for the shore, where he paced the white sands endlessly, a consuming fire of rage and despair in his breast.

Some few minutes after the chieftain had gone Morag and her brother said adieux at the Castle porch, but it was hours before the surgeon and his rival returned from their feverish pacings through the night. As luck would have it, the Highlander crossed the greensward from the east, just as Fraser approached from the fringe of the northward pines; and at sight of each other they halted as if suddenly turned by the moonlight to statues of black marble. Like black marble, too, the Castle rose beside them, grim and dark, save for a single light in the porter's window.

In his heart each said: "Then it was he!"; in his heart each felt the riot of the passions of the homicide. Yet they stood as if frozen in the cold moonlit air, and spoke never a word. At last Pennyfuaran shrugged his shoulders and, approaching the Tower's gateway, rapped and entered; and Fraser, waiting until he judged the chieftain had reached his quarters, knocked in turn and was admitted also.

23: The Rivals

"A Southern loon," sobbed Pennyfuaran, "a lousy mariner man, Drumfin. And me of the race of kings!"

They stood in a little glade of the Moy woods, Drumfin, cloaked and high-booted, leaning against a fir-bole, and regarding in silence the passion of MacKinnon, who marched to and fro as if in a stage-play, his hair dishevelled, his face begrutten. Although it was morning the close forest-roof of pine and spruce and larch made a twilight in the place.

"God kens," went on the young man, "it was little I thought of herself and much of the lands of Aros, when first I quested her. But now 'tis all another story, and it's the white truth I'm telling you. Had she but a single baw-bee, or had she the Arkaig gold, it were one to Pennyfuaran: rich or poor, sir, I love her to desperation." Unmanned, he hid his face in his hands, and rocking on his feet, groaned, "Her voice, her look! Oh, the eyes of her, the eyes of her!"

Drumfin held his peace, but picking up the other's bonnet from earth, he held it out to him; and MacKinnon, beholding the exile's impassiveness, snatched the cap indignantly.

"Have you bowels of compassion?" he cried. "Are you but frosted ice, Drumfin?"

"It's what's in my mind, I'll tell you," said the old Jacobite at last. "And its this: You've blasted every chance you ever had, by just being Pennyfuaran. The Lord He knows how you'll ever be other than yourself, lad; but there's no doubting but 'tis yourself stands in the way."

"Oh, damn your preaching!" cried the other, and went on inconsequently: "If it were but the old cause I lamented you'd be hearty enough with your sympathy."

"Where's the comparison?" said Drumfin drily.

"It's your idol, man, your idol! the thing you live for; a whimsy and yet your god! And here's mine, sir — here's mine — a woman as far above me as the stars, Drumfin — as the stars, man, the stars!"

"You've a touch of philosophy there," said his companion. "Ay, a lost faith, a lost cause — their glamour's on me still. But I see no need for greetin'. I lament the old cause; but the humour of the world sets another gate — as witness Conflan's ships the other day — and so the world and me, we disagree." He sighed. "Yet it never gets the length of me fleeching like a play-actor at the poor old world that kens no better, Pennyfuaran."

"My tongue is wild," said the chieftain. "You have the true word there; but see you, I'm Highland. And, oh, man, her face—was never face so bonnie! And this brock of a South-countryman —ugh! Just by the bridge there they met last night when the dance was barely over, and his damned sham of a broken arm was as good as a sound one to keep her safe and warm. The scunner of him .... spy and worse than spy!"

"Canny, lad, canny. After all's said and done, there's little tocher or lands to count on in Aros now. The wadsets are many, I fear," said Drumfin, watching narrowly the effect of his last words.

To his surprise the chieftain laughed loud and high in a fashion hysterical. "You surely think me play-acting with a vengeance, sir," said he. "That story you give me here and now may be true or false; but I tell you," he went on with passion, "tocher is a word of no meaning in this matter of mine. It's the lass I want, be her father laird or cottar."

"There now, there now," said Drumfin, clapping him on the shoulder, as he stood gripping and un-gripping empty hands, his wild eyes fixed on earth. "I tested you with a word I shouldna have spoken, poor lad. I but wanted to try your sincerity, yet I should have minded my teeth were before my tongue."

Pennyfuaran laughed bitterly. "Sincerity? That's your word, eh? Well, here am I, straight and clean; and yet it's this same spy she'll have before me."

"Spy?"

"You doubt it?"

"I doubt anything, as I said already—I doubt anything coming from the man, be he who he may, who carries Bas-Ondulé's likeness in his breast."

"I ken nothing of Bas-Ondulé, Drumfin; but I'll believe Norman MacLean before this toad. And I'll fight the rascal ere nightfall, sir, let me tell you, lame arm or no."

Drumfin sighed. "It's a weary world, MacKinnon," he said, "and a trifle *mélangè*, as we say across the water. If I were younger, I'd try dissuasion with you; but as it is, I must even let you gang your gate, and wish well to both of you."

And this is how it was that, when, a few hours later, Fraser and the chieftain met by chance in this same strip of woodland, Pennyfuaran drew steel at once. The surgeon, for all his weakness in the sword arm, was not slow to follow suit, and drew a hanger of young Moy's which he was wearing.

"It may be of interest to you, Mr. Fraser, to learn something of a side of this affair of which a Southron naturally takes notice when he goes a-courting," said Pennyfuaran darkly as he folded his plaid and laid it at the foot of a mossy rock. "I but heard it this morning, and it's this: Miss MacLean's father is a poor man, and her dowry will be little or nothing. Of course, I only mention this matter in the passing, but I thought it of interest, and so may you ... By the by, about this arm of yours that needs a matter of weeks for healing—I fancy I saw it used quite comfortably no later than last night, sir."

He rattled on, tightening the belt on his philabeg as he spoke, while Fraser divested himself of arm-sling and coat and rolled up his shirt-sleeves. At the first hint of commerce, the surgeon's face had flushed; but in the end the excited garrulity of his adversary lent no change to his features except an added grimness to their natural gravity.

"On guard, sir," said Pennyfuaran; and they bent their knees, their swords at the approach.

But no sooner had they begun than they ended, for at the sound of a low voice close at hand their arms were lightly sheathed; with one movement they crouched to earth, and, peering beneath the densely set columns of the trees, they saw the white leggings of King George's red-coats advancing stealthily. The quiet voice spoke again, and the tight-buttoned legs halted.

The duellists lay close together now, and the chief's dark hunting tartan covered the white shirt of his coatless adversary, as they screened themselves behind a fallen fir-bole.

"Listen," whispered Pennyfuaran. "There's a second voice: and I know him—the ferret! He's there—Callum MacQuarie, as I'm a Gael! And after all his oaths to me! ... Listen! — Drumfin is the name he is naming. Look to him washing his hands in air and laughing to himself and cringing to the captain, the toad! That's Fawkener—Captain Fawkener—Fort-William is his station —Look here, Mr. Fraser, this affair of ours can wait still longer." He gloomed regretfully into the surgeon's face from where he lay, not a foot off. "Fast to the Castle, and later so will I. Take the way of the sands. Warn Moy or his son. If you can find neither readily, lose no time but get to my bedroom, pull aside the hangings at the bed-head there, and rap seven times on the door you'll discover. Drumfin will answer, and you must tell him what you've seen here."

"You trust me?" said Fraser, smiling—"Me— a spy?"

Pennyfuaran flushed. "Yes," he said. "And God knows why I do it ... But fast! Not a moment to lose! Tell Drumfin I advise Kinloch as safest. And meanwhile I'll lead these hounds off the scent, and, if time permit, throttle one of them—a friend of mine, Callum MacQuarie by name. Haste, man, haste!"

24: The quarrel

On the afternoon of the day following the irruption of the red-coats, Morag took her accustomed walk with Belle by the side of quiet Loch Uisg, far from the bustle of the search at the Castle. Their converse was of Drumfin and his flight accompanied by Fraser; for the inner circle at Moy who knew of Drumfin's presence there, comprised both gentle and simple, and a secret bond of intimacy seemed to link all who were free of entrance to this magic ring.

"Puir body! and a cold day for him on the hill!" said Belle. "As kindly a man and as harmless as ever I saw. What the sorrow harm has he done them? What ails them at him, that they should harry him through the heather like a driven hare?"

"How you talk, Belle," said Morag irritably. "Is it not because he is aiding Drumfin?"

"It's Drumfin himself I mean," said Belle.

"Oh!" said Morag, reddening a little, "I thought it was of Mr. Fraser you spoke."

She walked on, brooding over the events of the night of the dance: her brother, Pennyfuaran, the surgeon, Drumfin—all in her mind's eye by turns; but oftenest she came back to Norman and his wild life. At their last meeting she had sought to learn the truth from him regarding the story of Fraser's adventures in Tiree, but all she had succeeded in eliciting were mysterious suggestions as to the danger of a Jacobite agent's task, and the need for secrecy. The interview had ended by her pleading with him to leave his perilous work for this broken race of Stuart, whose waning hopes he so bewailed. But now as she thought of Drumfin and his companion, hounded through the hills of Aros, her old compassion for the Prince renewed itself, her old hatred of Hanover revived. And yet — and yet the glamour and the grace were fading from her vision of a revival of the old clan-life; every day, indeed, her hopes of the cause were fainter; and hints of the wild ways of the Prince, which in former times she had brushed aside in scorn, were remembered afresh and dwelt upon. After all, the sleepy, orderly regime that Hanover promised might not be so great an evil as the reign of a Prince debauched, or a return of the stormy days of the chiefs and the clans.

"Would he had never left France!" she said suddenly to Belle.

"Miss Morag!" Belle stopped in her heavy lurching walk, and lifted her hands in horror. "Och, but I'm wonnerin' at you. It's Drumfin you mean now?"

"Yes, Drumfin," persisted the lady. "If the cause is so hopeless, why should he have so embroiled us?"

"I'm wonnerin' at you, Miss Morag! Och! I'm wonnerin' at you," was all Belle permitted herself to reply, and she shook her head and fell behind, casting angry glances at her mistress the while. Herself contemptuous of the Jacobite interest, she had her enthusiasms of sentiment for some among the supporters of this hope forlorn: Drumfin was one, and Morag was another. But here was a reversal of ideals with a vengeance, and she resented it, not so much because it suggested somewhat of disloyalty, as that she did not understand the hidden workings-that had brought about the change. Again and again she shook her head in disapproval, and finally sulking outright fell far behind her mistress.

Accustomed to these fits of vapours in her maid, Morag went on unattended, and soon was out of sight of Belle. The track rising and falling in hillocky fashion came close to the water's verge; on the landward side the hill rose steep and wooded, and the spot seemed loneliness itself, save for a hawk that soared as in menace, midway between her and the battlemented cliffs of the opposite shore.

Fraser and Drumfin, lying at watch, high on a spur of Creigaven beheld her figure come slowly into view around a promontory.

"A lady in a blue riding-habit, but on foot," said the surgeon. "It's Miss Morag, I think."

"Your eyes are young," said Drumfin. "I cannot recognise her from this height. But it's doubtless she, for she takes after her mother, that lass, aye given to lonely walks and brooding." He sighed, and seemed to dwell on old memories for a space. "It's scarcely safe, though," he went on, "for her to be so far from Moy and unattended, too — with the countryside so full of soldiery and gipsies as it is."

"Look," said Fraser suddenly. "That was a prophecy, I fear? Did you not see the birches move down there?"

He pointed to a wood on a hill-slope half a mile behind Morag's slow-pacing figure, where a single unit of the birch-planting tossed heavily, its leaves shimmering in a sudden sunburst.

"There's a man in that tree taking the lie of the land," said Fraser. "Wait ... He's down — Look there."

Far on the bare sunlit hillside, two dots of men emerged from the wood, and, running for a little, flung themselves prone on the heather, then crawled on again and lay flat once more.

"Is it the girl they're following?" asked Drumfin.

"There is none else to follow," said Fraser putting off his cloak.

"You are going?" asked the exile.

"Yes, keep us in view, sir, and help if need be."

What Morag's reverie was at the particular moment when Fraser brushed through a copse on the slope above her, she could never afterwards recall, but it seemed the most natural thing in the world that the surgeon in person should step into her thoughts just then. Yet she greeted him coldly.

"Sir," she said, "I give you a good evening."

"Madam," he said as coldly, "a fair evening to you. You are far from Moy to be unattended."

"Not so, sir surgeon, for it seems that you still play warden to me." Her eyes flashed angrily. "I go back even now," she said.

There was dismissal in her tones as she turned, and the whole miserable scene of the tiff at the assembly came back to him; but he wheeled about as if to accompany her. She halted smiling.

"I hope there will be no occasion for a further indebtedness, Mr. Fraser. There are Hanoverian soldiery enough in Aros to protect us all, I trust."

"And yet they were not far from Cameron Cave two nights ago?"

She flushed angrily, and walked on. "I should not remind myself so readily of Cameron Cave, sir, if I were you," she answered. "It sounds a trifle vainglorious."

"Madam," he said, "if it sounds warning also, I care not."

She stopped again. "I tell you I aspire to no further indebtedness, sir. Will you, indeed, thrust your company upon me?"

For answer Fraser set his face like a flint, stalking on ahead of her towards Moy; and at last she resumed her walk so that in a little they were side by side, pursuing the narrow track in silence and as if in haste to be rid of each other's company. It was thus that Belle found them when they suddenly came round a bend of the road face to face with her.

"Keep me! What's this? You've been crying, Miss Morag?"

"Nonsense, Belle, I'm hot and tired, that's all. Mr. Fraser and I have just escaped from the most dreadful band of brigands, you see." She was derisive in her scorn. "But now we are safe at last. Good-bye, Mr. Fraser."

The surgeon looked coldly at the little hand, and bowing over it, took his place at her side as she continued her walk.

"I shall go on a little way yet," he said.

They went forward again, and Belle followed gloomily; here was a further knot she could not unravel. Were these good folk and herself in their sober senses?

"Look you, Miss MacLean," said Fraser after a space, "I was rude to you at the dance in the matter of Pennyfuaran, but you have punished me already in a way you know nothing of."—He had a vision of a bridge with two figures on it, seen dimly in a moonlit glade—" You can add nothing to that if you torture me from here to Moy."

"To Moy?" she cried, halting once more.

"I go on to Moy," he said stubbornly, and was still.

"Oh," she cried. "You treat me like a bairn, sir."

"Madam, it's a whipped child you've made of me," he said bitterly, and they paced on in an angry silence.

It was just as they came in sight of the Castle that Morag saw Fraser glance round apprehensively at the wood on the hill above the road; next she saw him pause, and turning to look, she beheld the figures of two men slinking behind the larches on the fringe of the copse. Then the surgeon's hand went to his hanger; the two fellows instantly broke from the planting and made for the open corrie; a third, seeming to rise from the earth, joined them, and all were instantly over the hill's shoulder. They did not disappear so quickly, however, but that the observers could make out that they were wild unkempt fellows, wearing leg-coverings of rough hide.

"Why!" said Belle, "they wear cuarain. It's the Tiree men again, and the Sidier Roy not a mile off."

"Tiree men if you like, Belle," said Fraser smiling: "but Miss Morag will have it that they are brigands. And it's second sight she has, I think: for she was telling us of them before they even appeared."

He ascended the slope, as if in pursuit of the fleeing islesmen. "Goodbye," he called, waving his hat. "*A bas les brigands, mademoiselle!*"

Morag paled at the taunt. She beheld in a flash the cause of the surgeon's intrusion, and saw now what this forcing of his escort meant.

"Oh, stay, Mr. Fraser!" she called, but he was already out of sight over the rise of the hill.

"Oh, Belle!" said the girl, turning helplessly to the maid with tear-filled eyes; but Belle, scornful and puzzled by turns, received her testily.

"Och, what has come over you, ma'am?" said she. "You tell him to go when he'd bide, and to bide when he'd go. This day or two past you're beyond my comprehension entirely, Miss Morag— entirely."

25: Besieged

"Here is Craig at last," said Fraser. "Rest in the heather whilst I forage."

Ghastly pale from the exhaustion of continued flight, Drumfin nodded; the surgeon, despite his aching arm, had supported him for the last three miles. The disposition of the red-coats had turned them away from the short-cut by Loch Fuaran, and once more Fraser had to take the weary road by Spelve shore. Ardura passed, they felt safer, for now they had left the direct route between Moy and Duart, where the Fort-William soldiery had a temporary garrison.

A chill wind blew, it was dusk already, and lowering clouds were everywhere in the west, when Fraser, carrying a pot of milk and some bannocks, returned to the hollow where the old Jacobite lay. They ate and drank greedily.

"I'm for no more nights in the heather than I can help, Mr. Fraser, after this spell," said Drumfin; "though this, through your kindness, is pleasanter than I had hoped. But I tell you fairly, you risk much in aiding a man in my case. Why you do it, God kens!"

"Instinct, I suppose," said the surgeon smiling. "There is an evil face with those soldier-folk, a man named MacQuarie, and though it's four days since first I set eyes on him, even yet his airs make me grue. 'Twas enough for anyone of my way of feeling to know him on the other side to you; instinct, as I say,—instinct did the rest, and bade me take your part."

He stopped, astounded at the discovery of himself as fairly a rebel at last, aiding an insurgent in his flight from His Majesty's soldiers. Very far away, indeed, seemed his service on the old *Theseus* with its stuffy hammock-hospital, from this free life in the wind and the rain. And far away, too, seemed the Ian Fraser—the Whigamore of other days— from the present partisan of lost causes and broken hopes. He shrugged his shoulders lightly. As well on one side as another, he told himself, if that side could produce a man so clean and strong in action as Drumfin, so chivalrous, so responsive to every delicate overtone of fife. Yet, even as he reasoned, he flushed guiltily: for in his heart he knew that many motives had prompted his present course, and not the least of these had been Morag's espousal of the cause by which the old exile held.

"Instinct?" said Drumfin. "Instinct let it be. In any case my thanks to you again, sir. And new thanks also for the present fare—from the bottom of my heart, or of my appetite, shall I say?"

"That reminds me," said Fraser. "In the kitchen where I got these scones you praise so mightily, I saw a face I should remember, but cannot. I trust he was no unfriend; but he glanced at me like one while the goodwife poured the milk for me: a wild tyke, but I cannot place him. And, mind you, always his eye on this tell-tale sling on my arm."

He pushed a tuft of heather aside and looked down through the dusk at the huddle of thatched roofs beside the dim river.

"Surely not a King's man so far afield?" said Drumfin.

"Who'll say what strange crop will grow where gold is raining?" said the other. "Look at this MacQuarie, selling you as he did. If this new face is a traitor's also, we should have done better by starving until we drew Kinloch. Shall we to the road again? But bide you a little, and I'll return this pitcher, making that an excuse for sounding this fellow."

He was gone some time, and when he returned, it was by devious ways, although the dark was falling.

"No sign of him now," he said; "and the good wife has a new grip of her tongue. It looks black for us that he should have left the house, and the night so threatening. I'll warrant he's on watch for you or me, sir, but we'll stir for Kinloch, all the same. You know the road, you say, and you're sure the landlord there is friendly?"

"Yes," said Drumfin, rising and joining him on the rude path. "Friendly—friendly in half-hearted fashion like the lave nowadays ... Och, ochan, the weary road, Mr. Fraser, the weary road! ... Well, I've had my last taste of old Scotland, sir, and I'll soon cut ower the water again!. ... The weary road! ... But it's just the same heather and rock I'll see in dreams, lad, when I tramp the Paris causey, I'm thinking."

"I'm sure, sir," said Fraser respectfully, touched by the old man's emotion.

"Ay, ay. And I'll be thinking my little lodging in the Rue Roquette none so taking as a cave on Beinn-nan-Uaimh that I ken well. Oh, it's there I lay often and oft, dry and snug on my heather bed, and looked out on the sea and the hills of God spread pure and sunswept in the airs of the morning."

"I understand, sir; I understand," said the younger man softly.

"Do you think I'd open my heart to you if you did not?" asked the exile almost fiercely. Then his voice grew soft again, and he went on: *"Mo thruaigh, mo thruaigh!* my country, sir, my country! Oh, the glens and the bens and the children of them that are as nought and for ever!"

"'Twas over Aros township your cave, sir?" asked Fraser seeking to distract him from his melancholy.

"Ay, on the hill above Aros. Ah, Aros of the bens, where is the hill like Beinn-nan-Uaimh on a clear day of autumn, with all Albainn at my feet? Over Ben Shi ante you'd look to Moidart, sir; and beyond that, far and shining, like a dream of the heavenly places, the Coolins in pinnacles of white. But Ichabod, Ichabod—the red sorrow's at my heart for the days that will never return. *Mo thruaigh, mo thruaigh!* My longing and my pain, my longing and my pain!"

As they came down by the rushes and bog of the Goladoir, squalls and rain-bursts were added to the discomfort of the thick darkness. They held by the river's right bank till the ford was reached, and here, although the water came to their middles, Drumfin guided safely over.

"'tis fourteen years since I last crossed," said the exile, "and yet the stream's bed is but little altered, it would seem. Ah, the days—the old lost days!"

Two miles more of a tramping through the moss,, and then they stood, wet and cold in the gusty dark, knocking at the door of Kinloch Inn. The burly figure of MacKay, the landlord, made shadow and barrier in the fan of light that fell on them from the opened door; but when he saw Drumfin's face, pale beneath its tan, he drew aside instantly.

"Come in, sir, and welcome," he cried. "Bless you, you'll be the weary one with never a horse beneath you on this night of nights."

"Weary's the word, MacKay," said Drumfin. "Cold and wet and weary!"

Yet half an hour later—so assiduous was the Skyeman—Drumfin sat in dried clothes on one side of a roaring fire of logs in the upper room, and equally cosy on the other side was Fraser. It was well on for midnight now, and each felt his eyelids weighty; but the curious feeling of being too tired even for rest, which comes from extreme exhaustion, was heavy on both; and thus they sat half-drowsing in the warmth of the chamber, when a hammering on the hostelry door, woke them fully. Like a cat Drumfin was on his feet, and loosening his hanger, crept to the balustrade at the stair-head and leant over.

"MacKay," he called in a loud whisper, as he heard the landlord come into the kitchen below, "you ken me; and I solemnly charge you to ward your trust, for here's a youth with me, who has nothing to do with my affair. Let none enter unchallenged, man. You ken the price that's on me these fourteen years, but it's the last ditch, MacKay, and I'll die hard."

"Blessing on you," whispered back MacKay. "Keep you still, and I'll speak them fair. Trust me to manage them, sir."

"This is the work of your man at Craig with his eye on your sling," said Drumfin to Fraser. "He's got the red-coats on our track despite the nightfall. Listen—listen."

Leaning over the stair-rail, they heard the parley in Gaelic.

"Who is there?"

"Open."

"My door is open to every man with a name. Who is it?"

"Open and see: open speedily."

"What are your wants?"

"Open, MacKay."

"Unless you name your name, I tell you, your bed is waiting you elsewhere this night."

"Open, MacKay, open."

"Then if these be all your manners there will be no opening," cried MacKay in anger, dropping an extra bar across the door and walking away from it. He lifted his lit cruisie from the floor, and stood motionless at the stair-foot, waiting. There was a scurry of feet outside and a heaving of the door as several bodies fell full weight against it; but the great wooden bars did not give. Next came a musket report, a smell of gunpowder, and, with an oath, MacKay bent to grip his foot.

"The dogs!" he roared, and fell.

Fraser and Drumfin were by him instantly, and before the next shot came, they had dragged him into the kitchen.

"A bullet in the ankle," said the surgeon, examining hastily. "He has fainted from the shock."

Having nothing wherewith to attempt the extraction of the ball, he quickly dressed and bandaged the wound, and as he did so MacKay came to himself.

"Curse them," growled the landlord. "But gentlemen," he said, "I have guns, despite the Disarming Act. There are muskets and powder and ball under the middle flags of the inner room there."

With fire-irons for levers the fugitives prized up the stone and secured the arms and ammunition. As they replaced the slab a tousy-headed lad appeared from the back-quarters, rubbing gummy eyelids.

"Here, Hamish," called MacKay. "There are robbers outside, and it's shot I am. Help these guns upstairs and come back to me."

Though shaking with terror, and snuffling tears he strove to hide, the lad obeyed, and began bearing arms to the upper chamber; while with a run, for all his years and weariness, Drumfin passed him on the gangway, and reaching his room, commenced extinguishing fire and candles.

Fraser assisted, and when all was in darkness, the last ember black, they unfastened the inner shutter and flung wide the casement. A splatter of rain-drops entered; a cold blast ran round the room, and with it came the noise of waves; but for the rest there was deep silence everywhere. Born of the night there suddenly came a point of fire and a report, and Drumfin, taking quick aim at the dot of light, replied with his musket. The echoes roused on Ben More and called to each other fainter and fainter; but the Inn stood miles distant from any dwelling, and a thousand echoes could bring no succour in this lonely place. There were two more splashes of light in the outer blackness, and a bullet whizzed past the heads at the window, shattering the panel of the door of the room. Below them they heard a shot within the house, and MacKay called up that it was his serving-man at a hole in the shutter. And now the air bore mingled odours of sea-wrack and sulphur-fumes, and a sinister atmosphere of battle and treachery seemed to surround the besieged, so that they started at the scratching of a rat in the wall, or at a sudden onset of the wind.

"Do you think there are more than six in the attack, Mr. Fraser?" asked Drumfin. "To judge by their fire, I'd say four only. But in affairs of this kind I've always found it safer to allow a surplus."

There was the alertness of a young warrior in this man with the silver hair, as again and again after patient waiting, he took steady aim and fired. Forty minutes of give-and-take in this work was followed by a lull that lasted throughout the night.

"They save their powder," said Drumfin grimly. "Let them."

Daybreak saw the watchers in the upper chamber peering with grey and worn faces on field and shore that seemed untenanted by aught but the screaming gull and the wheeling tern.

"Have they gone?" asked the surgeon, crossing the window unguardedly to glance at the Inn's western side.

He was answered by a whiff of fiery smoke from behind a rock on the shore, and a bullet sang high through the room to bury itself in the ceiling. Immediately a second whipped out on the keen air as if from behind the house, and Drumfin, descending to enquire, returned with the news that the enemy were in the rear as well. It seemed that the serving-boy going to draw water at the spring in the walled patch behind, had found his few wits scared to none by a sudden bullet burying itself in the lintel above his head. It was only a little later that Fraser, opening the window of another room that gave on the east, had the shoulder-cape of his coat cut in two by a shot. And still nothing was to be seen of the enemy.

"Caution is not a word for it," said the old Jacobite, coming up to the room where the surgeon lay close by the window, adjusting a loose flint with a sliver of wood. "They're all around, and never a head showing anywhere. There, again!"—and a spatter of twigs and plaster from the ceiling came down afresh as a bullet took it. "It's you I'm wae for, lad," he said to Fraser, "tied as you are to a bodach with a price on his head. And I'll say this, that for soldier-folk, they look like earning that same price in easy fashion."

He reconnoitred from an angle of the window.

"By their firing now, I take it that they are certainly not more than six, Fraser, for if they were, they'd have more than four dispositions, as I said before. Now, if I made a feint to the west shore there, it should be easy for you to slip off to the hill unnoticed, lad. Then as for MacKay and the halflin—well, we could tie them hand and foot as if we had forced them. In the end there would only be old Drumfin to pay the piper."

"Tush!" said Fraser, smiling. "That's my answer, sir ...There again!"

Another patch of ceiling fell, and yet there was no sign of a marksman, only a little haze of smoke drifting over what had been the water-line at dawn. The tide was fast retreating, and where waves had rolled earlier in the morning, were now long slabs of wet grey sand, broken by dark dots and lines of rock and sea-wrack. The sun rose higher, and gradually all the gaunt hills were uncanopied—all, save Ben More, where a great cloud-roll drifted up the mountain-flanks to hang awesome round its summit. And still round the little block of buildings dropped midmost of this wilderness by the lochside, went the plopping of shot and the puffing of powder-smoke from the enemy, hidden and surrounding, with never a response from the house itself.

Fraser going below to where MacKay lay groaning and squeezing the halflin's hand, found him fevered and sweating profusely. The pain in the foot was agonising, but he controlled himself in order to ask the news.

"You shoot no longer, sir," he said. "And why?"

"Because there's not a head to see, MacKay. It's fell eerie to sit watching and listening there, and never a sign. Yet let me but show my face at my side of the house, and there's a slug for answer," said Fraser.

As he spoke a shot was heard in the upper room, and Drumfin's voice calling on him. He dashed upstairs, and at a sign from the other knelt at the open window.

"Who are these?" cried the Jacobite. "See: the fat fellow yonder."

Across the slobbered sands a stout man ran as fast as his thick legs could carry him. Like so many evil wings his coat of many capes flapped behind, and he trailed a musket with difficulty. Ahead of him, and passing the highest line of tangle with amazing agility was a rough fellow in trews and wearing unwieldly cuarain; and although half a mile off, Fraser marked him for the man he had seen the previous night in the cottage at Craig. He saw also that as these two ran, they looked over their shoulders and up the great glen. Somewhat belated, and coming at a rush past the Inn's west gable were five fellows attired similarly to the foremost of the flying figures. All carried muskets. As they came round the front of the house they tried to detour widely by the shore, but the swiftly incoming tide now prevented this, and they came easily into gunshot as they approached at a swinging run. Drumfin levelled his piece at the last man, but Fraser struck it up.

"Quiet," he said. "See how they all turn their heads one way, and that's up Glenmore. And see yonder, man, at the ford."

Stretching out of the casement and looking far up the mouth of the Strath, they saw little puppets of men neatly clad in red and white rise from the river's bed.

"The King's men?" cried Drumfin. "Then who are these who laid us siege; and why do they run?"

"Why they run is clear," said Fraser. "These are the fellows who kidnapped Miss Morag. The man in front but one—he with the cloak of many capes—is an unfrocked minister of Tiree, Deaf Alan by name in these parts—to give him his full title —Alan MacMaster MacLean."

"Ah! I know him. But what could they want with me?" said Drumfin.

"Nothing with you. But with me—everything," said Fraser. "And the reason for that is a long story that can wait till a fitter season for the telling. But now is your turn come, when the Sidier Roy are stirring so close, for they are making some speed in the glen's mouth there, and we'd be safer in the moorland than in this barrack."

"I'm fell tired," said Drumfin. "But I'm with you, lad! The east door, and forth again!"

26: A lady in a blue riding-habit

Just how Fraser and the exile came through Glen Seileasdair to Gribun, and took hiding with the fishers there; how in a night of storm the redcoats came on them; how Drumfin escaped to sea in an open boat; and how next day the surgeon was marched a prisoner through the wilds of Glenmore to lonely Strathcoil—is it not now all an old story in Aros Isle?

Fraser slept soundly that night, although his bed was but dried bracken and his roof a thatch that leaked, for his exhaustion was extreme, and if he were to be transported on the morrow he could not have waked a moment to commiserate his doom. He was still dozing deep in the early morning, when the officer commanding the company shook his shoulder. Captain Fawkener's face was red; his eyes like beads, hot and black; his gait shaky.

"Where's rebel?" he asked thickly.

"I know nothing of him," said Fraser wearily, tossing over, and half-asleep already.

"But you had rendezvous?"

"Oh, yes,"

"Where?"

The surgeon was silent, though far from sleeping now.

"Where, sir, where?"

"I shall not tell you."

Fawkener smiled foolishly and lurched forwards.

"Good fellow, good fellow! Tell me, now, tell me."

Then Fraser's continued silence made him tearful, and he declared the surgeon's conduct wondrous shabby, wept more copiously still, vowed his feelings deeply wounded, and departed.

Fraser slept again—heavy restful sleep, dreamless in abysms of unconsciousness; but in an hour's time the tipsy captain's return broke in once more on these slumbrous delights. Fawkener was still drunk, but more composed.

"Where's rendezvous?" he said, pointing a podgy menacing finger at his prisoner, while the two grenadiers behind him grinned at the figure he cut.

The surgeon still held his peace and to repeated queries gave no reply.

"Damned traitor," summed up Fawkener, and lurched past his men and through the doorway.

To sleep once more, but not for long, for scarcely had another hour gone, when the vinous breath of the captain was around him again as he wakened him with a grip on his shoulder.

"Come, sir, where's my man? Must tell me— must tell me!"

Fraser shook his hand off in disgust, and, unanswering, rolled himself anew in his cloak.

"Won't?—won't?" cried Fawkener, his red face darkening in passion. "Damned renegade! Damned traitor!"

He cursed erratically but forcibly for a spell, and retired to seek the sympathy of his lieutenant; but that phlegmatic youth was used to his captain's vagaries, and received his story with an ill-concealed yawn. The yawn, however, was not repeated, for Hodson found that the few words of soothing he had found potent in previous outbreaks seemed powerless here; indeed, the drunken officer was working himself to heights of rage his junior had never before witnessed, and a time came when the lymphatic lieutenant was roused to fear for the prisoner's safety. He knew Fawkener's temper on its lower levels, but this passion was new to him, and he dreaded the powers of wrath still latent. So, when at last the tippler drowsed, face forward on the table at which they sat, Hodson stole out to the sentry.

"Jenkins!"

The soldier saluted and came forward.

"Where is the man you spoke of following us last night for so long?"

"In the house by the bridge, sir."

"He seemed to know Mr. Fraser?"

"Yes, sir."

"Send him here."

It was Charlie Ruapais who came back with the soldier, and fearing some new danger, the little gillie snivelled dolorously, for the young officer, so languid in yesterday's march, looked very wide awake and business-like now.

"You are a friend to Mr. Fraser?"

"In a way, sir—a kind of a servant, sir."

"Servant or no—you are friendly?"

"Oh, surely, sir—surely."

"Mr. Fraser has other friends at Moy, has he not?"

"Many, sir, many."

"Then hurry to Moy with all speed and tell that Mr. Fraser is here and his life in danger."

"His life, sir? But—?"

"His life—his life in danger, and instant danger here, at Strathcoil," said the young man sharply. "Now, go at once."

The Ruapais looked to earth a moment as if in thought, and then swung round, taking Ardura Brae at the trot, while Lieutenant Hodson came back slowly and meditatively to the prisoner's hut. The surgeon no longer slept deeply: he tossed as in a nightmare upon his rude bed of bracken, and looking in on him from the open doorway, the erstwhile listless youth sighed heavily. But glancing hastily round at the sentry, witness of this involuntary exhibition of sentiment, he immediately elaborated an enormous yawn, and retired to his quarters.

It was noon before Fawkener awoke, and at once he made for Fraser's hut, his red face darker now, almost, indeed, a chocolate-colour.

"You dog!" he roared. "You will not speak, eh?"

Fraser could see that the man was mad with anger; he could see also that the faces of the guard accompanying the captain bore traces of some strong emotion suppressed: could it be fear? What was afoot? But he lay back on his bed of bracken, his hands underneath his head, and stared contempt at the bully. This look of disdain only enraged Fawkener further and with a sudden kick he sent bench and prisoner over in a heap.

"You dumb dog!" he screamed.

In an instant Fraser was on his feet and had him by the throat; and though his lame arm stung for a moment, he felt an infinite relish in the pang as he crushed the wine-stained face backwards. Yet the pleasure was short and sharp as the pain, for the grenadiers rushed in and pulled them asunder.

The captain glared at his assailant and then gave a quick command, and the next moment the surgeon found himself outside in the misty noontide air. There was a hint of frost abroad, and the nearer hillsides showed a faint apple-green through the thin fog that walled off the rest of the world. It was all like an ugly dream, and the pervading mist with the automaton-like figures of the Sidier Roy, moving in and out of it, enhanced the illusion. Out of the mist, too, came an order, and Fraser was marched up a little height to where four broken walls showed the skeleton of an ancient homestead. The faces of the men holding his arms, the prisoner noted, seemed suddenly to have turned the same chocolate-colour as their captain's, and they wetted dry lips constantly, exchanging covert glances the while. He saw the lieutenant expostulating with Fawkener; and saw him also thrust rudely aside as the captain went off out of sight behind the curtains of vapour.

There was silence for a little, then out of the stillness below came a throb of marching feet, and Fawkener appeared from the folds of mist once more, a sergeant with a file of six men following. Thirty paces off they halted, and set their musket-flints, and as they did so, the men at his side released their hold and left him standing alone against the broken wall. Then the full horror of the whole business flashed on him, as the captain's voice, cracked and unnatural in its excitement, came up to him where he stood.

"Still dumb?" he cried. "Go on, sergeant."

The sergeant gave a quiet order, and the six figures in front of the surgeon tapped some little black grains into the pans of their muskets, slinging their powder flasks aside in a clock-work movement.

"Ready," said the sergeant.

"Stop," cried Fawkener. "What in the name of all the devils is happening now?"

There was a noise of chopping and slithering hoofs behind the wall of mist to the south, but nothing could be seen, though the sounds chinked and clattered onwards at an incredible pace. All stood at gaze, and a waft of wind suddenly sending the fog from Ardura Brae, discovered the steep drove-track there, and three mounted figures on it rushing swiftly downwards. Two were women; the third was a man.

The leading horsewoman—a lady in a blue riding-habit—headed straight for the firing party, and her garron skimmed down the hillside like a deer to where Captain Fawkener, dumbfounded at the suddenness of these apparitions, stood with hand half-raised long after his first command had been given. He beheld the lady making straight towards himself, but he noted also that she was swaying in her saddle and, not fifty paces from where he stood, she slid heavily to earth under the very feet of her pony.

The group of soldiers stood a trifle dazed at the intrusion and its sequel, and when their prisoner, with the surgeon's instinct, started forward to aid the fallen lady, they felt no surprise at his audacity and gave no sign of interference.

"Damnation!" said Fawkener. "What's this?"

"Lord knows, sir," said the sergeant. "But her maid is coming up; and this man is a surgeon. We want nothing to do with sick women, sir, do we?"

"Surgeon?" said the captain savagely. "It's his last case, Townley."

The riderless garron intervening, hid Fraser from the view of the firing party as he bent over the girl. And it was well for him that it did so, for when he raised her head it was the grey eyes of Morag MacLean that smiled up to him; and instantly he had stooped to kiss her hand with a movement as passionate as it was unconscious. They heard Fawkener coming towards them, cursing audibly as he did so.

"Unhurt," whispered Morag to Fraser. "'Twas a ruse. Take the pony."

He gathered her meaning at once, and caught the garron's bridle, but stumbled against the bibulous captain ere he could mount. That officer saw his object and put out a shaky hand to stay him, but rage rendered him speechless. From all the many commands ranging through his fuddled brain he could select not one, and before he could speak, a blow from the surgeon's lame arm crashed on his chocolate-coloured face, and he fell. Fraser felt again the joy of his injury's stinging as his knuckles cracked at their task, but it was all so rapid that he was off and safe in the fog before the effects of his blow sent the captain to the ground at the feet of the amazed sergeant; and the solitary volley that followed him was as harmless as a salute.

27: Red rowans

AFTER the first mad rush, Fraser let the garron guide him through the mist. His mount was a Moy pony; its memories of its stable were acute, and accordingly the Glenmore track was soon found and the devious byways that led from it by Loch Sgunbain on the short-cut for home. Thus it was that by evening the surgeon was safely installed in the chamber of hiding so recently occupied by Drumfin. But the military continued to invest the district, and he had a prospect of enforced confinement for some time to the musty little room where no daylight came, but only the shine of peat and taper. In this cell he slept and ate and read for two long days, fretting the more since young Moy had brought him word that Morag, safely returned from her adventure at Strathcoil, was daily following the hunt with Pennyfuaran and some other guests still remaining from the dance. And he continued to fret till, at last, late in the afternoon of the third day, he risked a sally from his refuge, and, brooding over the news young Moy had given, stole out through the copse to the east of the castle.

"Pennyfuaran again," he said to himself, and gloomed.

A thin pale sunshine fell on the winter woods and on the grey plain of the loch's waters. Dull and thunderous, a sound came to the ear—the breakers on Laggan Sands; all else was still and dream-like. The cold air and the sea's salt tang lent his step a briskness that had long been wanting and he swung rapidly through the dark laurels, for the noise of the drumming waves was like a call of the old ocean to her lover, and a score of seascapes came to the summons. The dark blue leagues of salt water with a following wind and a wave ever breaking in the frigate's waist; the burning sky of the idle doldrum days withdrawn to heights immeasurable above a sea that glared back to it; the faintly breezy day with quiet surge and great white clouds on the horizon that always promised home, until the Needles came up and beckoned; he tasted them all anew.

Yet this was but a surface mood, for somewhere deep down in his spirit was a soreness at the frame of things—at this world so sadly awry; and dully he wondered if on occasions such as this, some evil humour were in the air, so that, it might be, all men felt at equal hours of the heavy day, this unbearable burden of their lot, this all-pervasive melancholy. It was a wild thought, yet he decided he would boldly probe the matter with the first chance-comer, discovering if he also felt the incubus. But he met no one; indeed, the place seemed untenanted, for it was late in the afternoon, and the Glenmore hunt had taken most from home.

Whilst he nursed this black mood, a turn in the path brought him suddenly on a lady pacing slowly in the direction he himself was taking. She wore a skirt and riding-coat of dark blue, laced with fine silver lines, and her hat was a tricorne in keeping.

Despite the averted face and up-pinned side-curls he saw her at once for Morag, and as she turned at the sound of his step, he noted with surprise that the quiet eyes were smiling.

"Sir, a good evening," she said. "Is it that you would still play the good Samaritan that I find you here? Is there a new danger?"

"I know of no further peril, madam," said Fraser stiffly, "and I did not expect you. I thought it was at the hare drive you would be found."

"I did but jest," she said.

"'tis your turn," he answered. "And 'tis mine to give thanks—"

"Ah!" she said, and her face flamed pink. "You mean your escape at Strathcoil? Pray, no more of that; for it were a sermon you gave instead of thanks, if you but saw my motive for the part I played."

"Your motive?" said Fraser quietly. "I know it."

"You cannot—you shall not," she challenged. "Indeed, you shall not."

"Was it not chiefly a desire to cry 'Quits'—to be even with me for any little service I had rendered you, madam?"

"Oh, a warlock, a warlock!" she cried in affected wonder. "You have it, sir—indeed you have." She was smiling mockingly now.

"And now, since you have paid off what you term your indebtedness to me, you feel you could forgive me anything, madam," he went on.

He could not help pluming himself on his sagacity, even though he felt the humour of the thing, and saw that he had only half the truth. Something in his face betrayed his satisfaction with himself; and the next instant he felt she had discovered his vanity in the matter, and was laughing at his efforts to read her.

"Forgive? Why, yes," she said. "Even my *bavardage*, Miss MacLean, about Pennyfuaran?" said he desperately, getting deeper into the toils.

She flashed round on him. "There is a deal too much of Pennyfuaran and Miss MacLean in the air,: it seems. Let me tell you, sir, and in one telling, that there is no truth in the story that links those names together."

Fraser halted as if he had been dismissed; and at sight of his doleful face she softened and said:

"Please you, sir surgeon, do not leave me. I go to see the waters coming in on Laggan Sands, and the approach is rocky. Remember my wrist. Will you not come?"

He stammered a glad acceptance, and they continued their walk.

"Of course," said the girl, a hint of mischief in her glance, "when Charlie came up with Belle and myself, half-way between Strathcoil and Moy, my first thoughts were for nought but saving the life of a friend. But that was momentary only, believe me: for soon there crept in this alloy; and ever after it was simply a case of crying ' Quits.'"

The words whipped, but he plodded on, unreplying: it was even as if he welcomed them.

"And again," she went on, "I remember thinking that I had done you the injustice of holding you for a spy. Yet here was the lie to that tale, for you were risking your life to shield the man you were credited with hunting to the death. And it seemed I might best atone by doing what I did—by coming to help you ... But again—" and she shook her head, smiling the while—" that vision was also too fleeting. The essential thought was ' Quits.'"

Still the surgeon took his drubbing in silence.

"Ah, enough!" she laughed—" enough of this searching of hearts. Like as not there were a-many motives in the business; and at last we ken there's more than one shuttle goes to the weaving of a tartan, Mr. Fraser. The matter is hardly worth the breath we spend on it, I jalouse."

He still kept silence. Indeed, although he heard her every syllable, he heeded her railing but little; for her disavowal of any troth with Pennyfuaran, unsought as it had been, seemed to him the only words of any moment, and he paced on, pondering them.

On the other side of the bay, and fronting them, were the headlands of the Laggan country: the little inlet whose shores they sought. But the path led now by rocky defiles between the cliffs and huge stacks of stone, winding in conformity with the landward steeps, so that the approach to the sands was indirect. Half-way, they came to where a spot of scarlet was visible high against a grey background of crag: a mountain-ash in full fruitage.

"The rowans! How lovely!" cried Morag; and then, "Oh, come back, sir! Your arm, sir!" for already her perfervid companion was high among bush and bracken, his sling over his shoulder, as he struggled upwards to the dot of red.

Breathless he came back, laden with a branch,, rich in glossy beads of vivid colour.

"How foolish!" she said with smiling lips. "And yet I thank you."

Breathless he was again as he watched her fasten a bunch in the knot of her coat, and look archly up at him as she did so. Then they walked on, and at length the sweep of the track was downwards, and they saw the white sands with the waters pouring in on them. Far out the billows curled, toppling into breakers of dazzling brightness, and these, myriad and incessant, sprawled shorewards and ended in thin lipping crescents of water that hissed into nothingness. They seated themselves in order to look on at this play of the surf. White and cold, the sunshine fell around, on rock, on sand, on wrestling waters, and, oh, so beautifully on the face of the woman beside Ian Fraser. He sat and gazed at that face, while she watched the inrace of the tide; and if there was fascination for her in the eternal mutation of grey water and white foam, for him, too, was there fascination in the play of changing moods on her perfect features. And so it was that as she turned with a sigh such as the vision of something in Nature at once beautiful and terrible may evoke, she met the man's earnest gaze. Her eyes wavered and fell; the faintest flicker of colour rose from cheeks to temples, and a sudden hush seemed to fall on her, so that even the waters' tumult was stilled and all was the profoundest silence in the deeps of her being. But with a flutter as of wings she felt and heard her heart-beats grow and grow, until the whole world was filled with them, for as she raised her shy glance to the man seated beside her, his hands were around her hands, and his eyes close to her eyes. His silken sling was tenantless now, and she did not speak, but looked at him and at the grey skies and sighed again. He tried to find words, but they failed him; and thought, too, was lacking. Only was he conscious of the song of the breakers, of her glad eyes, of the pale sunlight. Her eyes, her grey eyes, her glad eyes! ... Then the splash of scarlet in the bunch of rowans on her breast burned into his brain, and he found inspiration and voice at once.

"Pay me," he said, with husky voice and stammering—" Pay me a debt as yet unpaid. Pay me for the berries I gave you, Morag. Pay me," he whispered low, "with lips as red, as fair."

And all in a dream and a mist of gold, he saw her face come close, and felt her kiss, and oblivion seemed to fall on him then. But he awoke to the sound of the happy waves and the vision of the happy sunlight. The sea-pyat and the curlew were calling aloud for happiness; happy, too, the plover's cry on the bent yonder. Joyously the chariots of white cloud voyaged onwards in the zenith; and as the lovers leant towards each other, a little wind came from the sea, lifting the hair from their foreheads and sighing "Peace" to them before it went inland. Happily rose and fell her bosom; happily he gazed into eyes of happiness.

Surely the sun would stand still. Surely Time no longer mowed down swathes of space, for here was the beginning of the world and here the world ended. O Life, O Death, show to us the heart of your mystery, for now have our spirits understanding, and we are wise and strong with the wisdom and strength of gods. Who shall withstand us we mould old earth anew? We have learned the lesson of love; who shall oppose or sunder? Ah, Tir-nan-Oig! The happy sunlight, the happy waves!

28: Norman plays high

The enchantment of that hour at Laggan was not soon to be recalled, for that very evening Fraser had to seek the heather again, The soldiery were once more drawing to Moy, but in business fashion this time, and his only safety seemed that of flight. He went through the Croggan country, lying overnight at Leackruadh, ferried the mouth of Loch Spelve in the morning, and tramped to the Grasspoint change-house.

Had he but arrived an hour earlier he would have met Norman MacLean face to face as he left the inn on another excursion to Moy. Whatever fears of the Sidier Roy that youth had felt, these seemed groundless now; for he footed it blithely by Gleannan Mill and over the moors to Strathcoil as if the country held never a red-coat. Half of the way he journeyed with a horner, and when the poor man turned off at Glenmore he felt shamed at the profusion of thanks Norman gave him for his company. Yet for all his protesting he was at last convinced by this pale-faced young man, that though indeed his poverty was great, he was blessed with such a gift of ceilidh as was never before in the world.

"What's one he or a thousand of them if the man is made happier for a day?" said Norman to himself as they parted, "This night it's king of all the *seanachaidhean* he'll be in his own mind; and I'm never a whit the poorer."

Ever the actor, the born actor, he played pranks even on the shy Highland lasses he met the wayside. There was one carrying a cogie milk from Balure to a sick woman in Seanvaile, and he stopped to ask if she had seen his wife and heir maids go past. So circumspectly, indeed, did he describe their garrons and the fashion of their dresses, that for long and long the maid regretted missing the sight of such grandeurs. Her milk he tasted; and her kindness, oh, her kindness! how he praised it! And so the poor girl was left with an opinion of her own graciousness she had never held before, and for some days to come her new-born vanity caused not a few heart-breaks in Balure and Seanvaile.

But when he met Pennyfuaran by the banks of Uisg something warned him to withdraw into himself and lay aside his acting. The look on the face of the chieftain was new to him; indeed, Norman had never seen him so little susceptible to the influence of his mere presence.

"There is little need of your messages so pressing, if all the news you bring is as wide of the mark as your last," said Pennyfuaran.

"What's amiss?" said Norman.

"This man, Fraser. Your Tiree journey did you little good to send you so far astray about him," said MacKinnon. And he recounted the surgeon's dealings with Captain Fawkener at Strathcoil. "Then as for Morag—she is friendlier with him than ever," he concluded bitterly.

"So the man is no spy after all?" said Norman. "Now, what a fool I've been!" And there was the very essence of regret and anger in his tone, so that Pennyfuaran could have pitied him. "But who is directing Fawkener, if it be not he? For direction he must have, to move so close and sure as he does."

"Direction, yes. It's MacQuarie of Inshriff," said Pennyfuaran.

"Ay? MacQuarie?" cried Norman, and his anger was real. "He'll stop at nothing if there's money in't, will MacQuarie. Damn the man and his plotting!He's working years ahead of everyone, as they say hereabouts."

"The toad!" growled MacKinnon.

"The toad, yes, he's all that, for stillness and the dark," said the other. "But this turn it's better speed he'll come: it's the fox he'll be, Pennyfuaran, questing and questing quickly."

They parted then, Norman sending a letter to his sister by the hands of the chieftain.

"The chase is up," said the youth to himself, as Pennyfuaran stalked off on the shore track; "and it's a devil of a handicap MacQuarie has, Norman, my dear, for he's been days on the ground before us. But it's a race worth the running, and it's me that's the dog for *ventre à terre*."

He took the hill above Moy, coming to Glenbyre and waiting impatiently there throughout the short day; and when dark had fallen he was at the rustic bridge in the Castle woods long before his sister had arrived. When she came, it was a new Morag. Radiant her face in the moon's faint light; her voice subdued as if she feared to break the charm that made a new miracle of all the world since yesterday. Her kiss was strange to and he marvelled to see her blush as she gave Here was a transformation that perplexed, might have guessed the truth had not his clever brain on principle distrusted guessing: for his work of espionage had drilled him in the precise lines deduction from experience even in the smaller affairs. But experience could not help in this, for here was a realm whose ivory gates had never opened to his challenge—a city of dream whose streets his shadow would never darken. And so stood, silent and wondering, before this mystery, a woman whom love had blessed. Yet, perturbed as he was by the sight of this change in Morag, he held by the purpose of his tryst with her, and, before long, broached it.

"So it seems that after all I was wrong in the matter of Mr. Fraser," he said humbly. "How far astray, none but myself can feel or fathom, Morag; and at my first meeting with him there shall be full amends."

"Yes, you were wrong," she said quietly.

"It was but for Drumfin, I feared; and now that I find Fraser friendly, I am anxious to have his aid. For but yesterday there came a message from Paris for your exile—one that has never seen pen or ink; indeed, since it left France it has but travelled from lip to lip; and now there is no mouth but mine to speak it."

"Dear Norman, more danger?"

"More danger, little sister; and still and on I'd not have it otherwise, nor would you despite your pleadings. If I but knew Fraser's hiding I'd soon persuade him to guide me to Drumfin, I doubt not."

"Is there, indeed, a great danger to Drumfin, Norman, if he do not get your message?" she asked.

"There is a great danger," he repeated, and his voice broke in masterly fashion. "'tis a matter of life and death," he went on solemnly, "and I love the man—so helpless!"

"Then," said the girl, flushing and speaking with averted face, "I think I can discover some direction to him through Mr. Fraser."

"Ah," he said, watching her closely, a new light in his eager eyes. "You are still friendly with the surgeon? What a little conspirator it is; and all for the sake of a poor old exile?"

"And not at all for the sake of a poor young agent of exiles?" she asked, smiling.

He laughed and gaily kissed her hands.

"There!" he said. "I must lose no time. And yet," he cried suddenly, as if the thought had but come to him, "And yet we should go faster, little sister, if you sent a letter to Mr. Fraser, and your messenger brought back a note of Drumfin's rendezvous with him."

"Indeed, yes; and where were my wits not to see it? At the soonest you shall have Mr. Fraser's answer sent on to Glenbyre, dear Norman."

"Poor Drumfin!" said the youth, half-musing, his voice again tremulous. "Good-night, little one. *Beannachd leat, mo chridhe!*"

They parted. And Callum MacQuarie, crouching far up the woodland path, watched their parting and cursed them silently, for he would fain have followed both. Finding his spying on Morag the easier course, he turned to his task of shadowing her. He saw the return of the girl to the Castle, some coming and going of Belle, and another appearance of Morag as she stole out to the edge of the pine-wood in which he lay. She hid in the shadows of the great boles and waited: there were few people about, and these servitors mainly; but with a quarter mile of greensward intervening they seemed distant enough, though Morag would have felt them but a hand's breadth off if she stepped into the moonlight.

A little later a tall kilted form swung gracefully across the sands beyond the Castle green, his figure dark against the silver of the loch; for

Pennyfuaran had ever an eye for effect, and the sea-wind tossing his plaid on such a night as this, was just the necessary touch of storm which he could have desired. And it was this sense of the picturesque, so strong in him, that kept him to the sea-marge, the dark outline of his lithe figure skirting it longer than was requisite for his detour to where the girl stood in the shade of the woods.

"You're here before me, cousin?" said he. "I trust I have not kept you waiting? I was but on my way to Fawkener when Belle overtook me."

"Captain Fawkener?" asked the girl, shivering. "My cousin in his company?"

He laughed uneasily. "Oh, come!" he said. "We're both army men, you see."

"And yet with a difference, cousin. For you are friend to Drumfin, whilst he is but the bloodhound on his track."

Pennyfuaran tried to laugh, but failed to carry it off. "Well, I suppose the man's at his work," he said; "he but does his duty, I trust."

"Does he never exceed it?" asked the girl bitterly.

"As for Drumfin—well, has he not the best of aid in this wonderful Mr. Fraser?" said the chieftain.

"Kenneth, is it you that speak? Is it to this your anger is sending you—indifference to this old man's fate? Was he not friend to you and to your father before you?"

"Not that," cried Pennyfuaran. "No treachery to Drumfin, I swear! But," he went on quietly, "there are only Moy and some Campbell women in the Castle to-night, and be Fawkener harsh or no, at least he's soldier's company."

Morag sighed in relief. "Only that?" she said.

"Only that; and some dice."

"Ah," she said, "then I can ask the service of you that I came to ask."

This confession of the dicing had put the chieftain in good-humour with himself again, and he bowed low. "Your devoted servant," he said.

"Then it's this, sir. Find Mr. Fraser for me. Give him this note, and bring me an answer."

Pennyfuaran went pale, and stepped deeper into the fringe of the pines, moistening his lips feverishly.

"Madam, is it your lover's flunkey you'd make me?" said he. "Oh, beyond all bounds this— beyond all bounds!"

Morag turned pale also, and yet she found her voice. "You forget yourself, surely," she answered. "The affair is one of politics and not of sentiment, and concerns Drumfin's welfare deeply. Indeed and indeed, Pennyfuaran, it is life and death!"

He stood unmoved; his eyes were bright and staring; and a few beads of sweat caught in the meshes of his fair eyebrows, had taken a stray moonbeam and were sparkling eerily.

"You will not believe me?" she said in low rapid tones. "And yet here is Norman, but half an hour gone, begging me to have this done for him. And this is a note to Mr. Fraser asking for Drumfin's rendezvous; for Norman thinks that he will reply more readily to me than to another—since—" her eyes fell—"since the affair at Strathcoil.'

"The accident, as Fawkener names it," said the chieftain sourly.—

"As you will," she answered, and went on. "Norman says he has a message for Drumfin of the deepest import, that he alone can convey it, and that but by word of mouth. The very sky will fall, he says, if Drumfin have not the message in time."

Pennyfuaran was silent: he was thinking quickly. Here was news of a truth, but why had he not learnt anything of this from Norman six hours ago. Many things were putting themselves together in his mind; and, as in a vision, he beheld himself and Morag, and Drumfin and Fraser, as but pawns in the hands of Norman. He remembered now the youth's quick heat against MacQuarie when he heard that he also was on the track of Drumfin, and he guessed that here was a move of the most daring kind to gain a knowledge which would place him far ahead of any rival in the game of the exile's capture. Proof? -He had none: and even if he had, here was the man's own sister, pathetic in her faith, and adamant to any evidence against her darling. To refuse her asking were easy, but to cloak the reasons for refusal a task of less facility. Still harder was it to invent on the instant a sham ground of action, and to assume a vice of which he for the moment felt nothing; but he steeled himself to the work and acted the jealous swain to admiration.

"So! The sky will fall?" he asked. "Then let it, for all I care. You'll make no lover's flunkey of me, I tell you."

He went off abruptly towards the village, crossing the greensward with long steps, his plaid's shadow swinging gigantic this way and that; and with a fire of contempt in her grey eyes Morag looked after him; then, nodding her head slowly and decisively, she returned to the Castle.

When she had gone, a man rose from behind a little thicket close by. He had grey whiskers and ferret eyes, and he seemed to smile with his upper hp and nose rather than with his mouth, whilst he twisted his hands round each other, and gazed after the girl. For a little he stood motionless— faun-like and evil in the dark of the pines—and then, silently, furtively, swiftly, bored to the depths of the woods.

29: MacQuarie's cards

UNWITTING that his part of traitor was known to any, MacQuarie moved openly enough in the daytime among the Moy crofters; wheedling and flattering he came, all ears for any marketable news in the gossip of the place. And assuredly he lost no time in playing his cards, for on the morning following his eavesdropping, he set to work on the Ruapais. They met on the common grazing ground between the Castle and the village, and MacQuarie opened with a veiled compliment that took the breath from Charlie.

"Well, well, and here is Aros come to Moy at last," said he, smiling. "And your wife will have health, I trust, Mr. MacMorland?"

The Ruapais gasped in delighted amazement. "I did not get a wife yet, master," said he, chuckling nervously. "'Deed no, not yet."

MacQuarie's eyebrows went up, and then he laughed. "My blame, Charlie, but if I did not hear it somewhere, I'm sore mistaken."

"'Deed no, not yet," said Charlie, chuckling anew, and then laughing hollowly in a spasm that brought tears to his eyes.

MacQuarie joined him quietly as though by way of company, his head on one side and his eyes sharp in a watchful regard. There was something intimate, something of a compliment in this unbending of the tacksman to the gillie, and if Charlie felt gratified at the assumption of him as a married man, he was vastly more so at this union of their souls in vocal mirth.

"Well, well," pursued the man from Inshriff, "if not yet, still 'twill be some day, Charlie, I doubt not. Though it's not me that should be speaking, is it— an old man and a bachelor?"

"'Deed no," said Charlie, still delightedly pondering the thought of conjugal bonds. "'Deed no, not you—not you—MacQuarie—sir."

The tacksman's voice was graver when he next spoke, yet if Charlie had but noted, he would have seen laughter still in the little eyes. "Ay, an old man, Charlie, an old man! And a weary one, forbye; and to speak truth— for it's you I can trust if anyone, Mr. MacMorland—I've the weariest of weary work this very day. What do you think now of a message to a hunted man who may be anywhere in this isle for aught I ken—here the day and awa' the morn, you see?"

"Drumfin?" said the Ruapais, his pouched eyes wide, and his wizened face long. "*Och, ochan!*"

"Ay, Drumfin. And I'm an old man, Charlie, that's what I am," said MacQuarie. And he looked round helplessly on the hills surrounding, as if by chance he might sight the wanderer there. "You'll no can help me, Charlie, can you? And yet it's my very thoughts I'll give you, sir—it's what I was saying to myself was this: ' If Charlie MacMorland can help Drumfin he'll do it, for he never held by any but the Stuarts.' It's nothing but my thoughts I'm telling you, Charlie."

On Charlie's puzzled features a flicker of a vain smile played for an instant. "*Mo thruaigh!*" he said. "What a world! And you've a message for the poor man, and him harried by the red-coats? And you'll not know where he is?"

"What a world!" echoed the tacksman ruefully, and he ruffled his whiskers so as to conceal his mouth with his hand, while he pierced Charlie with his narrowed eyes. "Well, it's what I said to myself I'm but telling you," he went on in tones that implied a frank avowal of his inmost thoughts. "There's Charlie Ruapais," I said, "and there's Belle, and —"

"Belle!" cried Charlie delightedly as in discovery. "Belle will ken; that's it, Belle will do it."

"Well, well," said MacQuarie, "you tell me? Man, man, I wouldna have thought it. Well done, Charlie, say I. And you think Belle will ken? Wonderful!"

"It's just Belle will help us," said the Ruapais, excited and sanguine.

"And Charlie, lad," said the tacksman, sinking his voice to a whisper, while he laid an explanatory forefinger in a frayed buttonhole of the gillie's coat, "if not Belle, then I wouldna say but Mistress Morag would do. She'd be glad and more than glad to help Drumfin, poor man! No, no, not an asking, you see; but Belle could let a wee bittie hint drop, you'll understand." He half closed his ferret eyes, and wagged his head sagely.

More gratified than ever, the Ruapais smiled anew at the vastness of the confidence.

"She's anything but Hanover, you ken," went on MacQuarie with a sudden broad smile that almost hid his eyes but showed his broken teeth. He rubbed his hands vigorously together, and rocked youthfully, heel-and-toe, well pleased with this conclusion to their plotting.

"I'll see to't, Inshriff, man," said the Ruapais, grinning also. "I'm off at the word."

"Well, well," said MacQuarie, "but it's you that's the smart one, Charlie. Well, well," and he rubbed his hands with infinite zest, as he watched the quaint figure of the gillie depart at the accustomed trot.

It was in this way that the tacksman secured the promise of an interview with Morag; and the girl, with Drumfin's safety ever in the forefront of her thoughts, deemed it prudent to make the meeting secret. The tryst was for the Castle woods at gloaming, and she took Belle and the Ruapais with her as a precaution against further misadventure.

They hurried from the Castle, just as dark came on, Morag and Belle in front, and the Ruapais fifty paces behind. There was no moon as yet, but a faint starlight shone through the aisles of the woods from a sky cloudless save for one great bar that floated in fine with the course of the loch. Inland or seaward the waters were almost soundless, and only the waves of the distant incoming tide chimed feebly to these deeps of the forest, as they crossed the little bridge, and coming round a bend of an avenue, saw MacQuarie walking to and fro in front of them. He was wrapped in an old torn plaid, and a trifle of a swagger was observable in his gait.

A swagger, yes; and why not? Here already was a foretaste of gentrice, he was thinking; here already he was dealing with people of quality. And why not? he asked again. As good as they, he thought ... God! how he'd like to make them squirm—Pennyfuaran and the rest—if he but had the power ...And money gave power; and here was the road to it. Caution, now, caution ... Money was the means and power the end; let him play cannily!

Belle and Charlie had fallen forty yards behind, when Morag came up with the man. She was pale and a trifle breathless.

"You are Mr. MacQuarie?" she asked.

"Callum MacQuarie, tacksman in Inshriff," he said, bowing not ungracefully.

"And you have a message for Drumfin?"

"I have been so far trusted, madam."

"Is it a written message?"

"Written it is, Miss Morag; but no more can I tell you, if you'll pardon plain speech."

The sight of this girl so single-minded, so direct in her purpose, perplexed his shifty brain; he felt that unless she met him with methods as tortuous as his own, he would be on strange ground, and might betray himself at any moment.

"It's only plain speech I want," she said; "it's for that I'd be thankful. But this is my business: I also know of a message to go through to Drumfin, and I but wished to make sure that yours and mine were not the same."

MacQuarie smirked. "Well, well," he said, "if it's not the same message, at least it's the same cause, Miss Morag, I doubt not. My letter is from Dunkirk—that much I may say, but no more—and if we but knew where to turn for Drumfin, it might be the one sending we could make of both your message and mine."

"I have been thinking," said Morag, "that if we could but get into touch with Mr. Fraser—whom you'll have heard of—he would be sure to see to a safe ending of the matter, for he was Drumfin's close friend and kens his hiding, I should say."

"My very thought at this moment!" cried MacQuarie. "Well, well, and did not I discover Mr. Fraser's direction not an hour gone? It's even on the road to him I'd have been, had not your maid kept me back."

"Ah!" sighed the girl in deep satisfaction.

"Command me, Miss Morag," said the man. "One of your name has but to ask, you ken."

"Here is a note," she said. "Give it to Mr. Fraser, and return me his answer with all speed."

He took the packet, and then bent down of a sudden, looking under the brushwood to his right. "Hush!" he said, for a little rustling was heard, and a twig or two crackled. Then a hand came slowly through the birch leaves, pushed the branches gently aside, and Norman MacLean stepped delicately on to the path. Ironically he bowed with a glissade to MacQuarie, swinging his cloak gracefully, then came close and peered into the face of the tacksman, as if by way of identifying him to a certainty in that dim light. But despite his bravado it was evident that the stress of some emotion lay heavy on him, and that he controlled himself with an effort.

"Just as I had guessed," he said, eyeing the tacksman contemptuously. "I'd know his voice anywhere, Morag. I've watched all day, little sister, to guard you from something like this: your every movement I've followed, and yet this fellow had almost fooled us. He a friend! He a Jacobite! Traitor in one thing, traitor in all, Callum, the blackest of Callums!" He gave MacQuarie a push. "Off, wolf!" he said. —

The tacksman's eyes seemed to recede, his figure to crouch to smaller bulk, as he gave way; then in a sudden movement, he craned forward, shaking with passion suppressed, a forefinger pointing at Norman.

"And every word a true one, eh?" he sneered. "Every word a truth of the whitest, Miss Morag? It's me that's the poor man scheming to make a penny by selling the news of the countryside, eh? Well, then, let it be so: let me make a clean breast of it." He twined his fingers savagely around each other. "Hear Callum MacQuarie now," he went on. "Well, I did mislead you — that I'll confess — and there was no message from Dunkirk. And after all that, I doubt not, it's a spy Mr. Norman would be calling me?"

As much astonished by the fact of his recognition by MacQuarie as by his avowal of deceit, young MacLean hesitated for a reply. Then he laughed half-heartedly.

"Spy?" he said. "Why, yes."

"Well, well, wonderful," said the tacksman, sidling near, his head to one side and his voice very gentle now. "And your own name will be — what? — will be what, sir?" He smiled and shook his head as in reproof. "Oh, yes," he said softly and sadly, "just spy also — yes, just spy, Mr. Norman."

The youth retired before the close-pressed face of the old man, feeling that the brain behind those ferret eyes was master of cunning he had never sounded. He feared, too, the dusk of anger, creeping up over the high cheek-bones.

"Spy—just spy," said the tacksman in louder tones, "and a worse than the poor farmer in Inshriff ... Your very brother, Miss Morag,—oh, yes, your own brother—and yet a thing unclean!. . . God! I work crooked, but I never held the secret counsels of the Prince only to betray them; I had no hand in procuring the slaughter of Chisholm because he stood in the way of some blood-money in Tiree; and if I set myself to the death-hunt of Drumfin, my own father was never his bosom-friend, and my own sister like a daughter to him."

Norman drew off as if he had been slashed across the face.

"Lies, lies," he muttered, and silently fell back to where the pine's shadows were blackest.

Morag saw the movement, and putting her hand on the youth's shoulder she led him into the open and the starshine. Her gaze was steady on the face of her brother, but his lowered lids never lifted; there was only the faintest flicker, and still they kept lowered. MacQuarie, compressing and relaxing his lips alternately, breathed hard, and rubbed his hands as he watched them.

"Well, well," he chuckled underbreath—" well, well see you that now! 'tis not the first time she has suspected him, I can see. Wonderful the eyes of women! God! it's at me she'll be looking at next!"

"Norman," said Morag weakly.

He did not answer by the twitch of a muscle.

"Norman, this is true?"

"Yes," he said in a voice unstrung as hers. "True and untrue and part-true, but it will all come right. Oh, your eyes, Morag, your eyes, little one, I cannot bear them!"

He had fallen fainting in the shame of discovery so terrible; but his sister held his arm, and swung with him, shaking him from his stupor, so that he came to himself after a while, taking deep breaths like a swimmer returned to the surface after long submersion.

"Norman."

"Yes, little sister."

"Say this after me: 'It is true; it is past; it is done with forever!'"

He mumbled the words, shamefacedly after her, while MacQuarie looked on in open-mouthed astonishment, his eyes very bright, and his head craned forward. What would these strange people do next? he thought. But he started erect at a movement of Morag's—a movement he had expected and was prepared for. She turned to him, her hand outstretched.

"My letter," said the girl feebly, for she was exhausted by the emotions of the hour.

The tacksman took a folded paper from the breast of his coat, and ignoring Morag's hand, tore the note into shreds before her eyes. Then with a deep sigh that the twinkling of his ferret eyes belied, he drew his ragged plaid around him and departed.

30: The letter

As soon as a bend in the path had lent an added safety to that of the gathering dark, MacQuarie hurried his pace, his fingers clutching the prize he had won, Morag's note to Fraser, unspoiled and untorn. He reached a glade where the light of the moon, now rising, was sufficient to allow of his deciphering the writing; and unsealing the paper, he read greedily. There were only a few hasty lines from Morag asking Drumfin's whereabouts, and pathetically insisting that the exile's safety depended on an immediate answer, but to the tacksman the writing seemed incomparably full of humour, for he doubled up swiftly in a fit of silent laughter. Then he turned to a bypath leading to the hill-tracks and made for home.

It was an hour past midnight when he entered the great kitchen at Inshriff, and lit a lantern. He plied the fire afresh, and heating a knife-blade, roughly sealed the letter anew, then sat down to warm himself at the peats and ponder his good-fortune. His musings ended in his knocking loudly at a door on the other side of the kitchen, and in a little this opened, showing a steep flight of wooden steps, a pair of stockinged feet on them, and the owner of the feet descending. This was a man of middle age, whose apple-red cheeks and dark beard lent him a frank look that was not borne out by the sly glance of his eye. He walked a trifle in-kneed, and slouched forwards, smiling apologetically.

"It's just a nap I was taking, brother," he said. "'tis but this minute I lay down."

It pleased Callum to return the smile, and instantly the younger man's eyes were alert. Something of importance was surely astir, when the brother was so kindly.

"You'll need more than stockings, Murdo," said Callum, looking at the other's feet. "I have a letter for Grasspoint."

"To-night, brother?"

"Yes; and you'll be wise if you make as much as you can of the moon."

Murdo sat down obediently on a bench and drew a pair of brogues from under it.

"No matter," he said. "I've had a good sleep, and a waking before the dawn is what I'm used to."

"Tush!" snarled Callum of a sudden. "Have a guard of your tongue, or stay at home ... Man, man, it's only a moment ago that you told me you had but lain down. If that's all your skill, I'd better send the herd."

"There now, there now, who's your match for quickness in the uptake?" said the other, cringing.

Callum took out Morag's letter and handed it to his brother. "This note is for Mr. Ian Fraser at the Inn of the Grasspoint, you'll observe, and for no other. And the answer is from Mr. Ian Fraser at the Inn of the Grasspoint, and from no other, mind you. See you get it, man. You'll put on an old coat, and take some soot to your cheeks, for I'd not have you kent."

"And the pig as before as at Fishnish market?"

"And the pig as before, of course. What was I thinking of, to forget it? And your Gaelic be Kintyre of the best, too, for not a soul at the Inn must ken."

"Trust me," said Murdo, as he departed. "Trust me, brother, for I'll fool even my own collie, I tell you."

When he was gone Callum dozed over the peats till the laggard dawn appeared; then he went out of doors, circling the house and the yard, where the black cattle steamed in the crisp morning air as they took their dole of winter feeding from two gillies. Callum cursed these men roundly for a space, seemingly more from delight in the exercise than from any necessity, and then climbed the hill, and looked eagerly up the glen towards the wood of Benadd. But it was well on for noon before he caught sight of his brother emerging from the shade of the birches, the pig hobbling reluctant at the end of a tense rope of plaited heather.

"At length and at last," he said, hurrying to meet Murdo. "You have the answer?" he asked.

"No, brother, nothing."

"Nothing?" Callum's face grew dusky.

"Well, to be honest then," said the other, "a guinea was what I got. But that would be for my own trouble, brother?" He smiled appealingly to Callum.

The tacksman suppressed a curse. "Tell me," he said grimly.

Murdo recounted his adventures.

"Even the MacLeod woman at the Inn did not know me," he boasted, "but, of course, she'd never expect to see Murdo MacQuarie the worse of drink."

"Man, you were not drunk?" cried his brother.

"No," said Murdo slily, "neither me nor the pig, but I'll wager we both looked it."

"You fool, oh, you fool!" said Callum underbreath.

"And then I saw my gentleman, and he takes the note, and he glooms, and reads it, and glooms again, and looks me up and down."

"You fool!" said Callum underbreath once more.

"And then my gentleman says very sharp and quick 'No answer.' But I told him that of a surety there was an answer and an instant answer. 'Twas then he said the queer thing, Callum, for he said he did not doubt it, but he had none for me. So I begged a fee, and it was a guinea I got. It's here, brother, and half of it's yours if you will."

"You fool!" said Callum in a low tone of passion, and with a blow on the proffering hand he sent the coin spinning in the air. "Oh, you fool! Man, the pig is the wiser! And now the answer to that letter will be in Fraser's own person, I'll warrant, and the game is up. Oh, you fool, you fool!"

31: Perplexity

CALLUM MACQUARIE was right in his surmise: Fraser had decided to answer the letter in person, despite the danger from the continued stay of Fawkener and his men at Moy. He moved with caution, however, going by Croggan and Laggan, and circling back through the woods to the banks of Uisg, where he waited for nightfall. He had hoped to sight the Ruapais or some gillie from Moy Tower, who would take a message to Morag informing her of his return, but he found neither.

The evening airs were raw: it irked him this game of waiting in the cold and the dark, and at last as the night wore on, and a half-moon climbed the sky, he ventured nearer the Castle. With light steps and drumming heart he came down the pathway that pierced the belt of oaks and sycamores to reach the little bridge of logs. And, just as on a former night, he was brought suddenly into view of two familiar figures pacing slowly towards him: the woman silent, but the accents of the man's voice speaking contrition, remorse, assurance. The moon shone so clearly through the thin-leaved trees that he saw the kilt and plaid under the cloak of the cavalier, and noted the moon-rays reflected from a crystal set in the black knife handle close to a bare knee. But now the lady and her companion had caught sight of the intruder and had stopped in their walk, in order to scan him the more closely. The surgeon did not pause, however; with the same swift step, the same throbbing heart, as on that former night, he went on; yet now he did not flee, and his gaze held the woman still as a pillar of salt, while the cavalier, disappeared crashing through the shrubberies.

Something took Fraser by the throat just then, and a dizziness assailed him, as he rushed blindly forward. Yet his wrath, his jealousy, were as driven mists when he saw Morag's eyes brim with unshed tears, and her hands go out to his in a little helpless movement.

"Who is this man?" he asked.

She only sighed.

"Who?" he repeated, and of a sudden his pulses beat faint and small.

"You must not ask," she said brokenly. "I may not tell."

He dropped her hands and caught at an oak-branch unsteadily, and his heart was now hammering indignantly, painfully, as if some unjust thing held it checked.

"Ah, madam," he said bitter and low, "there is need for neither 'may' nor 'must,' for I can answer the question myself. He is the same you met on the night of Moy dance?"

She started at that, but was silent, and her look was downwards, as he took her hand again.

"Madam, it was the same?" he persisted.

"It was."

"And yet at Laggan Sands you had nothing but scorn for the gossip that linked your name with Pennyfuaran's? Faith! what a comedy, madam; and what a part I play!"

He swung her hands apart, but did not release them; and, distracted, the girl strove to set them free. Not a tear would fall; she could not even sob; her thoughts were all a-tangle. Two days ago it had been easy to acknowledge the stranger as her brother; but now that she knew of all his treachery, her shame seemed overwhelming. So much to do, so much to undo—alone in this worst of confusions, it was not strange if she kept silence. And still, Fraser held her hands and looked down on her.

"I had your letter," he said quietly, savagely. "The answer seemed safe only if I brought it in person, and so I came. I am glad I came. For where troth is held so light, confidences had best be few, or none at all—or none at all."

"A letter?" she said, amazed.

"This," said Fraser, releasing her hands at last, and drawing out the triangle of paper. "This, asking my rendezvous with Drumfin. It is your hand?"

"It is my hand," she faltered, "but I did not send it."

"You wrote it; yet you did not send it?"

"Yes."

"You will surely tell me why, madam; for this concerns the safety of my friend, Drumfin, does it not? Or is this also among the mysteries in which you deal nowadays?"

"There is nothing further to be said," she answered, her arms straight by her side, her eyes downcast.

"Ah! there is—there must be!" he cried, for something in her bearing had touched him, and now his voice was all faith and tenderness. "What is it, Morag?"

She shook her head sadly, and for the first time that evening a smile played on her lips—a little pitiful smile it was; yet when he saw it he breathed deep as in relief, and his eyes tried to read her eyes unfathomable. For reply she only shook her head again, and turned off on the homeward path without a word.

Fraser followed some paces behind until he saw her safely at the fringe of pines bordering the greensward before the Tower. Here he paused;

and she went out alone into the moonlight's pure austerity —a quiet drooping figure in a sober-coloured cloak and hood. He watched her eagerly, yet there was never a good-bye nor a turning of the head from her, and indignantly he wheeled, going back the way he had come.

But he had barely taken twenty paces when he heard the sound of fight running footsteps, and looking round, he beheld the girl returning. As she ran one of her fair side-curls tossed over her eyes—eyes that danced like stars in the wave— and a high colour flushed her cheeks. She halted beside him and taking a bunch of rowans from her waist, broke it in two, and shyly proffered him one of these lesser sprays. He hesitated for an instant, then took the berries, and as he did so, her eyes again lightened magically, and she smiled on him, her face transformed. Then she went swiftly away.

32: Deaf Alan

For a full day after his failure MacQuarie sat over the peats in Inshriff kitchen, blinking his cunning eyes, warming his writhing hands, cosy in deep communion with himself; and the more he felt the keenness of defeat, the more he felt the power of resources still untried. Let him wait, let him wait! a way would yet appear. Mentally he took up each puppet in the game, and regarded him intently for a time, testing this relation and that to another of the pieces on the board, and becoming surer of his skill, as he felt the zest of the trials he essayed.; And all the while, Murdo kept in the background, fawning in perpetual apology if the elder brother's eye but fell on him.

At last with a little purr of delight, Callum's face lightened—the vision had come. "If it's not me that's to snare Drumfin, at least I'll make sure that the other man does no trapping," said he, as he rose, his hands rubbing each other in a final twist of congratulation.

"Murdo?" he called.

"Ay, brother, ay. Coming, brother, coming."

"I'm for Rhoail, and I'll take the dun pony."

"Rhoail? Blessing on you, man, do you ken who's there?"

"See you that now? Do I ken who's there?" asked Callum in cold tones, the ferret eyes searching his brother contemptuously from under pent brows. He went as far as the porch, and turned slowly to regard the other from head to foot. "Do I ken who's there?" he snarled, and slammed the door behind him.

The afternoon was wet and cold, and the rain-bursts swept in long trails down the Glenmore valley from the west, obscuring and revealing by turns every contour of the hills, every winding of the river and its lochans. It was in one of the breaks of these vapours that the Ruapais—whom Morag had set on watch—perched high among the bracken of a little cliffy shelter above Inshriff, was aware of the near presence of a man leading a pony out of the sopping mists on the shoulder of the hill and making for Glenforsa. The mail's head was hid under a fold of ragged plaid, and turned away from Charlie, but the swinging of the fellow's shoulders seemed familiar. The bridle of his garron hung on his left arm, and he sheltered under the lee of the beast's head; yet from where he lay the Ruapais saw that the man's hands engaged themselves in a mutual wriggle that implied the reflective mind, and forthwith he recognised the stranger for his prey. He sighed reluctantly, however, for the lair he left was dry and warm, and as the mist drew closer between Ben Talla and Ben Vearnach, he must needs follow in a proximity that was hardly safe from discovery; and nearer he came and nearer, until he was but fifty yards from the figures of MacQuarie and his garron, ghostly and magnified in the fine spray of the fog. But as the rising ground was crossed, Glenforsa appeared clear of mist; and the tacksman, mounting his pony, drew further off, Charlie watching his movements curiously the while, as he followed him down the riverside.

"It's Ben Veon he's aiming at," said the little man. "What can he want there? Oh, Rhoail, of course!... My sorrow! if only the rain would come again till nightfall at least."

As if in answer to his wish, the mists came once more, stealing and sweeping down the strath in folds that lagged on earth and scurried in the heavens; and soon came gloaming also, so that the Ruapais' approach to the hay-tramp close to the little house of Rhoail was accomplished unperceived. Here he saw MacQuarie greet a stout man clad in a cloak of many capes and, after stabling his mount, enter a doorway, belching peat-reek in volumes blue and pungent. The door was left ajar, and presently there came from it a noise of shouting that sent the little gillie into a sweat of fear.

"God shield me!" said he, "that's Deaf Alan, I'll wager. My sorrow! I wish I were nearer home. But here's at them ... Poor Charlie!"

Coming up to the doorway, he peered cautiously in, but seeing nothing because of the smoke, he crawled to a gable-end, and by means of a pile of wet peats climbed to the opening in the soaking thatch which served for chimney. The evening light slanted through the gap, marking out from the surrounding shadow the smouldering peats, and the dim figures of two men crouching over them — MacQuarie and Deaf Alan.

"All," said the unfrocked minister in Gaelic, "all. They've gone to taste a new still at Gaodhail, and by this time it's beasts they'll be making of themselves."

He spoke in a soft voice, hissing his sibilants markedly, ducking his head in a deferential way; and the pouched lower eyelids, the flabby cheeks, the vacant look, gave the man a guileless air. "Yes, yes, quite alone. It's for hours we'll be undisturbed, I'll venture. Oh, yes!"

MacQuarie ducked and bowed in return, a smile that was almost imbecile in its bland good-humour gathering his features into a group of which the little twinkling eyes were chief. Then he slapped his steaming knees, and bent forward, his hand shaping itself into a trumpet around his mouth.

"In confidence—you understand—all this," he cried i a loud voice, and sank back smiling and nodding his head reassuringly, as if his exertions required excuse.

But the heavy face of the cleric remained unmoved, and his musing gaze at his shoe-buckles brought a trace of irritation to mingle with the wavering smile on Callum's lips.

"*Direach sin!*" said Alan at last. "In confidence, of course." He nodded his head in all solemnity, as if a communication of the gravest had been made, and drew himself up with a little movement of importance.

"It's about a matter in which you have some interest," said the tacksman loudly.

Alan nodded, frowning omnisciently, and combing his little beard with his fingers. His sleepy eyes seemed to have become suddenly half-awake.

"Indeed, and it's you that has an interest in it," went on Callum, putting his hands' palms together between his knees and swaying from side to side, well pleased with himself.

The deaf minister bowed again without a word. His eyes were changing for they were fully awake now, and the pupils seemed wider than formerly.

"And more—it's a matter of news you'd even be willing to pay for," said MacQuarie.

Alan was suddenly deaf in earnest; his look was of the blankest. "Ah," he said.

"Pay for—news—worth paying for," shouted the tacksman.

"Ah," said Alan, nodding. "Cattle?"

"No," cried MacQuarie, very red about the neck, and his ferret eyes flashing. "News—worth-paying for.—Mine —" He tapped his breast.

Alan shook his head helplessly.

"It's about Chisholm," said Callum.

The deaf man bent forward eagerly. "Alasdair Dhu who died by the knife in Tiree?" he asked, the words tripping each other, so great was his haste.

"The same, master. One of his slayers is here; and for ten pounds I'll put the name of his hiding in your ears."

"Here is the money," said Alan instantly, his pupils wider and blacker than ever. He drew forth a dirk from his oxter, and held it towards MacQuarie, as if asking his opinion of the blade.

The tacksman regarded it quietly, for he knew his man and had expected as much.

"Queer money that," said he.

"It will be of the best," said Alan with conviction. And they searched each other's faces in silence for a little.

"Well, well," sighed MacQuarie at last. "It will not be Angus MacLean that I know of," he said.

"No?" said the minister, testing the tip of his dirk with his thumb.

"And it is not Fraser."

"No?"

"But it is Cattanach," said Callum, with a slap on his knee.

"Ah," said Alan. "Who is this Cattanach now? Has he not more than one name?"

"I know nothing of that," lied the tacksman glibly.

"Where is he?" asked Alan.

"In one of two places: Glenbyre or Craig; it was Craig these last two nights. Get your men ready, I say."

"Get them sober, the brats!" said the minister. He sheathed his knife with a smack, and rose to his feet alertly, his eyes glowing. "We cannot move before Monday, for even if the drink has left them by to-morrow, it's a Sabbath, you see."

"Too good a day for a killing?" sneered MacQuarie, with a furtive look in his little eyes. "Who's to ken?"

The fat cleric eyed him solemnly and his paunch shook as he shivered in an access of emotion, while he raised the half-closed eyes of a fanatic to the rafters. "I ken," he said quietly and fiercely— "I—and my Maker."

"Well, well," said MacQuarie, surprised into an admiring glance at this transport. "Blessing on you for a queer mixture, Alan MacMaster MacLean." He rose to his feet. "Good-night! Blessing on you!"

"Good-night! Blessing on you!" said the other absently, for he was already preoccupied with his thoughts of vengeance.

The tacksman stole out through the gloom to the stable. But long before he emerged from it leading his garron, the Ruapais was speeding ahead of through heather and gall, in a darkness that was unfogged and starlit, his queer little mind guessing wildly at many things, his odd little heart beating strangely in the hope of service to his mistress-as intent on his task as any old-time knight performing in all reverence his lady's devoir.

33: The Clachaig pass

It was Sunday before the Ruapais brought his news to Morag, and she instantly despatched two piteous little notes by his hands, one to Pennyfuaran, and one to the surgeon.

"How to write," ran her letter to Fraser, *"how to tell you all: for the time is short, and the Danger great. But my Brother is in Peril from the Sunivaig macleans, and not a soldier in the Isle to say 'Stand you now,' for all the Companies have gone to the main Land. And I have not spoken of the Business to Moy or his people, for there are Matters in it that confuse it mightily. 'Twas none other than my Brother you saw accompany me in the woods but two nights ago—and O, sir, I'll warrant that you ken as well as his poor Sister why Deaf Alan has his Track.*

"I have sent Pennyfuaran to Glenbyre lest Norman should lie at that place. His other Hiding is Craig; and will you not, 0, sir,—for his Sister's sake—seek him there, and warn with all Speed. But I am come into a Flurry of Mind and can venture No More. Assure yourself that I am Your faithful Servant.

"M.M."

It was Monday, however, ere the Ruapais discovered Fraser's direction at Grasspoint Inn and coming there with the note found that the surgeon had gone north towards Aros that very afternoon. Like a sleuth-hound the little gillie panted after, and came up with, the traveller near Tigh-ban just as evening fell.

And thus it was that as on a former night Fraser found himself on the hills above Aros and making for Craig. Yet now it was to no happy tryst with Morag he looked forward, rather to a meeting with a man whom of all men he would have avoided. Because of the Sunivaig folk at Rhoail, Charlie had advised his taking another route than Glenforsa and so he crept onwards in the dark and the rain on the shoulder of Torlochan, and made for Maam Clachaig.

It was slow work as he slipped on the heather roots and the runnelled earth below their tough fibres, but coming to the lower slopes, he struck the drovers' track running straight for Loch-na-Keal, and stepped out briskly. When he reached the bridge of pine-logs over the stream of the Ba, he found the river swinging seawards in full spate, brimming from bank to brae. There was something sinister in the silence of its might, as it swept on heavily, speedily, steadily, as noiseless and gentle as it was powerful, and he fell to wondering if the next burn were bridged or not. It was too dark to allow of his consulting his map, but he heard afar the distant drumming of falling water and guessed it for that of a hill-torrent, not an uncanny stilly stream like this.

He crossed this new burn in a little with nothing worse than a wetting to his waist, and now he marched with the black sheet of Loch Ba on his left, a ghostly company of herded hills surrounding it. Yon would be the House of Gruline close to the shore, the manifold lights reflected from the murky waters of the lake. Midnight was past, he meditated, and yet they were awake yonder—the tapers lit, the fire roaring on the hearth, the punch-jug busy, the cards carpetting the floor. But no, it was kindlier even than that, for high and thin there wafted to him the skirl of the pipes and the call of the dancers. He halted for a moment to listen; then, shivering in the gowsty night, he plodded wearily forwards, and still and on a little laugh escaped him, for was he not as happy in the dark here as any in the warmth and light yonder, because the woman of his choice had trusted him?

Two miles more, and he came through the birches of Coille-na-Sroine, and over the long wet grasses of the slopes of Clachaig to where a spectral grey cottage with a single litten window stood high on the hill above him.

"Here also they are late of bedding," said Fraser to himself. "A cow calving, or a death-wake, surely?"

Between him and the house a torrent swashed and burred; the track went down to it, and in the uncertain light that held only a hint of dawn he saw a stepping-stone on the further side. But against the hither shore the water swirled furious, and no boulders could be seen; so for a space he groped up and down over rock and sand; and then, impatient, blindly essayed to ford. The chill and rush of the pouring waters about his middle, the sound of a sudden squall roaring among the trees of the corrie above, the dim forms of the giant hills shouldering down on him from every side—all these combined to fashion a horror that got hold of his soul as he lost foothold and was swept into a pool below the crossing; and an involuntary cry, strident and inhuman, went up from him into the night. But the shock of his fall chased the chill from his spirit, and when he crawled up the bank on the Clachaig side he was himself again.

As he rose to his feet and turned in the direction of the cottage, he noted another light besides that of the window, for now the doorway stood open and a fan of yellow radiance fell outwards from it on the grassy slope. He took a step or two forward, and as he did so a figure dashed from the house; ran clattering up the glen, the pebbles of the drove road skidding from the flying feet. Amazed, the surgeon paused and listened to the beat of footsteps, steady and rapid, dying gradually into the heart of the night.

Doubtless his cry of fear had alarmed someone. When next he looked up the door was closed, and he hesitated as to whether or no he should go up to the cottage. His goal lay farther on, and there was no need for a call here; but, nevertheless, more as an atonement for the coward cry in the torrent than for aught else, he advanced up the hill and knocked at the door of the tiny house.

It was open in a flash, and a young Highlander, big-boned and tall, stood before him, the black knife ready in his hand. Behind was a young woman, one arm holding a bairn asleep on the shoulder, the other upraised with a lighted cruisie.

"*Co tha sin?*" asked the man, ready to fall on this dark eerie figure, whose cloak glistened with dropping water at every tag.

"Ian Fraser on the way to Craig," said the surgeon.

"Then come in, even if you've a man's head under your arm," said the Highlander, and he stuck his knife in his stocking and turned hospitably inward, Fraser following.

"We are MacLeans from Tiree," continued the cottar, "and here but a few years." He kicked two collies from the hearth-front, and drew forward a stool for the stranger. "Neither kith nor kin to the Frasers, but owing them a debt all the same, I'm thinking. Give me your cloak, for I see you've been in the burn. It's the whisky he'll be needing, wife."

The round-faced bairn waked good-naturedly to play with his father, while the woman stirred a *cuach* of whisky-gruel.

"MacLeans of Tiree? Not of Sunivaig?" asked Fraser.

"God forbid!" said the man fervently. "We're Crossapoll."

"So you owe the Frasers a service?" said the surgeon, steaming stockings and shoes at the red of the peats. "Now, I wonder what?"

"Ay, but for all it was great, it's a kindness that I canna speak of," said the Highlander. "It was done to one of whom you'll never have heard—to judge by your Southron tongue—one Angus MacLean, tacksman in Craigmore. I'll say no further." He dandled the bairn on his knee, and added with a look of good-humour in his eyes: "It's well the teeth are before the tongue, as we say in the Gaelic."

Fraser unreplying, nursed his lame arm for a little, and his host observing it, condoled with him

"An ill thing an injured arm to cross the Maam with, the going is so steep. But you're not the first has climbed it in the night-time and in a hurry... My faith! but you're wet, sir. And if you werena gentry, it's a change of clothes I'd be offering you.",

"Here's the main thing to keep dry," said the surgeon, taking out a heavy pistol young Moy had given him some time before, and examining it. He found that the weapon had escaped soaking; nevertheless he recharged before returning it to the belt below his vest-flap. "That's of more import hereabouts, I'll wager, than water-tight shoes," said he.

"Faith! It's the true word you have!" said the big fellow, looking uncomfortable.

"You sit late, your wife and you," went on Fraser, the toddy-gruel loosening his tongue. "Did I not dislodge someone from your house when I cried out in my fall?"

The hillman eyed him gloomily, dwelling long on the stiff right arm, and the bulge over the waistcoat where the pistol lay, and the good-natured look faded wholly from the lean face.

"As the saying goes," he said dourly, "it's a big word the mouth canna hold. Here is food and fire and light; but for all your name of Fraser, I'll be glad to see your going, if your tongue is so full of life."

By this time there was evidently hostility also in the young wife's face as she walked up and down restlessly, the bairn asleep on her shoulder. Her black looks were rapidly infecting her husband, and he would have followed with still ruder words, had not Fraser risen, said good-bye, and taken the high road once more. Already the dawn-light was coming clear and grey, and looking back at the cottars, before he entered the next clump of trees, he saw them moody and silent, eyeing him distrustfully, the only hearty one in the group, the child once more awake and crowing in his mother's arms.

"Here's a ploy," said Fraser. "Smugglers, I doubt not."

There was another stream to cross and then the track zigzagged steeply up a cliff-face by means of the scree and rubble of centuries sloped across it from the flanks of Corraven. Westwards, the cliff ran in a stony spine to join the purple-black ridges, where, through films of mist Ben More upsprang in might, austere and sovran in the dawn. This was the valley-head, closed as by a wall of rock; and looking back in the dim morning light, Fraser saw Glen Clachaig scooped clean and fair to Loch Ba, its trees dwarfs, its river a ribbon of silver. He sat down to rest when half-way up the ascent, and prosaically enough sat to checking his bearings by means of his tattered map; then returning the papers to his vest-pocket, his left hand, somewhat awkward at the duties of his stiffened right, did its work so clumsily as to knock from his belt the pistol he had primed at the cottage.

It exploded as it fell, and there was an instant shattering of echoes on all sides, prolonging and terrifying. But ere they had died there came another report, and a bullet hit the boulder on which he sat, while the echoes ripped and ripped again. Fraser glanced sharply at the rim of the cliff above, then crouched with a swift movement behind a mass of detached rock; and as he did so his foot touched the fallen weapon over the path-edge, and it rattled far below in a small avalanche of grit. He bit his lip, for fifty paces were all he lacked of gaining the summit of the pass, and here was a barring of the way to some purpose. Yet his resolution was soon formed; for without a firearm, no course lay open but close quarters, and scrambling to his feet, he had rushed two of the serpentine turns in the path, before the next shot was fired. It also missed, and the echoes still mocked the marksman, when Fraser reached the last ridge, and saw him for a dark and tousled figure of a man, who suddenly flitted behind a great cairn some twenty yards off.

The surgeon's one thought as he emerged on the new country over the hill-top was the handicap of his stiffened arm, and at a glance he had marked the only place of shelter from further pistol-fire. For on this side the land fell gently away in moorland, and in its midst were the beginnings of a little glen, down either side of which went a division of the drovers' track marked by a cairn. Behind one cairn was his adversary, and forty paces off the other proffered safety to himself. But as he hesitated the hidden enemy's pistol spat out again angrily, and seeing his only hope was at still closer quarters, Fraser rushed for the source of fire. At the very start of his onset, he stumbled in a peat-hole and fell face forwards at the cairn's base, jarring his doubled right arm horribly, just as the dark mass of his assailant hurled itself on him, and a knife fleshed his shoulder. Yet the fellow drew off instantly as if in self-defence, and in that moment's breathing-space the surgeon had time to roll on his side and swing his leg in a savage hack against his opponent's shins. The man toppled downwards, and Fraser holding out his knife at the length of his left arm, received his opponent's breast full on it. Then as the slack body crushed down on him, he fainted slowly.

He felt as if ages had passed before he came to himself, yet the sky was still heavily grey, and the sun had not yet risen. As his shoulder twinged he recalled the fight dreamily, and rising to his elbow, stiff and cold and weak, he beheld his opponent crouching at the foot of the cairn. He was intent on some papers he had spread on his knees, but at the noise of Fraser's movement he glanced up, and rose to his feet hurriedly.

"Ah," he said, coming near. "As I thought. 'Twas but a fainting fit, *mon médecin*?"

"Cattanach!" cried the surgeon at sight of the familiar pallid features.

"And you?" said the youth smiling. "And you, my dear Fraser? The surprise almost exceeds the pleasure! I had no idea your leave was so extended, sir."

Fraser still too astounded to answer, could do naught but stare at the dishevelled figure Norman now presented, for he was dressed in some ragged odds and ends of attire, and looked as if he had but escaped from Bedlam.

"You pardon the déshabilé, do you not, my dear Fraser? 'tis only one of my few disguises But confide in me, I beg of you, the name of the maker of the knife you use, for I shall ever remember him in my infrequent prayers.

Indeed, had it not snapped like the trash it was, my account were ended, sir. Nay, nay, don't trouble to rise. My steel was good; your wound deep, and hence the fainting, is it not, my surgeon?"

Fraser moistened dry lips as the man babbled on.

"May I ask your business in this wilderness?" continued Norman.

"I sought—you!" gasped Fraser feebly.

"So? And why?"

"To warn you ... Your sister sent me. The Sunivaig men know of your hiding at Craig, and are on your track."

For a second the hard pale features of the youth softened, but for a second only; then he laughed shrilly.

"Admirably done," he said.

"You will not believe me?" said Fraser again.

"Admirable, admirable," chuckled the youth, shaking his head in a negative there was no misunderstanding.

"Her letter is here," protested the surgeon. "Read it, I beg of you. Your danger is great, I tell you."

"There is no letter, *mon médecin*," said Norman, still smiling reproof. "Here are your papers," and he showered the packets over the recumbent figure.

"My papers?" cried Fraser in angry surprise.

"Your papers, sir—from the breast of your coat, to be precise ... It is permitted, is it not?" smiled the other. "A privilege of the conqueror always, I believe?"

Fraser bit his lip. "There is no letter from your sister?" he asked.

"None!"

And so it was. Everything was there—map, notes, bills; but the one thing of importance for the occasion was lacking, and whether it had been lost in the torrent or on the cliff-face mattered nothing now.

"You are persuaded?" asked Norman, cynically polite, seating himself on an outcropping rock, and looking down on the other. Fraser, unanswering, turned on him an eye of loathing, and the youth caught the glance.

"There it is, that look again!" he cried. "Man, I've forgotten much but never yon turning of your eyes on me, just before we foundered in Aros Bay. And I've never forgiven it either, my surgeon."

Fraser closed his eyes to shut out the sight of this creature, for at last it was borne in on his brain, dulled though it was by the pain of his wound, that despite Morag's agonies of entreaty, despite his own pledges, this man was still the same he had known in Tiree, as evil, as treacherous.

"Listen," said Norman's cold voice, and now there was a new note of exultation in it. "Listen— whilst I give you a message that is not a lie, my friend—a message for your comrade, Drumfin, when next you see him.

Tell him, my worthy courier, that I had news from Paris yesterday; tell him that Conflans' fleet is broken and flying, and the great rising of 'Fifty-nine' as dead as the 'Forty-five.' And tell him also, I beg of you, who burst the bubble—myself and Pickle and the despised Bas-Ondulé—poor spies all of us: but with an achievement—an achievement, sir, to our names at last." He rose to bow mock-heroically. "Tell him also that I no longer pursue the chase of game as small as Drumfin—'twould be unambitious after Conflans, would it not?—but that I advise he seek the Rue Roquette as early as he can, for there will be many trustys in old Scotland before a week is past, believe me."

Fraser tossed on his side, as if to get beyond earshot of his tormentor, and stung by the contempt implied in the action, the renegade lost his cynical coolness, and in a sudden blind fury, struck with the scabbard of his hanger again and again at the prostrate man's wounded shoulder.

The surgeon could have filled every glen and corrie with his shrieks, had his bitten lip, his clenching teeth allowed, for the agonies of the poor battered wound pierced him to the marrow, and at last in a supreme effort to escape that amazed them both, he found his feet, and fronted the torturer unsteadily. Norman's face became contorted at the sight, and drawing his sword he backed to the cairn, while with a little staggering run, Fraser came after. A second knife from his belt had found its way into his hand in some subconscious fashion, and his eyes stared hate of the deadliest. But suddenly he halted, and eyed the weapon.

"No, no," he muttered thickly. "Morag, Morag!" and he tossed the knife far from him.

He saw it glitter in the dawnlight; he heard it clatter on the rocks; he felt the shock of combat, and knew his enemy had closed with him. Then they crashed to earth together, and the rest was blackness.

How long it was before he again felt consciousness and pain pour round him like a tide, he never knew; but when he opened his eyes, a trembling opal radiance in the sky bespoke the coming of day at last from behind the black crags in the east. From the sky his gaze came to earth, and turning his head he saw, close to his cheek, the shoes of a man who lay supine and motionless. He eyed the figure in sick horror, and crawling nearer beheld the face of Norman MacLean. The spy lay still as a waxen image, and the surgeon saw at a glance that he was dead ... Could killing a man be so simple a matter? ... There was a knife in his breast, and at sight of it he felt anew the wild-beast passion of the combat; again the blood flushed his brain to madness, and he tottered to his feet to look around for fresh foes.

Then with the regress of his emotion, he came to himself, and his thoughts ran clear ... How cold the grey sky empty of birds! How vast the earth untenanted by any living thing! How slow the break of day! Would the sun never rise? ... How blind his rage to have done this thing! And in sight of this cold clay what a mockery that casting-away of his knife! ... He had killed a man! ... He had killed ... Oh, Morag, Morag!

These and these only were his thoughts, repeated, repeated, as he drew nearer the dead man, huddled and horrible, and looked down on him. Here was the quarry of the Sunivaig clansmen; here was the man he would have shielded from death; here was the brother of the woman he loved, come to the dark ferry by this most tragic of roads.

Moodily he stood, pondering. Then, his decision taken as he marked a raven slowly winging down the little glen, he scraped a rude hollow with his hands by the base of the cairn, folded his cloak around the body, and dragged it with difficulty to its resting-place. A covering of stones was next lightly made, but strongly, too, for the raven had returned with his mate, and they were now circling high above the grave. To-morrow, or to-night it might be, the Aros folks would send, and the home-coming of Norman MacLean would be on a bier. But for the present, fitly guarded and fitly placed was the grave on this lone mountain-side, thought Fraser, as, clutching his wounded shoulder, he came slowly back to the descent on the Clachaig side of the pass; for even if the Sunivaig men should chance this way, surely the clansmen would be far to seek who would desecrate a foeman's burial-place set amid such solemnity of hill and sky, keened over by the winds from dark Corraven, enfolded by the weeping mists of gaunt Ben More.

34: The woman answers

HE fainted once again before he came to Clachaig, but recovered after a time and went on. The cottar and his wife were in consternation to find the strange visitant of the previous night—the man who had come in the dark, dripping from the torrent's bed— return in the daytime, blood-stained and tottering, and Fraser saw that they suspected an encounter with the traveller they had harboured before his arrival. But since they seemed as desirous as himself of avoiding the matter, he bound up his wound in silence, drank some spirits, and set off for Aros.

So great was his weakness, however, that he had to halt overnight at Killiechronan township, and thence he sent a message to Ulva House, the rendezvous Drumfin had given him at their hurried parting at Gribun. By morning light the old Jacobite had come and Fraser had told him the whole sad story.

"And you would have gone on to his father with this tale of death? You?" said Drumfin.

"How else?" asked Fraser wearily.

"You do not lack courage, sir."

"Ah," said the surgeon, smiling bitterly, "there is a still harder task."

The old man's eyes flickered in a sudden glance of comprehension; he saw much in that httle glimpse.

"Is it so, my friend?" he said tenderly, and his long brown fingers closed on Fraser's perspiring hand. "The world seems strangely made."

Fraser dozed a little then, and for some hours they did not speak, but on the surgeon's waking in the late afternoon, Drumfin suggested that he himself should go forward to Aros.

"You shall not," said the surgeon. "The work is mine," and he sat up in bed.

"At least let me help," said the exile. "I can go on to Moy?"

But Fraser was obdurate, and forthwith dressed. He was feeling stronger, and after an evening meal they set off together for Aros.

They found that the chief had gone to Quinish yesterday and that it would be the morrow before he returned; so yielding at last to continued entreaties, the surgeon consented that Drumfin should bear half the burden, and break the news to Norman's father, whilst he himself, after an interval of rest, would go on to Moy that night.

It was thus that Fraser and the Ruapais set out once more on their journeyings, and mounted on rough garrons, and well-happed in plaids, they went rapidly off on the Glenforsa road, in a cold night of cloud-free stars with a quarter-moon just rising. But the promise of the early night was not fulfilled, and before daybreak, squalls and rain-bursts from the south met the travellers in the teeth; so, when they came to Glenmore, the Ruapais advised that by a deviation eastwards to the longer Loch Uisg road, they would make quicker progress, and they turned their horses' heads accordingly.

As they came in by Loch Spelve, the sun rose, and at intervals flooded the winter landscape with its shining. The creamy torrents drummed and dinned everywhere through black rock and rusty heather down to a sea of spindrift and white horses—a grey sea, slowly and infrequently traversed by long shafts of pale illumination from the midst of the heavy cloud-drift. Sodden and weary, the riders jogged on.

They reached Kinlochspelve, and here Fraser thought it best to leave the Ruapais and the garrons behind, for the soldiery might have returned, or the Sunivaig men have circled back to Moy, and he would be safer if he went forward circumspectly on foot and alone. He made a strange figure, his dark plaid of tartan, mud-splashed and shrunken, hanging awry over the sling which his shoulder-wound had again rendered necessary; a gust of the night had left him hatless; his hair was plastered lankly on his forehead and tied with a shapeless bag-ribbon behind, whilst a pallid and unshaven cheek added to the uncouthness of his plain features, down which mingled rain and perspiration streamed salt to his lip. Yet he pushed on stoutly, leaning against the blast and the sheets of rain. Anon the sun flared out, and he steamed in it for a space, until the next downpour with its accompanying squalls broke sudden on him.

It was as he came through the larches by Loch Uisg to where the pathway parallels the shore that a movement at a point a mile ahead caught his eye, and he left the road quickly, disposing himself, aquake with cold and damp though he was, among the wet and fading bracken. Here he waited until the little group of travellers he had descried had passed. Moy himself, close wrapped in his plaid, his bonnet low on his brows, went by with his pony at a walking pace. Following him came some men on foot, whom Fraser recognised as the retinue of the chief—henchman, gilliemore, bladier, piper, and piper's gillie stalked down the track, their draggled plaids barely screening them from the sheets of rain.

"For Duart, I should say," said the watcher to himself, smiling at the pomp of the tiny procession. "A state visit, maybe."

He mused as his eyes followed the little company along the loch side: it seemed like the passing of the remnant of some brave old order of the world; and even while he smiled, he sighed, as lightfoot and silently, the chief and his little court disappeared through the slanting rain amid the pines.

Fraser took the road once more. And now the grounds of Castle Moy were reached, and the long avenue of oak and sycamore, running to where the burn came through the level, quiet and unbroken. There, where the stream swept to its turning seawards, was the well-remembered bridge of rough wood, and leaning on the balustrade of bark, was the cloaked figure of a woman, the sight of whom made the apple of his throat to swallow again and again.

"You?" she said in a low voice, and came to him swiftly. "Safe," she murmured, and pressed close to his side. "My heart!" she whispered, and kissed his wet cheek.

He looked away from her, and down at the eddies in the brown water and the red leaves falling there from the wind-tossed branches overhead. On this canopy of dying foliage the rain-drops pattered thickly, and sombre and sad seemed all things in the enfolding woods; no stirring of birds, no peering of flowers. Yet a bird sang in Morag's heart, and her eyes, lovelier than any flowers, looked up happily for the sunlight in the eyes of her lover. But when they turned on her there was no sunshine in them; fixed and glassy they were as the eyes of the dead, and at the sight she shivered and clung to him in fear.

"What is it?" she asked in a voice she hardly knew for her own. "What terrible thing is this?" He bent his head and was silent.

"My heart!" she said again, lifting the wet wisps of hair from his brow. "Wet and weary and broken you are; what is there else?"

He tried to find his voice, tried anew, and haltingly began his tale. Mostly he told it with his head bent to his arm on the beam of the bridge, so that she should not see his face. Mostly she heard it, bending over him, her hand straying over his sodden locks, while her grave eyes, set as in a trance, sought the forest depths surrounding. When he told of Norman's renewed treachery, she shuddered.

"Oh, be kind, dear heart!" she cried, "for the world slips from me, and here is bitterness and emptiness indeed. Oh, better a death for you from the Tiree men's knives than the old life, my brother!"

"It is death I have to speak of," said Fraser huskily. "Death?"

For a little he heard nothing but her deep breathing, and looking up, he saw her eyes still fixed on the far obscurities of the woods upstream.

"Courage," he said.

"It is Norman?" she asked.

He bowed his head.

Very calm and very pale, she repeated the words to herself in an undertone. "It is Norman," she said; and though Fraser strove to speak, he failed utterly at sight of that face so set and white.

"Go on," she said quietly.

His tongue clove to his palate, for her eyes were fire now, and her hand was raised from the folds of her cloak in a new gesture of wonder. Then of a sudden his voice came to him, but not for the work he asked of it.

"My God!" he cried. "You know—you have divined it!"

"It was you ... who ... killed him?" she said.

"I killed him," he answered.

At that she had almost fainted where she stood, but she struggled with her weakness, and moved off from him, her hands tightly clenched, her face averted. "Oh, brother—brother mine!" she whispered, even as if his shade might hear, and then fell silent for a space. And the man, sick unto death with the horror of it all, stood watching her, his every energy spent, the sweat of his agony breaking fast on him, now that his task was accomplished. But she turned slowly again, her grey eyes shining through her unshed tears, and came towards him.

"You ... killed him?" she repeated.

"I killed him."

"In fair fight?"

"In fair fight."

Her composure dumfounded him, so uncanny she seemed, standing there in the wet cold morning, the rust-coloured oak-leaves, the wind-showered rain-drops pattering around her—a figure alert and intense, a face pulsing with thoughts new-born and strange.

"And this is the tale you bring me?" she said, grasping his hands among the folds of his wet plaid. "And these are the hands that did yon?"

Unanswering, he quaked with a sudden fear.

But she kissed his fingers with a rapid movement, and then as quickly his lips that were dry with terror.

"Heart of my heart!" she said, her head on his shoulder. "You are my brother and my sister, my father and my mother," and at the word she swooned on the red leaves at his feet.

35: Drumfin goes fishing

FRASER had barely left Aros when Doctor MacNab arrived, Drumfin having sent for him because of his companion's wound. And on his heels came Pennyfuaran, still seeking the lost Norman—from Glenbyre to Craig, from Craig to Glencannel, and so to Aros.

"Well met," said Drumfin. "Friends crossing the ford are best near each other. Come ben and I'll tell you where the ford is."

He took them to the laird's study, where he gave them refreshment and told them Fraser's story. They heard it with grave faces and in silence, until at the mention of the surgeon's journey to Moy, Pennyfuaran's handsome face—now of a starker cast, a manlier grace—twitched as in sudden pain, and he rose and left the room.

A little later he could be heard in his chamber, executing little melancholy airs and runs on his chanter, while, miserable as men condemned, the other two sat on.

"Man, it's little sleep for me this night, Gillian," said MacNab at last. "I think I'll read a bittie physic." He took some heavy volumes of the laird's and drew into the hearth.

The exile rose and peered from the window into the dark; a fine smirring rain was obscuring all things, and at times squalls came through it in a blatter, rattling the pane.

"I'll not sleep either, I fear," said he, taking up a volume of the author medical and fingering it. "Humph! The learned Cullen. Well, well! Every man to his trade." He put the book aside. "And mine seems to be that of outlaw, Doctor—skulking in caves or fleeing through heather—a long apprenticeship, man, and it seems never to end. Even so, I'll take a turn on the shore just to keep myself in practice." And going to the hall, he donned his cloak and slipped out.

He took the road between the shore and Glenaros woods, and though the mist and the dark were thick, he felt again the hills and the glens of home around him. In memories of the past dreamed over once more, he tried to forget the tragedy of the present hour. But for the exile the past, too, was sad. Did he think of the woods of Morvern, or of the Speinne's slopes enfolded in these same soft vapours of the night, they brought to mind many an older sorrow—chief among them the memory of his lost love, a woman with the face of Morag. Did he recall the lands northward still, it was but to muse of Alasdair, the Bard of War, now grown old and peace-abiding—how on a day of days in Glenfinnan long ago, the poet's song to his Prince had hummed in his ears at its first chanting, and all seemed fair and bright, with never a hint of Culloden at the end of the road they had that day entered on. Sad memories all, and yet he dwelt fondly on them, bringing by some strange alchemy, sweetness out of bitterness. But not by any labour of thought would any such transmutation come to this new sorrow that had fallen on the house of Aros. "Blue are the hills that are far from us," he quoted, pondering the contrast. He strove to shut out the picture of his coming interview with Aros, but it would not be so easily banned; it returned again and again, and only vanished when a sudden necessity for action disturbed his mood of meditation.

For as he looked northwards in the dark, he saw far out, where the Sound should he clear, save for mist, for many a mile, a point of faint radiance grow to life and die again—blurred and diffused in the fog, a ship's light surely. Then, as he watched, there came close at hand the hollow rumble of a boat's keel on the pebbles of the beech.

"Here's mischief again," said Drumfin, and with the instinct of an old campaigner, he drew his cloak close, and laid himself prone on the wet earth to listen.

But for a full ten minutes there came no further sign or sound, till a clear voice close at hand spoke in Gaelic.

"It's the reef she's feared for: it's that keeps her out. And no wonder with that same reef, and the night so wild."

There was no answer, and after a pause, the Jacobite creeping behind some stony spurs that ran seawards, moved in the direction of the speaker. Could this be the soldiery on the move once more? he asked himself, and the next instant he had almost sighed audibly in relief, for the voice spoke again, and set his fears at rest.

"And now, good-bye to Aros Isle, say I. What hills, man, what hills!"

The tongue was the Gaelic; and in Gaelic the answer came: "Dry shoes catch no fish. The hills were worth the climbing after all, for the work is done at last. Show a light, man, show a light!"

A lanthorn was quickly unmasked, and Drumfin made out a group of men with the waves tossing up to their feet, as they stood around their craft, ready to launch. One he saw was a stout, silent man, who wore a coat of many capes. The boat splashed heavily as they ran her out, leapt on board, and pushed off; the lanthorn dipped with the swinging of the wherry, and against its halo only one dark figure now stood out solitary on the shore.

"Well, well," said this man, "a safe journey to you all. But see you now that you pay Rob, and not have him falling back on me."

Someone in the boat laughed derisively, the oars dipped in unison, and they were off—a yellow blur in the fog. He who was left, stood watching until the two points of diffused radiance approached, died into one, and gradually faded into the dark. Then he turned, chuckling, and crawled round the landward end of the rocky spit whence his late companions had embarked. He was making for the road by the shore, but forthwith he stumbled over the crouching form of Drumfin, who seized his wrists instantly.

The stranger gasped in terror, but struggling desperately, freed himself from the other's grip, and attempted flight. As he did so, he took something from his breast and tossed it seawards. Drumfin was instantly on his heels, and catching his arm again, swung into a wrestle which ended in a fall with the exile uppermost, and the other so far stunned that the binding of his hands by means of a hanger's belt was a matter of ease. The Jacobite then left him for a little and groped among the sea-wrack until he found the packet the man had tossed away: it was one of letters, tied with a ribbon. He struck flint and steel when he returned to his captive, and holding the lit tinder near the fellow's face, he blew on it till it glowed sufficiently to light his features.

"I thought as much," said he; "I just thought as much. Voices don't change greatly even in ten years."

The man answered by a groan. "What—what?" he asked.

"It's only Drumfin," said the Jacobite. "'Two hundred pounds and a crown a day for life,' you remember, Callum? You have had a long hunt for me, but here I am at last ... Do you think you can stand?"

He propped the dazed tacksman on his feet. "Try walking now," he said.

MacQuarie hissed a little as in anger, but did not move.

"Walk, Callum. Here is my sword behind you."

The man moved up the beach, and reached the shore-road.

"Quicker, Callum," said Drumfin. "The spray is on my hanger, and it is not good for it to be long unsheathed. Tramp!"

The tacksman trudged on in the wet darkness, his head hanging, a silly noise of moans and hisses coming from his lips; indeed, he seemed almost crazed with confusion. They came thus to Aros House, and the exile marched his prisoner straight to the laird's study where Doctor MacNab read his medicine aloud, intoning his author in tones liturgical. The physician stared in surprise at sight of the captive.

"Only a strange fish I picked up on Glenaros shore," said Drumfin smiling. "You ken him?" He brought forward a chair and pushed the tacksman into it. "Please you, MacNab, give the serving man a call, and ask him to send Pennyfuaran."

At the name of the chieftain, MacQuarie gave a loud hiss; his ferret eyes closed as if he suffered some inward agony, and he rose from his chair, walked round it in an odd movement, and sat down again.

While waiting the arrival of Pennyfuaran, the Jacobite opened the packet of papers he had picked up on the shore. There was a little torn map of Aros Isle with the print of Blaeu of Amsterdam upon it; the rest were letters addressed to Mr. Ian Fraser; and one had a spot of blood on it.

The chieftain came into the room like a storm-burst, the door slamming with a force that shook the dust from the long rows of books. His eyes shone with wrath; the patch of fair skin on his forehead was flushing and paling in rapid alternations, and he flourished his practice-chanter in a movement of threatening.

"You fox!" he cried: and his hands went out as if to rend the tacksman asunder.

MacQuarie gibbered in his face, hissed a little, and rising, broke out of reach. Then he came forward once more, made a little dance-step round the chair, and sat down again, the oddest of figures.

"*Dhia!*" cried the chieftain, falling back, very pale of a sudden. "The man's daft."

Drumfin nodded reassuringly, and signed to him to take a seat. "No, not daft," he said, speaking slowly and distinctly. "And I'll tell you why, Pennyfuaran;—Are you listening, Callum?—for if he be mad, as sure as my name is what it is, and outlaw though I be, he shall go to Bedlam; and God pity the poor souls there whether they be sane or daft! But if he be wise, and tell me truthfully what I ask—Are you listening, Callum?—I shall as far as it lies within my power, deal mercifully with him. I could say no more if I spoke till doomsday."

"Drumfin!" cried Pennyfuaran. "Is not this the man who sought to sell you?"

"That same man," said the exile gravely.

At that the tacksman's mouth stopped twisting, and the ferret eyes gleamed keen and steady. "Well, well! Wonderful!" said Callum. "Well, well! You saw through my bit ploy, Drumfin? And it's you are the man of your word, I'm sure."

"Fox, fox!" said Pennyfuaran underbreath.

"I shall keep my word, MacQuarie," answered the Jacobite. "But I warn you, I give it you here only as you speak truth to me. If you mislead, then—" He passed his long brown fingers through the air in a movement, as if all hope had gone from the world.

"There now—there now—it's naught but the truth you'll have. And if only I were free at the wrists, Drumfin, I'd be as happy here as in Inshriff itself, knowing you for the gentleman you are, sir. Ay, ay, and it's you are the gentleman, Drumfin."

The exile smiled at the flattery, and loosened the belt on his captive's wrists. Instantly the unbound hands were twining round each other, and it was as if the movement stimulated their owner to new life.

"Anything you ask, Drumfin—anything you ask. It's the truth you'll have," he said briskly.

"I don't doubt you," said Drumfin, looking away from him into the red of the peats. "Let us begin. I want to know about these letters.—But first, tell me this: Was it Deaf Alan and his men you parted from on Glenaros shore to-night?"

"It was, Drumfin—it was that. It's you kens everything, sir."

"And it was Rob MacAllister's smack that met them, Callum?"

"Rob's it was, Drumfin. That's whose it was, sir."

"And they spoke of their work as finished, Callum. Now tell me what they meant by that?"

The exile had suddenly turned his gaze from the peats and fixed it on his captive's face; and instantly the ferret eyes shifted to a downward, and then to a sidelong glance.

"Well, well," began Callum.

"The truth!" cried Drumfin, his eyes blazing, and his hand slapping the letters on the table.

The fellow became sullen at once, and still seemed to meditate a lie.

"The truth!" said the Jacobite again; "or—."

The lean fingers again tossed in air in a gesture of despair inexpressible.

"It's the truth you'll have then," said MacQuarie. "But God knows I had no part in the affair. It was forced I was."

Drumfin turned angrily on him. "And that's a lie," he said.

The tacksman beat his hands together wildly. "It's the truth I swear," said he, his anger also palpable. "Who is to judge between us?"

"Man, where was the forcing when you came to Rhoail?" cried Drumfin, recalling the Ruapais' story.

"*Dhia!*" said the tacksman. "You ken that, too?"

"I ken that: but I want more."

"We speak of different matters," said MacQuarie. "You ken of Rhoail; but I speak of what came after. For Alan and his men came back from Craig to Inshriff when they found Cattanach gone—Cattanach was the name, I think?—" and he gave a sly little glance at Drumfin's unmoving features. "And it's from Inshriff the forcing was, I tell you."

"I see," said Drumfin. "I admit I was wrong."

"They would have it that I knew where he was," went on MacQuarie. "They had already tried Glenbyre and found it empty, but I knew nothing further of their man."

"And then?" said Drumfin, finding the story halt.

"And then they forced me to guide them over Maam Clachaig to Glenaros, unsure of their ground as they were. Me, an old man, see you, and my hands bound, too! Well, well!"

"And then?" pursued the exile.

"And then it was on the Maam we found them, sir."

"Them? Who?"

"Cattanach and Fraser, both," said MacQuarie with a smile of deep satisfaction. "But 'twas only one killing."

"Ay?" said Drumfin drily.

"One killing," went on the tacksman—" one killing, for Fraser was stark in death when we got to him. I had no part nor lot in it, I say. My hands were bound, and that I'll swear to."

"I see," said the exile, leading him on. "I see."

"The way of it was this," went on the tacksman. "We were a full mile from the top, and the morning light was just beginning to show, when there came three or four shots on the hill above us. You could hear them echo long and long. And, old man as I was—bound as I was—mind you, the brutes pushed me on at the double. We came on those two—"

"Where?" asked Drumfin, testing his man.

"Right on the edge of the pass yonder, where the going is steepest—and they were wrestling keen. The dawn was but breaking, as I said, and we stole up to them and lay watching in the heather, not fifty yards off. It was no quarrel of ours, the fight was good, and they were too busy to notice us near. But when Cattanach killed his man, out we came."

"Only then? I see," said the exile, still plying him with a word to keep him garrulous.

"He tried the running, ay, did he, but Alan had him by the neck, and knew him for his proper game, and he sent his knife here." He tapped the left breast.

"Killed outright?" asked Drumfin.

"Outright, sir. Well, well, it's you has the very word, Drumfin. And—Dhia!—how pleased they were when they found that the other was Fraser! It's there was the toasting, I tell you."

"And these papers?" asked the exile, tapping the packet on the table.

"It's to them I'm coming, sir. For it was when they unbound me that I found them. And unbound I was, you may be sure, when the killing was over, for I must join them in their drinking. They were too busy at the horn to heed a burial or aught else, and when they hurried to leave the place, they overlooked these notes any sober man might have seen, so, thinking they might be of use, I just took them, sir."

"Of use?" said Drumfin smiling. "Worth money, you mean?"

"What else, sir, but the good money? And it's easy seen why I wanted riddance of them when you came on me, sir. It might have been someone else, and not so friendly." He turned to Pennyfuaran.

Drumfin glanced at the man with something of horror in his look, but the tacksman rattled on as glibly as if he but spoke of the price of black cattle at a Falkirk tryst.

"And then we came past Clachaig and as far as Loch-na-Keal. And still and on they wouldna let me go till I had seen MacAllister about his smack and bargained for his taking them off. 'Twas in Glenaros woods we lay last night and to-day, until Rob came. And it's me will have the trouble with Rob, for they'll never pay him."

"And that's all your story?" asked Drumfin.

"All, sir. And it's there is the truth. And I have your own word, Drumfin?"

"Your word?" cried Pennyfuaran. "This is murder, Drumfin."

In alarm, MacQuarie made a movement of appeal to the Jacobite. "See you that now, sir— see you that now! I have your word, Drumfin, have I not? It was two dead, and yet it was but one killing on our side, and till it was over, Callum MacQuarie's hands were tied.

"I believe you, I believe you," said Drumfin. "And though the dead may not return through anything you've told us, Callum, yet your story has broken a spell that was cast by the dead. Man, you've done what you never meant to do all your days—some good to another human, for your tale takes the blood-stain from innocent hands."

"Do you tell me?" said the man, his mouth agape in surprise. "Will I be paid for it, think you?"

"Ugh! Toad!" said Pennyfuaran. "Let me tell you, Drumfin, it's not me that believes him, for I'll take him for nothing but art and part in it. It's red-handed he is, and it's the gallows is hungry waiting for him. Man, was it not yourself he sold to Fawkener? And he'll sell you again. Do you forget Moy and Kinloch?"

"I forget nothing," said the exile gravely, handing the tacksman his bonnet and opening the door. "Yet he goes scatheless for me. Let him do his worst."

The ferret-eyed man retired, cringing, and rubbing his hands, and he smiled evilly over his shoulder at the chieftain who stood to watch him go. The door closed on him.

"Ugh!" cried Pennyfuaran in relief at his exit. "God send him his worst calamity!"

"Calamity?" said Drumñn, seating himself to gaze far into the fire's red heart. "But no. For what calamity can be worse than this man's: to be—Callum MacQuarie?"

36: "Beannachd leibh!"

Summer was come. Nine months had gone since Deaf Alan and his men had sailed from Aros, and passed for ever from out the ken of all who knew them there. But green Tiree never saw their voyage's end, nor any shore: the mist and the skerries had seen to that.

Summer was come. And from the churchyard beside the little ruined chapel on Pennygown rock there looked out on the blue Sound two little grassy knolls, where former summers had seen the turf smooth and unmounded. The headstones bore the MacLean quarterings, for Norman was buried here, and beside him Aros himself. It was but eight months since the chief had died: he had only survived the shock of his son's death by a week or two. Drumfin and Morag had spared him the truth, and he never knew his boy but as worthy of him.

Summer ... And still Drumfin haunted in safety his native isle, dreaming the old sweet sorrows over again, listening enchanted to the mavis, the robin, the fluting blackbird busy in Glenaros woods; hearkening on Glenaros shore the curlew's wail, so piercing, so intimate.

August was here, and a fair day for hay-making in Aros crofts; a mild sun and soft winds, the fragrance of the coils everywhere intrusive. But on this day propitious for seasonable toil, the fields were untenanted of workers, and the children, the brown-skinned rogues, had deserted the thickets of rasps on the hillside above Callachly for the pools on Ardmore beach. On a little hillock behind them sat a group of crofter women—the mothers mainly observant of the bairns' slipping feet and eager hands, the older people scanning under shaded brows the waters of the Sound.

Between Aros and Fiunary the waves were dotted with half a dozen brown sails, each little craft active beyond its capacity with passengers—the men-folk of the watchers on the shore. In the stern of one rude cutter reaching easily to and fro, Doctor MacNab was seated; while forwards at the mast-foot stood Drumfin. All were eagerly intent, watching a brig that tacked from Innimore to Fishnish and back again.

"With both wind and tide against her," said the Doctor, "she'll take time. It's two full hours since she left Duart, yet here is a sorrowful man, Drumfin—here is a sorrowful man, sir. What manner of a creature shall I be when she's gone, Gillian? ... And here is Aros Sound; but it's like a dream to me, and not the place it was at all, at all ... The bonnie Sound! the bonnie hills! Where in all the Carolinas will she find the like? .... Ah, well! her heart's desire to her heart, dear lass!"

Dubious and tearful, he shook his head, and after a silence resumed his plaint.

"A woeful country," he said, "yon America, with its Massachusetts' conventions and what not. Whatever takes them there? I say. A place and a time unsettled beyond comparison with this our native land, God bless it!"

"Ay, ay, Neil," said Drumfin, looking down the mainsail at him, and smiling grimly—"Ay, ay— here we are wonderfully settled, are we not? Never a rebellion nor a clan feud? We're vastly civilised under Hanover, eh? ... Give me, I say, the Indians of the Carolinas, and I'll match them with Deaf Alan and his men. Did you never hear of a night I spent in Kinloch Inn, Doctor?"

"Ah, Gillian, Gillian!" replied MacNab, shaking his head. "There's that night; and there are others I know of, when you slept safe as a babe in a cot. Do you forget that but two among a thousand in the isle have tried to sell the head of an exile they ken? And the price no small one."

"You do not take me," said Drumfin shortly, and flushing as he spoke. "It's not of my own race I'd speak ill. It's of misguided ruling of it, I'm thinking—But here's the *Bon Voyage* coming fair for us, and at the next tack it's the good-byes we'll be giving the young folk."

Surging to the forefoot amid showering sprays that took rainbow colours from the sinking sun, the great black hull and its towers of white sails came on.

"On the poop, on the poop!" cried MacNab, rising. "There, there!"

The brig went about grandly, a wonderful structure of wood and canvas, magnificent in full sunshine; her blocks creaked; a sailor yo-ho-ed; the rest was silent, gentle might. Splashing in her wake, came the little fleet of fishing craft, and there arose a babble of voices from their populous timbers, as the fishers and crofters caught sight of the dear ones on the sloping poop-deck near the wheel. Both were swathed in sea-cloaks that flapped in the breeze, but there was no mistaking them.

"He's queer without yon arm-sling of his," said MacNab. "But see! her handkerchief is a flutter yonder And there! he waves his hat ... My bonnie lass, my brave lass!"

They sailed closer yet, and still they waved their parting. The fishers sang *iorraman* while they put out the sweeps to keep their smacks closer to the brig, as she tacked across to Morvern again; and always the cloaked figures standing close together yonder signalled farewell. At times Morag's eyes could be seen a-glisten, despite their happiness; at times the twitching of the lips of the tall man beside her was plainly to be made out.

"A blessing on them!" said Callum Beag, pulling on a jib-sheet, and looking back to the dots of children playing on the rocks of Ardmore. He was thinking of a little brown-eyed boy with ruddy hair whom he had left behind. "It's the fool I am not to have taken the little one with me, for he'll never see them yonder. How beautiful the ships he carved for him! A blessing, a blessing on you!" he cried.

And so on they sailed far into the evening, a slow progress against water and wind. Then, as the hght failed, and purple clouds formed low in a saffron sky over Ben Shiante's shoulder, the cutters turned homewards one by one.

"*Beannachd leibh!*" cried a multitude of voices. "Blessing on you! *Beannachd leibh!* Good-bye!"

Thus they parted by stages until only one little craft toiled manfully in the great vessel's wake. The tide was now on the slack, and the *Bon Voyage* slipped on at a rapid rate, the cutter losing every moment. Fainter the glow in the sky, darker the low cloud-bars, colder the sough of the wind in the cordage: the night was come.

The forms of Fraser and his wife were no longer visible in the soft gloom, and the little boat's course was turned for the hills of home. Yet still those whom she bore, looked back at the brig's sails stencilled in black on the primrose sky, and spoke their good-byes .underbreath. Drumfin stood yet by the mast, a sombre figure, and gazed long at the distant vessel.

"*Beannachd leibh!*" he murmured— "*Beannachd leibh!* O hearts of gold! Would to God my Prince had known you!"

The Captain More

To Grace
In memory of the happy years in Eilean Aros

Time 1820-30.
Scene: Eilean Aros (Inner Hebrides)

Persons of the tale

Dr. MacCulloch	Country Surgeon in Aros Isle.
The Captain More	Retired Peninsular Veteran.
Draolinn	MacLean of Draolinn, a Highland Laird.
Grizel and Elspeth	His Daughters.
Garmony	Ewan MacPherson of Garmony, Tacksman and Sheep-farmer.
Carsaig	MacKinnon of Carsaig) Young Highland
Oskamull	MacCalman of Oskamull) Lairds.
Annalexa MacDougall	Oskamull's Housekeeper.
Alasdair	The Catechist's Boy, a daft lad.
MacLaren	Carsaig's Factor.
Philip Linnell	Naval Lieutenant, attached to Revenue Work.
Mr. MacLeod	Minister in Aros Isle.
MacKenzie	General Merchant in Aros Isle.
O'Brien	A Salt-Smuggler.

Contents

1:	Old Folk	187
2:	Youth	196
3:	Oskamull	207
4:	The Catechist's Boy	216
5:	Strategy	222
6:	Horses in the Night	230
7:	The Man from the Sea	237
8:	Taghairm	245
9:	Garmony	251
10:	The Thicket	259
11:	The Irish Schooner	268
12:	The Forsaken Orchard	273
13:	Eorsa	279
14:	A New Carsaig	286
15:	A Broken Man	294
16:	Hamesucken	301
17:	Salamanca	307
18:	Garmony and Grizel	314
19:	The Uniform	320
20:	Two Letters	325
21:	The Spanish Duel	332
22:	The Horse Fair	337
23:	The Langrets	343
24:	Happenings at Draolinn	349
25:	The Ride at Dawn	355
26:	Vale!	360

1: Old Folk

THE April twilight was darkening into night over the lochs and hills of Eilean Aros and her lesser sister isles, that, surrounding, warn and invite the passing mariner in the same instant by their savage beauty. A chill nor'-west wind, with occasional hail-showers, poured in from the Atlantic over the high cliffs of Loch-na-Keal, striking spindrift from the dark waters. On these it impinged in gusts regular and fierce, and then tore on and up the valley of the Ba so that the river frothed and surged to it, and the great cauldron of the Loch, which gave the stream its birth, chafed in its narrow confines under the volleys of the blast. A keen wind, it sang eerily in the ranked battalions of pines around the House of Draolinn, set on the river's northern bank; and the big trees rocked rhythmically, leaning as in confidence one towards the other, with all the assured airs of the besieged who know their might and safety. It seemed even as if their massed tops whispered encouragement to each other in the intervals of the onslaughts of the gale.

Something, indeed, of the attitude of these tall spires of the wood came kindly home to the breast of the only traveller afoot in the Draolinn policies at this hour—an elderly bent man, who trudged wearily down an avenue, with the bridle of a led horse on his arm, an animal conformably elderly and drooping. As squall after squall died away and hardly a branch fell to them, the old man chuckled; and at last, as if spokesman for the valiant pines, addressed the nor'-wester in an undertone of Gaelic. "So-ho! blusterer! ... So-ho! again, my hero! ... It's not from us you'll be looking for fear, eh? ... So-ho! ... Why, 'tis but child's play to us old ones, my bully!"

To judge by externals he spoke truth; for the dusky venules on his weather-beaten face, and the forward thrust of his shoulders, as if set to perpetual encounter with the gale, marked him as leading a life stormy in very literal fashion. He was the doctor to this West Highland countryside, and his present mode of progress with a led horse's bridle on his arm, was in his case a not unusual one. For he had some inborn incapacity for the art of riding, and, since he himself was vigorous of foot, had come to regard the animal more as a friendly travelling companion than a beast of burden. And now, as he emerged from the dusk of the wood and saw the sweep of Loch-na-Keal and the distant lit window of the Captain More's house whither he was bound, he said softly to the old brown nose beside him: "Yonder's stable at last, lad."

There was only a mile or so of wind-swept shore-road to cover before he entered the field that sloped to the little two-storeyed building set in the bield of a fir-wood at Killiechronan, where he was so sure of the kindly welcome and an installation for the night in "The Doctor's room." For in this scattered parish the long journeys of the country surgeon on his professional rounds usually involved a stay overnight at widely distant halting places; and so in every house of any size in the Isle there was a chamber dedicate to the lodging of the tired practitioner.

Darkness had fully come save for the faint radiance of a rising moon over Gribun, and the gale was abating, when he knocked at the porch of the Captain More's dwelling. The door opened swiftly, and Miss Belle, the Captain's housekeeper, a comely woman of middle age, cried greeting in eager Gaelic and begged him to hurry the stabling of his horse. "Haste ye," she said. "For it's at the cartes we are; and yet I should be setting supper. So you'll be taking my hand while I get the tea-table ready ... And indeed it's glad I am to see ye, Doctor; for it's long since we made *ceilidh* with you."

His horse's comfort seen to in a little lean-to shed that served as stable, Dr. MacCulloch climbed the steep stair, to receive a chorus of welcomes and handshakes from the Captain More and the other inmates of the room—four keen whist-players. There was a dark serious-visaged man at one end of the table, his eyes intent on the faded rosy cheeks and kindly brown eyes of his partner, Miss Belle, and on either side of them were their opponents, Belle's sisters: Miss Beta, the youngest, plump and ruddy and proper; and Miss Sheila, the eldest, a lady with features usually somewhat dull, but irradiated at intervals by a flashing smile that momentarily transformed them.

Small gentry—daughters of one James MacDonald, tacksman in the Rhinns of Islay, now deceased— they had drifted to Aros, by way of Lorne and many links of Highland relationship throughout the Isles, to this nest in the shelter of the larches at Killiechronan. What winds of sentiment, what struggles with the narrow ways of the household, brought and held them here, in the conjoint retirement and open hospitality of the Highland countryside, who shall say? In any case, one of their many helpful works was the linking-up of the gentry with the farmer folk and the crofters. (Not that the crofter is not of as good a family as the Chief, blessing on you! for he is of the same clan most likely, though not so far ben, it may be, as a tacksman.) And thus you behold to-night a tacksman's daughters playing cartes with a shepherd—" a good lad of honour," as we say in the Gaelic; while, out of the game and cosy by the ingle, sits a man who had held a commission in his Britannic Majesty's Army —Captain Duncan MacColl, late of the 61st Foot.

The Captain More—or Big Captain—as he was called, was a native of Eilean Aros; but finding on his return from the Peninsula, that most of his kindred had wandered to the ends of the earth (as is often the way with the Gael) he had taken up his quarters with the sisters in this kindly nook. He was a tall old man with military airs that were emphasized not only by the brass buttons on his fawn surtout, but by the carriage of his head; his neck, indeed, seemed more suited to the leathern stock, than the scarf of Indian silk he now wore. He secured the Doctor instantly, drawing him to a seat beside the fire, and at once diving deep into the news of the countryside; so Miss Belle was instantly ill at ease, divining that she had lost the surgeon's aid in her plans for escape from the whist now in progress. Her mind was thus divided between courtesy to her guests and a desire to get supper ready; and therefore whenever the trick then in play was finished she cried a halt.

"I'm sure, I'm sure," she said, "we're all so keen on the cartes, that it's supper we're forgetting ... I must be seeing after a bite now, and no delay ... Draw you into the fire, Mr. Morrison, beside the Captain and the Doctor, and be making yourself comfortable ... 'Twas good of you to come all the way from Frisa ... and the primroses are just beautiful, I think."

For all her faded cheeks, the little laugh with which she ended was a trifle coquettish. She lifted a posy of the flowers from the table, held it for a moment at her breast, and then placed it in a glass on the sill of the dormer window. The dark man flushed as he watched her, and bent his head to hide his emotions at the rebuff implied in the relegation of the flowers to a resting-place other than the bosom of her dress. "Aye, they're bonnie," said he, with assumed nonchalance. "It's a bit early for primroses ... but the place was sheltered, you see." And now the movement of chairs and the chatter of the sisters distracted attention from his confusion.

"Sit you round, and give us your crack, Doctor," said Miss Sheila ..." The cartes have made us a bit forgetful, Captain, I'm fearing."

"Aye, aye," said the veteran, rising to move his chair. "Supper did you say? .... Aye, the cartes arena bad for masking an appetite. They're the good friends to the sodger-man, the cartes ... If you're cold, a smoke and a pack to warm you; if you're warm, a pack and a smoke to cool you. ... I mind well now, Gillespie MacRae ... he was the hero at the cartes ... He could beat —"

"Gillespie that was in Garmonyneoch?" cried Miss Belle, busy with a white tablecloth and some platters of scones. "He that was so badly wounded in the wars, although his wife walked five miles on silver on her wedding-day."

"On silver?" said the Doctor.

"On silver she walked," asserted Miss Belle. "Did you never hear? ... On silver ... Five miles she walked to Kinlochspelvie to meet her man and the minister; and she with her shoes crammed full of crown pieces, and her poor feet raw with the blistering they made."

"What a world!" said Miss Sheila. "*Och, ubh, ubh!* ... and for all her trouble, never a day of good fortune has she had since then."

"Good fortune?" said the Captain. "And did she not get Gillespie MacRae that very morning for husband ...What better fortune could she be wanting?... the finest piper ever lifted chanter in all the West!"

"Piping?" said Miss Sheila. "Is it piping? ... When I was a young lass, for all his piping, I wouldna have married Gillespie, though you gave me Mull!"

"Aye," said Morrison of the heavy brows, "his piping never stacked his farm, look you! ... And his sheep so full of the braxy, too."

"Shepherding's one thing, John," said the Captain, "and warfare's another ... I can mind now when the turn of a battle—Aboukir, no less— was for either side, and Gillespie's piping helped to win it."

"Do you tell me!" cried the Doctor.

"To this very day I can hear the French six-pounders crunching among the sand on yon dark March morning down in Egypt ... It's true that was our warning; but there was something that bettered it ... Gillespie's pipes crying danger ... It was in between our left and right they were, and but for Gillespie's rouse, they'd have won through ... *Och, ille, ille.* but yon was the piping! ... And under the palm-trees and round the ruins o' Ptolemy's palace, look you! Gillespie from the rocks and rowans o' Craigaven, strutting it proudly!"

"To think of that now!" cried Miss Sheila, her eyes glowing.

"Man, man, John," went on the Captain, "life's big when you hear the like o' yon, and life's ending better than you thought, when you see men dying wi' yon music in their ears ... No, I'll never, never more hear piping like Gillespie's, not any more for ever, now he's gone ... And let me tell you this, Miss Sheila, whether his sheep were good, or whether his sheep were bad, it was nothing but the best o' luck came to the one with the blistered feet, the day she married Gillespie."

"Aye," said Morrison very slowly, all unmoved by this defence, "aye, I well believe he was the great piper .... Oh, yes ... but wasn't it just he that had the plentiful braxy?"

The Doctor laughed aloud. "Och, Captain, here you are at your wars again, and John at his black-faced sheep ... and we starving for the good supper that's waiting."

The ladies stirred, and chairs were set around the fair cloth of white, on which was spread a multitude of simple dishes—toasted scones, hot oatcakes, great cups of tea, fresh eggs parboiled, and a Coll cheese like a wee moon. Then, after a long grace in Gaelic from the Captain, they fell to heartily; and Gillespie, his magic pipes, his silver-shod wife, and his hapless sheep kept them busy till the meal was over.

As they rose the Captain was harking back to Aboukir and Alexandria. "And yon reminds me, Doctor," said he, "of my promise to show you the Wellington letter we were speaking about on your last trip here ... I came across it the other day, and laid it aside for you." He searched the breast pocket of his old surtout. "Tuts, I've mislaid it after all," said he ... "I'll have it handy for your next journey, however ... You've had enough o' sodgering for one night, anyway. Well, well ... it's getting late ... after eleven, I see .... Lights out, I suppose, Miss Belle ... Where are the Books?

But the Bibles for the night's reading had barely been produced when the douce Sheila broke in: "Och, well, well! and isn't it the great pity now!" She sighed, and her voice was a trifle tremulous, her face flushed.

"For why?" asked the Captain, turning slowly to a chapter in Ezekiel.

"Och, Captain dear, what but the wars ... the old, old wars ... What else is't but them that's upsetting me ... We're not Highland for nothing, I suppose ... And what wi' Gillespie's piping, and Egypt, and all the rest of it, it's little I'll sleep this night ... let alone that wonderful letter we havena seen as yet."

"So that's it," said the Captain, laying down his Bible. "Well, I'll be stepping ben, and find that same letter ... though there's nothing wonderful about it, that I can see."

"*Ubh, ubh!*" protested Miss Belle. "It's late, late ... getting on for twelve o'clock, indeed ... Let her be for a foolish woman, Captain MacColl ... She's like a lass o' twenty ...her and her sodgers."

But the Captain was off, and soon returned, bearing a small pocket of brown leather, with a bolt of hide for button, and traces of red sealing wax on four points of its surface. From this he drew forth a tattered missive, folded and addressed:—

H.M.S.
Lieut. MacColl,
Sixty-first Rgt.

J. Bathurst.

"Read it," said the old soldier.

And Miss Sheila, adjusting a pair of horn specs, and flushing and paling with delight, read slowly in the delicate script of the despatch:

"30th October, 1809, Badajoz.

"Sir,—

"*Your memorial of the 2nd October has been submitted to Lord Wellington, and I am directed to acquaint you that his Lordship is extremely sorry that it should fall upon you to lose the promotion for which you were recommended; but that he considers it as highly improper in the Commanding Officer who sent in a recommendation without stating distinctly the circumstances which occasioned the vacancy, particularly as it is well known to be totally contrary to the custom of the service to let any promotion go in a Regiment where the vacancy is the consequence of a Duel.*

   "I have the honour to be,
    "Sir,
      "Your most obedient humble Servant,
       "JAMES BATHURST.

"Lt MacColl,
"61st Rgt."

"Badajoz," said the Doctor, his eyes fixed, as if seeing beyond the dimity of the window curtains and over the moonlit loch and great fields of mountains to the distant South.

"Yes," said the Captain; "but that was written in 'nine, three years before the big assault was made."

"And a real duel! "said plump Miss Beta. "I declare! ... It sounds like a romance!"

"I'm wondering now," said the Doctor, "would that be the same duel where Oskamull's father was so sore wounded he had to leave the service?"

"Just that," said the old soldier quietly.

"Keep me!" said the Doctor, "but you've the silent tongue, Captain! ... You've had that letter all these years, and this is the first I've seen o't ... You and Draolinn and old Oskamull were in the same regiment, too ... the Sixty-First? ... And Draolinn, himself, never lifts a word about that business any more than you! ... That same duel! ... To think o' that now!"

"Aye," said the Captain. "It was young Oskamull's father and none other ... his right arm smashed, poor fellow! ...his pistol at the end o't, still smoking ... And the other man, scathless, look you!"

"My sorrow!" cried Sheila; "but it's just these duels I canna bear, with their cold-bloodedness and their counting o' paces, and the dour jaws o' them baith ... Oh, it's little sleep I'll be having, after all ... It's tossing and turning I'll be all night, thinking o' the good Highland gentlemen out yonder, throwing away their lives for a feather or a ribbon from the curls o' a Spanish lass ... Never a wink o' sleep for me this night, Captain, I'm fearing."

"Well, well," said the Captain. "You couldna well mourn worthier men, maybe, than most in those rencounters ... I'll no' say all, though," he concluded sadly ..."I'll no' say all."

Just then a dog barked out-of-doors, and Morrison, recognizing his own collie's voice, went downstairs to discover the cause, and returned in haste with the news that a gillie had ridden over from Draolinn House, asking for the Doctor. The Chief was ill.

"And me but parted from him, hale and hearty, a few hours gone," said the Surgeon. "I wonder what's amiss?"

"Plenty," said Morrison drily. "The lad below tells me Miss Elspeth has run off wi' yon wild Carsaig fellow ... And now her father's nigh demented wi' anger."

"He'll have a stroke, the old one, if that's the way things are turning ... I'd best be hurrying."

"What a world!" cried Miss Belle. "The poor man! ... She's the bad daughter, I'm fearing."

"And poor Grizel!" said Sheila. ..." A sore slight on her! ... Carsaig to pay court to the elder sister for a year and then elope wi' Elspeth!"

"Tach!" said the Doctor, securing his muffler around his neck ... "I wonder if Carsaig or either o' the lasses kens their ain mind ... First he danced attendance on the young one, then on Grizel, and now he's back to Elspeth again, it seems ... But I'll be stepping ... Good-night ... Be thankit! there's a moon." And descending to the stable, he decided that this was one of the rare occasions when he must really mount Fraochie, and so up-saddling, he rode off rapidly into the moonlit mists.

Round the curve of Loch-na-Keal's head came Fraochie at a rattling pace, and soon they were through the pinewood avenue they had already traversed that day. At the door of Draolinn House, a gillie took the horse, and the Doctor hastily entered the hall, where a man of middle height, with the white neckcloth of a minister under a little beard of grey, greeted him with a nervous, forcible hand-grip.

"It's you, Doctor," said he ... "I'll warrant you've heard what's afoot?"

"This runaway affair? ... It's true then?"

"True enough ... Garmony and I were staying overnight at Torlochan, and Miss Grizel, hearing we were there, sent for us as soon's the trouble began ... The Chief's like to burst wi' wrath, man! ... Come you in to him!"

He led the way to the Chief's den,—a little room lined with books, and known as "the Study." On a couch near the fire, lay Draolinn, a man of sixty, stout of build, with thick neck, short white beard and the wide-open fixed eyes that betokened a blindness of many years' standing. His face was empurpled, and the big veins on his high forehead stood out prominently as he breathed deep. "My head, my head," he moaned continually.

Garmony, a buirdly young farmer,—a distant kinsman of the chief's—sat on one side, holding a hand of the sick man and patting it soothingly; on the other, knelt Miss Grizel, busy with some cloths wetted in vinegar for the patient's brow. An exaggerated restraint showed in all her actions; and the persistent lowering of her eyelids, with the pallor of her plain regular features, gave evidence of strong emotions held in leash. Yet to Garmony, who followed her with lover's eyes, her mental agony was all too plain.

"My head, my head!" groaned Draolinn.

Dr. MacCulloch shook hands with Grizel, and then took the Chief's pulse. "Aye," said he ..."hard, hard ... A phlebotomy at once ... You'd best be sending in a lass with some vessels and hot water, my dear ... And you can be resting in your own room for a bittie, till we get this over."

When the lady had gone and the utensils come, the surgeon took out his lancets and bandages; and baring Draolinn's arm, set about the bleeding without delay. The little operation was soon over, and the limb bound up; and instantly the chief began to gabble incoherently regarding the runaways.

"Wheesht you, Draolinn," said the Doctor ... "Content you ... Rest you."

But the blind old man was now neither to hold nor to bind in the matter of talk. His brain seemed in reaction against the oppression of the past hour. Do what they would, they could not restrain him; and in the end the surgeon decided that it would excite him less if they let him have his way.

"From under my very nose, look you, Doctor!" said he. "Off with her in his arms, leaving me talking to the night-air! Curse him! ... I'll be even with him yet!"

On and on he rambled, and at last the tale of the elopement unfolded itself to his auditors. He had been sitting late in this very room with Matheson, his factor, it appeared, and after the man of business had gone, he had sat on alone till he heard ten strike. Then going out into the hall, he guided himself up the staircase by counting steps. There was a sound of some one moving on the first landing, and, thinking it one of the maids come down for some forgotten kitchen duty, he had said "Good-night." There was no response; his suspicions were stirred; and next instant he had collided with the conspirators. Both cried out softly in surprise, and he recognized the voice of each on the instant. On the instant, too, he guessed what was afoot—an elopement: the hour and the place could mean nothing else; and bitter reproaches fell fast from his lips. A softer mood followed, and, relenting, he had told them that this was an impossible affair; there must be no runaway matches from Draolinn. "Be putting off this daft business," he had said; "and since you're so set on't, ye can have the early wedding ... But, for Heaven's sake, by banns like the rest of the world." There was never a word of reply, and he had put forth a groping hand to find them gone.

"A waft o' cold air from an open door was all I got ... And ... indeed, I believe that before I began my fine sermon, he had her in his arms and was down the stairs and out, without a word o' mine ever reaching them ... He maun have forced her; for Elspeth would never have willingly passed her ain father without a word! ... Heard you ever the like? ... Curse him! ... And then my head went round and round ..."

"Wheesht you! ... Content you!" cried Dr. MacCulloch again. But there was no resting for that tongue so long restrained.

"Then I found myself here with Grizel, the dear lass ... And what, think you, did she tell me? ... (I had to drag it from her, you may be sure.) ... What, think you, but this? ... At the very hour I met Carsaig with Elspeth he was trysted to meet Grizel! ..." A volley of maledictions on Carsaig followed from the spluttering lips.

"Indeed then, if you'll no' be quiet, it's bleeding you again I'll be," threatened the surgeon.

"That a daughter o' mine should be so lightlied!" cried Draolinn, almost maudlin to tears now. "And by a wastrel like Carsaig ... a gamester and ne'er-do-well! ... Whatever did either of the lasses see in him?"

"I'll no' answer for you, if you go on at this rate," said MacCulloch.

But the Laird droned on, unheeding. "First Elspeth maun philander wi' him ... And then, when they broke a year ago, her sister, that's older and might have had sense enough, takes up wi' him ... And now he's off wi' Elspeth! ... By the Lord! blind though I be, I'll call him out, sir ... call him out!"

"Be resting now," pleaded the minister.

"Aye, man," sighed Draolinn, "I maun be resting ... But it's done me good to tell ye ... If only the Captain were here too! ... He's the good friend, the Captain, and the old one! ...Old? ... Aye, we're old! ... And we'll not be understanding the young folk that are growing up, Doctor, eh? ... They're young and thoughtless! ... We'll not be understanding one another." And so mumbling, he drowsed off into slumber, deep and stertorous.

2: Youth

IT was on the late afternoon of the same day, only some six hours before the chief's illness befel, that Grizel was discovered, tearful and disconsolate, by Elspeth in a corner of the walled garden at Draolinn. Long resisting the solicitous inquiries of the younger sister, she at last made full disclosure; and her story was not easy in the telling, for it was one of which Elspeth could hardly be a disinterested auditor. For a crisis had arrived in Grizel's affair with Carsaig (an elopement with him for that very evening, indeed, was in train); there had been much heart-searching on her part; and the result—dismay! She found herself bankrupt in all the essential ardours; and it was clear that her regard for him was greatly less than she had believed it to be.

Arm-in-arm, the sisters were slowly pacing the gravelled paths; but when the nature of the confession was made plain, Elspeth's steps took an impetuous turn, and her head bent low: clearly she was much moved. Taller than Grizel by some inches, her auburn hair, high colour and free carriage, contrasted markedly with the quiet self-contained airs of the dark, sober-featured elder sister.

"I've only been playing a part, it seems," said Grizel ... "But there's an end now."

The younger woman, breathing deep, kept silence, as she walked on; but her thoughts were crying out within her. Had Nemesis indeed at length arrived for this cavalier who had danced attendance on them both by turns for so long?

"It wanted only this," went on Grizel, "to show me how little I cared!"

There was a hint of weariness in the low voice, and at that Elspeth turned impulsively, and kissing her, said: "Motherless bairns! ... what else was to be expected, save ill-guidance for each of us ... To myself, in truth, the man's but a name nowadays," she added, inconsequently.

"Poor Alan!" said Grizel in weary tones.

"Oh, keep your pity for us women-folk," cried the other, passionately. "What right had he to propose a runaway business like this?"

"Good fortune for me that he did," said the older girl. "It has shown me clearly there was little o' the real thing betwixt us ... just romanticks, I'm thinking."

"It's long since I saw that was the way o't," said Elspeth, moodily. She might well have been years older than Grizel now, so did her mood of the experienced confidante become her.

The other smiled reprovingly at this assumption of authoritative airs; and said, "But it's what to do, we'd best be planning ... I had thought of a note to Alan at the Inns of Aros, where he's resting to-day ... But ... no, no!" and this came decisive ... "I'd best be meeting him and get by wi't ... I'll ride over and be breaking wi' him instanter."

Elspeth smiled. "Before all the township, lass?"

Grizel pondered. "I'll do't at the tryst then ... There's no other way."

"And where was that?" asked the other, quickly.

"At the east border o' Torlochan wood at ten."

"Then it's there I'll be, and at ten," cried Elspeth ... "and yourself safe at home ... I'll warrant once he's heard me, he'll never set foot in Draolinn again ... An elopement! ... Truly!"

"Indeed, and you'll no'," said Grizel, smiling wanly. "You wouldna ken when to stop, once you started your upbraiding ... I'll just dree my ain weird, Elspeth, if you please."

And so the matter was left for the moment; but after they had parted, Elspeth's busy brain continued to conceive new ways of shielding her sister from an encounter that would be torture; and at intervals throughout the evening, Grizel had to listen to various wild-cat schemes devised to this end. Smilingly she rejected each in turn, however, so that Elspeth chafed, and even secretly considered the desperate stroke of breaking confidence by laying all before her father. But the old chief was frail and prone to wrath, and any sudden access of passion in him might be serious. Besides, he had already given Carsaig to understand that his attentions to either of his daughters were unwelcome; since that youth, though a likeable enough lad and of good family, had the reputation of being but little less wild than most of the bucks of the period—a racketty, high-gaming, deep-drinking crew. And warnings to the girls themselves on this score had not been infrequent from their father.

Perhaps the old laird did not enough reflect that Carsaig suffered somewhat from the restrictions imposed by the scant nature of the social life afforded by a wild Highland countryside, and that he made up for this on his occasional descents on Edinburgh or London, by venting repressed energies in ways neither wise nor lovely. But thus it had fallen out, and the new vogues of killing time, acquired in town by Carsaig and his fellows in like case, were transferred, in some measure and in due course, to the daily round, on their return to their native haunts. A similar process had also been at work as regards the girls. For although their experience of tambouring and mitten-making during their annual two months' winter-holiday in Edinburgh was thorough enough, still there were a few dances and routs; and everywhere they met people who talked of Scott and Byron and quoted them interminably. The memory of those merry-makings bore a late harvest in the House of Draolinn; and the heady romantic spirit of the age's literary heroes continued to infect the girls' activities in Aros Isle during the succeeding ten months of the year, being unconsciously embodied in the outdoor life of wood and wave essayed by them there: riding, fishing, sailing and the like, pursuits none the less attractive that the young lairds of the neighbourhood generally assisted therein.

Thus arrived the affairs of the girls with MacKinnon of Carsaig, a youthful chieftain, recently orphaned, and therefore in as dire need of tutelage as the motherless sisters, daughters of a blind sire. Elspeth's attachment had lasted a year—a fervent business, ending in a funeral pyre of returned love-letters. Grizel's, as was meet, had been a gentler amour; but it was now come to a close with something of fierceness also. Life, lamented Elspeth, was nothing if not changeable; but she was glad that Grizel had at last discovered the hollowness of this man ... And yet, even as she framed the thought, her face flushed at old memories ... She felt herself weakening ... and instantly foresaw that Grizel also might relent, perhaps even at this final interview; for well she knew Carsaig's persuasive powers in pleading ... No ... her sister must not see him again; and it was this train of thought that decided her to make a desperate stroke ... Oh! she would save Grizel from herself ... from her own tender heart ... and to accomplish this would even do the thing she now planned. So she wrote Carsaig a note, addressed to him at the Aros Inn; and since the handwritings of her sister and herself were passably alike when naturally employed, she had little difficulty in making her own script still more resemble Grizel's, now that it came to a matter of artifice. *"Not Torlochan to-night ..."* so ran the letter. *"The pine-wood in front of my window instead. Grizel"*; and this was despatched at eight o'clock by the hands of a half-witted gillie whom she could trust to give no sensible answer to any questioning by Carsaig, if questioning there were.

Therefore, at a little before ten, Elspeth beheld her sister depart for the rendezvous at Torlochan, and five minutes later, she herself, with fast-beating heart, stole into Grizel's room in cloak and hood, and peered eagerly from the dark casement to the fringes of pines not a hundred yards distant.

The moon had not yet risen; but the stars were a fine dust of jewels in a dome of violet darkness, and gave light enough to distinguish the figure of the man she sought ... if he kept tryst. But no tall form in kilt and plaid emerged from the black wood; and already she despaired. Beneath the snood of dark velvet, her brow contracted anxiously, as she scanned the margin of boscage with narrowed eyelids. Surely her plans were not to miscarry after all? She trembled a little at the thought of failure, and listened for the sound of a footfall; yet only the chiming of moving waters and faint sighing of the pine-tops in the night-breeze fell on her ears ... But she could wait, and wait, and better wait, to unmask this man. Herself he had already deceived: he should not spoil her sister's life also ... She would confront him in Grizel's stead, and shame him from his plans for a midnight flight with her dear one ...

Would he never come? ... Again to the window ... And just then ... a faint tapping on the door. Hastily she pulled the hood over her head, and opened. Across the room the star-shine filtered palely, and in the gloom of the corridor stood Carsaig, a crystal in the brooch of his plaid glinting eerily. Tall, erect and dark, with an aquiline cast of feature, he looked anything but the weakling she knew him for, as he stretched arms to enfold her, while she held up a protesting hand.

"I could wait no longer," he whispered. "Why did you not descend at the hour? ... What's amiss? ... Come."

She had not reckoned on the meeting taking place beneath the very roof-tree of Draolinn ... Had Carsaig not estimated the hour accurately enough? ... Or was this only the impatience of the lover? she asked herself. For, even while she had watched the pinewood's margin, he must have already crossed the intervening sward, and stood silent beside the great door, awaiting his fellow-conspirator ... But now she prepared to descend with him, for in a flash she had envisaged the hall as the setting of the final scene ... the tossing aside of cloak and hood ... the fierce brief colloquy ... then the end, with the gesture of the opened door of Draolinn, and the cowed, slack figure of the chieftain shown to it! ... Nothing of the vindictive? ... No memory of the old love tossed aside? ... Oh, no; only the pure passion of devotion to her sister's safety! ... (She had smiled a little, she remembered later, at this last self-deception of the unmixed motive.) ... A rush of thoughts, half formed, coming back on her now, unsteadied her, and, unresisting, she let the chief take her hand.

Yes, she decided, they could descend to the hall in silence, and then the dramatic moment! ... Already they were moving downstairs but half-way they both halted in the same instant as the sound of a door closing softly came up to them; and a second later she recognized her father's foot on the stairs. Even then her courage did not fail, although she felt defeat desperately near. She would fight to the last blow for Grizel's happiness, come what might ... even to her father's hurt. Already the old man's fluttering fingers were on her cloak. But the meeting with Draolinn was but an affair of moments; for instantly she and her companion were in flight precipitate down the curves of the staircase.

The level of the hall reached, she looked back wistfully in the dark to where the blind man stood bewildered; but immediately she turned again, as if to shut off all thoughts save those of Grizel. She bit a quivering lip ... Not here the unveiling, With the good father so close. It must be in the open after all ... the final rupture.

She heard a bolt squeak, and suddenly the great door was opened a crack while Carsaig, peering out, as if to reconnoitre, glanced upwards at the stars, so innumerable and so steadily shining. To him they seemed to keep watch, eager and unwearied, over all the Isle—on the dim foldings of the hills and on the woods, dark as ebon carvings; but notably on this clearing where was set the roof he fled. And, when exultant, he flung wide the oak and ushered his cloaked companion out-of-doors, it was indeed for him as if every point of starlight centred on her.

They flitted noiselessly over a sweep of grass and gravel towards the dark tunnel of an avenue of pines, the woman slightly in front, with bent head; the man striding after her, silent and purposeful, his chin a trifle high. When they reached the margin of the wood he looked back swiftly at the sleeping mansion, bent an ear as if to catch any sound above the singing of the river and the soft fall of the waves on the far beaches of Drumlang; and then swung an arm passionate and masterful around the woman. "Beloved!" he whispered, and raised her face to his. A gap in the massed pine branches let through the light of the newly risen moon and it fell faint yet clear on her eyes as she lifted them and smiled tauntingly from the depths of her hood. Yet so impulsive was he, so glamorous were the night air and the witchery of the shining planets, that he had kissed her even on the moment of recognition.

"Elspeth!" he cried.

The girl touched her lips daintily with a trifle of lace.

"I didna bargain for a kiss," said she, bitterly.

For a moment Carsaig seemed dazed, then whispered in anger, "Where's Grizel? ... You're meddling where you've no concern."

"No concern in my sister's happiness? ... You spoiled my life, and now you'd spoil hers." The words came in a fusillade.

He stamped a foot testily. "Where is she?" he cried ... "You'll craze me with this dallying."

"Beyond your reach for this night, Alan ... I've seen to that, you may be sure."

"Madness! ... This is madness!"

"Maybe ... but I can go far for my sister's sake ... even to the tricking of an old blind man." Her eyes filled with tears at the memory of the meeting with her father; and her last words came in a little sob.

At sight of her thus moved, Carsaig paced to and fro uneasily. "Myself, I was sorry for him just there," said he.

"You'd good cause," said the girl brokenly. "My father! ... and him to be passed without a word from me!"

Now he thought to find her melting. "Come, Elspeth," he said kindly, "you'll no' be fretting ... It was a wild ploy, this; but it was the only way ... You ken how Draolinn looks on me?"

"I ken well he's wise enough to mistrust you."

"But you're surely no' the one to be hard on Alan?"

"And who has better reason? ... It's not two years since you shamed me wi' your wild routs in Edinburgh ... your name a byword in every mouth ... And what reply had I to my protestings? ... My letters unanswered ... and a jilting plain to be seen!"

"Tush! an auld story, that!"

"An auld story? ... Aye ... but one that was like to come true again wi' Grizel."

"I swear to you ..."

"Oh, often and oft you've sworn ... vowed to tak' tent and be wise ... And yet at the end, what was there? ... nought but a return to the gill-stoup and the dice!"

He growled, cocked his bonnet, strutted a pace or two, then faced her. "You'll tell me where Grizel is, like a good lass?" he demanded.

She returned his gaze steadily, and shook her head. "Oh, but you've been long daft!" she answered. "I'm wae for you both; but it canna be."

"The school-mistress scolding the weans!" he jeered: but there was now more than a hint of wonder in his voice at her courage and passion in attack.

"It's what the weans need at times," she replied ... "But I'll be going now." Her voice trailed off on a weak note, as she turned.

"I'll be seeing you through the wood," said he, following her steps moodily.

"Little need ... We're close at hand."

He halted at the rebuff; and relenting, she laid a kindly hand on his arm. She could afford to be gracious now, she felt, since the fight was over and the enemy so pitifully routed. "Look!" she said, and pointed across the moonlit waters of Loch-na-Keal, to where a white gable showed on the farther shore. "Yonder's Drumlang ... Rest you there till the morning, and sleep on a' this daft business ... You'll have clearer wits when you wake."

"Little sleep for me this night, I'm thinking," said he shamefacedly.

Something in his tone touched her, and instantly she halted. "Oh, Alan, lad," she said, "surely you'll be wise and have done wi' your roystering."

He stood with drooping head now; and her hand fell lightly on his shoulders. But at her touch, he shrank away. "Promise me you'll be wise," she said.

"Promises from me? ... And you but finished saying what you think o' them?"

"I'll take that back ... I've a quick tongue, I'm fearing ... But" (her voice shook a trifle) "you'll try, Alan." She fumbled with her cloak-clasp as she spoke; it had become undone; but her fingers were now as uncertain as her voice, and she could not coax the fastening to a hold.

"Let me be sorting that buckle," said he by way of evading an answer;

and his hands came about her shoulders as he deftly secured the clasp; while her face was very near to his.

She looked up pleadingly. "Be saying you'll try, lad."

He drew a deep breath. "Aye," said he, "I could at least be trying"; then tucking the cloak comfortably around her, he stepped back with face averted.

Some strong emotion surely held him? Was this repentance and remorse at last? she asked herself ... the suffering that cleansed and healed? "Poor Alan, what is't?" she said softly.

His hands clenched; "My God!" he groaned, and turned on her eyes that burned. Instantly her own fell before the ardour of his gaze; and she stood as if rooted there. The night-wind rustled softly jn the pines, and sighed away to the hill-depths far inland; the shine and shadow of the moonlit woods made mystery of all the world around; the long dying fall of the waves washing in on the shores of Drumlang seemed to interpret the very rhythm of their hearts. Of a sudden Carsaig clasped her, breast and lip to breast and lip; and bewildered and silent, she clung to him, swept out of herself by his passionate gesture.

"I have still some of the old-time letters," he whispered.

She was steel and fire on the instant, and withdrew from his arms' enfolding. "And the last two unanswered," she cried. "Oh! 'tis years away, but still a bitterness!"

"I should have written ... I did wrong," he said humbly. And now she wept, and unresisting, let him draw her head to his shoulder. "Elspeth! ... Elspeth! ... you've played with fire," he said. "Here is something that is stronger than either of us ... Little one ... Little one!"

"Oh!" she cried, "I never meant ... never ... meant ..."

He kissed her again; and again she sobbed, and leant on his breast, confiding utterly. "Of course ... of course," he answered, "you did not mean ... Ah! it's not the first time we've made up quarrels with a kiss ... Elspeth! ... white love!"

"But never before ... never before ... like this," she protested with dim eyes and quivering lips.

"Never before ... like this," he said, his eyes upturned to the stars as in a vow—the stars that throbbed and watched.

"Let us be going back," she murmured, and clung to him. "Let us be going," she whispered, and was still.

"Yes," he said after a space, "let us be going back."

But they turned away from the House of Draolinn and walked, enlaced, further and further into the mingled dusk and moonlight of the odorous pines; and a late hour found them pacing the lone resounding beaches of Drumlang. Later still, they embarked on a boat found snugly hid near the mouth of the Ba, and hoisting sail, were soon drifting far out on the moonlit tides of Loch-na-Keal.

"Hasty love, quick hate," says the Gaelic wise-word; and some measure of this truth soon appeared in several little bickerings between the lovers as they sailed the enchanted waters that lay between them and Oskamull, whither they were now bound. For on this night, Elspeth was nothing if not variable. At one juncture she bewailed her father's hapless lot, proposing an instant return to Draolinn; and Carsaig had even to free the tiller forcibly from her hand before his caresses had won a tearful submission to what seemed destiny in the most romantic of guises — the kilt and the plaid. In another phase she harped on her unfaithfulness to her sister. Later still, her brooding silence became as oppressive as had been her volubility in grief.

And although he succeeded in dispelling these unhappy moods by the tenderness of his assurances, the strain of the adventure was too much for his racked nerves long before the journey was over. Doubts began to invade him; the initial ardour dwindled as the journey over this magic sea drew to its close; and in the end, the vision of this fair creature — so full of whims and contrariness — inescapably linked to him throughout his life, seemed hardly so desirable as it had appeared two hours ago. Besides, Elspeth's frequent recurrence to the theme of Grizel rawed a very tender sore; and at the last he was amazed to find himself asking inwardly if his choice of the sisters had indeed been the wiser; if Grizel's partnership on the same voyage would not have been one less querulous.

Revulsion followed: he blamed himself for fears ungenerous, and so his mind oscillated, until, exhausted by the tension of the situation, he fell into a gloomy silence. And unhappily, this mood seemed infectious; for soon the case of the lady was not dissimilar. Thus the disembarking witnessed much less of fervour than did the setting-out; and, when Elspeth, now heavily veiled, was given over to the care of Oskamull's housekeeper for the night, the farewells between her and Carsaig showed but a tithe of the passion that had flowered so richly under the pines of Draolinn.

In the history of the mating of men and women, we may read that the strongest souls have misgivings when the crucial hour arrives. Poor Carsaig's fate was in no whit different from that of the strongest, but additional trepidations arose from the fact that his will was of the weakest, and his self-distrust very great. What wonder, therefore, that he sought assuagement for his unrest in an old ally? and his promise to Elspeth to seek wisdom, went down the wind with the first wine he took with his host. Glass followed glass, soothing his distracted mind to a deeper and deeper forgetfulness; and, if gleams of lucidity came at times, they but embittered, since they only revealed his broken word and fast warning powers of retrieval. Despair came next; then recklessness ... The coils of circumstance were too strong for him, he swore: he had made a fool of himself over this girl ... And now the tender love-passages of that night seemed naught but the wildest insanities ... Curse the woman! ... She had bewitched him! ... Ah! the cartes! ... A night of it! ... The rattlers! ... Let him forget! ... And so it came to pass that some four hours after his vow to eschew all folly, the dice were busy between Carsaig and his host in the dining salle of Oskamull, and they were deep in a game of hazard.

They sat by a table close to the fire, despite frequent down-draughts of smoke; while a whinnying wind and a blatter of rain on the window-panes testified to quite another world out-of-doors than that of the soft moonlight the lovers had left so recently.

"Isn't the gale rising every twist now?" said Carsaig as he threw. "Seven's the main ... Good Burgundy that ... What points?"

"Nine," said Oskamull, counting. "Chance to you."

"The play's as good's the wine," chuckled the other.

"The wine fair, the play good, and the lady worth the winning, eh?" said his host. He smiled and slapped his knee as if at some rare fancy; a slight man, with sly eyes and a heavy face, he was some years his guest's senior, and a distant relative.

Carsaig threw again. "Seven!" he said, bitterly, "and seven's the main! You've the devil's luck, Oskamull." He pushed over a small pile of guineas.

"Only twenty in my sporran now, so I'd best be stopping."

"Well, it's no' me that set the stakes so high, Alan, *laochain*."

Carsaig drained his glass. "Not you indeed, Colin—you were ever the canny one." He glared restlessly round the room; then rose to look at a chart of Aros Isle that hung on the wall-face between heavy window-curtains. "Here's Carsaig," said he, setting his finger on the map; "and here are your rocks and bracken. Damme! I'll set you Ben Iolaire against a swatch of yours: Coillemore, if you like, bully-boy—Coillemore, if you've pluck enough, Colin?"

Oskamull fidgeted. He was always indeed the careful one; but apparently his own Burgundy had him now well in hand. "What a pother about pluck, Alan," said he with an assumption of insouciance. "I'm your man."

"Agreed," said the other, sitting down heavily; and the dice rattled once more. "Chance to you ... Chance again ... And by Heaven you've got Ben Iolaire!"

Even Oskamull's heavy features seemed to show pity for the plight of his kinsman. "Nor stick nor stone of it do I want, Alan. Take it back, my hero ... I'll not have it."

"Have it you shall, man, unless the dice bring it again to me. Here! I'll set Ben Creach against it." The cubes were rattled and thrown. "And Iolaire's to me again, Colin!" He laughed hysterically. "God! it's the great game: Hieland hill-top to Hieland hill-top for stakes! Indeed and indeed it's the pretty diceing!"

"We'd best be stopping!" said Oskamull.

"No, nor stopping," said Alan, "as long's the wine and the hill-tops last. My throw, I believe." To it they went again, and far on into the night, while the winds from the very mountain crests they staked tore savagely at the roof-trees. As if aware of their desecration at the hands of the gamblers, they swooped at latch and lintel, and piped through transe and hall, the old walls shaking to their onslaught. Fully half Carsaig's lands had gone, when an unusually fierce onset of the tempest brought Oskamull to his feet.

"Take it easy, Alan," said he, moving to a window. "Are you hasting to part with all your birthright? Consider, man ... consider the lady in the case."

"I beg you'll leave mention of the lady. I told you ... did I not? ... that she was to be held incognita?" said Carsaig, brusquely.

"A happy ending to a stormy courtship!" cried the other. "You took the right way wi' a thrawn father, when you made it a runaway match ... She's a fine woman, is Grizel MacLean ... A toast, man! ... a toast!"

At the name of Grizel, Carsaig started, and gazed blankly at his host, then with a foolish look of cunning, joined in the honours. "I'm pleased you approve, Colin," said he. "It's indeed me is the lucky one."

"But there's more in't than that, Alan ... for you've brought me a share o' luck as well ... You've taken Grizel off the old man's hands ... I ay fancied, you see, he wanted the elder lass to be first to marry."

"And what then?"

"What then, man! ... What but Elspeth free for my own soliciting, you dog! ... So here's a health to Elspeth, and a speedy wooing for the randy! ... What ails you, man?"

Carsaig's face had gone pale of a sudden; and there was a quick twitching of his neck muscles that he could not control. He was sobering rapidly, and now rose to his feet, staring with brows perplexed at Oskamull, who kept his gaze fixed, as if fascinated by those eerie contractions beneath the other's chin. The air of the chamber felt suddenly foul to the younger man: it was heavy with spirituous fumes, odours of dropping candles, and sudden puffs of peat-smoke from the chimney's down-draught. Making for a recess, he shoved aside a heavy curtain, flung a window wide, and the salt tang of the shore-wrack and the clamour of the cleansing waves invaded the dingy salle. "Ails me? "said he. "What but the old tale ... the wine good and overly plentiful."

Dawn was breaking in a sky of mackerel-grey over the headlands of Gribun and Burg; and a fresh breeze fretted the steel-cold waters of Loch-na-Keal. Carsaig inhaled the sea-air deeply once or twice, as if he would free himself from the atmosphere of the room: for already his mind was clearing to a recognition of the madness that had possessed him there. "Alan, Alan," said he, underbreath, "it's dearly you must pay for the last five hours, I'm thinking." One pale lambent star in the southern sky held his gaze. "And there you are, the steady shining one,'" said he, "everything I should be and am not ... Ah, if I could but ... Tush! ..." He turned to his host, who stood with a tallow flickering, and took the light from him. "The bed-candle," said he: "that's the thing! ... I'm fell fond for sleep, cousin, and I'll be stepping"; and shaking hands, his eyes downcast, he passed through the doorway.

For a full five minutes after he had gone, Oskamull stood pondering this sudden change in his guest's demeanour; then smiling craftily, he poured himself another bumper of Burgundy, and drew in a chair close beside the dying peat-fire. A little table was near, and on this he set to tossing some dice, as if testing them. Not always, but with astonishing frequency, they fell cinque or six; and he chuckled as they did so.

3: Oskamull

AT Oskamull many of the upstairs rooms opened into one another—an old fashion in building that saved the space of a transe; and the door of the sleeping-chamber whither the strange lady had retired gave access to a middle room which, in turn, opened into the apartment of the housekeeper, Annalexa MacDougall, a poor relation of the chief.

At a stormy phase of the night's passing, when the whole house shook to an unusually threatening blast, Anna arose and dressed. Then she lit a dip and entered the middle chamber. "Shield us, God!" she said underbreath in the Gaelic. "The wind's rising and there's night; and there's darkness ... a night for witches, and for the riding forth of Ewan-with-the-little-Head." She paced heavily, and the boards creaked at each step; for she was a big woman, although comely. The place was full of shadows and little cold airs, that fought the thin flame of the candle at every turn; and the creakings of the planchings were of the eeriest. "This night o' nights!" whispered Anna. "*Och, ochan!* Veiled she came, and veiled she'll go, I'll wager. Who now can she be? With a storm like this, she'll no' can be sleeping: and yet not a sound from her ... And she to be tasting neither bread nor salt in the house! ... It is not to my liking, this ... Two shares of fear on her and the smallest share on me!"

She peered into an ancient dressing-mirror as she spoke, and it was a spectre of a face that met her eye—a shaking head and pallid lips. "*Och, ochan!*" she went on, "and downstairs there's the wine and the wine, and still the wine! Cartes and dice, cartes and dice! This house, this house! This night, this night!"

By reason of her heavy pacing of the room's length, the creaking of the floor-boards was loud and manifest in an unexpected pause of the wind's onslaught; at that the door of the chamber where the strange lady was bedded opened, and the girl came forward holding a lit candle in a sconce.

"Ah! "cried Annalexa softly at sight of her. "Now may the Good Being shield us! And is not this Elspeth MacLean of Draolinn? ... Oh! my dear, my dear, it's glad I am to see you; and yet maybe it's sorrowful I should be ... Whatever ploy is this? ... Treasure o' mine, put you your light down on the table there, as I'll do this; and sit you here ... *Och, ochan!* the cruel world! ... And never a stitch off you but the veil and the cloak as yet ... Ah, my dear, my dear!"

"Oh, Anna," said the girl suddenly, "help me!"

"My dear! ... To be sure, to be sure!"

"Anna, I've run away; and I fear ..."

"Carsaig, lass?"

"No, no ... not Alan ... but myself and my judgment and all that! ... And there's no time to think ... My mind's in a whirl. Oh, Anna, Anna, life's a terrible thing."

For answer Anna took both her hands and kissed them. Then they sat down on the edge of a great four-poster, and the big woman without more ado put the girl's head on her shoulder, and rocked and crooned to her as if to a child she would send asleep. Over Elspeth's drawn face a smile crept, and her weary half-closed eyes shut wholly. Anna sang softly, and the quiet ecstasy born of the unending refrains was communicated at last to the tired girl on her breast, till the look on the waxen features seemed that of utter peace.

"An end now," said the dame. "'Twas a song I often sang you as a babe." Raising the girl's head, she kissed her. At the contact Elspeth started as if from dreaming, and, with lips half-parted, blushed shell-pink. She smiled and was silent.

"But what I canna understand," said Annalexa, "is that I see no tears."

Elspeth's dark eyes regarded her steadily. "For why?" said she.

"For happiness, my treasure; or for ..."

"The other?" asked the girl. ..." Oh, woman, have not I put the world under my head this very night?"

"Left Draolinn, is it? ... Never!" cried Anna.

"My sorrow and my longing! but it's true."

"*Ubh! ubh!*" said the big woman breathlessly. "Tell me now."

Elspeth gave her story brokenly enough, for there were many tears.

"And the wedding will be when?" asked the practical Anna.

The girl hid her head in the good dame's bosom. "To-morrow, at Kilfinichen."

"Without banns! Are ye for the old Scots fashion, lassie? ... words o' present consent? ... Well, well, Carsaig was ay the wild one ... and never fond of ministers ... It's a daft business ... and I'd have a writing, were I you."

"Anna, Anna!" said the girl reprovingly.

"Well, there it is, and I've said it ... But what am I doing to be letting you starve this way?" she continued, rising. "It's down I'll go and bring you up the meat of each meat, and the drink of each drink you should have had long ago!"

"There is food enough in your wisdom, O woman," said Elspeth in the old language, with a smile that reassured. "Tell me ... tell me about the tears."

"Ach! it's not so easy as it looks," said Annalexa, shaking her head ... "Well, now, just listen to that wind tearing at the roof!" she went on, attempting another diversion. "And cold too ... it must be one of Fin McCoul's three coldest winds, I'm thinking."

"Anna," said the girl suddenly, "you're an old rigmarole ... And I don't believe you were ever in love, and so it's not to be expected you'll ken the ways out of a trouble like mine."

"Ah well," sighed the other. "Maybe, maybe! ... But even so—in love or not—it was just me had the fine lover once upon a time." She smiled quizzingly down at Elspeth, as she sprang this surprise; and the girl patted her cheek reprovingly in return.

"Tell me, Anna," she said.

"It was years ago at Laggan," said the elder woman. "And many a long day he spent there when I was a young lass, that same lad; hanging around, hither and yont, this corner and that. Och, and wasn't it just the great bother to get the work done, with me stumbling on him at every fank and byre and shieling."

"Ah!" said Elspeth, her eyes sorrowful. "And now he's ...?"

"No, nor dead," said Anna cheerfully, and folding her arms anew. ..." It wasna that ... It was just, well ... I'm sure I canna tell you why ... it just seemed it wasna to be, you'll understand."

Elspeth sighed. "Yes, yes, of course ... But it's not such wisdom I'm gaining."

"Well, then ... listen ... I'll tell you something," said the stout dame as in confidence and bending to whisper ..." He kissed me once ... just once."

Elspeth drew off a little, the better to regard the placid airs of Anna at this juncture. "Ah!" she sighed wistfully.

"And," went on Annalexa, lifting on her an eye, roguish though elderly, "I'm ashamed to say I liked it, my dear ... And that's all there is to tell."

"Now aren't you just the darling?" cried the girl, embracing her outright. "For that's what I myself could never have told, even to the stars."

"It's this way I'm seeing it," said Annalexa, bringing down a hand on her knee as in conviction. "Love-making is just a kind of a toy for a man ... So is hunting ... and gaming and drinking ... the same as they are downstairs even now, with a night and a wind like this around them! ... Just toys for big children."

"Gaming and drinking? ... Who?" asked Elspeth.

Anna blanched at the girl's tone—" Och, it's nothing ... just a toss of the dice between Carsaig and the chief."

"Drink and dice!" said Elspeth. "Oh! where now is his promise?" It was plain that to her the time and place were consecrate. The mood swept over her of an old-time tale of her father's of Peninsular days, where a convent church had been turned to the uses of a stable even while the nuns knelt before the high altar. "Dice! "she repeated bitterly, "and on this night of all nights! ... Oh, let us go," she sobbed. "Let us go: for it is in my mind to leave this place."

"And Alan?"protested Anna.

But at the name the girl swept both hands in front of her, as if clearing a path through high brackens; and the other understood. Then Elspeth disappeared for an instant into the inner room and returned, bearing mantle and veil.

"Wait you, till I see what's in it now with these men-folk," said Anna. She left the girl at the head of the stair-flight and descended into darkness. Nought came to Elspeth's ears but a sound of distant angry voices, and a hint of Anna's heavy footsteps as she moved uneasily below. It was some minutes before the old woman returned, breathless and agitated. "Come you back, my dear, come you back to the mid-room," she cried; and leading the way to the chamber they had left, she struck flint and steel with trembling hands, and lit a taper. Then she sat down heavily, and hiding her face in her hands, rocked to and fro, moaning uneasily.

"Oh, Anna! what is it?" The girl knelt beside her, taking her hands.

"What is it, but sacrilege and profanation! They're gambling away the very hills of God ... the fine lands ... the bread and life of the good kindly people! Ben Innigairt and Coillemore for stakes against each other! *Och, ubh, ubh!* Ben Creach and Ben Iolaire's lost to Carsaig already ... And they're wining deep ... And I fear ... I fear there will be bloodshed ere the mouth o' day. I darena move out of this house to-night, my dear. *Och, ubh, ubh!*"

"And it's no one will be asking you, Anna!" said the girl fierily. "Take me to them and I'll give them a taste of a Highland tongue." Next moment she was in a passion of tears.

Voices and the sound of good-nights in the Gaelic came to them just then; in a moment Elspeth was on her feet and had flung open the door of the chamber, as Carsaig passed with his bed-light guttering. He turned and gazed at her with haggard eyes; and on the instant Anna was by her side.

"Elspeth!" he cried ... "And weeping? ... Is it indeed to this I've brought you, my dear?" He passed a hand over dazed eyes. "But here's one that's downright sorrowful, lass ... "

For answer Elspeth hid her face on the shoulder of Anna, who instantly drew her back into the room, and closed the door.

Alone once more, they wept together, beguiling themselves with false hopes as only sorrowing women can.

There was little rest for either that night; but the noises of the wind and the shaking of the old walls abated as morning drew on, and at last, thoroughly worn out by the strain of their emotions, they contrived to doze a little in each other's arms. By ten they had made a show of breakfasting. After the meal, Anna set off to find a gillie who would set them on their way to Draolinn in a skiff; for the storm had now wholly abated, and the Loch had but the faintest ripple on its steely blue. The only evidence of the gale lay in the wrack washed high beyond tide-mark on rock or grass—great tawny cables and lianas of that submarine forest that is only revealed at intervals by the passion of the deep. To Elspeth at the open salle window came fresh odours from the tangle, and already on the Gribun shore she could see the kelp-gatherers busy at the harvesting of these gifts of storm. The sea had an air of repentance after last night's mood of angry debate with the island shores. Sunlight from an almost cloudless sky fell on the patient tides, and on the distant familiar shapes of the hills—protecting giants above her home at Draolinn yonder. Sea-pyats were calling along the beach, feeding to surfeit among the rich bladder wrack, and in mid-loch scart and gannet were busy swooping and plunging above the crowding herring shoals. The Oolava fishers had marked the birds' activities, and several tan sails were already hoisting. On Eorsa the wild goat were tracking the paths perilous of the cliff-face— mere specks for size; and on the Desaig shore some dots of russet-colour moved, too far to mark clearly; but well she knew them—the sturdy antlered fellows in their sappy gullies at Torr-na-Bhlar. Oh, home ... home! the dear fine place, so free yet so enfolding! There came a thin faint piping; and she strained to catch a glimpse of the foreland at Faolinvore, for that surely was the fingering of young Macrae—only he had such a lover's hand on the notes. Ah! the old, old Highlands, where was their equal? And yet ... and yet! only last night it was farewell to them, and with a sore heart. To-day it was another story, but the heart was still the same ... nigh to breaking, indeed.

She was cloaked for the journey; but her veil was thrown back, for the sea-airs were restful on a brow that ached; and so Oskamull found her, as he swung in, calling for Anna, and a late bite and sup. "Just a mouthful before I take the hill, Miss Grizel; and your pardon for my tardiness; but last night was a busy one for us, you see ... I trust you slept well?"

She turned from the window, and beholding her face, he stood in dumb confusion.

"Only Grizel's sister, Oskamull ... Or should I be calling you Carsaig to-day ... for by all accounts," and she glanced at the spidery crosses scrawled over the estate map on the wall, "you own more of that land than you did twelve hours ago ... nearly all, if the carte speaks truth."

Abashed, he drew himself up, put one hand to his haunch, and slipped the other to his sporran, where he fingered crumpled notes-of-hand for an instant. Then he was his swaggering self again almost at once. "Oh! the dice!" said he carelessly. "I didna think women bothered about business. That's men's work, Elspeth. And all's fair, madam, in love, war and gaming except cheating ... except cheating, you ken."

"Sir, you're shameless."

"Madame, you're my guest ... although an unexpected one." He bowed brazenly; and then Carsaig entered, a trifle wan and haggard. Elspeth caught her breath in a little sob and turned to the window again. Her sister ... her father ... this man? ... What a coil her thoughts were in! She would go; no, she would wait for Anna! But Oskamull's hard tones broke in before she could decide. "There you are, Alan, and it's you are the man to confirm me. I've just been telling Miss Elspeth here that it's an old saying and a true, that all's fair in war, in love and in gaming—except cheating—except treachery, Alan."

And unseen by the girl he crossed his right hand to his left hip and tapped where a sword should hang. His face was flushed; and regarding him keenly, Carsaig's face reddened also; instinctively his right hand also slipped to his left side and matched the other's movement. "I think I follow you," said he quietly.

"Then 'tis more than I do," said Elspeth, "so I'll be seeking Anna."

As the door closed on her, Oskamull turned with the teeth of a foumart. "Did you hear me, Alan?" he said with dry lips. "Treachery!"

The flush died from Carsaig's face. "Aye," said he drily, "I heard."

"You've played me false," said Oskamull. "Here you've come, cloaked and secret and in the shadow of night, with the very woman you were toasting as mine but a few hours gone. And you're my very good friend all the while? Damnation, man! explain!"

Carsaig moved languidly to a chair, and sank in it wearily. "Give me wine enough, Colin, and I'll toast her as yours all day long. I'm tired of all this."

"Look you, here is what is in my mind," said the other. "Meet me with a friend at the Traigh at Ormaig to-morrow at ten ... good footing and the sand neither wet nor dry ... and I'll do my best to spit you like the brock you are!"

"It's my excuses I must be making, Colin," said Carsaig, still languid, "for I'll no' can come. I've had enough of heroicks in the last twelve hours to last me a lifetime; so be sparing me yours."

"I'm inviting you to Ormaig to-morrow at ten ... you to bring a hanger, and me likewise," said Oskamull precisely and with determination.

Unheeding, Carsaig stretched himself, his hands deep in his sporran. "I'm fearing I'll be too far south by ten, Colin. For I'm just off to the Captain More for the good counsel before a long journey in the Service. I'll slog and idle no longer ... The Indies—the Levant—Muscovy—anything is better than this rusting here. I've a sword for that kind of work ... none for your ploy on the Traigh, man."

Oskamull's brow cleared. "And Elspeth ... and the Glen?" said he.

"Tach! are you blind? ... Elspeth gangs her ain gate ... As for the Glen ... you've nearly every peak that looks on Carsaig. And sorrow on the black thief, my grandfather, that broke the entail and let me do what I did last night."

The other's hand went to his lips in a movement of hesitancy and irritation. "And now you're for the Captain More," said he, "like a schoolboy to his mother's apron! See here, man, you'll no' be telling him about last night's gaming? He wouldna like the tale at all; he'd no' be understanding ... Not that it's any of his business, look you. ..."

Carsaig waved his hand in assent, smiling and a trifle scornful. "I think I ken what's fitting," said he. "I'm no tale-bearer."

"Not that it's any business of his, I'm saying," went on the other. "But it's just his good opinion I value greatly, and I'll no' have a hard word from him on any doing of mine if I can help it ... Ha! here's Anna, and dressed for a jaunt! ... Lord! are you all for leaving poor Oskamull? ... Will you also be seeking to the wars, Anna?" and he masked his drawn face in a smile.

"There's enough to do in this countryside, sir, let alone in the wars," said Anna. "But with your leave I was for convoying Miss Elspeth back to Draolinn; and since you werena down, I made bold to get out Callum with the skiff ... Will you be sparing him?"

"Surely, Anna, surely."

"She's a bit forewandered, poor lass, and we thought of making a call at Killiechronan in the by-going; for the Captain More's the old friend."

Carsaig laughed bitterly, his hands still deep in his sporran, his legs outstretched. "I'm saying, Colin," he said over his shoulder, "I'm thinking the Captain More will have a morning of reception. You'd better be coming with me, and we'll mak a day o't."

Anna bridled. "And indeed, sir, it may be a time for jests—but I'm not seeing it. Yet, I'll say this: I'd like well to see the Captain's face the day he hears you've gambled away your birthright."

Oskamull made a step and gripped her hand.

"Wheesht, Anna, wheesht! You've no right to be talking like this. And you've no right to the news you have ... for you got it from no lips o' mine." He glanced with black brows at Carsaig.

"Indeed and it was from your own lips, sir ... although a door was atween us. With the drink in you speaking as loud as it did last night, it was strange if all Aros didna hear it. And where else would I be but behind the door, and my poor knees shaking, when it's each other's throats you would be slitting, by the noise you made in your quarrelling? And how else could I help but hear?"

"So that's it," said Oskamull. ..." But you've the true word all the same about the Captain More. It's what was in my own mind; and wasn't it just that I was saying to Alan as you were coming in?"

He drew some scraps of paper from his sporran, read them by turns, tore them up, and cast them in the fire. "So!" said he. "Now there's Ben Iolaire and Ben Innigairt and Ben Creach and the rest o' them among the peats." Then he shook a threatening finger in the face of Anna. "And just let me ken that the Captain ever hears a sough of this ploy, and I'll slit the thrapple below the tongue that gives it vent, kin or no kin. It's truth, I'm speaking, look you!"

Carsaig was on his feet at once. "But, Colin, you'll never get my consent to the wiping out o' a debt o' honour!"

"Hush, man," said Oskamull, walking to the window to divert him. "There's a pibroch playing on Faolinvore: it'll be young Macrae. The pipes are like a morning dram to him ... And, Anna, here's your boat and crew and passenger waiting you at the rock-foot. Haste ye!"

Anna hurried from the room with a backward glance of bewilderment at the men, and instantly Alan was at the charge again. He gripped Oskamull's arm, and swung him forcibly from the window. "Is it a thowless man you're thinking me?" he said fiercely. "A debt's a debt, and I'll hold you to your winnings, be the bonds torn and burnt a thousand times over."

Oskamull turned his head, and his hand went to his lips, as a hint of the old crafty smile played there for a second. "It's no' me that's wanting lands of yours, Alan, and fine you ken it. We were too free with the wine-stoups last night, I'm fearing."

"It's a matter of honour, and it must stand."

Oskamull's lips had again the hint of a smile, cynical and evasive. "We'll see; we'll see! Let's consider for a bit, Alan. Meanwhile we'll say nothing anent it ... In a day or two you'll think better o't, maybe."

"It shall stand," said Carsaig.

"So be it, so be it!" said Oskamull airily. "We've had enough of bickering ... Only ... for the time being, this must be between you and me, Alan. Keep your rock and bracken for the present, sir; I'll let you ken when I've need o' them."

"What the devil are you driving at?"

"I'm driving at this ... Your word's your bond; there's no scrivener's parchment betwixt us; and when I want what's mine in Carsaig I'll ask for it, Alan, and not before ... We're both to be secret on the whole affair."

"You're a droll fish, Colin. It's no' to my mind at all, at all. I was never the schemer."

"Schemer!" said Oskamull hotly. "'tis the fine word for one who does you a kindness."

"Kindness here, kindness there!" said Carsaig. "Who's asking for it from you, Colin MacCalman? I've lost half my lands to you fairly, and there's the end on't."

"You're sore, Alan, sore; and your words are plentiful ... You can ay have your revenge when you ask for't."

Carsaig turned on him in a flash. "Then I'll take it! "said he. "I'll show you pluck enough, my bantam! Where's your rattler? I'll set you what's left of the Glen against all last night's hill-tops."

"Softly, man, softly," said the other, his eyes narrowing. "It's no' me will be denying your rights to you. But, whatever the upshot," said he as they sat down to the table, "we'll hold by the terms I've mentioned."

"Oh, hang the terms," said Carsaig. ..." Anything ... any terms ... Agreed, man, agreed ... Let's to the play ... Where's the Burgundy?"

Two hours later a lug-sail drew into the rock-foot, and Oskamull came down to it with his guest. Both bore the marks of deep wining. "Bonnie on the revenge!" said Carsaig grimly, well out of hearing of the boatman. "You canna give luck to the luckless! I've lost a bride and every rood of my lands. You've got the one: I wonder if your luck will hold with the other ... Listen to that water, Colin ... the withdrawing wave, mark you! Man, did you ever hear anything so wae as the suck and sob of an out-going tide?"

Oskamull took leave of him with a sardonic grin; and the boat sailed off to the west. Like a figure of stone Carsaig sat motionless by the gunwale, his temples throbbing, as memories of the night just over-past brought shameful flushes to his cheek. He turned to look at the far-distant pines round Draolinn; then covered his face with his hands. "God! but I've had my fling! . . ." he muttered between his fingers. "Whatna madness is this that's come over me at all, at all! ... Oh! Elspeth, lass! have pity on daft Alan!"

4: The Catechist's Boy

OVER Carsaig's head that morning there rose a tan sail with a white patch near the mast end of the gaff, as the boat slewed out of Oolava Sound; and the Captain More, daundering on" the height above his lodging, paused to note the marking as that of Callum Ruadh's lug-sail. "She's on a strange course," he thought; "I wonder where—" and the better to track the vessel's route past the great headlands, he mounted further on the hillside, and bent his footsteps to Tor-nam-Feinne.

That watch-hill of the old races of the Isle intrigued him, especially on mornings such as this; for the air, a trifle snell despite the sunshine flooding the great spaces of the fine Highland country that lay below him, tuned his every fibre to the alertness of his own martial youth; and he stepped out briskly. A clarity as of crystal was everywhere; the storm overnight had washed sky and sea and shore to a purity unearthly. The memories of the place called him as to a haunt of comrades dead and gone. Ancient warriors, of Ulysses-spirit like his own, had been here; they, too, had known leaguer and bivouac and the fever of wandering in lands remote; and after spindrift and sword-play and weariness,—exiles from Lochlin—it was here, like himself, they had found retreat. "Aye," sighed he, and underbreath he repeated the wise-word of the Gael: "To him that furthest went away, the sweetest music ever heard was ' Come home!'"

And yet ... and yet as he pondered the antique past, his mind swung nearer his own day; for the contours of the coast below him recalled Salamanca and the South, and he beheld as in a magic mirror his memories of that bloody day. In that distant corrie stood Pakenham in reserve, fretting his heart out for the word to go free; and when it came, how he swept into the mellay like a spate on the Forsa when it meets the scouring tides of the Kyle! Among the ravines yonder, scattered and half hidden by rock and fern, agonized the remnant of Hulse's brigade under the French battery's fire, like drowning men in a sea of long grasses; the old Sixty-first among them, sadly broken, but not beyond cheering even at the third of their charges that afternoon.

Then the sound of a voice fell on his ear like a dream within a dream; and he halted his fevered pacing, wiping from his forehead the sweat born from the stress of his imaginings, and came to himself. It was as if he awakened to a world empty in comparison with that memory of old Spain. A blackbird piped from an alder on the edge of the planting; and again came a high voice in a run of Gaelic. He topped a slight swelling of the ground, and his eyes fell on the figure of a boy on a knoll below and in front of him, who, unobserved, was in the very ecstasy of declamation after the manner of a Highland minister. Congregation there was none, except a somewhat critical robin on a whin-bush and two very restless rabbits, playing by their burrows some fifty yards away. A little cairn with some clods of turf surmounting it, so that it could be thumped with impunity, was, it appeared, the pulpit-desk. The lad's back was to the old soldier, and as the intervening turf was soft, and drying already, the Captain was able to approach within a stone-throw, just as what seemed to be the peroration was achieved to the accompaniment of two upflung skinny arms protruding from a short-sleeved jacket of hodden grey. A quieter tone followed as if a pendant were about to be elaborated; evidently the sermon was true to type—it promised fulfilment time and again, but there were many after-thoughts; and now the slight arms were thrown left and right, as the boy recited.

"Seamus Dhu, Donald Breac, Angus Thostary!" he called, "get you a-a-ll to the left—you're for among the goats, and let this be a warning to you— and to everybody! ... Charlie Crubach!—you may take a turn to the right, near the sheep, but be keeping on the fringes of them, for I'm none too sure of you just yet; it's sometimes well and sometimes, not so well with you; I'm fearing you're too fond of the dram, *laochain*. Are you hearing me?—Well, keep you on the edge of the sheep over there and no further than that in the meantime ... MacKenzie, the merchant! ... to the devil with you right away! And take your pass-books with you into the middle of the goats, my gentleman! See if you'll can grind the faces of the poor goats, MacKenzie! I'm thinking their horns will be interfering with your grindstones, my man ... And take your drunken housekeeper along with you; for, look you, her tongue was only meant for Yon Place.

"The schoolmaster had better be among the sheep, I'm thinking, although I could make out a good case for starting you on the Ither Road, mind you, Mr. Meldrum, if I was the least pernickity ... And the Man from the Sea can go to the left, blast him, the dark one!"

"And on which side would you be putting me, Alasdair?" said the Captain More, stepping forward.

The boy wheeled, showing a dark eye and a pale face that went paler on the instant. He feinted to escape the outstretched arm of the old man, then slipped to the other side suddenly, and was up the brae and out of reach in a flash.

"Come, come, Alasdair, is it coaxing I must be? ... Was it a sheep or a goat you had made me? ... I didna hear all your fine sermon ... only the tail-end of it."

The boy paused, his chest heaving, a wisp of mouse-coloured hair dangling close to his sharp brown eyes. "Och, it's you," said he, reassured, and returned with quick steps. A halflin lad clad in jacket and trews of rough woollen stuff too small for him, he was a strange mixture of the uncouth and the alert. His stockings of crotal colour were ungartered and slipped a trifle, showing pale knees that seemed never to have known the touch of sun.

"Preaching again, Alasdair! Man, you're sore on your congregation, dividing them as with an axe into the bad ones and the good ones! No wonder your kirk's so poor attended."

"It's what they're needing—the dolts!" cried the lad with spirit. "There would be as few in Aros Kirk itself if the minister spoke out. I'm thinking his business is no' to fill the pews but to empty them ... A sore handful, yon in Aros, look you ..." After a pause he added, "You'll be wondering to see me astir so early."

He was referring to his habits of the night-bird. For Alasdair, poor lad, had a twist of the mind since his youngest days, that sent him to bed when all the world waked, and to haunting the dreaming township, the empty roads, the darkness of hills and woods from gloaming to sunrise. He shunned mankind; and neighbours of his father, the Catechist, living within call of his cottage, had not set eyes on him for years. Sometimes a drover, late from fair or market, heard a pattering of footsteps on the road, and beheld an elfin figure pelting after him, only to halt suddenly, and disappear in whin or bracken, the moment Alasdair had vision of his scared face, had established his identity, and satisfied his curiosity by rapid guess-work as to his business and route. Often and oft the poachers in Glenaros woods divined his presence from a rustling in the scrub oak, or a snapping of a twig never made by deer; and the travelling tinkers got many an alarm from the glint of his white face in the camp-fire light as he peered in on them from the ferny brake. Never a midnight death or birth in Aros township, but his keen eyes were noting the scurrying, the softly opening and closing doors, the whispered colloquies by peat-stack and byre, as life came or departed; and had the old Catechist been gossip enough, he could from the boy's half-hints and asides, have provided chronicles that would have laid bare every thatched roof in the Isle as if to some aerial visitant. But the child was harmless; there were no pilferings or pranks; and the good folks of Aros slept soundly, although they knew to a certainty the daft boy was awake and prowling. " 'Tis only Alasdair Beg, blessings on his poor weary feet,"

said the goodwife, turning her face to the wall, as the fowls stirred uneasily in the hallan. "Only the Catechist's boy, I'll wager," said the crofter at the byre for a calving, as a quick late footfall passed on the dark highway.

"Aye, laddie, you're early; it's not often the sun gets a chance to give you freckles," said the Captain More.

"'Twas the Man from the Sea ... the bad one!" said Alasdair, "or I'd been bedded long ago. 'Twas he that started it."

"And who is he now?"

"The Dark One Himself, I tell you ... In a ship he came, and in a ship he went. A sword he wore, and a cloak to cover him. 'Twas at Penny-gown burying-ground, look you, and me thinking on MacPhail and the Roasted Cats ... It was a cutter, his ship; and all through the dark I followed her head-light; and when morning came, she passed out of sight, and me so far from home ... But I got in by Achadashenaig fank by the mouth o' day this morning, and Sandy *Cibeir*[1] was speaking to the new herd about the loss of Miss Elspeth of Draolinn; and it was come on me to find her. And so I searched and searched the Hill of the Cave, and I better searched ... And I came in by Glenaros wood where the white stag is, that will ay be grieving and mourning ... Man, man, I hope Miss Elspeth didna hear yon ... Och$_y$ ubh! ubh! but it's just yon stag that has the sore heart! So old, so old, he maun be; and his clan broken, and he the last of them ... his friends all dead! With him so lonesome, what else would he be doing but grieving, think you?" The dark eyes were appealing, and the thin voice shook with the sorrow of his meditation.

"Miss Elspeth is lost ... Is that what you're saying to me? "said the old soldier. "I was hearing something, but wasna just sure."

"What else but lost ... Sandy *Cibeir* was telling it to the herd ... the new man, Munro from Oolava. She's off with some fine gentleman; kidnapped, they were saying ... I hope she was under a roof last night, for at the start it was fine and there were stars, and a moon; but afterwards there was such a wind and such a rain, and I had to lie in the cave on Ben-nan-Uamh, watching yon evil ship's head-light ... And the hailstones so sharp on the nose, look you, they'd bring you nigh to weeping ... "

"And the Man from the Sea?" asked the Captain.

"It couldna be him that kidnapped her, think you? ... I watched him close ... close ... Unless he got her before he came to the burying-ground ... Aye! ... Maybe that's it."

"And I wonder now what was he doing in the kirkyard?" said the other cautiously. "Where did you first see him?"

"There was a cutter came round by Craignure, tacking to Innimore, I'm telling you, and then standing in to the bay at Pennygown. She anchored just at the mouth o' night ... I was at the burying-ground on my own ploy—setting the mark on my sister's grave ... Wi' shells ... and ye ken whit for ... Like this." He traced a pentacle with his heel on the turf. "It's the sure sign against all evil ... against the witch of Auchnabreae, and her of Achnacarry, and against the three Mull witches, and against Ewan-of-the-Little-Head. And every night that a moon is out, I'm for setting the shells in the shape of the good sign ... They shift the shells every time, or ettle to shift them ... the witches. They send winds and blow them far ... far; but Alasdair Beg puts them back; and sister Kirsty sleeps sound, sound ... " He dug his heel in the turf again and excitedly traced the angles of his charm.

"I had set them fair and straight, look you; when what should come out of the dark of the Kyle, but the beat of oars; and then there was a scraping on the stones in the hard sand, and whispering and the sound of fists; and up the beach comes my gentleman in a big cloak and a lanthorn under it, and the boat's crew following him ... And in they go to the old chapel-ruin, and start to the carrying out of bags from it ... Heavy they were, though wee, and down they brought them to the boat; then back again for more, whispering, whispering all the time! ... A strange thing yon! ... Maybe they'd found the treasure o' MacPhail, Captain ... What think you?"

"I'm sure I've no idea, Alasdair ... It was indeed a strange affair ... And what next?"

"And while they were taking off the bags, my gentleman with the lanthorn went walking up and down for a bittie; and then jumps the graveyard wall, and came in among the tombstones, looking at this one and that ... But when he came to MacPhail's, down he plumps at it with his light close to the lettering, that's all covered with moss and crotal leaf. Then he screeves out a cutlass from under his cloak, and he rasps off the moss, and he reads the lettering close, and writes for a little on a scroll of paper. Then down to the beach again, when his men had carried off the last sack ... Man, I wish you had been there to give him your mind about the defiling of graves. Back he goes down to the shore; and there was the beat of oars, and he's off to yon black ship o' hell!"

The boy's teeth showed. "And after that, it wasna one mark wad content me on my sister's grave. I put on other three." Again he traced the pentacle with his heel. ..." Then the storm came, and I went to Ben-nan-Uamh, and watched and watched his ship's light till the morning. Back he never came to Pennygown ... for, look you, there were four marks on her grave, and he daurna! He couldna ... the black one! ... could he? ... with four marks on it? ... By the screigh o' day they hoisted anchor, and up the Kyle she sailed; and I followed her to Ardnacross; then she went past Gualagu, and it was light ... light. I had to be thinking o' home and sleep ... Tach! ... the black one!"

"And what's truly known of Miss Elspeth?"

"*Och! ubh, ubh!* I dinna ken! I dinna ken! ... The kind lady ... the bonnie lady ... she's away ... away!"

There were tears in Alasdair's eyes. "She's away ... away! 'Twas all I coujd make out from Sandy *Cibeir* as he spoke to Munro ... me on one side of the dyke, and they coorying and smoking on the other, when they should have been at their work among the sheep ... the dolts! ... It's among the goats I'll be putting Sandy ... shepherd or no shepherd."

"And that's all you ken about the kind lady, Alasdair?"

"Aye, that's everything ... There was something about kidnapping ... but the memory's gone on me."

"Well, Alasdair, time you were bedded! Home now, and dinna bother about the black ship. She'll sail and sail, and sail foreign, I make no doubt; and they'll never come back to Pennygown Kirkyard, I hope."

"That's fine," said the boy, reassured. But with flashing eyes he added: "But I wish she'd founder deep, and send them drowned among the partans."

"Tuts! laddie, you're hard, hard. Off with you! . . ."

Hare-like, half-crouching, and with sudden skips and bounds, the Catechist's boy went over the brae-face on the flank of Tor-nam-Feinne, making for the moor-track to Aros.

5: Strategy

PONDERING this affair of The Man from the Sea, the Captain returned to his lodging; and at the door met Belle who recounted that Miss Elspeth and Anna MacDougall had come in his absence; but that the young lady had a headache and was resting upstairs.

"She seems in trouble, poor lass. I'm wae for her wi' a sorrow like yon in her eyes," added Belle.

"I was hearing," said the Captain quietly. "Where's Anna?"

Anna's self appeared from behind the door of the porch with a suddenness that was suspicious; she looked a trifle flushed and self-conscious, and her plump hands engaged one another in little nervous movements. "Is it me you were seeking?" she said. "I was just for going down where the gillie was at the skiff there, and him grumbling at a delay he didna count on. I've some word to send back by him to Oskamull. Will you take a turn, Captain?"

The Captain made a grimace and a gallant scrape that set the women smiling. "It's what I should be asking myself, Anna. It's little we see of you nowadays."

Gravity returned instantly, however, when their backs were turned to Miss Belle; and they went down the grassy slope in silence. They were nearing the beach, before either spoke; then the Captain said: "It was really Carsaig, I suppose?"

"Aye," said Anna. "But I'm wishing the lass were here to tell her own mind."

"If she's sore spent and bewildered, she'll no' can do that," said the Captain quietly.

"Oh, it's little enough after a' ... A bairn's ploy."

"Little enough may hold big burdens," said he. "It's a narrow strait under Gualachaolish but there's a strong water yonder when the tide's on the turn."

"And that's true," said Anna "Poor lass! . . It's a ravelled business." Then she told the tale of the night just past; but told somewhat more than she had intended, for she let slip a hint that Carsaig's losses at the gaming were heavy.

"Aye," said the soldier, when Anna had finished. "So that's it ... Hasty love, quick hate!"

"Hasty ... is it?" said she. "I wouldna say it was altogether just that; for there was an old story atween them before he took to wooing Grizel."

"Do you tell me? I'd heard that tale before, but didna think it well grounded ... In that case it's none so simple as I could wish," said he.

"And now her one cry is for Grizel ... Grizel ... And she's fair foundered with the fret and the strain."

"It's clear she must be going back to Draolinn in the end," said he; "but it's the way of it, look you, we must be thinking of ... It's the way of the going home we must be considering ... Should Elspeth come to Grizel or Grizel to Elspeth?"

"To hear you talk," said Anna bitterly, "you'd think Grizel was the perfect one!"

"'Deed, not I ... But she was never o' two minds in her love-affairs like her sister, was she now?"

"I'm no' so sure o' that ... For I can mind well when she kept Garmony daidling after her ... It was only for a month or two last year, look you ... And never a word from him, of course. It hadna got further wi' him than just glowering at her ... the great fool! ... But a body could see."

"And where then was Carsaig?"

"Just at the coming-on stage ... But my lady had an eye for both at the time I speak o'."

"It gets gey difficult this business," said he. "We maun consider well, Anna. But I think I'll be going over to Draolinn now."

Half an hour later he came through the avenue of pines that were roaring with thrashing tops in a northerly gale. As he rounded the hollies of the enclosed garden and became aware of the crying of the waves on Loch Ba close at hand, a gate clicked, and the cloaked figure of Grizel came up to him. "Captain!" Her voice was toneless.

"Oh, my dear!" he cried. "Whatna sorrow is yours! ... Come you indoors, and no' be grieving so sore ... The wind is cold."

"My father!" she said with a sob ... "He's at the end o' life, they say."

"Pity on us! ... The good Draolinn!"

"Garmony's there," she went on, "and the minister, and Dr. MacCulloch ... A stroke, they say ... They dread the worst ... "

"When did it happen? "asked the veteran.

"Late last night ... I've come out of doors, because I'm helpless, and the sight of him was crushing me ... We can do naught, the doctor says ... only wait."

"He kens best," said the Captain. "So e'en let us wait ... We could be walking to keep warm," he added, solicitous; and in silence they trudged off together under the swaying pines. They heard the wind, murmuring far away, as if gathering for assault on this, their sanctuary, and then, losing heart, die on distant corries. But at times it ceased this feinting, and trumpeting defiance, launched its full force on the forest where they sheltered. The river, too, was roaring at its outfall; and on Drumlang beach was the thunderous rhythm of breaking waves.

"It's wild," said the Captain.

"Ah, yes! ... But it's little he'll hear o' storm, the way he lies," she answered dully.

"Poor Draolinn! Many a battle we saw together out yonder, and yet Death ay gave us the go-by."

She took his arm, and over the soft pine-needles they now paced in silent comradeship, back and forth, time and again. In a breathing space of the storm she pressed his arm gratefully; and thinking this softer mood one in which he would find her responsive to his appeal, he said, "And so you've had no word o' her?"

At that he felt a young breast heave, and saw her head bend low. For a little she could make no answer; and when it came, it issued as from parched lips. "Nothing," she said.

"Aye, it's a sore trial, this o' yours," he answered ... "But it wasna just that I was considering for the present."

She caught her breath sharply, and halted. "And what then?" she asked.

"I was wondering in what strange corner o' a dark world poor Elspeth's heart was breaking."

She seized his hands wildly. "Oh, my shame!" she cried, "that I should be talking only of myself ... Is it indeed so wi' Elspeth now, are you thinking?"

"I'm sore mistaken if it's otherwise wi' her this night," said the Captain solemnly. "I ken the lass too well."

Forthwith she gave a little mirthless laugh, and though he could not see her face, he felt that it had again hardened to stony resentment against the errant sister; and so he resumed his pleading.

"Think you she has no longing for her father ... or for you ... this night of all nights? ... Think you she'll shed no tears, poor thing, to be so far from Draolinn?" said he; and his arm stole round her.

She softened instantly and wept outright. "Oh, Elspeth ... wee Elspeth!" she cried, going back in thought instinctively to childhood's days, when she had played protectress to a motherless sister.

The Captain kept silence while her tears flowed freely. Then, "Come, my dear," he said, when this outburst was spent, "let us go in. We'll find her, never doubt you that; we'll find her ... Maybe, even at this moment, she is on her way ... or if not, longing to be coming ... but fearing ... "

"Fearing? What is there to fear?"

"Nought that I can see, but she's young and glaikit ... and not understanding, poor thing!"

"I ken ... I ken! ... Oh, Captain dear," she whispered, "if I might but find her and take her to this heart of mine again, and bring her home ...

the poor lost one ... my dear, my dear! ... Ah, where are you this night ... this night, wee Elspeth, wee Elspeth?" And now she was about to repeat to this old friend the confession she had made to Elspeth in the garden yesterday, but all was so tangled now, that she despaired of making a plain tale of it, and so desisted.

"You're worn out, I'm seeing," said the Captain. "Be you resting now"; and nearing the house just then, he coaxed her indoors.

Subterfuge was ever alien to the Captain, but here now was necessity for it. Already he had played the part of ignorance regarding Elspeth's whereabouts, in order to a softening of Grizel towards the wanderer. The harder task of revealing a pretended discovery of the lost one at a period subsequent to this relenting still awaited him; and, as it involved his acting a part in very literal fashion, he boggled at it. Scheming was not his forte, he told himself, as he stood before a glass in the room allotted to Dr. MacCulloch at Draolinn, contorting his face into various expressions of excited delight which, in view of the chief's illness, he was far from experiencing. But when, half an hour later, the Doctor assured the household that Draolinn's seizure was not the apoplexy that had been dreaded, but only a prolonged fainting-turn, the old soldier felt elated enough to essay a dozen such unwonted tasks as that now before him. And so, ten minutes after the chief's recovery had been announced, you might have beheld the Captain perform an extraordinary series of antics.

He approached the door of the laird's study on tip-toe, and opening it a crack, pulled aside the sheltering curtain and peered in on Grizel sitting, brooding by the fire. He noted the grave features lovingly, even as if she had been daughter to him and not to Draolinn: the little tache of birthmark on the left lower eyelid, the strange quirk at the angle of the mouth, suggestive of the dawning of a smile that seemed never to come to fruition—all the small irregularities that gave liveliness to a face undeniably plain.

"And there she sits," said he inwardly, "the dear lass, so downright sorrowful and so true! and me to be acting a part to her, old fool! ... And yet ... and yet it must be."

He retired to the hall, rumpled his grey locks into a shock of hair standing on end, unloosened his kerchief and a button or two on his coat, and, murmuring to himself, "It's out of here she maun be, before she has time to question," burst into the room with a great appearance of haste. "Good news!" he cried. "We've found her! Get on your things, lass, and come wi' me! I'm off for the carriole ... She's at Killiechronan, I hear, wi' Anna MacDougall ... I had it from Anna herself. Hurry, lass, hurry!"

Dumbfounded, she rose to speak; but he was out of the room before she could utter a word. The smile that awaited birth on her lips broke forth at last—a queer little twitching smile; she followed him instantly, and with brimming eyes, whispered to herself as she sped through the transe to her room: "Elspeth ... wee Elspeth!"

What passed between the sisters that afternoon in the upper chamber at Killiechronan will probably never be known. The Captain More could have hazarded a guess; but for the confidences that accompanied their embraces and their tears he cared not a doit, as he beheld his end secure, when Grizel came down after half an hour and asked if the carriole could take them home instantly.

There was little of note on the journey by the wind-swept shore and through the pines still roaring; and by four o'clock a weeping Elspeth was kissing the worn hands of the old soldier in the hall of Draolinn. "Blessings on you, dear man," she whispered; "and it's just me that's the grateful lass this night."

"You randy!" said he. "To bed with you!

There was a scuffle of skirts on the stairs, and she was barely off with Grizel, when a tug at the sleeve of his old fawn coat brought him face to face with Doctor MacCulloch.

"My compliments, Doctor," said the soldier. "I hear you've brought him back to life."

MacCulloch sighed wearily. "Aye, so you say. But I'm wondering if I havena been too hasty ... Indeed and indeed, it's not often I'm regretting my employ ... but God! you should hear yon ... the oaths of him and the rage of him! You could boil water on his old bald head, he's in such a passion ... It's a sleeping draught he's needing how ... Such language! And he's for calling out Carsaig, to-morrow! Pistols and forty paces; and you and me for seconds, Duncan! ... Whatever can we be doing with a red-hot one like him?" He fingered a stubbly chin with nervous fingers.

The old soldier laughed. "A blind *bodach* wi' a duelling-pistol!" cried he.

"Man, he's thought of everything. He's for having Carsaig ... the eyes of him ... bandaged ...Whatever can we be doing with a rage like yon?"

The Captain laughed again. "What else, but be agreeing with him, Doctor? ... The duel's the very thing, says you. And a composing draught at once to make his finger steadier on the trigger tomorrow, man." He closed an eye in a flicker that might have been a wink.

"Ye've an idea there," cried Doctor MacCulloch, with a preoccupied air and making for the stairs at a trot .."an idea." But he turned on the first step, and came back, with a countenance wistful and imploring. "But his language, Captain! ... Man, could ye no' stay overnight and soother him a bit in the morning."

"Heaven be about us! I'm as tired as you, Doctor, and that's not a little," said the other. "But I'll stay ... No' but what I'm a bit curious too, you'll understand, about the language you speak o'; I havena heard a good swear-word since I quit sogerin'."

By ten next morning the angry chief had breakfasted before the rest of the house was awake, and despite the protestations of the Doctor that he must keep his bed, had installed himself in his study. Doctor MacCulloch interviewed him again there quite early, and retiring hurriedly, met the Captain More in the hall.

"I've had a morning with him ... what a morning, Captain! ... If he missed an apoplexy yesterday, he stands a good chance of hitting one to-day," he confided to the soldier. "Are ye for in to him?"

"Aye, I'll draw the badger," said the Captain cheerily, and knocked at Draolinn's door.

"Come in," roared the laird. "Who the devil's that next?"

"It's MacColl," said the Captain, entering.

Draolinn turned his blind eyes and flushed face on him. "Well, Duncan, what is it? ... I hear you also have been meddling in this business o' last night. It's ended, man. So what are your wants, now?"

Captain MacColl shut the door carefully, and stood with a finger on the knob of the handle. "Oh, my wants, Draolinn, are simple enough. I hear you're none so well; and I but wished to know if there was anything I could do for you."

"By God, there is!" roared Draolinn, half rising, the veins on his forehead swelling.

"And what will that be?" asked the Captain.

"Take yourself to hell out of this, sir ... that's what you can do for me," said Draolinn fiercely, sinking back exhausted in his arm-chair.

"I'll gladly depart," said the Captain, rattling the door handle. "I was never schooled under Cursing Picton, you'll understand, and this is what I'm no' used to."

"General Picton was a gentleman, sir."

"Oho," said the other softly; "so your general was a gentleman, was he? ... Well, it's more than I can be saying of one of his old officers this morning." He had the door open in a trice, and was on the other side of it, before Draolinn's voice rose in a cry of agony:

"MacColl ... MacColl ... MacColl!" The cry rang through a house apparently deserted save for the tall old man in the fawn coat, holding the door from the exterior, and smiling, as if in reminiscence, at the antlered heads round the oak of the hall. There was something of the eerie in a cry thus appealing in a place that seemed so untenanted. "MacColl!" came the high notes of the voice again; and with a rush of feet, a gillie from the gun-room, followed by the cook and Doctor MacCulloch, came down a passage at a run.

"What ails the man?" cried the Doctor. " 'Tis the voice of a spoiled bairn."

"It's just that," said the Captain drily, "and a bairn that has been getting his licks, look you."

"Go in to him, Captain, I beg of you; or the lasses will be in hysterics with his bellowing; and the Lord knows! one patient in Draolinn is enough at a time. Soother him, Captain! ... Soother him!"

"Wait you," said the Captain, and he opened the door a crack. "You were calling, Draolinn?"

"Come here," growled the chief from the depths; and the old man at the door, grimacing knowingly at MacCulloch, disappeared into the study.

"Come here, you limb," cried Draolinn. "You've done me, sir, ab-so-lute-ly ... I'm for crying your pardon, Duncan ... I'm sore trauchled, look you, this last twenty-four hours, and not altogether myself. You'll forgive me, old friend." He put out a groping hand, and the Captain More patted it approvingly. "Sit you down, Duncan ... Man, that last one was a wicked knock."

"Too bad of me, Draolinn; for it's just you have had the sore time ... But now, as you say, it's ended, and not unhappily, I trust."

"Ended," cried the chief, flaring up again. "It'll be ended when I've throttled yon Carsaig fellow ... ab-so-lute-ly."

"You may keep your wind, then, he's by wi't already. Oskamull's been afore ye."

Draolinn started erect. "Fighting, is it?"

"No, nor fighting. 'Twas cards or dice, and Anna tells me Colin has fleeced him fairly. Half Carsaig's lands are gone to the other, she says ... or something like that ... She was too flustered to tell me clearly; but it seems Oskamull has bested him to some tune at the gaming."

"Gad! he's his father's son is Oskamull ... a rare gamester! D'ye mind in Alverga how keen the old one was on the dice, the time Linnell pinked him in the right arm."

"I'm no' like to forget; I was one o' Linnell's seconds."

"A queer business yon, wi' old Oskamull and Linnell, eh, Duncan?"
""Aye, a queer business."

"I've ay wondered as to whether Oskamull— There was a petticoat in the affair, I heard ... a senorita in Robledillo, wasn't there?"

"It's what many folks have said," broke in the Captain stiffly; and if Draolinn could have seen, he would have beheld an angry man before him. "But in a duel, in our day at least, Draolinn, a second's tongue was ay tied."

"Tuts, man! it's no' inquisitiveness, this ... only my old tongue wagging too free, Duncan ... But what a shame that the Duke didna gie you your step when Oskamull had to go!"

"Aye ... a sore blow yon!" said the Captain ... "But it's no' complaining I am; though I think back on't whiles ... No later than last night even, when I read the Duke's letter again, look you! ... 'No promotion,' says he, ' in a regiment where the vacancy is the consequence of a duel ... ' Aye, a good Army order ... but a sore blow, man!"

"Tuts!" said the Chief; and here he roused himself, —" we're back in Spain, when we should be redding up Aros Isle, instead ... Gad! these lasses will be the death of me! ... What make you o't, what make you o't, at all, at all, friend Duncan? Here's Elspeth now ... as fine a lass— Tach! ... Tell me your way o't, for I'm fair bewildered."

Captain MacColl gave a version of Elspeth's adventures that was impeccably dry-as-dust; but do what he might, Draolinn's wrath against Carsaig could not be appeased. "To jilt one is bad enough; but by my way of seeing, it's both of them that have been slighted," cried the chief. "I'll poison the rat!"

"You'll make yourself ill again; and what is to come o' the lasses then? Let me ask MacCulloch to make you a potion."

"MacCulloch!" said Draolinn, in disgust. "I'm half-killed already by yon fellow. He disna ken a whisky-plook from the sma'pock."

"Send him down to Carsaig then wi' a tonic," laughed the Captain. "There's your revenge! For it's something uplifting that same young man will be needing after the go-by the lass has given him."

Draolinn chuckled. "Man, if the Doctor treated him as he has me, he'd have him in the kirkyard in a week's time ... But yon's a queer tale of Oskamull's lifting his lands from him, look you! ... He and his father ... a bonny pair! ... Pretty men both at the gaming, eh, Duncan?"

"They would need to be pretty at something, I doubt; they were gey ill-favoured at aught else," said the Captain More drily; and his soothering finished, he rose to go.

6: Horses in the Night

A MONTH passed, but Carsaig's fine words at Oskamull about seeking service for his sword in the Indies or the Levant came to nothing: he did not even venture South. There were wild tales for a time of his drinking-bouts and mad journeyings hither and yont, on the mainland and throughout the Isle. His extravagance at biddings at markets for bestial and horse was a byword, and it was even said that the Presbytery had him in hand. Doubtless his escapades would have been worse, had not MacLaren, his factor-man, taken to accompanying him of late. The story went that (by way of discouraging a too close attendance) he had led his henchman a dance on his last pilgrimage through the country-side, when every croft and sheiling within twenty miles had been visited. Mysterious whisperings between the chieftain and innumerable old wives and young skelps of lasses roused the curiosity of the man of business; for certainly something of import was to hand. But no interrogatory of the women-folk had any result; the chief had assuredly warned them; and they kept their vow of silence. At the end of it all, Carsaig emerged from a cottage one day with a closed basket in his hand. "Man, Gibbie, here it is at last," said he. "Three weeks' hunting, and not a *cailleach* would part with one until to-day."

"You're beyond me, sir," said MacLaren, a big gaucy man, with a white face and pale lips set in a beard of badger-grey. "What is't you sought?"

"A good clocking hen, Gibbie," said the chief, nudging him in the paunch mischievously— "what else would I be seeking?"

The factor had usually the eyes of a ruminant; here they flashed in anger for an instant; but quickly he became the sleek opportunist again. "What else, indeed, sir—what else?" he assented; and so went off, cursing his squandered hours.

There came a day when chief and doer rode helter-skelter down Glen Leidle on garrons that sweated and flung foam-flake to bridles. They raced through Pennyghael—hunched plaids and flashing hooves and a red cloud of dust all that was visible to the Loch Scridain fishers, busy at a mending of nets on the shore.

"Just that," said Alasdair of Burg, as the rattle and scurry died in the distance. "He'll no' stop till he finishes, will Carsaig ... That, now, will be MacCormack's pony—the one he paid so dearly for at the last market."

"Well, I wasna there, but I'm not for believing Carsaig was so foolish as to give fifty for her," said Para Ban.

"Indeed, and it's just what was given then," said Charlie Crubach; "it was the talk of the fair; but I didna hear the bidding."

"Look you," said Alasdair; "how many were they saying were at the bidding?"

"About forty," said Charlie. "And did you ever see forty people from Aros all together without one fool among them? ... Will you tell me that?"

The doubter tossed his head, and went on with his meshing in silence.

"And Carsaig was at the market," said Alasdair; "and where else would he be, but in the place of the foolish one, I'm wondering? ... There's only one man daft enough to give fifty for a shanker like yon; and that's my gentleman ... There was a day ... but ... *och* ... *och* ... . that's gone: and now he's like one possessed."

Carsaig and his henchman had meantime drawn up at the change-house at Kinloch, and the measures of aquavity were already emptying quickly. "Man, she's the good beast, Gibbie; say what you will of the price," cried the Laird, setting his glass to table with a thump. "Down the glen she came like a deer."

"Like a deer," assented the fat doer, nodding portentously, as if these were the ultimate words of wisdom.

"And by Heavens, it's to-night she'll carry me to Draolinn and back, that same wee horse, or there's no iron on my heel."

MacLaren cocked his ear, but was silent, pondering this new venture.

"Maybe, too," chuckled Carsaig, "she'll carry a double burden on the journey home."

The doer started. His mind was quick now, for he scented danger; and to loosen his master's tongue was instantly his sole employ; so agreeing heartily, he called for further draughts of Ferintosh. "Is it Draolinn?" said he. "Tach! she could well do that. Calgary too, if you wanted it, sir. She's wonderful ... just wonderful ... and swift, too ... like a deer ... yes, indeed!"

Forbes, the landlord, a big, fair-bearded fellow, brought in a fresh supply of drams, and, at the Laird's command, joined the others in a draught. The heat of the day and the hard riding had rendered Carsaig thirsty to a degree; he drank deep and free, and soon was maundering. MacLaren winked confidently to the tavern-keeper, got his assurance of understanding at once in a sleepy smile, and to gossip and drinking they set themselves in real earnest; so that presently the Laird's scatter-brained thoughts were bare to his table-mates.

"I drew the wrong suit last time, lads," said he, stretching long legs and hiccupping. "And now I'm for the other lass ... Oh, she'll come when I raise my pinkie, will Grizel ... like the mermaid to the harper on Scridain. I'll warrant she'll come fast enough!"

"I'll warrant she will," said MacLaren. "Health to the harper!" And thus they toasted and quaffed.

Twilight fell, and still they boozed and boasted; but now the chieftain's tongue failed, and he fell into a doze, head and arms on the sodden trestle-boards; while the factor and Forbes retired to the kitchen peats, and confabbed in Gaelic, whispering with frequent chucklings.

"It's now I'm seeing what he has been after this month past," confided MacLaren ... "soothing and soothing at old-time words: 'It's ill starting what's never ended,' and the like ... and here's the meaning of it at last ... He kidnapped Elspeth, and all he got for't, I'm hearing, was a sore ear from the lady's hand; and now it's her sister he would trepan ... *Och, och*, Iain, it's more than one halter he's weaving, if I'm to be at his shouther this night."

"Never you fear, ille," said Forbes. "He's carrying owre heavy a cargo already, believe me, without the weight of a lass. And he can have as much more of that same ballast as he cares to pay for."

"That's it!" cried MacLaren; "dinna stint the drink; and the later we leave, the better for both our necks, Iain! ... Be thankit! it looks like broken weather, and the stormier the kindlier for me ... A wet halter's ay a slippy one, lad." He nudged Forbes, and his belly shook with laughter suppressed.

It was well on for midnight when Carsaig roused and called for brandy. "Here's a downpour, Gibbie," said he, stepping unsteadily to the window, and looking out on a gusty onset of rain from Glenmore. "Scarcely a night for romanticks, eh? ... a black one and a wet ... But stirrup and saddle, man, all the same ... Haste ye, Forbes, and out with the beasts."

The garrons were brought round, shivering and steaming in the downpour, after their warm stable; the lawing was paid; the door-drink quaffed; and they were off to the Goladoir Ford, riding furiously. Pitch darkness lay on the bog-land through which the drove-track ran, and they slackened speed as they approached the river. For ordinary the stream was brattling noisily; but now it was eerily silent; and this stillness of the flood so imminent, coupled with the distant drumming of hillside waters far in the dark of Glenmore, foretold a spate at the crossing.

"For God's sake, sir, cannily!" cried MacLaren; "for it's swirling bank and brae."

"Not yet, Gibbie," said Carsaig; "but it will be in half an hour, or I'm not Highland."

"Stop you!" cried the doer. "You'll no' need to be crossing at all, at all, sir; for I've some news I'd have given you earlier, had you no' been so jinky at the riding ... Miss Grizel left Draolinn this morning."

Carsaig turned on him, furious. "Man, Gibbie, but a bit of gurly water's a grand jog to your memory," he said. "You lie, you dog!" And he slashed at the fat jowl of his servitor with his riding-switch.

The henchman quivered in every fibre; for an instant his hand sought a knife-haft in his waist-belt; but he recovered his composure quickly, and said in a quiet voice: "Have it your own way, sir. 'tis easy proved. It's only twenty mile to Draolinn, once the ford is crossed."

"You dare me?" cried the Laird, and dismounting in haste, he descended to the brink of the stream, and passed a hand over the face of a boulder till it reached the water's level. "The Tinker's Stone is only half-covered," said he.

"There's no footing for a beast that size then," said the factor.

"Man, I've done it at three-quarters on as small a mount, Gib," laughed Carsaig, as he regained his saddle. "Follow, follow!" he cried; and the next moment the garron surged into the sweeping current, and swinging head upstream for some minutes, drifted to a footing at a bend on the further shore, and rattled up a gravel bank. Almost automatically MacLaren followed and attempted to repeat this manoeuvre.

"Haud up your kyte," laughed the laird from the steep bank above. "Man, how I wish it were daylight, and me seeing the water bowffing at that wame o' yours."

The doer cursed him underbreath; but just then his horse took ground, and instantly he was the complaisant one, affecting to enter heartily into the joke. "Och," said he as he joined his chief, "there was nae breaking o' waves on't; they just played blaff and gaed by."

"Man, you're the droll one," hiccupped Carsaig, well pleased. "Tell me the truth now, lad; where's her ladyship?"

"She's at Moy, for all I know to the contrar'," said the factor. "At least, that was the gossip ... Thursday was the day fixed, and that was yesterday — for it's now past twelve, I jalouse ... And Forbes was telling me he saw a riding-party cross the Maam at noon."

"And what's to hinder a ride to Moy, you dog?" cried the chief. "It's one to me, Draolinn or Moy: she's in the Isle, anyway ... Follow you still, squire o' mine!"

He went off at a canter, and coming to the crossroads, turned to the right, on the Glenmore track to Moy. The heavy man followed as best he could, muttering malediction in a wet beard, blundering on over scree and pool that traversed this track through the great cleft in the hills. In the corries the wind whispered and whinnied; and great sheets of rain soused horses and riders till plaid and saddle were sodden, yet still the garrons' hooves danced on untiredly to the tempest's wild music.

By the fank where the route from Maam Clachaig turns off (just where, in the henchman's tale, Miss Grizel had passed some hours earlier), Carsaig drew up, awaited his follower, and sidling his steaming mount close, laid his hand on the dripping shoulder of MacLaren.

"Oh, Gibbie," said he thickly, "isn't it me that's the woefu' man? ... It's my duty I'm for doing by this woman, Grizel MacLean; for it's long and long since she had my troth." He lurched a trifle unsteadily. "Still-and-on, duty or no, it's Elspeth that has my liking."

"And that's true, indeed, sir," agreed MacLaren hastily. "She has your liking; and with reason too ... a fine lass."

"Maybe ... maybe, Gibbie, but"—he hiccupped— "I'm a man of conscience; and it's Grizel has my bond."

"She has your bond, sir, that's true! Miiss Grizel has it."

"But Elspeth—(Man, but you're soaking wet, *ille*. Have you been in the burn?)—Elspeth's the rare rogue, eh, you dog?" He prodded his doer's fat flank, and roared merriment to the floods and the darkness, while he turned his horse's head uncertainly. "There's Draolinn and there's Moy; there's Elspeth and there's Grizel; there's my liking and my word," said he.

MacLaren swung round his garron on its hindquarters instantly. "Then go to your liking," he cried through a squall that sent scuds of rain to their necks 'twixt bonnet and plaid. His mount stamped at a touch of heel; the movement startled the bemused chieftain to action at once; and back they thundered on the track by which they had come, with shoulders cowering to escape the blasts that whooped at a follow-on.

It was amazing how the horses kept their feet over loose boulders and rock-ribs, swept bare of earth by torrents new-born from the bog and heather of the hills that were like walls for immediacy and steepness; yet the dazed riders clung to their seats and tore on. Past the cross-roads at the divide of the Goladoir track, and down to the shore of Loch Beg they galloped. Ardvergnish clachan showed like a taper in the night, and that of Dererach was only to be recognized by the faint acrid odour of peat smoke, as they swept past. Never a halt till they came to the rise where the white walls of Kilfinichen Church showed ghostly.

"This was to have been the place," said Carsaig, stretching a damp hand as if in invocation; "and, by Heaven! 'tis here she should have come ... but for yon diceing-cogie ... My curses on the diceing-cogie, Gibbie."

"You were saying, sir," said MacLaren, coming up, hard-breathed.

"How many miles to Draolinn, Gibbie?"

"Twenty, sir."

"We'll make them short, my buckie! ... But first ... look at this! ... here's holy ground ... Put you up a bittie prayer now for our success ... Good lad, good lad!" He laughed uproariously; and then checked in a sudden calm, broken only by the ever-recurring hiccup. "Gibbie," he said solemnly, "I'm no' sure but I'm blaspheming ... For we'll no' can pray for aught but our duties, I fear ... And it's coming on me that my duty's to the lady at Moy, whatever liking I may have for the lass at Draolinn ... Pity on me! If only now I had the good advice of the Capta in More in this ... Yon's the man for that same ... But *ochanoch*, I'm fell sure it's my duty he'd be having me do ... and weary on the duty!"

MacLaren was sodden, and utterly outworn; but he brightened like a man shown suddenly bed and board and light and warmth in some invisible caravansary. "Just that," said he to the unsteady form, moving uneasily in the darkness, "then go you to your duty, as the good Captain would wish you." His heel prodded his poor garron's side as he spoke; the tired brute's hooves played cut-diamond on the pebbles, and startled Carsaig into a wheeling of his mount likewise. MacLaren clicked loudly with his tongue; and at once the garrons' instincts as to Kinloch stables lent new life to their heels, as they went helter-skelter southwards again, while the drunken chieftain whooped aloud for joy at the pace they made. Barely half a mile of this gallop had been run, however, when the Laird's pony shied, and the factor's mount had almost collided with it ere it was drawn up.

"Shield us! ... There's a light in the kirk-yard, sir," cried the doer. "And I'm not for passing it ... Be sure it's the little people of the hills!" Carsaig laughed drunkenly. "Little people or big," said he, "they'll tell me their business before I'm five minutes older, Gibbie ... Maybe they'll sell me a love-charm." And chuckling, he dismounted. "Come on, *laochain!*"

But MacLaren sat rock-fast, save for chittering teeth. "It's not to my liking, Carsaig," said he. "Get you on, if you will, and I'll mind the beasts."

The chief leapt a runnel, and took to a patch of bracken and brier between him and the kirkyard wall, advancing as noiselessly as the dark and his unsteady limbs would allow. He stumbled and cursed once or twice; but the light remained constant in a halo of rain-lances; and at last he reached the mouldering dyke and peered over. A lanthorn was set on a flat tombstone, sheltered in part from the wet gale by a headpiece reciting the names of the dead below. In front of it lay a sheathed cutlass; and seated on the end of the slab was the figure of a man in a cloak and glazed hat, who was busy scraping at the lichen-filled lettering on the monument with a gulley-knife. While he worked he sang a ditty to himself in a low and pleasant voice:

"We are three brethren come from Spain
All in French garlands;
We are come to court your daughter Jean,
And adieu to you, my darlings.

A bride, a bride she shall not be
All in French garlands;
Till she go through the world with me,
And adieu to you, my darlings."

The lanthorn rays lit the dark regular features of a young man, who suddenly looked up at a chuckle from Carsaig. Instantly he was on his feet, and seizing the lamp, turned it full on the intruder. "Is it you, Humphrey?" he asked, peering. "Isn't the cutter gone yet?"

"No, nor Humphrey," said Carsaig, leaping the wall, and brushing through a patch of nettle till he faced the stranger. "Nothing so Sassenach, my pretty man ... What's your business here?"

"His Majesty's," said he of the cloak and lanthorn. "What's yours, sir?"

"Only a Highlander's, whose forbears' bones lie in every kirkyard in Aros ... And by the same token that's a memorial to one of them you're after spoiling ... Put down your knife, sir."

The stranger had stooped to lift the weapon; and the chief advanced on him with nought but his riding switch; but stumbling, he fell fair across the tombstone and against the lanthorn, extinguishing it. The darkness that ensued for both was, by contrast, that of the pit to the fairy-like circle of lit turf, rain-gemmed and laced with shining gossamer, in which they had stood but a moment ago. Carsaig felt the grip of a wrestler pressing him face downwards on the tombstone the next moment, and at first thought that a combat was imminent of thew and sinew only.

But after the first surprise he recognized that a cautious groping of the other's left hand meant nothing else than the securing of the cutlass he had formerly noted as lying on the slab. Its pommel now bruised his lower ribs; he had therefore a clearer idea as to its whereabouts than its former owner; instantly he wrenched his right arm free, rolled side-wise to clear the weapon, and with an effort secured it. The other divined his success from the noise of the metal of the hilt as it rasped across the face of the tomb, and immediately disengaging himself, sprang free of his antagonist. Carsaig lurched to his feet, scant of breath; and unsheathing the weapon in a confusion of rage, took a sweep at random in the dark. Instantly came the shock of a blow; his wrist dirled; there was a faint cry; and a man's body fell into his arms, and went limply to earth.

The chieftain, suddenly sobered by these happenings, stood dumbfoundered for a moment, then dropped the cutlass, and stumbled back through nettle and brier to where his doer sat, shivering with cold and dread. "Cry up Dererach, Gibbie, and bring a litter at once," said he hoarsely. "I've killed your fairy, or come next door to it."

"But—" said MacLaren.

"On with you!" cried the laird, laying hands on the bridle of the other's garron, and turning the beast's head, "or, by God! I'll serve you a like stroke."

The factor went off in the dark and the rain instanter. "Now, look you, Gilbert," he muttered to himself as he rode, "he maun be rotten-ripe for the gallows-tree, that one; for I fear the halter's no' made that will slip twice in the same night."

Carsaig stood to watch him go; then buried his face in trembling hands. "Where will it end?" he groaned: "for now I'm like one possessed." He turned eastwards, and looking to the hills between him and Draolinn, lifted arms as in invocation. "Elspeth, Elspeth! "he cried: "Oh! this, surely, is no longer Alan MacKinnon."

7: The Man from the Sea

NEXT day the downpour had ceased; but succeeding it came a constant smir of rain and a seeping fog. At times there could be seen from Dererach, where the sick man lay, a swatch of Loch Scridain and a bit of scrub on the Aird; or the lower slopes of Benmore would unveil, and reveal, for an instant only, the boiling mist wreaths pouring from the high corries. Outside Seumas Og's cottage a group of fishers in dripping tarpaulins took the poor shelter of a peat stack, and awaited tidings of the progress of the wounded stranger. At length Seumas appeared clad in tarpaulin also, and in airs of importance.

"It's white he is and cold, and sighing and sweating, and the eyes of him like sloes; and it's not one spider's web will stop all the bleeding on yon head. I'm fearing that it's here he'll end, poor lad."

"From whom got he the knock, think you?" ventured a voice from among the group's second line.

"Well, he's revenue, it seems. At least, that's what Carsaig jalouses from his uniform."

This appeared to explain much, for quite soon the gathering began to melt away into the encircling vapours, divers excuses being proffered by this one and that, until at last only Finlay of Gribun remained — an old fisher with ragged beard and a pock-marked face that got him the name of the Gilliebreac.

"Revenue?" said Finlay. "Then whatever was he doing on this side, Seumas, when the salt was coming in so fast to Loch-na-Keal all last night? ... It was a great cargo the Irishman landed I'm telling you; and the carts waiting him for days."

"Aye, man; but I'm fearing, with a Government officer's head staved in, it'll be the dear salt, Finlay."

"You have there the true saying, *ille* ... Fifteen for the bushel's high, but none too dear, when it comes to keeping clear of the gallows; and even if we never pickled another herring, we'd still like to be in the land of the living, look you ... But where can the young man's ship be, at all, at all?"

"There you have me ... All I know is that she's the handy cutter and a ranger for speed. They're telling that she chased O'Brien's schooner from the Ross to Rathlin last trip, and just missed catching him ... *Och, och!*

weary on their salt-tax; for it has the good fishing spoiled on us, and the fine men broken or killed at the running of this Irish stuff."

"What beats me," said the Gilliebreac, "is this fellow coming here all by his lonesome ... Was he for spying, think you?"

"I wouldna wonder now; for they're saying he was venturesome; and that he's been in every change-house in the Isle this month back ... and always the ready tongue and the open purse ... He's the strange one anyway ... And what Carsaig could have to do with him in Kilfinichen graveyard in the middle of the night, beats me."

"By the same token," said the other, "here comes Carsaig, and with him the leech ... And doesna the old one look droll on horseback? It's the first time I've seen him higher than the beast's nose, *ille*."

The chief and the Doctor dismounted and hurried indoors; but soon after Carsaig reappeared, his face a trifle wan. "I had as lieve wait here, Seumas, even if it's wet," said he. "Yon's no' work I've any skill of," and he wiped a perspiring brow. "I wasna made for a doctor I'm thinking."

"Nor me," said the fisherman emphatically.

In half an hour MacCulloch emerged, pulling on his coat. "A big scalp-wound, wi' concussion but no fracture," said he. "He'll do ... But he needs a month's rest before we dare move him, Carsaig."

The chief swore in relief, and was fervently shaking the Doctor's hand by way of thanks, when they were startled by a high voice coming from the sick-chamber:

"Come back" (it sang), *"come back, you courteous knights,*
All in French garlands;
Clear up your spurs, and make them bright,
And adieu to you, my darlings"

"No doubt," said the Doctor, "he'll rave a trifle now and then."
The singing began again:

"Here's a poor widow from Babylon,
With six poor children all alone;
One can bake, and one can brew,
One can shape ...

The song trailed away; but a speaking voice ensued: "Oskamull ... Oskamull!" it said; then silence, save for the soothing murmurs of Silis, the wife of the fisher.

"Where got he that name?" cried Carsaig.

MacCulloch pursed his lips and smiled. "I doubt not but he's heard of the chief's fair-trading in salt."

"Salt be hanged!" said Carsaig, turning a wild eye on him. "It's not the first time, I ken, that smuggled stuff's been hid among graves ... But it was on the tomb of old Aeneas of Oskamull this fellow was seated last night, a-scraping at the lettering, when first I fell in with him."

"Well, I give the puzzle up. He has a fine taste in nursery-rhymes, and in kirkyards, it may be; but my business is with his calvarium, and not with his wagging tongue ... We'll get sense from him in a day or two, and then we'll make him out ... Patience, Carsaig ... patience."

"I'd better warn Oskamull; and see he gets his bolls well hidden," said the chief. "I'll letter him this very day."

The sick man made little headway for the first week but after this Doctor MacCulloch gave a decidedly hopeful outlook. "A man cannot have his brain shaken like a pea in a bladder, if only for a moment, look you," said the surgeon to Carsaig, "and no' be the worse for it. But he'll settle down now, I expect ... What's real droll, however, is his fancy for these children's rhymes. To-day it was '*Merry-ma-tanzie*,' and yesterday, '*Glasgow ships come sailing in ... come sailing in*,' as natural as if he were a bairn."

"Talking of ships," said Carsaig, "where's his own? ... They might well be foundered a week ago, for all the care they take of their master."

"No, nor foundered," said the Doctor. "From what I can make out from his talk in delirium, he was often ashore on a splore of some kind for days at a time ... Spying on the salt-runners, I doubt not ... By-the-bye, I've got his name now ... Linnell ... Philip Linnell,"

"Shield us!" cried Carsaig. "How came you by that? ..."

"From his own lips," said MacCulloch. "He's sensible enough at times, you'll understand."

"By Heaven, here's a light at last, then," said the chief, excited. "For it was a Linnell that gave old Oskamull the sorely smashed wing in a duel years ago out yonder in Spain, and made him leave the service."

"Because of the damaged arm?" asked MacCulloch quietly.

"There was more in it than that, I'll acknowledge," said Carsaig, a trifle ruffled.

"So I was thinking," said the surgeon drily.

"Tach!" said the laird, "it was only ... it was nothing ... nothing ... War Office intrigues and Bathurst's spite, I'll engage ... My uncle had the dour enemies in the Army ... But what ails this tyke that he's rooting round the graves of the MacCalmans like a French poodle after truffles? ... Linnell! ... And now it's sorry I am 'twas only the back of the blade he got that night, the dog!"

"Hush, man, hush! with your wild talk," said the Doctor. "The thing's bad enough as it is; but if young Oskamull gets your way of it, there will be more duelling ... It's a ravelled business; but I wouldna say but somebody can untousle it ... There's Captain MacColl now; he was a second to Linnell—this youth's father—in yon same duel in Spain ... Take your story to him."

Carsaig gloomed. In his cups, a week ago, he could have faced the Captain More's keen eyes; but, sober, the memory of his recent escapade with Draolinn's daughter gave him little stomach for an encounter with so close a friend of hers as the old soldier.

"Look you," said he, "I've much business these days with my doer, Doctor; and for myself a journey to Killiechronan is not to be thought of for the present ... But what's to hinder yourself, when you go back that way, stepping over to the Captain's, and telling him the tangle we're in ... He's the big man and the wise ... although, mark you, a bit severe on us young folks."

MacCulloch laughed cheerily as he thought of this sudden business assiduity of Carsaig. "Well, well," said he, "I'll take it up with the big one. There's little in it, I fancy; but we'll see."

He told his tale that same evening at Killiechronan in the high upper room, after the MacDonald sisters were bedded, and while the old soldier and he sat late by the ingle, discussing a toddy. "It's clear that Linnell's work is the stopping of this running of salt cargoes," said the Doctor. "But now it would seem he has also some private employ—this graveyard business."

"And it's not the first time he has been at that," said the Captain More; "for Alasdair Beg saw him at the same trick at Pennygown one night five weeks ago ... Yet why, even if he's Charlie Linnell's son, does he go poking round the tomb of the man his father helped to destroy? ... It's a queer business; but it's plain I must come into it, for I've no desire to see the sons carrying on the old feud ... And myself second to his father in his duel with old Aeneas, as you say! ... Indeed and indeed, I'm fearing that young Oskamull will be the red-hot one if he hears of your friend's interference with his father's burial-place."

"He kens nothing as yet," said the Doctor, "nor will he; I warned Carsaig against too free a tongue with him."

It was a full fortnight before the Doctor gave permission for the Captain to see the patient. But one of the rare days of sun came, and the veteran rode over to Dererach, and found the invalid out-of-doors, drinking in the good air from loch and glen with gusto. He was a trifle limp; and his bandaged head and thin white face were evidently serving as a peep-show and bogey all in one for a group of tow-headed children of the clachan, who were finding constant need to cross the patch of grass in front of him at a safe distance—slow, shy and observant in the first part of their journey; then with fast heels and flying skirts in the latter part of the adventure. Captain MacColl was introduced by Seumas Og (with the airs of importance now usual to him in all that pertained to his guest) as "one of the preencipal men in the place"; and was given a chair beside the sick man.

Linnell smiled somewhat self-consciously as they shook hands. "Sir," said he, "your kindness in coming here denotes you. Your name is not unfamiliar to me, for my father used often to speak of Captain MacColl. I expect you've divined whose son I am."

"There's no need to say more," said the Captain; "you're the very spit of Charlie Linnell"; and straightway made inquiry as to the young man's health. Would it be long before he could travel twenty miles in a post-chariot as far as Killiechronan? He must have lodging more suitable, and where else but with his father's old comrade?

Young Linnell smiled at the veteran's eagerness. "You're very kind, sir, but I'm already covenanted to convalesce at a place called Draolinn with the chief there ... a blind old gentleman I'm told." He lifted a note from the plaid on his lap. "The gillie's already half-way over the hill with my acceptance ... provisional, of course, on the Admiralty not recalling me."

"The devil take Draolinn for forestalling us," said the Captain. "It's at times like these that Highland hospitality gets a bit tiresome ... But I've little doubt he'll make you kindly welcome, for he also knew your father ... Besides he's no friend to the salt-runners."

"Well, I can hardly say I'm their enemy," said the young man ... "I'm only doing my duty by Government, and take little interest in the merits of this quarrel over the tax ... And so Draolinn also knew my father? Probably he guessed who I was as soon as my name got abroad ... I'm grateful none the less to you, sir, for your kind offer ... indeed my indebtedness is to many, since my mishap."

"How came it about this accident of yours?" said the Captain bluntly. "You'll pardon my abruptness; but I've good reason for asking ... And where's your cutter?"

"Refitting at Greenock, while I'm supposed to be busy making a few observes in this business of the smuggling here ... a task little to my mind, I can assure you."

"Whatever Draolinn may say," cried the Captain, "this tax is monstrous ... And I can well believe your heart's not in your work ... You know how things stand here? ... Salt's fifteen shillings to the bushel—a price the people can't afford—and yet salt they must have for their herring-pickling ... Last year the catch was big—a fortune for most—but it had to rot for lack of the wherewithal to cure it."

"Isn't salt duty-free at any custom-house on the mainland?" protested Linnell.

"Duty-free if you travel fifty miles to the nearest station of customs and take oath the salt's not to be used for aught but curing ... "

"I know there's hardship ..."

"And then you must give a bond that's not discharged, until you've come back home, caught your herring, salted them, and returned with the cured fish and the surplus salt to prove to my gentlemen of the customs that you've used it all lawfully ... Four journeys of fifty miles between the customs and Loch-na-Keal ... two hundred in all ... If the weather's dirty, of course it adds an extra hundred; for then your salt gets wet and useless before you reach home, and you must go back again for a dry cargo ... Oh, it's a wonderful government, isn't it?"

"As bad as that?" said Linnell; "then I fear I had not fully envisaged all the facts."

"The thing's an iniquity!" cried the Captain More.

"Well, it's never been work after my heart, but now it's less so than ever ... I joined in the line, you see; yet they take a lieutenant here and there just as they please, for this preventive work, willy-nilly."

"Tach!" said the Captain, "I'm not blaming you. You have your duty ... But, leave that, and look at this ... I was your father's friend when he was in life; and as your father's friend, let me have straight talk with you ... Now it wasna salt you were seeking in the kirkyard when you got the knocked head?"

"Well, no," said the young man, flushing and smiling as in reminiscence ..." not at the exact moment ... But half an hour earlier, my men and I were seeking salt even there ... and found it too; aye and with some brandy to boot."

"You tell me!" cried the Captain.

"Yes, the graveyards are favourite hiding-places with these fellows. We got six bags and twelve kegs among the nettles at the north wall yonder."

"Aren't they the bold ones now ... these smugglers!" said the veteran.

"My men took the stuff down the glen to the cutter ... leaving me behind ... She was due to refit at Greenock, while I was to remain in the Isle here, and keep an eye on things till her return ... I stayed on in the graveyard that night after my people had gone in order to have a look at the old head-stones."

"A strange hobby surely?" said the Captain sceptically ... "A wet night, and you peering with a lanthorn all alone among dead men's bones! ... I'd advise you to seek a healthier recreation in future."

"I fear I don't follow you," said the youth.

"Then, this is how I'm seeing it ... You're in a strange land, and I'd have you evade further calamity. Do you know that you were found misandling the tomb of a man your father brought down in a duel in the Peninsula; and that man's son even now in this very isle? ... You're in the Highlands, mark you; and we're a fiery people."

Again the pale lips smiled. "I know all is as you say, sir," said Linnell, "save that there was no mishandling. I but removed some moss from a description of the many virtues of the dead, in order to a better deciphering."

"For why?"

An air of brooding fell on the young man, and a glow came to his brown eyes. He moved uneasily in his chair, and his face flushed a trifle. "Oh, I don't know ... A fancy haply. You'll laugh at me, I'm sure."

"For why?" asked the Captain More again, his steady eyes on every movement of the other.

"Why?" said the youth a trifle testily—" why, Captain MacColl? ... Well, then, because I'm for ever wondering at the tangled splendour of things, at the stars and the seas, and the songs of little children—at life and death, and Oh! I'm a poor hand at revenue work, sir, I do assure you."

"What else?" said the old man relentlessly.

"Need you ask? ... Here was I cast up as by chance on an isle remote ... And old stories of my father's telling came back to me. I remembered that it was here should lie the grave of one who had long ago sought to kill him, while he in the self-same instant had striven to compass that man's death ... A strange thing old hatreds! ... And myself, unborn then, may now look down on the poor dust of both ... Shall I not then look well and ponder long?"

The mood of the speaker was infectious. "Shield us!" cried the Captain. "Have you not there the miracle, since that's the way you're putting it? ... Myself, I'm wondering often in the same way, but never finding words for it, look you."

The sailor's mood changed suddenly from passionate absorption in his theme, and he laughed gaily. "Beware then it goes no further than words, Captain, this same philosophy; for as likely as not you'll pay for it with a sore head like others before you ... Look at mine. Even now it begins to whirl a trifle, and it's time I lay down, I fear. I beg of you to excuse me." He rose to his feet, and extended a thin hand.

The Captain smiled too. "Well, well," said he, "if you will choose midnight (and wet at that) for your ploys in Kilfinichen kirkyard, you must just take your risks. Though why you should go there after dark on so innocent a task beats me." He hesitated, finger on chin, and then resumed in a matter-of-fact tone: "I opine you got off better the night you went to the graves at Pennygown." It was a very clear grey eye that now rested on the sailor; and the lips of the speaker no longer smiled.

Linnell started at the words, but did not lose countenance. "Pennygown?" said he. "So that's also in your knowledge, you wonderful man! ... I do believe this isle's enchanted, Captain, and you the wizard of it ... But hear Silis' tongue scolding me! ... I must be in now, or the Doctor will have a fine tale of my disobedience and what not, when he comes ... Pennygown's story must wait for another occasion, Captain MacColl."

They shook hands and parted, the sick man moving feebly indoors, while the veteran mounted, and rode off slowly. He turned in the saddle at a little distance and looked hard at the facade of the cottage, with the air of one counting on seeing a face at some of its windows. But there appeared no sign of the enigmatic occupant at any of the deep-set embrasures ... no visage smiling sardonically, as he half expected. "Tach!" he said, finally, as in reproof of his suspicions. "He maun be all right ... he's Charlie Linnell's boy."

8: Taghairm

THE second meeting of the stranger and the Captain More took place at Draolinn one fine day, some three weeks later. They sat on a fallen bole at the edge of a pinewood, and looked out contentedly on the sunlit waters of Loch Ba. Here was sanctuary indeed for sickness and for eld; and peace and healing came with the gentle hill-winds, the noise of falling waters, and the cries of distant sheep. The young man had doffed his bandage at last; and no trace of his recent illness now remained, save the pallor of his grave features. He wore his sea-cloak, and this, he declared, on such a day of sunshine and warmth was nought but the badge of the invalid. Yet Miss Elspeth had so decreed, and there was no gainsaying her.

"She's not easy to withstand, I'll allow," said the Captain; "I've tried it more than once. She's through ither, as we say in the north."

"She's ... she's ..." (the pale face flushed self-consciously) "... well, she's Elspeth," concluded the young man haltingly.

The Captain More smiled. "I don't think you could better it," said he. "She's a' that."

Then they both laughed at the impasse they had discovered, and were silent for a space, regarding the lapping waters on the shingles below them, as if probing the profounds of some great philosophic truth they had happened upon in company together. But their meditations were suddenly broken in upon by a scamper of tiny feet, and a half-grown kitten, known as Jock in the Draolinn kitchen, sped down the beach, and beholding them, turned at bay. Following this apparition came a crashing in the elder brake, and an elfin figure darted on the little beast, and clutched it. In the same instant the Captain More had his arm out and grasped the newcomer by the coat-collar.

"It's you, Alasdair," said he. "This looks well now; for it's twice running, of late, I've found you astir in the daytime. You'll be for giving the go-by to the night-prowling, I'm hoping, and taking a taste of the sun now and then."

The boy did not answer, but stared dully at Linnell.

"Have no fears," said the old man; "he's a friend o' mine and Miss Elspeth's." Yet Alasdair still regarded the stranger in steady fashion, without replying. "Tut-tut! ... your manners, laddie," said the Captain.

"I'm no' feared," said Alasdair, at last. "I ken him ... He's the man that sings on Drumlang shore at nights to Miss Elspeth ... I like his singing fine ... They didna see me."

Captain MacColl's eyebrows went up; and Linnell flushed once more.

"I like yon one best ... 'Seven long years,' " said the boy, hugging the kitten close, and drawing near to the youth. "Sing it to Alasdair."

"It's only a children's rhyme, my boy," said Linnell; a reply meant chiefly for his older auditor.

"I ken," said Alasdair. "She said that was why she liked it ... And I liked it fine ... fine; but what for I dinna ken ... Sing it to Alasdair."

A trifle flustered at the revelation, the sailor cleared his throat and sang a verse in a fair baritone:

"Seven long years I served for thee,
The glassy hill I clamb for thee,
The bluidy shirt I wrang for thee;
Wilt thou no' wauken and turn to me?"

"It's fine, isn't it, Jock?" appealed Alasdair to the kitten now purring on his knee, as he sat on the bole by the side of the Captain More.

"What for the kitten?" asked the old soldier. "Are you thinking of a *taghairm*, Alasdair?"

The daft boy grinned, unreplying.

"*Taghairm*?" asked Linnell.

"We have him there, Alasdair," said the Captain. "He kens everything about us in Aros, he thinks; but there we have him ... Tell him about Lachie and Alan long ago ... A story for a song's no' a bad bargain."

"I'll tell him," said Alasdair; "but I'll no' tell Jock ... Hame wi' you!" he cried, and setting the kitten to earth, he sent it scampering into the shrubbery. "It's the only *taghairm* I ever heard of," said he: "but this is it! —

"It was years and years ago; and there was Alan, and there was Lachlan; and on a night o' nights they started a *taghairm* at the mouth of Glenforsa. They wanted to ken something that they didna ken.

"It was near the year's end, and it was stormy and wet, and the Forsa was in spate. And the spate grew and grew, and swept and swept, and broke the banks at the height of it, just under Callachly. The tacksman at Rhoail was drowned, they're saying, and his body never seen. Yon was the wild flood, the trees sticking out o' the swift water like big wet feathers, and the drowned sheep, bloated as big as meal-sacks, caught in their branches. Like Noah's flood was that same; and after the water had gone down, and the sun come out, like the plague in Egypt it was, with the stink from the carcases in the tree-tops yonder.

"There were wild-cats in the glen in those days." The boy looked round furtively to see if Jock were near, but finding no sign of him, he went on.

"Wildcats ... and they're saying they fed on that same carrion ... And the people of the Isle, they're saying, were shooting them with arrows, or trapping them.

"Alan of Leitir was at the trapping, and so was Lachlan of Scallasdale. Alan was a little man with a wee face, and staring eyes and a big brow, and as bald as Ben Talla; he was the silent one, they're telling. Lachlan was a big red-haired fellow with golden eyes; and he was the one to talk.

"Now there was a steading at Callachly, and for years and years no one was tenant there, for that same was the place where big Murdo's ghost used to be walking on nights o' tempest. But where else did Lachlan and Alan meet for the trapping? And people were saying they were the great trappers, and making a fortune from the furs o' wild-cats that they were selling on the mainland ... It's busy they were under cloud o' night, bringing peat-creels on pony-back: and in the daytime they would be searching the shore for drift-wood. Folk were saying there was more than peats in the creels; for a cottar o' the Big Glen had passed them one night on the shore-road after dark, and heard something in a creel crying out like an evil spirit. And then there was talk of witches! ... One day Lachlan the son of Neil, said to Alan the son of Ian: ' It is to-night we will begin.' But Alan shook his head. ' Well then, neither to-night nor to-morrow, *ille?*,' said Lachlan; 'but let it be between the two ... ' And Alan nodded.

"So by eleven that night they went into the big barn of many rafters at Callachly, and kindled a great fire. Peats began it, but it was the red pine and the fine drift-wood that gave the big blaze. Oh! it's just there was the great fire." The daft boy's hands were outstretched as if to the warmth he saw in his vision of the tale.

"They worked hard at it, sweating sore in the smoke; and always Lachlan talking and cursing; but Alan with never a word.

"Then they brought out two strong turn-spits of iron, and many chains of fine steel, and got them ready. And at the slack of midnight they carried in a creel from the big house, and" (he glanced round as if to catch the bright eyes of the kitten) "and they took from it a live wild-cat, and chained it with the fine chains to the turn-spit, and set it by the fire, and Alan turned the spit, and there was the wild-cat roasting alive ... It was Lachlan did the chaining to the spits; and they're saying it was easy work, for the beasts were starving and weakly ... And always while Alan was throng at the roasting with one spit, the noisy fellow was tying on another cat to the second spit.

"The first cat yelled until it died, and then they roasted a second, and they're saying it was this one that made the sore wailing, so big it was, nearly the length of Alan himself when its tail hung down. But it wasn't till the roasting of the third beast that an evil spirit in the form of a black cat, came into the barn, and sprang to the rafters, and spat at Alan and cried: 'Alan, son of Ian, that is bad usage to be giving a poor cat ... ' Alan never spoke, but just looked up at him with his big eyes, and then went on with his turning the spit, while the poor brute grat sore ... 'Lachlan, son of Neil,' said the black cat on the rafters, 'that is bad usage for a cat ...' Lachlan gave him his answer. 'It is not cold he is anyhow ... Come you down and try ...' And Lachlan said to Alan: 'Be you turning swiftly, *ille*, and heed not the black fellow ... Stop not you, or the spell is broken.'

"So Alan turned the spit swifter than ever; and the great black cat on the rafters took to wailing, and there came other evil spirits in the form of black cats up beside him on the rafters, and called out loudly, lamenting sore; and what with their crying and the roasting one shrieking, there was a great noise and a terrible in the house at Callachly ... 'Turn you, turn you!' cried Lachlan, tying on another fellow that spat and scratched as he put the chains round him. And Alan turned harder than ever; and the sore lament of the wild-cats and the cries of them could not be held within the four walls of Callachly, and the whole Glen was filled with the noise.

"At last a great black cat that was like a calf for size, called down from the rafters: 'Alan, son of Ian, if you cease not before my big-eared brother come, it's just you will never see Paradise ... ' And then Alan spoke for the first time: 'My hand is to my task,' said he; 'and finish it will I, even though all Hell came to me ...' And again the cats roared wi' greetin' till the Hill of the Two Winds echoed back to them.

"They kept the spits turning for four nights and four days, and at last every rafter was crowded with black cats wailing and begging them to stop, and all the Isle was aquake with the noise and the yells of them. The crofters up the Glen and all along the shore kept shut doors, and prayed night and day, fasting—for those were the days o' real fasts they're saying—and they were thinking the Judgment Day was on them, for the roars of the black fellows could be heard over in Morvern. But Alan, son of Ian, and Lachlan, son of Neil, would not stop.

"Then the Hairy-Pawed One came in the form of the biggest black cat of all, and it was Him Lachlan and Alan wanted; and when they got Him there, they asked Him the question they were for putting to Him. But what that was I never heard, and what answer they got nobody kens ... And that's the end of it." The boy sat hunched, breathing fast, and staring into vacancy.

"Yet you have a guess what it was—the question, I mean—eh, Alasdair?" said the Captain More.

"Oh! I can jalouse; but it's no' in the story," said the halflin.

"Tell us your way of it," said Linnell.

"I'm thinking they wanted to ken where the treasure o' the MacPhail was hid," said the boy.

"I've heard of him," said Linnell, "a queer fellow ... a kind of a pirate, wasn't he? A strange part for a Highlander to play."

The Captain turned a wondering eye on the sailor. "Man, but you're well-versed in the history of the place ... And I believe you're right. He's buried at Pennygown, that same old rover."

"I fancy I've seen his tomb," said the youth, smiling.

Instantly the Catechist's Boy sprang to his feet, and peered into the sailor's face. "I ken you now," he said in a low voice that trembled. "And there's your sea-cloak, but where's your lanthorn? ... It's you were the Man from the Sea." He shook a puny fist in his face. "It's you were the defiler o' graves ... Poor Kirsty! ... Poor Sister Kirsty!" and in a moment he had swerved and vanished with a leap in the thicket of high elder. They heard him crash through the bushes, the snapping of twigs denoting his progress long after he was lost to sight.

"Now there's the fat in the fire," said the Captain, bitterly, "and I fear you've made an enemy, sir ... Will you never be wise? ... MacPhail's treasure! ... a fireside tale! ... And you must be howking for it like a schoolboy! ... It's on a par with your nursery rhymes."

"Just on a par, Captain," said Linnell. "You know the old rant. 'Here come I Galatian.' ... Well, I was no more treasure-hunter that night than I was Galatian in the days of childhood. I but played at the thing."

"Tuts!" said the veteran testily.

"In any case I was on my lawful business of tracking the salt-smugglers that evening. We got ten bags stowed away in the old chapel; and while my men took them off, I made a tour of inspection of the old place ... And oh, Captain! what content it brought! ... The lonely shore, and the misty dark; the broken wall; the sepulchres of ages past sunk in quiet turf, and among them the bones of the old sea-reiver."

"Aye, you'll be for making a ballant of it before you've done, I suppose," said the Captain sardonically.

"Then the story of hid treasure in his native glen ... the glen where he'd once ranged a bare-legged laddie, innocent of aught more piratical than the capture of butterfly or troutling," went on the youth with enthusiasm. " 'Twould have been criminal to have gone yonder save at midnight and with a lanthorn. And I'll wager that, in essence at least, your own thoughts are not greatly different in broad daylight in any parish graveyard, between the services of a Sunday ... The boon companions of your childhood; and there they lie ... How varied the tale of each! ... Oh! I fear I'll never be growing up, Captain, and never get beyond the halflin's sentiment of things, you see ... For me there's more wisdom in a graveyard epitaph or in the songs of bairns, I tell you, than in all this damnable brooding over the rates and taxes of the good citizen," he concluded passionately in a fine inconsequence.

The Captain More regarded him quizzically. "No," he said at last, "your father never went that length ... Still-and-on, I've kent him try his hand at verse-making now and then ... Have a care, sir, or you'll maybe fall into that vice also." He paused, and then added, "But I'm sorry you've got at cross purposes with Alasdair. I trust he'll carry no tales."

"Never fear," laughed the sailor. "I'll make it up with a song next time you catch him for me."

9: Garmony

NEXT day at dawn the hapless Linnell added to his disabilities by his efforts at extinguishing a half-burnt kitchen-wench, who had risen to poultice a toothache, and had, poor lass! to endure a far worse agony before her remedy was half prepared. It seemed the sailor's arms were soon to emulate his sconce in the matter of bandages, for the sisters were already about him, and busy with oils and dressings. Every one was but half-clad at that early hour, and the young man's eyes dwelt secretly on the bloom of sleep scarce lifted from Elspeth's eye and cheek, and on her hastily coiled masses of red-gold hair. From an upper floor the voice of the blind chief came booming, wild in Gaelic imprecations, and demanding the meaning of the uproar below.

"*Ubh, ubh!*" cried Lexy, the second serving lass. "Poor Sheena! ... Well I knew it; well I knew it! ... Did she not hear the first cuckoo while she was fasting? and the first lamb she saw this year had its tail to her! *Och, ubh, ubh!* ... Poor Sheena!" The gillies from the gun-room quarters joined in the gabble of lamentation, and still from above rumbled the thunder of old Draolinn. Indeed the only silent one now was the burnt lass who had ultimately fainted. A fresh wailing from her friends resulted in new notes of discord from the old man above stairs, who now raved with threats lurid and manifold; and Linnell mounted to allay his wrath, while Elspeth saw to the bedding of the injured maid.

Grizel, distrustful of any useful service from the excited gillies, decided that she herself must seek Doctor MacCulloch, so running bareheaded to the stables, she saddled her garron, and rode off on the road to Coillemore, a farm where the Doctor was known to have been in recent attendance. The little mount spanked easily through the arcades of the pine belt, whose dim recesses and darkened vistas showed like the abode of warlocks in the dawn-light just breaking. Out on the shore-road to Killiechronan and past Drumlang came the pony on a noble stretch of hooves, the girl encouraging him with a good word of Gaelic in his prinking ear. The morn was fresh; a light mist lay on the Loch and on the low grounds; but the mass of Gribun rock showed above this grey scarf of vapour like a battlement of iron, and from it swept upwards the great hills, herding to the knees of gaunt Ben More. Grizel patted her loose-knotted hair, and again bent to the ear of her horse, coaxing, promising, adjuring. "Corran, Corran," she whispered, *"suas e ... suas e,"* and the fine fellow rattled the faster. Redshanks and curlews waked to the beat of hooves and sounded a warning to the little peoples of the shore; sea-pyats protested — wheet-wheet — on quivering wing; one or two early herons rose, royally indignant, from the orange of the sea-wrack.

At the bend of Kellan, where she had taken the turf, and Corran's shoes plyed silently though swiftly, they suddenly fell into the midst of a council of beasts and birds (so Grizel named it) — a brace of grouse, a comical little fellow of a rabbit, and a roe-deer of rather solemn aspect. For all the world these creatures were doing nothing but gossip in the bare middle of the highway, since not a scrap of pasture or a grain of corn was near. They fled instanter, and Grizel laughed low at her conceit of a parliament of beasts, as she swept on and into a little pool of mist in a dip of the road. She was still smiling when she emerged from this; when all at once she beheld a stranger thing. A gulley deep in fern ran back to the moorland on her right; folded there she saw a flock of sheep, a couple of startled dogs standing alert on either lip of the cleft; and scampering to hiding behind some gorse in the background, the figures of three men. Another veil of mist, and the picture was gone like a dream. Subconsciously she felt her hands pull on the reins, but the memory of the shrieks of the tortured kitchen-lass came back at once; so no halt in a task so urgent: it was on and away for Coillemore and the good Doctor. Other incidents of the morning's alert came back to her as she rode; and now she found herself laughing at the thought of the rueful countenance of Linnell as he regarded the burnt patches of his handsome boat-cloak, in which he had enswathed the scorched serving-lass. Clearly the spoiled garment had more of sympathy than his flayed arms. "The dandy, even then," she thought. "But up and away, Corran; for here's the last stretch, and yonder's Coillemore's first reek just rising."

At the farm she found fresh trouble, for the Doctor had left overnight for a case of some urgency at Torlochan. The girl grew dispirited: Corran was spent, and Torlochan was now eight miles off; but the good farmer put all right by instantly upsaddling a gillie on a fresh horse, and sending him back the way she had come, with orders for the Doctor to betake himself hot-foot to Draolinn. He was for pressing Grizel to dismount and rest, but she would not; so, drinking a cup of milk, more from respect to Highland manners than from need, she returned at a slow walk. Half-way down the brae above Kellan she heard a great crying of sheep take the air, and at a turn of the road she beheld in the light of the dawn, now flooding sea and hill, the gully of bracken near Kellan.

The skulkers in the fern had left their hiding now; their cries rang out strident and angry, hounding on the yapping dogs at the flock streaming across the roadway, and down through broken rock and slippery tangle to a beach of pebbles. The leading figure in a philabeg, she at once made out as that of Oskamull; there was no doubting the strut of him and the port of his chin in air. She saw that, with a collie, he had detached three ewes, and was sending them straight for the water. Bewildered and mute, the poor beasts entered the shallows, breaking this way and that in short rushes, yet ever plunging deeper; already one was afloat on a seaward current, and battling silently. In fancy Grizel saw the dark eyes beseeching, and her cheek flushed in shame that one of her race should decree this torture. Was the man mad? Would he seek to destroy the whole flock in this savage fashion? She slid from her saddle distraught. A waft of wind brought the chiefs laugh to her, and floating across the still spaces came his shout in the Gaelic: "We'll see if they're swan or seal." As she turned to mount, the quicker to make her protest, her eye fell on a tall figure of a man racing down the moorland slope above the gully. He disappeared in the dip, then broke cover from high bracken, and staggered down the rock and weed to the beach of pebbles, while at his heels flew Oskamull's collies. But his cromag was busy, and they fled howling. He stumbled throat-high into the sea, swam a stroke or two, and dragged an imperilled gimmer to safety by its ear; then the shepherd's crook came into play again as he stood knee-deep, this time piloting the other two ewes to safety.

Hand on haunch and nose in air, Oskamull waited composedly for the rescuer as he waded ashore, glistening with sea-water. An encounter of some sort would surely follow, thought Grizel, and she felt turned to stone at the prospect. For in her own heart she felt strangely near to bloodshed for requital of a deed so cruel, and now endowed this knight-errant, so opportunely come, with thoughts of her own. She saw the man was John Morrison, the shepherd at Frisa, an outlying sheep-farm of Garmony's, for his stark ascetic figure was in profile now ... the long knee breeches, the sharply pointed beard, and the rest; and she could have cried aloud for joy: "John Morrison, John Morrison, my dear!" Pity on Oskamull if it comes to play with staves! she thought, for John was the dour one and the strong. And now the new-comer went up to the chief, his hand outstretched to the heavens, crying down maledictions in Gaelic. But the kilted figure took to the tonguing also; there was a pantomime of raised fists and of cromags that flourished in air; and Oskamull's two gillies were slouching nearer, when there came a shout from the road, and there, sure enough, was Garmony himself, big and burly, leading his pony by the bridle. Grizel sighed contentedly, for the quarrel was certainly now equally matched, and the poor ewes safe from further mishandling.

The big tacksman made no haste, and advancing as easily as if he went to kirk or change-house, bore down on the disputants. Oskamull met him with high words, his fist rapping on his palm; but Garmony made no answer, only signing by a movement of his head to Morrison to take the sheep off the shore and southward. With difficulty the shepherd obeyed, since his dog was lacking, and the sheep were still a trifle scared; but at length, by dint of much running and shouting, he gathered them clear of the beach, and moving off some little distance, awaited his master.

On the shingle, Oskamull raved and ranted; and Grizel saw that the tacksman, still unreplying, was listening patiently to the plaint of the chief, tracing figures idly on a slab of wet sand the while with the point of his cromag. She beheld him look up at the laird, still storming, and fancied, though she could not see, the slow incredulous smile he always had with such a lift of the head; that and a twinkling eye always went together, she recalled. The next moment she was flushing to find her memories of Garmony so intimate; her shoulders shrugged as in self-contempt; and patting her disordered hair a trifle, she dashed a finger at the little speck of a birthmark below her left eye as if to remove it instantly. Yet all the while her gaze was on the men on the shore.

Oskamull still gabbled, but never a word did the other give to my gentleman in the kilt, and finally swinging on his heel, he turned slowly, and passing the chief with as much ado as he would a threatening bubbly-jock, went steadily up the shingle to where Morrison waited him with his flock. Grizel nodded her head, well pleased. "And that's a lesson to me; for I'd have knocked his bonnet in the sea ere now, I fear ... That's Garmony! What a will the man has! . . ." She ceased her musings suddenly. "Eh, Grizel MacLean, what's this of it, now?" she whispered to herself. "It's you are the silly lass, surely!"

Oskamull stood for a moment, looking after the receding figures, plainly taken aback by their businesslike airs, then strode across to his henchmen; and, followed by their slouching dogs, all three instantly made for the drove track that led from the gully to the inland hills.

The whole affair had appeared but a pantomime for the girl; the bawling of Oskamull and Morrison had been too distant to be intelligible, but so well did she know the characters of the actors, that she had read nearly every thought of them in the mimic show she had witnessed. All except the motive for the torture of the beasts; what could that mean? ... In any case there was Garmony in front, and, lest the search for the Doctor had miscarried, she might as well secure his aid. She mounted, therefore, and pushed on towards the convoy ahead.

The sun was now peeping over Torlochan, and some warmth was in the air. A cock crowed distantly in a croft near Kellan; and the thrushes in the woodlands by the wayside began to essay their practice songs for the day. Gone were the lakes of sih mist in the hollows of the land, and the loch's surfac was now also clear of vapours, as it ruffled into ripples like fish-scales for shape and iridescence. Corratí shook his mane, snorted at the day new-born, and breaking into a trot, soon brought her into sight; of the sheep and their deliverers, just beyond the Pedlar's Halt. The flock of ewes was cropping by the roadside; Morrison couched in slumber on a stretch of heather, his master's garron lying unsaddled near-by; and the tacksman pacing to and fro, a vigilant sentry.

Garmony smiled broadly at sight of the lady, and signed to her to walk her pony on the greensward past the sleeping shepherd, lest he roused. As she obeyed, Grizel flushed a trifle at his assured air of command, and his eyes twinkled mischievously as he divined her irritation from the queer little twitch of the nether lip. He took her horse's bridle, and walked Corran to where the river scoured in a little shallow in which he might drink in safety. "I just thought it was you," said the big man, turning a roguish eye on her.

"For why?"

"Oh," said he, rocking heel and toe as was his wont when pondering his words—" well now, for cantrips at dawn, commend me to a Draolinn lass."

Her brows came down; he saw his error, and hastened to explain. "It's clumsy I am, as always," said he. "You surely ken me better than to think I ettled an impertinence."

But his false step had been made; and all her thoughts were instantly back on that terrible night of her sister's escapade in this same airt; for indeed here was the very road down which Elspeth had returned. But seeing the good fellow's distress, she smiled, relenting. "It's plain you've still the hankering after the courtier's tongue, kinsman," said she.

"I'm ay the 'prentice hand, it seems. Or should I have said 'prentice tongue now?" said he ruefully.

"The eyes of you are beyond the 'prentice stage anyway, Ewan," she replied. ... "Where did you see me first?"

"On Kellan Brae, when the collieshangie between John and himself began. You were at gaze and in wonderment as to what all the palaver was about."

"Well might I be that, for never a word could I hear plainly. Nothing for me but the shouting; and that was all from one man's throat as soon as Morrison left."

"Good reason too, for John had given him plenty to think about before I came into it."

"And then?"

"Oh, well then" (he grasped his cromag tightly and his face lowered dark), "Lord kens I had plenty to say to yon fellow with something else than my tongue, had you no' been on Kellan Brae."

"Keep me!" she cried, "and me admiring your restraint, Garmony! ... I thought it was nought but contempt for the bully, yon silence o' yours

... Me envying you your strong will; and all the time it was but parlour manners before the ladies!"

The tacksman looked again discomfited; and then laughed outright. "It's me that's the unlucky one," said he; "for there was the chance to shine, it seems. *Ochanoch!* ... I'd like to be the one you thought me yonder ... But I've given ye the truth o't ... and I'm just plain Ewan, you see." He fell to glooming, and kicked the pebbles at his feet in aimless fashion.

She strove to make amends. "And you knew me so far away ... at dawn, and dishevelled too?" She patted the dark coils on her head.

Garmony's face shone once more. "Still-and-on I've eyes," said he. And frank admiration shone from them now.

"Ay the courtier!" she cried, smiling and went on to explain last night's trouble at Draolinn, and her journey at dawn for the Doctor.

"Oh, the Doctor's at Torlochan, sure enough," said Garmony. "It's myself that saw him last night on my journey out here; so it's there that Coillemore's *sgalag* will find him ... Yet we'd best be getting on to your father; for he'll need some soothering, I'm thinking; and I'm an old hand with him at that ... Wait you." He went back to the sleeping shepherd, roused him for a word of instruction, and saddling his garron, rejoined her.

As they trotted on, she told of what she had seen on her outward journey, the folded sheep in the gully, and their skulking attendants.

"It's just as I guessed," said he ... "Yon's the man sore pressed for money."

"You mean—?"

"I mean sheep-lifting," he said bluntly.

"But he would have had them drowned, it appears?"

"No, nor drowned ... Play-acting yon ... He made out Morrison or myself on the hill; kent he was caught; and to screen the theft, was for pretending anger at these sheep o' mine taking to his ground ... And, oh, so angry, look you ... so angry that he would drive them—the trespassers!— drive them to their death in the Loch! ... Oh, a cunning fox is my gentleman! ... But he must be fell hard pressed for money ... MacKenzie, the merchant, has him tight, I'll swear ... He's deep with O'Brien too, in the salt-smuggling. (Though there's no crime in that in reasonable amount, you'll understand, no matter what your father says.) ... And it's often he's south at the gaming tables, I'm hearing ... What next ... what next, poor man!"

"It's fortunate you were so near," said Grizel. "What chance brought you all the way to Frisa in the nick of time?"

Garmony pulled himself up suddenly, checking his pony in the movement; the lady also halted her garron; while the man raised eyes that burned, and regarded her steadily; and just as frankly she returned his gaze. Then with a little heightening of colour, she patted her chevelure again, and touched Corran with her switch, so that he moved on at a walk. Garmony's whole aspect became dull at once; his head sank moodily, and he followed.

"Well," said he presently, "I never was good at chapter and verse for all my doings ... I had a notion to come this way ... that was all. I'll stay overnight at Frisa, thinks I, and look in on my kinsman at Draolinn in the morning." He laughed gaily at the thought. "And here I am," he added, "but a trifle earlier than I had intended."

"What a rover! "cried Grizel.

"The wildest," said he. "And so, about the turn of the night, I came to Frisa, and found Morrison gone ... Thinks I, 'Here's a truant shepherd ... He'll be at the cartes with Miss Belle at Killiechronan again.' ... But I did him an injustice ... For I waited, and better waited, and at three in the morning, in he comes panting, and snatches at his spy-glass on the wall, and out at the door before he sees me dovering by the hearth. I called him back, and he gave me his story ... What think you it was? ... Oskamull's shepherds—these two MacLiver fellows that we saw this morning—had got John across to Bellart for a dram and some piping, and after the splore was by, they insisted on his bedding there till the morning ... As you may have noticed a little ago, John's a sleeper of one eye; and about two of the clock he heard a stir in the kitchen below his chamber. He peeps down; and there they were, the MacLivers pulling on their brogues, and Oskamull with a storm-lantern. He guessed their business instantly, and was out of the back-window, and home to Frisa for his long-glass like the deer of the hill. He found his glass, and he found me, and we hunted the hunters ... They made a bonnie *creach* of a hundred, and we followed, as you saw ... Oh, John's the rare shepherd, despite his weakness for the cartes at Miss Belle's."

"He's the fine fellow," said Grizel, "and I only wish Belle thought as much of him as I do."

Garmony's eyes opened wide. "And what then? "said he.

"Oh," said the girl, a trifle confused at astonishment so manifest, "I suppose she'd look kindlier on the poor man."

The tacksman sighed as in relief. "Now, wasn't it there I got the start?" said he. "Why, the man's for an instant wedding and nothing less ... 'Look kindlier,' says she! ... Well, well!"

Grizel laughed. "Still-and-on," she said, "when it comes to courting, an old maid's little different from a young lass, believe me ... And John would come better speed if he werena so downright ... Is he no' gleg enough to see that, this model shepherd of yours?"

The tacksman pursed his lips in an assumed profundity, to hide his bewilderment; but at last gave in. "I'll no' say I follow you with perfect clearness," said he. "The man kens what he would be at; and he's honest and straightforward."

Grizel bent to her saddle in an ecstasy of merriment. "Straightforward?" she cried amazed. "Oh, man! man! ... Tell John to watch the swallows at their courting in Achnahully some night o' summer ... They're downright enough, it's plain to see. But ... straightforward . . .? No ... no." And off she went at a canter through the screen of the Draolinn pines.

Garmony followed slowly and smiled grimly as he did so.

"Nearer it you never were, Ewan," he said to himself, "and a sad mess you'd have made of it. ... It's you are the lucky man to have had John for a warning and a sign ... Poor John, poor downright John! ... Why, it seems the fellow's ruining his every chance by taking after his master!"

10: The Thicket

ON a Sabbath morning a fortnight later, Linnell came over the Hill of the Cave, long after the kirk-hour at Pennygown. He had half a mind to attempt a call at Garmony's farm if his strength held for the miles of heather he must traverse. He felt, indeed, a trifle guilty in making such a venture, for he had secured abstention from the day's kirk-service on the score, not only of his Anglican upbringing, but of his invalid state; and here he was, breasting the mountain-side, and leaping the burns like a schoolboy. The crossing of the Forsa River had to be made by the bridge at Pennygown, close to the church, so he made a slight détour, lest a wandering glance of Elspeth or of Grizel through the dusty panes of the preaching-house should fall on him as he passed. A faint sound of singing came from the place of worship, an ugly square of whitewashed stone set on the shore below the poor old ruin of its predecessor in an earlier form of the faith, now lying half-buried in the grassy swell of ancient graves that flowed like a tide round it and the islets of grey tombs. The blue sound slept as in a dream beneath a sky of blue in which a high sun shone fierily; and despite a gentle breeze, only the tiniest of waves chimed faint on the shore. A few gulls planed silently; and silent, too, were the terns in their magic swerves as if in accord with the holy time. But the pippits whistled persistent on the sea-marge; and at intervals the plaint of lambs took the airs appealingly, for, as far as the eye could reach, the low grounds were dotted with ewes and their young.

"The sheep upon a thousand hills," said Linnell, after he had covered a mile or so, and turned to look round on a scene so different from the penned sheep-folds of his Southern England; "and among them"... he listened intent ... "the essential lost one." A lamb's voice protesting innocence loudly, came from the midst of a bramble thicket close to the shore-track.

"Coming, my darling," cried the sailor playfully, and he set to running awkwardly, arms held stiffly from his sides, the better to evade a rawing of the flayed wrists. But the tangled bush was dense; his knife soon blunted; and his bandaged arms served him so badly at his task, that at the end of half an hour, he had made only a yard of progress. He noted, however, that he was not the only one interested in the lamb's plight; a glimpse of a tawny coat, a black brush, and a beady eye, denoted a weasel's momentary presence; and a snorting drew his upward gaze to the wild-maned head of a Highland pony, who seemed mildly curious, and somewhat tamer than his fellows when afield. There were other sounds also in the vicinity of the thicket—hard breathing and a rasping that indicated the munching teeth of Highland kine, perhaps. "A wonderfully social animal world this, leaving out the weasel, of course. Have they all come to see me perform the rôle of Father Abraham, I wonder?" thought Linnell.

The lamb evidently misunderstood her rescuer's intention, for, when next he essayed further tunnelling, its movements and bleatings increased in frequency. He feared the poor thing would involve itself deeper in the thorns if he did not hasten, so setting himself to work like a negro among lianas, he was soon within a foot of the imprisoned beast. Another five minutes and his work was ended; when to his amazement he beheld a brown sun-burnt hand reach for the captive from a point of the compass exactly opposite him, and peering from behind this, a bearded face above a minister's white stock. The face was scratched and bleeding, but the eyes and the lips were smiling, and a screed of compassionate Gaelic was addressed to the little lost one.

"Who the devil are you, sir?" cried Linnell. "This is my thicket, let me tell you; and you're not in the play ... 'Tis I am Father Abraham."

The bearded face with the many scratches gaped at him, and then withdrew down a dusky tunnel of thorns, a lingering hand coaxing the scared lamb through the same exit. Immediately there came a triumphant bleat, and the answering voice of an ancient ewe announced deliverance and reunion.

The sailor disengaged himself, and moving his cramped arms gingerly, rose to his feet. Then, full of wrath at this forestaller of his task of mercy, he rounded the thicket to find the rescuer still kneeling before his handiwork; a great gully-knife in his fist, and a business-like pile of severed brambles neatly arrayed by his side: a man of clerical aspect, with some severity of visage that was belied by brown eyes now twinkling to a pipe he was preparing. He regarded the young man steadily for an instant, then knocked the back of his knife-blade on a flint held over a tinder-box, and, this rite successfully accomplished, lit his weed and puffed with great smackings of his lips. At last the ignition of the tobacco seemed satisfactory, and critically gazin at his pipe-bowl and Linnell by turns, he said, frowning: "Swearing and blaspheming on the Sabbath ... Man, man, who can you be at all, at all?"

For answer the sailor put out a hand as if to raise him to his feet, when a sudden twinge of pain in: his rawed arm gave him check. "I would rather you were in a more suitable posture for converse," said he.

"Converse here, converse there," said the cleric. "I'd liefer you were on your knees beside me, asking the Lord his pardon."

"You forget your pipe," said the other, smiling.

The lambent brown eyes twinkled, and the old man scrambled upright. "Man, man," said he, and he laid a friendly hand on the arm of the sailor, who shrank from him, wincing. "Och, I had forgotten your bandaged arms; and me staring at them all the while ... Yes, yes, I can understand a hasty objurgation, when you're suffering like that ... But Abraham now? ... that savours more of light-mindedness, you see ... You'll leave Abraham to the ministers, if you please."

"Then let the ministers leave my lamb alone," said Linnell. "It was mine; I was first at the thicket."

"Doubtless it was yours by right," said the old man, puffing with a hint of the whimsically judicial in his air. "But I didna hear you until I got hold of the poor beastie ... You were first at the thicket; I was first at the lamb."

The sailor assented with a good-humoured laugh.

"You understand," went on the other, "I'm fell smart wi' the knife; and I'm in good fettle, for it's my third lamb this morning ... And then, look you, your bad arms were the sore handicap ... Man, man, it's fair ridiculous the way the ewes bring up their young nowadays! ... Here am I that should have been at the service at Pennygown Kirk half an hour ago, playing pastor in too literal a fashion on Leitir shore ... And Lachie Dubh — that's my precentor — will be leading them well on into Psalm a hunder and nineteen by now ... Aye, aye! Lachie kens; it's no' the first lambing time wi' Lachie and me ... Lachie kens."

"You've a weakness for lambs," hazarded Linnell.

"Aye; a strong weakness, as the auld wife said. , . . Sympathy's like to be my undoing some day ... A queer thing sympathy ... Look you now" (he puffed energetically at his pipe and his voice took a pulpit sing-song), "the reverend Mister Chisholm of Kilninver once said what was very, very precious ... Oh, yes, he said what was very, very precious ... He said he had a little girl, and when she laughed, he laughed too ... Aye, man, a powerful thing is sympathy ... Not that you could say the lamb was laughing," he concluded, with a smile that suddenly faded, when he regarded his now exhausted pipe. He looked at Linnell critically. "Sailor? "he asked.

"Yes, sir."

"Come and have a bathe," cried the old man exultantly, and seizing the youth by the lapel of his coat, he dragged him across the shore-road before a word of dissent could be uttered. They were at the water's edge ere a halt was called.

"You're forgetting your congregation," said the youth, protesting.

"Not a bit ... Lachie kens ... But," said this droll cleric, releasing him regretfully, "I was overlooking those poor arms of yours again."

He proceeded to undress swiftly. "Wait for me," he cried, as he plowtered deep, circling wide with amazing power for so old a man;

and ducking like a seal time and again, he reappeared snorting in evident enjoyment. Then, making shorewards for a sandy spit, he knelt behind some rocks, whence presently there issued sounds of passionate pleading —a Gaelic prayer. The petition was long enough for the bright sun to do all the work of a towelling, and soon he was donning his blacks again. This done, he filled and re-lit his pipe. "There's an end even to the hunder and nineteenth," said he, "and I must be going ... Lachie's voice is not what it was; and I doubt if he'll can hold out next year's lambing ... But we'll see," he added cheerfully— "we'll see," and he called his garron, which the sailor now recognized as that of the intruder at the thicket earlier in the day.

"My name's Linnell, sir," said the youth as he held a stirrup while the minister mounted. "I'm a guest of the chief at Draolinn."

"Just what I was jalousing," said the other. "I've heard tell of you ... Mine is MacLeod, minister of this parish, and very much at your service, sir."

"I take you at your word then, Mr. MacLeod; it's a service I would crave ... I'm in as close a thicket as that the poor lamb tenanted so recently."

The minister's eyes moved restlessly up the Pennygown road, and the young man took the hint. "I can wait for your return, if you come this way home," said he eagerly.

"Man, you're thoughtful," said MacLeod in evident relief, his eye roving to the beach. "Meet me here in three hours' time, the tide will be much better by then." He waved a hand, and turned on to the road in no great haste, for he was now regarding the glow in his pipe, as if to time his pace by so much of the herb as was still unconsumed.

Couched on the short turf, Linnell rested for nearly two hours, watching some sea-pyats teaching their young to swim, then walked slowly back in the direction of Pennygown. Coming to the change-house set close by the church, he found it closed; but a herd-boy lounging near told him in poor English it would open when the kirk skailed. And so he found; for the bonnets of thrum separated from the snoods and mutches with a stealthy rapidity as the congregation emerged; and, the inn-doors opening, they disappeared within. The sailor took care to be among the first of these; and if he failed to join in the numerous hand-shakings and gossipings in Gaelic, he did justice, however, to the general interest in Ferintosh, buttered oat-cake and cheese that was the staple fare of the day. After a hasty consumpt, he stole out quietly lest the Captain More or any of the Draolinn party should arrive and discover his presence. At once he set off to his rendezvous with Mr. MacLeod, but had still half an hour of waiting, before he saw a mounted figure approaching from the Pennygown brae; and ere long the smoke of a well-puffed pipe assured him it was the minister.

"You'll excuse me for five minutes, I'm sure, Mr. Linnell," said MacLeod, as he drew up and emptied his pipe-bowl, "but just now is the moment when the tide's a treasure. Half an hour later, and there's a current as cold as a dog's nose." He stripped quickly, and the morning's performance was repeated, the prayer possibly a trifle shorter. "And now," said he, when he was re-clad, and his pipe lit anew, "what about this thicket of yours."

"Sir," said the young man, "the matter is a bit ravelled; and I cannot see my way to a fair beginning—"

"Give me the bones of it —the heads of the sermon, as we would say in these parts."

"I follow. The argument then, in playwriter's phrase, runs this fashion ... My father many years ago wounded another man sorely in a duel in Spain—"

"So-ho! then you're Captain Linnell's son, and it was old Oskamull was the other in that duel. Portugal it was, to be exact, I believe."

"You know the story, it seems?"

"Bits of it ... bits of it ... It's little that Aros folk dinna ken of their own people's doings in the big war."

"Well, sir, this man's son is in the Isle even now."

"Young Oskamull? ... At kirk this very day," said MacLeod; adding gloomily— "a place he's in not ower often."

"I've been considering what reparation I owe this man's son."

The minister slowly removed his pipe and his mouth fell agape. "Another duel? ... And is it to a minister of—?"

The young man's smile checked him. "I was thinking of the other thing," said Linnell somewhat awkwardly. "I gather that this Oskamull is in some kind of business embarrassment, and that the family fortunes went steadily down after the father's disablement, and went deeper still after his death. That crippled arm meant the loss of his profession to the father, and so on to I know not what involvement of the estate ... I've a fondness for the old rhymes that children sing; and there's one:

"' For want of a nail the shoe was lost; for want of a shoe—' ....

You take me?"

"Aye," said MacLeod. "There's a world o' philosophy in it ... Consequences ... Aye, man, aye ... from the fall of Adam right on, you might say ... And so you're for playing Providence to yon fellow at Oskamull ... It's a strange world."

"I might help," said the youth, reddening a trifle. "I've neither poverty nor riches, yet ..."

"The thing's by no means so simple as it looks," said the minister ... "I must consider it ... Have you aught against my taking counsel with the Captain More, whom you'll ken?"

"Nothing at all, except that perhaps he's by no means quite disinterested, for he was second to my father in the duel."

"Oh, I'm understanding that; for, as I have already said, there was little happened in the war that was not abroad in Aros two months later ... Oh, we're none so backward here awa', Mr. Linnell."

"I make my excuses again," said the sailor, smiling at local patriotism; "and I leave myself in the hands of yourself and your friend ... But I trust you'll soon be able to help, for a recall may come from the South for me any day now, once my cutter has finish patching."

"I'll make what speed I can; though it's a far cry from my manse at Gualachaolish to the Captain More's lodging ... And," he added warmly, shaking the sailor's hand, "blessing on you for your kindly thoughts for a fellow-creature. It's in that way, sir, we become scholars of Christ ... *Beannachd leat*, Mr. Linnell."

He trotted off; and the young man turned back on the road he had come, for it was plainly too far on in the day for the walk to Garmony now; the sun was westering fast, and folds of mist were already midway to the hill-peaks. He passed the church and the change-house, and remarked how vacant their aspect to that at the kirk-skailing an hour ago. The podgy landlord of the inn was in his shirt-sleeves, and sat out of doors, watching his bairn toddling to roadside adventures; a barefoot lass brought home some active kine; these were all the humans visible just then. But at a turn of the road through a belt of larch and hazel he came in sight of the bridge over the Forsa, and saw two figures seated on its low wall. Their outlines were plainly lifted against the sunset sky; and the scraggy arms and flitting movements of one, as he rose and stole off into the woodland, recalled the Catechist's Boy. The other remained seated; he waited some one surely, thought Linnell, for the figure raised a hand as if scanning his approach.

The noise of the river's outfall at the sea-marge half a mile below the bridge now took the sailor's ear; the angler in him stirred at the sound, and he turned aside to gauge the water's possibilities in the matter of salmon. When his arms recovered a little he might, perhaps, try a cast here with profit. He came to the pools; and there were the grey fellows leaping at the creaming downpour that dashed them back to a linn teeming with fish. The energy of these athletes of the waters, the tragi-comedy of their failures to ascend the fall, and the rare success of one long-trained and powerful, enthralled him for a time. But evening was fast coming on; his absence from Draolinn for so long a period was unusual; the duties of a guest pricked him; and reluctantly he turned away. He saw that the solitary figure on the bridge had moved and was now approaching him over the intervening dunes. The sun shone on some tassels at mid-leg of the man; and the sailor instantly guessed at Hessian boots. From that to officialdom was an easy leap for his mind ... "Here's Admiralty again," he sighed. "My recall, I suppose; and good-bye to Aros for me." Yet, trusting he might be mistaken, he affected not to see the new-comer, and descended to the last tawny pool, whence a snowy torrent slid, eager and roaring, to the tides of the Kyle.

The stranger came nearer, hurrying. He wore drab stocking pantaloons above his half-leg boots, a Jean de Bry coat of brown that showed a tartan vest at the tight waist; and he carried a flat blue bonnet in his hand. "A North-country buck," said Linnell to himself, "all in his Sunday best!" The fellow looked about thirty, bore his chin high in the air, and the youth noted that his face was flushed and angry, the jaw-muscles atwitch.

"Sir," cried the dandy.

"You called," said the sailor, turning easily and coming up with him.

"Your name is Linnell, is it not?" asked the other, planting himself stockily before him.

"Lieutenant Linnell at your service, sir ... What's amiss?"

"This," cried the stranger, slapping him full in the face with the blue bonnet. "Defiler of graves! ... Mine is MacCalman."

The sailor staggered from the clout, and put his hand to where his cutlass was wont to hang; then squared himself against further attack, biting his nether lip. "This is Alasdair's doing, of course," he thought. Then after some moments had passed, and he had gained control of himself, he said quietly, "I understand."

"You do? ... Then you know where to find me, and you can send your man to Oskamull at midnight, noon, or cock-crow, as soon as you've done malingering with your blistered arms ... I'm ready for you any day for a month on," cried the other, and swinging on his heel, went off at a rapid walk.

The other sprang to follow, but with an effort halted and stood as if rooted. "Stop," he cried; and Oskamull came back, glooming. "I said that I understood ... I would further have said that you do not understand ... For I have defiled no grave; and when I stood by that of your father, my thoughts of you and yours were not unfriendly."

"You've a long tongue and a pretty one," said Oskamull. "So had your father, I've heard, to the undoing of mine."

"Sir, I'll brook your bonnet in my face; but leave my father's name untouched."

"I'd willingly touch nothing that has Linnell to it, save with steel or bullet."

The sailor's fingers flexed tightly, but he kept silence.

"And," went on the chieftain, "this is not Spain, my burnt hero; so the fight will be fair this turn." He made to go once more.

"Stop," cried Linnell; and his hand on the other's shoulder spun the fellow round till the sand whirled at his feet.

"Take that back, sir."

Oskamull crouched, and drew a knife from under his coat.

"Off," said he. "Your time's not yet, my pretty man."

They stood tense and breathing hard for a moment, watching each other cautiously. Then Linnell spoke. "Bah! "he said. "We're like children, squabbling thus ... But it seems you will not comprehend ... Your words are hot; and indeed what else should they be, since the matter is not yet made clear to you ... I must see to that ... Meanwhile we had best say good-day, I fancy."

Oskamull slipped his weapon behind his coat-tails, smiling grimly. "A long tongue and an oily one," said he bitterly ... "Well, I'll leave you till you're healed ... But contrive no more burnings, I pray you. The sword-arm always suffers most in such accidents, I've heard ... And the Draolinn ladies are the rare plotters, eh? ... Elspeth's the cunning one!" he concluded, grinning.

The girl's name had barely passed his lips when Linnell's arms were round him; it was too late for the knife now. The sailor held him in what was scarcely a wrestling grip; for he was crushing him, arms and chest caught sideways against his body. The prisoned man's cry was strangled, his face empurpled; —Linnell found himself amazed at his own strength; but reason enough was left him to fear it, even in the midst of this great flood-tide of anger; and so his hold relaxed when the man's eyes glazed and he came dead-weight in his grasp. Then he trussed him as easily as a fowl, and tossed him to the swirling pool below. "Make your cleansing there," he muttered; and waited to see the red face come up: gurgling, and sink again. Instantly the sailor leant down and clutched a disappearing hand, while he clasped a rowan stem to steady himself against the water's sweep to the fall, whither the body trailed; then by main force he dragged the burden to the edge of the rocky basin, and so to the reedy shore, where it lay motionless. He put an ear to the breast, and waited for a sign of returning breath. At length this came fitfully, and by the time Linnell had secured the waist-knife and tossed it in the pool, the respirations were as regular as those of a sleeper. After a little the half-drowned man groaned, and Linnell went off a few paces, patting his arms, as if to allay the twinges of the torn flesh beneath the encasing bandages. He watched his opponent narrowly; and very soon a muttered word or two from the figure in the sodden brown coat announced that full recovery was not far away.

"Get up," commanded the sailor, and the ducked dandy struggled to hands and knees. "You're not dead, you see," went on Linnell. "You'll live to lie another day, I make no doubt."

"Damn you!" said the chieftain feebly.

"And damn you, sir," said the other heartily, swinging off over the bent. "Good-day to you!" A moodiness came over him as he walked. "It was not in this fashion I had planned to get clear of my thicket," said he underbreath; "nor was this exactly Mr. MacLeod's method, I'll wager ... A pretty start for a man commended for a Christian hardly an hour gone ... At heart now—at heart, my dear Linnell, you're nought but a murderer." Yet this phase passed quickly; soon he was singing; and the notes of his chant came feebly to the shivering buck on the river's edge.

> *"Birch and green holly* (it ran),
> *Birch and green holly, boys,*
> *If you get beaten,*
> *'Twill be your own folly, boys."*

11: The Irish Schooner

LINNELL returned through Aros township, a straggle of crofts, the menfolk gossiping at gable-end or peat-stack, the women indoors, save for those calling to the children that it was bedding-time. Gloaming was long-drawn; yet there was sufficient light left, as he crossed the stepping-stones at the Preacher's Burn, for him to descry the distant figure of MacKenzie, the village trader, seated on a cask before his store. The man had become well-known to him in his hours of official observation; he was suspect in the matter of smuggled salt for long; and with the old sleuth-instinct reviving, the sailor at once discarded his intention of an immediate return to Draolinn, and sauntered in the direction of the merchant. "How droll!" he said to himself: "MacKenzie in an evening reverie! ... Has the poet in him overcome the trader for the moment?" Rounding a knoll, he recognized his error: a small schooner lay in the bay, and from a punt at MacKenzie's stone jetty, a man in thigh-boots and brown jersey was stepping. Of a sudden the figure on the cask leapt to earth, glanced hurriedly at Linnell, and then hastened down the little pier to meet the newcomer.

"I wonder now ... I wonder," said the sailor. "That ship looks for all the world like O'Brien's."

The figures on the jetty were already moving towards the little two-storey block of building, set on the fringe of the Glenaros woods, where MacKenzie had dwelling and business-house in one. They reached the line of casks flanking the store, and seating themselves, awaited Linnell's approach. He came up nonchalantly enough, but he knew MacKenzie's reputation too well not to hold himself alert inwardly. The man's life was a blot; buying and selling provender, fodder, fishing-gear, timber, wool, and rough-woven stuffs, he contrived to have crofters and fishers for miles around, thirled to him by debt; always the balance at the year's end lay with MacKenzie the creditor. The poor folk paid in kind—cheese, stirks, tweed from their rude hand-looms, dried ling-fish, and even peats for his firing—nothing came amiss to the trader; and little did the crofter have in return. Chieftains like Draolinn of long descent held the poor folk by strong bonds of sentiment and liking; MacKenzie knew a stronger power. The sailor was acquainted with the type: it was not confined to the Highlands; he had found it in the Levant; he had seen it in Ireland in the gombeen man. And to-night the very odours of the place, as he approached it, seemed to cry out its infamy; for the smell of fish and kebbuck, of tar and seal-oil, brought up, not visions of prosperous commerce blessing him that gave and him that took, but of independence crushed out of life, and of avarice gluttoning on the labours of broken men.

"Taking the air, Mr. Linnell?" cried MacKenzie. "Come away and rest." He indicated a cask-head by his side. "It's long since we had the pleasure ... Aye, aye, and what's this I hear about burning your arms. You must be careful, sir; good people are scarce, you ken; good people are scarce ... You'll have met Mr. O'Brien?" The merchant's fine white teeth showed, a strange contrast to the squint eyes, and smashed nose above them.

The sailor glanced at the big fellow with the thigh-boots and brown jersey. He had a frank open countenance—a man of about fifty, with profuse dark hair in curls, and a grizzled beard. One ear carried a little ring of fine gold. "I've heard of him and of his schooner," said Linnell. "The *Maggie,* isn't it?"

MacKenzie pealed laughter. "No, no, that's another man altogether," he cried. "He's taking you for the salt-runner, Dominic, you see ... No, no, Mr. Linnell ... This O'Brien is the decent one ... His schooner's the *Janie*, and a fine bit boat she is."

The big Irishman grinned. "I've heard of the *Maggie*," he said; "and I think I saw her once. But I work Portaferry and Strangford way; the other fellow deals more to the north, I believe— Rathlin and 'Derry and that run."

"What's your cargo?" asked Linnell.

"Odd ... tar, keel, sugar, some sheep, building-stuffs, and salt—customs salt, of course. Taking wool back, though a trifle early."

"Come in and look at the King," said MacKenzie, rising; "I've some rare Ferintosh."

"Thank you kindly," said O'Brien with alacrity.

But the other shook his head. "I must keep better hours with my host," said he. "I'm off."

"Well, well," said MacKenzie, his white teeth showing almost as if in sarcasm. "Ours is the loss ... Good-night, sir."

The sailor took the hill-path, and at a faster pace than any he had made that day, for his arms cried out for fresh dressing. He was thoroughly tired when he reached Draolinn, in time for the evening meal.

Dr. MacCulloch was there, fuming to have had to wait overnight, because of the youth's delay. "It's at Torness I should have been by this time; and you stravaging the mountain moors like a shepherd."

"A shepherd indeed," said the sailor, and told the tale of the lamb in the thicket.

"Aren't you the odd man?" cried Elspeth; "and Mr. MacLeod another!"

"A pair of us," said Linnell whimsically, "can never be odd."

"Forfeit if you quiz me," said Elspeth. "What shall it be, Grizel?"

"We'll not show him the snipe's nest we found to-day," said her sister.

"So be it," said Linnell; "yet I've found a nest of my own; a mare's nest, perchance ... But I shall not hold it for forfeit"; and he recounted his meeting with the man from the schooner.

Draolinn growled. "Of course it was the salt-runner," said he. "That's the cut of him, I've heard: a dark man in a smock of brown worsted ... Ab-so-lute-ly! ... They bluffed you with half the truth ... Know what I mean? Gave you the name O'Brien to surprise you into belief of their story ... Cozened ... eh, MacCulloch?" The Doctor hummed and hawed. "Well," he concluded, "anyway I would never go behind the door with one word MacKenzie gave me. The man's dark, and not to be trusted."

"We'll see more of him before we're done," said Linnell grimly.

Elspeth's quick eye was on him at once, and a faint flush swept her brow. "Father, forbid it. He's for more adventure ... Dr. MacCulloch, we'll never have enough fine oils left for those arms of his. He'll be into the thickets again, if we do not restrain him."

"Unless you promise to show me that snipe's nest; I'll go back and kill those two rascals instantly," said the sailor merrily.

"Tush! be wise," said the girl, plucking at the stagmoss at her breast.

"Agreed then; the snipe's nest, and I spare their lives," said Linnell ... "But back I must go to-night; for something's afoot ... This MacKenzie fellow sets my teeth on edge."

"Mine too," said the Doctor. "Oh, he's deep, deep, is Duncan ... Did ever I tell you, Draolinn, how he prigged on me for months to sell the horse the good Countess gave me, and buy what he called 'a wise-like' beast—a Uist pony ... Of course I paid no heed to him—Fraochie and I winna part. But long and long I puzzled as to what he was after; and then I found—after two years of puzzling, look you,—that he had an old pony-chaise at Arle for sale ... 'Twas Tearlach Voulin told me of it. ' Nothing but dry-rot covered wi' red paint,' said Tearlach. ' Depend on it, Doctor, it was meant for the new pony you were to be buying.' ... And I'll wager Tearlach was right ... Oh, Duncan Merchant is the cunning one, let me tell you, sir."

"But Mr. Linnell is not to go moss-trooping to-night, is he, Doctor?" put in Elspeth.

"Well, he's a King's man, isn't he, lass?" said Draolinn; "and there's his duty, isn't there? ... Cut off to your books, you girls ... And the rest of us will have our punch over the study fire, and discuss things."

The girls retired; and the men drew into the cosy corner of Draolinn's den. "There's truth in what the lass says," concluded Dr. MacCulloch, after an hour's consideration. "You're none too fit for work of this kind

... But something's afoot, and we should have knowledge of it ... I think you must go; but I'm with you. I'll be at Torness sometime to-morrow, I suppose ... Weary fa' MacKenzie! ... We can watch from the wood above his house; and the thing shouldna be difficult ... For if cargo goes, or cargo comes from O'Brien's schooner, we'll soon ken what cargo ... That's all we want, to begin with."

A moon like an orange-slice hung over Corraven as they started; but by the time they had reached Tom-a-Chrochaire's slopes, it was tangled in a fold of purple vapour and its light almost gone. "A great bother the moon failing so early," said the Doctor, "we'll be making more noise than we need."

"Take the gorse patch," whispered Linnell. "I hear a foot."

"He's on the hill-track ... Come this side: and we'll see him against what little light there is," said MacCulloch quietly; and down they sank on the heath behind the whins.

"There's some one also to the north of us, and running, too," said the sailor, with his ear to earth. "Are they ranging the hill? ... Have they seen us?"

"Hush! here's the first fellow, on this very track," said the other; and they lay close, scarcely breathing. Haltingly, as if wearied, a man came along the old drove-road, planting a cromag heavily to earth at each step. Something familiar in the poise of the head's outline against the faint radiance momently thrown by the surging of the crescent moon to the top of a cloud billow, took the eye of the sailor. A sparkle of light on tassels at mid-leg clinched his suspicion: it was certainly his opponent of the afternoon. When the soft beat of brogues on turf had utterly died, MacCulloch spoke. "That's Oskamull," he whispered, "but not so jaunty a step as for ordinar'."

"I heard he had some accident recently," said Linnell. "A fall, I think."

"Any way, it's my gentleman," said the Doctor. "But what ploy is he after? ... He's thick with MacKenzie this year back ... deep in his books, I should say."

"We can move now," said the sailor. "The other man's steps are quiet also."

They stole silently on again, the Doctor leading the way, and at length came to a little wood of birch set on a cliff, down which a tiny fall of water went tinkling, steps and stairs fashion. Below them was a screen of scrub-oak, with a light peeping from the midst of it, where MacKenzie's house lay; then came the dark outline of the shore with a wash of little waves; and on the Sound, further out, a swinging light that marked the schooner. The moon shone fitfully at intervals, and they could descry on the jetty some grey patches that looked like bales of merchandise. Figures moved indistinctly on the beach; a boat sculled in to the pier; the bleat of a sheep took the air; and a dog whined. The seeming bales began to move.

"Sheep!" whispered MacCulloch in surprise. "Why, man, it's a hanging affair! ... He had better have stuck to salt-running ... I wonder if they're Garmony's ewes again?"

They watched the shipments in silence—the moving of the boat in and out from the schooner, and the quick handling of the cargo by wool and horns. At length the last load was gone; the light in MacKenzie's house went out; and Linnell rose. "I've a mind to see this merchant again at closer quarters," said he.

"Tush! you'll risk your neck," said the Doctor. "Leave it for the present; and let's mark the schooner's course. We've time enough ... What's that?"

Dusky figures rose from the undergrowth around. MacCulloch fell to the blow of a bludgeon at once; but the sailor struggled for a tortured two minutes, his arms crying out agony. Then he was hooded with a sack and knocked senseless; a bag was also drawn over the Doctor's head; and their assailants took them, thus bundled, by a steep path to the pier, and aboard a punt that shoved off instantly for the schooner. A little later O'Brien came down unsteadily from MacKenzie's house, and embarked on the returning punt, while a figure with tassalled Hessians waved him a farewell, and watched to see the schooner hoist her sails and head slowly down Kyle Aros.

12: The Forsaken Orchard

THERE was a feeling of uncertainty abroad at Draolinn on the morning after the departure of Linnell and the Doctor, when it was found that they had not returned. The ladies wandered uneasily from garden to hall and back again. Draolinn fretted and growled; at first he was confident that the absentees still held watch or followed a trail, but by mid-day he was frankly anxious. "Ride you round by Aros, Grizel," said he. "Ask if they've been seen, and mark if the schooner is still off MacKenzie's pier, or to be heard of anywhere."

Grizel was off and back by three; no news of the missing men; and no schooner in all the Kyle. They were still debating the situation, when there was a noise of horse's feet; and presently a serving maid brought news that Carsaig was below, and asking for a word with the chief.

Draolinn was red-hot on the instant. "He dares me!" he cried, gasping, the big veins prominent on his temples, his white beard a-bristle. "The hound! ... Bring me a pistol, Grizel ... Give him into my hands, and I'll strew his four quarters to the winds!" He rose, groping for the door. "I'll shroud him," he cried. "I'll trap the beast ... That's it, poison, d'ye hear ... poison for the vermin and a bowl of punch ... I'm blind, maybe; but somehow I'll shroud him!"

The girls strove to soothe him; but still he roared malediction on the intruder. They suggested that the chieftain might have news of the absent men ... a message perhaps; something of import had surely transpired, or he would never have set foot in Draolinn policies. But the blind old man would have no excuse, and muttering curses, devised such strange tortures for the visitor that even the sober Grizel could not restrain a smile.

At length Elspeth called strategy to her aid. "Well, then," she said, relieving him of the poker he flourished. "I'll send word that you refuse to see him. Of course, he may have news of our friends; but we must let that chance be going, rather than have you murder him."

A fresh outburst followed, directed chiefly at Linnell and MacCulloch — "fools that must go night-prowling"; and he sank to his chair, exhausted. "Well, have him up," he said. "As you say, he may have news of them ... But clear away, both of you, for I'm sure you've seen enough of the dog."

The girls retired; and shortly after, Carsaig was shown into the laird's sitting-room. He wore top-boots; his coat was dusty; he had ridden fast and far, it seemed; and his face was lined and care-worn. Draolinn turned unseeing eyes on him, as he stood tapping his thigh with a riding-switch. "Well, sir?" he growled.

"I am not here at my own instance, Draolinn," said the young man. "My cousin of Oskamull sent me to-day with an urgent message to your guest, Lieutenant Linnell. As your servant said he was not at home, and could not tell me where he was to be found, I considered it best — in view of the serious nature of my task — to make inquiries of you personally as to his whereabouts."

"Now, here's a well-read order of the day," sneered Draolinn. "So many fine words! ... No, sir, Lieutenant Linnell is not here, and I regret I cannot direct you to him. If I could, I'd do so gladly, for your manner of speech clearly indicates what your business is ... And I'd be pleased to hear the end of it, when he's done with your cousin ..."

"I fear I cannot discuss my business with any but Lieutenant Linnell."

"Oh, hang your primness! I never heard the like but that it only meant one thing ... It's likè a minuet for precision ... And that same is a music you yourself would have danced to long ago, let me tell you, had I but had eyes enough to see your waistcoat buttons at forty paces, my man."

"I shall report your answer, sir, to my principal."

"And tell him I trust that when the Lieutenant has given him his due, he'll serve you the same turn, sir ... I'd give much to see that meeting."

"I thank you," said Carsaig, twisting a slip of paper nervously in his fingers; "and good-day to you, sir."

By way of reply Draolinn growled in his beard: "*Marbh phaisg ort!*" and the chieftain slipped from the room.

On the landing outside, he beheld Elspeth descending towards him. He hesitated, but, impassive and silent, she passed, her dark eyes taking him so steadily that his head bent in shame, as she went on to Grizel's door. Memories of that night of ecstacy — so long ago it seemed now — swept through them both. For here was the very stair where had begun that mad adventure, and pictures of the moonlight through the pines, of the soft night-winds on the loch, of the orgy at Oskamull, came swift to the mind of each. A few steps down, he dared to lift his gaze in a poor appeal for mercy, but it met eyes relentless, as she stood, still as marble to watch him go. His head sank again, and he stole on and out of sight, like a man in a dream.

The girls were beside their father the instant the outer door had closed on the unlooked-for visitor. "What news, father? Where are they?" asked Grizel.

"Oh, he knows nothing," said the chief ... "Had called to see Linnell ... Didn't know he wasn't with us."

"What did he want?"

"He wanted Linnell I tell you ... Well, he isn't here, is he? ... . Well then ... well ... nothing," fumed the Laird.

Elspeth stooped to pick up a scrap of paper from the floor, glanced at it rapidly as she unfolded its twist, and then signed to her sister to retire with her. They left the old man spluttering about boobies that went night-wandering, and came out on the landing. Elspeth held the paper towards her sister; it bore a rude drawing, a map with the legend "Sands at Ormaig in Oolava"; a cross was placed at the north end of the bay, and a note of hours and dates below this was marked "Ebb-tides."

"What is it?"

"It's in Oskamull's hand," said Elspeth with blanched lips ... "Ormaig has been an old meeting-place for years ... Don't you see?"

"A duel?" whispered Grizel, paling also.

"What else?" said Elspeth bitterly. "Their fathers fought; and these madmen will have it that their sons must do likewise ... A birthright ... Well, we'll see"; and her head went high. "Keep you by the good father, Grizel ... I'll have this out with Carsaig."

She took the stairs in long leaps, ran to the stables, saddled the garron, and went off at a canter down the avenue of pines. But clear of the trees, she beheld the road empty for a mile on either hand; and, judging Carsaig had gone east by the Torlochan hill-route, she whipped round, raced back to Draolin and plunged into the forest track beyond. The road was narrow, and she must needs go slowly, so did it wind among the birch and hazel; but after ten minutes of threading these devious ways, a clearing came, where lay an old orchard and garden, long disused. The path ran now by a high beechen hedge; from behind this came the sound of a champing bit, and instantly the girl guided her mount to an opening in the close-set leafy barrier. On three sides this wall of beech rose dense and high, but on the fourth, there was only a low rail, with wild rose riotous over it, marking the boundary, where the old orchard looked out over an open stretch of park to Loch Ba, and took the sun. One little unhinged gate of decaying wood was in the thicket of wild-rose, and still served for entrance. Within, hay grew prodigal over the ancient flower-beds, and scattered here and there were some isolated apple-trees— moss-grown and aged, all that remained of the olden plenitude of fruit-bearers. The broken box-wood borders, the moss-covered paths, the draggled patches of lupins still persistent, and the tumble-down summer-house in the far angle yonder—all told a story of neglect and decay. Behind the great hedge, rose the tall protectors of this deserted sanctuary, elm and oak, plane and pine, close-ranked and enfolding, walling out the outer world from this once-favoured spot, with its airs of loneliness and brooding peace.

But for the sound of the champing bit and of slow hooves on the old garden-paths, there was silence. The horse was a saddle one, Elspeth saw; probably that of Carsaig. But where was he? She tied her garron to a pine-branch, and loosening the rickety gate, entered the place of dead memories. Almost midmost of this little sheltered square that had once been radiant witfc simple blooms, was an apple-tree, half-uprooted, but still gallantly flaunting its topmost boughs in air, laden with early globes of red and green; and, seated on the sloping trunk, his head in his hands, was the man she sought. Long-limbed and swift the girl strode forward. The slatting of her dress in the high grasses roused him; and he started up, his face very white, his hands clenching.

"You left this behind," said Elspeth, pale and out of breath, handing him the paper he had dropped on the carpet at Draolinn.

He received it with a sigh of recognition, and then looked at her, his eyes questioning.

She nodded in reply. "Yes, I've seen it," she said. "I understand."

A fit of trembling took him momentarily; he turned shrinking from her challenging figure, and walked a pace or two away on the mossy path; then, returning, sat down suddenly on the tree-trunk, and bending his head to his hands, hid his face.

At sight of him, so stricken, the girl flushed, and a moisture came to her eyes. "You are ill? "she asked.

"Not bodily," said he. "But sick to death within."

"Oh, Alan," she cried, "you hate this thing as much as I ... It must not be ... Evil enough. that their fathers fought."

Carsaig looked up, his visage blank, his eyes without expression. "My will is sapless," he said ... "You canna understand ... I think I do what I would not."

She sat down and put a hand on his shoulder. "Tell me," she said.

"It's easy asking," he replied bitterly; "but my lips are bound ... And it's killing me your eyes were, when we met by your sister's door this morning ... Oh, my dear, something is happening to me; for here is nought but blankness of soul ... Not torture of spirit, even that a body might bear; but deeps of isolation ... emptiness ... where there is nothing. Not madness, not that ... only an endless sinking to where no mind is ... What is it has come over me ... what is it?"

"Poor Alan!" she said; and patted his shoulder as she would a fretting child.

"Oh, the thing I am become!" he whispered. "The poor slack thing! ... And it's me that should be on my knees to you, asking pardon for wrongs long past ... But I've neither spirit nor words for that even."

"It will pass, cousin," said the girl. "Have faith."

He laughed low and bitter. "In what?" said he.

"In yourself, first of all."

"A sick, exhausted spirit like mine?" He swept a despairing hand; and she grasped it in her strong freckled fingers.

"Listen," she said. ..." I at least believe in you ... I've seen your worst, and I've seen your best ... Bring back your best, Alan, the strong hours of your youth, the clean days, the fine days. It's there I'd be putting my trust ... And it's in my mind to tell you what I'm for doing always when I'm sore bestead myself, Alan ... I just think of the bonniest glen I know; and what's that but Glen Lussa on a sunny day in autumn, the burn swirling among the hazels, and the birds there, and the big hills around? ... Or maybe, I think of a windy day on the Beallach, looking out past the headlands to the skerries wi' the blue sea making fountains over them, and the ocean stretching and stretching beyond ... It's a deal easier than struggling wi' dark thoughts, let me tell you; and when you've finished making pictures in your mind like that, the black care's gone, you'll see."

"You're more than good," said he, "but—"

"And when the black care's gone, then you'll have a heart in you ready for a kindness to somebody, I'm thinking ... And you'll say: 'What shall it be?' ... and the answer will just be this: 'This evil must not happen; these men must not fight.'"

His eyes gleamed. "You're the rare doctor," he said; "and you give me back my courage ... But you canna see the net that's round me."

"Break it!" she cried.

"There are twenty behind it."

"There's a weak mesh in every one of them, if you but look for it," she answered with conviction.

"It's easy talking, lass," said he; "but something has come over my very soul and centre; I'm as thowless and pithless as a played salmon." He stretched slack arms like a man in slumber, an sighed. "I canna put a name to the thing: I'm just done and by wi't."

"I tell you I believe in you, Alan MacKinnon," cried the girl, fiercely defiant of his protests.

This hint of anger roused him. "Aye," he said$_s$ whimsically, "I was once Alan MacKinnon." He looked at her steadily; saw the tears flood her eye of a sudden; and the sight of them brought him to' his feet. "Tears for me?" he cried in wonderment. "Then by the grace of God I may be Alan again.".

She smiled tenderly and shook her head. "Tears for you, and myself, and all of us; but it's myself that needs them most, I'm thinking; for I've made but a tangle o' life, so far."

He smiled wistfully. "Oh, my dear, my dear! for me you're ever the flawless one ... Put not your name and mine in the same breath."

"Have done your havering," she said merrily. "You'll have me as feckless as yourself ... Here's your garron fidgeting to be off. Through the nets wi' you, and stop this murder." She gripped the pony's bridle, and placed it in his fingers.

He caught her strong hands to kiss them before he sprang to the saddle. "You've put new heart in me," he said. "I'll set an end to this mad business ... And all the blessings in the Good Book on your head, Cousin Elspeth."

She opened the gate to him; and he trotted off on the woodland track, and was lost to sight amid the birches. The girl returned to the reclining trunk of the old apple-tree, and seated there, looked round helplessly on the forsaken orchard. Even the birds were few and silent, as if they approved the forlorn airs of the retreat; the only living things, indeed, were the tiny wrens in the trailing wild-rose thicket, and they were voiceless. The secret desolation of the place seemed to chime with Elspeth's mood, and bowing to the lichened bole as in despair, her breast heaved with sobs that were now tearless. "Poor Alan! "she said in a whisper. "Oh, my dear, my dear, will you never be wise?"

13: Eorsa

"PRACTISE the phlebotomy; then give whey sweetened with honey, and add decoction of tamarinds. Bathe the bruised part with spirits of camphor; and apply a poultice."

Linnell wakened to the chaunting of Dr. MacCulloch's voice. Bright sunlight shone on a dancing sea beyond the shore on which he lay. Distant cliffs and far green isles, an ocean horizon and a blue sky with clouds like scattered feathers were before him. His head burned and ached; his limbs were heavy; and as he turned painfully on his side, something clanked.

"Ah!" said the Doctor's voice. "Awake? ... I've been rehearsing a prescription for you, which in circumstances of civilization, might be procurable and useful ... Yet I think I'd forgo the bleeding in view of the haemorrhage you endured when the cutlass wounded you at Kilfinichen ... For myself —only a little hack on the temple—I should prefer a slice of the agaric of the oak, and possibly some caddis lint; afterwards the unguent we call the yellow basilicum, would be proper, I opine." He lifted himself from a bank of turf a yard away; and again something clanked. "Ship-irons on a schooner so small," said he, shuffling near, and exhibiting heavy padlocked fetters on his feet. "Heard you ever the like? ... But I daresay they're handy things among a wild gang like O'Brien's."

"Where are we?" asked Linnell faintly.

"On the island of Eorsa—its west side; six miles from Draolinn."

"What's the meaning of it?"

"Wait you, laddie; and we'll reason it out when your head's sounder. Have a mouthful of *drammach* for they've left us a *cuach* and some meal." He made a mixture, and the youth drank greedily. "Sleep you now, while the sun is here. We can talk at nightfall."

Linnell drowsed again; after a while, so did the old man beside him; and it was late afternoon before either stirred. The sailor rose wearily, hopped a pace or two on his close-shackled feet towards MacCulloch, and looked down on him pityingly. The good Doctor's weather-beaten features smiled back with boyish glee. "You laugh, sir," said the youth; "but I fear I've led you into a pickle ... I'm sorry."

"Now, now," said the old man, fingering a scrubby chin, "where's that wonderful philosophy of yours in the ballants o' bairns? Strike up a stave, man!

'Fortune will be fortune still,
Let the wind blow as it will?'

For myself I'd be heart-content, were it no' for thoughts o' yon poor woman at Torness, ay waiting her doctor ... But that clour on my head was none too heavy; only a *commotio cerebri* at the most; it might have been worse ... You likewise; so we'll leave the poultices till we're home ... In any case, I'm lucky to have a holiday; and the body at Torness was not in real danger, I fancy ... It's seldom I'm off the mill-round, I can tell you."

"A holiday—this?" said Linnell. "You puzzle me"; and he sat down disconsolate.

"Maybe I'm thoughtless," said the Doctor; "but, look you, I'm in my own country, not in Barbary; and, though shackled, I think I see the way things are working ... There's Gribun cliff; there's Inish; there's Oolava and Colonsay; and Staffs should be yonder. This is Eorsa, and nought on it but ourselves and some wild-goat. If we had flint and steel now—but they've taken them from me— we could make a smoke that might be of use as a signal. Or if we could get to the top of the headland here, doubtless we might be seen against the sky from Scarsdale or Coillemore; but that we'll never do with these irons—that's why they're on us, I jalouse. There's a chance, too, but a rare one, that mackerel will come up the Loch, and then we'd have the Gribun fishers after them, and coming close in here ... Oh, we're none so badly off; they're not for killing us, you see. It's only a case of keeping us out of the road for a bit."

"Why?"

"They're running a fresh cargo of stolen sheep, likely; and if we'd been free, we'd have warned the countryside, I suppose."

"But the owners of the sheep will surely do that."

"Aye, round their own doors; but a schooner like yon may make a wide sweep in a little time. Neither MacKenzie nor Oskamull is a fool. 'In for a penny; in for a pound,' that's the word for them and their like ... North, south, east and west—a day between liftings; who in all Aros Isle could stop them, if they're swift and daring enough? They'll run a hunder and more at a time ... And then they've the mainland to harry, likewise."

"How do you know they've but a day between?" The old man tapped his nose comically. "By induction, sir ... a doctor's business, that," said he. "Look you, you were snoring like one in an apoplexy, when they bundled me ashore last night, and I was then but coming to myself in yon dusty meal-poke ... I've a watch here"(he showed a mass of silver and crystal like a small turnip for size); "it runs down in forty hours, and I wind it every day at noon or thereabout. It was fifteen hours wound when we were clouted in Glenaros wood at three o'clock yesterday morning. Fifteen from forty leaves twenty-five; and the watch was for stopping, if I'd let it, at four o'clock at dawn to-day, when they dumped us ashore here. I'd sense enough left to look at her after they were gone. At four o'clock this morning, therefore, it was only twenty-five hours since they felled us. A day between liftings, I argue; therefore, they're off on another sheep-run."

"And after you came to consciousness?"

"Oh, then, I'd also wit enough to notice that it was through an empty ship they carried me, poke or no poke ... Never a ewe yonder, trust me!"

"That rules out an Irish trip; they'd take more than the twenty-four hours to that," said the youth.

"Aye; for the present we rule it out," said the Doctor eagerly. "Now, look you, they've sailed half round Aros. They left the east of it with sheep; they reach the west of it with none. That means that they've discharged the sheep somewhere betwixt east and west. And they've marooned us—that's the term nautical, I believe—in order that we may not give alarm. That means fresh cargoes of other folk's sheep, until they've made their total. Ah, believe me, there's a great gathering of some poor folk's ewes in a secret place ... And where's that? ... Somewhere on a course 'twixt the east and west of Aros Isle, as I say; and not as far as Ireland ... there was not time enough ... And where's the safest place for them," he went on, in evident relish of his reasoning, tapping his palm with a forefinger.

"You're beyond me, I fear," said Linnell. "I know the coasts hereabouts, but not from the shepherd's point of view."

"Look at it rather from the view-point of the stealer of sheep," said the other ... "It's a wee island they're on, I'll swear, man ... an island ... well out from the coast. And where's that now?"

The sailor shook his head.

"It's there I stick also," admitted the Doctor. "If she went north when she left MacKenzie's, I'd say it's one of the Treshnish the sheep are on. If south, then it's on one of the Holy Isles they are gathered."

"You're wonderful at diagnosis," said Linnell admiringly; and the keen eyes of the little old man lit up anew, as he beheld a fresh chance of exposition.

"And how is it done, sir—the diagnosis? Quite simply ... Ask yourself how you'd feel if you were in the position of the patient—the sheep-stealer, I mean?"

"A good deal less cramped about the legs, Doctor," said the other, and he hummed a stave:

"Malbrouck s'en va-t-en guerre
Ne sait quand reviendra"

"French?" said the Doctor. "What does it mean?

"It means that we looked for trouble, and we found it."

"You rascal! ... But it's glad I am to see that you've got back your philosophy ... Well, I'm going to look for something more to my mind than trouble—a lodging for the night." He rose gingerly, and went off hopping, bird-like, round the foot of the little bluff behind them. Presently he called Linnell; and the sailor following in like fashion, although a trifle less steadily, because of his still singing head, found his companion before an aperture in the rock, part fissure, part cave, which promised better quarters than the open during the dark hours. So they busied themselves for a little, collecting heather for a couch; and having removed the *cuach* and the package of meal to their new quarters, settled down for the night, A four-hourly watch by turns was arranged, in case of any fresh happening; and thus their first day in Eorsa ended, the sun sinking red and oval over a point of Oolava. Its last rays struck a sudden reflection from something high on the northern hills of Aros, and Linnell, on his first spell of sentry-go, had the Doctor out at once to ask its meaning.

"It might be the sun's rays on a window, but no house is in that airt," said the old man, hopping back to his bed of heather.

"Or a glass," hazarded his companion.

"A spy-glass?" cried MacCulloch eagerly. "Then we're watched ... Man, they're feared for what they've done to us. It's of good omen, lad: and I'll sleep sound."

When he awoke Linnell in the morning at the end of his watch, the Doctor was full of theories about the sheep-lifting. "I'll warrant it's the Holy Isles," he said ... "Eileach a' Naoimh, I fancy: not so far from Ireland, either. They'll have a thousand ewes there in a week: and in a week more they'd have them in Ireland—aye, in less than a week, if they'd more boats than one ... Aye! Oskamull 's the daring man! Last year—he marches with Garmony at Frisa, you see—last year these MacLiver fellows came as shepherds to Oskamull; and at the lambing time, there wasn't a ewe of their master's but had twins, and never a lamb to Garmony's sheep, though full of milk ... Lifted the very day they were born, you may be sure, and given fosterage on Oskamull's beasts ... They're smart boys, the MacLivers ... There's bad blood between them and Garmony's man, John Morrison; for one night (they didna stop at lambs, you see) John was down by the march-burn; and there was the youngest MacLiver half-way across it with a wether o' Garmony's on his shoulder. John seized its hindquarters; MacLiver had its horns: it was pull devil, pull baker; but John was the stronger, and landed the sheep on its own ground, and gave the rascal who was for stealing it, a sore drubbing ... Aye, man, I wouldna wonder but it was Garmony's ewes we had for fellow-passengers yon night."

"It's a hanging affair, I understand?" asked Linnell.

"Aye, for the little men ... the poor ones ... the fellows with but a single kail-pot to fill. But the men of the big liftings go scot-free, often and oft ...

You need good dogs, though ... that is if you're working on the mainland. I'm no' thinking o' boats and schooners, as in O'Brien's ploy ... that's new in the game ... I mind once of a whole flock lost in Lochaber, and sold at Falkirk tryst within the week, while Lochaber was scolding Badenoch ... He must have had good dogs, the man that carried through yon *creach* in Lochaber now ... Sleeping at daytime in corries o' Black Mount and hags o' Rannoch Moor, and travelling at night, I doubt not." The old man's eyes were as ardent as those of a schoolboy nest-harrying; his figure had the alertness of an old-time freebooter as he recounted.

"Why, you're the devil himself, his advocate," said the sailor.

Dr. MacCulloch's zest vanished instanter. "Well, no," he said apologetically, "but the dogs must have been good dogs, you see ... I'll be looking at those arms of yours now, I think," he added inconsequently. He dressed the burns with strips of linen torn from shirt-sleeves, damped in spring-water, and overlaid with broad leaves of the iris. "'Twill serve as well as the oils; and besides, you're healing fast," said he.

The day drifted by, the tedium broken by further tales from the Doctor of sheep-stealing and smuggling. The old man's philosophy of patience and the merry heart was not, however, so manifest as on the day before. He fidgeted, and watched the glint on the hill of Coillemore uneasily. "It's a glass, sure; enough; but I think the fellow has moved," he said in the afternoon. "He was at that patch of scrub-oak in the morning, and now he's higher up the hill and in the heather. You see it glittering yonder now?"t

"There's neither heather nor scrub where I see him," said Linnell. "The glass I see is shining on a bit of bare rock, a mile inland from his post of yesterday ... I hate this being overlooked in my every movement," he added testily. "If I'd his coat-tails within reach."

"Man, man!" cried the Doctor, excitedly, "you're right: he's on the scaur; but there's another in the heather—the one I first spoke of."

"You have it, sir," said Linnell. "There are two of them. What can it mean?"

They watched both reflections make eyes of fire in the sun and die away, time and again; finally the higher ray disappeared, but the single glint in the heather remained until the going down of the sun, and then went out. It was as if they had lost company of a kind; and, somewhat dispirited, they returned to their cave, and prepared for the night-watches. Dark came slowly on; it was MacCulloch's turn to do sentry-duty in the first four hours; and towards midnight, he found himself a hundred paces away from the sleeper, shuffling his feet cannily to keep them warm, without undue noise. From the gloom of the water's face came the soft beat of oars; and instantly he hailed it. An answering call reassured him, and presently out of the dark there stole a boat that grounded on the shingle below. Some figures sprang ashore, and soon the tall form of the

Captain More stood before him; and Elspeth was by his side, weeping for gladness. "My dear," she cried, "my dear!"and kissed the old captive's unshaven cheek.

"And Mr. Linnell?" asked the Captain.

"In a little cave, a hundred yards to the north. I'm afraid ... My feet ... you see?"

Elspeth was kneeling instantly, and feeling at his fetters. "How terrible!" she cried.

The old soldier passed a rapid hand over the irons and his teeth gritted. He called the gillies, and two of them carried the old man to the boat. "I thought as much," said the Captain; and off he went in search of the sailor.

The youth awakened to a hand on his brow. "Mr. Linnell, we've come," said Elspeth.

He sprang up, stumbling in his bonds, peered in the face of the girl, then in that of the Captain More, and laughed cheerily.

"We've a boat," said the old soldier, "and the Doctor's already aboard ... You're merry enough, it seems."

"Pardon!" said the youth. "But I was thinking of Miss Elspeth. There's a scolding in store for me, you understand."

The girl, unregarding the banter, was patting the wall of the cave, cold and wet with dew. "And to sleep here!" she cried.

"Madam, a palace," said the sailor. "In very truth, this is the house that Jack built." He lifted the meal-poke. "And this is the malt that lay in the house that Jack built ... And I'm the man all tattered and torn" (the girl drew back, flushing angrily) "that kissed the sheep with the crumpled horn," went on the youth without flinching ... "from early eve to dewy morn ... in that vile schooner of O'Brien's ... What? Carry me?" he cried, as the gillies hoisted him. "Well, well, so be it ... Forward, my braves." And down they trooped to the boat of rescue.

They rowed the six miles of quiet water to Drumlang in a soft darkness, for the young moon was now behind Ben More. The Doctor was all agog to hear by what means their prison had been discovered; and the Captain recounted how he had taken a walk on Coillemore hill with an old Army telescope in his oxter, on the second day of their absence. "And what should I see but somebody else with a glass lying in the heather half a mile below me."

"Aye," said the Doctor, "did we no' see two glasses glinting, just at sunset?"

"The fellow was looking steady on at Eorsa," continued the Captain, "so I took a vizzy in the same airt; and there were the both of you under the west cliff busy mixing a *drammach*. I could make out the meal-poke plainly, and I saw your legs were bound ... But what amazed me was the fellow in the heather down below. There he lay, kecking and giggling, vastly amused as he spied on you; plainly an unfriend. So, after watching him for a bit, I got up the hill to the corrie, and gave him the slip, unperceived. Then back I came to the boat at Drumlang, as fast as my auld shanks would carry me; and here we are."

"Well, I'll name no names," said the Doctor bitterly; and he nodded to the gillies at the oars, "but I'm thinking now your man in the heather would be wearing tasselled Hessians, Captain MacColl?"

"Just that," said the Captain briefly.

"The gillies have little English," said Elspeth. "You can tell the rest with safety."

"Oh, the rest of it is even worse," said the old soldier in a low voice. "For not twelve hours ago, my man in the heather sends a challenge to Draolinn for Lieutenant Linnell ... Do you see the devilry? ... He's for saying, as it were: 'I've nothing to do with the Lieutenant's disappearance, look you, or I'd never be sending him my second.'"

"Aye," said the Doctor, "but he's even deeper than that, the fox. He's for also saying, as it were: 'Good reason, indeed, for his disappearance, for have I not sent him my cartel?'"

Elspeth's fingers clutched at Linnell's shoulder, where he lay couched at her feet, and he turned to find her peering at him with eyes imploring. "Promise me," she whispered, "not that, not that ... You will not be foolish?"

He laughed back reassurance. "Oh, I've the rare motto for all such quarrels," said he.

"And what, sir?"

"The children's, madam ... It runs this way, I think"; and he trolled some lines of a Lowland rhyme in a voice so loud and hearty that the startled sea-birds on Scarsdale rose in the night with petulant cries, protesting.

> "My grandfather's man and me cast oot,
> How will we bring the matter aboot?
> We'll bring it aboot as weel as we can,
> And a' for the sake o' my grandfather's man"

"Aye, just that," said the Doctor grimly. "Well, we'll see ... we'll see ... But here's Drumlang at last; and if the smith's at home, my poor ankles will be glad of his services."

14: A New Carsaig

HIS shackles clear, the Doctor's thoughts turned at once to his patient at Torness; his mind, indeed, was set on going off to her that same night; and it was with difficulty that Elspeth persuaded him to rest at Draolinn till morning. "I maun be early astir then," he growled; and so it fell out; for by ten he was well up Glenforsa, leading Fraochie as of old, well pleased to be again at familiar tasks. By noon he reached Torness; and a stout, apple-cheeked woman met him smiling at the cottage-door.

"Were you for giving me time to get well or to get really ill, Doctor," she cried. "It's three days since I sent for you."

By way of apology he laid out for her some part of the story of the sheep-stealing, and his marooning on Eorsa.

"You poor man!" she cried, "and me blaming you! ... And the sheep stolen a' airts! ... I was hearing o't from Carsaig's doer this morning ... Ardchoil, Auchnacraig, Laggan and Moy lost badly the first day, he was saying; and yesterday Carsaig was robbed of over a hunder."

"Yesterday?" he cried. "Are they still at it, the rascals? ... But if his sheep are being stolen over there, what brings Gibbie hereabouts?"

"Seeking his chief at Aros ... And now they're both gone back to Carsaig but half an hour past, and riding hard."

"I'll be after them, then," said Dr. MacCulloch.

"I've a patient over their way; and they'll be company for me."

But, little used to saddle-work as he was, and the road through Glenmore being poor, he did not sight the travellers ahead for many weary miles, not indeed until he was nigh his goal. They were walking their horses up the steep slope of Glen Leidle, when he gave his view-holloa; and Carsaig halted to wait for him, while MacLaren looked round only to push on hastily again.

"You're for the sick lad at Feorlin?" said the chief, and the Doctor assenting, he went on eagerly, "You've heard the news? ... My hills stripped o' sheep by that black Irishman last night!"

"I've heard ... And all the rest o' the Isle well harried before that," said the surgeon.

"Well, thank God! we've tracked ours," said Carsaig ... "Gibbie's no' slack."

"Ye tell me!" cried the other. "Were they on Garvelloch?"

"You have it ... How did you guess?" The Doctor hastily recounted his adventure on Eorsa, as they toiled up the brae, and rehearsed the deductions he had already made regarding possible hiding-places for the stolen sheep.

"Violence!" cried Carsaig ... "As bad as that? ... Well then, if it comes to blows this night, the Lord help O'Brien!" and he told how MacLaren, guessing the Garvellochs as the resting-place of the spoil, had crossed over there, and found the lost flock on Eileach a' Naoimh.

"No easy job landing sheep yonder," said the surgeon, "or getting them off either."

"No; the skerries are bad ... But Gibbie's the rare one ... It's been a calm spell for some days back, and so he borrowed a fishing-gabbart from Loch Scridain, and set my men to ferrying back the ewes. They've been at it all day, it seems ... Slow work, wi' nine miles o' water to cross ... God send we get them all safe before O'Brien returns!"

"Oh, it'll be dark before he shows face," said the Doctor. "He's a bird o' night."

"I'm no' so sure that he'll wait for dark, though," said the chief. "He has the skerries to get past ... But, night or day, I'll be ready for him, and he'll find something else than ewes on Eileach a' Naoimh, I'm thinking ..." The last words came through set teeth.

The Doctor cocked his ears: here was a Carsaig vastly different from the dispirited fellow he had known of late. He took a side-glance at the tense figure in trews and plaid striding swiftly uphill beside his horse's head. "A bundle o' nerves," said he to himself, making a mental professional note. "Soon down; soon up." Then aloud: "You're for putting out your hand on him strongly, I see."

"I am that," said the other, grimly. "I've had troubles enow of late, without this Irish tinker adding to them ... It's past bearing ... The cup's brimming, and he'll get the fill o't, let me tell you ... "

"Indeed, then, and I bear him no goodwill myself for yon jaunt to Eorsa," said the Doctor.

Carsaig laughed delightedly. "Come you then over to Garvelloch wi' me, Doctor; and we'll lead him a dance ... Your lint and bandages will likely be handy; for there'll be broken pates ere this is finished; be sure o' that!"

"I'll come, and gladly," said the old man, his eyes flashing ... "But first, I maun be seeing Angus Dubh's lame leg ... When do you start?"

"In half an hour's time," said Carsaig, mounting, for they had now reached the head of the brae. "Haste you, Doctor ... You've little time to lose, if you're no' to miss this horoyally."

The surgeon followed him; walking the steep declivity slowly, his horse's rein on his arm, and so coming to Feorlin, saw his patient, and then pressed on to Carsaig House. Here he stabled Fraochie, and instantly went down to the pier, where a smack was unloading a batch of the rescued sheep. The chief soon joined him, and embarking with gillies to the number of nine, all armed with stout cromags, they set sail. To the south, rose Jura's peaks faintly outlined, as if limned in a delicate pastel of varied blues; nearer, Scarba loomed sphinx-like and dark; while, behind them, on the hills of Aros, shadows presaging the oncoming of evening were already deepening in the valley-clefts. But the low scattered isles of Netherlorn were bathed in light, their soft greens and greys and whites etherealized by sun and wave and sky as into something heavenly fair; and the tonic breeze, the boon air, the silent dreaming isles and seas caught the old surgeon up into a vision of *Tir-nan-Oig* ... The Land of the Ever Young ... Forgotten his weariness, forgotten his business here, the secret ineffable of life's meaning seemed plain in such surroundings. Elusive, intangible as sunlight on spray, this vision of beauty and power and good at the heart of things had again .come to him, as it had come in earlier years; and boy-like now, he stretched himself happily, dabbling fingers in the cool waters racing past the gunwale. Suddenly he heard a merry laugh, and looked up to find Carsaig gazing at him with glowing eyes. Had he, too, felt this kindly magic of the place and hour?

"The Highlands for me, Doctor!" cried the chief ... "Is it not now the noble country, this!"

"My own thought, indeed," said the old man ... "I just feel as if I could write a book, and all the wisdom of the world in it."

"Come to trying, 'tis another story," said Carsaig, with a sigh; and a trifle shamefaced at his outburst of sentiment, he turned off to take a vizzy from under the foresheet.

The Doctor followed him with a curious eye. The fellow had changed, surely! Eager, purpose ful, high-spirited, he gave his orders and scanned the boat's course in masterly fashion. "A new Carsaig with a vengeance," said the surgeon to himself. "I'm glad indeed I ventured this trip ... I wonder what has come over him." Had he been able to read the chambers of imagery in Carsaig's brain just then, he could have answered the riddle; for ever before the youth's inner eye that day was the picture of the forsaken orchard where Elspeth bent over a stricken man; and the memory of the sequence of that meeting ... a stormy interview with Oskamull when Carsaig had declined, despite many threats, to act further in the matter of a duel with Linnell, and so won to a peace of mind long sought for.

The gabbart was now rounding the southern spit of Eileach a' Naoimh, and already she felt the flood-tide running strong against her bows, as they opened the channel between the Isle and the Black Skerries. But the wind was fair, and if not in the teeth of the tide, at least, stronger than it; so, easily and surely they drew to the landing-place below Columba's Well.

MacLaren and his men leapt ashore, and scattered along the gullies to capture the score or so of sheep still to be recovered. No dog had been taken, lest he gave tongue inopportunely when O'Brien's men appeared, and thus the gathering of the ewes was an arduous task. Meanwhile Carsaig and the Doctor climbed Dun Bhreanian and looked down on the rich, grassy glade beside the ruins of the old Columban settlement, over which seemed to brood the spirit of utter peace. Around the isle lay the blue plane of the sea fretted to the south-east with the rocks of the Black Skerries, and the racing whirlpools of the tides.

"God! But it's bonnie!" cried Carsaig. "They chose well, those holy men of old ... Man! it's sacrilege! O'Brien bringing his spoil to a place so hallowed!"

"And yonder he comes, most likely," said the Doctor, pointing.

Far on the ocean's rim to the south, a speck was now to be seen; and instantly Carsaig was down the hill to his men, hurrying them on with their task. They had all the ewes close to the gabbart by now, and soon had them embarked. "Take her up to Geodha Iain, lads, and anchor there," said the Chief ... "We'll lower the mast, and they'll never see us."

They sailed through the northern channel cautiously, brought the boat into the creek Carsaig had named, and her crew, creeping ashore to hide in the clefts of the rocks or the long grasses, awaited O'Brien's men.

It was now well on for dusk, but the strange bark was already recognized by MacLaren as the quarry they sought; and as she sailed nearer it was plain that she was indeed the *Maggie* again bent on the old ploy. Already she was checked by the tide-race, but the wind held, and forging slowly past Am Port, where Carsaig's people had landed, the schooner came well up channel, took in sail, and with a rattling roar that sounded eerily in that still place, dropped anchor. Then she backed a little and lay, riding easy. Dusk though it was, the watchers now beheld a dinghy launched; dogs were heard barking as they were dropped into it; a lamp was lowered; and her men took to the oars.

"Send your gillies over to these fellows now, and see what you can make of them, Gibbie," said Carsaig. "The Doctor and I have business here."

As MacLaren and his men disappeared in the shadows, Carsaig turned to the surgeon. "Isn't he the daring one?" said he. "He's come right up to three fathoms ... But did you ever see aught luckier for us?" he whispered ... "We'll have a closer look at her now ... Come, you! . . ." He scrambled southwards along the beach, and the older man followed, panting. The rocks were rough, and the chief was breathless when he halted opposite the first of the skerries, where the tide ran fastest. "I'll can do't," said he ... "I'm no great swimmer; but here's the chance o' a lifetime."

"What is't you're at?" asked the Doctor.

"Cutting yon hawser," said Carsaig, briefly, beginning to strip. "We'll see if she'll make Rathlin this trip without a crew!"

"Bethink you!" cried Dr. MacCulloch. "That tide-race is no' canny, and there's danger from a breaking rope ... it may brain you, man!"

"You're right there," said Carsaig, "so I'll just have to cut it from aboard ship; and then dive clear."

"I'm telling you that tide's running like Corrievrecken," persisted the old man, nervously.

But Carsaig, now mother-naked, was buckling on a waist-belt with a sheath-knife in it. "The chance o' a lifetime, this," he repeated ... "I'll risk the tide ... Be you getting back to Gibbie, Doctor, and tell him what I'm after."

He plunged and the swirling waters took him. A faint phosphorescence showed in the growing gloom as each stroke of his circling arm took him athwart the race; and MacCulloch, watching his progress, swore softly. "Oh, hang your theatrical touches!" he said, inwardly. "I'm fearing you're just the old Carsaig after a'!" Yet he relented; for he muttered as he turned off in search of MacLaren and his men: "Still-and-on, it's a good work you're doing, *ille* ... But, man, I wish you'd drop these flourishes you're so fond o'."

Out in mid-channel, Carsaig wrestled with innumerable small whirlpools and undertows that took him unawares; yet the main current was with him; he held his course, and bore swiftly down on the dark bulk of the schooner. By dint of careful strategy, he reached the cable unhurt, though much buffeted, and testing it, found it so taut, that it would be madness to cut it from the water. To do so, he must needs support himself by it as he sawed, and the breaking strain might come unawares, the severed rope stunning or enwrapping him as it snapped.

There was nothing left but to go on board the ship and do his work from behind the protection of its timbers.

It was darkening fast, although a faint light still lingered in the west, as he drew his dripping body up the side by the rope lately used by the dinghy's crew, and crept on deck. Crouching, he listened ... the ship was now untenanted, he was sure ... Not a sound ... all were certainly ashore. Suddenly he noted how the vessel sheered with the tide, and he chuckled ... another thought had come to him ... He knew that once the cable was cut, the schooner would come gradually broadside on, as she drifted with the current. The chances were that she would keep in mid-channel and float derelict to open sea; but, if he cut her hawser as she sheered to starboard, there was every likelihood she would cant towards the southern point of Eileach a' Naoimh and go aground. The worst skerries were there ... knife-edges for abruptness ... and with that swift flood against the schooner's side, she could hardly miss striking. Then half an hour of those rough waters and keen rocks, and her back would break!

He ran swiftly back to the bows, his knife ready. But an adze lay handy; and with it he drove forcibly at the great rope as the ship swung in the desired direction; then skipped aside, while the severed end lashed back like an angry snake. Already the schooner was sagging down channel towards the reef below Geodha Bhridhe; so, mounting the rail, he dived, and swam shorewards. A westerly current took him fortunately close to the spit above Am Port, and none too soon, for his strength was spent, as he crawled out on the slippery weed-covered rock and lay, panting for breath. His chest was still heaving painfully, when a crash from the darkness to the south fell on his ear; and he laughed aloud despite his labouring ribs.... The *Maggie* was indeed now anchored in strange fashion by the shores of Eileach a' Naoimh.

Breath regained, he rose shivering and listened for some sound of conflict from the interior of the isle, but nothing save the noise of contending waters was to be heard. As to the upshot of the meeting with his men and O'Brien's, he had never a doubt; they were nine to six, and the issue could only be one way. So he stole slowly back along the beach for a space, and then taking to the turf, came north to Geodha Iain, where his discarded raiment lay. Towelling with his plaid, he was quickly aglow; and re-clad, he set off inland on a cautious reconnaissance.

A faint radiance lit up the north wall of the old Columban ruins, and here he found his people bivouacked round a fire with five of the Irish squatted beside them, all with bound wrists and two with bloody heads; the cromags had evidently been at play ... But the surgeon and MacLaren were absent, and he learned they had gone south of Am Port seeking himself. A faint halloo coming out of the dark just then, he set out in the direction whence it issued, and found his friends on the rim of the creek at Geodha Bhridhe.

The Doctor approached, stumbling on the rough ground, and peered anxiously in the dark at the Chief's face, while taking his wrist to feel a pulse that still throbbed too strenuously. "Keep me!" he cried, "your heart's hammering fit to break, lad ... It was too big a strain, that awful water ... You might well have been carried out to sea! Did you board her?"

"I did that."

"I saw her sweep by like a ghost ... She'll be well on the way to Ireland by now," chuckled MacLaren.

"She'll never more see Ireland, Gibbie ... It's on the skerry I sent her ... Her deck's well buckled by this."

"And what came of O'Brien?" asked the surgeon.

"O'Brien?" asked the Chief.

"He's aboard," stammered MacLaren.

"But I thought her dead empty," cried Carsaig, aghast.

"And well you might ... Senseless wi' drink in his cabin he's been, since they left 'Derry ... So his men say."

The chief's teeth gritted. "We'd best be going down to her then," said he.

"Where, sir?" asked the doer, trembling.

"Where O'Brien is ... Be putting your best foot foremost," said Carsaig, and went off southwards into the night. The others followed clumsily over the alternating bog and rock, and came upon him half a mile farther on, close to the water's edge, where the rock lipped sharply to a sea that raged like a mountain stream in spate. Above the sound of the contending waters, there came a grinding noise from out the blackness, and a dark hulk was to be seen indistinctly some seventy yards out from shore. By stooping they could make out the swaying masts of the wrecked schooner against the faint light still lingering in the southern sky; at times a report like a shot came from her as a deck plank started. Carsaig took off plaid and tunic.

"She's buckling 1" cried MacCulloch. . "You'll never reach her in time."

"Ye'd be ripped into skelfs wi' breaking timbers, even if ye did," pleaded MacLaren.

"The man's dead to the world wi' drink too ... What could you do wi' him?" moaned the old surgeon.

Carsaig, unheeding, stripped without undue haste, his eye on the schooner, as if testing her chances of holding together.

"Bear witness, Doctor, I advised him against this," cried MacLaren, in desperation, as the Chief took the water.

For reply MacCulloch sank down on the wet rocks and buried his face in his hands ... his brain awhirl ...There was no high-falutin here, indeed ... only a plain duty simply done.

The current took Carsaig sou'-west at once; but he came up slowly against the breaking water with strong strokes and forged slowly across, gauging his distance with wonderful accuracy, as MacLaren could see from the faint phosphorescence round the swimmer's arms. Now he stood on the reef, finding slippy footing below the rending hull; the dinghy rope still swung handy; and he was soon on deck by its aid. Groanings and cracklings came from the bowels of the stricken ship; it behoved him to pick his steps carefully, for the deck seams gaped at intervals below bare toes, and at any minute a limb might be thus imprisoned. At one instant there was a tearing noise and several planks flew up with a sound like a cannon shot not two yards away, and instantly the main mast rent free and crashed thunderous over the bulwarks. That gave him check ... he knew he had not long for his task ... the knife-edge of the skerry was cutting keenly and surely. And yet he dare not hasten ... every move must be certain ... He found the hatchway to the cabin clear of wreckage, and descended, testing each step; at the bottom of it, to his relief, his foot touched the heavy bulk of the senseless O'Brien. Dragging him on deck was hard work; but elated, he thanked Heaven the fellow was still in a stupor, and incapable of struggle: it would be an easy matter launching that inert figure, for the schooner had now listed so that the port bulwarks were awash. O'Brien also had a good shock of hair, a fine handful when it came to the crossing. But now he must rest to recover breath, so, sitting down by the snoring drunkard, he scanned the swirling flood and waited. The night was still fine, he noted thankfully, for with a stormy west wind meeting that tide, what chance would he have had! ... But ... time to go ... more deck-planks were starting, so, slipping the body of O'Brien to the water, he pushed off easily; and at once found the task harder than he had bargained for ... There was but a quarter mile of coast left for him to land on now, for this was the extreme end of Eileach a' Naoimh ... and the current long pent in its narrow channel was here bursting over the sill of the strait to open water as if rejoicing to be free. Half dazed, he plied his right arm, his left extended, towing the heavy bulk beside him ... And now he saw the folly of this adventure. He had been too sorely spent by his former exertions in wrecking the schooner ... This last ploy was madness ... madness ... nothing but madness ... the rest was a roaring in his ears as he sank ... His knee hit a jagged rock just then, and instantly new life sprang within the tired brain! He struck out with failing limbs, breasted sea-tangle, heard the voices of his friends, and fainted in their arms.

He came to, laughing hysterically, to find the surgeon chafing limbs that were agonizingly stiff and almost powerless. "Quiet you, man, quiet you!" said Dr. MacCulloch.

But Carsaig laughed on, pointing a shaking finger at the hull still faintly visible in the gloom. "What for" —he gasped—"what for did she no' break, as soon's I left her deck, Doctor, eh? ... It's spoiled ... spoiled any story you'd have to tell, man!" O'Brien groaned just then, and as MacLaren hastened to pour something from a flask down his throat, Carsaig, chuckling anew, crawled on hands and knees over to the rescued man. "There you are!" said he ... "A braw sheep-lifting you've made o't! ..." And rising he staggered off, to don his trews and plaid once more. Re-garbed, he came back to them ... "I'm for the fire yonder," said he. "I'll send down some of his own lads to carry him ... A braw sheep-lifting, aye!" and he laughed wildly once more as he stumbled up the beach.

"He's clean daft," confided the Doctor to MacLaren, as they knelt in the weed, rubbing O'Brien's face and hands. "And he'll pay for this the next few days, I'm thinking ... Soon up ... soon down ... that's the way of all the Carsaig folk."

"Maybe, maybe," said MacLaren, crossly, "but he's my own chief, look you ... And up or down or roundabout, he's a good lad, and it's a good night's work he's after doing."

Just then the *Maggie* bent in two with a roar, and a wave rose on the beach, drenching them ... MacLaren got up, swearing, and dragged O'Brien out of danger. "Look at that now!" he cried. "Chief or no chief, wasna he the fool all the same? ... He might have been trapped like a rat yonder."

15: A Broken Man

WHAT to do with the sheep-stealers was soon settled. There was no room in the gabbart for them; and indeed, if there had been, there was no proof definite of sheep-stealing against them, for they claimed to have only come ashore for a refilling of their water-breakers, and the casks in the boat were there to bear witness. Besides, the marooning of the Doctor and Linnell had been so carried out, that not a tittle of clear evidence lay to hand. And so O'Brien and his men were left on Eileach a' Naoimh with their dinghy, to make Craignish or Rathlin in the morning, as they thought fit; while Carsaig and his folk set sail for Aros Isle.

Draolinn fumed when, next day, the Doctor told him his story. "What for did Carsaig bother about saving the skunk," he cried, "if he didna mean to put his neck into a halter? ... Evidence? ... Plenty! ... Let them seek for't in 'Derry ... There are five hundred witnesses over there in the shape o' black-faced ewes, I tell you ... We'll get Linnell to say a word on't when he goes south to-morrow."

The sailor had to leave for Greenock to see to his cutter and report on the salt-smuggling; but, as he explained to Dr. MacCulloch, the sheep-stealing was another matter. "I fear I can do nothing," he said to the surgeon, who rode with him part of the journey next day on the way to Grasspoint Ferry.

"These Navy people will touch naught but my proper business, the preventive work against smuggling of any kind. They'll tell me that sheep-stealing's a matter for the sheriff ... But I'll try what can be done ... In any case, O'Brien's been well hit by the loss of his swift schooner ... And there'll be less salt-running for some time in consequence."

"Well, whatever happens," said the other, "be canny wi' Oskamull's name, for we've no real proof of him being in it. The Captain More saw him spying at us from Coillemore Hill ... and that's the most of it ... O'Brien's your quarry; see to him, lad ... All the same, I wouldna like to be Oskamull; for it's plain to me that the Captain's full cry after him in some private fashion ... Haste ye back; for we'll maybe have news for you when you return."

The Doctor was right in his surmise; the old soldier's thoughts were busy with Oskamull's recent activities, and when, one day, a week later, the minister rode over from Gualachaolish, and related the odd request of Linnell at the thicket on Leitir shore, he found the veteran unsympathetic.

"That young man will be the death of me," said the Captain. "What for is he wanting brotherly love and the rest of it wi' a fellow like Oskamull? ... He's as ill to place as a grasshopper—that sailor-boy ... now here, now there ... Come you up the hill a bit, Mr. MacLeod, and I'll tell you a tale." They were walking in front of the Captain's lodging after the mid-day meal, and turning his steps to Tor-nam-Feinne, the veteran told the story of Eorsa and the spy-glass, and of the challenge sent through Carsaig.

The minister sighed, and lit a fresh pipe. "Man, it seems as if nothing but the Old Dispensation were fit for a case like Oskamull's," said he. "And it's clear that we're on different ground from where we were when young Linnell spoke to me ... It's difficult ... difficult ...; and yet I had some hopes."

"Difficult?" cried the Captain, casting an eye on the slopes below them, and halting to mark a figure on the edge of a birch-grove some distance below. "I'll warrant I ken a minister would make another story of it ... See yonder!" He pointed to the slight form of Alasdair Beg, gesticulating in the pantomime of one of his out-door sermons at the fringe of the wood of birches.

"Keep us!" said MacLeod. "What's come over the lad? It's the Catechist's Boy, isn't it?"

"Let us take a slant," said the Captain, "and come on him from the west through the trees yonder." He recounted the former sermon he had heard in the same spot. "If Alasdair kent all I've learnt in the past week, I've no doubt as to how he'd be for dealing with Oskamull," he concluded. "He'd have him among the goats, sure enough."

But the preaching was past and over by the time they reached the boy, and he was busy removing all traces of his improvised pulpit-desk of stones and turf. The Captain More made a swift step from the shelter of the birches and had him by the arm before he could escape. "You'll ken Mr. MacLeod, Alasdair?" he said.

The boy strove to set himself free, his face white, his look that of a snared animal. "Let me be!" he cried in Gaelic. "It's not against him I was preaching."

"Surely, Alasdair, surely we'll let you be," said the soldier in the old language also, as he released him and sat down on a tussock. "Go you, if you will go ... But I'm for resting for a little in this bonnie kirk o' yours, and looking out on the splendour of God ... His good hills and the loch; better preachers than any of us, I'm thinking ... Sit you down, Mr. MacLeod."

The minister stretched himself on the soft turf, and smiling invitingly at the daft boy, patted the grass by his side.

Alasdair retreated a pace or two, and regarded them both sullenly for a little in silence; then he came forward eagerly. "There's one law for the rich, and one for the poor," said he; "but what sort o' law is yon?" He pointed down the hill.

"Where? "asked the Captain.

"At Cladh Phobuill, last night."

"Whatever can you be meaning, laddie?"

"Says he, 'There's no law to compel you; but do it, you shall'; and the other just groaned, and turned on his face among the *canach*."

"A queer thing that to say, eh, Alasdair?" said the Captain cautiously.

"Oh, but he's the wicked one, is Oskamull ..." cried the boy. "You dinna ken how evil ... I thought him fair-dealing till last night, when I heard yon ... Just a word or two from him, and there was the broken heart down yonder at Cladh Phobuill."

"It's the strange world, Alasdair," said the Captain soothingly. "Who now was the other man?"

"Who but Carsaig? ... And to hear him pleading would have made you greet."

"When did you say this happened?" asked the minister.

"Yesterday at the mouth o' dark. I came down to Cladh Phobuill, where the graves were once so plentiful, and are now but bits o' broken stone among the hazel roots ... It's a by-ordinar' graveyard yon, so old—so old! ... Alasdair likes to sit there at the time o' dusk and lateness, deep in among the hazels that cover the house o' death. It's where they buried, hunders and hunders o' years past, you see ... And the head-stones have mouldered and mouldered, and the hazel shoots have crept in, and now the trees come up among the dead, and cover them and shelter them so bonnie."

"And indeed, it's often I've wondered what its story was, Alasdair," said the Captain.

"Oh, mony's the story to it," said the boy; "but you'd be forgetting there were ever graves yonder, if it hadna a name: Cladh Phobuill; so far back the buryings, so close the hazel shaw. It's fine, fine, the way it kens to hide the dead folk, yon wee quiet wood, ay growing leaves and shedding them on stones so old and mossy ... And when the wind is up, it's the great harping it makes among the trees o' Cladh Phobuill ... Lucky the sleepers there; grand their dreams! ... Never a kirk-skailing to bother them; never a tomb wi' lettering left for reading; never a new burying wi' its trampling feet! ... It's just old and quiet and done; and Alasdair likes it fine."

He paused in his eulogy, and regarded the minister seriously. "What for did you bring him here?" he asked the Captain after a moment or two of silence. "For, if he werena here, it's now I could be swearing."

"I trust you'll no' do that, Alasdair," said Mr. MacLeod gravely.

"What for no'? ... What else should I be doing when I mind o' yon devil, so near a place that's holy and solemn?"

"Alasdair, Alasdair!" cried the Captain soothingly.

"... And tearing Carsaig's heart out wi' his bitter words."

"I see," said the Captain, seeking to lead him on to the marrow of the matter. "You were in among the stones and hazels when you came on them?"

"No; I was in Cladh Phobuill, when they came off the path to a hollow on the edge of it (to be private, as it were); for they were argy-bargying as they rode; and up there they came to finish it in secret; so they tied their horses to the big oak, and sat down to the debating. Money was Oskamull's cry. He was being pressed by MacKenzie; and he must have money. And Carsaig must clear his crofters, and put on sheep and sheep and sheep; and so have money enough for yon hound. It was the only way to raise the guineas nowadays, he said. Year in, year out, Carsaig was to pay him. If he didna, then Carsaig's lands were to be taken; and the beast said he'd soon clear the crofters, and show him what a sheep-run should be like."

"And now, Alasdair, are you sure o' that?" asked the Captain eagerly.

"As sure's you're sitting before my two eyes," said the lad. "It was in the old language they spoke, and it's every word I heard ... Carsaig's lands were to be Oskamull's if he didna do as he was bid by yon black one ... But the strange thing was that Oskamull said he'd never take the law of him. 'You're Highland, and that's law enough for me ' — he says (What sort o' law is that? thinks Alasdair). And then poor Carsaig almost grat, and begged him to think o' something else than clearing the estate ... Fancy you that devilry at *Cladh Phobuill*, minister!"

"And what then, laddie? "asked Mr. McLeod.

"And Oskamull just made mouths at him, and mocked and laughed, and left him at the wood-edge,face downwards in the *canach*, a broken man ... 'I'll give you till next Martinmas,'says he of the high chin; 'and if you'll no' move afore then, by the Lord I will at the term! '"

"The dog! "cried the minister. Alasdair turned on him swiftly. "Swear if you like, Mr. MacLeod," said he; "Alasdair'll tell nobody ... But is it not a wonder, look you, that the spirits of the dead came not poking through the hazel-trees of *Cladh Phobuill*, and tore him to bits? *Och, ubh, ubh!* the bonnie place, spoiled on me for ever with yon one's grief!"

The Captain More exchanged a look with the minister, and they rose to go.

"You're the good lad, Alasdair," said Mr. MacLeod; "but it's a sore world for good people ... So let you and me and all of us be trying to lighten its burdens ... Was there aught else that you can call to mind?"

The boy shook his head. "You've all of it," said he, "and is there not enough? ... The poor man lay like dead for an hour, and then trailed away, leading his pony by the hill-road to Aros.... And it's me must be taking that same road now: it's dovering I am, for I've slept little since I heard yon ... *Feasgar math*! "ˣ

"*Feasgar math*, Alasdair," said the others, and the boy slouched off.

"Heard you ever the like?" said the Captain. "Here's Carsaig a hero one week, and a poor thing the next ... It's the strange world!"

"It looks as if Oskamull were taking revenge on Carsaig for the way he served O'Brien's schooner ... He would have shares in her, of course," said MacLeod.

"Maybe, maybe," said the other. "But it's clear from Alasdair's story that we maun go further back to get at the root o' the business ... MacKenzie has some kind o' hold over Oskamull, it appears."

"Ah," cried the minister, "he's the dark one, is Duncan Merchant."

"It's like steps and stairs," said the other; "MacKenzie holds Oskamull, and Oskamull has a grip on Carsaig, and Carsaig ..." Elspeth's name had been on the tip of his tongue. He stopped in a confusion his companion noted, and instantly did his best to allay.

"I think I follow you," said MacLeod, "and we need say no further there. But leaving that score to one side, there are the crofters to consider. They're to be out by Martinmas, according to Alasdair, if Carsaig doesna pay. A black winter in front of them, and hovels to build on the rocks of the shore like others before them, I'll wager. Their roof-trees burnt, as like as not, and bloody murder before the day is done. The thing's like a plague for spreading among the lairds, since Farr and Kildonan were cleared; but who'd have thought tq§ have seen it in Shire Argyll? "

"Aye, it's bitter, and a' for the sake o' supplying Oskamull wi' yellow Geordies that take wings at Crockford's gaming-tables, almost as soon as he gets south."

"Humph!" said the minister. "They're telling me the great Duke's often at that same club."

"But no' for gambling," cried the Captain hotly. "Wellington's no fool."

"Maybe, maybe; sometimes he's wise, and sometimes no' so wise, the same man ... But, look you, here's our own affair. Whoever pays the piper, it looks as if it were MacKenzie that's calling the tune. And it means ruination in the end for the poor folk on Carsaig's lands. Is there no way out of it?"

The soldier's jaws set hard, and he halted. "You're right," said he. "Oskamull may be black; but it's this brock of a money-lender that's at the root of the thing ... And by Mary! if I were a younger man, I'd beat him myself. As it is, I must wait for Linnell."

The minister fired at once. "Linnell here, Linnell there! what about me? I'm only fifty-four," said he eagerly. "Linnell may come next week or never ... And, Captain, I'm fell keen to turn the tables on Duncan." He was pleading like a schoolboy for a share in the games of his comrades.

The Captain smiled grimly. "Well, myself," said he, "I wouldna just call fifty-four a young man's age,"

"I'll swim Linnell any day and beat him," said the other, ruffling.

"Oh, you're grand at that, I well believe; but it's of a possible hamesucken I'm thinking, and I'd back the sailor any day against you, when it comes to that kind o' sport, minister."

"Violence? "cried MacLeod.

"And what else is more fitting, if we're to withstand violence. The uprooting of these poor crofter-folk, and their slow slaughter by the winter! what else is that but violence? ... Call it law if you like; but it's nothing else than sentence of death to some innocents, believe me. I've seen what was done in the Strath of Kildonan, and in all my life of sodgering I only saw one thing worse ... a new-filled burial-trench in Spain, the earth covering it, and it heaving."

MacLeod regarded the veteran with horror for a moment and then, seeking his usual solace, produced his pipe and *fleurisch*. "Aye," said he, puffing with an attempt at philosophic calm, "a hard life a soldier's, and bitter memories too ... But I'm for putting forth my hand strongly on yon fellow, if you tell me there's no other way to stop this evil ... They're saying that Columba himself made some journeys wi' a claymore on his shoulder."

The Captain's gloom dissolved in a smile. "Well, if neither of us is just what you would call young, Mr. MacLeod, still-and-on we've something that youth lacks plentifully, and that's wits ... And I think we'd be a match for Duncan Merchant, the two of us, either in blows or in cunning ... When's your next preaching at this end o' the country?

"I'm to be in Pennygown Kirk on Sabbath week, ten days from now."

"Come you to Killiechronan then on the Saturday before, and stop overnight with me ... And talking of lambs in thickets, I suppose we could get a lamb on the north side of the township, as easily as on Leitir shore?"

"Man alive, yes; the low ground is thick with them ... But who was talking of lambs? What are you driving at, you droll man? Are you for sheep-stealing as well as hamesucken? ... And this business is no' for the Sabbath, surely?"

"I see no other way," said the Captain calmly. "A Sabbath it must be, or not at all ... But if you've a conscience in the matter, I'll just wait for Linnell."

"Oh, botheration on Linnell: if there's a lamb in the ploy, he's bound to be in it, of course."

"Aye, and it was on a Sabbath that you stretched your hand to save a wee sheep from a wheen scratches on its nose; but now you'll no' put forth your hand on the Lord's day to save a hunder poor folk from misery and starvation?"

"Do you tell me then, that of a surety we can thus set this thing right?"

"Under Providence, I believe we can, Mr. MacLeod."

"I could come quite early on Saturday, you ken," suggested the other feebly.

The old soldier turned off with a gesture of despair, and instantly the cleric capitulated. "Sabbath be it then! Hamesucken be it!" he cried angrily. "But, look you! I'll make Mackenzie pay for this, once I get my nieves on him."

16: Hamesucken

DURING the following week the Captain More found occasion for two visits to MacKenzie's house: reconnoitring expeditions, as he termed them; and on the first of these he went straight to his quarry.

"Come away, Captain MacColl, come away," cried the merchant at sight of the grey beaver and the long fawn-coloured coat. "Glad to see you; but it's driving you should be, not walking the long miles in this hot sun ... You must take care of yourself." Followed the usual compliment. "Good people are scarce, you ken; good people are scarce!" He stuck his hands in his big belly-band pockets, and hugged himself, his swivel eyes blinking, his white teeth flashing.

"So they're telling me, Mr. MacKenzie; and that's one reason I'm glad to see yourself so hearty."

"Come in and look at the King," said the merchant, and led the way past barrels and boxes and bales of webbing, through the counter, to what he termed his back-shop.

The old soldier had chosen his hour carefully; there was no customer in sight, and they sat down to a dram from a black bottle, designed to represent George the Fourth squashed sideways, pouring Ferintosh liberally from the peak of an Admiral's hat. The talk was of weather and crops, the prices of cattle and the new leases; then it declined on countryside gossip.

"And were you hearing of Callum Crubach's latest?" asked the man of business, smiling broadly.

"No," said the Captain, his eye ranging the files of papers hanging from shelves everywhere. "What was that? He's a droll one, the Crubach."

"Aye, he's all that. And, you ken, he's sore bothered wi' the cailleach, his wife's mother, that stops wi' them. Well, one day lately, Callum heard that Angus up at Arle had been taking his grannie —Mary Vore—taking her out an airing in a new trap he was, when a wheel broke on them, and down they came, and the old wife's head sore hurted (a fracture of the skull, the Doctor was saying), real bad the poor old body was, when last I heard. Well, when he got word of it, what does Callum say, think you? ' I wonder now,' says he, ' if Angus wouldna give our *cailleach* a drive? '" The merchant laughed uproariously as he concluded, hugging his belly-band.

The Captain was unresponsive; he had just noted that one of the two chests by the fireplace was covered by a drugget screen, which was sufficiently displaced at one end to reveal a padlock with hasp; yet he was alert enough to answer casually: "Poor body! An accident like that! And at her age!"

MacKenzie's manner changed rapidly, and his laughter ceased. "Poor body indeed," said he. "A queer business that wheel breaking on them ... A new trap too, as well I know; for Angus bought it from me—and cheap—but two days before. I canna understand that wheel."

"Oh, I've heard of that trap before now, if it's the one you stored at Arle," said the Captain. "Wasn't it the thing you were for selling to the Doctor a year or two back?" His gaze fixed the least deviated of the squints of MacKenzie, who was sipping his glass reflectively, and instantly the merchant was seized with a paroxysm of coughing. Making big excuses by signs he retreated through the store to the open air, clearing his throat loudly as he went.

"Aye! and it's well all the keys of the world are not at your belt, my man," said the Captain More to himself, as he looked after the fellow to make sure that he was out of sight. He laid his hand on a desk that stood by the window and tried to lift a flap that resisted. Still the well-acted coughing went on intermittently out-of-doors; so the inmate of the back-shop proceeded to test the fastenings of the two trunks that lay on either side the fireplace. They held firmly, however, and he went on to a hasty survey of the sheaves of papers on strings and wires around the walls. "Twenty years of accounts and invoices, I should say ... They must be bonnie as pictures to Duncan Merchant, and him doting on them ... Nothing hidden among that lot, I fancy ... But here are a desk and two kists; and the one with the hasps is my fancy, Mr. MacKenzie: something nice and handy to the shop where you sell your soul every day ... At night now, a different story ... a strong box lifted from there up to your sleeping-den? Most likely that'll be it, I'm thinking. And here you come again, my beauty!"

The merchant returned, still clearing his throat ostentatiously. "A bad hoast that, Duncan," said the Captain, rising. "Well, you canna blame the dram for it; it's prime stuff, I can assure you ... Not a drop more, thank you. And I'll be saying good-morning."

The second visit of the veteran, two days later, did not involve a personal call; indeed the reconnaissance was wholly masked this time. He came out from the edge of Glenaros wood to the little cliff that overhung the store-house, and, cowering behind an alder-tree, surveyed the outbuildings of MacKenzie's dwelling through his battered telescope. Then entering the wood again, he emerged half a mile further on, and noted carefully the presence of several ewes and their young on the grassy ground near the shore.

As he returned on the homeward track through the heathery knowes, he found himself short of breath at the brae-top that gives the first vision of Loch-na-Keal. "I'm fearing you're too old for a game like this," he said to himself. "But you'll never let yon minister body cast that up to you ... And you canna just turn back because you're ganting for wind more than ordinar', can you?"

On the Saturday evening the minister arrived, solemn exceedingly, despite many pipes on the way: and, after the manner of Highland womankind, he was duly idolized by the three sisters at Killiechronan. The Captain smiled at the tip-toeing and lowering of voices among the ladies, and said in a mischievous aside to the cleric: "It's clear they've no suspicions of what a desperate character you really are, Mr. MacLeod."

The minister flushed furiously, but said nothing until he went out-of-doors with the veteran to take a breath of air before bedding-time, "My shame and my melting! "he cried then. "Isn't it me that feels the hypocrite with those good women, so gentle and kind, ever about me, tending my every need? ... Och, Captain, now, couldna we be putting this thing off till Monday?"

"What a trimmer!" replied the other. "Light would be the breeze you couldna sail in, minister. But it's to-morrow it must be; and at the very hour of your service, moreover, when you should be pulling a long face in Pennygown pulpit, sir."

MacLeod flung up his hands in terror, and groaned. "And now," said the Captain, "do you not see that the best time will be when all Aros is at worship? If any remain they'll be busy at their kitchen fires, and hardly one will be stirring as far as Duncan Merchant's. There's Kirsty, his housekeeper, to reckon with; but she takes turns about with her master at your preachings; and as you must well know, it's Kirsty's day for the kirk the morn; so my gentleman will be quite alone."

"Indeed and indeed, you're the masterful man," said MacLeod. "Be telling me no more, or I'll never sleep the night ... Still there's one thing I'd forgotten; you were asking about a lamb in a thicket ... What o' that?"

"Man, you're as keen as a laddie making his first pee-oy," said the veteran gaily. "But I've no more news for you this night, my youthful friend. So let us to our bedding."

They returned to their quarters: the minister to toss uneasily for a full hour before he slumbered; the Captain to sit long by candlelight, adjusting something that looked like a dog's muzzle of leather, and, thereafter, testing and priming two old pistols that had seen service in Spain. When this was finished, he, too, retired, and sighing contentedly, fell asleep the moment his old grey head touched pillow.

In the morning they were up betimes; by eleven were off, the minister leading his pony; and half an hour later they stood on the cliff down which went a little fall of water to a stream running past MacKenzie's back door. Smoke rose thinly from a single chimney in the merchant's house; and presently the kitchen door opened to let out Kirsty MacIver with some breakfast remnants for the hens. Ten minutes later she sallied forth in curch, Sunday blacks and creaking shoes, on her way to the preaching at Pennygown. Worshippers in groups of twos and threes were already passing on the high road in front, crofting folk from the outlying townships of Glenaros and Frisa. A clear sun shone; the wee waves glucked on the rocks; a Sabbath peace was over all.

"Just look at them," sighed MacLeod, pointing to the wayfarers. "If they but kent their minister was spying on them from behind an alder-tree, or about to lift his hands in assault on the Lord's day, I wonder."

"Have done wi' your havers, and get on wi' you," snapped the Captain. "There need be no violence, if you'll but do what I ask. See you here." He held up the muzzle. "Take a turn ahint, and seek me out a strong bit lamb, and clap this on his nose, so that he'll can greet none at all. Bring it here before twenty minutes are by; and the job's half done ... And keep you out of sight of the shore-road, and these douce parishioners o' yours," he added.

MacLeod stared in amazed protest at the tone of command; but it was not for nothing that the Captain had served in many a campaign; so, meeting the clear blue eyes of the old soldier, the minister obediently picked up the little contrivance of leather, and set off, the most docile of subordinates.

Immediately on his departure, the Captain took up his telescope, and carefully studied an outhouse close by the gable; then, well-satisfied with his observe, lay down on the turf, soothing "*Cogadh no Sith.*"

MacLeod was back well within time, a fine ewe-lamb, well-muzzled, with him; and at once the veteran looked at his watch. "Five minutes from noon," said he. "We'll just wait till we get them all well-gathered into the preaching-house. Ten minutes'll do it ... A bonnie morning, and the Sound so blue, minister! Just look at Killundine and Fiunary yonder ... the fat crofts of those Morvern folk! ... Happy days now; but what's before them, if they're soon to have a swatch of the Sutherland devilry, as well as Carsaig's people?"

The cleric's eyes blazed. "For the Lord's sake, Captain," he groaned, "stop it; or I'll be doing more harm to Duncan than I was ettling ... Can we no' be going on wi' the business now? I feel foolish, sitting here nursing a wee lamb on my knee, like a wean wi' her doll ... And me thinking of the sound o' fists all the time, and almost wishing for them; may God forgive me!"

"Stop you with your fists, the sound of them," said the other. "I hope and trust there'll be no need for that. It's easier to keep a man out, than to put him out when he's in; and I'm for getting Duncan out from among his filthy papers before I make a mess of them."

He briefly explained his plan to the minister, who received it with murmurs of strong approval. "There's only one thing more to say, Mr.

MacLeod," concluded the Captain as he passed a piece of cord round the lamb's forelegs, and tied it firmly; "and that's this: as your commanding officer, I must ask you to leave your pipe with me. It has a way of delaying you at times, you'll understand."

Without a word further, MacLeod glumly complied. "You can go now," said the other, "and I'll keep my glass on the road ... There's the oil." He handed over a little phial.

The minister slipped into the wood, the lamb in his arms; and a few minutes later came out silently at the cliff-foot, leapt the burn, and proceeded towards an outhouse, which was invisible from the main building, since it faced a blind gable to the north. This was a cellar, formerly used for storing hides, but now empty; its one door was half-open, and a key stuck in its lock. The minister drenched the bolt in oil at once; next, removing the key, he treated it in similar fashion and re-inserted it. Then, his face white and perspiring, he deposited the lamb on the floor of the shed, slipped its muzzle, and closed the door softly. Instantly he skipped, the oddest of figures in white stock and flying coat-tails, to the rear of the cellar. Thence he glanced upward to where the Captain More held post, and beheld only a disc of brass-bound glass staring at him fiercely from among alder leaves.

Presently a bleat sounded from the depths of the lamb's prison; then rhythmic calls for release took the air insistently; and after some minutes the back door of the store-house opened, and MacKenzie appeared in his wincey shirt-sleeves. Unkempt and unsabbatical in each detail, he yawned and stretched his arms. The lamb's appeal went up more lustily than ever at the sound of the door's unlatching; and the merchant, cursing in Gaelic, went back for his brogues, and stepped across the clutter of the hen-yard in the direction of the sound. He paused at the door of the isolated cellar, put an ear to it, and flung it open. Amazed at the sight of the shackled animal within, he entered in order to get a closer examination. Doubtless, indeed, he already saw free provender in the poor brute. But just then the Captain More waved an arm wildly, and MacLeod tip-toeing from the rear, propelled the merchant violently farther into the interior of the out-house by a wild blow between the shoulders, banged the door to, and turned the well-oiled key with ease. MacKenzie's fists were hammering on the planching at once; but the minister's only reply was a most unclerical snap of his fingers. Meanwhile the Captain had descended the cliff-path; and together they now made for the merchant's house.

"Lachie Dubh will be at the hunder and nineteenth by this time," said the minister gleefully. "The congregation'll be wondering at his fondness for it."

"Bother Lachie Dubh," said the Captain. "Let us get to work. You'll be at your preaching in ten minutes from now if your pony's any use: for two minutes are all I want here ... But stop you at the window there, and keep your eye on yon door; for, if he breaks loose, it's more than the hunder and nineteenth'll be needed at Pennygown the day, I'm thinking ... And, look you! "(he showed a pistol). "If you hear a shot or two, don't be put out; it's the soldier's picklock, you ken."

He strode through the transe and entered MacKenzie's back room. A pistol nozzle was put to the desk's keyhole, and following the report, the lid lifted easily. Here were papers enough; passbooks, receipts, bills of lading, and so forth, but nothing of importance; so he turned to the drugget-covered chest, levered the hasps free with a poker, and opened the lock with a bullet from his second firearm. It contained some clothing, a stand of blacks and such like, and, buried among these, was a box of walnut-wood, brass-bound. Reloading, he fired from keyhole to lid of this receptacle, so as to save the contents from damage; and lifting the flap he hastily rummaged over the contained papers. "Here's the nest, I'll warrant," said he; "and I'll just be taking all the eggs, Mr. Merchant, so as to be sure of one good one."

He crammed all the papers into the deep inside pockets of his old coat, and turned to go; but finally reloaded again, and blew the lock of the second chest. Ledgers, account-books and clothing were there ... nothing of use to any but MacKenzie apparently; so, buttoning the fawn surtout carefully over his spoil, out he came and found the minister watchful of a battered cellar-door that still held stoutly. "Hear till his drumming, the roll of it," said the Captain. "Man, it sounds not unlike a salute of the French I once heard in Toulouse. It was for their colours, if you please; *Drapeau*, they called it; and they beat it on the *tambour* ... But man, even if French, their hands were clean; while the fellow's—" He tossed his head contemptuously and set off for the path up the cliff-face, followed by the minister. At the top MacLeod's garron, tethered to the alder, stood waiting placidly; an unhitching the animal, the minister turned an appealing countenance on his companion.

"For the dear sake, Captain, give me my pipe, and *fleurisch*, or my nerves will never be settled by the time I win to Pennygown. I'm fearing it'll be a poor sermon and a short one they'll be having from me the day."

The old soldier turned on him in a flash. "A poor one if you like," he cried; "but never a short one. Give me time to get to Killiechronan with my treasures, man. Make it as long as Lachie Dubh's psalm if you please; but keep Kirsty MacIver from too early a discovery of your crime."

"Crime! "cried the cleric, halting in the act of lighting his tobacco.

"Hamesucken, I tell ye! I had counted on nothing but a house-breaking; but you spoiled a' when you first gave him yon ... Hamesucken! ... violence to a man in his own house ... and the penalty's capital punishment, no less!"

"Man, I'm sorry I didna get to his face. My nieves on the skelly eyes of him is what I'd have liked best of all," said MacLeod. And so he trotted off, while the Captain More made once again for the moorland track that led him home.

17: Salamanca

IT was at Leitir, some days after this, that the Captain More made his famous answer to Seumas Dubh; and it was on the way back, at the cave at Rudha-na-Leitreach that he opened the eyes of Grizel MacLean by a chance observe—not a bad day's work for an old soldier. The ten Highland miles between Killiechronan and Leitir were the least of it; the riposte to Seumas was a small matter; but the revelation to Grizel was what she'll ay be grateful for. There was also, it is true, the story of Salamanca Fight told to the Catechist's Boy—but that was in the by-going, as it were.

Seumas Dubh has nothing to do with this tale, but here it is that he must come in, for in Grizel's mind he will always be nought but the hand of Providence. Had Seumas not quarrelled with the widow of Corrie, the Captain More would never have come to Leitir that day, and Grizel might never have found content on this side Paradise.

The Corrie widow was from over Drimnin way, and thus Catholic; but Seumas was true Mull, and that means much since the days of Lachlan More, as every one knows. Therefore it was that, as the Captain came in by Leitir, he went warily, and took care to halt in neutral territory—at MacMaster's, the first house by the burnside, where a mixed marriage had resulted in a following to each of the rival sects. Here he found the goodwife and her daughters busy carding wool round a fire of peats. Three sonsie lasses they were, these young ones, full-breasted, and with tawny hair that fell fiercely tousled over straight brows, like to those of the kyloes on the braes above their dwelling.

"Shield me! "cried the Captain; "so many women! ... Now, isn't it me that's the lone man and the unprotected! ... Where's Seumâs and the widow? "The girls tossed their red locks at this, and showed white teeth, smiling.

"Come in, and with a blessing," cried the lusty mother. "Seumas will be here in a breath, for I saw his long legs on the Rudha shore five minutes gone, and him hurrying to overtake you. Till he comes, it's myself will be warrandice for your safety, poor weak one that you ar'"; and she glanced admiringly at the upright six-feet of the old soldier.

Seumas came in, stooping, a match for size with the Captain—a black-avized young man with a melancholy air; and immediately the story of his wrongs was laid before the veteran. Never was there such a cow for breaking fences and trampling corn as the widow's—the camel of the desert itself had never such an expanse of foot-pad. Never corn so golden as that of Seumas', nor so tall—in comparison the cedars of Lebanon were but a very little thing. The Captain listened for a while in silence, and then interrupted the spate of declamation.

"I'm thinking we should be waiting the widow from Corrie," said he. And the jury of tousy-haired MacMaster girls nodded their heads in approval. But on the young man rambled, and still no defendant appeared.

"What can be keeping her? Did you tell her I might be here by ten?" asked the arbiter.

"Well, no, Captain. But I was for stepping over to her, and asking her to have you for middleman, once we had gone up the hill to see the damage that wild beast is after doing. 'Twould be only the one journey, Captain, you see."

"Now, Seumas Dubh, is that right?" asked Captain MacColl, tapping him very gently on the shoulder. "You bring me ten miles, and yet you've never had word from her as to whether or no' she'll agree to my giving judgment. No task is to my liking, look you! where the play is not fair; so you'd better be getting some one else, Seumas; for it's not me that's caring for this kind of sport." He rose to his feet, an angry man; and Seumas Dubh laid appealing hands on his shoulders on the instant.

"Och, it was the agitation, Captain ... Now, be reasonable, sir, be reasonable. For who else is there better fitted to be middleman in all the Isle than you, will you tell me? ... Yes, indeed, for it's you are the good Presbyterian, and the wise man and the old—"

The Captain's eyes flashed, and he strode to the door. "Call me an old man, and so many lasses listening," said he. Three red-gold tousled heads ducked as his glance fell on them; through the tawny fringes peered eyes mischievous; and Seumas could have sworn they were giggling—at least their necks were very red, he saw, and their ample shoulders shaking. "An old man! "cried the Captain again. "Och, Seumas, Seumas! and me a wanter! Man! I've done wi' you! "and the door shut behind his exit, just as the good dame's laughter skirled to the rafters, her hands clapped to her sides for the heartier merriment.

Captain MacColl chuckled as he turned the gable-end, well pleased to have escaped embroilment in a quarrel, petty in its beginnings, maybe, but one that held promise to go deep in the old strife of the religions and races of the Isles before it ended. "That kind of thing's best strangled at birth," he muttered, and took the road for home at a swift pace.

It was a day of sun and shower, with some sharpness in the air; and little cold gusts came regularly from off the water. Ben Shiant wore a tiny cap of mist, and there were scurrying veils of vapour dragging long sweeps down the Sound. One gathered and swelled; he foresaw a downpour when it reached the Aros hills, and so made for the shelter of the cave on the Rudha.

A stretch of sward lay before the fern-fringed arch and the scattered stones of the old croft of Ian of the Glen—haunt of the Captain's schoolboy days when the cave was stable and byre. Many a scamper he had had, bareback on Ian's Uist pony; many a heather rope he had plaited for its tail, when the rude ploughing of those old days was due. Then were the golden hours when colours were fresher than to-day; green was green then; and oh! how blue the waters of Kyle Aros; how creamy-white the torrent-falls on Innimore in that ancient time! For him the wood-violet, the hyacinth, the primrose were still sources of deep joy; but a quantum of their first magic had departed; their tints so delicate, so elusive, were fainter ... Some old association thrilled him at the thought; for, as a sunburst came through the trailing mists, up went his fingers so that he might behold the marvel of the rose-pink of flesh and blood illumined by the splendour of those eternal fires ... a prank of his earliest years that matched with boyhood's sense of miracle in the frost's feathery crystals on window-panes of long ago ... Yes, colour and beauty and light were dimming ... He shivered, pondering what this resurrection of early moods might portend—was it, haply, the second childhood of the aged? ... The hands, uplifted to the great glory, fell; and he beheld them many-veined and worn and ancient ... hands that had once been strung to the work of youth in deadly fashion in the distant war-time. Involuntarily, at the old memories, his jaw squared, and his shoulders set; but he came to himself to find he was soothing '*Crodh Chailein*' before the dark recesses of the cave of Iain a' Ghlinne.

A rank growth of bramble, reeds and bracken, fed by continual drippings from the cavern's eaves, partially masked the opening; and the Captain pushed his way through this thicket to emerge on the sloping floor of the shelter, just as the storm broke with a hiss of close-ranked rain on the waves of the Kyle. In one corner lay a pile of heather the colour of rusty iron, and topping it some branches of green pine. "A tinker's bed?" queried the old campaigner, noting the woodcraft, evident in the traversing of the layers of the heather, and in the setting of the pine-shoots with resilient arches uppermost. "Tinker—tailor—soldier—sailor, "said the old man, musingly—"and here he is, whatever his calling"; for a quick patter of feet sounded on the earth overhead, and next moment a small figure dashed into the cave-mouth. It paused irresolute at sight of the visitant, and had scrambled back out of sight among the rushes before the Captain found voice.

"Alasdair! Come you here, you randy.—It's only me sheltering for a bittie," he cried. And, shivering in his soaked clothing, the Catechist's Boy returned.

"I ettled sleeping here the day," said the lad.

"We'll have to dry you first then," said the Captain. "See you, I've a *fleurisch* ... Bring you some heather and fir over here."

From the depths of an inner pouch, he produced flint and steel and tinder, and soon the boy was steaming his sodden rags in front of a blaze just inside the mouth of the cave.

"And here's a bannock to divide; and we've shells for *cuachs*, and it's not to-day we'll be thirsty, I'm thinking. We've bread and we've water, and it's what we were promised, *laochain*," said the old soldier.

"I wadna ca' the king my uncle," said Alasdair, munching with zest and taking a glance up the Sound, where nought was to be seen save sea and land drumming under the rods of the rain till they smoked.

"'Tis a bivouac complete," said the Captain, equally content, "and a drier one than most I've seen, laddie."

"Is this like the storms you had before the big Spanish battles you were telling me of?"

"And whatna storms now, Alasdair? for they were many."

The bog fidgeted uneasily. "Ach, the thunder-plumps that Sir Arthur ay waited for, to make the ground slippy for the Frenchmen."

"God forgive me, laddie, if ever I vented such nonsense to you! For why should he have done that?"

"Because our sodgers were better used to sappy ground ... A night's rain, and then, fall on— clinkity-clank! "The lad's eyes gleamed; and he raised a skinny arm in fanciful sword-play.

"Och, och, and yes! ... Maybe ... maybe ... ! But if I were you, laddie, I wadna be too cocksure of that view of it. And wherever you got it, of this be certain, it was none of mine, Alasdair ... The most I could tell you was that we had often a storm before a big victory ... For why, I dinna ken ... Salamanca was one like that ... Yon was a tempest the night of the twenty-first, look you."

"Tell me Salamanca, Captain."

"A strange fight it was, and a deadly one for the Glo'sters that same; but the strangest thing was the marching before the fight. For days we footed it parallel with the French—well within musket-shot we were, yet never a gun sounding ... And then the officers on either side, saluting each other on the march; and at the bivouacs, the men down at the burnsides, changing tobacco with the Mossoos ... 'Twas queer, indeed."

"What for did ye no' blast them when ye got the chance?"

"The chance never came till the twenty-second, laddie ... Salamanca Fight."

"What for did ye march yon fool's gate then?"

"'Twas like a game on the dam-brod, you'll understand ... You've seen a race for the crown-head?"

"Aye, it's my father's the swift one at that."

"Well, Salamanca was our crown-head, Alasdair; and it was in front of it we sat down ... Look ... See you the burnie there, running straight' from us, and then to the left—like a shepherd's crook ¡ Well, Salamanca lay at the end of that crook, on the far side of it, where the big stones are heaped—that's Salamanca for you ... At the top of the bend yonder was the ford—Huerta they named it—and it was there the storm I mind of, fell on a division of ours as they took the water. There was a spate on, and the lightning was in sheets, and the thunder just terrible. Hundreds o' horse were stampeded and many killed by flashes, and some men too; but our fellows went over as quietly as if they'd been at drill. It was by that ford most of us crossed—all, in fact, except Pakenham's division—and we came well into the crook of the river, and lay down in front of Salamanca—alongside the shaft of the cromag, you'll understand ... Look you now." He peeled a twig on one side only and laid it on the floor. "That wand is Wellington's line—the white wood his front, to my right; the dark his rear, to my left ... Swing on that"; and he clutched the ragged end of the bit of wood nearest him, and pivoting on it, turned the line of the twig to his left till it reached an angle of ninety degrees with its first position. "Now, see you, the white is looking away from us, and what was his rear's his front now ...

"And where is Neddy Pakenham, will you tell me? ... Neddy's up and away through the big stones yonder—Salamanca, you'll understand—and across the bridge, and round the folds of the hills, and through the woods on the Frenchies' left, just as they try to flank our right ... Oh, man, but their left was too eager; and there was a gap between them and their centre, and Wellington flung at that same gap, before you could say knife ... He broke them there; and then the fight was right along the line. He broke them, Alasdair; but back they came, for they're game-cocks, the Johnny Crapauds; and then there was a bloody business on the French Arapile—that's the wee bit o' grey rock yonder—and it was there the Portugals got it sore—Pack's men ...

"Our turn came after that—Clinton's division. He had Hulse on his right, and Hinde on his left, and we'd Portuguese for the second line ... Hulse was our man; and—och, but it was just like the deepest pit in Yon Place, laddie—smoke and dust and blood and gloom—the night coming on fast, and the musketry gey hot. Then it was three cheers and a charge with the bagnet,—up and away!—and the French division was off the hill and in retreat ... There was rye-grass yonder—a terrible thing rye-grass, laddie, when it's three feet high and on fire. Pity on the poor man that's down then! It was there that Barlow and Downing dropped, I mind well.

"We halted beyond the hill, but the Frenchies came on again wi' skirmishers, and a new battery of guns; and then there was an infantry charge threatening, and we'd cavalry moving on our left. But, man, our fellows were parade-steady—the old Sixty-first! and the Eleventh by our side! Four divisions, two deep, we were; and we went at them with the bagnet for the second time. Hot work yon; for we were hardly breathed, when we saw them massing in front of us wi' a hill and some woods behind ... So at them we went once more, cheering like mad. This time the colour-sergeants went down, and the ensigns were out of sight; but not for long, look you! for Coulson and Crawford had up the old flags before you could whistle, and we wrestled on to the top of the hill and planted them soundly there ... Oh! ... Clinton's men ... Hulse's men! ... Find me their like, Alasdair; find me their like!

"Night had come on, and the grass was alight; and there was the glare and smoke o' the guns; and: round us were sheets of musketry fire ... I tell you, yon ridge looked like a burning mountain, topped with shining steel, and the old banners waving dark and terrible above it.

"Pakenham had crushed their left; and now their centre was smashed; and into the woods they went —Foy and Ferez and the rest. And—by God!— we'd have broken every bit of them, if the dark hadna fallen, and the Spaniards had but held ... And save a wheen bruises, Alasdair, never a scratch for the Captain! Wasna it wonderful? Yet we went in wi' twenty-seven officers, and four hundred and twenty men, and came out with only three officers and seventy-eight of the rankers that were good for aught ... Oh! it's long ere I'll forget the Spanish ryefields, Alasdair, and the good men who fell there in the mouth o' night so long ago ... Yon was the sore day on the plain of Salamanca!"

"And," queried the daft boy gaping at the veteran's fiery declamation— "and that was the end of it ... And ye won?"

"Now, mark you, here's fame! ... Salamanca? ... Of course we won, laddie! ... D'ye think I'd have told you as much if the other fellows had come off best?"

"What for no'? 'Twould have been a grand fecht all the same," said Alasdair; "and a fine lot o' killing going on."

The Captain gnawed a thumb reflectively. "Ye have me there, laddie."

"What like a man was Sir Arthur?"

"Like no single man I ken. He'd an eagle's look and an eagle's neb no' unlike Carsaig's, but he'd energy enough for ten o' his kind, and brains for a hunder. A steady, strong kind of a man, wi' a fire inside him."

Alasdair giggled. "That's no' true," he said. "He'd be burnt."

"I don't mean that sort of fire, laddie. I mean a real man like Garmony— true and strong in the depths o' him. As for outward looks—well— Carsaig, if you like."

There was a step on the gravel, the bushes were parted, and a woman's face peered in between the high fronds of bracken.

"Keep me! Miss Grizel! Are you, too, for sheltering," cried the Captain. "And it's wet you are, indeed! ... Stop you, Alasdair; it's only the lady from Draolinn."

But the boy was through the screen of fern and rushes in one wild dive, and instantly on his way to the woods again.

"And I had but got him dry," said the old man regretfully, as he raked the fire anew for Grizel. "Now, is not he the untamed one?"

"It's what I jaloused might happen," said Grizel, flinging off her wet cloak, and revealing the day's business in the shape of a basket filled with primroses. "And wasn't I weary, and me dripping, waiting fo£ the tail-end of your story! For I knew that if I stirred before the finish, Alasdair would never hear it out ... It's seldom I ever felt so near martyrdom, Captain dear." She stretched cold hands to the blaze new-kindled, and smiled archly over her shoulder at her friend.

The Captain More smiled also; but it was a trifle grim that smile of his, she thought, and she turned away from his searching gaze. "Aye," said he guardedly, for he was recalling the references to Garmony and Carsaig, which she musfc have overheard—"Aye. But I'm fearing we'd got past the tail-end and were at other things than battles, just when you appeared. Indeed we were descended to countryside gossip, if you'll credit me."

Grizel's cheeks flushed, and she bent lower to the fire. "Oh, then, my coming was opportune, even if I did scare poor Alasdair," said she. "I'm glad I stopped you; for there's nothing so dangerous as gossip in douce Aros Isle."

The Captain bit his nether lip. "Well, you've scared more than Alasdair, Miss Grizel; for, when you entered, my tongue was wagging a trifle too freely even for a cave of the desert like this."

Grizel's plain face lit in a happy smile that transfigured it. "Your tongue said nothing amiss, dear Captain MacColl," said she, with a strange uplift in her voice. And instantly, unheralded and unforeseen, it was as if a bird sprang up in her breast and carolled gaily. Instantly also, her face was turned to the fire in such a fashion, that it was securely hid from the kindly gaze of her inquisitor.

And for the rest of that day Garmony was much in her thoughts.

18: Garmony and Grizel

FROM Leitir shore a wood of scrub-oak and birch climbed the lower slopes of mighty Dun-da-Ghaoithe—The Hill of the Two Winds; and in its depths lay hidden vast boulders, spoil of the centuries' weathering of the great mountain. A. crotal grew on these, famed through all the Isle fori the rich red-brown it gave as a dye; and hither one summer's day, a week after her visit to the cave of Iain a' Ghlinne, came Grizel on her garron, with gathering creel and scraping-shell. Already she had harvested many roots of sand-rue from the dunes at the Forsa's mouth; only remained now, before her return journey to Draolinn, the collecting of some of this rarest of the colouring-stuffs.

A fine day it was; the Sound like a shining scimitar, curving from Kilchoan to Innimore; and the white cots of Morvern over the water, gleaming cosily among their patches of young corn. To the north Ben Shiant towered glorious, its water-courses lacing its green velvet with braids of silver. Across the clear blue of heaven white cloud fleeces sailed slowly; and in Leitir wood the mavis and the blackbird fluted and trilled in triumph of the warm and golden day, while curlew and redshank and pyat on the shore fringes piped back assurance of accord with praise so masterly and magical.

Grizel herself was singing as she dismounted to explore the recesses of the boscage; and, tying her garron to a twisted oak, she deposited her basket, already treasure-laden, by the side of a streamlet brattling noisily to the beach. From it she took her scraping-shell and a square of white linen for the lichen, and then, her fine contralto still pulsing in happy content, she thridded the woodland paths to the heart of the grove, where lay the boulders with the coveted crotal. "*An Gillie Dubh*" was what she sang, and the rich notes came from midmost of the wood, through the still sunlit spaces of summer air to the ears of a man tramping the high flanks of the Hill of the Two Winds, and searching for strayed sheep. He paused, irresolute, as the full vibrant notes came floating up deliciously in pauses of the gentle wind from the Kyle.

"And now," said he, "if that's not the voice of her, my name's not Garmony." An ardour glowed in his dark eyes and his firm lips took lines of tenderness and humour. "And she's for singing '*An Gillie Dubh*' the rascal ...! Well, well, Ewan, your shepherding's finished for the day, I'm thinking," and calling on his collie to follow, he set off swiftly downhill in the direction of the voice.

Coming to Leitir wood, he skirted it to the south, and reconnoitred cautiously the fringes of young oak that looked shorewards. The singing had ceased for a moment; but the harsh grating of the clearing-shell on the boulder rock mingled with the still vigorous carolling of the woodland birds. Then the noise of the scraping-shell ceased; even the birds' song fell silent, and instantly Garmony regarded the forest marge with suspicion. "She's surely moving this way now," said he, "since the birds are so quiet," and he peered into the aisles of the thrusting birches.

But no sign of the longed-for one appeared? "They've marked a hawk," said Garmony. "And' thinking of birds now, that reminds me of her parable of the swallows at Achnahully ... Strange creatures women! ... It seems the roundabout and swerving way is what they're fondest of ... I wonder if it's the adventure in the business they prize; or is it that so great a treasure as themselves must be approached with a deference that's plainly to be seen ... *Och, och,* Ewan, you're used to the other fashion in most things; but now it looks as if it must be the crooked path in this." He sighed dolefully. "Well, we can but try," he concluded; and calling his collie, he pointed homewards. "You'll be in the way, Hector," said he by way of apology; and the obedient beast, with a regretful glance of farewell, trotted off.

A moment after, Garmony came on the pony, munching the young grass under the oak, and in the same instant almost, spied the basket of rue-roots ... "Just that," said he. "I thought it was dye-hunting you were, when I heard your shell, my lady"; and he scowled at the little creel and the garron with jealous eyes, meditating their significance for a little, finger on lip. Again he listened for the sound of the scraping-shell, but it did not come; the birds, however, had resumed their glad hymns. He still regarded the fringes of the grove distrustfully, but at length, impatient, he decided to risk the chances of the situation, and with a sly movement of his foot, he toppled the creel and its contents into the burn. The pony was his next concern; and, unloosening its bridle from the low oak branch, he led the little mount over the stream to the soft wayside turf where its hooves were noiseless, and so skirted the edge of the wood till he had covered half a mile. Then, cutting a briar, he pelted the flanks of the poor animal, and sent it scampering down the shore-road, round the turn of a knowe, and so out of sight.

Forthwith he came back on his tracks to the burn, where the little basket now lay in the shallows and empty of its treasures. He contemplated it critically for a moment, then went down to seat himself on a rock of the shore and await the appearance of Grizel. The sound of her voice again made melody in the wood-depths, and at intervals the shell was to be heard at work. "It's 'Mull of the Bens' she's singing now," said he. "I couldna have been better served if she'd asked me for my favourites ... So far, it's you are the lucky one, Ewan." He sat entranced, a happy smile on his broad features, his great bulk stretched easily, his eyes closed in the sheer delight of listening to this song of home sung by so dear a voice. When the air ceased he sat up, alert, his gaze on the fringe of oaks, and at last beheld her emerge, a goddess of the forests in his eyes. She was clad in a dark green joseph, and a little beaver hat of the same colour cocked itself jauntily on her dark hair with a slight incline to the left, as if to shade the tiny birthmark of red on the lower eyelid of that side (a minute stain that ever loomed portentously large in the mind of its bearer). She carried a crooked switch of hazel on her shoulder, and from this depended a square of linen knotted in a packman's bundle, some grey crotal peeping from its folds; her colour high, her step sure and free, she looked the woodland rover to the life.

"Garmony! "she cried, flushing a little, as he rose to meet her. She flicked at her eyelid's tache with her free hand, and stood the very picture of the oread surprised. "Who'd have thought to find you here!"

"And where else would I be in all Aros on a day like this, with yon fine singing in the forest going on — the merle and the blackbird and Grizel MacLean? Believe me, I'll never be saying nay, when I can have, music without a fiddler's fee."

"Where now is my garron? "cried the girl suddenly and in dismay, looking round at the tethering oak.

"What garron? "asked the farmer with all the appearance of innocent ignorance. "Is it riding you were?"

"And here, too, are my dye-stuffs all gone," cried she, stooping to salve a basket wet and empty.

"Indeed and they are that," said Garmony, gleaning a stray root from the sedges. "The beastie has broken loose, you see, and kicked them over in the by-going, I'm thinking."

"Half a day's work gone," said Grizel regretfully; "and the pony still to seek."

"Let's consider," said he, bending down to examine the hoof-marks. "There, he's gone south, you'll notice ... I'll take a step up the hill, and see if I can mark him anywhere. Stop you here, and we'll soon have him."

He went off up the braes, and in twenty minutes returned round the shoulder of a distant knowe, running beside the ambling truant. "Here's your friend," said he. "And now let us see what we can be doing about the other thing ... It was sand-rue you were digging, wasn't it? ... And it's just me that's the great hand at that same."

"Indeed, and I'll not hear of you at that, Garmony. 'tis women's work."

"I'm not saying it's no'," said the big man, his eyes twinkling. "I was but offering my help by way of paying for the concert in the wood."

"Go on with your nonsense!"cried Grizel. "I'm for Forsa banks again; but I'll not hear of your coming with me."

"Yet you'll never forbid me Forsa banks, if I tell you I'm just hunting a strayed gimmer there," persisted the farmer,—" a black one that's been missed since morning. I've been all day on the hill for her. You didna by chance see her in the wood?"

"Not a live thing there, but the birds, and one wee roe-deer."

"Then it's on Forsa banks she'll be," said Garmony with conviction: but inwardly he was praying that the ewe was farther afield.

Grizel mounted: and they journeyed on to the dunes at the Forsa mouth: and here for a space he left her, whilst he scoured the shores reluctantly, pretending a zeal in shepherding, of which he felt not a moiety. Back he came to her in half an hour, high-spirited, for his search had been fruitless. She made no protest now when without a by-your-leave, he started digging some distance off; and so they worked on, all alone in a solitude of bent and sand, with promontories of oozing mosses intersecting it. A thin crying of the distant surf mingling with the muffled roar of the river's outfall was constant; breaking across these monotones came the weird calls of the seagulls wheeling above them, sometimes with a laughing note—*lookahlookahlookah!*—that made the girl start guiltily and angrily, as if conscious of spectators of the comedy enacting in this wide and lonely place. The man also was scarcely at his ease; yet they worked in a fervour of silence, until Garmony, raising himself to stretch his limbs after the unwonted stooping, found his companion standing erect some hundred yards away, and watching him with wrathful intentness. She flushed at his surprisal of so flagrant an interest in him, while he came up to her, awkwardly enough over the slipping sands, and deposited a handful of roots in her basket.

"You were calling? "said he.

"No," she answered, "I was considering whether we had not despoiled the shore too much already by taking what we have. You know this plant keeps the sand from drifting."

"Hoots! "said he. "There's little loss of binding-power for all we've taken ... Besides you havena yet the half of what you lost." He could have bitten his tongue the next moment, for he saw he had declared outright his complicity in the overturning of the creel. But the girl seemed not to have understood that his words implied a knowledge which was practically a confession of his misdeed; and not a sign did she give of suspicion.

"Maybe you're right," said she. "We'll take some more then."

In half an hour the basket was well-filled; and they set off over the dunes, to where the garron browsed near the roadside.

"A fine song that, '*An Gillie Dubh*,' "said Ewan, as they stumbled along in the loose gliding sands. "The lass had good cause to be lifting a lilt so joyful, with a lad so much to her liking."

She answered him curtly. "It's the air I'm fond of. The words of it are no great matter."

"Grizel!" he cried; and as they halted, she turned on him a stern eye that abashed him utterly. "Shield us!" he said inwardly. "This way of it will never do. I'm forgetting again the roundabouts of the swallows at Achnahully."

"What is it, cousin? "asked the girl coldly.

"Och, it just came on me in a flash," said he lamely, "that maybe the black gimmer's been stolen ... The Irish schooner—you see—" He waved an arm vaguely.

"No, nor stolen," she said, as she turned to move on. "I'll wager it wasna." This in a tone of decision that convinced him instantly of her utter disbelief in the existence of any such animal; and now he beheld how terrible was her faith in her power of feminine clairvoyance.

Such a deadly oppression next assailed him that he searched wildly for some hint of a compliment that would swoop on swallow-like lines, and give him time to collect his forces for a clear indication of his attitude to this woman of his choice. He must make haste; a hundred yards more, and they would reach the pony. But the moments of opportunity flitted fast; and in a maze of mind he found himself holding his hand for a step, as she sprang to the saddle; even then speech was lacking save for a formal good-bye. She moved off on the homeward road; and white-lipped and parch-tongued he stood at gaze.

"Grizel," he cried at length; and as she turned smiling, a half-humorous twinkle came to his eyes, as he recognized how ridiculous his efforts in the struggle must seem, how foolish his final words must be; for even while he strove to hold them back, he saw them shaping as foredoomed to bathos, and knew he must utter them.

"It's—it's been a fine day, Grizel," said he shamefacedly.

But despite this anti-climax, she was tenderly serious, and shook hands once more with a fine gravity for which he inwardly blessed her. Then she went off at a rapid trot; and he stood to regard her for a time, as she neared the hazels round Forsa bridge. Here she would disappear from his vision, and as if divining his desire, she looked back to give, by a waving of her switch, yet another farewell. But; she made some false movement with the reins as she did so; and instantly the pony was on his knees; The girl leapt from the saddle in the moment of the fall, however, and had the little mount on his feet in a trice. Up came Garmony, wildly racing, and eyed her eagerly to make sure she was scatheless.

She stood flushing with excitement. "It's well we were not cantering," said she, laughing, "or my neck were broken ... Poor beastie! ... Look at his knees, Garmony."

The farmer passed his hand over the bruised and bleeding limbs, then taking the bridle, led the pony to the river, where he bathed the wounds;

the girl looking on from the bridge above. The rough toilet was soon over, and patient and healer returned to the waiting lady. Trees sheltered the approaches of the high arch on either hand, and the three occupants of the old grey lichened span were shut off from the roadways north and south; nought could be seen from it save the blue sky, the brown dappled water, reflecting it, the green belt of larch and hazel, and a stretch of the Forsa's banks seawards. The man had come up from the stream with determination writ on every line of his great frame; the bridle of the pony was on his arm; and, with its nose on his shoulder, it now regarded with dark reproachful eyes this mistress who had twitched the reins so suddenly, bringing disaster on a faithful servant. And now Garmony planted himself stockily before the girl, who leant back on the parapet, her hands behind her, her eyes wide and far-seeing, fixed on his face.

"I'm thinking life's too short for this business of the swallows at Achnahully," said he. "Grizel, will you be my wife?"

She eyed him frankly without a change of feature, and put her strong hands in his.

"Gladly, Ewan," she said.

For some minutes following, the brown eyes of the garron. took deeper hints of reproachfulness; for the kindness and petting lavished on him but a little ago had vanished as suddenly as surely; and here were these two strange beings, settling down to whispers and caresses such as he had witnessed never before.

"There's one thing, my dear," said Garmony, when at last to the pony's delight, they prepared to move on to Draolinn; "and that's this (I may as well confess it here and now) ... Myself it was that destroyed your gathering of the roots of rue, and set your garron wandering ... You'll be understanding why?"

Grizel's mouth twitched at the left corner as she nodded acquiescence. "And indeed, if it comes to confession," said she; "well ... I saw you at it from the edge of the wood ... Maybe I should have told you before, but ..."

Garmony silenced her with a kiss; and waved his disengaged hand gaily to the pony, who hobbled behind at as discreet a distance as the reins would admit, but now with more of pity than reproach in those doleful eyes of his.

19: The Uniform

AMONG the papers in the box of walnut-wood abstracted from MacKenzie's, the Captain More did not find what he had hoped for: some written evidence of the complicity of the merchant and Oskamull in the sheep-stealing. He was greatly crestfallen at this, for ever since daft Alasdair's story of what had happened at *Cladh Phobuill*, he had hoped to turn the tables on Oskamull by some such discovery, and so relieve Carsaig of his oppressor. Still, there was one paper among many worthless, that looked as if it might be regarded as fair spoil, although it did not concern the affair of the stolen sheep; and if skilfully used, it might help towards the end he desired. This was a bond for eight hundred pounds over some farm lands belonging to Oskamull, and drawn by that chief in favour of MacKenzie.

The Captain had qualms for a time about touching a quasi-legal document like this; but in the end he decided that the merchant was none the less a rascal at heart, however imposing the parchment he used for his trickery; and so the bond was held as fit booty. MacKenzie would only lose eight hundred pounds as unfairly as, no doubt, he had gained them, argued the Captain; for if the bond were returned secretly to Oskamull, that wily schemer would certainly destroy it in order to relieve his burden of debt. And so eased, who knew but that he might be less insistent in his demands on Carsaig? This was but a hope; yet the plot, though a poor one compared with that involved in the finding of evidence anent participation in the sheep-stealing, seemed better than inaction, and so was carried out.

Were he thus to help Carsaig, the Captain knew, he served Elspeth also; for she (wilful lass!) was again on lover's terms with the volatile chieftain. The Doctor's story of the happenings at Eileach a' Naoimh had done not a little to rehabilitate Carsaig in her eyes; and of late they had often been seen together in the summer gloaming, deep in Draolinn woods, or wandering on the white beaches of Drumlang. "Queer folk, women!" said the veteran, discussing this matter with the minister. "After all she's come through! ... Maybe, she'll make a man o' him yet, however! ... And indeed he didna do at all badly, look you, in yon affair o' the schooner, when you come to think o't."

The two ancients were basking in the morning sunshine by the wall of Pennygown churchyard, some ten days aftèr their forcing of MacKenzie's house, and in schoolboy mood were living their adventure over again, and trying to calculate the probable outcome. The immediate sequel of their freebooting had been a lack of any complaint by the merchant: he maintained a silence that was enigmatic. So, too, did Oskamull, although the Captain had made sure that he received the bond under cover of a muddy envelope, and by the hands of a trusty crofter friend —Neil of Kellan. Neil's story to Oskamull was that he had picked up the packet in the roadway in front of his own door; and it was certainly true, for the Captain More made sure that he happened to be passing at the time, and beheld him discover it. It was clear the chief had received the deed. That he would now relent towards Carsaig did not follow.

Another difficulty was one suggested by the minister: namely that the transaction might have been legally regularized before a Notary Public; and in that case the holding of the bond by Oskamull went for nothing.

"Keep me! "cried the Captain More. "I hadna thought o' that! ... An instrument o' sasine on the bond? ... But there's no' a Notary in the Isle ... And he'd grudge bitterly paying a fee to bring one from the mainland, would MacKenzie."

"Aye, he'd grudge it, I ken ... But he's cautious ... aye, mean, but cautious, that same man. I wonder now if he didna get it attested?" said MacLeod.

"I misdoubt we've boggled this affair," went on Captain MacColl. "We've no track of the doings of either Duncan Merchant or Oskamull. It was a shot in the dark."

"Hoot-toots! It was fired in a good cause, anyway," said the minister, puffing at his accustomed solace; "and it's more than likely Carsaig's crofters will sit the easier for it."

"Hilly-hoy!" cried a voice from below the grassy bank where they reclined, and rising, they beheld Linnell, resplendent in full naval uniform, descending from the hiring garron belonging to the Grasspoint Ferry. The youth tethered the pony to a thorn-bush, and unstrapping his cloak from his saddle-bow, climbed up to them. Then, after greetings and hand-shakings, he laid the mantle carefully on the short turf, and deposited himself daintily in the mid-length of its folds. The Captain regarded his dandiacal bearing with a critical eye, and the sailor flushed hotly under his gaze. His coat was of bright blue with lapels and collar of white; the knee-breeches and stockings were of white, and over all was scattered a plentiful supply of gold anchor-buttons. A black tricorne with cockade, and a sword on a shoulder-belt, completed the rig, which had an outlandish air in this rustic nook, beside the worn fawn coat of the old soldier, and the minister's threadbare blacks.

"Fine feathers, Captain MacColl?" said the sailor, smiling uneasily.

"Indeed they're all that," said the veteran drily. "You'll be on leave, I'm thinking?"

"How did you guess? "cried the youth in surprise.

"Ask the Army," said the Captain grimly. "They're just like the Navy, never so kenspeckle as when on furlough ... But in war ... well ... as plain as pease-brose, most of us."

"It's a kind of a celebration," said Linnell. "I'm out of Revenue now ... thank Heaven! ... appointed to the *Dromedary* ... a seventy-four, and they say we're for the Archipelago in twenty days ... The Greeks and the Turks again ... And we'll be in, too, before long, I hear."

The Captain smiled at the youth's ardour.

"He smelleth the battle from afar," quoted MacLeod, strangely belligerent in countenance for the moment.

A hush fell on them after that, as if each dreamed futurity even then, beholding this old conflict of warring faiths, its blood and tears, its exaltations and its agonies, as a thing predestined to re-birth again and again, terrible yet beautiful.

"Ah," sighed the Captain, "well, what maun be, maun be I But warfare's a fool's game, when all's said ... I'm for believing, indeed, that daft Alasdair has more sense than us all ... What think you was his verdict on Salamanca Fight when I tellt him it the other day? ... 'A fine lot o' killing,' says he ... Castlereagh should have heard him at it."

There came a silence again in that sheltered spot, and the three men stared aimlessly at the hills encircling Aros Sound to the north. Scarves of ever-changing mist drifted round those mountain flanks, and even so did the thoughts of the watchers wander, vague and various; the youth thinking of white-sailed frigates threading the sea-paths 'twixt the Grecian isles, or beating off Levantine coasts, rich in mosque and minaret; the old campaigner rehearsing bygone battles on plains of Leon and Castile; while the cleric, repentant already of his bellicose outburst, beheld a vision of the Galilean cornfields of long-ago, and the Nazarene teaching peace to his followers. Yet swift as the melting of the grey wreaths round Ben Shiant's shoulders, these moods passed, and soon they were back to their workaday world, giving and taking news of Aros Isle.

"Tell him of Carsaig," said MacLeod; and the Captain recounted their fears of Oskamull's pressure on Carsaig, and their plot to help the latter. At the tale of hamesucken the sailor laughed gaily, and the minister hung his head abashed.

"Yet," concluded the Captain, "there's something wrong about the business; but where the false step is, I canna just make out ... What think ye, Philip?"

"'Tis plainly seen, sir," said Linnell. "You relied on Oskamull being knave enough to destroy the bond and advantage himself at MacKenzie's expense; and you were right in my poor judgment ... But if he were rascal enough to do that, he'd be rascal enough never to give up his grip on Carsaig because his money difficulties were eased."

"You have it," cried the old soldier in frank admiration. "You're grand at the foresight ... just like your father, lad ... Man! and to think I missed that!"

"Of course, you're right," said the minister, "and it's to myself I take blame, that I was so sin-blind as not to see it ... For thus might I have escaped this hamesucken business that still weighs on me like a rock."

The Captain laughed, and turned to the sailor. "Well, well! here we are at your feet, Gamaliel ... And now what would you be advising, so as to get Carsaig clear ... and his crofters free ... poor bodies!"

"Go straight," said Linnell. "Find out from Oskamull or Carsaig what's the secret understanding between them. From what you tell me of Alasdair's story, I take it to be a point of honour ... But, save by accident, we can hope for nothing from Oskamull; and as for Carsaig in such a matter, you'll also get nothing from him, unless ..."

"Unless . . ." said the Captain eagerly.

"Unless you show him clearly the duty he owes his tenants ... He might say something then that would help us to lift him from this trap."

"Stop you! "cried the veteran. "I'm none too sure, but I see a way to Carsaig's mind."

"Miss Elspeth!" blurted out MacLeod, and could have bitten his tongue, for the Captain's eye of scorn was on him instantly, as they beheld Linnell's face blench to a death-like pallor.

The youth wetted dry lips. He saw in a flash that during his three weeks' absence there had been new happenings of which he was still unaware. The implication in the minister's words was plain to see ... some bond of friendship again existed between the chief and Elspeth, something that would allow of her approaching him on a business so intimate as that they now discussed. He tried to smile, but it was an affair of a wry mouth. "What? "he cried in an attempt at the humorous that was pitifully feeble. "Is the old feud patched up again? ... Oh! the Highlands, the Highlands!"

Subterfuge on the part of the others was now useless, so the Captain turned to him frankly. "The lass is glamoured, Philip; and although I sometimes think Carsaig's naught but a wisp o' straw on a windy day ... still-and-on the man has good in him, if he'd but give it a chance ... So there the thing is ... Her father will never consent, of course; but you may as well ken now as later that they're together on Scarsdale banks every night for a week back ... And God kens what ploy will be next to the fore."

The sailor's face went haggard. "My thanks, Captain MacColl," said he, and arose, making pretence to yawn and stretch weary limbs. "By-the-by there's a cave hereabouts, isn't there?"

Perplexed at the query, the soldier pointed out a buttress of cliff, on whose seaward face was a cavern where the tinkers sometimes made their home. Linnell thanked him mechanically, picked up hish cloak, and unhitching his garron, went off through some patches of rush and iris towards the rocks.

"Poor lad!" said the Captain. "He's sore hit, I'm fearing."

In twenty minutes the youth reappeared round the cliff-end, his naval finery gone. A plain travelling suit of brown, close-fitting and with ankle-straps had replaced the uniform, evidently now snug in the valise on his saddle-peak.

"Just as I thought, poor lad! I'll wager he's been reading that fellow Byron. Poor lad, indeed!" said the Captain, half to himself.

The sailor came up to them: his calm had returned; the wan look was gone from his eyes; while he swaggered a little as he approached and sang in a low voice:

"Braw news is come to town,
Braw news is carried,
Braw news is come to town,
Draolinn's Elspeth's married"

"Scarcely," said the Captain, grimly endeavouring to carry off the poor jest.

"Well, as good as married," said the youth with an assumption of breeziness his slack looks belied. "And here I'm off to Draolinn to give my humble duty to the lady ... Good day to ye, gentlemen!"

20: Two Letters

LINNELL took his slow way through the Aros crofts in a brown study, his face impassive, his eyes fixed ahead, unregarding the distant salutes of the cutters and carriers of peat in the wayside fields. So abstracted was he that he overshot the turning of the Draolinn road, and pulled bridle only when he heard the bridge at the Preacher's Burn sound boss under his pony's hooves. Coming back to his true route, his spirits did not revive until he reached the heights above the Black Rocks that overlook the fall of the road to the shores of Loch-na-Keal. Here the sight of open water in full sunlight, and the touch of a volleying breeze on his cheek brought back somewhat of liveliness to his features; so at a fast trot he passed Drumlang, entered the pine avenue of Draolinn, and ten minutes later was taking a hearty welcome from the blind chieftain in his den. The old man was all agog for news of the south, and especially of the progress of the case against the Irish sheep-stealers. And thus gossip about Queen Caroline and the Spanish revolution was mingled with his outcries against O'Brien and the dilatory revenue men; while queries anent the Glasgow radicals' new treason, and Castle-reagh's quarrel with Metternich were interrupted by cursings of MacKenzie and Oskamull. On the last-named, whom he conjoined with the treasonable Lanarkshire weavers, he wished fervently, it appeared, to make a good use of his favourite rat-poison.

The sailor gradually soothed the old roarer, wooing him from his eloquent expletives slowly and by stages, through the medium of further tit-bits of London news, until he found opportunity to plead toilet and letters home as an excuse for retiral. Once in his chamber the moodiness of the earlier morning returned; he unpacked his valise, and, spreading the various items of the bright uniform on the bed, sat down to regard them regretfully, his mind almost vacant save for some dim soreness far within. A full hour passed thus, for he was still in a daze from the blow received at the hands of the minister that day. Before his inner eye there ever ranged the girl's image: her clear gaze, the glint of her auburn hair, the tiny freckles at the temple, her free swinging step ... What it was that Draolinn had said regarding her and Grizel in response to his politenesses of inquiry on entering, he could not now recall ... He felt weak enough for self-pity: but a sudden clearness of mind came to him at sight of a water-jug, and instantly he was stripped and sluicing himself free from the sweat and dust of travel.

Sheena, the serving-lass, meeting him at the stair-foot as he descended, shepherded him to the dining-salle. "At last," he said; and braced himself for a meeting with Elspeth. But the long dark room was untenanted save by the chief, who again deluged him with queries regarding "the fools down yonder." The youth, however, hastily gulping some scraps of cold venison and a dish of tea, escaped anew — this time by professing a desire to take a look at the salmon-pools on the Ba; and soon he was striding through a woodland short-cut that lay to the south of the walled garden. In parts the path was almost paved by traverses of half-buried roots of the beeches fringing it, and his footsteps rang hollowly on these from time to time.

It was thus he roused Elspeth from a reverie, where she sat on a bench recessed among the trees, and looked out on the white horses of the tides below Kellan. At once she left her retreat, and so came on him suddenly and face to face, as he rounded a winding of the woodland track. "I heard your step," she said, extending a hand and smiling. "I thought of you; but I missed the ballad you were ay for humming, and so was unsure ... You are recovered? ... Welcome back to Draolinn."

She wore a screen of MacLean tartan on her shoulders; her dress was of green taffety, and her wonderful hair had but a fillet of dark velvet for ornament, that barred the brow and enhanced the wanness of her face. He caught his breath, less in surprise at the swiftness of her descent upon him than at her beauty, still beauty despite this mood of sadness. "You startled me," he said in a low voice. Then with an effort he essayed a cheerier note. "Oh, yes, I am whole again."

They talked for a little of commonplaces — her father's health, the infrequency of the Greenock packet-boat's sailings which had caused him delay, and so on. At the last she mentioned Grizel's betrothal to Garmony, the faintest of flushes stealing to her temples. He opened wide eyes at the news, but ventured nothing save some formal hopes for the happiness of the plighted. An awkward pause ensued, but in the end, beholding weary eyes and a shadowed face, he said, "You are tired. Let us go back to your arbour."

She turned with languid airs. Where now was the free springing step he used to know?...They seated themselves, and gravely and in silence regarded each other for some instants.

Then Linnell leaned forward, elbows on knees, his hand, clasped tightly. "Miss Elspeth," he said slowly, "it is a strange thing I wish to ask ... but ... you have told me of your sister and Garmony—"

He ceased, and his head continued to move deliberaately as it had done while he spoke, like that of child reciting its lesson.

Pity for this confusion of the halting tongue shone in her dark eyes at once. "Yes, Mr. Linnell, pray go on."

"It is this, Madam, I would ask very simply ... Are your affections engaged?" His gaucherie was immense, he felt: it was, indeed, far otherwise; this should have fallen out. Some harsh necessity seemed to compel his utterance; but, at least—he told himself—at least she should have sincerity.

For an instant the girl's eyes opened in wonderment; then she glanced aside, and gave a little uneasy, colourless laugh. "Why do you ask?" she said, her lids downbent.

"Because I wish words of your own for answer."

She rose, flushed and annoyed. "I must go," she murmured.

"Oh, never that ... never that," he cried, leaping to his feet. "No word of anger from you to me I ... Indeed, I ask because I must ... It is the straight path ... You will tell me?" he pleaded.

She was now in a whirlwind of emotions, smiling mechanically to check a rising anger she felt unreasonable in view of their philandering of some weeks ago in the woods of Drumlang. Her eyes turned away uneasily, as if enumerating the beech-trunks surrounding, and so flitted back to him again, their excursion completed ... She could only murmur: "You ask ... but why?"

At that his gaze became unsteady as hers: already he felt himself defeated, yet clung wildly to a hope forlorn. "Because there is no other way to discover if ... if I have the right to say I love you."

There was a steadiness in the utterance that seemed alien from all emotion; but, even so, the earnestness behind the words came to her with all the greater might. This calm was witness surely of the deeps of passion, and here was a revelation for her that blinded and overwhelmed. Pity and terror struggled within her for an instant—but never love ... and terror won. "I must go," she panted, and fled.

For a space Linnell stared dully at the beeches that had encircled her but a moment since, and then began walking aimlessly to and fro before the little arbour, dead to all else but the consciousness of existence. But after half an hour this merciful dulling of his faculties passed, and he sighed as if awaking from a trance. "Ah, well! "said he with a philosophic air, as who should say "Spilt milk," and so set out for a long tramp by the shores of Loch-na-Keal.

The philosophic air was only a matter of some minutes, however, and he was amazed to find himself back in the profounds of a melancholy that bred murderous waves of anger, blotting out sea and sky in red surges that blinded him time and again.

Betwixt these tides of barbaric emotions he would repeat "Ah, well!" as if it were some sorcerer's charm against the rioting blood. A full hour was thus spent, wandering up and down the shingles kicking pebbles fortuitously, before his grave features resumed something of their earlier serenity, and he set his face again towards Draolinn. To-morrow he would say good-bye to the pines and the shore, and look his last on Aros hills. He now had wha^k he came for ... an answer, although unspoken. Old Briny would have him ere long ... whi sails and southern waters, and he would work to make himself such a sailor as his country had not seen since Nelson's day. Nothing like the Service after all ...!

His meditation was broken by the sound of hooves and, glancing up, he found himself at the Drumlang cross-roads and MacLaren, Carsaig's henchman, posting past, making for the Oskamull road at a swinging trot. The sight of the fellow took hi* mind back to his master: and anew he was filled with a jealous rage. The story of the Captain More was true! And what a fantastic world it seemed! How ill the cards had been shuffled that brought this fine woman to the arms of such a fool and idler! ... He strode on, swinging his switch savagely, many a lovely iris falling to his blind ardour of envy, and only desisted when he once more beheld Elspeth come into view. She was now seated on a grassy wayside knoll, and approaching close, he saw eyes brimming, and features pallid with misery. Linnell stooped to lay a compassionate hand on her shoulder before he had recovered from his surprise; and to his amazement she did not shrink, but wept silently.

A letter fluttered from her hand, and lay unregarded in a tuft of iris leaves.

"Let me help," he said.

She shook her head. "The world's become a maze, I'm thinking, and all of us lost in it," she murmured brokenly.

"Let me help."

"You cannot," she answered. "Read," pointing to the paper.

He picked it up. It was a single sheet, first doubled and then folded in treble in the usual fashion; it had been fastened with a seal, now broken.

"I'll come to see you soon; by the week-end most likely, but have pity on me, Colin" it ran. *"I had never a thought of diceing away the honest folk here. The lands are yours, and my honour the bond: but on my honour also I'd never have touched the cogie had I thought there was the least chance of your mind turning to these things. Have pity, I beg of you, for already I am for seeing nought but the future here: a desolation, I do assure you—the larach and the nettle everywhere; the stranger's sheep; and my kindly people scattered and wandering.*

"ALAN."

"Why, it's for Oskamull! "cried the youth.

She nodded, distraught and tear-blinded.

"Did MacLaren bring it? ... I see ... And he has given you the wrong packet, and the letter meant for you goes on to Oskamull ... I can set that part of it right at least. He's but a mile ahead, and there's a fresh pony at Draolinn, I suppose. I can meet up on him instantly."

He turned the packet over to look at the address. It ran:

To Miss ELSPETH,
at Draolinn.

At that instant the paper seemed to break apart, and at once it was clear that there were two letters, the seal at the back of Elspeth's having adhered to the front of Oskamull's, covering the inscription:

To MACCALMAN,
of Oskamull.

Linnell handed her the packet addressed to her, and flushing, she slipped it, unopened, into her girdle.

"I'd best be after Gibbie with this, I think," said he, holding up Oskamull's note.

She rose, her eyes again downbent, her fingers plucking at her dress in an agony of indecision. "Indeed, it is what seems best," she said in a toneless voice, and then bitterly: "My grief! and but little good will it do with dark Colin. It's just he has the heart of a stone, I well believe."

Her spirit fired the sailor, yet he kept silence. She was again his dear lady, he felt; and despite her troth to another, already he was framing a vow in secret to serve her in this contest with Oskamull. Her lover was feeble enough, God wot; but instinctively he was now for appraising him more generously, since he saw himself as a possible benefactor to them both. The next moment he beheld the meaning of his thoughts, and was inwardly amazed at this infection of egotism. Here was a Linnell he had never yet known, and an abasement of soul that was plumbless fell on him. Indeed, this business of the rejected lover was a strange affair! ... But he must be stirring if he was to catch up MacLaren, and so, folding up the letter, he saluted without a word, and turned to go.

She called him back, and he saw eyes tearful yet starry. "Oh, Philip," she cried. "Be you still the good friend."

He bent to kiss her hand, yet could find no word of adieu, so swung off, switching once more at the unoffending *seilisders*. Once out of sight behind the pine-trunks, he took to running, gained his room at Draolinn, and with a heated knife-blade re-affixed the almost unbroken seal on the letter. Next in haste to the stables, where he borrowed a pony of Draolinn's, and so off on the track of MacLaren.

Passing the kitchen-quarters he left a message with Sheena for Draolinn. "Tell him I've business with the Captain More, and will sup at Killiechronan. It may be late or I'm back," he said.

The henchman had reached Coillemore before the sailor overtook him, and already the sun was westering fast. Linnell explained his business briefly, and delivered the letter.

"See you that now," cried the big fellow. "And it's sticking together they were, is it? ... That comes of a stout man on a warm day for messenger, and nothing but one inside pocket. Man, man, but it's myself is the glad one and the grateful! ... You can fancy Oskamull, when I told him my errand, and showed him an empty pouch. It's just he has the ready tongue! ... And indeed, Carsaig himself is not the easy one to deal with nowadays, sir, let me tell you. He's no longer the slack one, is Carsaig ... Indeed and indeed, a changed man ... a changed man! ... And all since he came across yourself yon night in Kilfinichen Churchyard ... Aye, a matter of weeks, you might say, and he's another man ... quite the sober, wise-like laird nowadays ... How in all the world did you bring him to the right tack, sir?"

"Oh, to the devil with you! "cried Linnell, gritting teeth in a sudden gust of jealousy, and riding off noisily, he left the big henchman open-mouthed. Glancing back after a little, he beheld him statue-like, dark against the sunset on the hill-road, a figure of comic interrogation.

"Poor Gibbie," said the sailor. "Doubtless he, too, finds the world hard to understand."

He did not draw rein until he reached the Pedlar's Halt, half a mile from Killiechronan, where he had merciful thoughts of his mount, and let him cool at a slow walk; then passing the path diverging to the home of the Captain More, he made for the shallows on the Ba where the garron might drink fetlock-deep before stabling at Killiechronan.

The rosy gloaming was fast deepening, dimming all around him, and the guiding of the beast over the broken ground between road and river, difficult enough in the daytime with a wary rider, was ten times more so in twilight with a horseman sunk in a brooding melancholy. And so, just where the salt-sodden turf met the shingle, the garron's forefoot sank deep in a bog-hole, and the sailor was tossed from his saddle. He fell heavily on the beach, and his head striking a boulder, he lapsed unto unconsciousness.

When he came to himself next morning he found himself at Killiechronan installed in bed in a tiny cam-ceiled room, his head enswathed, and Miss Belle and the Captain More in attendance.

"Aye," said the veteran, crossing his long legs, and regarding the youth critically. "And what next? ... The Lord alone knows! ... You're never out o' a pickle, it seems; for you've done nothing but ram-stam into trouble since first I set eyes on you, my man."

"And what else would I be doing," said the youth, mimicking the island idiom with a smile, "when it's yourself that's always by to lift me out of it? "He yawned in delicious ease as he ended.

"And that's a gey broad hint," said the old man, grimly regarding the other's open gorge and turning to depart. "Like your father, I see, in the matter o' teeth; a good mouthful ... Good-night!"

Next day the youth's spirits returned, and although his bruises felt worse, he insisted on dressing and hobbling downstairs and out of doors with the Captain, for a walk in the morning sunlight. They went as far as the lee of the larch-wood behind the cottage and stretched themselves on a grassy bank.

"There's one thing I've a mind to ask you now, sir," said Linnell. "And that's about this duel of my father with old Oskamull in Spain. I never got more than a hint of it from my dad."

"And it's just what I've a mind to tell you," said the Captain, smiling; "though, indeed, you'll be the first to hear o't from lips of mine. Many have asked, and often they've asked; but never a one save yourself had the right of asking, and never a one, save you, but would have misunderstood ... < Aye, a twisted thing they'd have made of it. ...

"It happened, however, not in Spain, but in Portugal—Alverca was the name of the place ... Yet the folk in Aros ay speak of it as the Spanish duel ... That's a detail; still-and-on, you see, it shows how they get even the start o' a story wrong. Can you wonder then that I keep a knot on my tongue in the matter? ... Besides I was a second, you'll understand ... And to crown a', here's the other man's son next door to us, at Oskamull ...

"But this is how it fell out."

21: The Spanish Duel

"YOUR father and Oskamull never hit it off after an affair in Robledillo; some difference of opinion about a girl in white on a balcony there. She jilted both, it's true; but there it was, an old rankling sore for each of them. Most of us thought that this had something to do wi' Oskamull sending the wine in your father's face that night in the old hospice at Alverca, where we were then stationed. But we were wrong, as I learned later.

"The hospice was a disused part of the convent there, right in the face of the Sierra d'Estrella; and a more unlikely spot for a duel I never saw. The men were in village billets; but the officers messed and slept in this old lazar-house, flanking the convent garden. Opposite us was the nun's church, and at the top of the square formed by the garden was the convent itself, where twenty women still stayed on, despite the unsettled condition of that countryside. And thus, you may conceive, we saw more of religion than for ordinar'; and the good folk (while we were there, at least) saw less of war than they did for many a long year after that, I'll warrant. It's true we were neither blate nor blameless: there were one or two of us that beheld the bottom of our glass too often for our good; and I could never fancy the slap o' cartes and the chink o' dice fit music for the inside o' convent walls ... But for wartime we werena bad ... We were dog-tired waiting for word to move; the air was either trembling with heat, or there were thunder and lightning and lashing rains—an evil climate for men fidgeting to be stirring. Still-and-on we held ourselves in hand. Stuck for three weeks were we at Alverca, I tell you; and yet but one duel in all that time, despite the sultry weather. I suppose it was the holy life of those douce folk kept us in leash. There they were at prayers and rosary, gardening, tending their little cemetery, or teaching a dozen or so of orphan lasses. And across the lawns and the flower-beds, our men ... the folk of the jest and the song, of the sword and the epaulettes. Even the wee bit fountain tinkling at the feet of the gilt Madonna, set midmost of the quadrangle's flowers, had something of the peaceful in it that helped us through, I fancy."

"Then there was the church, a marvel o' white stone, finely sculptured, and full of clear light; a good and holy place it seemed to me (that boke at most things in their religion) where the solitary soul might maybe win ben to the grace we ay crave, even in war ... *Ochanoch!* and often I tried yonder, but there ay sprang up a kind o' shutter in my mind that left me powerless and empty, 'spite of a' my striving.

"Your father looked then as you do now, a bit of a sobersides with a long face, but in reality frank and merry enough. Oskamull's father was a young, red-cheeked, stout fellow, with a jaunty cock of his chin, and sharp, sly eyes."

"What I can't make out," said Linnell, "is how all you Highlanders came into a Glo'ster regiment?"

"Oh, common enough: we drifted where promotion promised best, and for a Scot that was ay to be seeking south. Oskamull's father came the same gate as myself—Argyllshire Fencibles, and Middlesex Militia, and then the Sixty-first. How your father, who was half-Scotch, though Lowland, got to us, I never made out.

"Well, there we were in sultry weather, as I say, inactive and grumbling. Cartes and dice, drink and singing; sometimes a wild-boar hunt; sometimes yon stamping dances with the lasses in the village. It was in 'nine, you see, and there was some waiting before we joined Cameron's brigade at Oropesa, just seven weeks before Talavera ... a different story that from loafing in a convent, I'm thinking.

"Well, as I said, after dinner at nights in the big salle of the hospice, it was cartes and dice and wine in lashings. The place was like a tavern wi' smoke and noise, the calling of points, the jingling of glasses, and staves of song from every other table. On this evening Oskamull and your father were in a corner, nearby where I sat by my lonesome. The dice were busy between them when the brulzie broke out. There were some words, the both of them on their feet; then came a glass of liquor in your father's face, and over went the table and wine-stoups. Your father had given him the lie direct, we understood. There was only one way of it, and that was a meeting.

"MacNutt and myself were your father's seconds, two others were got for Oskamull, and it was arranged that the affair was to be there and then, since we didna ken the moment we might get the route. It was a clear moonlight night after the rain of the afternoon. The place was to be the Raised Road, a kind of viaduct, centuries old, that ran from the end o' the garden terrace down a wee valley to the home farm o' the convent. Here there lived another community of nuns ... of the same order as ouf friends; I don't know what it was, but they wore black gowns and a cord of peacock blue. The Raised Road was as broad as the walls of 'Derry; once or twice in its half-mile were parts that were fairly flat; on one of these we could measure forty paces and that was enough. So we roused the regimental doctor, a fellow who wined early, and slept much in consequence; and out we trooped like romping schoolboys. If it wasna exactly the Plains of Maida it was at least distraction, and as near war aft we could come ... Like schoolboys, you understand. ...

"There were twenty of us that stole down the garden to the gate .that gave on the road to the farm. And then came the eeriest turn; for though it was well after midnight, there was the sound o' spade and mattock from the graveyard, close by the convent church. We halted, fear-gripped every man of us; for we were bent on a duel, and here was a grave already a-digging: I tell you it was a sound o' dread, yonder in the moonlight. The gate came heavily to on the last of us, and just then the head of a woman with coif and hood looked down from over the wall of the graveyard, to where we were standing in a group fully thirty feet below her. It was the Mother Superior—a wise-like woman wi' specs and bad teeth—and she asked our business. But before we could answer, up popped the *dispenseira* (or housekeeper) by her side, the merriest face I ever saw on nun or milkmaid, and teeth of the finest in all the world—ay laughing she was. We pretended not to have enough of their language to understand, but assured them we were not going near the home-farm. That seemed to relieve them somewhat, and they informed us that one of the sisterhood had died that day. As was their custom, the nuns themselves were digging her grave; and the good Mother asked our prayers for the poor soul's repose. The sound of the mattocks had stopped, and there we stood staring at her, and she at us: ourselves uneasy, and she the least bit suspicious. Down in the valley among the cork and olive trees the nightingales were now singing in a way to break the heart, and once we started, every one, at the wail of an owl. Then even the birds fell still, and all you could hear was the river crying at some broken water far below, among the corn and vine-fields. We looked, doubtless, to those poor women peering at us from the ivied wall, like some traitors conspiring a deed o' blackness. At last the Mother spoke. ' Go with God,' she said. So off we trooped, wrapped up in our cloaks, and our heads hanging, uncomfortably aware we were worthy of no such grace. And immediately there began again the *tack-tack* of the spade and pick as the women's heads sank behind the dyke.

"Half-way down the mounded road we halted; the footing was good; the moon lit everything as clear as day; and the elevation of our chosen ground made it like a castle's battlement, so did the men stand out against the sky. You'd have thought that neither could miss; and indeed, I was thinking one grave might be little enough that same night. But a miss there was; and it was not your father's; for Oskamull had dropped, his right arm smashed ... And now down the road there came four of the nuns, wi' protesting cries, their robes kilted and their feet heavy wi' red clay. Then the *dispenseira* must needs quarrel with our surgeon, who was none too sober, about the bandaging of the splintered arm ... A strange sight yon! ...

"I came back with your father; and up to hia room we went, a wee bit place over the salle. It had a sloping roof, I mind, and we looked out of its dormer window at the bringing in o' Oskamull. They had stopped at the fountain o' the Madonna in the middle of the garden, and were bathing the wound. The air was heavy with the scents o' rosemary and myrtle, and your father remarked on them. ' A bonnie night for a killing,' said he. 'God! what animals we are! ... Go down, Duncan, and see how the poor man is.'

"Down I went, and found him sitting on the sod, quite joco', cracking jests wi' the housekeeper sister, who was binding his wound afresh. 'A flea bite,' says he; 'I'll be about in a day or two.' I came back and told your father how things stood. ' I'm glad he thinks so lightly o't,' said he. ' I'm sorry for the poor thief.' ... ' Thief! ' said I ... ' What else? ' he answered. ' I'll tell you, Duncan, what I've told to none ... Look at this'; and he took a dice-cube from his pouch, and tossed it several times. It fell cinque every throw. He followed with another; and it fell six each cast. He picked up the cinque. 'I found this under our table the night before last, after the gaming was by wi',' said he. ' I'd done nothing but lose then. To-night we had a second bout. Thinks I, I've got his false dice, so he's harmless! But there he was, no end to his winnings; and at last I challenged his six, picked up the ivory and threw it thrice. It fell six every time. I put it in my pocket with never a word, and rose. He was equally silent, but he knew there was no witness; so what does he do but turn the tables on me. "Cheat!" says he; and flings his wine at my head. "Liar," says I ... You know the rest o't. He said nothing, and I had no proof. The men will think it's the lass at Robledillo again ... Let them ... It's little I care, and he'll never say no to that story himself.' I was mad wi' anger at the trick Oskamull had played my friend; but could do nothing. In any case the cheater was well served; for the arm was hopeless, and two days later, when we got our marching orders, he was sent back to Lisbon, for the road home. It was his right arm, and before a week the bones were rotten; the hand withered in a month; and by the autumn there was a captaincy vacant in the Sixty-first ... That's the story then; and you're the first I've told it to, laddie."

"I'm grateful, Captain," said Linnell. "It helps my understanding of a thing I often have brooded on."

"Come you indoors, and I'll show you something," said the Captain, rising and extending him a hand. Linnell scrambled painfully to his feet, and, returning to the house, they mounted to the room of the old soldier.

"And here now," said the veteran, going to the topmost drawer in a high chest of mahogany, and fumbling there,—"here are the false dice themselves, given me that same night by your father, in case of trouble afterwards. We never knew the chances of battle, and he had a fancy that I should guard them for him in case of inquiry, and he gone. ... But nothing happened either of us in all that bloody campaigning ... and the things went the round o' Spain wi' me ... It's odd when you come to think o't."

Linnell picked up the cubes and tested them; they fell cinque and six nearly every throw. "They're a trifle bigger than ordinary," said he.

"Take them wi' you," said the Captain, "if you've a notion o' them. It's all o' your father's I have; and who better than you to heir things like that wi' a story ahint them?"

Linnell thanked him and pocketed the ivories. "I suppose he would have doctored cards also, a man like that," said he.

"I'll wager he had," said the Captain. "And plenty other false dice too, I make no doubt; for there was a whisper about his gaming being twisted, later on: before he was out the Service even ... between Lisbon and London, you'll understand."

"And the poor creature, his son," said Linnell, moodily. "What chance had the fellow with a father like that?"

The old soldier laughed. "Man, you're Charlie Linnell all over," he said. "He was for pitying old Oskamull night long as he hung out yon dormer window at the convent in Alverca ... Man, it was a bonnie night ... and the teeth and laugh o' the *dispenseira* woman—I can fancy them yet ... a fine lass! ... And I never smell rosemary to this day, but I'm for seeing yon fountain in the garden, and the moonlight on the gilding o' the statue o' the Virgin, and her looking down, surprised-like, at the cloaks and spurs o' our folk, round the wee wifie in the white coif, busy with a bandage that soaked red at every turn."

22: The Horse Fair

Dr Macculloch arrived at Killiechronan in the afternoon in response to an urgent message from the Captain, and was able to assure the household that the sailor was little the worse of his accident. "That head of his would withstand Ben More itself if it fell on him," said he ... "Fancy you! Carsaig's knock; and then another from the sheep-stealers; and now this one! ... The man has a charmed life, I'm thinking."

But Captain MacColl, drawing him apart indicated forcibly the undesirability of Linnell's returning to Draolinn. He recounted the scene at Pennygown when the minister and himself had revealed to the sailor the renewal of the love-affair between Elspeth and Carsaig. "Crestfallen wasna a word for it," concluded the Captain. "The man was almost melancholy-mad, look you ... He's been sore hit, and the kindest thing is to keep him here."

With astonishing celerity the Doctor at once went back on his favourable prognosis. "I think,' said he to the sailor later in the day, "it's a quiet life you must be leading now. You'd best be keeping that sconce o' yours at peace for a bittie, and you'll no' go over the doorstep here for a week to come ... at least, not beyond the lea-field anyway ... Rest, man, rest is what you want."

Linnell, guessing conspiracy, glared gloomily at him and the old soldier. The Doctor, however, pretended not to see these sour looks and went on cheerfully: "I'm for Gribun now, so I'll look in at Draolinn in the passing, and explain to the Chief, and ask him to send your baggage across without delay ... Wi' a head like that on you, there's nothing else for it but your stopping here."

During the next few days the sailor profited by the wisdom of these sages, for his spirits revived somewhat, now that he was out of immediate danger of further rencounter with Elspeth. And soon a new interest opened to him, for he had revealed to the Captain the purport of Carsaig's note to Oskamull, and immediately the old fellow was on a fresh trail as to a solution of the tangle.

"Look you," said he, "I made a mess with that business of MacKenzie's bond, and despite all our trouble ... hamesucken and the rest of it ... I misdoubt but that Carsaig's folk will be cleared from their crofts once

Oskamull gets possession; Carsaig himself ruined, and others. . . others wi' broken hearts." (He was thinking of Elspeth, but wisely forbore mention of her name.) "At length and at last, however, I'm seeing a way out o't. I'm loth to take it, but I see no other."

With this mysterious saying he departed in the direction of Draolinn. Here he had an immediate interview with Elspeth in her beechen arbour, where she now sat daily, brooding unhappily. This conference was an arduous one for him; all his powers of persuasion and tact were called for; at times the debate was stormy; and indeed the girl left him at last in petulance and with a tear-stained face. But the Captain came from the parley with a countenance radiant. At last he had the secret key to the riddle of Oskamull's hold on Carsaig, for he had forced the girl to confession of all she knew.

"What think you," said he to Linnell on his return. "Oskamull has Carsaig's lands, but not a scrap o' parchment covering them ... Heard you ever the like?"

Linnell smiled. "Oh, the Highlands," said he. "Nothing surprises me in this strange country."

"It seems that Carsaig's word is the only security," went on the Captain ... "That explains yon saying in his letter to Oskamull—the one Miss Elspeth opened by mistake—'my honour the bond,' or something to that effect."

"Oh! the Highlands! the Highlands! "said Linnell, still smiling.

"But best of all my news is yet to come, Philip ... The lands were lost by Carsaig to Oskamull ower the diceing-cogie ... You take me?"

Linn ell's smile vanished in a flash; and his brows came down in horror, as the Captain's meaning lay clear before him. "Heavens!" he cried. "Cheating? ... You don't think . . .?" A stare of interrogation concluded the query.

"Aye," said the Captain, with a hint of sadness in his tone. "You have it ... That's just what I think ... But we maun get farther than the thinking, lad, if we're to be of any service in this."

"By all the stars!" cried the sailor with conviction, "you've got Oskamull's bearings at last ... You're the great wonder, sir! ... However did you manage all this?"

"By asking those that kent," said the Captain briefly, and turning away his head. "I had to do't lad ... There was nothing else for't."

"Ah! "said Linnell, flushing painfully, as he saw the covert reference to Elspeth. "That was not in my mind, sir," and a fit of melancholy ensued that took him for an hour from the Captain's company.

By the afternoon, however, the two were once more on the trail together like sleuths just blooded. Long colloquies ensued; much pacing to and fro between the cottage and the larch-wood, and at the end of the day their decisions for action against Oskamull were taken. "The horse-fair is our only chance," concluded the Captain with conviction, "and a good one too. I wouldna ask for a better."

Aros horse-market was in early August, and lasted two days or three. It wanted but a week of this when Linnell and the Captain concluded their pact, and the time went quickly enough. One fine morning the sailor awoke in the little cottage on the hill to other sounds than the song of the lark and the sea-gull's strident cry—a drumming of hooves multitudinous on the shore-road. He leaped to look out from the skylight. Bay, roan, white, black, dapple-grey, and piebald; gelding, mare, foal and filly, there were the horses at last. Heavy of fetlock and long of mane, they looked a trifle wild-eyed, as if they had not yet recovered from the scare of their sea-journey from the outlying Hebrides. In most cases the breeders made use of the isles as stepping-stones on their route: the Barra and Uist folk had landed their convoys in Tiree or Coll a week ago, rested there, feeding their stock for a day or two, and then ferried the ten or twenty miles to Calgary Bay or to the Ross. Thence, travelling the length of Aros Isle by easy stages, they sustained their charges in freebooting style by foraging in wayside fields, and so made for the fair. Failing sales at the market now due, there were still other fairs in the South, and the next stepping-stone would be Kererra, ferrying from Grass-point; from Kererra to the mainland was but half a mile of water; then nought but dry land and good grazing all the way for a hundred miles by Lochowside and Inneraora, through Glencroe, and past Dumbarton town to Falkirk Tryst.

The horsemen looked as unkempt and savage as their charges; voluble in Gaelic, they praised the points of their stock, or decried the baseness of low offerers. As a rule they slept by the roadside or high on the moorland in all weathers, close by their tethered beasts.

A red dust rose in clouds as they went through Killiechronan; whinnyings came frequently; the hooves thundered back to the breaking surf's clangour on the sunlit shores; and the sight stirred Linnell and the Captain to an approach to the roadside to watch the passing of the cavalcade. The sailor remarking in some of the beasts a wild beauty in neck and eye and pastern he had not noted before, the veteran interpreted.

"Arab blood, I well believe," said he. "We had strays from the Armada shipwrecks, they're saying, all along the coasts of the isles ... Spanish captains and their chargers ... Set them up! ... And who so grand as the Don, will you tell me with his horses on shipboard? ... I've heard they fed their mounts from golden salvers, too—the braggarts!—But talking o' Spain, our business winna wait, and we'd best be going over to the market itself."

They took the hill-road for its greater freedom, and looking down into the valley on their right, saw the dust-clouded caravan ranging the whole length of the narrow isthmus between Loch-na-Keal and Kyle Aros. The sun rose warm; odours of crushed gall hung around them; the red grouse rose whirring from their feet; above, the lark quired melodious, and the busy scene below held the eye like a pageant. It was with mounting spirits that Linnell followed the Captain on the descent to the township by a path that took them close to Mac-Kenzie's pier.

Making for the change-house, they went slowly, for the roads were thronged with men leading horses, jostling, chaffing, commercing, or hailing friends unmet since last year's fair.

"Look at this," said the Captain, "here's the bargain-maker."

A group had gathered round two tousy old men, whose right hands were held by a red-headed, lame fellow. A horse on a halter surveyed the scene morosely from over the shoulder of one of the principals, his price evidently the matter of dispute. The bargain-maker, cajoling, jesting, and pleading in Gaelic, dragged the hands towards each other by main force, and, time and again, endeavoured to make the palms meet in warranty of agreement; but on the instant of close approach, each of the old fellows pulled backwards with might and main, shouting denials in the ancient tongue. At times they relapsed into English and the sailor then noted that the substance of their appeals were to moral considerations.

"Och, man, have you no conscience at all, at all," came indiscriminately from either side, as price after price was named. But at last, in an unlooked-for moment, the bargain-maker touched their palms, and turned off, smiling broadly, plainly well-pleased. Not so his clients, however, who violently abused him, neither consenting and both protesting. But impassive as a sphinx, the maker of bargains regarded them silently. Custom was stronger than their pleadings; the die was cast; and the horse was now bound to change owners at the price last named. So the three went off, still wrangling, to the change-house to conclude the sale and settle the bargain-maker's luck-penny over a dram.

"Yonder's Carsaig's man, MacLaren," said the Captain pointing as they turned off, "also John Morrison; and that means their masters are at the fair. And here now is Callum from Oskamull. We're in Fortune's hand sure enough, for I'll wager his chiefs not far off, if Callum's at the market."

Though early in the day, it was evident that the gillie had been indulging in strong waters, and the Captain stood to regard his movements. Callum, sixty if he was a day, had seized another ancient by the lapels of his coat. "And they're telling me that it's Rory the Pilot you are," he cried. "Man, it's long since I saw you." He swayed unsteadily as he spoke.

"And who now may you be?" asked the other, clasping with equal unsteadiness the shoulders of Callum.

"Just Callum MacFadyen, that would be putting the stone with you often and oft in his young days in Glenforsa, *ille*."

"Man, man! "said the Pilot, "and is it you that's in it, Callum? It is indeed long and long since the good days of youth."

"Long enough and a tail to it," said the other ..."And how's your father?"

For a space the Pilot regarded him in amazement, and then said slowly, as he uncovered: "Well, Death took him from us thirty years ago, and I havena heard a word from him since."

The group surrounding the quaint figures broke up smiling, and the Captain took Linnell's arm. "The stoups gang ower freely on a day like this," said he ... "See you that over there." He pointed to where, under the shelter of a bank and hedge, a youth was combing carefully at a horse's fetlocks, and another brushing its rough hide. "Last fair, I mind well, there was a Torloisk man came over wi' a pony, and sold it to a Glasgow horse-couper. The Glasgow man barbered the horse, just as these fellows are now doing; maybe too, he used a trifle dye. And then in the gloaming, what does he do but meet the same Torloisk crofter (now far gone in the matter of aquavity) and sell him the very beast he'd parted with in the morning—sold it, too, for five pounds more ... Aye, aye, there are too many pinkies cocked at the inn, I'm thinking, on a day like this."

"Let's hope it's a custom may have its uses to-night," said Linnell with meaning. "Where's our quarry now? Let us try the change-house without delay, for I'd fain see the thing moving."

The day was early yet for any signs of general fuddlement: but the islesmen were coming and going from the inn-doors like bees about a hive. One or two of the Aros lairds were already arrived, Oolava, Morenish and Moy, keeping an eye on their factors and their dealings with their stock. These the Captain and Linnell duly saluted as they passed on into the change-house. Here they went through a tap-room, and climbed a stair with a shaky handrail to a wide, low-ceiled room reserved for the gentry, but finding it empty, they returned to the open.

"Try the parks," said Linnell; and they pushed their way once more through the huckstering groups and the horse-holding mob of gillies, until they reached the seaward side of the inn. Between this and the Kyle, was a bit of flat moorland, where were scattered clusters of bargainers, with their charges. In some places men ran ponies on halters to show their paces. Near the shore was a field where a game of shinty was in progress. Here and there by the rocks were dots of men retired from the bustle of the fair for a space.

"Is not yon figure Dr. MacCulloch? "asked the sailor, pointing to a man in a long-skirted coat and black beaver hat, moving swiftly from group to group of the horse-dealers. "Whatever is he after?"

"None other but the same good man," said the Captain. "And what else will he be after, think you, but a payment of one or two of last year's accounts, long overdue? ... It's a soul-destroying business; but what other can you do wi' the two or three scurvy ones in Aros Isle (God be thanked there are so few!) who winna settle the bill that should ay come first—the Doctor's? ... So, if there's one of these dark fellows sells a pony, the good Doctor duns him politely, as soon as the cash is handed over by the buyer ... And he gets paid too, for the thing's done privately, yet in public, if you'll understand ... "

"A hard life," commented the sailor.

"Hard? ... It's a crucifixion, I tell you, for that man to take aught for his work, let alone in this fashion," cried the Captain with a flashing eye ... "But look at those fellows down yonder—the two with flat bonnets—close to the water-line," he said in a whisper. "Let us move nearer ... Yes, it's Oskamull; I can see the cock of his chin in air ... and Carsaig's wi' him ... Best go no nearer, in case they vizzy us ... We have them safe; for they'll be here all day watching their stock; and they'll stop overnight if they keep to custom ... The evening's our time, lad; so let's be taking the moor again for Killiechronan—and a restful afternoon; for it's coming ower me that I'm no longer young; and I'm dog-tired with all this dust and heat."

23: The Langrets

IT was nine at night before they set out on their return journey to the township, this time by the glen road. A moon rode high on silvery cloud-billows, and a thin mist lay on the lower grounds, from which emerged, ghost-like, the forms of grazing horses in the wayside fields, and the plaid-wrapped attendants on the high-road margins. From unwonted quarters, low voices sounded unexpectedly; in Glenaros woods a single shot rang out ... no doubt but that there would be venison and to spare at some moorland bivouac to-morrow. It was indeed strange to behold this countryside, for ordinarily tenanted only by a few field-workers, become on a sudden so populous by reason of this invasion of men and beasts. They rested now in the moonlight and the mist, like some army on a stage of its journey to great doings far away; it wanted but the bugle's note, the flapping of canvas, and the sentry's challenge, to render illusion complete.

An elfin figure with skinny arms flitted from behind a whin-bush, peered into their faces and vanished into a birch-grove. "The Catechist's Boy," said the Captain. "'Tis he has the rare ploys on a market-night. Many a strange thing he'll be seeing at times like these ... the wee rover! ... I could almost be envying him."

Lights were showing in front of the dark bulk of the straggling buildings of the change-house as they drew near the village; shouts and laughter came from its busy doors; and a faint sound of a Gaelic chorus recurred at intervals from the direction of MacKenzie's pier. Entering the inn, the Captain led the way through the tap-room, and whispered a word to MacMurchie, the landlord, a little grey badger of a man, who furtively signed them to the upper room.

"Tostary and Oolava are there," said he; "Carsaig and Oskamull also; and they're all for bedding here to-night ... Aye, aye, Captain, it'll be Ferintosh of the best; I'll see it's sent up to you ... Make yourselves cheery, gentlemen!"

They ascended to the first floor, and opened the door of the wide, low-ceiled room they had already visited that morning. The chamber lay in shadow save where a faint light from a peat-fire shone ruddily on a stone hearth, or where a candle in a sconce lit a corner holding a table strewn with cartes. Tostary and Carsaig sat by the fireside, supping toddies that steamed, and discussing market prices. At the card-table were Oskamull and Oolava, a fair youth with curly locks. Their empty glasses told a clear tale of absorption in their game.

Linnell seemed to stumble as he entered this place of rich glooms, but instantly he was steadied by the hand of the Captain More, who led him towards the fire. "A bittie tired by the long walk from Killiechronan, gentlemen," said the veteran, making a significant movement with his hand to his mouth, behind the sailor's back. "After his recent illness it's not quite unexpected, so to speak."

The youth, it appeared, was suddenly become as one drunken, and staggering to the fireplace, he fell against the jamb, and then subsided neatly into the chair vacated by Carsaig, who had risen on the entry of the new-comers. The Captain presented Linnell to the company with much seriousness, as who should say: "Let us humour the lad, gentlemen, for you see how things are." The sailor, without rising, grinned vacantly at each of the lairds in turn, and flourished an unsteady hand in salute.

Carsaig and his friends were plainly flustered, but all kept silence except Oskamull, who said in bitter tones: "I think I've met Mr. Linnell before; and, I fear, Captain MacColl, there's not a room in all Aros big enough to hold us both."

The drunken man was as if deaf, however, and made no answer, but extending his hands to the fire, set to crooning and talking to himself. He seemed, indeed, already half asleep.

"Let be ... let be," said Oolava, "the man's maudlin, and will soon be dovering."

With a frown and a grunt, Oskamull sat down to the cartes again, and the Captain, drawing in a chair to the ingle, joined in the gossip of the fair with Carsaig and Tostary; while Linnell showed immediate signs of bearing out Oolava's prediction, by partially slipping from his seat as he fell deeper into his drowse. But on the arrival of the liquors the Captain had ordered, he was instantly broad awake, and silently absorbed half the contents of his glass with a droll solemnity and precision that brought smiles to the faces of his companions. Then, despite the clamour of song and shouting from the tap-room, he sank to a profound slumber, still sprawling ungainly.

The night drew on, the trio by the fire deep in the discussion of tacks and leases, market prices, and new sheep runs on the mainland. At times Carsaig went to the broad uncurtained window that gave on the shore and the moonlit Sound. He seemed ill at ease, the Captain noted; and he remarked also that at the window, his eyes were always skywards. "Is it a weather change, you're fearing, Carsaig," said he, "or have you turned astronomer, I wonder?"

The chieftain laughed nervously. "Neither," said he. "But the stars are the great friends to me, I'm ay thinking ... They're the constant ones ...

Keep the mind steady when it fain would be wandering." He returned to his seat, sighing, his restless eyes anxiously regarding Oskamull.

Somewhere about eleven the gamesters ceased play; some money chinked between them as the final winnings were paid, and Oolava joined the others at the fire. "Draw in before you bed, Oskamull," cried he, "and warm your toes."

"I'm near enough," said the other sourly, keeping his place at the table, and glaring at Linnell's slouching figure. He bundled the cartes as he spoke, and laid them aside. "Will you play, Tostary? "said he. "Let's try the rattlers." He drew forth a diceing set, chinking the box; and Tostary, an elderly man with grey haffets, took the seat vacated by Oolava. But twenty minutes had hardly gone when he called a halt.

"I've but ten guineas left," said he. "The luck's against me, and I maun be stopping. It's you are Fortune's favourite sure enough, Colin."

"And high time I was, too," said Oskamull: "for at the cartes I did nothing but lose."

Linnell stirred just then, and sat up stiffly. "Cartes? "said he, with a hiccup. "Who said cartes? ... I'll play cartes, Captain ... shertainly ... You spread cartes, Captain, an' I'll keel-haul you all night at cartes, sir ... Cut your cartes at onsh, man! "His voice rose unsteadily, and as he stood up, swaying, his half-filled glass was knocked over.

"Tush, Philip," said the Captain, "there are no cartes a-playing ... Sit you down and be civil."

"Plen-plen-plenty money, y'know," said Linnell, pulling out a handful of loose gold. "Who says I'm afraid?" ... He staggered to the dicer's table. "Where's pack? "he demanded.

Tostary put a restraining hand on the youth's shoulder; while Oskamull rose, with dark brows. The Captain came across the room to them. "They were diceing, man, and you're interrupting the play," said he. "Come, sit you down by the peats, and we'll have up another dram."

"I want dice, Captain MacColl," said the sailor, doggedly insistent. "Must dice, y'know." And thrusting off the hand of Tostary angrily, he plumped heavily into the chair the old chief had just vacated. Slowly he fumbled in his breeches pocket, and then, producing a handful of gold, he placed it with a thump on the board, and glanced at Oskamull without a hint of recognition in his eyes. "You take other fellow's place, Captain," he said, pointing a commanding finger at the old soldier.

"Never a bit o' me," said the veteran. "Come you back to the fire, lad ... You're disturbing the company, I'm telling you."

The youth smiled foolishly, and rose as if to go, shaking Tostary's hand warmly, and murmuring, "No offensh "; but the next moment suddenly sat down again in sullen defiance. "Must really rattle a bit," said he.

"Oh, for Heaven's sake take the fool on yourself," whispered Tostary to Oskamull. "It will be the quicker to bed for us all, and in peace, too."

The chief nodded, his eyes fixed eagerly on the guineas among which the sailor's fingers strayed; and assenting, with a supercilious smile as if sacrificing his pride to the cause of good company, he said in an aside to the old laird, "By all means ... no quarrelling ... Nevertheless, let him pay the honours, tipsy or no'."

He rattled the dice box, and laid down three guineas. Linnell capped these with three from his heap. Oskamull called the main. "Eight," said he, and cast. Two sixes had been thrown. "I nick," said he, and moved the staked guineas to his side of the table.

The others retired to the fire and their talk again, with sometimes an anxious glance at the players. An occasional boozy chuckle from the sailor reached them as he won; but Oskamull kept silence, except when the game required his voice. From below singing and bursts of laughter still ascended. Then twelve struck ponderously from a hidden eight-day clock somewhere downstairs; and shortly after, a shuffling of feet and a slamming of doors, succeeded by a gradual fading into distance of the singing, indicated that the change-house was ceasing business for the night. Thinking of retiral also, the group by the fire rose, and crossed the room to look on at the final stages of the hazard.

"Time we were stopping, my hero," said Oskamull, turning to smile at the others. Three-fourths of Linnell's pile of guineas had gone over the table already.

"Right, little bird! "cried the sailor cheerfully; and he counted his remaining gold. "Twenty-two," said he. "The lot against twenty-two of yours, sir."

"As you will," said MacCalman. "My cast, I believe ... I call seven." He rattled and threw two cinques. "Chance," he said, and threw once more: again two cinques. "Chance again," said he, and raked the money over.

Linnell stood up. "Cheat! "he cried.

The chieftain's face went white: and he made a move, as if to fling himself at the other's throat, that would have sent the table flying. But the Captain More's strong left hand intervened and thrust him back to his seat, while his right steadied the table, so that the dice and guineas lay unmoved. "Leave the table untouched, gentlemen," he cried. "Mr. Linnell has made a charge, I believe."

The sailor, astonishingly sober, turned to the other lairds. "Will one of you test the dice," he said quietly.

None stirred; the accusing dice lay waiting. "I say that either of the pair will fall cinque at nearly every cast," said Linnell. "He has played a double set."

"Nonsense," said old Tostary, putting the cubes in a glass and rattling them. He threw, and each came up a cinque. "Nonsense," he gasped again; and once more rattled and cast. Two cinques lay plain for the second time.

"He's palmed them off on me," cried Oskamull shakily. "By Heavens, sir, you shall answer me now with weapons."

"An untruth, gentlemen," said the sailor calmly. "For he has two others in the left pouch of his vest ... both sixes ... Let him empty the pocket if it is not so."

With pallid lips and frowning brows, Carsaig stood, awaiting his friend's denial. But it did not come. "There's none here man enough to ripe pouches o' mine," cried Oskamull in a cracked voice, as he rose to his feet defiantly. "And I'm little likely to empty them at the bidding of a halfiin ... It's sufficient for all of you, if I say there's not a rattler on my person ... And if the dice on the table are false, then I say I know from whom they came; they're none o' mine." He pointed a quivering finger at Linnell.

"Come, come!" said the Captain More calmly and gravely, "there's none here would be picking pockets, I'm thinking." His left hand was now on Oskamull's shoulder, as if he feared a fresh attempt at violence. "If the dice arena there, they arena there, Colin, and that's an end on't." He clapped the angry chief on the back with his left hand in a fashion that disarmed suspicion, while his right hand passed appraisingly in a rapid movement over the contour of the waistcoat-pocket. To the amazement of the beholders the challenged gamester stood as if mesmerized at the boldness of the move. "All the same, laddie," went on the old man, "the memory's a treacherous thing; and, indeed, speaking only for myself, you'll understand, I would say you have there something no' unlike a pair o' dice." And as he spoke, his worn fingers dipped swiftly into the pouch, and withdrew two cubes of ivory. He tossed them on the table, and they both fell six.

"Curse you! "cried the chief. "You'll hear more of this"; and ducking beneath the Captain's outstretched arm, he made for the door and clattered downstairs.

The remaining lairds regarded each other with white faces; while the Captain More lifted the ivories, and tossed them time and again with the air of a connoisseur. Then he examined the ace side of the sixes and the deuce side of the cinques carefully. "As I thought," said he, "they're langrets."

"What are those? "asked Carsaig in a half-choking voice.

"Only dice with a small matter of inequality in the sides, the larger side being opposite that you're wanting to come uppermost ... Nothing so crude as loading, you'll understand. They're never so certain as the loaded ones ... but they'll fall as planned often enough for their purpose."

"You'll have seen the like before, Captain, I take it? "said Tostary, turning away to hide his crestfallen airs.

"Oh, yes; but it's years ago, here and there in Spain and Portugal."

"Horrible, horrible!" said Tostary. "Who'd have believed it?"

"Aye, it's bad," said the veteran, drily ... "Well, Philip, we maun be stepping ... Goodnight, gentlemen."

Going out-of-doors, after paying the lawing, they beheld a horseman turn the inn corner from the direction of the stables, and take the Draolinn road at a canter. "There he goes," said the Captain. "A done man! ... God be thankit there's no' a wife at Oskamull to be dragged down wi' him!"

At the start of their journey they kept silence, each brooding on the scene just overpast, but half-way the Captain swore audibly. "Damn Carsaig!" said he. "A stock-fish would have shown more in his face than he. Not the least sign that he saw reason for thankfulness in the exposure o' that scoundrel. It has freed him from his promise to beggar himself at Oskamull's bidding; yet never a token did he give that he jaloused as much, the dolt!"

"Maybe," said Linnell, thoughtfully. "Yet he couldn't but see whereto the matter pointed, surely ... the plain conclusion that he had lost his lands by those same false dice ... But did you mark his face? ... I could almost love the man' for it ... for there was nought yonder but horror at the thought of an old friend lost to him and for ever."

24: Happenings at Draolinn

NEXT morning the Captain More was up betimes; and when Linnell came down to a late breakfast the old fellow was nowhere to be found. The sailor was now eager to be moving south again; he had hoped to have a forenoon of leave-taking with his friend, and then to set off towards evening to Grasspoint Ferry—the first stage of his journey, There was no reason for further delay: he knew how he stood with Elspeth, and could look calmly back on what was now a sealed page in his history. Then, too, the strange tangle of his own and his father's life with the house of Oskamull seemed at last as clearly unravelled as by the hand of Destiny itself. His return to Aros had been indeed worth while; but it was time for the road again, and the new career on shipboard. He chafed at the Captain's absence, therefore ... a very young old man, he thought, to be so early stirring ... as restless as one of yesterday's market colts.

The truant appeared just after the mid-day meal was over. "I had a bite and sup at Draolinn," he explained to Miss Belle. "Come you out for a daunder in the lea-field," he said to the youth.

They went out-of-doors into the meadow where Belle's two milch-kine basked drowsily in the hot sun; and the Captain looked over the waters of the Loch to the smoke of Draolinn House rising thin and blue above the embowering woods. "I've had a devil of a morning," said he, "wi' that blind *bodach* again. He's given me the makings of a headache ... Such language I havena heard since my Spanish days!"

"What's amiss?" asked Linnell.

"I met Neil of Kellan on the shore-road this morning early," said the Captain. "He was seeking the Doctor for the old laird, but could give me no account of what was wrong; and so I went on to inquire."

"Another seizure?"

"Scarcely that as yet; only a big fright, so far ... It seems there was a stampede of some horses returning from market. They were on the Drumlang road, and one of them turned into the Draolinn policies. Up the avenue he came, a big thundering roan fellow, his halter among his feet; and the blind one fair in his track, helpless and swearing and waving üis staff ... Carsaig happened to be about that bit of the wood just then," he continued, significantly lowering his voice; while Linnell flushed painfully; "and Carsaig it was that ran for the halter, and brought down the roan just under Draolinn's nose. The lad's hands were a trifle spoiled with the rope, otherwise he got off scot-free, save for a tonguing the old chief gave him for daring to be about his grounds ... It seems Draolinn had forbidden him the place long and long ago; and the ungrateful old rascal could think of nothing else but to curse him up hill and down dale ... Never a word of thankfulness for saving his own scurvy life, the dotard! ... Of course the man's blind; and had he seen his own danger fairly, and the courage that went to the stopping of yon mountain of a roan, it might have been another story."

"Surely," said the sailor,

"But, by Mary! if he hasna the use of his eyes, he makes up for it wi' his tongue ... Such an old volcano you never saw or heard ... spluttering fire and brimstone on everything and everybody ... Carsaig, the horses, the dealers, and the market generally, all got it in turn ... A full hour I spent trying to soothe him; but he was by ordinar' obdurate. His bellowing had sent his daughters nigh distracted; the serving-maids were in hysterics; and at last I despatched another messenger for the Doctor; for I well believe if he's no' bled soon, he'll burst."

"Falstaff in a kilt," said Linnell, smiling.

"Something like that ... Poor Carsaig hadna a word to say in reply; so I led him off to the kitchen where I mended his skinned palms, and then to the garden, out o' earshot of the old fellow's howling ... I improved the occasion by taking him to task about his foolishness in gambling away his lands to Oskamull; and showed him I knew everything ... He was clean dumbfoundered at my story; and is grateful indeed to you for your part in the affair. I said I hoped he'd not let any folly about a word of honour to a cheat stand in the way of his denouncing the bargain; and what think you he replied? ' It's done already,' says he. 'I rode over to Oskamull at dawn to-day, and gave him my mind on the matter, telling him I held myself free of a promise got by cheating ... ' Man, I'd dearly have loved hearing him at it ... He's getting quite a mind of his own, is Carsaig ... You should have seen the set of his jaw when he'd done telling me.

I "Oskamull, it seems, was on the point of stepping into Callum Ruadh's smack, his malles packed and all the rest of it, when Carsaig arrived ... He'll be for Loch Feochan and the String o' Lorn, I'll wager, and so south without delay. I can see as plain as day what he's after: Crockford's gaming table, before word reaches them of what's happened hereabouts. He's desperate, and if he's no' caught red-handed, he'll make a mint o' money in a day or two; and then it'll be the gambling-hells of the Continent for him ... Poor man, poor man! ... and so down and down and down! ... Aye, man, aye! ... ' an horrible pit' ... ' the miry clay,' as the Scripture has it ... And, oh, it's a sore task he's setting the good God that made him, to howk him out o't!"

"That settles it, then," said Linnell. "I can't go to-night."

"Go where? "asked the Captain, blankly.

"On my journey south ... I've no relish for four days in the same stage-coach as Oskamull, I can tell you; and that's certainly what awaits me if I start this evening ... I'll let him get a day ahead," said the lad. "But I'd gladly have stayed longer to hear the end of your hamesucken business, and help lay these sheep-stealers by the heels."

The Captain smiled broadly. "Oh, the hamesucken," he said ... "We'll hear no more o' that."

"You're sure?"

"Quite ... Didn't Mackenzie come to consult me secretly but two days ago anent that same. He mentioned no names; but a friend of his had lost a bond and so on ... No instrument of sasine ... Did I think the bond gone for good?... Could nothing be done? ... ' Nothing,' said I; and off he went glooming, the rascal!"

Linnell chuckled. "He saved a notary's fee there," said he. "But here's a topsy-turvy world! ... The house-breaker as lawyer!"

"As for the sheep-stealers," said the Captain, with chagrin, "we were clean beat by them, I'm fearing, despite their wrecked schooner; and we may as well acknowledge it ... But in any case, we've bested Oskamull and Duncan Merchant in some ways. Two out o' three's no' bad fishing; and O'Brien's time may yet come."

"I'm loth to go without seeing him in the net also," said Linnell.

"Philip, maun you indeed go? "said the Captain, his eyes dimming the least bit.

"To-morrow, sir ... I must," said the youth, laying a pleading hand on the old man's shoulder.

"Well, well," said the veteran, turning away to hide a countenance of dismay. "I'm sorry, lad; but you ken your duty best." The next instant he wheeled round, and said, smiling broadly: "Oskamull's done me one good turn after all, since he's given me an extra day wi' you."

As he spoke, he mounted a knoll, the better to regard the figures of a horseman with a woman on a pillion behind him, passing on the shore-road below. "There goes Anna MacDougall," said he ... "She's not the one to lose time, is Anna ... As soon as Oskamull's away, she snecks up, and is off on a jaunt among her friends ... I wouldna wonder now but she's for Draolinn ... A fine woman that! And if any one can smooth down yon old blind bird's ruffled feathers, it's just Anna."

It was indeed for Draolinn that Anna was making. Rumours of Grizel's betrothal to Garmony, and of Carsaig's renewed court to Elspeth, had reached her of late: and now that Oskamull had gone on his travels, she found instant opportunity for taking a spéll of holiday to seek out the truth of these matters.

On her arrival at Draolinn she found the blind chief still storming; but she gave him soft answers unweariedly, and went calmly forward with her rôle of the good kinswoman intent on an inquiry regarding every relative, near or distant, common to the chief and herself through the numerous intermarriages of the island families. And at last she drew nearer home, and got confirmation of Grizel's engagement. But at this she stopped short, judging the affair of the second daughter too delicate a matter for the formalities of a state visit such as the present. There were other ways.

And so, later in the day, she manoeuvred Elspeth into a walk in the twilit fields, as the mist folds settled heavily on Corraven, and the peace of night drew on. They came through the darkling woods to the meadows lying between Torlochan and the highway to Aros. Snipe wheeled, bleating thinly in the upper air; head high and numerous the bats flickered; and the midges' dance in the rosy light by the burnside was a thing of faery. A brooding calm was everywhere; the last sun-rays lay level and long on the Black Rocks; the gloaming invited to the unburthening of hearts. Elspeth's eyes were shining; and her step was free as air: some miracle had surely fallen on her spirit since yesterday.

"And now, my treasure," said Anna in Gaelic, "be telling me if all stories are true."

"What stories, O woman of the questions?" said the girl archly.

The other smiled and pressed the linked arm of Elspeth, then halted to face her. "Look at me," she said. "I'm Anna MacDougall; and it's the truth I'm wanting, and the truth I'll have. I'm one as you well know, to cheat the heron of her eggs, even if her two eyes were fixed on me ... So you'll hide nothing from me, my dear, and you may as well be telling me without delay."

"Is it Alan you're meaning?" asked the girl faintly, her eyes downcast.

"Carsaig was name enough for him, the last time I saw you together, and that not so long ago," said the other.

Elspeth sighed contentedly as if from a full heart. "It's thousands of years since then," she said.

Anna compressed her lips: her love for the lass would let her abate no jot of this probing of old wounds. "Then he had need of those same years ... all of them," she said stoutly; "for it takes long for a weak carle to grow into a king that's strong."

The girl laughed happily. "Maybe," she said. "Anyway it's just Alan that's king ... But if it's the whole truth you're craving, I'll say nothing about the strength of him."

Impulsively Anna kissed her, and said: "Well, your head's no' turned if you can say that ... I feared you were at your romanticks again. But now I'm satisfied; and it comes on me that you've spirit enough for two, if that's how you're taking it."

And then Elspeth flung quivering arms around her neck, and burying her face on Anna's breast, sobbed out confession. "I ken, Anna, I ken, he's weak and all that; but ... he's just Alan, and there's an end on't."

"My dear, my dear! "sighed Anna, caressing her.

"And you remember what you told me o' yourself and the lad at Laggan, a long time back ... 'It seemed it just wasna to be,' you said."

Anna's eyes glowed and her head went nobly high. "It's not me that can forget, lass," she said very simply.

"Oh! "cried the girl, "'tis cruel to remind you in this fashion ... But it was wi' me even as wi' you ... yet strangely otherwise ... For although I fought hard against it, here was a thing that was to be."

"My treasure! "said Anna: and they walked on again.

Gloaming was now darkening fast into night; and, leaving the dewy fields, they came back by the dusty highway, speaking no more with the voice; for their clasped hands now seemed to transmit every pulsing mood. The kindly time, as the ancient folk called it, was never kindlier: an air from the sea came in sighing cadences through the trees; the little furry tribes in grass and stubble and copse betokened their myriad activities by tiny noises on either hand; a white owl startled them by its slow flight across the forest-aisle; in distant Kellan a dog barked at intervals; and high on the hillside they saw 'twixt the tall columns of the pines, an orange square of light come out, marking the cottage at Killiechronan.

Elspeth paused to note the lit window. "See yonder," she said. "Oh, is it not the fine, brave world; and has it not the good kind folk in it! ... A blessing on all in Killiechronan this night!"

"This night and always, a blessing on them!" said Anna ... "But," she added, "isn't that Linnell man still there? My cousin of Oskamull had no good word for him this morning ... far from it. Something came between them last night, I jalouse."

"Like enough; men-folk are ay bickering," said the girl. "And we'd best keep clear o' that, whatever it be; for Heaven kens I've enough ado wi' a quarrelsome father." She spoke hastily, anxious to screen the misdeeds of Oskamull from his kinswoman; but added in a sudden gush of feeling: "Yet I will say this, that Philip Linnell's been the good friend to me; and whatever difference your chief may have wi' him, Anna, neither his name nor the Captain More's will ever be missed from prayer of mine or of Alan's."

"Well, well," said the big woman briefly, "then his name will be in good company ... But if you're really for marrying Carsaig this time, my dear, I'd ay be putting the name of the Captain first in your prayers, were I you."

Somewhat earlier the next evening, the two women took the same walk through the quiet fields and by the burnside; and further confidences were but beginning, when they heard a sound of horses' feet on the distant highroad to Aros.

"It's the Captain," said Anna: "I'd ken yon grey beaver a mile away. It's no' often he's in the saddle ... But who's wi' him to-night ... a man in uniform ... Blue and white, and shining buttons like gold ... the dandy! ... See ... they're waving ... Do they want us, I wonder ? "

"No," said Elspeth in a voice, the least hint tremulous; "for they're in a canter now ... It was a good-bye ... I fancy it's Mr. Linnell setting out for the South ... And, like enough, the Captain's giving him a convoy as far as Grasspoint."

"Set him up!" grumbled Anna. "Him and his buttons!"

25: The Ride at Dawn

FULL-ORBED, the August moon hung over Aros Isle; hill and loch and river slept as in a dream enchanted, and in long-drawn rhythm of unvarying tone, the wave swelled and lapsed on the white sea-beaches. It was past midnight; the air was still and mild; and only seawards were the stars plainly visible on the dark horizon line, so softly pervasive were the mingled lights of moon and dawn of a summer of the north. A faint sighing of pine-tops, the voice of distant inland streams, and the murmur of the surf were the only sounds that fell on the ear of Elspeth as she unlatched the great door of Draolinn House, and came out into this world of unearthly radiance. Very pale in the moonlight was her face as she glanced upwards at the facade of the home she fled once more; and for an instant her eyes closed as on some inward vision, while she halted in the shadow before moving off in silence. Tiptoeing, however, seemed little in accord with the passion of her mood, and presently she resumed her customary swinging step, the gravel crunching noisily till she reached the path below the pines; it was as if she would go freely or not at all. Out of the trees' shade she strode, and so to the footpaths through the dewy cornfields, sibilant and ghostly, that lay between Draolinn and the river at Knock. She crossed the sharp arch of the bridge over the Ba, a dark flitting figure in her heavy cloak, unwonted lights in her red-gold hair, bare save for a fillet that made a dark bar of velvet across the wide brow. On past the graveyard she pressed, to the long barrow of the old Vikings that looks out on the Scarsdale skerries; and here, under the shadow of the great burial-mound, stood a man with two horses ready saddled.

She came up to him with energy, put out her hands to grasp his, and peered into his face with eyes that showed pain and passion blended. Long and long she looked, and he, flushing a little at the searching gaze, smiled féebly, and then stretched welcoming arms. At that the little constricting lines on the girl's brow and lip vanished and instantly she was all tenderness, her lashes tear-fringed.

He kissed her. "My brave lass," he said, and gazed at the wonder of the moonlight on auburn hair ... glints of a bronze iridescence.

She laughed quietly, her head on his shoulder. "What nonsense! "said she. "I think I ken where all the bravery is ... That you should trust me again is the great marvel!"

"Oh," cried he, "what is't you're saying? Defection on your side, I'll no' hear o' ... Mine was the blame." His eyes shone, and he looked upwards to the starless zenith, and then swept the violet dusk of the sea-line to where a single planet's eye of red fire seemed to watch them unweariedly. "And it's an unstable one like me you're for having?" he whispered.

A rogue's smile lit her lips, as she dashed a hand across her eyes, and taking him by the shoulders, she shook him playfully. "I'll not have you fishing for compliments, Alan," she said ... "Whatever your faults or mine, it's come on me that it's just you are ..." She halted and hung her head.

He bent low. "And what, now?" he asked cajoling.

"My man," she whispered. "Mine to me, since the beginning o' things."

For a time they were in a land of faery, and the old language with all its lover's endearments flowed freely between them, until a tugging bridle and a stamping hoof brought them back to the world of roads and travelling. "It's to be the marriage-tree at Pennyghael," said Carsaig; "and the minister from Bunessan to bless us at four this morning. Poor man! An early start for him! But let us be going on now."

He held his hand, and instantly she was seated like a queen, the reins in her hand. He mounted also, and, moving to the shore-road, they broke into a trot that held as far as Desaig. Here the morning light came grey and clear, and they halted to rest the horses; to watch the big seals fishing salmon in the sea oif the burn mouth; and to make further talk of love. Then on past the Druge, and round the Gribun cliff that rose in castled crags like towers of the Feinne, their horses guided to the wayside turf, as they came on the fishers' crofts, so that they traversed the hamlet unperceived. They dismounted to walk the Beallach rise to the watershed, and at the height of the pass turned to look oceanward and watch the waves fountain in spray over the Skerry of the Sword. The dawnlight on the grey plain of the waters, the distant mist-enfolded heights of Aros and Oolava, the gaunt bastion of the Wilderness Headland with the sea-foam lacing its iron roots, the chiming of the multitudinous voices of the surge, and a little singing wind in the heather at their feet, made a vision of the old Hebridean world so starkly lovely, that it held them both at gaze.

"Now here's one that's happy and sad at the same time," cried Elspeth, "and for why I couldna tell you." She drew to her lover, and put her hand on his shoulder, looking out to sea; and he, too moved for speech, contemplated her wind-swept figure with delight. She turned her eyes to Loch-na-Keal, but a buttress of cliff hid Draolinn now; and tears were brimming instantly.

"No time for grief, lass," said Carsaig. "It's not long ere you'll be back there and welcome too."

She shook her head. "It's me that kens the father I have, Alan. He's dour and he's bitter still, although it's but a fortnight since you saved him from certain death."

They rode on in silence to the watershed, and coming to the slope that led down to Kilfinichen with the Aird and Loch Scridain showing ghostly far below, Carsaig found her weeping quietly, and strove to comfort her. "Look you, lass, there's no need for tears. Did we not agree a week ago that your father would never consent to my suit?"

"Why, yes," said Elspeth, marking some unusual note in his voice, and drawing bridle.

"Well then," said Carsaig feebly, and, avoiding her eyes, he stretched deprecating hands, as if to call the heathy solitude to witness that all was as it should be. Then he wheeled his mount as though he would resume the journey; but she sat her horse like a statue and did not move.

"Alan," she cried; and back he came. "What else? "she said.

"Surely never the lovers' quarrel already, my dear?" said he.

Her face paled. "What else, Alan?"

"*O, ghaol mo chridhe!* did we not agree to the old story over again, wi' a happier ending and you at Carsaig table-head in the morning?"

"Alan, you're holding something back. Tell me."

He laughed uneasily. "Well, it's nothing but a happiness I was keeping in store as a wedding gift, lass ... I asked your father's approval of my suit yesterday. There was a stormy hour, but in the end I won."

The girl blenched, and constriction came again to lip and brow. "Although we had agreed you shouldna ask? "she said, icily.

"My dear, my dear, what's this o't? Have I boggled again? ... Surely, surely, 'tis as plain as a cow's horn, Elspeth. We had indeed agreed that we shouldna ask his consent since his refusal was certain ... But yesterday I found him in a kindly temper, risked his anger, and was well repaid. And then thinks I: ' Since we're trysted for midnight, the minister warned, and all the rest o't, let's e'en go on; and once the writings are signed I'll send back a gillie wi' the news to Draolinn.' "

"And if he'd refused? "cried the girl.

It was now Carsaig's turn to grow pale. "Do you doubt me? "he said in a low voice that trembled. "Do you doubt but that I'd have kept tryst if he had refused?"

The girl's head sank, and in helpless' fashion her hands hung down, the reins idle on the horse's neck. "Why not have told me the instant you had his word? "she said. "Did you fear I'd break the tryst, because I thought you over-cautious? "

"God knows," cried the chieftain. "I thought of naught but a new happiness for you. Yet it seems I'm still the blunderer! ... I dinna ken what you're driving at, lass; but have care before you say further!"

"It's a strange tangle," said Elspeth, sighing wearily. "I think I'd best be turning back to Draolinn."

He put a hand to her horse's bridle. "No, nor back, Elspeth MacLean"

"You're forgetting your manners," said she; fingering her riding-switch. "Let the bridle be."

"No, nor back, was what I was wishing to say, ... till you've heard me speak ... I think I can unravel this tangle for you; and do it I shall before you go."

"I'd rather be riding back."

Alan's eyes flamed. "Here's your fankled skein to be sorted out first of all, I tell you," he cried. "You think when I speired your father, that, had he refused me, I'd never have kept tryst? You think I did not tell you of my speiring him, since I dreaded your guessing I'd have failed you had he said ' No'? But I'm for telling you, madam, that I wished naught but a speedy bridal, and the joy o' surprising you wi' your father's blessing, fast on the heels o' the priest's."

Elspeth shrank and held up a protesting hand.

"And now," he went on, bitterly, "it matters not a docken to me whichever tale you choose to believe. I may be all that's weak, Elspeth; but, by God, I protest I am not this!"

"Alan," she cried, tears in her eyes, but with lip smiling.

Unheeding, he turned her horse's head towards Draolinn. "Ride fast," said he, "and you'll be home before any are stirring. I'll follow to see you safe."

"Take your hand from that bridle, Alan MacKinnon, and listen now to me," she said huskily.

He halted to hear her words; but there was only a flood of tears, and, dismounting, she cast herself on the dewy heather.

"White love of my heart! "cried Carsaig in dismay. "What is this I've been saying?" and instantly he was kneeling by her side. But at his touch, this strange girl sprang up, laughing, despite wet cheeks, and kissed him daringly. "Oh, Alan, *laochain*, where now is the weakness of you fled," she said proudly, "that you should have such words for me!"

"Forget them," he cried.

She laughed merrily; her face radiant. "It's what I'll never forget; and, indeed, I should be thanking you for them; although you're no' for understanding me at all, at all ... I'm only a woman-body, Alan. ..."

"The queen o' them, my dear," said he, taking her in his arms.

"And, indeed, indeed," she murmured, "it's no' clearly in my head now what I've been thinking; but chiefly it was a silly repining that I had missed a bridal wi' pipers and a procession; something better than this ... a foursome only ... the priest and his beadle, and the pair of us under a marriage-tree on a raw morning, wi' nought but the birds o' the shore looking on ... Oh, I'm fearing I'm but a glaikit lassie still." And now her smiles vanished momentarily as she sobbed quietly on his shoulder.

The chieftain cast a bewildered glance about him at the bog and heathery knowes surrounding, as if imploring their aid; then heaved a deep sigh of relief, and strove to soothe the weeping girl.

"But now," said the repentant Elspeth, "let it be Pennyghael, and the sea-spray on the marriage-oak, just as you wish; for it's proud and happy I am to be going there; and if it's cold and wet we'll be, I canna be worse than I am, for my brogues are soaking even now." And again her tears gave way to happy laughter.

"As bad as that!" cried Carsaig in alarm, but smiling at last. "Then the brogues settle it; and it's time you were back in Draolinn wi' Dr. MacCulloch for your minister. Let us be going at once, lass. And before a week is out we'll have the pipers and all the rest o't, I'm hoping."

He lifted her to her saddle; back on the way they had already come they went at a wild canter; and the red sun peeping over the ridge of Torlochan half an hour later, smiled broadly down on them as they kissed farewell by the edge of the Draolinn pines.

26: Vale!

ON a day in late Autumn several years after Linnell's departure from Aros, the Captain sat by the wide ingle in Killiechronan kitchen, his eyes a trifle bleary, his frail hands withered and tremulous, outspread to the blaze. He had been ill for months; but was now, at last, regarded as convalescent. Yet the old fawn coat shrouded a shrunken figure, and the red bandanna was knotted carelessly under an unshaven chin. Belle, busy at a baking of bannocks, cast wistful looks at him, as she passed to and fro from griddle to table.

"You're no' sleeping your ordinar', Captain, I'm fearing," said she.

"Maybe no', Belle, and it's tired I am to-day. Night long, I'm thinking and thinking: my brain as busy as a millwheel."

"Thinking?"

"Aye ... wondering and wondering on and on at the chances of life and such like havers."

"You should try counting in the Gaelic," said Belle. "Nothing like it for coaxing the sleep that's sweetest."

"Counting? Is it counting? It's often I'm at that; yet still-and-on I canna manage." His weary eye fell on a small chest set near the hearth as he concluded. It had a covering of red-haired cowhide, worn in many places, and was plentifully studded with many brass domes of strong nails, for it had travelled far in old Peninsular days. The Spanish sierras and the tides of the Tagus knew it well, and it had even made an odd voyage or two as far as Sicily and Calabria in the first surge of war ... "Aha!" he chuckled in a flash of recognition at a linking of his thoughts. "Counting? ... Is it that? ... We'll show them how to count, my beauties! ... And it's at you I should be even now."

Fumbling in a breeches pocket and producing a bunch of keys, he selected an old rusty fellow, unlocked the trunk with some difficulty and smiled at the vision the uplifted lid displayed. Three-fourths of the box showed packets of blue envelopes and some beribboned parchments with traces of red seals still evident ... official documents of his days in the Service; but the remaining quarter of the space was occupied by small packages of doubled greasy papers showing humped backs. He unwrapped one of these from its ceinture of black braid, and brought to light the Scottish bank-note of his time, a thing of dingy blue and green that he tested carefully 'twixt finger and thumb.

"Yes, indeed; yes, indeed! Damp as peatmoss," he mumbled. "We maun see to that, Belle, eh?" He dragged slow steps to the window, and peered out with blinking eyes. "Sun enough and the wind no' up yet," he commented. "I'll plant them in the lea-field."

Belle looked on and sighed. Many a time and oft had she protested against this ritual, but unavailingly, and she was silent now. The Captain tottered to the doorway, a handful of notes in one hand, and passed into the sunlight, pausing for a moment to pluck a spray of southernwood from the clump at the gable-end before he came out on the stretch of grass in front of his cottage. For a little he regarded the blue sky-depths and the still waters of the Loch; the cloud-shadows flitting over the sun-bathed contours of Ben More and its stalwart supporters. A heron flapped from the orange weeds of the tide-mark to her nest in Kellan wood; from the Aros road, far inland, came a creaking of distant cart-wheels: a sleepy sunny world, with just breeze enough from the northern hills to freshen its drowsiness. He stooped with difficulty, and spread a square -of the green and blue paper on the short herbage, a pebble serving to keep it in place, and, so proceeding, he strewed his handful of notes side by side, anchoring them against the little flaws of wind by small bits of sandstone or shingle. Then laboriously straightening himself, he returned to the fireside, and securing another bundle of the precious tokens, resumed his task. For an hour he toiled, latterly on hands and knees, till the green of the lea-field in a small portion of its upper stretch disappeared gradually under the sad colours of the precious papers. And next he unfolded the commissions of the regiments of his youth.

"Argyllshire Fencibles," he read, setting down the parchment outspread with a chip of sandstone at each corner. "(You're moist enough; yet I'll no' say but that a certain humidity is fitting for the Argyllshires; eh, you rogue?...).... Cheshire Fencibles ... (And that's an auld story) ... Middlesex Militia ... (You're in good company, Middlesex) ... Cornwalls ... (And blessings on you, Thirty-second) ... South Glo'sters ... (Steady, Sixty-first, and lie you there)." Hands behind back, and head bent, he paced the length of the field, musing while sun and wind caressed his mouldy treasures. There they lay, the warrants for his fitness in the work he had done, and a good swatch of the rewards for the same. They spelled battle and leaguer to him, voyages and marches when he sailed foreign, and many a homelier memory, too, of tramps through the island hills, and ferryings from Grasspoint, when he had travelled to the burgh on the mainland to lift the quarterly pension that was fairly his due. Nothing of the miser in this gloating: these smudged papers were first and foremost the pages of history as he chose to read it, where, for him, history was liveliest ... the days of his youth.

Again he halted to regard the changing aspects of the farther shore, as the cloud-carry sent its shadows flitting over the bold sweeps of Gribun cliffs. The sunlight and shade on the torn rocks there recalled just then an early encounter in the Spanish Estremadura in old fighting days, and he pondered the scene, repeopling the crags with the tobacco-coloured figures of the native guerillas, the blues of the ambushed French, and the scarlet and dark tints of the oncoming British. A fire lit in his eyes; his step quickened, and he left the lea-field for the moorland, in order to obtain a better view-point of the distant hillside. "Aye," said he, "I mind me well. 'Twas just such a day ... Yon was a great stroke, MacPhail! Ower your shouther! ... The bagnet's the hero in a narrow place, lad."

Forgotten the ingle and the kist, Belle and her bannocks, and down came the Captain More like a wild deer through the birch and hazel that drape the hillside above Kellan. He struck at branches that tore at ear and brow; he stumbled and recovered, and sped forward leaving wisps of the fawn coat in bramble and briar; for it was on and on to a better vantage ground for the vision of the rocks of the Estremadura, where MacPhail had delivered his mighty thrusts. But still the birches intervened, and a trail of tall pines he had forgotten came like a line of grenadiers to block his outlook. Higher he must climb now and higher, until half an hour after leaving the cottage, he fell, ragged and bleeding, in a swoon among the braeside bracken, just as he broke cover afresh, to find the Gribun rocks again transfigured, and the Spanish hills of the good ancient time vanished like a mirage.

Belle, busy at her griddle, did not discover his absence for some time; but, instantly she was aware of it, she set to reconnoitring planting and thicket, lamenting loudly in the Gaelic that on a day of days such as this, her sisters should be absent on a jaunt to Aros township. The near country scoured, off she must run to Kellan, bareheaded and befloured, to ask for tidings. But the good-wife at the croft there, invalid for many years, had not been over the doorstep that morning, fine day though it was, and her son was up the Loch, fishing mackerel.

"Peety on us! "she cried. "The poor Captain, Belle! ... And his pound-notes lying open to the face of the sky, you say."

"*Och, ubh, ubh!* "cried Belle, "and it's me that was forgetting ... And his kist open, and the door wide, and the bannocks burning ... What is't I'm thinking of, at all, at all! ... And so many homers and orra men on the road! ... The good money ... the good money! ... It's back I must go at once ... Send you Hugh up to me, Mhairi, as soon as he puts toe on threshold, for it's all night we'll be searching, I fear, I fear."

Lightfoot she sped home again, and found all safe ... no unchancy visitor around, and she instantly harvested the bank-notes and Army papers from the lea-field. Breeze and sun had done their work, and the precious things were no longer damp, save for a tear or two of Belle's, as she locked them away once more in the trunk of red cowhide.

By nightfall Hugh of Kellan had collected his search-party of crofters and fishers; and towards the dawn, they found the old soldier, stiff and cold, lying in the ferny brake on Coillemore hillside, maundering about some one named MacPhail, and a strange place called the Estremadura.

For long after he was never the same man; the tall figure stooped; he was gaunter than ever; his memory failed somewhat. There was a day when two schoolboys from Laggan met him on the twist of the highway below Killiechronan, at a point where a planting hides the cottage. They were neither better nor worse than any schoolboys since schools began, and so they grinned at the frail figure of the old man who was said to have been a warrior of great parts once upon a time. It was too droll a fancy for their slack minds, and they smiled anew and nudged each other, as he acknowledged their lifted caps with a military salute. Then the elder of the rascals had an inspiration, and winking at the other, he went back brazenly, to twitch the sleeve of the old fawn surtout.

"Captain, dear, you're far from home, and night's coming on." (It was full noon by the sun over Knock.)

The veteran paused irresolutely, and bewildered, looked round for the white gables of his lodging! and found them not. He shivered. "True, laddie; and it's you are the kind one ... Be you taking me home now, and here is a white penny for your; goodness."

It was some fifty paces till Killiechronan was in view again; yet the Captain might have wandered as many miles, so extravagant were his thanks to the sniggering youngsters, who had grace enough, however, to refuse the proffered coin, well rewarded as they thought by the success of their ploy.

And so the news spread among these light-thinking laddies, and often after school-skailing at Laggan you might see the figure of an old man in a military coat of the fashion of thirty years back, hirpling hastily along the shore-road below the cottage of the MacDonald sisters; his hand, tremulous with fear of night and wandering, on the shoulder of a giggling schoolboy; his eyes eager for sight of the sanctuary that would protect him from a world grown too vast for his comprehension, and thronged with terrors hidden and innumerable.

Yet the Doctor did not lose hope, and was arduous in devising means to lead the sick mind back to its former vigour, and to coax the worn frame to take sustenance sufficient for its recovery: for months on end he fought for his old friend's restoration to health. And in the end he won, aided not a little by a certain number of the *Edinburgh Courant* containing Codrington's despatch regarding Navarino, in which was Philip Linnell's name, mentioned with honour. "His father's son," said the Captain ... "Of course, of course ! ... What else were we to be expecting, I wonder"; and from that day onwards he made rapid progress. Throughout the winter he kept the house; by summer he was taking his daily walk to Tor-nam-Feinne, and in the fall of the year he ventured as far as Draolinn, tempted thereto by an event of some importance.

For the chief's daughters weie on a visit to their father, and the occasion had been seized to bring their children together for a measuring of heights, and a discussion as to family likenesses; Anna, now housekeeper at Draolinn, was to be mistress of ceremonies, and the Captain to act as judge. It was a fine morning in late September, when he came through the pine grove and approached the house; the hillside bracken already showing its winter red, the leaves of the scattered oaks fast yellowing. Just at the turn of the avenue, he halted to take breath, glancing furtively round, as if in fear that some chance-comer might perceive his weakness; then straightening his shoulders, he advanced to the door of Draolinn with all the martial airs he could command.

Elspeth and Grizel met him in the hall, each accompanied by a romping boy. Alan, Elspeth's child, dashed at him instantly, seizing a hand. "Captain, I'll be five next Tuesday," he cried.

"Me too ... only a bit more," shouted Grizel's boy, Duncan, so called after the Captain himself. ..."I've four months' start of him ... so I have"; and he also caught a hand.

Thus encumbered, the veteran was fair prey for the sisters, as they kissed his worn cheek; then linking arms, the happy group burst into Draolinn's den.

"What a racket!" growled the chief ... Ah! it's you, Duncan ... Come you in now and rest ... Well, well! Great days ... great days to see you here again!"

They sat and knelt round the fire, a merry group, recounting this old memory and that, until Anna came in with inch-tape and ruler, and announced that the hour of testing had arrived. The children sprang up, doffed their shoes, and were instantly back to back.

"Steady," said the Captain. "Wait you now! "and the ruler was levelled over dark hair and auburn.

Alan ducked suddenly and looked sideways. "Aha! He's on the hearthstone! "he cried ... "And I'm only on the carpet."

"Look at that now! "said Anna admiringly. "Isn't he the sharp one?"

"Will we be giving you a sheet o' notepaper under your heels to make up for't, Alan? "asked the Captain. "Or no ... You'd best be on the carpet, the pair o' you ... for this is a pernickity affair, let me tell you ... It's sweating I am over it."

And so the great business proceeded, spun out with jest and subterfuge, until the mid-day meal drawing near, the old soldier gave a cautious decision in favour of Duncan. "He has it by less than a quarter-inch," said he ... "But never you mind that, Alan; he's four months ahead o' you ... So you can be putting it down that you're really the same after all, you see?"

Alan gloomed. "He shouldna have stood on the hearth," he said. "But I'll be making up on him next year ... Just you wait till then, Duncan."

The happy day sped on; then by four the Captain said good-bye to the chief and set off homewards, the sisters insisting on convoying him part of the way. Anna came behind with the children, and at the edge of the pine-grove, they took leave of the veteran, Grizel and Elspeth promising him a return visit next day.

On the way back, Grizel and the boys having gone quickly ahead and around a bend of the road on a butterfly chase, Anna and Elspeth found themselves alone of a sudden, and each as if inspired by the same thought, turned to glance backwards at the tall figure in the fawn surtout, plodding somewhat wearily towards the short-cut through the woods of Drumlang.

"He's failing a wee bit, Anna," said Elspeth sadly.

And just then the Captain turned on the fringe of the yellowing oaks to wave farewell once more. A moment later he had entered the screen of trees, and so was lost to sight. A tear glistened swift in Anna's dark eye; a strange proud look came into the strong face, and instantly Elspeth understood.

"Oh, Anna! "she cried, her arms around her.

"It was the Captain More ... the lad at Laggan ... long ago?"

"Aye, my dear," said Anna, softly, and with head erect, "... at Laggan ... long ago."

Strawfoot

To
Neil Munro
Master of those who know the Gael

Contents

Book One   371

I:	Gibbon	373
II:	The city	377
III:	The man with the straw in his boots	384
IV:	The pickaxe	388
V:	Music	393
VI:	Marion	400
VII:	Work	406
VIII:	Snow	412
IX:	Brass buttons	419
X:	Curlew-Curlew	424
XI:	The new nurse	434
XII:	The pipes	440

Book Two   443

XIII:	Pause	445
XIV:	The gloves	450
XV:	A late post	454
XVI:	Take-in	459
XVII:	Personnel	463
XVIII:	The happy war	466
XIX:	First room on the right	474
XX:	The rally	480

XXI:	Leave	488
XXII:	Sister Mary	491
XXIII:	The wine of Aubepierre	496
XXIV:	A fire is lit	504
XXV:	Race	512
XXVI:	Roundabout	519
XXVII:	At the Lion d'Or	525
XXVIII:	The pine ridge	532

Book Three		541
XXIX:	The return to Aros	543
XXX:	The sanctuary	552
XXXI:	Locum tenens	561
XXXII:	Afterthoughts	565
XXXIII:	The gathering	580
XXXIV:	Spring cleaning	588
XXXV:	Cause célèbre	596
XXXVI:	Mary	607

Book One

Pre-War

I: Gibbon

"FOR you, Dr. MacLeod," said the buxom Sister of the women's ward, handing a telegram, and turning off with an air of unconcern the least hint exaggerated. After all, a telegram was a telegram, and as Sister trotted off to sterilize her hands preparatory to the next dressing, who shall blame her if she glanced back momentarily, hoping to read in the house-surgeon's face something of the purport of that exciting pink paper? But a brief glimpse told her nothing, and she passed into the side-room almost maternally anxious; for did not the fortunes of her house-surgeons reflect on the honour of her chief and the surgical service of her flat? Meanwhile MacLeod, white-gowned and bare-armed—a bearded youth with the air of a medical Captain Kettle—read his message, conscious that from twenty beds twenty pairs of eyes were watching its effect on him. The little stir that went around the ward pleased him: it was as if his patients had awaked to a new sense of importance, because their doctor had received something so unusual as a telegram; in fact, they basked in a reflected glory. He finished reading the wire, then pocketed it, and made for the wash-up room; and sharp on his disappearance arose a confused murmur of conjecture from the beds, for this was an hour when no junior nurse was on duty.

"Somebody's deid," said Bed Eight, a romantic appendicitis of eighteen.

"Havers! "said Bed Ten, a philosophic leg-amputation. "He's juist backit the wrang horse."

Discussion followed; here and there a trifle shrill, but for the most part in low tones of commiseration; and finally, since the doctor's countenance had been "gey solemn," opinion veered decidedly towards confirming Number Eight's conclusion that death was the culprit.

Scrubbing his hands alongside Sister in the side-room, MacLeod kept silence at first, but in the end, feeling it was only comrade-like to confide in her, said: "I'm offered a job."

"Oh! Any good? "she asked.

"Don't know. A Highland parish."

"What? You?"

"Yes. I'm hard up. Always have been. There's a salary right away—a hundred a year; and no opposition."

"You'll take it then?"

"Oh, I'll think it over. The trouble is they won't want much doctoring up there. Horribly healthy, I expect."

"Well, well! "she mourned. "After all your training with us! A Highland parish!"

"But starting practice is just a lottery. And I must begin somewhere."

"There was a man here at one time," said Sister reminiscently, as she dried her hands, "Gildard by name. He went to something like that."

"Oh, where?"

"The Yorkshire moors, I think. And he did very well. Quite like you in appearance, too. Yes, he did quite well. But then, he had no beard." And she sailed back to her white sunlit ward, while MacLeod followed more slowly, puzzling over the ambiguity in her last sentence. "No beard?"

Dressings over, he retired to his sitting-room, gazed again at the telegram, tossed it aside, and looked from his window for a moment at the off-duty residents, busy at tennis in the quadrangle far below. Then turning to a mirror on the mantel, and fingering his moustache's fiercest curl, he regarded his own image intently. "No," he said at last, "I daren't. I hate the bally beard—but it must stay. And, of course, these women will never understand." For, unknown to his immediate world of the hospital, there lurked beneath that hairy mask a boyish countenance—so innocent and rosy indeed, that no self-respecting matron would repose a single confidence in the possessor of those cherubic cheeks. Here lay his guilty secret: to look older than his years by abjuration of the razor. Yet already the wisdom of this renunciation was challenged by these few words of Sister Carroll's. Yes, life was very difficult. He must consider this further. Should he shave for beginning practice? After all, he was older than he was a year ago. Should he, after all, take the practice? A thinly scattered population—long distances —many days of waiting between cases. What about it?

His chair and pipe invited. He sat down and smoked. Something hard intervened between his back and the cushion—a book; but he was too engrossed to mind, and besides, books—which he tossed everywhere—could be circumvented by a little wriggling. Thus he ended with his feet on the mantel and his spine at the horizontal. But one corner of the tome still edged his left ribs, and lazily inserting a hand under his back, he withdrew the offender: volume one of The Decline and Fall. He scanned a page or two; read some surging lines: Maximus enforced his exhortations by a liberal donative, purified the camp by a solemn sacrifice; and then ... And then the whole current of his thought was changed. Indeed, had he but known, his life swept in that moment into fresher, wider channels, simply because he had sat down upon immortal Gibbon.

The book he now held was one of a twelve-volume set, bought—second-hand, of course, and for an old song —when he had reached the ripe age of eighteen. He recalled his first delighted browsing in its pages; his decision to read the great work through and through, and not only that, but to check every note by the original authorities; for Gibbon challenged so much, and here was the man to pick up his glove.

This projected study of Gibbon marked, indeed, a critical stage in the young man's development. A Scot, and dour at that, he had in quite early days discovered —with the assistance of Thomas Carlyle—that life was a serious business; and had then made up his mind that he at least would do something worth while therein. But doing meant, first of all, knowing what to do. "As a man thinks, so is he," he told himself again and again. Like most lads of his time and country, the old obsession of his race with theology held him firm: and he must square accounts with all the ancient oracles before he set out for open sea. "Fate, freewill, foreknowledge absolute," had to be wrestled with; he must know the stars of all the heavens, ere he marked out his course. Useless for Carlyle to tell him: "The end of man is an Action, not a Thought," and: "Do the duty that lies nearest thee. Thy second duty will already have become clearer ": for the duty that lay nearest in his case was clear thought as to the meaning of life.

That involved study and books and acquaintance with thinking men; and opportunity for all these was not easily come by in the case of a poor costing-clerk in a shipping-office, with his home only one remove above slum-level. Affrighted by the immensity of the task he had set himself, and tongue-tied by shyness, he could not voice his thoughts to his fellow-workers in the drab office at the docks. Decent fellows, they had their own interests, and regarded him as "a bit odd." Thus, in Carlylean phrase, he had "a fire in his belly "—but must consume his own smoke. And so, taciturn and moody, he read and pondered, without tutoring or guidance of any kind. But suddenly he became aware of the need for concentration if any progress beyond Carlyle was to be made; and, stumbling in his reading upon a magazine article on the origins of religion, he was led on to Gibbon, and fascinated by the magic of the rolling periods and the vast panorama of the ancient world unfolded before his eyes in that great history. Could he but absorb something of the knowledge and wisdom of this master, surely he would gain some safe standing-ground whence he could survey life more steadily and fully ... And then? ... Well, then back to the Infinities, to challenge them with clearer eyes ...

Yet he sighed at this conclusion.

For the task was immense; and he had a plentiful lack of leisure. How should he find time for it all? Yet he must. Where could he turn? ... Enter a profession that would take him away from his present slavery amid ledgers and accounts? ... More toil, and years of it too. A profession, of course, must only be the means to the end—to wit, the study of ancient history with special reference to the origins of religion ... But he must take care that the means did not become an end in itself. Oh, the thing was without limit! ... But to get down to brass tacks: what should he choose for profession? ... Medicine? ... Yes, that might offer leisure: one had to sit around a bit and wait till people took ill, or at least till they had sense enough to send for him ... And medicine kept one in touch with the human side of things— with real live men. He must beware of abstractions and get closer to his fellows; link up his studies in books with his observations of raw life. The one would balance the other; and he would jolly soon discover at first hand if the theologians' estimate of mankind was right. Original Sin—Pascal—Calvin—all that lot would be well weighed, once he got to work as a doctor, getting in touch—intimate touch—with human nature in the rough ... A great idea, this of Medicine as a career!

He cooled, however, as he approached the outworks of the fortress he would storm. But nerving himself to his task, he had, after many years, at last achieved his end at no small cost of energy, by means not unfamiliar to the Scots lads of his time. Winter at College; summer in this dingy office or that, doing holiday-duty to gain money for next winter's class-fees; paying for the spare time of the future by six years' lack of spare time. And yet—great Gibbon was still to read.

But here at last came opportunity. For this out-of-the-world practice was just such as he had dreamed of in the old days when first his big resolve to master The Decline and Fall had been made. Leisure enough and to spare in the Highlands, surely. Yes, that" sharp-edged corner of Gibbon in his ribs had indeed been a spur to memory—haply also to conscience. Let him be about his duty.

And so he arose, alert and joyous, reached for the telegram and wrote his "Reply Paid ":

MacLachlan, Inspector, Torness, by Oban—Accept appointment—MacLeod.

Next day another wire arrived while dressings were being done; and again the ward buzzed with surmise as the young doctor opened it. Come at once, it said.

II: The city

MACLEOD, however, could not leave just at once.

He had first of all to finish his term in hospital, which did not end till ten days later; but he secured a week-end of that time for a hurried visit to his widowed mother in Edinburgh.

"Weel," she said in her broad Scots (for she was Lowland by birth, although a MacLeod by marriage), "they're fine folk in the Hielan's, if they're a' like your father, Finlay. And it stands to reason that, wi' a name like his, they'll draw to ye." They were sitting at a window on the fourth floor of a working-class tenement which was their home.

"They'll have to," said he, looking out as confidently on Holyrood as if he owned it. "Even if my name were Habbakuk, they'll just have to draw to me."

"Keep me!" she cried: "you're no' blate, laddie!"

"Dr. MacLeod, if you please. Forget this 'laddie' business, mother. Otherwise, when you come up to keep house for me—next year, say—you'll be talking to my patients about 'the laddie,' when they ask for me. Always say, 'the Doctor,' remember. Like this: 'The Doctor is engaged with the Earl of Bennachie, but will be with you presently.'"

"Aye, aye ... We'll see—we'll see." And she rose abruptly to poke the fire, and hide her emotions.

He followed her to the fireside. "You'll see nothing but what I see, mother. Give me only a year, until I've saved a little money. Then you'll come up to Torness, and we'll have great times. What else would you see, woman, but yourself in the best chair?"

"A lassie, laddie."

He reddened, and turned away awkwardly. "Tuts!" he said. "I'd have no time for the lassies. It's yourself, or nobody."

On the Monday he returned early to Glasgow. This was to be a day at operations with his chief, and he must acquit himself well, for MacIver, the sub-chief, was off duty, and MacLeod would therefore have the honour of assisting Elliot—his ideal of all that was big and fine and thorough among surgeons. Elliot was a man of much work and few words; and, apart from his surgery, his mind was a closed book to his staff, whom he kept at arm's length, as rigid in discipline and as reserved as the commander of a battleship. Unsparing of himself, tireless at operations, his energy that of three ordinary men; with faultless technique, and results amazing in their perfection, his example was infectious to the staff, who slaved themselves to the bone in his service.

The morning's work started with a head case—an extensive depressed fracture of the skull. The lower jaw had also been broken, and some teeth loosened; but these latter had been extracted by the anaesthetist, and all had apparently been accounted for. The man was greatly shocked, his pulse not good; and the anaesthetist was not happy over his task. Elliot trephined, and after some ten minutes' work, asked a nurse to rotate the head on the sand-pillow, so as to allow of his working further round. The slight movement resulted in a sudden block to the respiration that was complete. Some obstruction —a loose tooth after all, perhaps? Gag and forceps were used at once, and the anaesthetist quickly explored the throat with his finger. Something was there, but he hadn't got it. "Leave it," said Elliot. "Tracheotomy." The cyanosis on the man's face became deeper. Quickly and securely the operation wound on the skull was covered in with towels, and the chief proceeded to cleanse the front of the neck.

The patient's face grew darker and darker; yet still Elliot cleansed and cleansed. Would he never have done! The tension was too great for MacLeod; and before he knew what he was doing, he found himself saying: "Best make haste, sir, or you'll lose him."

"I'm making all the haste that is necessary," said Elliot quietly, still cleansing carefully. Then the towels were clipped in place, and the chief performed the tracheotomy with deftness, yet deliberately. The silver tube was slipped in; a slight pressure on the man's chest, and he breathed again; while the white-gowned workers turned to the wash-up, and cleansed anew for the interrupted trephining.

MacLeod was a trifle rattled by the incident, and this may have accounted for a technical error on his part as he assisted at the second operation—an abdominal. Elliot halted at once. "Wash your hands, MacLeod," he said.

MacLeod turned off abashed, and rinsed his gloved hands meticulously in one lotion after another, before he resumed his assistance. But his two errors that morning had not yet had time to leave their lesson very deeply imprinted on his mind; for, five minutes later, the chief again halted and said: "Keep—your—hands—out of the wound, MacLeod." And then, as if in mitigation:

Bad enough that my hands have to be there."

Poor MacLeod washed his paws once more, and glanced piteously at the clock. Hard training, but of immense value to all who experienced it— this of asepsis. For in Elliot's wards the longest way round was oftenest the shortest road home. And always the patient came first.

The forenoon's work over, he saw the chief to the gate. On this progress downstairs and across the quad, nothing was spoken of as a rule except the cases in hand; but MacLeod felt he must say something by way of apology for his errors that morning. Too bad that on his last day but one, he should have made so many bloomers ... Dare he break the rule? And what should he say? ... But his own shyness and his chief's taciturnity settled the question; and they parted with nothing more than the usual "Good morning," and "Good morning, sir."

There was a symposium of the residents that night to celebrate the end of term, but MacLeod was so full up with work that he could only spare an hour there; and it was late before he got to bed. Next morning, before the round of wards was made, Elliot asked him, while they donned their surgical gowns, as to the results of the tests on some fluid from a pancreatic cyst operated two days before.

"Not done yet, sir."

"Why?"

"Busy with reports for to-day, sir."

"Yes. But the tests aren't done."

MacLeod's face flamed scarlet. He was dead-tired, and the repressions of yesterday had rendered him irritable.

"I was slogging at reports till three this morning." he burst out, and then halted as he saw the chief's moustache twitch suddenly, and his dark eyes light up with a quizzical humour.

"Yes," repeated Elliot. "But the tests aren't done."

MacLeod was answered. The patient came first, no matter how tired the resident surgeon might be.

Elliot went over and tried the lock of the door, then said quietly: "This is between you and me, MacLeod." He was choosing his words, it was plain; and he took a pace or two up and down, before he went on: "I think, you know, that if a man works all out for somebody else for a spell, he'll be better able to work all out for himself some day."

"Yes," said MacLeod, and was dumb.

"All right," said the chief, unlocking the door. "What about the gastric cases in Twenty?" And they were out of the room and on their way to work again.

Two hours at reports and examination of cases in wards, then back to the chief's room, where Elliot doffed his surgical kit. (He was off early to-day: some private operation, surely.) Then downstairs and across the quad to the gate, MacLeod—bare-armed and white-gowned, according to the ritual of the place—accompanying him. At the gate Elliot said: "Well, good morning," as usual.

"I'm afraid it's good-bye, sir."

The chief wheeled on him, frowning. "What?"

"My term's up to-day."

"Why on earth didn't you tell me?" said Elliot, chagrined. "I wanted you out for lunch before you left. No idea it was so near term. When do you leave town?"

"To-morrow."

"Awkward," said Elliot, pondering. "Where are you going?"

"Eilean Aros. You remember you gave me a testimonial for a post there?"

"Yes, yes, that wet place ... Well, sorry I didn't know earlier. Be sure you look us up when you're south again."

As they shook hands, MacLeod blurted out: "Of course I'll do those pancreatic juice tests before I go, sir."

Elliot's lips shut close, but his moustache-tips twitched, and his eyes were smiling. Then a renewed hand-grip, and he was gone, quiet and purposeful as ever.

MacLeod felt moved as he went back to his work. How intense the concentration of that man on his job, and how heedless of the little things of which the everyday world made so much! Ah, but it was not a little thing that, a few moments ago, his eyes had lit up—the eyes now, not of a master only, but of a friend. Heavens! how he longed for that return from Eilean Aros in a year or so, when he and his chief would meet again! How they would talk, and talk, and talk!

It was now after twelve; an unwonted stir was in the corridors and on the stairs; and luggage stood at many doors. New residents were coming in, and old ones going: some, like MacLeod, leaving hospital for good; others only crossing from surgical to medical side, or the other way about. In any case a new life was beginning for all next day; but the men leaving hospital were the heroes of the saga. Last night, at symposium, how they had shouted and sang, ragged and blethered, and toasted everyone and everything their wild fancies had suggested! For subconsciously they had felt their days in hospital the happiest they would ever know; and for one night at least they must celebrate their passing. But now came hurried good-byes in many wards; and soon taxi after taxi, with luggage atop, drove tragically across the quadrangle, a crushed Hamlet in each, with bowler low upon his brows; while Ophelias at high ward-windows sighed "Well-a-day," more numerous than the Hamlets.

MacLeod's ordeal duly arrived. He went round the wards with the new resident who was taking over, and said good-bye to his nurses, to one of whom he most unwisely gave more of his time than even to Sister Carroll, for there was something about Sheena MacAlpine's face that played havoc with many hearts. Also she was Highland, and since MacLeod was bound for the Isles, they had had many talks about Eilean Aros, which Sheena had once visited.

And so with his trunks to the hoist, where Sister Carroll bade him a second farewell, and thus put Nurse MacAlpine in her place. Then came the drive to the station to deposit luggage against a departure in the evening, for his train so fitted in with the next day's steamer; after that a crawl round shops for odd medical books till it was time for lunch.

That meal over, MacLeod did an unwonted thing by taking train to the east of the city, and walking out to the Cathkin Braes—the nearest approach around Glasgow to his loved Pentlands that looked down on Edinburgh. He told himself that up on the hill he would say farewell to the cities of the plain; for he had begun to ask himself whether this break he now made with the past had not its origin in something deeper than a desire for leisure to read Gibbon. He was, indeed, not so much reaching forward to a new life, as seeking escape from an old one: his real motive a passion for flight from the dirt, ugliness and clamour of the city; from the hustling crowds, and the smoke and fogs that shut out the life-giving sun; from the "ante-chamber of Hell," as one of his hospital friends had described the black belt of coalfields that ran across Scotland from Clyde to Forth. There was surely something wrong in this life in the big city: The hell-for-leather struggle-to-flourish for eleven months in that dense mass of stone and lime with its canopy of soot and then the summer or autumn rush for a month purer air on the moors or by the sea, as instinctive as that of the buffalo herds to the salt-licks of the prairie. A month only of sun and wind and clean rain, in each year! Only a twelfth part of their lives! What madness! ... Yes, he would go up the Braes and consider this.

There were few people on the hill of Cathkin that October day, sunny though it was, with a blue sky and fleecy clouds; and he had the vantage ground for an outlook over the Clyde valley all to himself—a grassy rampart whence the ground fell away to the woods around Castlemilk. Farther off a tower and a tumble of house-roofs showed dimly through a smoke-haze where Rutherglen lay hid. Then came the fields around Cathcart, and the patches of smoke and grey blocks of stone that meant Glasgow. Not a good day for a view. (Was there ever indeed, save at the holiday season— the Fair—when for a fortnight the city was almost smokeless?) Even the river's course was obscured. Some tall smoke-stacks and church spires did pierce the haze here and there—a symbolic association. But his own hospital and the University steeple were befogged ... The smoke-stacks and the churches had it ... Poor old hospital! ... Poor old University.

A single window in a high tenement of Garnethill became a sudden glory in the rays of the westering sun, and glowed and flashed as insistent as an army heliograph. What could it be signalling, if windows had souls? Jollity, gaiety, of course; for was not Garnethill the home of Bohemians, play-actor folk on tour, vivid vital people? And, of course, the soul of that window was signalling that the barnstormers behind its panes were birds of passage, full of delight that they were not tied to great cities, since at times they could flee them, and speed off to homelier places—market-towns and such like in the heart of Old England, where green fields could be seen not a mile from the little town's centre.

But here was no little town. This city in the valley was immense—ten miles by ten of brick and lime—a hundred square miles, and still growing; eating its way into the countryside ... London, too, was at the same game—thirty miles by thirty, probably—sending out its octopus arms. Where would it end, this folly?

Yonder, however, beyond the city, were the green hills, smoke-free and with shining faces: the little ones were the Kilpatricks; and was that white spot on them Qochno House? No higher were the Campsies; but then the bold spur of Dungoyne marked them out so splendidly as outliers to the great fellows on the skyline, the real Highlands—Ben Lomond, Ben Venue and the next one—Ben Ledi or Ben Voirlich? Westerly too there were big hills, Cowal, most likely ... Well, it would be long enough before the jerry-builder pushed Glasgow out as far as Ben Ledi ... Perhaps he'd get stuck at Stirling—half-way to Ledi; for Stirling of the castle and the kings would surely have something more than words with which to defend herself.

So MacLeod brooded. And now the legacy of his race descended on him, and the moralist came uppermost. The great city, he told himself, had ever been the seat of evil, according to the prophets—not only of Israel. Density of population had always bred crime. Bunyan's City of Destruction was a very real thing; the City of God only an ideal ... But wasn't an ideal also very real, if it stirred a man to such effort that he transformed a City of Destruction into a City of Life ... And was he doing any better than Christian (whom he had always been dubious about) if he fled this city of Destruction, instead of remaining to ght for a better—a continuing city? ... Or was Christian the wiser in fleeing, since, if he was to help, he must first of all see to it that himself was not destroyed? ... Here he became confused, as even a Scot may at times become ... Yes, the instinct in him for flight was strong; he must have peace, far away from all that pell-mell down there—peace to think things out. He felt intensely his own youth and rawness; he must read and ponder. History must be studied ... Gibbon might help, after all ... And now he saw in a flash, how motives might merge. Queer, that! ... It wasn't then a case of "Either-or," it seemed. Both motives were good: the desire to flee the city, and the desire to study Gibbon ... Also perhaps it wasn't a case of "Either-or "in the matter of town or country? ... Both had their parts to play ... "But God knows there's room for improvement down there," he said half-aloud and with passion. "I'm fed up with it." Yet the next moment he admitted there were good men in it—old Speckle-Belly, his former chief on the medical side, for one. But, ah! his chief on the surgical side, there was a man! Where but in a great city could such a surgeon find scope enough? ... He wondered if he was operating just now—snatching some poor devil with one foot in the grave back to life—doing the big daring thing that other men funked.

The window up in Garnethill blazed now more gloriously than ever (the play-actors' window he named it), and caught his eye again ... What a contrast! the actor's and the surgeon's lives: the player in the crowded theatre, miming life, and taking his curtain-call from applauding thousands; while the surgeon bent in silence to his grim, delicate task, half a dozen white-gowned figures his only appraisers: a real man among real problems ... And yet again, both player and surgeon had their parts in this strange world that seemed bent on flinging infinite variety into life at every moment: artist and scientist, business-man and lonely shepherd, crowded street and homely Highland croft.

There was no end to this discussion. Anyhow, he wasn't going back there: something was wrong in it; he felt it in his blood. For all their science and all their art, they were blind in many ways, these city-folk. Habit had made them insensible to the evils that jostled their very elbows: to poverty, to disease, to the frightful slum-life he had seen when he had ranged the dark wynds as a student, doing maternity work. Unspeakable things he had then noted came back to memory: the verminous walls; the evil-smelling single apartment; the only bed a "shake-down "(and sometimes not even that, nothing but a blanket on a heap of coal-rubble); the back-lands making density more dense; the stairs on wet nights, crowded like a rabbit-warren with sprawling children: what a nightmare it all was ... He must come back some day from the Highlands, and help to put that right. He must study hard, up there in the North—learn something about economics. He might squeeze that in with the other things he meant to read —history and so on—Gibbon, especially ... Queer that his search for leisure to read the great historian had combined with this desire of his to flee the city. And, of course, both his motives worked into one another's hands, so to speak. "Funny how all roads lead back to old Gibbon," he thought, as he took the path downhill towards the city, which, strangely enough—by means of a railway station—itself provided the means of flight from itself.

III: The man with the straw in his boots

THE afternoon of next day found him, clad in oilskins and sou'wester, crouching on the leeside of the purser's box on that ancient paddle steamer, the *Cateran*, as she thrashed a devious course through a westerly gale in the Sound of Aros. Yet in spirit he was far away from the mist and tempest that now enfolded him bodily; for in fancy he was in his old wards that hung high in air between the huge towers of the city hospital. But that happy, busy life was gone. What new service was this that now claimed him? Well, the die was cast: let Fortune turn her wheel.

A sudden yawing of the vessel brought him back to his immediate environment; he clutched a stanchion; and, peering through sopping banks of fog, noted they had gone too far inshore and were veering off suddenly. Monstrously magnified, the ruined Castle of Ardtornish was seen momentarily in dim outline. Again the veteran steamboat rolled heavily as she swung farther out: MacLeod lurched, lost grip of the stanchion, and found himself in the arms of a little man wearing a double peaked cap.

"Steady! "said the stranger. "This tub's light in draught, isn't she? That's a fine old castle we've just passed—Ardtornish."

"Oh, yes," said MacLeod. "Didn't Scott write it up somewhere?"

"You bet! "said the other. "Sir Walter had the very word for these old Highland keeps. You know the passage?—

Each on its own dark cape reclined,
And listening to its own wild wind."

The young surgeon stared at the little man; for he seemed the last person in the world to spout a verse of Scott. A trifle grubby, with untidy grey beard, and ragged upturned cuffs on a sodden ulster several sizes too large for him, he cut an odd figure. But what took MacLeod's eye most of all were several wisps of straw protruding from the eyelet-holes of his heavy footgear. "Yes," said the stranger, "Scott got it pat now and again." MacLeod agreed and sought around in his memory for some further lines from *The Lord of the Isles* to cap the quotation. But presently the steam whistle gave a continuous blast, and together they joined the general movement forward of the other passengers —crofters, sheep-farmers, and a sprinkling of Highland lairds and shooting-tenants—curious as to the cause of this alert.

"It's nothing," said the little man, after a brief glance aloft that betokened a knowledge of the ways of the *Red Funnel* steamers. "I know that old whistle: the spring's gone." And so it was; for a fierce squall had bellied a wet cord and pulled open the valve of a rusted throttle that refused to close until a deck-hand applied a mop's shaggy head to it. "Primitive, but effective," chuckled the stranger. "I know this tub. Yet she does her job."

"Whereabouts is Torness? "asked MacLeod.

"Over there," said the other, pointing to some phantom-like gables on the western shore, now fast receding into mist. "Pity she can't take it to-day. With a Westerly gale she never gets that pier." MacLeod was alarmed at the news, for it was there he should have landed. He explained matters to the little man, who sympathized, but added: "After all, it's only a matter of a ten-mile drive back from the next pier—Torlochan." And so the white gables of MacLeod's new home faded into the mass of gaunt hills behind; then a fog bank came down and even the hills were lost to sight, while the steamer's whistle boomed and boomed as she groped her way into the mists.

"Eerie, isn't it, all this fog? "said the little fellow. "But allow Captain MacPhater. They're good men, these *Red Funnel* chaps; and he enlarged on the merits of the masters of that famous fleet. He seemed to know its every unit; and details -followed of this vessel and that; when to come on deck for the beauty spots; when to go below to avoid a dull swatch of a journey. And at one point he used an odd expression when speaking of the stretch of water they were then traversing—the Sound of Aros; for he called it "Heaven's Sea-Pathway," and to MacLeod's ears the words had a foreign ring.

Some desultory talk followed; later, the stranger drifted off; and the young doctor watched his queer figure move easily and familiarly among the motley crowd of farmers and peasants aboard, as he exchanged greetings with this one and that. Who could he be? He looked like a tramp, might be a "simple-lifer," was certainly a Bohemian, but indubitably, in the end of all, a gossip. For as he passed from one group to another, it was obvious that MacLeod himself was the subject of debate; and the many eyes now turned in his direction indicated that his status and business were already common property and possessed uncommon interest. Shy glances from kindly faces came every now and again; some of the oilskin-clad figures drew unostentatiously nearer; whispered colloquies in the Gaelic became more frequent; and at last a broad-shouldered fellow of Viking type accosted the young man heartily:

"Well, Doctor, it's a rough beginning for you, this; and you missing your pier, too," said he; adding that he was in like case. He gave his name—MacCormack, the hotel-keeper in Torness; and after a brief talk, introduced MacLeod to some neighbouring farmers who would share a wagonette with him on his drive back to his new practice. Simple folk and cordial, inquisitive in the courteous Highland manner that makes curiosity itself a compliment, they quickly put the young practitioner at his ease, and he heard much of his future duties and environment. The population was a scattered one, oh, yes; but the roads were good, oh, very good. "And you'll be having a bicycle, of course? No trouble on the roads with a bicycle; och, no, none at all, none at all."

MacLeod acknowledged that a bicycle was coming later by the cargo-steamer, but, cautiously enough, did not add that as yet he could not ride it. Their enthusiasm for the new-comer was, he felt, too lovely a thing to chill by such a confession, and this was not the time for any ardours of exactitude.

And now the little man with the straw in his boots drew near to the outskirts of the levee MacLeod was holding, saw that his protégé was happy in his new-found importance, and drifted off again. The doctor asked MacCormack who he was.

"Och, is it Mr. Gurney?—Well now, who he is or what he does, I just couldna tell you—not if you gave me Mull. They're saying he writes for the papers away up in London. And sure enough he's often at the post office with big bundles of letters. He's the strange one. But real fond of the Highlands—oh, yes, real fond of the Highlands, he is, Mr. Gurney."

"And has he not the good reason? "said a cattle-drover. "For was he not telling me yesterday he could be living cheaper here than in a model lodging-house in Glasgow?—Just fancy you!—Och, no pride about Mr. Gurney at all, at all! And it's only scones and milk they're saying, that he lives on, down in Arle yonder."

"Aye, aye," said MacCormack, "real poor he must be. But quite the gentleman all the same, you'll understand—och, yes, quite."

The *Cateran* was now under shelter of some high cliffs, the sea was less rough, and they were heading for Torlochan pier. The sodden passengers stirred, deckhands pulled tarpaulins aside and sorted out luggage; fat harbour gulls came out to greet the vessel, squawking a tame town-bred note, the vessel slowed into still thicker mist-curtains, and gangways rattled on quays invisible.

"Cold?" asked a voice at the elbow of MacLeod, and he turned to find the little stranger stamping feet close beside him.

"Very," said the surgeon.

"Aha! You should try straw," said the other, looking down at his boots. "Nothing like it for warmth and softness."

"Indeed?"

"Nothing. See those hills?"

"Faintly," said MacLeod. "I feel them, rather. They're foreboding enough."

"Nonsense. Great fellows when the sun is out and the mist has lifted. Straw's the thing for them." He stamped wisped feet. "I've tramped twenty miles on those tops, and never a toe chafed, with this stuff under me.

"Not the very tops surely? "said MacLeod, smiling.

"The very tops. What else are the Highlands for? Uphill and down dale on straw. It's a great country! — Well, good-bye for the present. You know what to do when you get ashore. We're tying up now. Here's the gangway. You go to the hotel with these fellows. Have a meal there. Drive back to Torness with them in the wagonette."

"And what about you? "asked MacLeod.

"Oh, I'll stump it: Shank's naggie, as the saying is. See you later in Torness some day." He pointed triumphantly to his straw-shod feet, smiled merrily, and clamped ashore.

IV: The pickaxe

"WE get sun and shower here—especially shower," wrote MacLeod to Sister Carroll a week later. "But you don't feel the rain as you do in a city. The worst of this place, of course, is its infernal quietude; and even if there is a burn, musical enough, in a wee glen below my windows, it only intensifies the general drowsiness of the village. I miss operations dreadfully. How did the chief's last interilio-abdominal amputation get on? All right, I'm sure. Do you know, I had got so used to the surgical gown with my arms bare, that I sit here with jacket off, and sleeves rolled up, waiting for these good people to get ill; but they simply won't oblige."

In a later letter he admitted that practice was improving. "I haven't been in bed for three nights, so that's something," he enthused. "Not that I was working all night. Most of the time is spent in getting to your patient, thirty miles off frequently; and one drives a good deal through the night—or rather is driven. And that's a worry; for the fees here only run to a shilling a mile, while hiring costs one and six a mile. That won't pay! The roads run mostly along the shore, and you have the sea and the hills always with you. Cold, naturally; but my beard is a great asset." (He chuckled as he penned the last words. "One up to me," he thought.)

"I have good rooms where I lodge with two old ladies —sisters: a Miss Flora and a Miss Silis MacDonald —that's Highland enough, isn't it? Fine people, so homely! I play whist and 'Catch the Ten' with them sometimes in the evenings just to get into their old-world atmosphere. But, of course, I shall have to drop that as soon as I get a course of surgical reading mapped out for my Fellowship exam. Also I mean to get back to my reading of Gibbon. I don't know if I ever told you that I was studying Gibbon when in hospital." ("And that's a whopper," he thought. "But I meant to.") "Worried about my bicycle—hasn't arrived yet. When it does come, these hiring charges for driving will fade out."

The bicycle he had ordered was not a motor-bicycle; but an ordinary push-bike ironically named a Safety. It duly arrived, and the day of his first real acquaintance with it was marked for him by a white stone—by many white stones, in fact, for the roads around Torness were pebbly. A message from a patient at Laggan, ten miles away, had arrived; in his eagerness to save further hiring fees he incontinently mounted his steed of steel, and fell off all the ten miles of the way to Laggan. He could ride when he came back.

His route by the shores of the Loch-of-the-Cells looks across that fine fiord to the Gribun headland with the waves breaking lace-like on its iron roots; while above that gaunt bastion the slopes of high Ben More aspire, sun-flecked and cloud-dappled. It is one of the loveliest roads in the Hebrides; but for MacLeod that day it was a Via Dolorosa. In later years he was to rejoice in the vision of those great spaces of free air and hill and water, rich in wild life—heron and seal, deer and mountain hare; the wheeling tern, the plunging gannet, the larks so numerous, the blackbird and the mavis so golden-throated; the many-tinted heath, the iris, the primrose—a magnificent country; but that day, bruised and breathless, he staggered onwards and saw nothing of all its beauty.

And even when, on the return journey, he had somewhat mastered the foibles of the torturing wheels beneath him, still did he hardly dare lift eyes from the brown ribbon of road that stretched eternally on and on. But just at the turn of the way near Kellan, an unwonted sound from the hillside on his left took his ear; and, involuntarily looking up to discover its origin, he found to his astonishment that a somersault over handlebars did not result. He was even able to dismount decently, and hail the stumpy figure of Mr. Gurney, minus his ragged ulster, and wielding a mattock vigorously, high on the slope above him, where an old path stole snakily through the heather.

Gurney dropped his tool, looked at him under an uplifted hand from afar, and came downhill with astonishing swiftness. MacLeod, leaving his machine by the roadside, went to meet him; and, greetings over, they sat down on a bank of heath.

"So, so," said the little man; "we progress. A bicycle, heh?"

The doctor explained his morning adventure. "And you?" he inquired. "Still tramping the mountains?"

"Oh, pottering around! I discovered an old road on the hillside here this morning. Great things, old roads! They shouldn't be neglected, you know. And strangely enough, I found a pickaxe close by. So I trimmed up that road a bit. Fine exercise. One neglects one's arms, you see, when one tramps a lot, like myself." He produced a large-bowled pipe as he spoke, and lit it.

"Where does the road go? "asked MacLeod.

"Lord knows. It's been a drove-track at one time. And before that an ancient Fingalian path; and before that again neolithic man's bare feet pattered down it often enough, I suppose.—Not so? You see how it makes for the gap in the hills yonder: the shortest route when men knew how to use their legs. Nowadays we haven't legs; we all run to belly and brain."

"You're pretty deep in archaeology, I suppose? "said the youth, lighting a cigarette.

"Heavens, no! I've read a bit. But it takes a lot of knowing before you do any digging for stuff. You surely don't think I'm after buried treasure? No, no: my operations are only for the fun of the thing—rank sentiment! Had I not found that old mattock, I believe I'd have been over the Loch and up Ben More this morning. Rank sentiment, sir, for an old neglected road! One of the finest things in the world, an old road —almost as fine as a little glen."

"A glen?"

"No, sir, a little glen. Emphasis on the 'little,' if you please." His eyes twinkled as he puffed his pipe, regarding the youth humorously. "None of your great canyons for me—although Glen More over there is very good. No, no, it's the little glen with its tinkling burn, its hazels and its birches, its brown pools and its fairy grottos; the little glen that no one knows—the one you discover for yourself—it's that I am after praising (to use an idiom of the Gael). No matter how scorching the sun, your head is cool, because you clamber up the water-course under a screen of foliage. And your feet are cool, for they wade in running water; that's one place where straw comes in. Feet as wet as you like, but there's always fresh straw for to-morrow. Aha! Straw and the glen, I sing."

"You seem to get quite a lot of fun out of life."

"Meaning that you wonder how I'm able to make a living, pottering around this way?"

"Oh, no; I really wasn't quizzing you."

"Well, I don't mind telling you, all the same," pursued Gurney. "I'm a journalist of a kind—write for the raggiest of the rags, you know. Describe a different ' little glen' every month for a different paper each time. The women like it—the nature note, you see. Then I do birdy articles, weasely articles, and articles as to how the lobsters fight their duels. Ever seen lobsters fighting?"

"Not I."

"Great stuff that for an article in *The Weekly Flip*. You get a lot out of a description of how they seize claws —pull devil, pull baker—till one chap's claw breaks off. The swirls of sand, the desperate give and take, the cautious creeping for position—quite like a human tug of war, you understand. Oh, *The Flip* loves it. The readers write the editor for further details. It isn't *The Flip*, of course: that's only my name for it."

"How do you manage your observations?"

"Egg-box with a hole in its bottom. Get out in a boat—invert box—peep through hole. You get quite good visibility of the sea-bottom that way. I'll show you later on. Come and see me at Arle some day. I've a room at MacLaren's, the shepherd's."

MacLeod agreed.

"Piano at your place? "asked Gurney presently.

"Yes."

"Play?"

"No. Do you?"

"A tiny bit. Chopin-mad, you know."

Further talk followed for a little, and then Gurney rose. "I'm afraid I'll have to be off. It's a long tramp over the hill to Arle; and I've some scribbling yet to do; for *The Flip* won't wait. So long."

They parted; and MacLeod, stiffened somewhat by his halt, mounted with difficulty. Indeed, he was fain to walk the next mile—a stretch of road that took him out of sight of the hillside where he had met Gurney. But at the end of the mile the road rose steeply, and, ascending this incline, he paused on its summit to look back. Faintly there came to his ears the sound of a mattock being plied regularly once more, and faintly too he descried the figure of the strange little man again bending to his toil with ardour. "Queer," he thought. "He must have changed his mind. Or could it be that he wanted to be rid of me? "And he mounted gingerly to coast the slope on the other side with caution.

The rest of the four miles was uneventful until he crossed the bridge over the Burn-of-The-Preachings, and met MacCormack, the hotel-keeper, whose acquaintance he had made on the deck of the *Cateran*, on the day of his arrival in the Isle.

"Well, well! "said the big Highlander, "and you're at the biking already! It's little hiring you'll be wanting from me now, I'm thinking." Village gossip followed, and MacLeod ventured an inquiry about the little man with the straw in his boots.

"Queer chap, Gurney," said he. "I met him out past Kellan—digging at an old road. The man's a mystery. What is he really after?"

"Godsake! Is it there he is? And digging, did you say? "said MacCormack. "Myself, I saw him leaving Arle with a pickaxe when I passed there at five this morning with a hire for Torlochan. He was just making for the pass that would take him over to Kellan."

"But he told me that he found the pickaxe on that old road."

"Then I'm fearing he told you what was not true," said MacCormack, solemnly. "For it was a pickaxe and nothing else he had on his shoulder, and him climbing the braes long before MacLaren was stirring."

"MacLaren? "asked the doctor.

"The shepherd he lodges with. Now, what does an incomer like him want with a pickaxe at five in the morning on an old ancient road that nobody ever uses, will you tell me? "And the big man combed his long beard with his fingers, and stared hard at MacLeod.

"Oh, he writes for the papers."

"Well, he'll not do much writing with a pickaxe," said MacCormack with conviction.

"He might write about his experiences as an amateur digger, of course?"

"Aye, he might well do that," said the big Highlander. "But before long, I well believe, he'll be writing about his experiences in a lunatic asylum, if he keeps on as he is doing. Good evening to you, Doctor!" and he sauntered off.

"Good evening," said MacLeod, and then swung round suddenly. "I say!—Any stories about buried treasure hereabouts?"

MacCormack grinned as he came back slowly. "Och, yes," he said; "plenty of stories, and plenty of treasure. But I'm thinking the treasure's buried very deep."

"I see," said the doctor, smiling encouragement to a jest so feeble; and five minutes later he reached his lodging. Here he found Miss Flora at the door of the wood-shed, talking to a misshapen old woman with a load of faggots on her back, and a hatchet in her hand. Giving them good evening, he passed into the shed to stable his mount, and as he dusted his machine, could not help but hear a little of their talk.

"Well, well; and it's a great loss to you, Mysie," said Miss Flora's kindly voice. "But maybe you'll be finding it again before long. And you're welcome to the loan of the axe. No hurry at all for the bringing of it back, no hurry at all."

"Och, but it's good you are," piped the other in high tones—"good, good. And I'll take care that no one steals this one, anyway."

She hobbled off, and Miss Flora came into the shed to turn a wheel for MacLeod as he cleaned the machine. "Poor Mysie!" she said. "She's the hard-working one, that. She's after borrowing a hatchet to break up her firewood; and I'm sure she'll find it a deal easier to handle than the old pickaxe she used to have for that same."

MacLeod started. "A pickaxe?" he asked.

"Just that. Too big a weight for an old body like herself to handle. But it's gone at last, and a good riddance; for somebody stole it from her back door last night. Aye, aye, too heavy for old Mysie—a pickaxe."

V: Music

IN the week following his first adventure with the cycle, the young surgeon was busy, and so became quite expert in the management of the machine. His last run, indeed, in the north of the island, was a round of forty miles, and at the end of it he felt supremely happy, not only because of the ease with which he now covered his ground, or the addition of several new patients to his list, but in his discovery of the beauty and grandeur of the country he travelled through. The seascapes especially sank deep into his chambers of imagery, and their loveliness recalled was a constant delight when a slack time came and he rested for a day or two, sitting with uprolled sleeves, smoking a good deal, and toying with volume one of Gibbon. This day-dreaming alternated, however, with a meditation on the affair of Gurney and the pickaxe, a matter regarding which he could come to no more definite conclusion than that of MacCormack. "Yes," he said to himself —"yes, dotty, poor chap!—-that's the explanation." He looked out of his little side window at the stretch of blue sea-water fretted by white horses from a fresh wind off the flanks of Ben Shiant far away to the north. "But that yarn of his about the London papers? They're fond of Highland scenery—the little glens and so on, are they? Possibly there's something in that line for me as well as Gurney. Maybe I could swot a guinea or two out of them, myself ... Nature notes?...

I've enough spare time for it, anyway." And setting Gibbon defiantly aside, he took up pencil and paper. "They pay so much the thousand words? By gum! I'll give 'em a few thousand! "Thus it came about that a week later Sister Carroll received a letter from him, which began as usual by asking about the results of certain major operations just due after he left hospital, and then went on:

"You would enjoy this island if you holidayed here. You should really think of it, if ever you want a good rest. I wonder if I could describe some of its beauties as I saw them on a long cycle run I recently made in the course of a round among my none too numerous patients.

"An October day of warm sunshine and cloudless sky; and at the setting-out my road lay along the shores of the Sound of Aros. On the other side of that lovely strait great fields of mountains stretched from

Morvern to Duror, away up to Ben Nevis and far beyond. A noise of falling waters in the hazelwood under the roadside cliffs was constant, and from those woods came also the blackbird's song, so masterly, so magical. On the orange-coloured wrack of the sea-beaches, gulls and sea-pyats fed happily; a heron, immobile yet watchful, stood ankle-deep in the salt tide to see that I passed in friendly fashion. The old ruined fortalices of former days, Castle Aros, Castle Ardtornish, Caisteal nan Con, rose from the fringe of the wave; and—forlorn—looked out like eyeless skulls on a world they were done and by with, their old days of feud and foray gone for ever. The great sun shone, the falling waters drummed, the tide lisped on the shore; the bog-myrtle and the asphodel gave forth their faint incense, the larks were at their psalms on high. ' A day for putting the seven bens and the seven glens and the seven mountain-moors under the feet,' as the old Gaelic saying has it. Up Glenaros I sped by the side of a tawny river that swept seaward with the silent gentle might of the Highland stream in spate—up to the watershed, and down Glen Bellart's green grassy solitude. Dervaig's white cots, Celtic church-tower and dark embowering woods were like a dream of the Middle Age as I raced past. Then through the forest to Calgary's white sands and cool waters of limpid green, on to the headland that looks out beyond Rudha na-Caillich to the wine-dark sea, the cloudless sky-spaces and the great shadowy isles of the west. Far away rose the pinnacles of the Coolins as if done in delicate pastel of varied blue; and Rum, nearer and darker, with its gloomy peaks of grey—Allival, Ashval, Trallval—ancient Viking names every one, and in each of them the magic of history, with pictures of the old Norsemen fleeing Harold Fairhair and seeking new homes in the west. Nearer still, too, lay Eigg, its great sphinxlike form traversed by shadows and boding mystery.

And yonder—"

There were many pages more of this; for MacLeod, cautious youth, was trying his 'prentice hand on Sister before attempting invasion of editorial sanctums in London. Of her cool sanity of vision in many things besides the multitudinous crises of work in the surgical wards of the great hospital, he had seen abundant evidence; therefore it was that he now turned to her as to a trusty touchstone in this matter of commencing author. Yet not without craft; for he desired a spontaneous verdict—one in no way influenced by any knowledge of his desire to attack the outposts of literature. These purple patches were to appear in the most casual fashion, as merely those of an enthusiast for his newly discovered Highlands; thus would her unguarded comments be a hundredfold more useful in the way of valuation of his literary powers than if he had revealed his real ambitions.

A conspiracy, he admitted, but really a quite innocent one.

Sister's answer was also innocent, but overwhelming —for, among other things, she wrote: "I enjoyed your fine description of the island scenery. You are certainly developing in unexpected ways. I never thought to find a poet among our house-surgeons. Who is the lady?"

And with this cryptic query her brief note ended. MacLeod's teeth clenched angrily as he tossed the letter aside. "Well, that's that," he said. "No journalism for me, if that's all she sees in it."

After all, the place was a dull hole; and he did miss the daily skirmish with his nurses in the old hospital, all the more delightful that Sister's vigilant eye had to be evaded. There was that MacAlpine girl, in Ward Twenty-Two, with the face of a Celtic Madonna. Yes, something was lacking in his hermit-like life here. But, thank Heaven! Gibbon was always a friend to fall back upon. And taking up the book he read till dark.

Yet later that evening the old restlessness returned; and, undeterred by the tap of the rain on the window, he donned his oilskins and sallied out aimlessly. Must keep fit, he told himself—had been cooped up all day —a walk would do him good. He took the road leading away from the scattered lights of the village and trudged into the dark and the rain. In front he dimly felt the forms of the brooding hills; from behind came the myriad noises of the sea, and loneliness descended like a pall. In the cots of Torness, he knew, the crofters were now at *ceilidh* over the glowing peats, happy folk! And farther inland were the big shooting-lodges, with fashionable house-parties busy discussing the day's deer-stalk or the enormities of yesterday's politics. From both groups he seemed shut out by the taboo of caste; one would confuse with shy silences, the other oppress with empty condescensions.

He trudged now in the gloom of the Black Rocks; and an owl startled him as it swept noiselessly over his head, busy with the nightly search of its hunting-ground. It took his eyes momentarily upwards, and thus he beheld a solitary star, unwinkingly bright, peep out of the cloud-wrack above Ben Buie. Instantly he sensed the great earth swing on through space and time —felt himself swept far from that old Rome he had left so recently in his lamplit chamber. Where now were the Praetorian Guard— where Pertinax—where Severus? Immensities enfolded; he was crushed by their might; and turning on his tracks he strode back towards the lights of the village, where kindly folk still had wisdom enough to shut out the dark of a world so alien.

Music seemed to be a stand-by in more than one wee house. Passing the smithy he heard Big Rory at his chanter practice, playing *The Grey Wife of Raasay*—a good reel surely for a night so wet; at the post office house an accordion bleated. Singing too there was: from Angus More's thatched cottage came the chorus of *An t-Eilean Muileach*, and he had a vision of swaying figures seated round the peat-fire, holding hankies to beat time. But it was at the inn, before whose lit sitting-room window he paused at the sound of a violin accompanied by a pianoforte, that he warmed suddenly; for thence came the notes of a Highland air, passionate and pleading. Here surely was something that fitly conjoined with that sole star above Ben Buie in crying out against night's blackness and all loneliness of spirit; against old Time that would not wait, and the wild spinning of the earth unresting in its toil through space — something that called to comradeship and a rally in the fight ... Yes, he would go in here. And so, leaving the wind and the dark, he entered the tiny hall of the inn, turned down a passage on his left, and knocked at the door of a little room.

Instantly the music ceased and the landlord's wife, a comely dame with a roguish face, opened to him. " Come in, Doctor, and put off your wet things," she said. "And is it for travelling you are again; and it such a night of storm?"

"Not this time," said MacLeod, hanging up his coat and sou'wester in the lobby; and entering, he bowed to her daughter, a shy graceful girl of eighteen with a violin in her hand. "I won't bother you much for hiring in future, you know. I have a bicycle now."

"So I was hearing. Did you not go to Laggan one day on it? "Her glance was mischievous.

"Oh, you've heard of that? "said he, uncomfortable.

"Who hasna'? "cried Mrs. MacCormack. "They're saying the road needs quite a lot of repairs now, the way you were falling all over it."

"Show me the man who told you," grinned MacLeod, "and I'll fall on him."

"Rank murder that would be," she replied. "But where are your manners, Marion? A chair for the Doctor. Well, well, sit you down, and let us be thankful you came in through the door, and not through the window, as you nearly did yesterday when you skidded out there."

"Never heed her, Doctor," said Marion. "She doesn't know where to leave off, once she gets going."

"Just like some bicycles I know," said her mother, smiling archly. "But how are they all over at your place, Doctor?"

And so the homely talk of countryside affairs continued until MacLeod asked them to go on with the music. "What is it you were playing?" he asked.

"Only the airs of some old Gaelic songs," said Marion shyly.

"But that last one — what was it all about?"

"Och, just about a lass on an island, and herself at the herding of cattle," said the young girl. "It was nothing at all."

"Ah, no," said MacLeod with conviction. "It was about everything that matters. There was life and love and death and all the stars and the flowers in it. Play it again, please."

The young girl raised her bow delicately; the magic air soared again; and profounds of emotion held the youth once more. The stately woman with her fingers on those charmed keys; the youthful face of Marion, lit with dream as she swept her mystic bow; that heavenly appealing melody: here was what his inner being had craved for these many days, although he did not know it—music and youth and womankind by a fireside that was truly homelike. They played on and on; and "Another," cried MacLeod, as each simple air breathed softly to its close. His eyes were on Marion, so sweetly secure of herself; her every gesture, every word, bringing healing to his troubled mind. And when a tap came to the door, and big MacCormack looked in showing great teeth in a massive grin, he started angrily as if an intruder and not the master of the house had appeared.

"Well, and it's the great concert you're making to-night," said MacCormack. "And here is Mr. Gurney, who was just passing and heard you at it. And now he's begging to hear more."

He stood aside, and the strange figure of the little man appeared, his face a trifle flushed as he bowed with a grace MacLeod envied.

"Your pardon," said Gurney, "but may I ask a favour, Miss Marion? That fine air I heard from out-doors a few moments ago—would you be so good as to play it again?" The light in his eyes seemed to transform his face, his bearing was that of a courtier; and, his ragged cuffs and straw-wisped foot-gear notwithstanding, he looked a guest for whom no honour could be too great, his few words of pleading naught else than a command.

"Come you in now and welcome, Mr. Gurney," said Mrs. MacCormack. "Of course, Marion will play for you. It will be *The Skye Fisher's Song* you're meaning."

"It goes so," he said, and trolled a few masterly notes.

"Godsake!" cried the big landlord from the doorway. "And isn't it you that has the fine voice, Mr. Gurney! You must be singing to us some of these nights. But you'll excuse me. There's a man for Ardvergnish wanting a trap," and so departed.

"Singing?" said Gurney. "No, no." Then eagerly: "And now, Miss Marion—?"

The wild air again uprose and throbbed, crying out against the loneliness of great waters: a call for patience in hard toil—of wistfulness for home and rest such as only poor fishers far out at sea can know. Mysteriously, softly, came that cry, inweaving with the pulse of waves, and the vision of wide horizons. Then, just as strangely and as softly, the noise of surges ceased, the mirage of the wild Coolins faded.

At the last notes' dying fall, MacLeod saw tears in the eyes of the little man. "Ah," sighed Gurney, as Mrs. MacCormack rose, "the Gael and his dreams! it's there —it's there we're lacking. It will take you far, that! "He broke off suddenly; and with an air of suspicion glanced hurriedly round at each face in turn, as who should ask, "What have I said?"

"And now, you'll play, yourself," said the older woman.

"May I? "he said eagerly; and sitting down before the keyboard, he gave out very simply the air just finished, then with variations, and at last with crashing chords that rose to a masterly close. He ceased with an air of disappointment. "But no," he said. "It is best as you give it—simply. This way is foolishness. I bow to you, Miss Marion; you are Gael, and you are artist. What more?" He flourished a hand in an indescribable gesture of defeat.

"But something of your own. Come now," cried the landlady.

"Of mine—nothing," he answered. And again his hand tossed upward in token of abject surrender; but soon his fingers strayed over the keys as if seeking direction. "But of the great ones—the clear-shining ones —of them we might supplicate. Not so?" He slowly lifted a head like a king come at last into his inheritance, and turning to the instrument called forth from it a victorious pasan as of acclaim to heroes in some great conflict of the ages. Yet scarcely had he begun, when he ceased, stole a shy glance at the others, and saying "No—not Beethoven to-night," crashed into a polonaise that caught them up into a wild mood of fantasy. A slow movement followed—the very spirit of peaceful night in a far land of romance. And now it was Marion's eyes that filled, as, rapt and trembling, she listened to all the loveliness evoked by the little stranger.

The music ceased, and Gurney sat silent, his head bent as if in meditation. But presently he wheeled on his stool, and with affected gaiety cried, "What a man, that Chopin! Poland and France—the very soul of both! And what a pleasure you have given me in letting me recall him." He bent to kiss Mrs. MacCormack's hand. "I must go; it is a long five miles to Arle, you remember." He shook hands with Marion and with MacLeod, and bowing once more, retired with the landlady, who protested she must see him to the outer door.

The young girl and the youth sat on in an awkward silence. MacLeod's mind had in some strange way conjured up a likeness between her face and that of his Celtic Madonna in the hospital; and he was now lost in a transport of dream where were music and clear skies and the forms of fair women. The girl toyed with her bow, balancing it this way and that. At last MacLeod rose.

"Good night, Marion," he said, taking her hand.

"Good night, Doctor," said Marion.

They were standing thus when Mrs. MacCormack entered.

"Keep me, Doctor! and are you for going already? "she said, as she tidied her sheets of music.

"Yes," said the youth, with the girl's soft fingers still in his. "Good night, Marion."

"Good night," said Marion.

"That poor Mr. Gurney," cried Mrs. MacCormack, turning to bid MacLeod good-bye. "I don't know what to do with him! It's such a night of storm; and yet he's that proud I couldna well offer him a bed, the way he is with those old clothes of his, could I now? And I doubt he would be angry if I offered him the bothy or the hay-shed—a man that can play the way he does. Whatever kind of creature is he at all, at all?"

"Yes," said MacLeod abstractedly …"Good night, Marion."

"Good night, Doctor," said Marion.

VI: Marion

THE inn was busiest, of course, in summer and autumn, when tourists and salmon-fishers most abounded. But with the coming of winter, these stole away south, and were replaced by a mere sprinkling of guests—two or three farmers on their way to mainland markets, or a few commercial travellers on their rounds throughout the Hebrides. And so, since winter was the season for friendly visitation among the people of the Isle, MacLeod drifted of an evening now and again into the cosy living-room of the MacCormacks; and latterly, as if by some recognized arrangement, every Thursday night found him tapping at their door.

Ostensibly he came for music and a talk, but in reality to be near Marion, to listen entranced to her playing of Highland airs, or to pass a word or two with her. But she had few words for anyone. A glance or a smile indeed from Marion conveyed much. And more than speech was the strange sense of balance in all she did, of unconscious grace, of instinctive ease. MacLeod, in her presence, felt life to be, not so much a fuller, as a finer and rarer affair than elsewhere. Ordinarily he met each day with a sense of frustration, "as if the edge had been taken off things," he told himself. But here in this little room where Marion was, there came to him an alertness of spirit that surprised by the discovery of new values even in those humble surroundings. Colours and shapes had now a new beauty; the fire-glow was richer, the shadows on the wall quainter and more clear-cut; the piano's ivories a creamier white. And when Gurney would steal in furtively, accept a seat on the music-stool, and finger his way delicately into the heart of some heavenly melody, MacLeod watched with a new intentness the eloquent lines on the face of the queer little man.

Back in his own lodging, however, he was moody and miserable. He fell off his food. "He only picks at his meals nowadays," lamented Miss Flora to her sister.

"Drink or a decline," said the practical Silis.

"Drink! "cried Flora. "Silis MacDonald! whatever are you saying!"

"Ah, well, we'll soon see," said her matter-of-fact sister.

Night after night MacLeod opened his books, but—medicine or history—it was always the same—the volume was tossed aside before a single page had been read. But one evening he sat long over a book on operative technique, then rose to close it with a bang ... Yes, that was it ... Surgery. The big cities. And a triumphant return to claim Marion ... But the years between? ... Damn the years between. He could not wait: he would speak to her at once.

He went to bed chanting *Grows the Yarrow in Yonder Grove*; and, hearkening to strains so unwonted from below-stairs, his landladies clung to one another in affright for a moment before they extinguished their solitary bed-candle. Then Silis chuckled: "A decline! No, no, it's the drink after all, Flora. What did I tell you?"

Soon a sick old woman in a croft at the Black Rocks gave MacLeod his opportunity; for Marion at times visited her after dark, doing good by stealth, it was to be supposed; bringing her some little delicacy in the way of food, a wing of chicken or a pot of bramble jelly, and easing her weariness with a little gossip. And so it happened one gusty night that, as the girl stepped from under the dripping thatch of old Anna's cottage, she saw a bicycle lamp draw near; and presently, as she closed the cottage door, MacLeod dismounted close beside her.

"I thought of asking for Anna in the passing," he said; "but you can tell me."

They walked on, and old Anna, the weather and the possible early advent of a new teacher at the schoolhouse, provided subjects for a constrained conversation. He felt that the girl was on her guard; and in her presence his strategy seemed now the clumsiest of make-believes. They trudged on, the wet gale flapping his waterproof cloak and the skirts of his companion; their talk of the scantiest. At the bridge over the Burn-of-The-Preachings, he halted to lean his cycle against the wall. "Excuse me," he said, "a stone in my shoe"; and bending down he retrieved a wholly imaginary pebble from between stocking and sole.

The wet wind suddenly came in a gust through the autumn night. She instinctively drew to shelter under the alder-trees that thrashed boisterously above, and the movement brought her close to him while he struggled with his lace. "Does it hurt? "she asked.

For answer he stood up and reached for her hands. "Marion!" he said huskily.

"What nonsense, Doctor," she said, and drew a little way off.

"But, my dear—won't you come to me?"

"No, no." She turned to look at the distant lights of the village. "Let us be going." She moved away slowly.

He took up his cycle and reached her side. "I'm sorry," he said.

"Och, it was just nonsense," she quietly answered. "I'm not minding it at all."

"There's somebody else? "he asked despairingly.

"Nobody, Doctor," she said in even tones.

They plodded on in silence through the rainy dark until they reached his lodging. "Good night," she said.

"But I'll go up with you," said he, hoping for some relenting on her part before the hundred yards to the inn were covered; but never a word passed until he opened the porch-door, and the light shone maddeningly on her fair hair, a trifle wind-tossed.

"Good night," she said again, and gave a firm hand, her clear eyes steady and friendly.

"Good night," he muttered thickly, and turned off, stunned.

Entering his little sitting-room he sat down, exhausted by the tension of the encounter, stared vacantly into his fire until it was stone-cold, and then until his lamp had guttered and gone out. He never had believed his world could be thus overwhelmed. Surely this was another Marion—one impossible to fathom? And surely in himself were depths dim and undreamed of—powers that worked far beneath the threshold towards this upheaval of all clarity of thought? A nightmare madness all this. Without undressing, he tossed himself on the bed, to pass a sleepless night.

The days that followed were a long misery, his work mechanically done; and at last, so incredible became the memory of that night's experience that he must needs test its reality by a renewal of his suit. Therefore, a week later, on a cloud-free night of stars with a hint of frost in the air, when Marion again visited Anna, she found him awaiting her at the gate of the croft, this time without his cycle; for he had vowed there should be no further dissembling.

"You're surely often this way, Doctor?" she said calmly.

"Not often at present," he answered. "I only came to see yourself. May I walk in with you?"

"Yes " and they faced homewards.

"And may I speak of what I spoke last time?" he said as he walked on.

"Och, I'm hoping you'll not do that."

"But I must."

"I'm fearing you're troubling yourself for nothing," she said, glancing at the sky.

"But you said there was no one else," he went on, struggling hard to speak in low tones. "Please don't be wilful. Please let me reason with you."

"Och, it's not reasoning that's in it," she said softly. "It's just the way things are."

"The way things are? "he repeated. "Have you troubles of your own?"

"No troubles at all, Doctor. It's just that this should not be the way of things between you and me at all, at all."

"And why?"

"Well, isn't it little you or I know of life as yet? And we werena at the making of ourselves, were we?" She looked upwards again at the myriad stars.

"You don't care for me?"

"Not in the way you're seeking."

"But maybe you'd care that way some time?"

"It's little like. You and I are a bit lonely in this wee place; but there's no call for us to be foolish, just because we're lonely, is there?"

"Not foolish. This is true earnest."

"Aye, but the world's big, Doctor; and God has plenty of time," said Marion very simply.

A few paces farther on, and they were at the door of the inn; and her smile as she wished him good night gave him courage to bear this second buffet. He left her, indeed, with an inward glow as if he had come through some tonic experience that was for his good. Not that night any bemused melancholy or self-pity; he slept soundly, and in the morning opened his Gibbon resolutely. But the old oppression returned before he had read half a dozen pages; and had not a sudden call to Dervaig, some fifteen miles away, turned his thoughts to outward things, he would have again sunk to sullen depths of self-solicitude. But for some days after this he was much in the open; and long journeys kept him physically fit; while study of his cases employed his mind in healthy fashion, and saved him from too much brooding over the pranks of Fortune. And at last there came a night when he felt stoic enough to go over to the inn once more, telling himself he was heart-whole again.

He entered the cosy room to the sound of the piano's notes; and seated himself quietly. Gurney, rapt as in a trance, was at the keyboard, his eyes half closed, and playing with the ease of a master. He struck great chords and MacLeod understood as he had never understood before. These men surely knew what he had felt — the man who wrote and the man who played. Here was the great conflict; here was the field torn with the strife, and all the ardours of the battle with destiny. Protest and challenge; the quailing of strong hearts in sight of a victory that ever eluded: then renewed combat for some high purpose; and in the end a paean of triumph that crashed and thundered. Surely, something more than Chopin this!

So wonderful was the music in the way of interpreting his recent experience, that at the moment of his entry he gave Marion but a glance. Yet he noted that she was listening so closely as to be almost unconscious of his presence; and indeed, he himself was soon swept into dreams of his own. At a pause in the playing he looked again at the girl, and was startled by the intensity of her gaze at Gurney. Her eyes devoured the little man's every movement; something akin to adoration was there. Her brow, too, was flushed, and a wild air hung about her. A strange surmise possessed him. Surely there was more than the enthusiasm of the artist in her looks, as she leant forward, elbow on knee, one hand supporting her cheek? But he checked the thought as unworthy, moved uneasily, and turned to watch Mrs. MacCormack crocheting.

When the close came, solemn in its impassioned restraint and might, Marion sighed, while her eyes fell and a pallor came to her brow. MacLeod again sank to sullen brooding. But the next moment Gurney was on his feet, saying good night and thanking Mrs. MacCormack for the pleasure the evening had given him. Then she saw him out; and their departure from the room left the girl and youth in an awkward silence. Marion rose to lift her violin from a chair and place it in its case.

"But won't you also play?" he asked.

"After that?" she asked with burning gaze; and he felt rebuked.

Mrs. MacCormack returned. "Well, Doctor," she said; "and haven't you been the busy man these days? We've seen little of you of late."

He made some lame reply; and the two fell to discussing countryside affairs, of which the arrival of Miss Murdoch, the new school teacher, was the chief; while Marion silently took up her mother's discarded crochet work and went on with it. From time to time he tried to draw the girl into the talk, but without success. She only smiled wanly in reply, all airs of radiance fallen from her of a sudden.

"You're quiet to-night, Marion," he said at last.

"Och, she'll be thinking of the fine times she'll be having in the north very soon," said her mother. "She's for Inverness on Monday."

"Inverness?" said he in alarm.

"Yes, it's her only holiday—two months at her aunt's up yonder, once the season is over, you see."

Marion continued her crocheting in silence; and MacLeod was inwardly perturbed. "And what's to come of us with no music?" he asked, affecting gaiety.

The girl's clear eyes lifted for a moment and rested on him gravely; then without a word she let them fall again to her busy fingers.

"And what's to hinder Mr. Gurney and me making the fine music, all the same?" said her mother. "Although we'll ay be wishing Marion was here," she added tenderly.

"And maybe it's myself that will be wishing that same," said Marion in a low voice, her head bending over her crochet. It was the first word she had spoken since her mother had entered; and there was something so startling in her tones, that a silence fell on the others. She continued her work for a little, then rose and said good night.

Two days later she left for Inverness; and when a fortnight had passed, a letter came to her people asking their consent to her taking a post as probationer-nurse in the Northern Infirmary. A place was vacant, and if she was to get it, she must apply at once. "Aye," said Mrs. MacCormack to MacLeod, "we're just letting her have her own way, for she'd have it in the end, that lass, quiet though she is. Besides, she was ay keen on nursing, you see."

After a month had passed MacLeod wrote. Marion, asking how she liked her new work and so on—a little tentative note from which he hoped a correspondence with something of a glow might result. But week followed week and no reply came; little news also was to be had from her people; and his visits at the inn began to intermit. A time came indeed when they ceased altogether, since he had discovered a fresh source of interest in the Isle. For the new school-mistress—an alert, town-bred girl—cycled a good deal, and had quite a liking for history—especially Roman history.

VII: Work

ROBUST and self-possessed, the lady of the school-house had a dancing eye. She had also a sense of humour, and a gift of incisive speech that accorded ill with MacLeod's sentimental broodings; so the affair was soon at an end. The breach began with some banter of hers as they cycled together one Saturday down the shore-road to the south.

"Well, and how are the tin hats getting on? "she asked.

"The tin hats?"

"The Romans—old man Gibbon," she explained.

There followed an exchange of sniping. She was all for what she termed "living history" —the life of her own day—socialism, Shaw, Wells—the future of women in politics—aviation—the new India—the new science; while he insisted on the triviality of all these as viewed by the light of ages past. He was the more resentful perhaps, because his knowledge of the light of ages as represented by Gibbon partook more of intention than of deed; and he felt uneasy. For although this girl had physical charm—a dark Atalanta on wheels—she had a hidden hardness; and he divined her as uncannily intuitive of the artificiality of his present pose of a misunderstood talent for deep thinking. In a week or two both had cooled; and the early dark, and rising winds of oncoming winter, conspired to curtail opportunities for further expeditions by cycle. Soon there came the break; and MacLeod's weathercock mind veered instantly to memories of his earlier attachment. He would write Marion once more.

A tame gossipy letter he knew it to be, once he had posted it; but he envisaged it as only the first of a correspondence that was to flame steadily to ardours inconceivable. Again no answer came; and when the days passed, still letterless, a deeper self-pity fell on him, as he beheld himself lonely and uncomforted, in work that grew increasingly hard, and in a countryside wilder and more menacing every day, as his first winter in the Hebrides drew on.

Throughout the dark months the Storm-fiend held the Isle in its grip; and high winds, heavy rains and sleet that whipped and seared the face had to be fought daily. Mentally, too, he was ill at ease, for although the niceties of medical diagnosis and treatment were scarcely to be expected from a man exhausted by thirty miles of cycling daily against Atlantic gales, yet he worried as he found himself less alert at his work than when in hospital. Another source of depression lay in his isolation from the brotherhood of his craft. There were, it was true, two other doctors in the Isle, but they lived miles away; and should he require their help in some case of urgency, they would probably be many more miles farther afield, since they also had long distances to cover between patients.

The work would have been less harassing had his duties ended with long journeys and doctoring single-handed; but at times there came other calls on him, as when an overworked district-nurse broke down while tending some case of acute illness, and he must take a spell at her task for a night or two, until a deputy-nurse arrived from the mainland. There was, for example, the pneumonia at Glenba, half-way round the shore-road between Carsaig and Moy: a shepherd-lad housed in a squalid hut set above á beach wherè ocean rollers crashed thunderous the livelong night. Little fear of MacLeod falling asleep at his vigil while the ranked battalions of those billows were ever at the onset in Loch Moy. Yet young Duncan slumbered soundly through all that uproar as the carefully estimated doses from the doctor's hypodermic tided him over his crisis.

Other troubles were the occasional cases of madmen; the last two also in Moy. Here he had to arrange the transport of these poor folk to the south—work no one but himself would undertake, for the islanders had an almost superstitious dread of these afflicted ones. Indeed, the parish doctor's job was no sinecure in Eilean Aros, for when a hefty builder of dikes and bridges like John MacColl went off his head, John's strength was multiplied tenfold.

"Doesn't he suspect that you are taking him to an asylum?" asked Mrs. MacKinnon of Moy, as the doctor finished tea at "the Big House," where he had made a duty-call before removing his patient.

"Oh, yes; he knows where he's going all right," said MacLeod cheerily; "for I told him. Always best to be straight with these people, you see. He'll come quite quietly, I expect. And if he doesn't, I've six stout crofters outside."

"Outside," grunted the Laird of Moy from the depths of his arm-chair. "Yes, that's just where they would be. But it's you that's got to go inside, my boy."

"And all alone," sighed Mrs. MacKinnon. "I can't think how you manage those wild people."

"Oh, it's quite simple," said the youth lightly. "The power of mind over matter, you know," and departed to his task.

But it fell out that when he entered the bothy thus jauntily to prepare his patient for the long journey to the asylum in the Lowlands, a change had come over John; and John forthwith proceeded to strangle his good doctor across a ramshackle bed, his grip only relaxing when MacLeod's sou'wester fell off in the struggle, and the lunatic recognized his victim.

"Och, and it's the Doctor, is it?" said the madman, regretfully disengaging a powerful knee from the other's abdomen. "Well, well! And me not knowing you in them oilskins!" And quite tamely now, he set about dressing himself warmly for the drive to the south-going steamer.

MacLeod tottered back to the House of Moy for some much-needed stimulant. "Brandy!"he said thickly; and his white face alarmed the good lady.

"Whatever has happened?" she cried; while Moy himself joined in with, "Well, didn't I tell you? What was it, eh?"

"The power of matter over mind," said the youth, with a ghastly smile, as he tossed off his glass, and took his leave somewhat shakily.

In the case of the mad Colonel, a winter-shooting tenant, there was perhaps less excitement; for luckily a missing revolver, although arduously searched for by the Colonel, was never found, or there would be here no tale to tell of MacLeod.

As the winter wore on, the doctor's rusty push-bike became still rustier, since it made many strange journeys. Once he crossed Mam Clachaig in a hunt for a short-cut home from Glenmore; and on the ascent to that pass found many frozen burns where the water had lapsed from under sheets of ice that now roofed tiny gorges. These had to be crossed spread-eagle fashion, by crawling belly-wise over ice not too strong in places, the cycle being dragged ignominiously after as it lay on its pedal. But at the summit of the pass the cycle had its revenge, for on the glassy path that wound down a sudden precipice it took command; and it was the cycle that brought MacLeod down the cliff-face, rather than he the cycle. How he descended that wild escarpment he knows not to this day; and to this day no one in Eilean Aros will credit the tale of a feat only fit for the Feinne. "Whoever heard such nonsense!" they say. "A cycle crossing the Mam! ... No, not even in summer, let alone in a frosty winter! ... Och, no, no!"

About another adventure of his the islanders were only half-sceptical. "But surely nobody in his senses would ever think of saving ten minutes by wading half a mile at the Ford with the tide coming in!" they argued. "And they're saying that Lachie Dubh saw him waist-high in the water with his bicycle on his shoulder. But no one would be so foolish as all that, surely! ... Aye, true enough, old Duncan was deadly ill when he sent the telegram; and they're saying the Doctor was just in time ... Still-and-on a man'll no' die till his hour has come ... But who ever heard of anyone crossing the Ford, and the tide coming in! ... What foolishness people will be talking!"

Yet accounts of what MacLeod regarded as more dangerous journeys were received as credible by the islanders, for these were made by accustomed methods of transit, as in fishing-smacks when crossing Loch

Spelve and Loch-na-Keal, wild fiords in winter, swept by fierce gusts from Craigaven or Ben More—squalls that too often broke the rotten tackle or burst the ancient sails. During that winter indeed the doctor had good reason to dread the care-free ways of the Aros fishermen. "It's the ground-swell that kills," said one of them placidly, as he peered into the mouth of night, looking for water breaking on hidden skerries. "It's best done in the daylight, this crossing. We should have started earlier, look you."

"Then why on earth didn't you say so before we started? "asked MacLeod, aggrieved. "You're not wise, Donald."

"Och, her ladyship told me I was to take the Doctor over. And I would not be disappointing her ladyship," said the seaman easily ... And, returning next day, when a squall took a cap overboard, Donald calmly put about in broken water, and tacked and tacked till he recovered the cap.

Assuredly these travels through the wilds made the life a nerve-racking one. At times he covered a hundred miles in a day; but there came other days when he never crossed his doorstep; and thus his daily average was only about thirty. Yet thirty multiplied by the three hundred and sixty-five days of the year gave quite a respectable annual mileage. And long cycle journeys were made doubly exhausting by cold weather. Therefore, when one night he was foolish enough to taste whisky at a wayside croft while still ten miles from home, was there any wonder if, dazed by fatigue and ardent spirit and a keen wind from the north, he lay down to rest on the steps of Pennygown churchyard and ran a real risk of death from exposure?

But despite all this physical strain, MacLeod, by midwinter, was certainly twice the man he was on his first coming to Eilean Aros. Bodily he was stronger; and the necessity for doing his work single-handed had bred in him courage and resource ... Self-reliance: that was the great thing, he assured himself ... Reliance? ... At the word a vision of a girl's clear eyes came before him, and all his self-approval fell into dust as he beheld how little this crumb of virtue would avail him with Marion—how petty its aid where most he had need of it.

And now the Spirit of Storm fell on the Isle with redoubled might. In one day the Forsa River burst its banks and swept away part of the road, barring his route to the south. Then followed a night of frost which broke down great masses from the brittle cliffs of Gribun, so that the highway creeping humbly between the headland and the sea was blocked, and a passage to the west of the Isle also shut off. Even so, in the restricted area left, he had his tasks; while wind and rain and sleet tore over the waste places of the seaboard to buffet him as he worked. And rest at that season was not easy to be entreated; so great was the clamour at nights of the wind around his dwelling, tearing so fiercely at door and at window, that sleep was often denied him, and he had to fall back on his bed-candle and his Gibbon, until a wild dawn beckoned, and he must set out on a weary round once more.

It was about this time—just after the south road had been cleared—that there came a day when, on his return journey from Moy, dark found him on the hill-road near Balmeanach, hearkening in the pauses of the gale to the churning of the Sound's angry waters far below. High in the corries of the great hills above whooped the winds as in a Ride of the Valkyrie. A sleet-shower stung nose and eyes; and bending to the blast, he trudged onwards, pushing his cycle, until his lamp blew out in a mighty onset of the gale; and he staggered to the shelter of a roadside wall, utterly spent. For a little he lay on the lichen-covered stones, breathing hard, then turned to discover if he could glimpse a light in the croft of Balmeanach that should lie somewhere on the slope below. But no light was there: those good people must have bedded early, as was their wont in winter. He could see the outline of the little house, black against the grey-black of the waters of the Kyle; he knew that he had only to step over a wet field and knock, and bedded or no, old Murdo would rise with a warm welcome to stir anew the smoored peats, and make ready his poor table with generous hands. Yet, shivering in his wet overalls, MacLeod did not stir from the cold stones where he lay exhausted. It was no thought of avoiding a disturbance of old Murdo's slumbers that now held him; only that of a sudden the world seemed more strangely alien than ever, and himself become more acutely aware of his miserable plight. Here he was in his first practice, after six years of schooling in college and hospital; and yet he now lay, sodden to the skin by a dikeside, like any tramp. The noble profession of Medicine! Surely this was too quixotic a venture for any man with a spark of sense. The romantic Highlands! Romantic indeed for him — with only twenty pounds for capital, and a push-bike for transit over the rude roads of this stormy coast! Fatigue immeasurable to-night; and to-morrow, fatigue again; and the day after, fatigue once more.

Wild gusts tore round him as he peered into the dark, and the rain drummed incessant on his oilskins. Within those four walls, so close at hand, were shelter and comfort for the asking; yet, storm-battered though he was, he knew he would do no asking: too well he recognized his mood of bitter pride ... And then in the midst of these musings, the rain suddenly changed to a sleet-drift that whipped his face like a torture of the damned, so that the pain brought tears to his eyes ... "God! what a life!" he muttered; and as if evoked by the contrast, a picture of the warm, soft-lit wards in the hospital in the southern city arose before his mind's eye, and so unmanned him that for the moment his tears had almost a source other than physical. "Tuts!" he said, swinging his machine round to the homeward track. "This will never do."

But on the instant he shrieked aloud and let his cycle crash to earth; for he had stumbled against a shaggy hide, saw dimly above his head great antlers and wild eyes, and heard a scurry of hooves as a tall stag and his hinds galloped back to their mountain fastnesses. Even the wild creatures of the Isle, it seemed, on a night like this sought shelter near the haunts of men. Surely the Storm-fiend was doing his worst: surely the witches were out on the winds of the tempest—busy with their dark orgies on the steeps of Corrie-na-henachie ... Those hammering hooves, that hurricane in the hilltops, whinnying, moaning, baying by turns, as if Fionn and his Hunters were abroad, awaked old memories of the race in his blood. Instantly he was the outlawed, making for defiance and flight; and with a fist flung momentarily skywards, he raced for the sanctuary of the larch-wood behind him. As he did so, the tree-tops thrashed and tossed before the gale in rebel agonies, so that he halted at the sound, half-crazed by wild imaginings ... Yes, rebellion! that was the thing ... Yes, a challenge from the hunted ... But the shrieking squall smote through this sham courage like a lance, and, cowering as in fear of the nameless, all his training in science gone down before these spectres of old time, he turned on his tracks, and plunged madly over bog and heather to the shelter of the sodden dike once more.

And here it was that reaction came; for, as he leant over the wall's wet stones, an instrument-case, dislodged from a breast-pocket, fell clattering on the cycle's handlebars. It opened as it struck the steel, and its contents dived into the drenched heather. He felt gingerly for the knives and retrieved them one by one, but the delicate surgical needles eluded his groping fingers. "Damn! "he muttered. "Just when I needed them for to-morrow's job ... Must wire to-night for a fresh supply." Professional instinct was suddenly uppermost again, and all his hysteria swept aside. "Surgical needles," he mused. "I wonder if Marion sees much surgery up there." Once more he swung his cycle to the road and, mounting with difficulty, slogged heavily homewards in the teeth of the gale.

VIII: Snow

MACLEOD sat before his fire. It was a November morning, not cold for the time of the year, but cold enough for him to be thankful that he need no longer don the short-sleeved gown of the surgical wards. He had just breakfasted, and was now "reading-up" the article on Chlorosis in Allbutt's System of Medicine. There were forty pages of it: that seemed a lot to read for the single case he had under his care just then. His mind strayed from the task; he fell to dreaming of the wards in his old hospital, and soon to dreaming of a certain nurse therein.

For of late he had found solace for his loneliness in letters to and from Sine MacAlpine—Sheena, she pronounced it—quite a beautiful name, and one that somehow seemed fitting for a woman with a face of such grave Celtic loveliness. Sister Carroll had not been appreciative of his literary powers in the least; but this girl was Hebridean and seemed to understand when he wrote about the island ... Sheena—really a lovely name!—What about a run south at New Year to see her and the old place again? But thoughts of departure recalled another truant from Aros—Marion; and he flushed a trifle as the names of the two girls came together in his mind. Instantly there was added the humble one of Kate, hers of the schoolhouse—an appalling contrast, commonplace indeed, beside the music of those others.

And now he saw himself on the steep path of the philanderer—an unthinkable thing. He must go carefully. Work was what he needed, he assured himself, or he would drift God knows where: therefore, back to Allbutt once more. Even if there were forty pages on Chlorosis, he would know that subject well before he finished with this particular patient.

He glanced out of the window as he resumed his study, and beheld a sunny winter landscape—Ben Shiant looking very close at hand under a sky of steely blue, and the waters of the Kyle hardly ruffled. He read doggedly on; but half an hour later drew closer to the fire, for the air had become appreciably chilly; a little wind, too, was singing in Glenaros pines. He observed also a darkening sky; grey clouds had gathered from the north; on the water spindrift was already flying, and a snowflake or two floated down. A little later he saw that the snow broke into fine powder, and, mixing with the dust of the road, looked a trifle grey. Later still it fell more swiftly, and about eleven o'clock was lying two inches deep under the hedges, where the sweep of the rising wind could not penetrate. Just then the garden gate clicked, and he shivered as he saw the post-office girl run up the path with a telegram in her hand. "It's a 'come at once,'" he muttered, and rose to take the message. "Leackruadh," he said to Miss Flora. "Old Iain ill again. Why hadn't he the sense to get ill yesterday—a fine day and nothing else to do. I must hire, of course."

Hauling on a coat, he went up to the inn. MacCormack was dubious about sending out a trap, however. "The horse's feet will get balled in that snow, look you, and he will be sure to come down. And there will be great drifts, Doctor, with a wind like that. It's thirty miles, too. Maybe you could wait till the morning?"

"No," said MacLeod sharply; "it's a 'Come at once.' I must just cycle the bare bits and tramp the rest."

"You might well do that, if the snow gets no worse. For one thing, you'd have the wind behind you."

Returning to his quarters, the doctor donned his overalls, and took out his cycle. "Keep me!" cried Miss Flora, who stood with her sister at the gable-end to see him off. "You're not wise; you'll get your death of cold." But he was mounted and away before there was time for reply.

"Well," said the stout Silis, "that little beard of his will be some use after all, on a day like this." And smiling and shivering in the keen wind, the sisters retired indoors.

Meanwhile he flew before a tearing blast through a village apparently deserted. At the end of it he met the Draolinn stalking party, leaving the hill with their only hind; they had evidently had enough of it, although the day was young. Pink faces, pink hands, pink knees under kilts that lashed in the gale as they bent to its buffets, they halloaed greetings, unintelligible in the storm's uproar, as MacLeod dashed past.

At the keeper's house he came upon his first patch of snow and crunched through it without skidding; then on to another wind-swept stretch of road for a full mile, never pedalling a stroke as the blast bore him onwards. Over the Forsa Bridge safely; but, on the far side, the road cut through a sheltered hollow under trees, and cycle and rider plunged into a snow-wreath that took him to his middle as he leapt. Knees lifting high, he waded through, carrying his cycle over his shoulder, and was soon on terra firma and mounted again. Hoo-hoo! piped the wind in his spokes as he free-wheeled at an incredible pace, carried onwards by the rushing air.

But by this time he was forewarned of the treachery lurking at turns of the road, and braking at the next bend, he dismounted just in time to avoid another fall into chill depths. He skirted the snow-filled hollow by shouldering his mount again and climbing a fence that took him on to some rough heather. But, after a detour, he came back to the road that now ran by a sea-beach where the wild cries of gulls and the clang of breaking waves bore him company.

He had barely covered four miles, but a full hour was already gone, and he was the least bit fatigued. He halted by a dike to rest, and some black markings on the snow close to it catching his eye, he found they were the breathing-spaces of a few Glenforsa sheep, already buried by the heavy fall. Poor brutes! he could do nothing for them; but if only the snow would hold off until he had warned the shepherd's father at Bal-meanach, they might be saved. Meantime he must hasten to his own task at Leackruadh; for the dark comes early in a winter of the north.

The hill at Finchness was not so bad; for the gale had brushed that bit of road clean as a ballroom floor ... But, oh, so cold the dancing there! Snow again at the larch-wood, and here he must walk; and again at the Bullhouse Burn, where the road crossed at a little ford —a frozen ford now—a deadly slip under its mask of snow, had he not remembered it ... Only six miles covered thus far. This journey would beat him, he feared. But up the brae to Balmeanach, where he must leave a warning about those sheep; and soon he was knocking at the door of the poor croft of Murdo Dubh, the cobbler.

"Come in, come in, Doctor," cried Murdo, his old eyes lighting up as he sensed adventure. "God! what a wind!"

MacLeod shook his head. "Sheep," he cried. "In the snow—near the fank—beyond Leitir."

"Aye, aye," shouted Murdo above the gale. "I'll warn Colin. Och! who now would be a doctor!"

"Good-bye," cried MacLeod, and mounted to the sound of a hastily slammed door as Murdo stole back to his fire of warm peat, thanking Heaven he was a doctor of shoes and not of men.

On now to the uplands, where the wind was doubly keen; whence, too, he beheld the Kyle tempest-torn, its currents making strongly for the tide race at the Big Isle. And the hills!—the hills seen from this vantage ground, so stately and so coldly white—how gloriously changed from their grey beauty of yesterday! He had laid his cycle down and was swinging cold hands and watching a snow squall flit down the Sound, when suddenly he became aware of something moving through the heart of that dark veil: something ghostly grey and massive—a battle-cruiser, terrible in its might, yet stealing on so quietly, a dreadful, hushed, menacing thing. The snow-veil swept past, and another leviathan appeared some lengths behind, equally appalling in its sinister might; then another, and another, spaced with beautiful precision. At first they seemed to go slowly, but he noted that already the first great ship was far away; for the silence of their progress gave the man appearance of tardiness—either that, or the sureness of their passing.

Well, it was a big world: they had their duty out there; but here was his, on the way to Leackruadh. He cycled on, and soon a dip in the road took him out of sight of the Kyle and the great warships. The powdered snow hissed in his wake or preceded him in little dust-storms, as if urging him forward—its monotone almost hypnotic to tired body and brain. Another rise now—Garmony Hill; and despite the following wind he must pedal here, so steep the ascent. But at the summit he was too fagged to risk coasting the downward side; his hands were numb, and a sleepy feeling increasingly heavy on him. Sleep? Yes, sleep would indeed be welcome, when he had won through. And so, in a doze, he trudged the bare declivity to find, on the low-lying ground, snow once more. Crunch, crunch! not too deep this. Sleep—sleep! that was the thing. And now what wine of gladness glowed in his veins that he should feel elated, although drowsy? What could it mean? For here was but the old picture already so familiar—the eternal hills, the dark waters of the Kyle, a stag and some hinds like rusty splotches on the flank of Ben Veon; and he, the parish doctor, staggering onwards to his task. How bald and bare the stage, how humble the sole actor in the scene; and yet how overpowering this sense of happiness! He struggled now against increasing coma; but the sense of well-being persisted, suffused indeed his every fibre; and in the end he felt himself slowly subside into a couch of delicious softness. At last came sleep, the magic restful thing; he drifted deeper and deeper into dream, and the snow covered him.

Ages thundered past; he beheld the old legions marching, marching; Gibbon came, furiously chariot-driven, the bays on his head and a Roman sword by his side; Allbutt, incongruous, followed fast, bestriding a pale steed named Chlorosis, his toga streaming far behind; while Gurney in a very short ulster, but with the legs of a giant, strode from one white mountain-top to another, a pickaxe on his shoulder and a sack of treasure trove in his hand.

Gurney?—Gurney?— And then Gurney's face really peered into his own, and Gurney's voice really cried: "Wake, man!—wake up"; while a very material pair of field-glasses depending from Gurney's neck knocked MacLeod on the forehead, as the little fellow bent to give him a sip of brandy from a silver flask.

"Good man! "said the youth. "More."

"No, no," said Gurney. "Time enough. Can you heave a leg? "And he hoisted him to his feet. "Mary Vore's cottage is only a hundred yards off."

"Mary Vore's," said the doctor. "So it is. I had forgotten Mary. Where's my bike?"

"Oh, damn your bike," said Gurney. "It's in the ditch. Come on."

"Fancy me forgetting Mary Vore's," mumbled MacLeod, and staggered onwards, with the little man supporting him.

At Mary's cot there was a great fire at which the good crofter woman made a steaming toddy; and, while the doctor thawed, lying on a rug before the glowing peats, Gurney set off to the manse, and in an hour was back with the minister and his trap.

"Well, well," said the reverend one—a portly gentleman, MacPhail by name—as he fussed over the spent youth, "haven't you doctors the long journeys now! Fancy a minister travelling thirty miles in a snowstorm like this just because old Iain of Leackruadh had a pain in his conscience! But you're too big a handful for Mary here, and her house so small. You must be coming on to the manse."

"Och, what need! "cried Mary Vore. "He's just fine where he is; and glad I am to have him."

There followed a contest in Highland hospitality: Mary shrill in her protests that all was well; and MacPhail insistent that, while he cast no aspersions on her goodwill or the smallness of her cottage, the manse was the more fitting house of reception for such as Dr. MacLeod. "And I could give you good scripture for that same, Mary," said he, "if I werena in such a hurry— 'The stranger that is within thy gate,' and all that," he added with a twinkle in his eye. "And where are your gates, Mary?—Tuts! get a blanket and hap him up, woman, and we'll take him off at once."

Grumbling still, Mary Vore obeyed; and although dark had now fallen, and the blizzard from the north still tore onwards, the minister and Gurney presently drove off with the doctor encased in wrappings, and packed cosily between them. As they tucked him into the bed at the manse, MacLeod insisted that he must rest only for a little while, and then get on to his patient at Leackruadh. "I never failed old Iain yet," said he; "and I must see him to-night."

"Well, we'll bring him up here, and then you'll see him," lisped the minister's wife—a thin little woman with russet apple cheeks and toothless gums, adding with a smile: "And I'm thinking that, ill as he is, he'll be better able for the journey than yourself."

"Och, but is Iain truly ill? "asked the minister. "He's maybe not really ill at all, at all. Is it only the rheumatism now, that he suffers from; or just the great laziness? Well, he has the laziness anyway."

"We could wire down and ask if he's really bad," suggested Gurney.

"Right," said MacLeod. "Got a pencil?"

So a telegram was sent: *Nurse, Leackruadh—How is patient?—Am very exhausted. Will to-morrow do?— Doctor.*

And an hour later, while the surgeon slept, and the minister and Gurney sat at watch over him before a roaring log-fire, and discussed in low tones the genealogical trees of the old families of the Isle, there came the reply: *Doctor, Torosay. Patient recovered. No need for your coming.—Nurse.*

Next day the storm continued; and MacLeod was clearly still too fagged to move from the hospitable manse unless the steamer going north was able to call for him. But Gurney insisted on returning by road, then and there. He loved snow, he assured the minister, who pressed him to wait; and he would be all right, halting as he intended to at this house or that when the blasts were too bitter. Besides, he had work to do at Arle: "Some writing for the London press, you see." And so they let him go, but reluctantly, for he had been an inspiration to all of them by his eager interest in everything Highland.

"An odd wee man," said the minister's wife. "It's 'Straw-Feet' they call him hereabouts. But hasn't he the fine manners on him! I wonder now, is he French or what?"

"He's fond enough of French music anyway," said MacLeod. "Chopin's his great favourite."

"I might well have put a stitch in that old overcoat of his before he left," said the good lady regretfully; "but I just couldna get courage enough to hint it to him, when he was becking and bowing all the time. It's hard to see a skilly man like him so poor."

"Poor? "said MacLeod. "Yes; but he must have been well-to-do at one time; for the brandy flask he brought out when he found me in the snow yonder was of solid silver."

"Are you sure now? "asked the minister, suddenly alert, his grey eyes all eagerness.

"Oh, I remember well enough," said the doctor. "And come to think of it, he had a brand-new pair of field-glasses hanging from his neck. I'll bet he's not so poor as we think. The straw in his boots and the ragged ulster are just a pose, I fancy. A Bohemian, you know."

"Field-glasses! "cried the minister. "You were surely mistaken, and you half dead with cold?"

"Well, my head is still sore where it was bumped by them last night."

"God!" said the minister.

"Andra MacPhail! What a word to say!"cried his spouse.

"I'm sorry, Ailie," said he. "It just slipped out. But here's a coil."

"What is it? "asked the doctor.

"What is it? You may well ask. Did not our battle-cruisers go through the Sound yesterday?" demanded his host.

"Yes, I saw them. But where's the connection with Mr. Gurney?"

"Mr. Gurney be hanged. Haven't you just done making him out to be a Frenchman. Well, what's a Frenchman doing hereabouts in the middle of a snowstorm like yon, if he wasn't watching them?"

"And what then?"asked his wife. "Were they not worth looking at? And had you not now your own old telescope on the study table, and you seeing nothing of them, because of the verdigris on the brass of it?"

"Tuts, woman, I'm no foreigner," said he testily.

"Woman! "she cried. "First it's 'God! ' and then it's 'woman!'—Andra MacPhail, whatever has come over you? There have been no such words on your lips since ever I have known you."

"I'm sorry, Ailie," he said again. "It's this Mr. Gurney is doing it—not myself at all, at all."

"Aye, blame it on Mr. Gurney, the poor wee man! As if he would harm a rabbit! And him with yon ragged cuffs to his coat. It's nothing but your own bad temper." And out of the room she flounced.

"Damn!" said the reverend gentleman; and then thanked Heaven she had not heard him offend a third time.

MacLeod, finding the air a trifle electric, did not reopen the matter of Gurney; and therefore tactfully led the irate clergyman back to his favourite subject of Highland genealogies. A session on that matter followed to the accompaniment of much tobacco over the study fire—a session which continued, indeed, with intermissions only for sleep and meals, for several days.

For daily the *Cateran* came into the bay, her smoke flat on her funnel-top, the spray leaping over her bows; and daily she looked hard at a ferry-boat that dare not venture out, then steamed on, contemptuous. But on "the fourth day the wind abated and the ferryboat did go out, and in it MacLeod with his rusty bicycle. As he stepped on board and the old steamer thrashed off again, he waved a good-bye to the handkerchief tossing from a window of Torosay Manse, and wished he were a minister with antiquarian tastes and a weakness for strong words. "There," he said to himself, "is the kind of job for a man who wants to read Gibbon."

He paced round the deck, and taking up his stand on the lee side of the purser's box, recalled that it was on this spot he had first met Gurney. "A queer fish," he reflected. "But, hang it all! he saved my life in the snow yonder. There can't surely be anything wrong with little Straw-Feet." With which generous *non sequitur* he closed his mind on the subject.

IX: Brass buttons

MACLEOD felt that winter lonely; for the liveliness of his correspondence with Nurse MacAlpine soon wilted in the absence of personal encounter; and finally she had ceased writing. The coolness, too, between himself and the lady of the schoolhouse continued. Of course there was Marion; but he could not find courage to write her again, since no answer had ever come to any of his letters after months of waiting.

Of Gurney he saw little, and latterly nothing at all; for just with the first hint of spring the little man had suddenly taken passage on the south-going steamer and vanished from the ken of Aros Isle. Whether he would return or not was unknown: the shepherd at Arle with whom he lodged was uncertain; Mr. Gurney had simply said that he must go off in a hurry, and that was all—a bit of news that somewhat mollified MacLeod's irritation at the little man's omission of a farewell.

It was about two weeks after Gurney's disappearance that the registrar of the district, a retired schoolmaster, laid before MacLeod the sad case of a blot in his books —a vaccination defaulter of some two years' standing. "It's in the Long Glen, Doctor," said old Chisholm, "near Craig—and that's the black end of the world. But if the doctor before you had done his job, you would not have had this bother." It was indeed a long journey for all the fee MacLeod could claim—half a crown, so authority decreed, was the payment for a vaccination in those days, be the patient distant one mile or many In this case the mileage was fifty; and the visit of inspection ten days later would make another fifty—a hundred miles in all. But the thing must be done some time, and why not now?

So, on a cold drizzling morning in late February, clad in his customary oilskin overalls and sou'wester, he took the shore-road circling the great bens on whose farther side lay the house of his patient at Craig. There was mist both seawards and landwards as he left the village crofts behind and came athwart the mouth of Glenforsa —an eerie place that day, for into the great strath the grey sea mists sucked and swirled like smoke in a city lane, and from its depths came the timorous cry of ewes dreading their approaching travail.

For the next ten miles he met no one, the road skirting nothing but sheep-hirsel or deer-forest; the only signs indeed of anything human were the roadside larachs —happy homes of olden days, that now had nettle and bracken high over threshold and hearth. Time was, he had heard from the older islanders, when this countryside had teemed with the former inhabitants of these cots; when on a Sabbath the roads had been thronged with worshippers trudging to service miles away. But now—a world desolate—a nightmare of a world—nothing but mists and waves and sea-birds. Was there truly aught alive in it, he wondered, but the shepherd's wife and child at Craig, and himself, sodden and steaming, pushing on to them through the steady rain? The ghosts of old-time crofters seemed to jeer at him from the mist-wreathed hillsides of Finchness and Allt-Criche. "See to him," he fancied them saying. "Hard was our work at the foot-plough, and little our reward. And for this man as little. A hundred miles on the devil's wheels; and a fool's pay in the end of it all!"

Fourteen miles from his base he came to Torosay, where his friend, the registrar, had his home; and here he rested for a few minutes. "*Och, ochan!*" said the old man, "and why did you take a day like this for it? There was no hurry at all, at all." Yet the kindly soul rejoiced inwardly that his registry books would show one page the fairer very soon. And now, on once more. Past Torosay's crescent of crofts, the moorland was gained and held for five miles; then the highway again descended to the shore; and finally the jaws of the Long Glen opened up to receive him. The road here was rough and little used, climbing through birch and hazel copse to run slantwise on the foothills of towering bens; and in some parts the track lay over shingle as slippery as a sea-beach—places where the torrents had taken their will of the road, and swept it to the river below. The hills on either side now drew darkly nearer; the river brawled more loudly in the mist of the valley's depths, and the noise of those hidden waters fell uncannily on his ear.

> *"Let me in, for lood's the linn*
> *That's roarin' ower the Warlock Craigie,"*

quoted MacLeod under breath, as he hearkened to that yammering.

The Long Glen measured thirteen miles; and the house he sought was half-way through it, indeed the only dwelling at that point. But the route was new to him, and so he feared the enfolding mists would hide the cottage. What if it lay aside from the road? He might pass it—might already have done so. But even as he questioned, a gale came up from the Atlantic side of the glen, sent the fog flying, and wailed mysteriously in the high corries far above. With the next waft of wind a hint of peat-smoke came to his nostrils; soon he saw a chimney peep over a high bank of the stream; and in a few moments he was before the door of the little thatched house of Craig.

He dismounted to find a melancholy fellow leaning against the porch and looking out dejectedly at a rain-sodden world. Doubtless he was thinking of the sheep he should be tending. But he had an easy-going master, who was miles away; besides, the mortality in flocks was accepted as high for those wild hills—and who cared? MacLeod greeted him, entered to meet a buxom wife and lusty child, and at once set about his task. Then a hurried cup of tea, some countryside gossip, and he prepared for his return journey.

The shepherd came to the door to see him off. "Did you now, I wonder, see any sailors on the road? "he asked.

"Sailors? No.—Man alive! what would sailors be doing in the Long Glen?"

"I'm sure I don't know. But there was a sailor passed me at Ardvergnish this morning early, just at the mouth of day—and him drunk. He was making for the north, so he was. I wonder now, who could he be?"

MacLeod was in haste to be off. "I've no idea," he said shortly. "What made you think him a sailor? "

"Well, he had a navy uniform, you see. Some kind of an officer, I'm thinking," said the shepherd; and in Gaelic he wished him a good journey, and went indoors.

MacLeod mounted his cycle. It was three o'clock, five hours since he had left home; and the short winter's day would soon close: he must hasten. And now he did not retrace the way he had come, but pushed on over the second half of the circling road which swung around the base of the great ben that formed the core of the Isle. At least there would be variety in this new return route, if nothing else.

At the height of the pass that brings the road over from Loch Scridain to the Loch-of-the-Cells, dark found him. Here he lit his lamp; and so round the mighty bastion at Gribun, under cliffs of basalt in whose fantastic buttresses the gale harped loudly as it set him flying before it like a bird down the wind. At Derryguaig rocks the seals were already nosing for their beds; and the wise hinds at Tor-na-Vlar were sheltering from the gale in the gullies there; while at Scarsdale he noted that the sea-mews were plaintively calling around a broken bit of wall half-way between shore and road.

Now MacLeod was no naturalist; but he had already acquired some little sense of the ways of the wild life of the countryside, and he knew that sea-birds were not on the alert on the sea-marge at such an hour of the dark without cause. He instantly pulled up, therefore, and detaching his lamp, laid his bicycle aside, crossed a patch of bog—leaping from tussock to tussock—and so came to the ruined dike. Close to it lay the figure of a man in a suit of blue serge, his face to the earth; beside him was a square-hipped bottle with a familiar brandy label. "So here's our sailor," he muttered, and setting his lamp on the wall, he twisted the body round, cleared the nostrils of ooze, and slipped a finger to a pulse that flickered feebly. He noted the odour of alcohol as the slow sighing breaths came irregularly, and taking down his lamp to mark the pupils' reaction, found himself staring into the features of Gurney—features now dreadfully altered, grey-blue and deathly. And in a flash he saw that the suit of navy-blue was really a uniform: there were brass buttons on coat and vest. But to work! And instantly he was stumbling back to the roadside where a freshet promised water clean enough to risk a solution of a hypodermic tablet. He returned in haste; the chill forearm of Gurney received a dose of strychnine, and presently the pulse-beat was less feeble and more regular.

"So that's it," he mused. "Drink! Who'd have thought it! And he comes here in retreat, for a while. Then the breakaway to the big cities—a carouse—and back again to safety. Poor devil!"

He hoisted the sick man to a reclining posture where he could breathe more easily, covered his body with his oilskin coat, and splashed back through the bog to his cycle. Ten minutes more, and he was at the gamekeeper's house at Knock; and half an hour later, with the assistance of MacRae and his gillie, had Gurney in bed. Hot coffee, hot water-bottles, and warm blankets were ready at the kindly hands of the keeper's wife; very soon the little man's colour approached normal and his sighing respirations became more regular. "He'll do now," said MacLeod, and sank exhausted into an easy chair before the blazing kitchen fire.

"And isn't it tired you are, poor man!" said Mrs. MacRae. "A wee cup of tea? Yes, yes.—And haven't you doctors enough bother with decent folk without all this stramash over a gangrel body like this one!"

MacLeod accepted the tea gladly; but, as he sipped, was sensible of some uneasiness in the bearing of MacRae and his wife—was aware, indeed, of certain nods and glances between them; and at last turned a questioning eye on both. "Come away, MacRae; out with it. What's the trouble?" he asked.

"Och, never mind him, Doctor," said the good lady. "Another cup? You're real tired, I can see."

"Not a drop more, till you tell me what's the matter."

"Well, look you," said the keeper, a trifle flustered, "we were thinking that it's still a good five miles to Torness; so maybe we'd better be driving you the rest of the road; and you so worn out. And we could be taking your bicycle in the trap as well."

"But I'll wait up with Mr. Gurney. Time enough for Torness in the morning. You good folk cut off to bed now. I'll do all the nursing that's necessary."

"Och, the wee rat!" cried Mrs. MacRae. "We can manage him ourselves, I'm thinking. We've seen plenty of his kind at cattle-market time—drovers, ye ken. Och, just you be leaving him to us. We'll manage him fine."

"No, no," said the surgeon. "There's something behind all this. What is it?"

"Well," she said, "we didna like troubling you, and you so tired. But just half an hour before you came in on us, there was a message asking if you'd passed."

"Where from?"

"From Callachly."

"Not the goodwife at last, surely?"

"And who else? Aye, her time has come to her, poor body! But she's all right; and the baby home an hour ago."

"Then why on earth didn't you tell me earlier, woman? "cried MacLeod, springing to his feet. "Get out your trap, MacRae."

The blackavised keeper showed white teeth in a grin. "No need to get it out, sir," said he. "It's just waiting at the door."

Callachly and other townships near by saw much of MacLeod that day, for a small spate of work had suddenly arrived; but early next morning he returned to Knock, and found his patient gone.

"Just as sour and bitter as a man could be, when I came in to him this morning," said Mrs. MacRae. "But the next minute he was like the Duke himself for politeness. Och, he's not a bad wee man at all, at all. And we were for driving him over to Arle; but he wouldna hear of it. So off he went on his stumps, as if there wasn't the least bit wrong with him."

"In a cold wind too," said her husband; "and him with never a button on his coat."

"Yes, indeed," said Mrs. MacRae. "And if I put one pin in his vest, I put a dozen. And him laughing and joking so pleasant, you'd think it was he that was doing us the favour, and not the other way about. He's the queer one, yon."

"But he had buttons on both coat and vest last night," said MacLeod in amazement— "brass buttons. Hadn't he, MacRae?"

"'Deed now, and he may have had gold ones, for aught that I can mind," said the keeper. "I was too busy putting him to bed to notice. Still-and-on, there was something about him and his clothes that was different this morning from what they were last night. But what it was, I couldna for the life of me tell you now. All I noticed was that he did not have the straw sticking out his boots the way he used to have. And I missed yon ragged ulster of his."

"But he did have buttons—brass buttons, last night," persisted MacLeod. "And I'll swear the little beggar cut them off, first thing this morning!"

"Och, him and his buttons! What matter about buttons!" cried Mrs. MacRae. "Come you in to the fire, Doctor, and warm yourself. And how is the good-wife of Callachly? And is it, I wonder now, a boy or a girl?"

X: Curlew-Curlew

GURNEY, clad once more in old ulster and peaked cap, was soon a familiar figure again on the roads of the Isle; and a few days after his return met the doctor near Arle. "Ah, good morning," he said casually, "you see I've got into working kit without delay ... By the by, what did you do with my arm that night? It's been devilish sore ever since."

"Strychnine," said MacLeod, nonplussed by the other's nonchalance. "I had to take hill-water. I'm afraid there was no time for strict asepsis."

"Just what I guessed," said Gurney. "Well, I'm much obliged. You've saved a pretty worthless life, I'm afraid."

"Nonsense," said the other. "And anyway, what about that business in the snow near Torosay? We'll cry quits, if you like."

"Well, I must be getting on," said Gurney. "I've another 'Little Glen' article to finish." And off he tramped, the straw wisps dancing around his ankles; while a bewildered MacLeod addressed himself to climbing the steep hill-road to Torlochan.

A certain coolness sprang up between them after this. For the surgeon resented the airy way in which the little man treated the affair of his rescue. Some explanation was surely his due, he considered. And so it fell out that for a time they saw little of each other: a condition of affairs not bettered by the early arrival of Marion, and a consequent return of Gurney to the inn parlour on most nights of each week. And presently it became known throughout the village that the girl had given up all thought of continuing her training as a nurse. It was plain too that all her enthusiasms were now for her violin; and her evening leisure was wholly spent in practice, with Gurney as accompanist.

MacLeod held aloof from these meetings for a little, but at last the old spell of Marion drew him back. It was the same Marion he met, the same poise and grace and tact in all she said and did; but he noted that her knowledge of music had been enriched by her stay in Inverness. She spoke now to Gurney about the great masters with an understanding that was amazing; it was clear also that when he talked of music she took his meaning in some finer, deeper way than any MacLeod could attain to. And Leipzig, Prague, Vienna—the great conservatoires and the teachers there—were discussed by the little man with complete mastery. Could it be that Marion's thoughts were on another flight from home—this time to the Continent, for the further study of her art? In any case the surgeon soon felt that he was outside the magic circle in which these two now ranged; his visits to the inn became irregular and presently ceased, except for matters of business. His coolness to Gurney was indeed now fast passing into dislike.

So the last days of winter passed. Then came spring, and with it a visitation wholly unexpected; for one fine day of shower and shine in early April, a somewhat ancient paddle-steamer with yellow funnels anchored in the bay; and presently, when a boat put off, Torness discovered itself to be honoured by a visit from the Navy that would last for many months. For *H.M.S. Alligator* was engaged on a hydrographical survey, and would begin with the waters around the Isle.

The officers of the *Alligator* were busy all summer; and although sea-fogs hindered their work a good deal, they made quite a stir in the Isle, since they were often ashore, and their parti-coloured poles, measuring-chains, and theodolites were soon familiar objects on the roads around Torness. The liberty men of the crew hobnobbed with the villagers; the officers got to know the lairds; visits and return visits between the ship and the castles or shooting-lodges were frequent; and the commander's wife and daughter came to stay at the inn. Altogether it was a bustling time for Eilean Aros, this advent of a Government ship; and the constant coming and going of the naval men, occupied with work that was really scientific, brought a sense of the far-away big world into that sleepy countryside.

But MacLeod noted that there was one member of the little community who reacted strangely to these new arrivals; for Gurney had suddenly become quite a hermit, and stuck so close to his lodging that the doctor only caught rare glimpses of him when his work took him near Arle, where at times he saw the journalist sitting out of doors, busy at his scribbling. He surmised that the little man was avoiding the new-comers by reason of a shyness natural enough in one come down in the world: he would not, of course, care to mingle freely with upper middle-class folk (a caste to which he so obviously belonged), since old memories might thus be rudely awakened.

About this time, however, a new interest took Gurney out of his thoughts; for he had decided that the first profits of his practice should go to the purchase of a motor-car; and already piles of makers' catalogues hid his discarded Gibbon. Eagerly he studied strange designs of engine, chassis, and motor-body; and by every post fresh bundles of booklets arrived which assured him that his only chance of happiness depended on his placing himself unreservedly in the hands of this agent or that. Also he corresponded voluminously with friends in the south—connoisseurs and fanatics in all things pertaining to motors. Now to this design, now to that, he swayed; but at the end of a fortnight's delirium he came to himself, and discovered that for him the matter of price was really of greater importance than the make of any engine. Regretfully he recognized that his ninety pounds would only reach to something at second-hand; and in the end he cast himself on the mercy of a friend in Glasgow, described his needs and the shallowness of his purse; urged him to do what he could without delay; and, making a bonfire of his catalogues, moodily returned to Gibbon and Clifford Allbutt.

In the matter of cars, however, there is, as all the world knows, a considerable interval between ordering and delivery; and so August had already begun before the long-awaited telegram arrived announcing shipment. But at last on a pleasant autumn evening MacLeod heard the siren of the *Claymore* as she drew into the bay of Aros, bearing his new acquisition on board; and, not without a sense of importance, he walked down to the little pier just as the steamer tied up, and beheld his purchase on her deck. A breath of the car's expected arrival had got about, and quite a reception party of crofter folk was present on the quay; among them he noted with a qualm the local repairers of all things in wood or metal—the blacksmith and the joiner—already eyeing his machine with professional interest.

He had heard from Young, his friend in Glasgow, that she was "eight-horse power, magneto-ignition, and solid tyres"; but it was only the last-named of these wonders that had any meaning for him. Young, who had something of a literary bent, also wrote that the seller had made an important concession in price as soon as he had heard that the buyer was a doctor in the Hebrides — "those remote places of the earth, where distance, winds and rain conspire to keep medical adviser and patient apart, just when they most desire to be together," were his words.

"Doesn't he lay it on!" growled MacLeod when he read this purple patch; but as he gazed fondly at his car on the deck of the *Claymore* he himself fell into a lyrical mood, and beheld her fair as the moon, clear as the sun, and terrible as an army with banners to all obstacles in her path.

Lascelles, the laird of Draolinn, then on holiday, had lent him the services of his chauffeur for a fortnight's initiation into the secrets of motor magic; and that worthy now stood henchman to him as he awaited the ceremony of the car's disembarkation. This was, after all, a bald enough affair, consisting as it did of a jerseyed pack of seamen trundling the machine down some planks on to the pier, and forthwith abandoning her without a single glance of regretful adieu. Then MacLeod and his borrowed driver wheeled the car slowly by hand off the pier and set her at last on good Highland earth.

John, the chauffeur—a native of the Isle—had only recently qualified as a motor expert (having previously been family coachman to the laird of

Draolinn), and did not therefore claim an extensive acquaintance with cars of other types than that he drove himself. He now confessed that he had never seen one of the same build as the doctor's. These magneto-ignitions were queer things, he added; for himself he preferred accumulators. "And where now is her tail?" he asked, walking round the machine, with the starting-handle in his fist.

MacLeod pointed out a possible attachment on the near side. "Och, and is that it?" said John. "Well now, you see, in a proper car the tail should be at the front."

"Anyway, we can twist this and see what happens," said the doctor cheerfully.

John regarded him with sorrowful eyes. "I'm thinking we'll have to find the 'out' notch first of all," he answered sceptically; and experimented forthwith. After some difficulties in the way of restraining the car from backing again to the deck of the steamer, the required notch was discovered; and John invited him to step into his very own car, that now throbbed and groaned as if eager to be off. He mounted; the gears were changed; and—oh, joy!—they moved slowly forward. Again a change of gears; she moved faster and faster, setting up a wail as she did so—a cry piercing and appealing that re-echoed from the far inland hills. As he heard the sound, inspiration descended upon MacLeod, and he named a name. "That's it, John," he said. "That sound settles it. It's the call of the curlew. And *Curlew*, therefore, is her name."

"*Curlew*?" said John. "Only one, is it? More like a hundred curlews is that same noise, and every one with a bad cold in her head."

But the happy owner heeded not. "*Curlew-Curlew*!" he murmured, as they sped wailing onwards to the garage at Draolinn, four miles away.

On the day following, the lessons in motor driving began, and went on for a fortnight. MacLeod's progress m that time may be gauged from a letter to Young.

"I can drive about five miles an hour," he wrote, "that is when we are on a road with a good soft grassy bank standing well up on either side. I don't think I've done much damage as yet. But really her vices are legion and familiarly feminine."

Young's reply was commiserating. "Your teacher can't be up to much. Chuck him and bag another. Then keep at it, and you'll get right before long. I admit the car's an iniquitous antique; but there are still quite a lot of that dog-cart type messing about down here. She's certainly worth eighty pounds at second-hand. As you say, the left front-wheel tyre cannot be called exactly solid since it opens out an inch at the joint; but you'll find it spreads out all right in the first mile. What about speed? Fourteen downhill with the wind behind her, I fancy."

Some weeks later MacLeod wrote again; but this time in a spirit of elation. "I buzz along all right now; and find the *Curlew* a great help.

Looking back at the beginning of my acquaintance with her is a horror, however. There was one day I must tell you about. It was just after the arrival of your last letter and I felt a bit stung by the way you put things. So, although I was still a novice, I decided to take her out all by myself on a journey to a patient thirty miles away. I cycled over to Draolinn, where the car was stabled, and found that John was from home; but I opened wide the garage door and backed her out. Unfortunately, I came too far, got off the cement-floor and bogged badly in some soft ground. I was a bit excited, you see, John not being with me.

"She wouldn't budge; so I foraged among the kennels and the square, and collected one plumber, one gamekeeper and one gamekeeper's mother—the last-named aged but powerful. Four of us in all, we pushed with the wheel well slewed round, and finally pushed to some purpose, for the car moved forward suddenly and started firing. I had left the gear in and the switch on! Anyhow, in a second the *Curlew* was in rapid flight, while three desperate men and one desperate old lady clung to the tailboard, the silencer, the door handle, the springs—to everything, in fact, except the wheels that were scurrying like things possessed. But not for long did we cling; soon she was off, without captain and without crew.

"By a miracle she dodged the kennel-wall, and at twenty to the hour, she charged incontinently at the estate's dancing pavilion. ' Valiant' is too weak a word, nor will 'heroic' serve to describe that onset. If you are to imagine her justly in her eagerness and *furor*, you must recall the ceaseless buzzing of the blue-bottle, as it strives to pass through the window-pane—thus the *Curlew* against that wall. She even reared on her hind legs, as she laboured to climb cement and corrugated iron. But just then I reached her switch, and with a wail of petulance she subsided to earth once more.

"My patient, however, still awaited me; and my blood was up: the *Curlew* must take me to him. So I wheeled her carefully to the roadway and started the engine anew. But her whole character was suddenly changed. Formerly she had sailed off with a sweeping movement, no less a curlew in her grace of action than in her plaintive cry. But now as I changed gears, she made a sudden leap forward, ran a few yards and stopped dead with a growl. I repeated the starting, remounted, again changed gears, and once more came the leap and the grunt as of agony, followed by a cessation of all motion. In this wise and no other, labouring much and sweating sore, did I come half a mile of the homeward journey. Then, leaving her ignominiously by the roadside, I walked back to the inn, hired their recently acquired Darracq, and got to my patient in record time. That day I renamed my car *Jumping Jaguar*, for only so were her leaps and growls to be fitly characterized. But next day the wise John set a fired clutch to rights. So the little beast is the *Curlew* once more; and I fervently hope her days of adventure are now over."

But MacLeod had no gift of prescience in the matter of the *Curlew*'s taste for adventure; for one night, as he sat over his Gibbon, a tap came to the door and Miss MacDonald ushered in Marion. Her face was pale, her eyes bright, her breathing hurried; she wore a screen of dark tartan thrown hastily over her head. "Your car, Doctor? "she said quickly as soon as the door had closed. "Is it all right?"

MacLeod rose, confused; old memories of other evenings came back; and, besides, he had avoided meeting her for many weeks now. "Oh, the car" he said, affecting a gaiety he did not feel. "It never was all right, and never will be, I fear. Just some bits of old wood and iron, you know ... Won't you sit?"

"No, no ... And please don't jest at a time like this ... Can you—can you run a friend of mine down to Croggan to-night—at once?"

"Certainly. I'll do my best. But what's happened to your Darracq?"

"Nothing. Father won't let him have it. There's some trouble. It's Mr. Gurney. He must cross to Oban to-night. There's a cattle-boat leaving Croggan about twelve."

"Yes, the Otter is doing a Croggan run."

"You mustn't say I've been here, or that I've spoken of this?" she said, eagerly appealing, her hand on his arm.

MacLeod had only to look at that white distressed face to know his answer. "I promise, Marion," he said.

"Not to anyone—not even to my father? "she went on.

"Oh, yes. I'll see to that. But, let me help you, my dear. What's wrong?"

She smiled wanly. "You're the kind one," she said. "But there's no time to lose ... I must be going. Good night, Doctor." She pressed his hand.

"Good night, Marion," said he, remembering another such parting. Then she was gone.

Donning an overcoat he went out into the dark, crossed the road to the little shed where the *Curlew* made her nest, and tested her thoroughly. He had barely been there ten minutes, when big MacCormack loomed into the glare of his headlights.

"For the road, Doctor? "said he.

"Not yet," said MacLeod warily. "But I may have a call to-night; and I'm just making sure that everything's ship-shape."

"You'll not be expecting to go near Croggan, will you?"

"Well, that's one of the places I may have to visit."

"Look you, there's something troubling me," said MacCormack. "It's that little devil of a tramp—that man Gurney. I canna make him out at all, at all."

"What's up?"

"Well, he came around the bar this evening, and, after his drink, he was asking me how the survey was getting on—the Admiralty folk, you understand. And 'Is there any truth,' says he, 'in the story that they found a new rock in the Sound last week?' Well, I just told him what Captain Moseley himself had told me, that it was no new rock at all that they had found, only one that had been there from the foundation of the world, as the saying is; but that, being a kind of peak, and well under the water, the old survey of sixty years ago had missed it."

"It wasn't charted then?"

"Isn't that what I am saying? It being a kind of solitary steeple, so to speak, right in the middle of the Sound, and its top well below the surface of the water, the ships of those days could just sail over it, high tide or low tide; and so the old survey had missed it. But nowadays these big heavy cruisers of ours are not so light in draught» look you, as the old wooden ships, and it's a real danger to them. It's a feather in the Captain's cap to have discovered it. He's the clever one, yon."

"But what's Gurney got to do with all this?"

"That's just what I'm wondering. He was for knowing where was the rock, and all about it. And fidgety he was, in a way I've never seen him before, putting so many questions to me about that rock, till I snapped him off. 'Och, to hell with you and your rock!' says I at last, and just walked off and left him."

"He must have been very troublesome," said MacLeod.

"But that's not the whole of it. Away he goes back to Arle. Johnny Post saw him there about seven, so I know it was home he went. And I think I know what he went for—money. I'm sure that was it—just money. And the Lord alone knows where he got all yon bagful of notes. Well, back he comes, and says he was sorry if he had offended me. Och, as oily as you like. And would I hire him the motor to take him to Croggan? Och, very polite he was; and out he brings a pocket-book and takes some pound notes from it, just to show me he had the price of the hire, you'll understand. Well, thinks I, you'll be making a song and dance about that rock in the papers, my man; and then there will be trouble for John MacCormack; me having told him what the Navy was telling me, you see. ' No,' says I, ' the motor's not for hiring this night, Mr. Gurney—not this night, anyway.' Then he pleaded on me with this and with that, until I got fair angry and ordered him out of the inn. And now I'm warning you that it's here he may be coming, and asking you to take him down to Croggan. But if you'll take my advice, Doctor, I'd have no dealings with him at all, at all. He's not safe—him with his digging out the old roads, and looking at the sea's bottom through an egg-box, and all that —he's not safe, so he's not! There's something queer about yon one."

"Oh, never fear; I'll send him off with a flea in his lug if he comes my way," said MacLeod, suddenly busy again at his engine; and MacCormack, satisfied and growling agreement, drifted off into the night.

He had barely gone, when the strange figure of Gurney appeared out of the darkness.

"Car's all right," said MacLeod abruptly: "Marion has told me. Wait till I get the rugs." He dashed into the house and returned with some waterproofs and wraps. "Boat's at twelve, isn't it?"

"Yes," said Gurney as curtly. "And it's half-past ten at present. Can you do it?"

"We'll try," said the doctor, wheeling out the car and locking the shed door. "It depends on what the surface of Ardura Hill is like." He started the engine. "Get up."

They took their seats; and the *Curlew* wailed through the village. MacLeod caught sight of MacCormack at the inn door, peering vaguely after them; while at the gable-end he glimpsed Marion's figure huddling darkly. As they lurched round bends of the road he sometimes touched Gurney's shoulder with his own, and, as he did so, discovered a tremor in the body of the little man. "You're shivering," he said, "and it a summer night?"

"It's nothing," said Gurney. "For Godsake, hurry!'

MacLeod accelerated; they spun onward along the shore-road; and for the next ten minutes they were both silent. But, at Finchness, Gurney said with an effort: "This is very good of you, you know."

MacLeod grunted: "Oh, that's all right."

For the next half-hour they sped over moorland roads, but swerved at times to the coast or ran through the foliaged tunnels of wood6. At last a dark mass loomed in front.

"Here's Ardura Hill," said MacLeod. "This is where the fun begins. It's one in six at the top."

"Can you do it? "asked Gurney anxiously.

"Sometimes. Depends on the surface. If it's washed off, or very soft, my sprags won't hold."

"Sprags?"

"Yes. Hansom-cab arrangement. When she sticks, I rest her on her sprags and race my engine. But sometimes she backs over them. Still, there's a good ditch near the top that always stops her."

"Hadn't I better walk it?"

"Yes, I'll shed you here, if you don't mind. It's only half a mile to the top."

Gurney got down stiffly and followed on foot; while the *Curlew* panted slowly upwards; then her sprags dropped and tinkled on rock, as rounding a turn of the road, her lights disappeared. Gurney toiled up the steep track, which had many windings; and near the summit came on a cheerful MacLeod, with the *Curlew* comfortably ditched.

"Sorry," said the doctor gaily. "Sprags wouldn't hold; but it's all right. I'll take you down to MacLeay on the other side of the hill, and he'll ferry you over the loch in a jiff. Saves a twelve-mile drive round the head. You really have bags of time."

They left the car and trudged over the summit; then by a gradual descent came to the shores of Loch Spelve and saw the riding-light of the Otter at Croggan Pier tremble bright across two miles of water. Old MacLeay was not yet abed when they reached Seanavaile; the night was fine; and he made no ado about so late a ferrying. MacLeod helped them launch the skiff, and stood on the shore as they pushed off. All was still save for the lapping of dark waters, the sound of oars in the rowlocks, and a faint lowing from the herds far away at Croggan. "Good night and many thanks," called Gurney, from the boat.

"Good night," cried MacLeod; and then, a spirit of mischief seizing him as he recalled MacCormack's surmise about a newspaper deal, he added: "Hope you'll make a good yarn about that rock." He had hardly raised his voice, but the night fell miraculously still at that moment and his every word rang clear.

Instantly he heard a voice from the boat. "Stop," said Gurney, and the soft beat of oars ceased. "Go back." MacLeay's oars swept the boat shoreward; and a minute later the little man sprang into the shallows, and wading ashore, scrambled hastily over the pebbled beach towards MacLeod, and peered into his face.

"What do you mean? "he asked harshly.

"Oh, sorry," said the surgeon, taken aback by the suddenness of this return. "I shouldn't have said that. A silly joke."

"A joke about what?"

"Oh, well—the papers—I mean your articles."

The little man looked searchingly into the youth's eyes, then suddenly grasped his hand. "You're a good lad," said he. "But it's a strange world; and I wish to God it were otherwise."

He stumbled back to the skiff, which now drew off on the still water, and moved towards the Otter's lights.

MacLeod, puzzled, paced the shingle, watching the boat till it faded from view in the shadow of the Croggan hills, then turned to trudge back to the ditched *Curlew*. Something throbbed painfully within him as he recalled the incidents of the night; and it beat to the tune of "Marion?—Marion."

His musings were suddenly interrupted by the familiar sound of a cycle bell, and he stood aside as the rider dismounted close to him in the narrow road, and peered at him in the dark. "Fine night," said the newcomer, and then: "Godsake, if it's not the Doctor! And me just coming to meet you."

"It's you, Lachie," said MacLeod, recognizing a small-farmer near Moy. "Who's ill now?"

"A tinker lass at Laggan, in a tent on the shore. There's a child coming to her, and the nurse is with them."

"But how on earth did you know I was here?"

"The telegraphs. We heard you were down this way. But have you not the car with you?"

"Stuck on Ardura."

"Take you my bicycle then, and I'll be tramping back ... Man, man, and wasn't I the lucky one, finding you so near!"

XI: The new nurse

MACLEOD rode the ten miles to Laggan in the warm dusk, to find the babe born and the nurse departed. The young mother, freckled and tawny-haired, smiled happily as the doctor knelt by her couch of fern. A tang of seaweed odours hung about the place, and a salt-laden breeze entered as a gipsy crone lifted a flap of canvas and brought in the child. "And wasn't she clever now?" said the new-comer. "Only two hours, and then this big fellow." She held out the baby for inspection. "A real MacAllister, he is: look at the wee nose of him."

"His hands are wet," said the doctor, testing their grip.

"What else? Am I not just after coming back from the shore, where I was letting him have a feel of the wave? We're MacAllisters, look you."

Recalling the tribe's preference for sailing skiffs to caravans in their travels round the coast, he made a pretence of remembering the ritual, completed his examination and took his leave. Outside the tent he found the youthful father, to whom he gave assurance that all was well.

"Yes, yes," said the youth shyly; "that is good, and very good.—And the nurse asked me to tell the Doctor that his bed was ready at the Big House."

"Right," said MacLeod; "and I've need of it"; and so set off for the House of Moy. Absence from home, entailed by sleeping overnight at this place or that when urgent cases so demanded, was routine with the island practitioner. And if work was hard and journeys long in Eilean Aros, there were compensations for these drawbacks in the fine hospitality of the countryside. Often enough the nature of his immediate tasks, such as a serious case at either end of his many miles of shoreline, kept him from accepting these kindnesses, and he must push on through the dark to keep tryst with his patients. Yet there came rare occasions when he could relax, and spend an evening twenty miles or more from home in Big House or manse, or in the humbler dwelling of a crofter. Indeed, it was a tradition in some of the older families of the Isle that a chamber be kept free for such visits. This was usually known as the Doctor's room; and many were the tales told MacLeod of the foibles of its former occupants—his predecessors in practice there.

Yet in the wayside cot, where household ways were narrow and no special chamber set aside for such use, he was none the less welcome.

"The bed will be a trifle hard, maybe," said the crofter's wife at Benadd once upon a time; "but sleep is sweet anywhere to a tired man." Yet never were pillows more downily soft, or sheets more fragrant, than those in homely Benadd. And next morning how kindly the adieux as, heartened and refreshed, he sped up the Long Glen, taking the trail joyously, for life seemed fair and good with friends like these.

No less did he enjoy spending a night off work with one of the lairds, and most of all a night at Moy; for there the oldest family in the Isle had its seat; and the chief, a MacKinnon, was full of ancient lore regarding his forebears, who had held sway for centuries over the bens and glens where himself was now master. But that night he came to the House of Moy too late for any gossip in the laird's study; and in truth, even had his arrival been earlier, he was too tired for anything but bed, and soon was in his chamber and drowsing deep.

He wakened to the sound of the pipes playing *The Big Spree*, as Para Mor paced the green sward under his high window. Later, at early breakfast in the dining-room whose great windows gave on the sunlit Loch of Moy and its guardian headlands, he was joined by the chief, a portly man of sixty with boisterous airs.

"Hullo, Doctor," said Moy, shaking hands heartily. "Well, things all right at Laggan, eh? ... And what's the news from your end of the country? How's that hydrographical survey getting on? Hydrographical! What a name! ... Wish these beggars would come down here and liven us up. Haven't had a Navy man about the place for years, you know."

MacLeod thought they would soon work down the coast to that part.

"And is it true old Wilmot's at Draolinn again?"

The doctor believed he was.

"Good! Hope he'll take a turn this way, when his visit's over at Las'celles'. Nice chap, old Charlie Wilmot. Was in the Guards with me at one time. Now he's in the Tower. Has charge of the Beefeaters there. Used to be in waiting on the King. My word! how I used to rag him then. Kept me kicking my heels in a side-room at a levee once. ' Patience, my boy, patience,' says he; ' and don't forget I'm in attendance on the King.' — 'Oh, damn the King,' said I. 'Tell him MacKinnon of Moy is here.' You should have seen old Charlie's face. Thought he'd have had a fit, ab— so—lute—ly—!"

Court news, politics, talk of shooting—lets and local gossip—a farrago of odds and ends, poured forth from the old man in an unending stream; and finally: "By the by, seen Tuesday's paper? Austria and Serbia at loggerheads. And Germany just gasping to have a hand in the game. Don't like that. I know Germany, by gad! Well, I hope she will come in; and if she does, we come in too, mark my word. War is what she wants, and by the Lord! war is what she'll jolly well get. For we'll lay her on her back for two centuries at least. See if we don't."

"But—war? "said MacLeod. "In Europe? Surely not? We're not Zulus!"

"Too civilized, eh? "asked Moy. "Skin deep, my boy—only skin deep."

He rambled on, pitifully wrong-headed from the young man's point of view. "These old fire-eaters! "thought MacLeod. "How dangerous."

But to his relief the chief struck off on a new line of inquiry. "Chap called Gurney up your way, isn't there?" he asked. "Kind of a tramp, eh?"

"Yes, a queer lot."

"Hum! "said Moy. "Well, you can keep him up there. Don't like him. He was down here last autumn, staying at Alasdair's, my shepherd's, at Laggan. Used to sit up all night, they said, writing stuff. Slept in the daytime. Don't like that, y'know."

"A journalist, I believe."

"All my eye, that journalism. He's up to no good. Cheeky beggar. What do you make of this? Mosley was here: Stormberg Mosley—a Colonel—South African War, y'know. Stayed with me. Well, he got the idea that Gurney was a gentleman down on his luck. So he called on him one day, with half a thought of giving him a leg up; and blest if the little beggar would let him put a toe over his doorstep! Stood in the porch, most polite, and just bamboozled Mosley with talk about climbing in the Alps. Told Alasdair—that's my shepherd—told him afterwards that an Englishman's house was his castle, and nobody was going to get nosing round his premises! Blast him! Englishman? He's no Englishman. He's some damned foreigner, as sure as God made little apples!"

"He's certainly odd, sir."

"Odd! "cried Moy, his face purpling with angry memories. "Well, by gum! I'll get even with him some day for his treatment of old Mosley. He's no good, that chap. All this German business going on, and mouldy foreigners prowling around! Won't do, y'know—won't do!"

MacLeod smiled uneasily, deprecating further discussion; and taking his leave shortly afterwards, walked over to the cottage, half a mile along the bay, where the nurse had her quarters. She was a new-comer, only a fortnight on duty so far, and as yet he had not met her. The little house stood strangely quiet in the strong sunshine on the fringe of a larch-wood; and he wondered what its new occupant would be like: if she was as efficient as the last one, she would do. Only the hum of bees and the lisp of waves on the shore broke the stillness there. Strange to think, that behind that fuchsia-clad wall was another adventurer in this wild island life. How would she take to it? A woman's cycle leaned on the gate, its polished steel-work a rebuke to carelessness in the matter of his own rusty mount, luckily at home that day. "She's tidy, anyway," he mused. There came a stir in the shaded depths of the little house as his feet crunched on the gravel, and a strongly built girl in nurse's uniform came to the door. She was dark, and had a humorous eye.

"Nurse Yarrow? "he asked.

"Yes; and you'll be the Doctor," she answered, her Irish accent unmistakable. They shook hands. "Well come in," she said, sighing; "for I suppose I must ask you. You'd be sure to find me out some time, anyway. This room of mine is always like a rag-store."

He entered and discovered the truth of her confession; for the little place was indeed in disarray. Breakfast dishes were still on the table, a dressing-gown hung over a chair, and on a desk by the window was strewn a mass of letters and journals, with which were intermingled several medicine bottles and a stray bandage or two. A nurse's handbag lay open on the floor; the girl immediately knelt beside it and proceeded to pack it hurriedly. "Did you ever see the like?" she said. "You'll excuse me going on with this bag of mine; for if I stop setting it to rights I'm done for. I'm always misremembering something I should be putting into it till I'm ten miles from home." And she attacked it furiously.

"Take your time," said he easily.

"And did you have a good night's rest? ... And how is ould Moy this morning?"

"Oh, going strong."

"Isn't he the ould darling? I could sit all day listening to his lies," she said casually, snapping the catch of her case at last, but with difficulty. "Well, that's that!—Though," she pondered, gazing round dismally without rising, "I'll be bound I've forgotten something I'll be needing badly before an hour's gone. Och, will you look at this room! Like a pawnbroker's after a burglary!" She got to her feet. "Are you for Laggan now? Well, let's get out of this chamber of horrors."

They came out of doors, and he halted by her cycle. "But you'll want to ride," he said. "I can easily walk, and get over by the time you've finished your work there."

"But isn't there a wee hole in the back tyre! And I can't find my repair outfit, the way things are in that room of mine. Och, I'll just be walking too." And they set out, MacLeod carrying her bag. "If I'd only time, I'd get things to rights in that wee house; but there's so much nonsense in this place, you never can call a minute your own," she explained.

"What kind of nonsense?"

"Ould Moy's kind. I have to massage his sore leg; and he makes me cut the grandchildren's hair; and now he's wanting me to catalogue his library. I told him yesterday it wasn't a nurse he wanted on this estate, but a blooming cornucopia."

"Serve him right," chuckled MacLeod. "But why do any of these extras? They're not your job."

"Och, the man's poor, and he's seen better days; and he's such a one for the blarney, you're doing all he wants before he asks for it."

"But shouldn't your district work come first?"

"You're right now—you're right. And I'll just tell him what you say."

"Good Lord, no. Don't bring me into it."

"Look at that now." She halted to survey him scornfully. "You're as fond of the ould villain as I am myself; and you wouldn't cross him for anything."

"Yes, I would. And you can tell him what I've said, and tell him I said it.".

She smiled. "You're quite sound, I can see. I was just trying you. But I'll give him the rare dressing-down one of these days. I'll just up and I'll say: 'Look here, Moy, I'll catalogue your library, or I'll cut the children's hair, or I'll massage your bad leg. I'll do one of the three; but I'll not do all. Now which is it to be?'"

"That should do him good," he said.

"More like it would give him an apoplexy—for he has a temper if ever man had. I'd best leave him alone."

"Oh, come now! I think you should try it."

"I'll not now, so don't be tempting me. Didn't I see him one day last week, and he was that angry, that if ye'd poured cold water on his ould head, it would have boiled?"

"Indeed?"

"Yes, he'd met that wee man they call Straw-Feet down here, that day; and it seems he'd passed ould Moy without 'good day' or ' good evening,' if you please."

"Who's that? Mr. Gurney?"

"I don't know now. I only saw him once—but he's the wee man with the straw in his boots. Stays up your way, I'm hearing. You'll know him yourself?" Her regard was intensely curious; and it was clear that the spell of Gurney was on her also.

MacLeod frowned. "Yes, I know him; and yet I don't know him," he said. "He's a queer fish."

"A wee moody man that goes nosing along—thinking —thinking, all to himself—yes, he's just right queer. Maybe the poor wee fella never saw ould Moy, and meant no harm—him being that busy thinking. Well, now, but wouldn't the world be a dull place if there weren't some queer people in it—and nothing but plain doctors and nurses?"

MacLeod laughed outright, and they resumed their walk, getting in the end to a discussion of their work and their patients which lasted till they reached the tinker's tent at Laggan. And here he noted, as she set about her task, that if her housekeeping was a trifle untidy, her nursing duties were performed with a technical precision and a tender care he had never seen surpassed. Her training had certainly been good.

"Isn't it the wee darling, that baby?" she cried in a burst of enthusiasm, as she proceeded to pack her bag once more, with the perplexed air he had already noted in the cottage—a perplexity that increased as she suddenly dived for something in the depths of the case. "Och, will you look at that now? "she cried, retrieving a small object from among some bandages. "Here's the blessed repair outfit, after all." She laughed wildly. "When I get that ould bike punctured all over like a pepper-pot, I leave these things at home. And now, when I've no bike with me at all, the wee devils are sure to be turning up."

They came out from under the canvas into the sunlight and the breeze, and threaded their way through the whin bushes back to the road. "Isn't it the rare day!" she said. "And the loch just lovely! You'd never think there was a great world of towns and people beyond all them big quiet hills ... Is it true, d'you think, what ould Moy tells me, that there's going to be a murdering war?"

"So he says," said MacLeod lightly; "but I can't believe it. He's just letting off steam, I fancy. We're not fools and savages, are we?"

"I wonder now if we're not just that," said the girl, all her merry airs gone on the instant, her face gravity itself.

He stared at her in amazement. Her voice had changed and in some strange way her manner recalled something of Marion's.. She had the air of one who had sunk to some deep of the inner life. "Whatever do you mean?" he asked.

She turned to glance back at thé column of smoke rising stilly above the dark clumps of gorse, where lay the little encampment they had just left. "Did you never live in a garrison-town?" she asked fiercely; and then: "Man alive! there's more sense in yon wee tinker's tent than in all the great cities of the earth."

XII: The pipes

IN the afternoon he got back to Ardura Hill with the aid of a lift in a friendly farmer's trap. The shallow ditch where the *Curlew* lay was on the side of a steep gradient, a spot where he had already experienced not a few adventures. He knew every inch of the ground indeed; so with the aid of his companion was able to coax the car back to the highway; and soon she was wailing homewards once more.

As he drove back, his mind turned gloomily to Marion and her part in this last escapade of Gurney's. He pictured a tragic interview in which he "had it out "with her. Whatever Marion might think of himself, he must let every chance of his own go down the wind, rather than that she should be further involved with this stranger.

His last thought that night was a further registration of this decision—he would act at once—to-morrow, indeed. But next morning all remembrance of his vow was blotted out when he awoke, still a-dream. For his dream was not of Marion, but of Mary Yarrow, as one moment she jested, and the next so gravely indicted the great world of their own day. Then memory jogged him, and Marion was again recalled. But he fell back, nevertheless, to thoughts of the dark girl with the quaint incisive tongue, among the whins on Laggan shore, do what he would to force his mind to its former track. What a muddled business! He must do the Oolava visit that morning and see if a breath of fresh air would help clear his brain.

Yet, as he swung over the hill-top at the Black Rocks in the bright June sunshine, and came upon the long coast downhill to the Draolinn cross-roads, a sudden bugle-call rang out, re-echoing among the mountains; and all his dreams were shattered. For, as he rounded the bend above that lovely fall of country which leads to the Loch-of-the-Cells, he beheld a great fleet of warships on those placid waters. Was this then the meaning of the *Alligator*'s recent survey of the seas around the Isle? Possibly old Moy was right after all about that trouble in the Near East. What now was afoot?

A little way on he came upon a party of blue-jackets, led by a petty officer, foraging in the wayside crofts and buying up poultry and general provender. On the rest of his journey he passed many more such groups bent on the same errand; while from the roadside cliffs he beheld the floating city of the Navy; the crews busy as ants; a band crashing out brassily from the deck of one; signal flags busy on all; and numerous motor-pinnaces darting in and out between the great grey hulls.

Donald of Kellan cried out on him as he passed: "Here's the end of the world, Doctor."

MacLeod pulled up his car on the instant. "Is it war?" he asked.

"What war? "said Donald. "I never heard a word of it. No, no; it's just that they've bought up every sheep I ever had—fifteen of them, no less. Man, man! they'll eat up the whole island, these fellows."

No, it was not war—not yet. Three days longer the great ships were at anchor there; then one morning no fanfare of bugles broke the stillness, and the Loch-of-the-Cells lay unbroken by any sign of life save the tiny lugsail of Donald of Kellan, fishing mackerel off Eorsa.

The last week of July, 1914, arrived; and looking back on it from later years, MacLeod saw that in the secluded atmosphere of Eilean Aros it had appeared comparatively uneventful. There had been some scattered paragraphs in the newspapers of the "startling sensation" variety; but, of course, it was just the modern newspaper's job to exploit that kind of stuff. There had been trouble in Ireland: gun-running at Howth, near Dublin; some Irish Volunteers had been shot. On the Tuesday Austria declared war on Serbia over that Serajevo affair. (Nothing would come of that, surely?) And some traveller from the mainland, at the inn, had brought over a bill advertising John Bull, a cheap weekly paper, whereon the legend ran: TO HELL WITH SERVIA! (Why couldn't people keep their heads?) All the same, the papers stated a few days later that Russia was mobilizing, and that Germany had asked her to confine her mobilization to South Russia. (Tuts! it would all fizzle out—a flash in the pan!)

But on the Monday a local farmer, just returned from a trip to Kintyre, brought word that he had seen no less than eight destroyers in the Campbeltown waters, obviously watching the Irish coast. And next morning young Lascelles of Draolinn was hurriedly motored down to the pier to await the south-going steamer. A second car brought much luggage—an unusual quantity indeed for the young laird at that season of the year, so near the opening of the grouse-shooting; and it was rumoured that he had been r«ailed post-haste to rejoin his regiment —the Scots Guards. Later in the day, sundry men known to be reservists began to arrive in the village— humble folk, crofters and fishermen from different quarters of the Isle, hardly recognizable at first in their smart Sunday clothes. They had been called up suddenly, but knew nothing as to the wherefore of the summons: the big steamer from the Outer Isles was to make a special detour to Torness in the evening for them; and they were to report at their depots—that was all.

Now the village began to buzz: at the inn-door groups gathered, at the pier, and at the smiddy ... Of course, it might only be coincidence, but it was strange young Draolinn going off in such a hurry, and at the same time, too, as the reservists ... Maybe it was only this Irish horoyally — maybe not even that; just a surprise practice drill or a review or something. Strange things happened down in the south, in the big cities where there were all kinds of queer goings-on ... Nothing serious, whatsoever, you may be sure! ... But for Godsake, don't let the women hear you talking, all the same. You never know, you see ... Och, yes, nothing serious ...

What most struck home to MacLeod, however, was a story told by old MacKichan — a shepherd from Burg, in the extreme west of the Isle — who had come in to Torness the same night to visit some of his kin there. Looking out to the Atlantic from high Burg Head, he had seen eight destroyers tearing north at full speed that very morning ... Could these be the watchdogs from Kintyre, released from their vigil on the Irish gunrunners? thought MacLeod. There had been eight at Campbeltown; and eight was the number old MacKichan had seen steaming full pelt northward. Something of greater moment than the Irish trouble was surely afoot to cause so sudden a departure. (A false alarm, most likely. Those silly rumours about mobilization on the continent. And Germany at her old game of bluff. Nothing more, to a certainty!)

But there came a night when, sleeping sound after a tiring day, he was awakened by a loud knocking, and through a chink of his door beheld a bed-candle a-tremble in Miss Flora's hand. "Whatever can be wrong, Doctor? "she said. "What noise is that? — Listen."

He heard only the brattle of the burn in spate below his window. "I hear nothing," he said.

"But listen! "she said. "It's the boys down at the smiddy; and it one o'clock in the morning. And they're shouting; and I thought I heard the pipes. There's something in it that is not right, for the lads to be abroad at such an hour of the dark."

"Nonsense," he said. "It's only the wind."

But faintly now there came the sound of a distant cheer; then more firmly the sound of the pipes, and the tune was *Cogadh no Sith*, an old battle-field rouse. He leapt barefoot to the floor. "Then it's war! "he cried.

"Poor lads, poor lads!" said Miss Flora, and the candle shook again in her hand — " them and their piping!"

Book Two

War Time

XIII: Pause

ON the 1st July, 1916, MacLeod was wounded at Gommecourt. During the preceding years of war the world for him had been a nightmare; but in the hospital ward where he now lay, looking out through open windows on the sunny Berkshire downs, he was pleased, despite his smashed knee-joint, to allow the world a certain measure of sanity. Even the dread clarity of the steel-bright operating theatre, the assured airs of surgeons and nurses, the ritual of dressing and X-raying his wounded leg, brought a longed-for peace of mind. And doggedly he was again forcing his way into Gibbon: already he saw volume two beckoning him, for the first was almost three-fourths conquered. Indeed, after the first month in Blighty, although he knew himself maimed for life with a knee as stiff as a poker, his spirits rose. The Boche had been held—that was the great thing. And the war would soon be over: two years were surely enough for any old war.

But as the long days of battle dragged on, the vanity of this way of thinking dawned on him; the war need not end, of course, because Finlay MacLeod had been laid aside. Ironically he recalled the entries he himself had made at Army boards on the papers of other wounded before he had crossed to France; and now he pictured the possible entry on his own sheet: "Became noneffective by G.S.W. Left knee." Soon, however, he emerged from these broodings, and turned to his book of old Rome.—*But the operations of the campaign,* he read as in a dream, *though wisely concerted, were not executed with ability or success. The first of the armies as soon as it had entered the marshy plain of Babylon, towards the artificial conflux of the Euphrates and the Tigris, was encompassed by superior numbers, and destroyed by the arrows of the enemy.* He looked up from the page in amazement ... "Arrows? "he said, and then, tossing the book aside: "Why ... it's Gibbon!" Passing his fingers over cheeks now beardless and no longer cherubic, he meditated: "Wonder how often those old chaps shaved in the trenches at Babylon?" And his thoughts drifted back to the cold nights in Eilean Aros when a beard was really an asset of some value.—Aros? —Marion?— Where was she now? He had heard over a year ago that she was then serving in some hospital near Bethune, but never a word of her since. And that Irish nurse at Moy? She also had disappeared into the blue;

was serving with the French—the rascal! Weren't our own people good enough for her? Of course, she was Dublin—that might explain it. A queer lot!

And the *Curlew*, poor old 'bus, where was she? She had been sold to a maker of bobbins down in Dumfries, who fixed her stationary, and ran her engine to drive a turning-lathe. An inventive genius; but what a come-down for the *Curlew*! In any case a restful conclusion to her strenuous youth in Eilean Aros—if she ever had a youth, or a conclusion.

Eilean Aros? An isle of desolation nowadays of a surety; for scarcely a clachan in it but had paid toll to death. Those two fine chaps at Draolinn, the keeper's sons, killed at Thiepval; and big Archie of Callachly gone down on a mine-sweeper. Torloisk and Tostary had been sorely hit; and Dervaig, Torlochan and Calgary; Moy village also. But it was good to hear that the chief's son, reported missing, had at last turned up, although badly wounded ... When would it end? And how would he himself now fare, once it was ended? How should he tackle the practice in Aros again with a lame shank like this? ... Yet things might have been much worse; and Aros was still a possibility if he could afford a modern type of motor-car. What a nuisance this money business! But wait and see! ... Wish they would hurry up with his dressing to-day. Must have some idea of the leg's progress before he started planning what to do once he was out of hospital. But why deceive himself? The knee was stiff as a gun-barrel; and a limper wouldn't have much chance of getting overseas again, as long as the present lot of mandarins ran the Medical Service. More likely they'd send him to inspect railway passes at Nigg. Or—horrors!—send him to look after a garrison of six on the Bass Rock. Maybe neither. Wait and see ... No, they wouldn't even send him to Nigg—they'd write him down as noneffective, sure as fate; since the Permanent Home Service for damaged goods like himself was fairly well filled up at present.

His last surmise proved correct; for six months later a Medical Board in Edinburgh discharged him with a pension. He admitted a partial justice in the decision, saying: "After all, a game leg and a uniform don't go well together"; but added, "Still, men are running short; soon they'll be wanting everybody. See if they won't be glad to have me later, lame leg and all." He returned to Eilean Aros for a short holiday, and made inquiry as to Marion's whereabouts; but all he learnt was that she was still in France and moving about a good deal from one hospital to another. And then his stay in the island came suddenly to an end; for, as he visited the scattered crofts, he found wellnigh unbearable the tale of good men gone—at Combles, at Guillemont, at Delville Wood—and soon returned to the mainland.

Back to Edinburgh, to find his frail mother much concerned over his eagerness to get overseas again, if not in the Army, at least in some auxiliary service— with one of the Quaker Ambulances, perhaps. Her strong suit was that he had had enough of it, and that nobody in their senses would want a lame man anywhere near a battle-field. In reply he gave daily demonstrations in her tiny kitchen to show that the injured leg was quite serviceable; but she would not be convinced. On one occasion, indeed, he thought it wise to manoeuvre some furniture between himself and her as he performed his exercises; but she protested. "I canna see through a table, laddie." And when he insisted that the leg was now really all right, she retorted: "Aye, aye: so ye say. But it's a pity ye hadna that table atween you and the Germans, when they shot ye. Man, they'd never hae seen ye."

All her cajoling was useless, however, and after a week at home, he set out for London, where he did some study in war-surgery, and sought service in various "fancy units" overseas—hospitals of an auxiliary type mostly manned by crocks like himself, and attached to the medical service of one or other of the Allies. Desperately he pulled several wires that promised to open magic doors of preferment; but there were many in like case to himself; and no door opened, pulled he ever so hard.

But suddenly, one day in the spring of 1917, in the midst of a sunny shower in Regent Street, he beheld the portly figure of Moy bearing down on him—Moy unmistakably, although transformed by the smartest of town kits; and scarcely had MacLeod's inquiries as to the health of the chief's wounded boy been answered by the assurance that he was out of danger, than Moy pronounced an "Open Sesame" to just such a door as he had for so long striven to force. "Know any sawbones wants a job in the French Red Cross?" he asked.

"I do. Myself."

"Well, there's one going a-begging just now."

"I've no graft."

"Don't like the word, but know what y'mean. You shall have that job. But—Lord! I'd almost forgotten!—you speak French, of course?"

"I read it easily. I speak it very little, and that badly."

"You're too damned honest for this war, my boy. Fancy telling me that! Here, let's get a taxi and we'll find one of these Berlitz johnnies at once."

"The Berlitz men are all across the Channel, sir. But never mind. What you want is a surgeon who can keep silent in several languages. And that's me ... When do I start?"

The chief fumed. "But, my dear chap, I am serious. All your wounded will be French. It's a good hospital attached to the Army of Verdun; and it's run by a Comité Brittanique or something like that in town here. All the staff are British, and all are crocks or over age; and all speak French. You must speak the lingo. There's no getting away from it."

"I do speak French," said MacLeod hastily. "What I mean to say is that I'm rather better at reading it."

Moy grinned delightedly. "You are a lovely liar," he cried, taking his arm and hailing a passing taxi. "Who said we weren't going to win this war? "He bundled him into the car, and gave directions to its driver. "We'll lunch at Gustave's down Soho way; and it will be a long lunch, let me tell you. There's an old Swiss waiter there who'll give you French while he waits ... I wait—thou waitest—he waits—we wait"; and his Falstaffian girth shook with happy laughter.

But when they reached the little restaurant in Soho, Moy's Swiss friend was found to be off duty—a fortnightly holiday, it appeared; and so the project of a free lesson in French had to be dropped, for no other alien except the Swiss was now on the staff at Gustave's: all were overseas and engaged in slightly more exacting tasks than those of waiting table. During lunch, therefore, the talk drifted to other subjects than the speediest methods of acquiring modern languages; and finally to affairs in the chief's home country—to the fortunes of this family and that in the dread lottery of war: poor crofter folk and proud aristocrats, alike stricken sore. Then into the midst of the survey came a name long-forgotten. "And to think that three years ago," said Moy angrily, "that little swipe, Gurney, was hobnobbing with most of those poor lads that are gone!"

"Gurney? Was he really a twister, then?"

"'Course he was. Didn't you hear when you were home?"

"Well, yes, I did hear some stuff about Gurney—I forget what; and thought it only the usual spy-scare story."

"Story! My dear chap, that little devil had really been busy staking out hiding-places for petrol for Boche submarines, all over the island, two years before the war started, blast him! "

"Good Lord!"

"Clever, eh? Two years before they started. Fancy your thinking it all bilge! Didn't you see the posters in Edinburgh when you were there? Bills offering rewards for the discovery of secret dumps in the Outer Isles—the lonely ones, y' know?"

"Nary a bill," said MacLeod; "or I'd have told them of one hidie-hole at least. For I saw old Gurney prospecting on the hill above Kellan once upon a time."

"I know. Making sure he had enough soft earth. Yes, we got that one. But the Boche never touched it. Know why?"

"No idea."

"Sorry I can't enlighten you then, my boy. Reasons of state, y' see. But we got two others, right on the shore, bungfull of tins of spirit; both of 'em on spots where friend Gurney used to study so scientifically his nice little crabs on a shallow sea-bottom."

"They're thorough, aren't they?"

"No flies on Brother Boche—at present. But we'll see what happens later on, sonny." And the old fellow indicated his knowingness by a series of nods suggesting the profoundest secrecy. "But fancy that chap watching the Admiralty survey, and guessing jolly well what it was all about! Sending home reports and giving away our case! Faugh!"

"That survey meant the Fleet's visit to Loch-na-Keal later on, of course?"

"Sure. And a good thing we did have that survey. Imagine one of our ships falling foul of the Steeple Rock."

"You mean the new rock they found in the Kyle?"

"Yes. And big MacCormack tells me Gurney was on to the news like billy-oh."

"I remember," said MacLeod, flushing guiltily as he recalled his complicity in that affair; yet relieved to find Moy oblivious of it. "But whatever had the discovery of the reef to do with his clearing out at once?"

"Why, man alive! everything. Don't you see that some of their blasted U-boats might have smashed on that rock, if they'd been working on the old charts that didn't have it marked?"

"But their submarines were surely not out before war was declared?"

"Oho! weren't they? Austria and Serbia scrapping, and the Boche doing no preliminary scouting, eh? No, no, my boy! Old Gurney knew his job all right, even if he knew dam all about manners. Little blighter! I always said he was a wrong 'un, after the way he cheeked old Mosley."

"Yes, you were right," said MacLeod. "But it's strange MacCormack never said a word about all this to me when I saw him a fortnight ago, although he knew I was interested in Gurney."

Moy chuckled. "Oh, well," he said, "a Highlander never gives you a sore heart, if he can help it, does he?"

"But, Gurney "

"Oh, damn Gurney! Let's clear out of this, and get right on to the chaps in charge of that old hospital."

XIV: The gloves

MOY had many interviews that afternoon with people whom he described as "live wires, ab-so-lute-ly "; and on the following day MacLeod saw the British representatives of the Croix Rouge Francaise, and at once tabled his application and credentials, prominent among the latter being a letter from Moy. The post was that of surgical assistant to the Médecin-Chef of an hospital at Arc-en-Aulnoy, housed in a great château close to the Vosges, and some five hours east of Paris; the service being attached to the Army of Verdun, whence its wounded came. Taken altogether, nothing could be more inviting to a man of MacLeod's outlook; and the C.R.F. officials seemed as eager as himself to settle the business there and then. He was asked to undergo an immediate examination as to physical fitness; and this having proved satisfactory, it was intimated that he would be formally appointed at a meeting later on the same day. Meanwhile he was to hold himself in readiness; he would most likely be required in a week's time.

"Most likely!" cried Moy, when MacLeod recounted this decision. "The skunks! No nominee of mine was ever held up for a week. Are you sure they saw my letter? Never heard of such a thing!"

"The whole affair's getting rather big for them, I suppose."

"Well, there's that to it," admitted the chief reluctantly. "But in the old days all my man had to say was, 'MacKinnon of Moy,' and the affair was settled. A whole week! Tut-tut! Why, I got that Yarrow girl off two days after she spoke to me."

"Nurse Yarrow? Is she at Arc?"

"Not exactly. But in the same lot, you know— Croix Rouge. I tried for Arc, but they sent her to Orange. She likes the Frenchies. Fine patients, she says."

"Trust you've a good nurse in her place at home?"

"No, we haven't. Regular alligator of a woman. By gum! I do miss that Irish girl. Kept things lively, if you know what I mean. Well, well, another of the sacrifices of the war. We can't get all we want." And he sighed.

"She knows her work, Nurse Yarrow."

"Doesn't she. She'd tackle anything. Why, just after you left she yanked out some old tooth-stumps of mine beautifully. Saved me a fifty-mile journey to a dentist. And a fee ... Hillo! Must you go? All right. But look me up at Moy if you get a leave, will you? Stay with us and all that. And if you've any trouble out there, just mention my name. Bye-bye."

There now came a week of waiting, during which MacLeod returned to his studies; then came further delay because of submarine activity in the Channel; but at last a wire arrived saying: *Boats running. Cross to-night.* He caught the six-o'clock train at a rush that evening, and boarded the steamer at Southampton at once. His leg ached because of the unwonted bustle over luggage and visés and permits to travel—necessities for mere Red Cross people; and so he turned into his bunk forthwith.

Next morning he found the vessel still at her berth. A light mist lay on the water; but whether it was this haze, or the submarines of the enemy, that held the boat to the English shore no one seemed to know: "Admiralty orders "was the only explanation given. She did not venture out in the daylight in any case—did not, in fact, sail till seven that night, several hours before the usual time for the night-crossing; and so had to lie outside the closed gate of the protective boom at Le Havre until early morning—fair game for torpedo attack by any questing U-boat. The cessation of the engine's throb had awakened him, and he now paced the deck in a drizzle of rain, watching an unusual activity in the shore-signals—whose meaning only became plain later on, when there emerged from an opening in the boom farther north a chain of hospital ships, making for home with their quota of wounded. Decked with rows of challenging lights in red and green, each with a great luminous red cross prominent at prow and amidships, the big vessels seemed almost festal in their brilliance. But not even the knowledge that those flaming crosses ensured to the stricken men behind them a protection from attack ungranted in ancient wars, could lighten MacLeod's depression at the thought that even now new convoys of wounded from torn battle-fields were preparing for this same voyage ... The thing was interminable!

Dawn came at last and the formalities of disembarking. Then, as the Paris train did not leave till five in the afternoon, he walked leisurely to the Hotel Normandie —an old rest-house of his before Gommecourt lamed him. The Normandie was a quaint place, he remembered, with an odd salle-â-manger in a glass-covered court away behind the main building, where they served rather good meals. And you reached that salle by a long corridor with all kinds of queer little rooms opening off it. Yes, he recalled these now, as he entered and burrowed his way through a crowd of the khaki-clad in the porch. And the first door on the right led into the smoking-room, of course. He looked reminiscently into this room in the passing, and as he did so was aware of a keen scrutiny by a tall man in civilian dress, standing slightly back in the room. Something in that glance irritated—a slight hint of the supercilious, perhaps. "Only a brass-hat in mufti could afford a glare like that," thought MacLeod as he passed on to his roll and coffee. But the sense of irritation from that look remained, and several times that day, as he came and went, he slowed down to discover if the fellow were still there, but did not encounter him again.

Coffee over, he wandered out to the heights above the town; round stout fortification of an older generation, and huge gravestone manufactories of the present. There seemed miles, indeed, of these latter, and they appalled; for he remembered that the French did not publish their casualties. Yes, but the French were not too busy with the war to forget commemoration of their dead: and for a little this thought brought home to him a quiet confidence.

From the heights he limped down to the docks and the Grand Quai. The lame leg ached, but the immense ennui of this waiting-time rendered him half-oblivious of his wound. In the outer harbour a vessel lay sunk, only its blistered funnel and salt-encrusted masts above water. "Torpedoed," he thought, picturing the stricken ship struggling harbour-wards, only to fail within reach of safety; and his mind went back to the hospital ships he had seen leave port a few hours ago. Surely the enemy would never attack them; the Red Cross must still mean something. Yet even that might come if they grew desperate. Skin for skin then; and they would stop at nothing. Hospital ships?—Hospitals?— Marion?—He wondered if by any chance she had been transferred to work at sea. She might even have been on one of last night's ships—those big fellows with the red and green lights. Three years since he had seen her. And Gurney—where now was he? Queer the fascination that old chap had for a mere girl like Marion. What in all the earth could be the bond between them? Art, he supposed— no barriers of race for art. But strange that the link should be so strong. He could not get the hang of it. Well, wherever Gurney was, he was the enemy—had always been, most likely. With the submarine lot, too! Good God! he might at this very moment be sinking her ship—Marion's ship!

Tuts! he was dithering; his imagination was running wild. There was no reason to think she had left the Bethune sector. Busy enough there, poor girl; a far cry for her nowadays to the quiet of Eilean Aros. And what was there in this Gurney affair, after all? Nothing, except some gossip of Moy's; and one knew, of course, how legends grew in the Isles. Spy mania—that was it. All nonsense most likely.

And yet—? Faugh! let him get out of sight of that rusty funnel, or he would go daft. And then he did the daftest of things; for he wandered back to the bleak town, and, entering a shop, bought a pair of gloves for Marion. As he came up to the counter and its fussy attendant, he did not know what he wanted: distraction seemed his only need—he must buy something for somebody. And here he was, ensuring a closer focusing of his thoughts on the one subject he would most avoid. The gloves were white and had wattled gauntlets. Celtic, this wattled business—she'd like that. The size was probably all wrong, the price high; and a war majoration, only disclosed when it came to payment, made it higher still; but the gloves were now Marion's. He might never have a chance to give them to her, but they were hers—a gage he could flaunt in the eyes of a spectral Gurney, daring him to do his worst. Futile enough all this; yet he felt comforted, as he took his seat in the Paris train that afternoon, with the little parcel still in his hand.

It was dark when he arrived in Paris, and he made at once across town in a taxi to deposit his luggage at the Gare de l'Est against to-morrow's journey. Here he found the approaches to the station lined by the recumbent forms of soldiers in horizon-blue, ghostly in the light of a frosty moon: some new move was to a certainty being made on the French front. And the hotels were packed with the officers of the *poilus*, so that it was with difficulty he secured a bed. Next morning a scurry for the Chaumont train; and, later, a descent in that town in the midst of a heavy snowfall. Then another cold wait till the starting time of a train on the little sideline that ran close to the Aulnoy hospital. But his journey was now nearing its end: this was to be the last of railways for him for many a long day; and when the voice of a Cockney chauffeur hailed him at Latrecy station, he sighed in relief. Instantly he was whisked off in the auto through miles of poplars and snow-banks showing fitfully in a night now moonless. Then came the château gates, and he entered a huge porch decorated with the stuffed heads of wild-boars that grinned forbiddingly at him in a faint lamplight. An elderly French servant appeared, and, announcing himself as the gardien of the château, led the way upstairs and down a corridor to a great room, where MacLeod, now thoroughly tired by his long journey, sank at once into an arm-chair set before a stone fireplace where glowed a fire of logs.

"Monsieur is fatigued?" asked the old man in poor English.

MacLeod admitted that he was. "But this is good," he said, stretching himself luxuriously. "What a big room!"

"But, yes, monsieur," said the attendant, busy with hot water and towels. "The room is perfect, except for the mirror."

MacLeod looked up. A long crack ran across an upper corner of the great glass over the stone mantel. "Oh, that's all right," he said. "The crack's nothing."

"Ah, but yes, M. le Major, it is something. It was made by the Boche."

"Good Heavens! They haven't been here, have they?"

"Not in this war, monsieur; but in the last—in 'seventy. But this time they shall not pass."

"Jamais! "cried MacLeod, flourishing Marion's parcelled gloves at the shattered glass. "Â bas tous les Gurneys!"

Puzzled, the old man halted, then bowed. "Of a certainty, monsieur," said he, and departed.

XV: A late post

THE room was indeed large; but, more than that, its walls were decorated by a pattern of golden fleurs-de-lis on a ground of blue. He remembered that the château belonged to an old Orleans family, and that royalty itself was claimed by those lilies of France. Certainly a change from the trenches, this—almost worth a stiff knee; and he chuckled as he set to his toilet. As he finished dressing, he noted that the big windows were vibrating; and he applied the usual test: on opening one the vibration ceased, on closing it the tremor was renewed—a bombardment at some distance evidently.

A knock came to his door, and in response to his "Come in," a tall stout man in khaki entered. "Bowlitt's my name," he said: "Médecin-Chef here. Glad you've come, Doctor." They shook hands. "You'll want a bite, of course. We're just finishing dinner, but we'll scrap up something for you." MacLeod declared himself well fed, having had a good meal at Chaumont. "Well, come and have a coffee; and let me introduce you to our lot."

He led the way to a corridor on the ground floor, pushed open a door, and brought MacLeod into a rather badly lit salle where three women and a dozen or so of men sat at table. Introductions were made, and he sat down to coffee. The ladies were the Directrice of the hospital and her sister—English gentlewomen, who looked after the business side of the unit, supplies and money matters generally: alert, pleasant people of fifty-five or thereabouts; the third was the Matron, a cautious Irishwoman, a little bewildered by the fact that nursing in war-time meant so many men, other than patients, about the place. Bowlitt's aides were Henson, a young American, lanky and untidy, in a dingy volunteer uniform of the U.S. Red Cross (for as yet the States had not come into the war); and Leclercq, a French Army doctor, a youth in horizon-blue, invalided home from Salonika because of a bad chronic malaria, but now almost convalescent. The Frenchman, grave-faced but with a quaint humour, was talking to the Directrice, excusing the lateness of that day's post, as MacLeod entered. He had also to reply to a general charge by the lady of procrastination in all things French, even in peace-time. "No, no," said he earnestly; "the post will come to-night. It is the railway that is embarrassed because of the movement to Berry-au-Bac: that is all. And we do pot procrastinate. Myself, I was never late for a train in all my life! "Then, with a smile, "Or, if I was late, I catch another train that get me to my place, before the one that I miss." He sipped his coffee, and grimaced as he did so. "Pas de sucre! "he cried. "And no post! ... Quelle guerre!"

MacLeod glanced round at the others—orderlies or chauffeurs—all over age, or with disabilities that kept them from acceptance by the British Army. Among them were several elderly artists of some note—a solicitor from Rangoon; a retired Civil Servant from the Straits Settlements; a public-school boy of eighteen with congenital cataract; a Canadian youth, weak-chested and slightly deaf; two elderly Irishmen—one a civil engineer from Belfast, the other an industrial magnate from Dublin — both said to be high-speed wonders with motor-ambulances; and a scion of the English nobility—the oldest of the company, but a younger son—all the way from a ranch in Montana.

The Directrice, with a smile, apologized for her inability to present more than one historian, a slight dark man of fifty—an authority on matters Napoleonic; but she added that quite recently she had, as chief-orderly, the author of a six-volume history of France, now transferred to the Intelligence Staff in Whitehall. "And I'm sorry we have no poets just now," she said, "although six months ago we had several." She mentioned two quite considerable names in English letters, and jestingly added: "We must really order a few more poets, Dr. Bowlitt; they are always such good carpenters. Those last fracture-beds were very good, weren't they? But that dreadful Intelligence Department has such a liking for poets, we don't have a chance nowadays." It transpired, however, that Edwards, the Rangoon lawyer, was quite handy with plane and saw, although his strong point was cleaning the château windows; and the Honourable from Montana could make a nurse's table quite passably, although his special field was the kitchen garden. MacLeod was, indeed, a trifle dazzled by this recital. Not quite the *Arabian Nights*, he thought, but jolly near it.

Kelsall, the half-blind public-school boy, now claimed his attention. "Ever play rugger? " he asked in his hoarse voice, sizing up the surgeon's build peeringly.

"No," said MacLeod, "but I used to push-bike a lot. Country doctor, you see."

"I know," sympathized Matron. "Hard work."

"Yes, but keeps you fit," said Kelsall, and returned to a description of Morse signalling he was giving to his neighbour on the other side, the Canadian. His voice was naturally strong, but his auditor's deafness seemed to suggest the need for his raising it still further, and he so dominated the table that all had perforce to listen.

"Once got me into a beastly mess—knowing about Morse. Last year, that was. I was motor-biking down in Cornwall—"

"But wasn't motor-biking dangerous? I mean, do you see well enough for that?"

"Oh, I dunno. The other chaps keep out of the way, if you go fast enough. Well, it was a hot summer, that; and when I came up to the house of a chap I knew at school, I thought I'd touch him for a drink. So I barged in. It was hot, I can tell you: the french windows were open; and I went in to look for him. Nobody about. But there was a wireless set tick-ticking on the table. ' Hallo!' I said,' Morse? ' So I sat down to it. Knew the chap well, you see. And, just to give him a hand, I started taking down the message. It was a wireless from the big station, Poldhu, and I'd just nicely begun, when Flitter—that's my friend—well, Flitter comes in, and half-strangles me. Didn't recognize me at first; but even when he did, he kept on getting excited, and asked me to clear out. Not the least chance of a drink; so I had to go; and not a word of explanation of all the fuss he'd made. Not like a chap who'd been to school with you, was it? And I came away, quite cross. Then, in the afternoon, he came over to my hotel in the village, and explained things. Told me he was in the secret service, and that I'd been butting into his stuff. Funny chap! How was I to know what his job was?"

"Which side was he on? "asked the Montana rancher quietly. "What do you mean?"

"I mean, was he British or Jerry?"

"British, of course. He was at the same school as myself."

"Don't see what his school had to do with it. Queer name, Flitter."

"Well, as a matter of fact, he had Jerry connections, but those were away back in his grandfather's time. And that was quite useful, for he was in both secret services, British and Boche. Quite common for our chaps to be in both, you know."

"And how do you know which side Flitter was really for? "asked Scales, the historian.

"Man alive! he was at school with me," persisted the youth.

"Well, I think you should let our lot know about that chap even yet," said Featherly, the rancher. "They'll jolly soon make out which side he's on."

Kelsall relapsed into an angry silence at once; and the stillness after so much shouting was awkward. But Lang, the Dubliner, broke in in his rich brogue: "J'ever notice a fellow in the smoke-room of the Hotel Normandie in Havre?" he asked. "Always struck me as likely to be one of them secret service boys. Tall chap with eyes like gimlets—standing well back in the doorway."

"Saw him last night," said MacLeod. "Gave me the shivers."

"Did he that, now? "said Lang. "Same with me. I'll bet he was one of them fellows."

"But which side, d'ye think? "queried old Featherly.

"Oh, give it a rest," said the American, Henson. "You guys have been reading dime novels. You make me feared. I'm sweating like a nigger under oath." He grinned and cracked a walnut, adding to the huge pile of shells already beside his plate.

There came suddenly into the quiet of the dim-lit room a sound as of great iron doors being slammed in the heavens. "They begin," said Leclercq. MacLeod looked an inquiry. "Verdun," said the Frenchman.

"Thought it was fifty miles off?"

"Yes; but we stand high here—five hundred metres. It gets across all right," boomed the Médecin-Chef.

"Something of poetic in that sound—at a distance," said Leclercq, shrugging shoulders cynically.

"You been there? "asked MacLeod.

"With the guns, yes. But not at Verdun, as yet. Perhaps later."

"No, no, M. Leclercq," protested the Directrice. "You must stay with us a little longer. You are so useful with the Minister of War. And just presently I want another franc a day for each of our *poilus*—an additional grant."

"Ah, mademoiselle, then you must find someone who knows a Deputy."

She affected horror. "Politics! "she cried. "No; that kind of thing is not for us. We will avoid the Deputies, if you please."

Aristocrat, he bowed at the compliment. "It is delicious, that," he said. "You understand to perfection, mademoiselle."

The ladies rose; and, soon after, the men drifted off to their billets throughout the village, or to their rooms in the château.

"You won't mind not seeing the wards to-night," said Bowlitt to MacLeod. "Most of the men are asleep very early here. But come into my office and I'll give you the hang of things—papers and all that." He led the way to a little bow-windowed room, where the lamps shone as feebly as elsewhere in the building, yet were able to light an arc of snow-covered shrubbery out of doors. "Snow?" said the Médecin-Chef, looking out. "Yes, no wonder the post is late. Well, here are the forms—bags of them—more than the British by a long chalk. Just fancy! a special sheet for the kind of metal that lays out a chap." He tossed over a paper. "Hope your French is good. Mine isn't. Hallo, here's the post-bag all the time! Why the devil didn't Henri tell me! "

He grabbed a sack and emptied it hurriedly on a table, searched for his own letters feverishly, and picked out a journal for MacLeod. "Care to see the *Daily Mail*? Paris Edition, of course. Excuse me while I run through my little lot. But I must take the rest to Henri, old fool! He'll have the devil of a job, distributing them so late." And he departed hurriedly with the bag; while MacLeod took off the newspaper's wrapper languidly enough, and opened the sheet. Flaring head-lines were everywhere; and one gripped his attention instantly: *Red Cross No Longer Sacred*, he read ... *U-Boat Sinks Hospital Ship in Bristol Channel*. Mechanically he ran his eye down the list of the missing, then started to his feet to come closer to the lamp and make sure he read aright ... Yes: it was Marion's name.

Dazed, he crushed the paper in his hand, and stared out at the snow-shrouded shrubbery. Now and again the big iron doors slammed in the sky over distant Verdun; but between-whiles all was very still. A telephone bell rang suddenly close to his ear; and just then Bowlitt entered, and took up the receiver. "Chaumont, I expect," he said. He began to answer the call in slow bad French, then set down the instrument. "A take-in," he said. "Twenty cases at Chaumont about one-thirty. You'll be too tired to go, of course?" "My God! no," said MacLeod, smoothing out the newspaper nervously, and returning it to him. "Work! —that's the thing! "And somewhere deep within he was telling himself again and again that this thing could not be ... Marion ... Marion ...?

XVI: Take-in

HALF AN HOUR after midnight four ambulances set out from the château for Chaumont, and he went with them. Work—work, at last. Anything to hide that vision of Marion's head sinking in dark waters.

The quiet of the snow-clad country, the straight white roads with their flanking lines of black poplars, the stillness of Chaumont asleep—mediaeval it looked with its irregular gables winding streets and wide Place: all these, and the silence now of the Verdun guns, accorded little with thoughts of war. But at the great station all was changed, for close outside it were newly dug trenches, hacking the carpet of snow. What could this portend? Chaumont stood on the next range of hills west of Verdun. Was the fall of the great fortress imminent? and was time being taken by the forelock here? Was the next stand against the Boche to be on this ground? ... Inside the station all was bustle, for the train with the wounded had arrived before time. All kinds of sous-officiers moved rapidly about, pencil and paper in hand. The station commandant appeared at a corridor entrance in the train, and beckoned to Bowlitt, who saluted and went in with him to select his cases. The Aulnoy bearers brought their stretchers on the platform, only to remove them almost at once to allow passage to some *poilus* blinded by tear-gas, who, linked arm-in-arm in groups of four, stumbled along, shepherded by orderlies. They were to await a train taking them to a hospital in the south, set aside for such injuries; for the French had at length found time to create special centres for different types of wounded.

(Marion ... Marion!)

"Gee! "said Henson, coming up to MacLeod. "See that? Nix of that lot for us. I'd have liked a few of them. Haven't seen any tear-gas as yet."

The young surgeon said nothing in reply, but looked after the disabled men hobbling past on scorched feet, their legs encased in uncouth wrappings improvised from old newspapers and bits of string, their heads enormous with white bandages, their swollen eyelids thick with gummy pus—forlorn and helpless all of them. He was thankful they had fallen into other hands than those of Henson and himself: clearly they were better off in the care of specialists.

"I hear we're not to have any jaw cases, either," went on the American gloomily. "They've got some blamed special hospital at Langres for them.

Stomatologic they call it. Damn all experience we'll get here, if they start that game."

"Oh, blow the experience."

Henson grinned. "You make me squeal," he said. "Think we're going to win out?"

"Yes."

"Say," said the American, "what about this battle of the Marne? Who got best there?"

"We did."

"Gawn! What makes you think that?"

"Jerry went back."

"He was just tired, I guess."

"Yes, and we weren't."

"Gosh! Queer guys, you Scotties."

He sauntered off, a strangely dispassionate colleague, but with an engaging quality of frankness. Clearly he did not make the common mistake of discounting the strength of the enemy; and he evidently saw much on the side of the Allies that amused by its futility. But the stretcher-cases for Aulnoy were now being conveyed from the train, and the American and MacLeod were separated for a little as they busied themselves adjusting dressings before the removal of the men to the ambulance-wagons. A secondary haemorrhage in one of the last cases, however, brought them together again; and, as they finished the final bandaging, Henson took up the discussion once more. "Say, Mac," he said. "Ever hear of the Alaskan boundary quarrel?"

"Yes, States and Canada, wasn't it?"

"Yep. And I don't know why our people didn't let you have it in the neck, that go!"

"Don't you know why? "asked MacLeod.

"Nope."

"'Cause you weren't Boche."

"Gee!" said the American, "I'll hoot no more"; and off he went, somewhat shamefacedly, to take his seat in the ambulance next to MacLeod's.

(Marion ... Marion!)

Back at the château, the wounded were ranged hurriedly on the floor of the porch, and given some *bouillon* by Matron, while the Médecin-Chef inspected the red labels detailing the nature of each casualty, and ordered the patients to this ward and that.

And now a strange figure came downstairs—one that might have stepped out of a portrait by Holbein: a little lady in a gown of cherry-coloured silk, a loose jacket of grey brocade, and a coif that matched the latter. She had with her a very ordinary and un-Holbein-like pail of zinc and a supply of feeding-cups, one after another of which she dipped in her pail and handed to the wounded.

"Pinard! "cried the *poilus* joyously (their slang for *vin ordinaire*), and faces, dull a moment before, brightened marvellously.

"A moi—pinard!" came from every side, and cups were held up greedily for replenishing by the lady in the gown of cerise. One striking face among the soldiers did not smile, MacLeod noted, a dark-visaged man, who drank his portion philosophically, and on returning his cup said: "Ah, la guerre heureuse!—Merci, mademoiselle!" The surgeon bent over him, and asked his name, just as the bearers came to take him to his ward.

"Koechlin, sergeant," said the man in good English, adding, "—of Alsace. Not much wound. Shrapnel, right leg, M. le Major." And, grave and composed, he was borne away.

Bowlitt, coming forward, found MacLeod staring in perplexity at the strangely garbed little lady, and grinned in amusement. "Let me introduce you to Mademoiselle Pinard," he said; "at least that's what our fellows call her"; and he brought him forward. "Miss Torrance, this is our new aide, Dr. MacLeod. Another Scot, so I need say no more." He smiled again, and departed.

The surgeon found himself looking down into the clear blue eyes of a woman of forty-five or so, as they shook hands. "I'm Forfar," she said. "What are you?"

"Argyll. More exactly, Eilean Aros."

"My dear! "she cried, "you're a sicht for sair e'en. And you know MacKinnon of Moy, I hear?"

"Yes; he got me this job."

"Me, too. Then you know Nurse Yarrow, of course? She's from Moy."

MacLeod started. "Is she here? "he asked.

"No, no, still at Orange. I was there for three months before I came on to this place. I say! we must start a Scots Society here."

"A Society of Two? "he asked, smiling.

"Why not? Two Scots are more than a match for a pair of the other kind.—Save us! here's Dr. Bowlitt again! If he heard that, he'll slay me." And picking up the now empty wine-bucket, she ran off, her cherry-coloured skirt an oriflamme on the great stair.

"Just wanted to say we won't need you further to-night," said Bowlitt, coming up. "You must be dog-tired. I'll take you round wards in the morning. Yours are Salle Foch and Salle Kitchener. Glad you've found a countrywoman of your own here."

"Who on earth is she?"

"The Honourable Grizell Torrance of that ilk, as your people say. Jolly good sort; but she lives 'way back in history. Mary Queen of Scots, the

Auld Alliance, and all that sort of thing. Hasn't forgotten Flodden yet. And we English haven't a chance when she gets down to The Border Ballads. That dress of hers came from France about Mary's time, I'll bet." "Why don't you put her in uniform?" "My dear chap! consider the assortment we have here—poets, historians, artists and. so on. And see what a mess they make of their uniforms. Well, if you ask me, they're no longer uniforms; they're fancy dress. But they all work damn hard, and we'd be glad to have 'em, even in straw hats and pyjamas. Talking of pyjamas, what about bed for you now, right away?"

They said good night, and MacLeod departed brooding on his strange entourage, a motley assembly of people bewildered by the catastrophe of war, and seeking peace of mind in service of any sort.—He wondered if Gibbon had any instances of the kind. Sure to have. Who was it that said all history was modern history? Not bad that. He turned up his lamp, rootled among a pell-mell of books and surgical instruments, found the volume, and sat down by his log-fire to read once more in the tale of ancient Rome. History? That Mississippi of fiction, Arnold had called it. Let's see: where was he at his last reading?—The tremor of his windows was again audible. Four o'clock in the morning; snow everywhere; and yet the big guns were once more busy. Well, those guns weren't fiction, anyway; nor that crack in his mirror, witness to the conflict of fifty years ago. The logs gleamed generously; and, extending himself on a couple of chairs, he read for a little; then lulled by the drumming of the distant bombardment, he drowsed. The volume slipped from his fingers to lie open on the hearth of stone, and register by tiny shakings of its leaves the tremor in the air from the Verdun guns. A little later and the vibration, by its repetitions, detached a crumble of hot wood-ash from the fire. It fell on the pages of august Gibbon, scorching the paper a trifle before it died. One way at least, contemptuous perhaps, for Verdun to leave a mark on history.

(Marion in his dreams ... Marion!)

XVII: Personnel

THERE then was MacLeod's new post: sub-chief of a type of hospital known as a "mixed unit"; and with all kinds of odd people serving under him.

Henson, his American aide, intrigued him by the aptness of his slang, his strange oaths, and his humour. A difficult surgical dressing would be described as "scuffling around that wound for twenty minutes, and hot as the hinges of Hell." The epilogue of his recipe for a strawberry shortbread was no less picturesque: "Wal, having made it, you jest give thanks to the Almighty and hoe in." But his summary of President Wilson was his masterpiece. "Gosh! he's a champion at spilling words! And as for doves of peace—why, he's a reg'lar incubator."

Leclercq, hearing his last saying, capped it irrelevantly but in language almost as quaint: "Ver' American. Ah! A thing that remembers me!—an American whom I have found. He say that it was a great day for the worl' when America discover Europe in the person of Christopher Columbus."

"You've rimmed me there," said Henson.

An unusually interesting group were the stretcher-bearers—men who fetched and carried all day long; their heaviest tasks the transport of the wounded into the sunlight of the park, and back again to the wards at night, or the transfer of casualties from train at Chaumont to ambulances and thence to hospital. But there were also the stoving of uniforms temporarily discarded by the soldiers, sanitary duty, scrubbing of corridors, or cleaning of windows—all hard work for elderly litterateurs or artists. Then they had an infinity of small tasks—the transit of wash-baskets to the laundry, attendance on chloroform-sickness after operation, amateur carpentry, storage of wood-fuel, collection of eggs from the neighbouring farmers, or shopping in Chaumont— work that the constant rumble of the Verdun guns seemed to make a mock of, growling insistently as they did, that only up there was the real thing—this petty stuff down below only skiddle. Nerve-racking all this; and these men, counting the years of their age with wry faces, set about their jobs with an assumption of gaiety they were far from feeling. But at times even small tasks became scanty, and then the brancardiers prowled around inventing new ones, lest *cafard*, the Frenchman's black dog of *ennui*, should perch on their shoulders. At such seasons steam was usually let off by denunciation of the politicians at home. "Don't you think, Doctor, we should hang Asquith?" asked Hemingway, a dark gipsy-like man of fifty, an artist whose serious face was belied by a simplicity of mind almost Pickwickian. MacLeod thought such an execution wouldn't mend matters; and immediately Hemingway appealed plaintively: "But I do think Lloyd George ought to be hanged—-don't you?" His dark eyes implored agreement, but receiving no answer except a smile, he departed, meditating gloomily on his dream of politicians pendant.

Regarding the war's progress Hem was definitely pessimistic; and his conclusion on that score he confided to MacLeod. "It would be much easier to pray for a mild winter than the end of this war. Because, y' know, that would take a lot of people and a long time." But his difficulties about politics and the war were as nothing to those he experienced in matters of religion. "Y' know, Doctor, when I begin to think about these things, I get all tied up in knots. Well, it's a queer world, and on the whole I don't think I like it."

It was, however, on Barling that slack seasons of work told most of all. He was a young Canadian; and, deaf and weak-chested, he felt himself specially helpless in slack seasons as he mooned around, occasionally playing a little on the dining-room pianoforte, oftener loafing by himself in some dark corner. "Don't you know," he tried to explain to MacLeod, "sometimes you want to be alone, and sometimes you'd rather have someone with you." And the irony of the affair was that the doctor could only console by promising him a fresh batch of wounded before long—people so badly gassed that their chests were worse than his, or robbed of their hearing by shrapnel as thoroughly as he had been by disease.

Street, who had care of the dispensary as well as duties as stretcher-bearer, was an offset to Hem and Barling. In civil life he was a painter, and here, in the war-zone, he was still supremely the artist at heart. Fair-complexioned, hook-nosed and prematurely bald, his mind belied his odd exterior; and in his off-duty hours he was ever busy with his crayons, making rough drawings of this odd gable or that quaint line of poplars — notes of line or light repeated again and again, how speedily and yet how fastidiously. And to all the talk that flowed around him about the changed earth that was to arise from the ashes of the war, his only comment was that his one desire was to get back to old ways of work. Revolution itself, it seemed, could make no change in the world of visioned beauty wherein he dwelt. Shyly he quoted a brother-artist: "Friend of mine says there are only two things in life, y'know—painting and not-painting."

Leclercq answered him gravely: "Ver' true. And the not-painting include the war, which is a serious war. Also the question social. After Mont Corneille in the Chemin des Dames there is trouble—revolt, you say— in our Army. We shall have Socialism. It must come. And the people must have some to lead. Also it is we who must lead—the young men who are educate. But we must study Socialism first—that is our task—so that we shall be able to lead."

Then there was talk of *Le Feu* by Barbusse, of Duhamel's *Vie des Martyrs*, and of the need for a true picture of the war being broadcast to the world. The nations must know what this thing really meant.

These moody ponderings on days to come were frequent among the hospital's personnel; and were resented not a little by Lang, the Irish civil engineer turned ambulance driver. No sooner did he discover such a conclave than he swooped down on its gloom. "What's all this grousing?" he would cry breezily. "Sure, this is a beaucoup place. And I'm that happy I don't know if it's to-day or to-morrow. Here! have some of these cherries picked by the sweat of me own brow" —or some such tomfoolery. A regular antidote to *cafard*, old Lang.

The nurses too had conspiracies for brightening up the staff: there was, for instance, a group whose special duty when off work was the organization of stunts to this end, one of their tasks being "cheering up Chumley"—a nurse unusually despondent about the universe generally. Their work was ghastly enough at times, poor girls! and reaction from it was really at the root of much of their playfulness when off duty: a gaiety too often misunderstood by the grave villagers, who wore black every Sunday, and remembered their dead. Gayest of all among the nurses was little Harvey, whose laugh was often heard the moment MacLeod entered her ward; some mistranslation of a patient's French, perhaps, having aroused her sense of the world's topsyturvydom. "Oh, Doctor," she would cry, shocked at her own levity, "if I hadn't been a Methody parson's daughter, what would I have been!"

XVIII: The happy war

IN his first days at the château, thoughts of Marion were often with MacLeod; and he was amazed to find himself so greatly moved by her death. He had seen so little of her—only came into momentary contact with the fringes of her life in the ordinary boy and girl romance. Yet there had been a strange spiritual quality about the girl—something fey, as the old Scots would name it; and he felt that he had been in touch with an experience rarer than he had guessed in those earlier days. Her mere presence then had seemed to lift his world into a finer air; and now the memory of her made great issues appear less unlikely from a life so poor in spirit as his own. Duty seemed easier, and the mystery of all things could be more confidently faced, because he had known her. Strange the persistence of that influence-—a compelling power of stillness and resource somewhere deep within.

Thus he came to his new task with an elation of spirit long foreign to him; and soon was eagerly busy with the routine at the château—ward-visits, dressings and operations in the mornings; official papers and administrative work in the afternoons; while every two weeks or so a discharge of convalescents, or a take-in of new wounded, had to be dealt with. And occasional surgical cases from the civilian population around had also to be operated; for there were comparatively few native doctors left in the district, so great had been the holocaust among French medical men at the onset of the war.

About a month after his arrival, Bowlitt, who suffered from some cardiac trouble, had to resign in order to return to England for treatment; and the responsibilities of a Médecin-Chef now became MacLeod's. But, except on the official side, these added little to his work: receptions of the French authorities inspecting the hospital, or the decoration of some wounded hero, made up the most of it. The biggest worry in his relations with the French was perhaps with the authorities at Marac, in their supervision of the English personnel at the château; for they seemed unduly nervous as to espionage, fearing the inclusion among the rather unusual staff there of some enemy agent, and so were strict as to the movements outside the commune of the hospital workers. But an offset to this restraint came about this time with the arrival of American troops in the Aulnoy district. The Americans were easy as regards discipline of any kind; and as they ultimately took over the policing of the village, le Capitan Bee at Marac relaxed restrictions considerably, and contented himself with occasional *communiqués* to MacLeod regarding possible spies in the persons of applicants for the post of masseuse: adventuresses, it would appear from his letters, of quite melodramatic type.

Administrative details, however, were secondary considerations for MacLeod; his work for the wounded interested him most. Good patients—slight, dark, alert fellows mainly, they were cheerful and well-behaved. Their disabilities were largely shrapnel requiring removal, or septic fractures of arm or leg—comparatively simple work; but at times cases of more difficult type appeared, where brain or nerve operations were necessary, and MacLeod had good cause to bless the surgical training he had undergone in London, scanty although it had been.

The oddities among his patients especially intrigued him: Joseph, the Breton, who in fine weather played child-like with toys, and when thunder was in the air hid under blankets, and cried that the devil was abroad; Aubré, the thigh-amputation, who had a passion for surreptitious cycling on a borrowed bike in the avenues of the park; Quatrecóte of the Chasseurs Alpins, who sang *Sidi-Brahim*—the wild battle-hymn of his regiment—so softly to himself in all kinds of obscure corners, while he fondled his wounded arm with savage care—a legacy of hate still to be avenged. Then there was Koechlin, the Alsatian, grave to melancholy, whose almost only words were: "Oh, la-la, la guerre heureuse!" MacLeod had one day asked this man the meaning of his oft-repeated phrase, and the soldier had explained that it was a saying of the Crown Prince's on the eve of a special attack upon Verdun. "At last" — he was reported to have cried—" at last we shall have a fresh and happy war! "Beyond this the Alsatian said little; yet MacLeod felt that something lay behind his habitual sadness greater than mere bitterness at the cynicism of the German princeling. But what that was did not come to light till some six weeks later, when, Koechlin's leg having healed, he was allowed out of doors, with the freedom of the village as bounds, and so set in motion a train of events that might well have seemed fantastic to an observer from any other area of the army zone than this secluded backwater of Arc-en-Aulnoy.

Koechlin had been quiet at first, showing little of the restiveness of other patients in like case, some of whom at this stage disappeared for a whole night of jollification. The Alsatian seemed the last man of whom such a breach of discipline could be suspected; but one evening he was reported as indubitably "pas couché"at the hour of retiring, and by morning he had not returned. The fellow's moroseness was perhaps significant of dark things. Recently one of their patients had taken his own life, two days after his return to the trenches—a man just as reticent as Koechlin.

MacLeod was alarmed—not only for the safety of the man, but for the good repute of the hospital. An English unit under supervision of the French military authorities had to be carefully nursed: there were so many misunderstandings. Also the factor of racial difference had entered so much of late into his people's dealings with the French; and petty jealousies had abounded. A mess-up about Koechlin might involve them all in a row with that fool of a captain at Marac —might ultimately end, indeed, in the relegation of the hospital from Class A to Class B. From simple perturbation MacLeod passed rapidly to a condition of extreme neurasthenia ... An all-night exposure of Koechlin in the woods would play hell with his wounded leg ... All kind of wild fancies possessed the surgeon ... An amputation might be necessary—and God knows what else!

But he pulled himself together, made inquiries with as little fuss as possible, and at length learned that the gate-porter was thought to know something about the truant. MacLeod went to see him at once. "What's this about Koechlin?" he asked. "Where is he, Renaud?"

The old fellow stammered a rambling tale. He had heard that the gendarmerie had captured a Boche near Courlévéque yesterday, and that the fugitive had confessed to his companion in adventure being still in the woods near by. The porter confided this news to Koechlin, who in turn told him that he believed the Boche was in hiding in the Calvaire Wood, close to the château. He had seen traces there which were suspicious—a bed of fern and so on. Then the Alsatian had become excited, and, swearing Renaud to secrecy, proposed taking a lone hand in the hunt. The porter tried to dissuade him; but Koechlin borrowed a revolver— indeed forced the old fellow to give it up—and disappeared.

MacLeod returned instantly to hospital to take counsel with Leclercq. That officer had also been making investigations, and could now tell him that Koechlin had been seen early that morning leaving Aubepierre, a village some six kilometres away. They agreed to set about a search as soon as feasible, but for the present to keep the matter to themselves; the fewer who knew of Koechlin's adventure, the easier would be their relations with le Capitan at Marac. If they were to do anything, however, they must hurry the afternoon's work; for the morning's operations could not be postponed, and it was a full morning. But the afternoon turned out almost as busy as the morning—there were many official papers to do, as well as a discharge of some twenty patients, now healed and *en permission.* At eight they were clear, and set off—Leclercq to Aubepierre, and MacLeod to the Calvaire Wood—both to meet at the château by eleven that night and compare notes. A daft business, the surgeon told himself, but the only way to save their faces before that Marac crowd.

MacLeod knew his lame leg would hinder him in the undergrowth of the forest, and remembering a central clearing of plough-land, he made for this. By careful scrutiny of the fringes of the wood with a field-glass he assured himself he could do better work there than by exploration of the forest paths. He had, however, to cross a section of the wood in order to reach the clearing, and at one spot where anemones flowered profusely, there came a crashing in the brake that alarmed. He grasped his loaded whangie in readiness for attack; for the escaped Boche had still to be considered. But in the dim recesses of the undergrowth he glimpsed a lumbering animal form, and presently came upon signs of rooting in soft earth—a wild-boar for a certainty. The encounter set his nerves on edge, and he proceeded more cautiously as he reached the side of the clearing on the hill-top—an expanse of broken soil that dipped to the south over the crest of a hill with a sky-line that was treeless. Far away on this rim of earth the silhouette of a peasant unyoking his team of horse and bullock from a plough showed plainly, just as the Angelus chimes floated up from the valley. No use hailing that fellow, thought MacLeod, for if Koechlin were in the wood, he too would be watching the labourer's movements. He seated himself on a fallen trunk, and taking up his field-glasses scanned the arc of the forest's edge. But no hint of uniform appeared, although he repeated his survey again and again, hoping that at some moment the Alsatian would emerge to cross the open or to reconnoitre.

The Angelus ceased; the horizon-line was unbroken now by the figure of the ploughman; stillness was everywhere save for an occasional rumble of distant guns. The sky darkened a little, a drizzle of rain ensued, and visibility was distinctly less good.

Patience—patience. He must wait. And then came the sound of a wood-cutter's axe in the forest some distance off. "Funny thing—working after the Angelus," thought MacLeod. "Best investigate" and, skirting the forest margin, he made for the direction of the sounds. At the point where they were plainest he burrowed in the undergrowth. The wet thicket was close-set, and soon he was half-sodden; but his eagerness made him oblivious to this, for he heard more clearly now; and he could swear that this was no charcoal-burner busy beyond the usual hours of work. No axe or chopper ever gave blows so dull: plainly they came now to the ear—the strokes of a spade digging in heavy earth.

He pushed stealthily farther into the wood-depths; all at once there fell a silence; and he waited till some minutes had passed—still as the fir-bole he leant against. Then came the sound of twigs crackling. Something or someone was brushing through the thicket on his right. He peered in that direction; an opening in the branches caught his eye, and beyond the opening a patch of blackened earth—the site certainly of a charcoal-burner's activities at some time or other. He moved his head to bring more of the tiny clearing into his eyes' range, and checked suddenly, for there was the spade. What else? The gloom here was trying. What could it be? At last he saw—a mound of clayey soil, and beside it a grave.

He turned to the right, seeking the cause of the other sounds he had heard; and, as he turned, beheld the face of the man he sought, peering in bewilderment through some boughs of larch. On the instant the Alsatian advanced timidly, a scraggy figure—his uniform clay-stained and torn. "Ah, c'est M. le Major," he said, standing at attention.

"What foolishness is this, mon vieux? "asked MacLeod. "You know you are breaking bounds? You know that I can order a fortnight's cells for you once you return to your regiment?"

"But yes, M. le Major."

"What does this mean? "He pointed to the pit of clay.

"Voilà!"said the soldier. "He is there." He pointed to the obscurities under the low fir-boughs he had just left.

MacLeod crossed the blackened space and peered into the thicket, where lay the figure of a man clad in dark fustian. No need to ask who he was: the mark of the Courbon prison-camp was there—a patch of bright blue sewn into the cloth of the right knee. He touched the slack eyeball. "Dead," he said.

"Oui, monsieur, last night ... The gendarmerie capture the first man ... This is the second."

"There will be all hell to pay for this, Koechlin. Was he dead when you found him?"

Koechlin hid his eyes with his hands, and his shoulders heaved; then he uncovered a face of anguish. "C'est Armand, monsieur. C'est mon frère."

"Brother?"cried MacLeod.

"Oui, monsieur. I go to bury him. Pas Boche, Armand. He must lie in the soil of France."

The surgeon understood now. "Alsace," he said. "Of course, that's it."

"Monsieur comprend?"

"Yes, yes. Terrible."

"Oh, la, la! the happy war!" said Koechlin, seating himself on the mound of sods, and covering his face again with his hands. MacLeod stood silent, waiting; and after a little the soldier spoke. "In July, monsieur—before the war begin, I see that the war will come; and I hasten from Alsace to la Suisse, and then go from there to France, in time for the mobilization. But my brother is too late; he try to do the same, two week after; and he is seized at the frontier and forced to take arms for the Boche ... I hear from my friends in la Suisse, you see."

"And you also heard from them about his being a prisoner at Courbon?"

Koechlin smiled bitterly. "Ah, not that. Some things I have heard, but not that. He would not now be dead, if I hear that."

"But why hunt the woods for him?"

"Why do I hunt for the Boche, you mean, M. le Major ... C'est pour la France. I did not know he was Armand ... I think him Boche ... And why do I hunt Armand ... C'est le destin ... The worl' is ver' small. And it happen so—it happen so." He rose to pace restlessly back and forth.

MacLeod was puzzled; many questions rose to his lips; but before this tragic figure moving aimlessly in front of him he was dumb. Koechlin seemed to divine the meaning of his silence, and halting said: "Monsieur asks himself if I kill him?"

The surgeon bent his eyes to earth, and did not answer.

"But, yes," said the Alsatian, "it is so. I have kill."

MacLeod shivered. A row with the Marac people was nothing to this. Poor devil! he must see him through.

"Not with intention, M. le Major. But I have kill all the same. It happen so. Yesterday I hunt the Giey woods, and then come here. And by chance last night, just at darkness, I see a man asleep, sur la rive. I go to him quiet—quiet—then suddenly make false step and noise. He awake and run away. He go uphill —through the wood. He is feeble—exhaust. Sans doute he is sick and has hunger. He fall, and I come to him. But I also am exhaust, and I faint. Then I regain myself. I light allumette and look at his face. Oh, la-la, monsieur, it is the face of Armand!"

"My God! "said MacLeod, and his lips were dry.

"Yes. Et c'est moi, son frère, who have kill. His heart go out—pouf! like allumette—not so?"

"Yes, yes; his hunger and weakness killed him."

"But it is I that kill—for I have hunt him like a dog."

MacLeod turned away uneasily. The drizzle had ceased now, and beyond the tree-tops he saw in the west grey billowy clouds with a sea of golden fire below. Verdun was silent; yet there came from a distance the roll of a drum; and Koechlin started in alarm ... But MacLeod reassured him at once, by recalling that Roche, an invalided *poilu*, simple in his wits since a head-wound received in the early years of the war, had a passion for the tambour, and took lessons now and again from a veteran military drummer, retired in Aulnoy.

"Oui, oui," said Koechlin. "C'est Saumade who teach. He was in last war with the Boche. But I did not know he come here. You are certain—no danger, M. le Major?"

MacLeod assured him there was no danger, and explained that Roche took his instruction in retired places like the Calvaire, since it was necessary to get far from the *poilus* in hospital who must rest and sleep much.

"So? "said Koechlin. "It is why I have not heard them."

"Well, never mind: they won't trouble us. Let's get this business of your own clear ... Why didn't you come back straight away last night, mon vieux, and report to me? You've put us in a devil of a hole. We could have arranged things all right with the Sùreté Générale."

Koechlin shook his head with conviction. "Non, non," he said. "They would give Armand the burial for the Boche. But his grave must be of France—here, in the wood of the Calvaire—sacred earth ... So this morning I go to friend in Aubepierre, and borrow this." He touched the spade. "Then, when the man who plough the field over there is downhill, I dig. When he come up the hill, I stop. It is ver' slow."

MacLeod was moved, yet held to his point. "But I will make explanation," he said. "Myself, I will go to the commandant at Marac. I will even, if there be need, make requisition to the Minister of War. Your brother must not be buried here. His place is in the cemetery at Aulnoy with the others of France, the tricolour at his head."

But Koechlin was not to be dissuaded. "It will indeed be difficult that! Le Capitan Bee is nervous; he see a spy in everyone. And the Minister of War! —Non, non—too much noise!"

MacLeod had to confess he was right; the difficulties would be enormous. Indeed, now that the first glow of pity for poor Koechlin's sad case had faded, his thoughts were all for hushing up the whole wretched business. The Marac authorities would be sure to put the worst construction on it; they must never hear a word. The good name of the Arc hospital was at stake. Mismanagement ... another instance of English slackness ... and so on. That was the kind of charge he would be up against ... Why not risk the burial of the dead man as Koechlin proposed—just there, and right off? Before three weeks were gone the lush undergrowth of fern and briar would invade the freshly turned earth, and the grave be completely hid. "Very well," he said.

Between them they lifted the fragile body into the pit; and, covering it with branches of green pine-boughs, dug back the mounded clay, using the single spade by turns. They were barely half-way through their task when the roll of drums again rang out, but now hardly a hundred yards away.

"Only Saumade and Roche again," said the surgeon. "We can wait till they go."

"Ah, he is très militaire, le vieux Saumade."

As they waited, roulade followed roulade on the drum, sounds of terror in that desert place. Well, indeed, that those two chose retired spots for their hobby! MacLeod recalled having met them quite close to this quarter a week or so ago; Saumade had then proposed playing him a special salute—one suitable to his rank—and had been chagrined to find that the surgeon's grade was that of Major. "Ah," he had said, "c'est comme le chef de bataillon—le major," and explained that he had salutes for captains and colonels, but had forgotten that for le chef de bataillon. His last war was long ago, and he was very old. "And the memory evades one nowadays." MacLeod smiled, remembering the old fellow's eagerness.

The drums fell silent at last. "Perhaps they're gone now," said the surgeon. "But we'd best make sure."

He threaded his way to the edge of the wood, and, safely screened by the thick undergrowth, saw that Roche's drum hung on a pine branch, while Saumade explained certain technicalities as to the holding of the drumsticks. He stole back quietly to rejoin the *poilu*. "Pas fini," he said.

Just then there came a preliminary roll of the drum. "Listen," said Koechlin excitedly. "That is Saumade who plays; and it is the salute: it is *Drapeau*! ... What could be more fitting for the burial of Armand, M. le Major! It is not like the bugles and the firing-party; but *Drapeau* is something of great." And he moved to the side of the grave, where he stood immobile, his right hand at his *képi*. "It is even as if they knew."

MacLeod took place by his side, as the great symphony of the tambour pulsed through the darkening air. And such was the magic of the drums that in fancy the surgeon saw the grey-blue legions of France—the steel casques so Grecian above the tanned faces of the *poilus*; heard Petain's great word: "On ne passe pas!" and the thunder of the captains and the shouting. They called and called, those drums, to thoughts of great endeavour, crying up and on to the heights, rending apart every obstacle, chanting of glory yet to be. Then a last thunderous roll of acclaim—and *Drapeau* had ended ... Nothing now but the dark forest, the half-filled grave, and the broken man by his side. He heaved a sigh and said," Come, mon vieux, let us finish."

In silence they completed their task: soon every sod was in place, and a thick covering of larch-boughs hid the scar in the soil where the dead man lay. The sound of the tambour came faintly now in a last long rumble, as Koechlin and he descended the hill by the skirts of the wood; and the guns of Verdun growled brokenly for a little, to burst out ultimately in a sudden violence that shook the air with giant throbs. At the immense concussion, Koechlin, turning with a bitter smile to MacLeod, lifted his clay-stained hands in a gesture of hopelessness, then plodded on, muttering to himself. No need to ask him what he muttered ... "The happy war! "to a certainty.

Leclercq had not returned when the surgeon arrived at the château and sought the quiet of his own room. Vacantly he surveyed its walls as in a dream, for his mind was still back in the Calvaire wood. "Armand," he repeated to himself, as he bathed aching temples —" Armand." By a simple transposition of syllables, how like Marion's name, if one spoke it French fashion! ... "Armand—Marion; Marion—Armand."

As he towelled his head roughly after bathing, his eye caught sight of several maps of the Western Front which he had tacked to the walls of his room. A zigzag of blood-red ran across each, marking this or that sector of the battle-line. "Happy! "he muttered. "Like hell it is."

XIX: First room on the right

SUMMER came to the army zone in France; and not all the thunder of guns in Verdun or in far Champagne could retard the blossoming-time of the flowers in the Aulnoy countryside: dogwood, gentian, orchis, lily of the valley, narcissus bloomed lavishly. In the evening the massed croaking of frogs in the Aujon marshes was constant—answering the dread voices of barrage and bombardment with assurance of the persistence of life, even if grotesque and puny as was theirs. And in the lake near the château the carp bubbled and splashed in the early dawns like miniature saurians: life in plenty here, whatever was happening higher up the scale, where men made noise and smoke for a time, and then lay in a strange silence, and were not. Life persistent too in the river where trout and *poisson blanc* flashed and drowsed in the sun-clear pools; in the sky where the lark's song pulsed and the dark hawk hovered; in the woods where nightingales called and answered so magically, and the owl flitted ghost-like. And on quiet evenings, above the red tiles and the church spire where Aulnoy lay as in a cup, shrill voices would take the air—an old woman scolding in an orchard on the hillside while children ran from her, clutching stolen apples. Yes, great Nature went her way, despite the blood and flame across half France.

Something of all this came into MacLeod's mind about this time; and he busied himself affixing several new maps to the walls of his room. First he set up a chart of the little commune, then one of the department —the Haute Marne; there followed a map of France, next one of Europe; and above all these a Mercator's projection of the world. He had wished to acquire something astronomical to finish off with—a plan of the Solar System, or such like; but it was only after considerable delay that he procured it, for Paris booksellers were little concerned about astronomy just then. But at last a Solar System chart did turn up, and he was busy attaching this to the wall, when Leclercq entered and regarded the collection quizzically.

"Something of superior, not so?" suggested the Frenchman.

"Priggish, you think?"

"Salon planetaire—salon des siècles," said Leclercq, waving a declamatory hand. "It is an idea, but not for a serious war."

MacLeod flushed. "No, but I'm trying to get the damn thing into perspective. Kind of a happy war, you know," he said bitterly.

"Pardon ... I had forgotten," said Leclercq. "But I am not philosophe enough to see the connection."

"Neither am I. All I can see is that the war's big, but the solar system's bigger ... Oh, come on, let's get out of it"; and he led the way to the door.

"Out of the solar system?—out of the worl'? "asked Leclercq, following him. "Ver' easy in a war, that ... You have only to make an ask of the Ministre de Guerre ... Then front line—et fini."

They passed out into the park, where the wounded lay under sun shelters surrounding the big oaks. Nurses flitted around with Carrel solution for the two-hourly dressings, or with meals; stretcher-bearers came and went with special cases not yet habituated to the full day out of doors. There was a murmur of happy talk with plenty of soldiers' slang in it, a clinking of glasses and laughter: for a little time at least these men were out of the mêlée. The two doctors walked across to an avenue of elms beside the river while the grave twilight fell. Close at hand the grillon rasped its high note in the long grasses; from a ward in the now-distant château a gramophone tinkled; and the Verdun bombardment rumbled from far away.

"Listen!" aid Leclercq. "What did I tell you? ... The guns have a sound of sollenel—of noble at a distance. But up there, it is a tearing—arrache—not noble."

"I've seen very little of war," said MacLeod. "Five minutes was all I had—then I got this." He slapped his lame leg with his cane. "How does it feel, the real thing?"

"In the departs—the over-the-tops?" MacLeod nodded. "Ah, it is terrible, the departs—horrid. You have expectation of death, and you must hope only to be wounded. It is a way of looking—un point-de-vue. In a battle, there is barrage. You are mad. What do you want—what do you expec'? In a battle a man may represent himself—how do you say? You are away from your body. You are not afraid, but your teeth are going. It is perfectly horrible to come to your commander, and your teeth going. And you say to your body: ' Dammy fool! ' and yet you cannot help your teeth going. Sometimes, too, you walk over the ground, and there is noise of obus—of shell everywhere; éclats—shrapnel everywhere; but there is nothing in your mind excep' some music of Beethoven, or something as so. An' then, tout-de-suite, your dammy teeth click-click! ... It is strange."

They went on in silence for a little, then Leclercq resumed in a meditative tone: "It is bad with France at the front just now. I think I must go back there. My malaria is not too much at present."

"Nonsense! You're not fit by a long chalk," said MacLeod.

But the Frenchman insisted. "I shall ask for the artillery of the field," he said. "If I want, I could go in ambulance; but if you take your duty—no, I do not like that word—if you take a high way of looking, the most useful place is the place of danger. For you may keep your brancardiers from staying away. They are only men, and you with your little rank may save three hundred life. It is not high surgery—only a garotte on a man's arm, but you may save him. Not much honour." He considered for a little and then: "But I cannot go to the artillery of the field until I first of all pass examination for higher grade." He burst into droll laughter. "The silly board! Yes, I must look up my measles for my medical examination."

"Oh, chuck it," said MacLeod, "you're not going just yet. You're not fit until you've had further treatment. A fortnight more of those quinine injections, and then we'll see. Besides, I must go on leave next week. Mother ill, you know, and I shall want you and Henson to carry on till I get back."

"Ver' well," said Leclercq; "I stay.' But I will make my ask for the front as soon as you return."

"Nonsense! We can't do without a liaison officer. But we'll talk of that later on. Meanwhile I expect to get off on Thursday next. Back in two weeks."

And Thursday saw MacLeod on leave and in the train for Paris. The railway service was bad, and he had to stay in Paris overnight, getting the Havre train next day. In his compartment the only other occupant was an elderly Englishman, who turned out to be, of all queer things, a commercial traveller for English hats. Odd businesses there were in the world, but this of selling foreign hats to France, during war-time, seemed one of the oddest. However, it was to be supposed that some kind of trade must go on in the midst of all the turmoil.

Pleasant, tall, broad-shouldered, Mr. Crossthwaite was a typical Yorkshireman, even to a slight accent. They chatted freely, and MacLeod spoke a little about his work. The big fellow became enthusiastic at once. "What? English people—English aristocrats nursing French wounded! Fine! Of course, you'd require people of quality to get good French, eh? That's the stuff to give Brother Boche! "Enthusiasm indeed was the note of all his talk. The Allies were all right, he declared, indicating profounds of knowledge whose source he dared not reveal; and the surgeon smiled, remembering old Moy's foible on this score. "You'll see! "said Mr. Crossthwaite in a confiding whisper. "In another week Jerry will get the fright of his life. He thinks he's going to take Amiens, does he? Well, he's going to take a jolly good hiding instead. You'll see! "And he puffed furiously at his cigar—a veritable war-horse. At the Havre terminus they parted. "See you on the steamer," said Crossthwaite. "I've got some business calls here before sailing-time."

MacLeod hailed a porter, and sending his kit on to the Hotel Normandie, where he purposed resting till the time for embarking, limped down the station. Now that Crossthwaite had gone, he found himself puzzling as to where he had seen his face before, but could not place him. The lame leg had been cramped by the train journey; so, deciding to exercise it by a turn round the town before seeking the Normandie, he drifted on aimlessly until he found himself in a familiar scene—the docks. Yes, there was the outer basin, and there that forlorn yellow funnel of the torpedoed vessel, still above the tide. The place, indeed, had altered little since that memorable day when he learnt of Marion's death.

The gloves? That little parcel lay as yet unopened in the depths of his trunk in Aulnoy. Of a sudden he saw the whole misery of the world focused in Marion's tragedy. And yet, away inland there—in the battle-line—fresh tragedies as bitter as hers were being enacted. A maelstrom of madness, and he and everyone whirled helpless in it! This sad grey city, that murderous haze-covered sea, those heavy spiritless faces of the quay-workers—God! how he hated the mess war made of life! But soon the old Scots dourness came obstinately back. The cause was just; they must win through.

And now he pitied the grey city. How else should she be but hushed and forlorn as she sat beside these waters so perilous—that pathetic hull out there, surely a fit symbol of her plight. He recalled a previous crossing to England from this port—the secrecy as to time of sailing, the zigzag route whose details only reached the captain a few minutes before gangways were drawn, the patrol signals, the many halts, a dropping of anchors even on one occasion. Then there was the story Kelsall had told in the Aulnoy mess one night, of a steamer he had seen on fire when half-way across. No, the Channel, despite all our watching, was still treacherous; little wonder that Le Havre sat hushed there in the evening greyness.

He turned and walked slowly towards the *Normandie*. The boat would probably sail about ten, so there was time for a meal and a look at the papers. As he approached the hotel, there suddenly came back to him a memory of the broad genial face of Crossthwaite in other surroundings than that of a railway carriage. Yes, he remembered him now—the man he had seen in the Normandie, on his last visit to Havre—the fellow in the first room on the right who had stood scrutinizing the passers-by so keenly. Other Aulnoy people had also remarked him, he recalled, and set him down as a secret service man. He chuckled as he imagined their surprise when he revealed the true nature of the old fellow's business—a commercial traveller for English bowler-hats! Of course, there was always the chance that he did belong to the secret service, and that his talk about hats was all camouflage; for you never could tell who was who nowadays. And, he concluded as he entered the hotel, it would be rather fun discovering what his real game was, when they met again on the steamer.

Spaciousness was not a strong point of the Hotel Normandie; and its tiny entrance-hall, thronged by young officers in khaki, was stuffy. A buzz of voices, much laughter and the tinkle of glasses came from the little private rooms on either side the corridor which burrowed through the ground floor of the building to the offices and grand staircase at the back. Behind the offices was the glass-covered court transformed into a salle-â-manger, a place not unfamiliar to him in former crossings from Havre.

As he made his way through the crush of soldiers, noisy with stale army jokes, he caught a glimpse of Crossthwaite's head above the press of people in front; and, with some idea of sharing a table with him, he struggled after the big man. There he was, just approaching the door of the smoking lounge. Would he turn in there, and resume his curious scrutiny of people, just as formerly? A queer thing, habit, and a queer hobby for a hatter, watching the little foibles of his fellow-mortals—ironically or sentimentally, which? He might instantly have accosted Crossthwaite, but the humour took him to hang back, and see if he would enter the lounge to take up his usual post there. But, no; he passed on with a muttered word or two and without turning his head. MacLeod instantly halted in confusion; and, to hide this, struck a match and held it to a cigarette already alight. Something in Crossthwaite's demeanour and in those few whispered words was all wrong. The syllables had a foreign ring in them although unintelligible, so low had been his voice; and MacLeod sensed that they were in the nature of a hasty reply to something muttered by a man standing back within the shelter of the lounge's doorway. The surgeon looked cautiously round, still struggling with his cigarette, to see if any others in the crush of army men had noticed anything amiss; but those youngsters were busy with chaff and story, and clearly had observed nothing unusual. He fumbled further with his cigarette therefore, and lit another match. Crossthwaite was now well ahead and about to enter the salle-â-manger at the corridor's end ... A secret service man, after all? ... But, as old Featherly in Aulnoy might ask, on which side—British or Boche?

His cigarette was now too plainly alight for him to halt longer without attracting attention; so he moved forward, and, as he passed the first door on the right, looked into it with what nonchalance he could command. What he saw there made his heart race violently; but he kept on his way apparently unmoved, his one object to gain the end of the corridor and slip aside into the office-bay before Crossthwaite—now taking his seat at a table in the dining salle—should turn and discover his presence. By good fortune he moved out of the big fellow's line of vision just in time, and approached the office window to ask some foolish question about the night boat's time of sailing.

"One never knows exactly, monsieur," said the clerk. "C'est la guerre."

MacLeod picked up an *Echo de Paris* from a bundle on the counter, paid for it, and sat down in a chair close to the desk. He strove to appear quite at ease, but in reality was trembling with excitement at the thought of what he had seen in the smoking-lounge—a sole occupant, and therefore the man who had passed those few muttered words with Crossthwaite. A little man, clean-shaven, dressed in a dapper suit of grey and wearing glossy pointed shoes of the familiar French type—glossy shoes that looked strange because no wisps of straw protruded from their eyelets. Despite the transformation, it was Gurney.

XX: The rally

WHAT next? ... Gurney was a spy without a doubt; and espionage was a matter for the Assistant Provost-Marshal. He must obtain direction to that official's bureau without delay; for he required the affair settled some way or other if he was to get that night's boat. And so, with every appearance of casualness, he bought another paper—*l'Humanité* this time —and how ironic its title to his eye as he beheld himself planning Gurney's doom. He got into talk with the clerk, and after a few inquiries learned that the A.P.M.'s quarters were easily to be found about half a kilometre away—a hut near the extreme west end of Rue Victor Hugo—monsieur could not mistake—one passed a barber's salon, then some vacant ground—and at last one came to the house of wood such as the English soldiers make. MacLeod recalled the quarter; he had suffered under the razors of that barber during his last passage through Havre and believed he could reach the place even in dimly lit streets. "One," he said to himself, and suddenly recognized that he was using the method of rallying-points in difficult operations, where the surgeon halts to revise his landmarks before going on to the next part of the dissection.

This memory calmed MacLeod automatically; he emerged from the confusion bred by thoughts of his old association with "Gurney in Eilean Aros; and henceforth Gurney was nothing more than a malignant root, to be extirpated with caution but without delay. A little ago he had been obsessed by the sense of the night outside, with its furtive officialdom thronging the quayside to watch the ship prepare for another gamble at a crossing. Now he was far from Havre and its docks; for his mind's eye saw only the steel-bright operating theatre and the white-gowned figures busy at their task.

Stage one—the location of the A.P.M.'s office—was already over. Two—the setting aside of the affair of Crossthwaite for the time being—was easily met by rising and turning his back on the *salle-á-manger*. He limped down the corridor, dreading a hail from the big man every step he took; but none came, and he reached the door of the little lounge unchecked.

"Three," he breathed involuntarily to himself as he stepped into the room to find his quarry still there and —thank Heaven!—alone. As he entered, the little man turned, cigarette in hand, and glanced keenly at him. The surgeon smiled wryly and extended a hand. "Good evening," he said. "Mr. Gurney, is it not?"

The other hesitated for a second only, then shook hands with great heartiness. "Why," he cried, "if it isn't Dr. MacLeod!"

"Yes"; and already the coolness of the fellow had brought a chill to the heart of MacLeod. Could it be that Gurney was straight after all? But within him something said: "Three—stage three," so persistently, that he smiled in confidence and came back to his task on the instant.

Gurney wagged his head vainly. "Aha!" he said, "I knew you at once. The voice, you understand; I never forget a voice. Otherwise I should have had difficulty in placing you, for you've stopped one, I see." He glanced at the stiff leg. "And—another difficulty —the golden beard has gone."

"Oh, yes," said MacLeod, taking a proffered cigarette and lighting it. "But more than mine has gone, it appears."

The other fingered his shaven chin. "Well, one grows older. And while I don't mind grey hairs, I draw the line at white." As he spoke he eyed the doorway for an instant with the least hint of apprehension; it was clear that he feared an intrusion by Crossthwaite. "And what's happening to you?" he asked, with a sharp glance at the blue facings of the other's uniform. "Invalided out, and then joined the C.R.F., I suppose?"

"Right," said the surgeon. "And you? What's doing?"

"Oh, the old stuff—journalism—war-correspondence on the usual lines. The looker-on sees most, you know —and all that rot. I'm sick of it; but how the public swallow it!"

"Yes, don't they?" said MacLeod absently, pondering what move to take next.

Gurney provided it, however. "You crossing tonight?"

"I hope so."

"Had dinner?"

"Not yet."

"Well, what about a little do at Tortoni's, across the way?" And again his eye turned anxiously to the door. "This place is packed. No good anyhow. And Tortoni's truffles! Nothing to beat them!"

"Delighted," said MacLeod: Tortoni's suited his plans admirably.

"Good man! "fussed the little fellow. "We'll have no end of a binge." He made for the door instantly. "My things are in the hall." He led the way to the porch, where he donned an Inverness cape and a deerstalker cap that made him as odd a figure in MacLeod's eyes as the ancient ulster and the straw-filled boots of former days. Gurney grinned at the curious regard of the Scot. "Quite Highland, eh?" said he, as they passed out into the night, and began to cross the Place Gambetta to the lights of the café opposite. "And warm," he added; "for the evening air here is what you call snell over yonder—yes, snell is the word."

"You're a great linguist," growled MacLeod grudgingly.

"Oh, a hobby—a hobby only," said Gurney, chuckling gnome-like at his elbow in the dark. "Well, well! —Just fancy meeting you again!— Well, well! "The old fellow's coolness was amazing; he bombarded the surgeon with queries about his work as they walked, and asked carefully the location of his hospital and the stations on the way to it where trains were changed. "Latrecy? —that's near Chaumont, isn't it? I see. Change at Chaumont for Latrecy. I get you. Must look you up there, one day."

MacLeod's teeth gritted. "There may be difficulties," he said; and then pulled up short. He was going too fast. The little devil! Did he never dream of a firing-party before a chair wherein a man sat with a white disc over his heart?

"Difficulties?" queried Gurney, trotting on.

"Oh, well, our place is in the army zone, you see," said MacLeod. "And civilians don't come our way —that's all."

"Yes, yes, but—again to use a Scotticism—there are ways of managing."

"As how?"

"Oh, one passes: that is all." They had halted at the entrance to Tortoni's. The light fell from the doorway on the face of the little man; it was pale and enigmatic, a look in the eyes, too, that showed him on guard, his mind as taut as that of a duellist in parry. "But, come in, come in," he said, "and give me all the news from the isle of the little glens."

They entered. The dining-room was fairly full: many British officers, a sprinkling of French and a few civilians; but they secured a table for two, and agreed as to food and on Beaune for wine. Gurney gave the order in amazingly good French, passing a word or two of *poilu*'s slang with the waiter; then turned to his companion. "Tortoni's for truffles, as I remarked already. Best in France," he said, sighing luxuriously, and leaning back to regard MacLeod with such an air of affection that the surgeon's heart smote him. "Well, at last we can talk. And what's the latest news from Aros?"

The aplomb of the man was magnificent; and again MacLeod was disconcerted. Hang it all! the fellow wasn't surely such a bad lot? It might even be that he was one of our own Intelligence Staff. There were always Scotland Yard men on that job, of course; and naturally they didn't give themselves away to everybody. And yet—and yet? That sudden flight from Aros in pre-war days, when the Admiralty survey was on? Old Moy's story of the caches for enemy submarine petrol on the shores of Loch-na-Keal? That strange encounter with Crossthwaite in the *Normandie*? No, he must not let himself be hypnotized by this agreeable table-companion. The logic of the affair was clear as crystal; and this man through his work for the submarines was as surely responsible for the death of Marion, as if he himself had launched the torpedo that sank her ship. A mad thought, but there it was, all mixed up with hatred of the Boche and championship of his own side. But he must be on guard. Not a single word about Marion. True, the mere mention of her name might reveal something of the man's real character; but better that the first word on that score came from Gurney: then he would see how the land lay. Could he have heard of her death? Strange that from one who had been so intimate with the girl no inquiry regarding her had come as yet. He must be careful.

"Oh, news of Aros? "he said. "Well, I'm afraid that's a sad story." And he briefly related the disasters war had brought to that countryside—the many young lives lost at Loos, on the Somme and elsewhere.

They chatted on, Gurney quizzing him keenly about his surgical work. He trusted the morale of the French wounded was good? It was? Glad to hear it. And the Americans had at last arrived in the Aulnoy sector, he understood, and were busy at machine-gun practice, weren't they? Yes. And what about discipline among them? Getting better, he hoped? Fine. Glad to hear that too! Splendid chaps!

Over the liqueur Eilean Aros again came into the talk. Gurney had heard of some mines which had drifted ashore there and damaged a pier. Was it by chance Aros Pier itself? Strange to think of the old place being knocked about!

"No, it was the pier at Archie Voulin's," said MacLeod. "But you're surely well up to date? That never got into the newspapers, you know."

"Oh, I had it from an Aros boy—a MacLean of Callachly. He was in the Gordons, I think. In hospital in Rouen last year. Shrapnel in shoulder. Pretty bad. And by the by, he told me that fine girl at the inns— Marion, you remember—had nursed him somewhere before he came down the line. At Bethune, I think it was. Was she nursing in the Bethune sector, do you know? "There was the faintest tremor in his voice and a little eagerness in his glance.

MacLeod bent his eyes to flick his cigarette free from ash. "She may have been at one time. She isn't there now," he said.

"A fine girl. Where is she, I wonder? "The little man's hand moved a fork aimlessly to and fro on the white tablecloth as he spoke; but MacLeod could see that his fingers trembled ever so little.

The surgeon raised eyes that blazed, and the other seemed to shrink from them as the answer came slowly: "She went down with her hospital ship in March. Torpedoed—although they had half a dozen red-crosses from stem to stern."

Gurney's face went ashen grey; his slack hand dropped the fork he toyed with and swept some glasses from the table with a crash; he slithered back in his chair, eyes staring, mouth gaping. A waiter came running and caught him as he fell; a manager and some officers crowded round.

MacLeod rose and put them aside. "I'm a doctor," he said. "Stand back. Lay him flat." He took Gurney's pulse, loosened his collar, and waited till his eyes showed signs of returning consciousness. "Only a fainting attack," he announced. "I had to give him some bad news, and it was too much for him. Some brandy, please." The circle of curious watchers gabbled their sympathy as he held the glass to the lips of the man on the floor. The little white-faced fellow sipped, rested, sipped again, and at last sat up. "Get me a taxi," he whispered. "A taxi," MacLeod repeated to the waiter, who departed instantly for the doorway. Gurney's eyes met the other's just then, and were at once averted. MacLeod noted the evasion, and for him it clinched matters definitely. "That settles it," he muttered to himself. "Fourth point next."

Gurney seemed to sense danger in the silence of the surgeon and his brooding airs; he stirred uneasily. "Take me to the hotel," he said plaintively.

"All right, all right," answered MacLeod, now on edge lest his prey should make a last-moment escape, "a bus is coming," and turned aside to pay the bill.

The taxi was announced; and with MacLeod on one side and the manager on the other, Gurney was helped down the hall and into the machine. A waiter brought his cap and Inverness mantle; and while he was being tucked into these, the surgeon gave a hurried direction to the driver, then took his seat beside the bundle of nerves that was all now left of the brilliant talker of ten minutes ago. Both were silent during the short drive; but when the little man stepped out unsteadily from the taxi he gave an exclamation of dismay. "What is this?" he asked huskily, peering into a dark deserted street which showed no sign of the Normandie's crowded porch.

"Just a moment," said MacLeod, settling hastily with the driver and watching the machine drive off. A feeble light came from a broken window mended clumsily with brown paper, and discovered to them a hut-like structure of wood to whose door worn steps of plank ascended; it stood alone on some waste ground, the whole surroundings secret and sinister.

Gurney leant against the clinker-built boards of the building, the picture of dismay. "What is this?" he asked again querulously.

MacLeod gripped his arm, and leading him up the steps, opened the door. "Office of the Assistant Provost-Marshal," he said. "Get in, you swine."

Gurney stared at him with the blank eyes of a rabbit before a weasel, then turned and entered the doorway, followed by his captor. However dingy its outward aspect, the office of the A.P.M. was tidy and business-like inside; stacks of files neatly labelled covered its walls, and before a roll-top desk sat an officer in red tabs, busy with a card-index of many colours. He swung round at their entry—pink and white cheeks and a small neat flaxen moustache his chief features. "Hillo, hillo! "he said in a gentle voice, as Gurney sank down exhausted on a bench. "Your friend's ill! Wants a doctor badly, doesn't he?"

"I think not," said MacLeod. "I'm a doctor myself. He's only frightened. A case of espionage."

"I see, I see," said the A.P.M. softly; and he rang a bell. An orderly appeared. "Room three for this man, Carson, please. And would you mind getting him a little cognac or something? "He handed the man a bunch of keys. "And just go over him, will you? Papers or arms, you understand." Carson helped Gurney to his feet, and they disappeared through a door at the back. "Have a seat, won't you? "said the officer. "I don't think we've met before, have we?" and he offered his cigarette-case.

"Sorry," said MacLeod. "I should have introduced myself, of course; but that little rat put me off my balance"; and he briefly gave details of himself.

"Yes, yes. You don't mind if I make a few notes, do you?—C.R.F. Hospital—Arc-en-Aulnoy—Médecin-Chef—" He wrote precisely for a moment in a clear script. "And what's the trouble?"

MacLeod began his tale. "Well, it goes back to pre-war days, but I'll cut it short," he said; and in a few words he told of his acquaintance with Gurney in Aros, and went on to what Moy had revealed to him of hidden bases for enemy petrol in sites that had been frequented by Gurney at one time or another.

At mention of Moy's name the suave A.P.M. became suddenly alert. "I think, if you don't mind, I'll get on to Major Whittaker—the Intelligence Officer. You're sure you don't mind—really? I hate keeping you; but this looks as if it might have something in it, you know." He took up his 'phone and spoke for a minute, then set it down. "Yes," he said, "old Moy's no fool. Whittaker will be here in a jiff. So sorry to keep you waiting."

MacLeod explained that he hoped to cross that night. A case of illness— his mother.

"Yes, yes; but we shan't be long, really we shan't. Whittaker will have his C.I.D. man with him—Burton, a wonder. Knows all that lot"; and he jerked a finger towards the door through which Gurney had disappeared. "In any case, the boat won't sail for an hour yet; and you'll get off in ten minutes, once Burton has had a look at your man." MacLeod acquiesced. "Good of you," , murmured the A.P.M., and took up his pen. "Suppose we just get down the rest of your story before they arrive. Save time, you know. We've finished that bit about the Hebrides, haven't we? And what next?"

The surgeon gave his story of what had happened in the Hotel Normandie between Crossthwaite and Gurney —the few words of muttering between them at the lounge door; and then described the scene in the Café Tortoni when he revealed the fact of Marion's death to Gurney.

"Oldish man for a love affair with the girl, don't you think? "murmured the A.P.M. softly, as he finished his writing and dotted his period with care.

"Good God! yes," cried MacLeod. "I'd never dreamt of that! At least I had thought of it, but —"

"Well, you never know," said the other softly. "But you don't mind my asking, I hope? "and his voice was really a wonderful instrument for tones of persuasive courtesy. "We find all kinds of information useful in a job like this. The facts are that at mention of this girl's death the old boy fainted. There must be a reason. Was he, do you think, by any chance a relative, although not known to the girl as such?"

"My dear sir—"protested MacLeod.

"I know—I know. You think I'm making a romance of it"—laying down his pen, after cleaning its point meticulously. "But we had recently a case of a German father and a Scots mother. Hadn't seen each other for years. Unmarried, of course. And what must the fond father do, but choose the middle of the war for getting over to Aberdeen to look up the woman and ask for his boy! Gave us no end of a bother. We got him at this port on his way back. Not a young man either by any means ... Oh, yes, there's quite a lot of sentiment still about this old earth, war or no war."

MacLeod felt reproved: the soft-voiced A.P.M. knew his work. "Well, you stump me," he said. "I really can't make out anything in Gurney or the girl to suggest a resemblance, except that they both were daft for music."

"Not much in that," said the A.P.M.; "but I'd better note it. You never can tell, you know. Old Burton may see something in it"; and again he put pen carefully to paper. But he had hardly written a word, when the sound of a car drawing up was heard, and the door opened to admit the two men they awaited.

"This is Dr. MacLeod, sir, about whom I 'phoned. Major Whittaker, Doctor. And Mr. Burton." The Major shook hands with a pleasant smile, almost boyish: a red-haired man of forty with alert eyes that showed little flames at times as he read the report by the A.P.M. Burton, a tall man of middle age, looked like a ship's mate on shore leave; and wore a new serge suit he was rather careful of, to judge by the buttoning and unbuttoning of his reefer jacket, as he waited for his turn at the report. He read it rapidly when handed over, and when he had finished Major Whittaker said: "Well, shall we see him?" Burton nodded; the A.P.M. led the way to the door at the back, and showing them through, turned to say to MacLeod: "You don't mind waiting a minute, do you? The Major may want a word with you. Your boat's all right. Just a jiff, you know."

He went out; and the surgeon chafed for what seemed an interminable time. Neither of those men had said a word to him, only smiled enigmatically and shook hands. What a mystery they were making of a business as plain as a pikestaff! He knew now why that fellow had fiddled with his buttons. Saved him talking. He looked at his watch; only half an hour now left for him to cut back to his hotel, pick up his traps and get aboard. And what about Crossthwaite? Would he have to go into his case also with these people? Further delay! Should he vanish without waiting longer? Leave a note on the desk for the A.P.M. perhaps? And yet he would like to know what was happening to Gurney, and the upshot of the whole affair.

Just then the door at the back opened, and the A.P.M. came in. "So sorry to have kept you. Major Whittaker won't need you further. And would you please make use of his car to get down to your boat. His chauffeur will have you there in no time." He led the way to the front door.

"Yes, but what's happening to the little man? "said MacLeod, confused by this off-hand dismissal.

"Oh, well, you know, these things take time. But we're really awfully obliged for all the trouble you've taken. And if we want you, you'll be back in a fortnight at your hospital, won't you?"

"But can't you tell me anything definite?"

"Well, really, you know there's nothing to tell, is there? You don't mind my putting it that way, do you? Oh, here's Johnson! ... Johnson," he said to the chauffeur who appeared out of darkness suddenly, and switched on the car's lights, "Major Whittaker wants you to take Dr. MacLeod to the night boat at once ... Oh, your kit, of course! It's at the hotel? ... Yes, Hotel Normandie, Johnson, first of all; and then the steamer." Already the door of the car had closed on MacLeod, fuming at this evasion of all his queries; and the next moment the motor had whisked him out of earshot of the A.P.M.'s soft voice, still protesting polite apology for official discretion.

Late that night he paced the steamer's deck and saw the long line of Havre's lights fade gradually. A confused medley of emotions possessed him as he reviewed the events of the day just gone; but one was dominant, and "Poor little devil!" he said time and again, stamping angrily on the wet planking.

XXI: Leave

EDINBURGH at last. Edinburgh in war-time, alert yet unflurried, her high castle watching for whatever might betide. A few more pennons streamed above the city's reek than in peace-time; soldiers were more numerous in Princes Street; the bugle and the pipes called oftener across the valley of the Gardens: but—MacLeod assured himself—Scotland's rock looked on unperturbed. No new thing this. She had known war from of old.

The taxi stopped before the building where was his home. The sight of that drab tenement—a "land"is the name for it in Edinburgh—irked MacLeod not a little after his experience of Aulnoy. And so, greetings over with his mother—whom he found just recovered from a pneumonia—he set to work persuading her to leave the old place for better quarters. But she had the pride of her caste: her people had been working-folk, and she had no wish to appear otherwise. "Na na," she said caustically, " it's guid enough for me. There's maybe no' so many Honourables to the square yard as in that grand hospital o' yours; but I'm just fine here"; and she became busy on the instant, making him a brew of tea.

But as she did so, he noted a tremor in her hands that was new to him, and saw that she had become more fragile. He quizzed her, and she admitted that the doctor had said her heart was "a wee bittie touched."

Oh, no, nothing serious: she was "juist fine." And she riposted by inquiries as to his own health in general and the damaged leg in particular, also as to the degree of dampness in the beds in the châteaux of France, and the state of his woollens.

He refused, however, to be put off; so, after tea, he left to call on the doctor, who allowed that her heart had been badly hit by the pneumonia, but said that if she would only rest for a couple of hours in the middle of each day, she would soon be herself again. MacLeod returned with this as ultimatum.

She heard it with horror. "Rest!" she cried. "And how could I rest, wi' the hoose to look after?"

"Nonsense!" he said. "There's only yourself to fend for. Off you go, and lie down for an hour. I'll do all the housework—if I can find any. Come on, I'll time you." He glanced at his wrist-watch, and her eyes followed his.

"Keep me," she cried. "That's no' the watch I gied ye, Finlay. What hae ye dune wi't?"

He flushed, then fumbled with a watch that was no purchase of hers, but one he had bought in Chaumont only a week ago, hoping its resemblance to her gift would blind her to a loss he could not account for. "Sorry," he said, "but I lost the one you gave me. I must have taken it off at an operation somewhere, and forgot to pick it up again. It's all hustle out there, you know."

"But did you no' put a notice in a grocer's window, or something?"

"No; but I'll do it yet—I mean, not in the grocer's, but in the post office. Tell you what: I'll make a deal with you, mother. You lie down for an hour, and I'll write straight away to France this very minute and have a notice put up. That's fair, isn't it?" And, protesting, she was led to her room, where he tucked her into bed, and exacted a promise for a renewal of this midday break for every day thereafter.

Then he forthwith scribbled a note to Hemingway, and among other things wrote: "Here's something you might do for me at once. You remember that wrist-watch I lost in Arc—a gift from my mother? Well, the old lady won't give me peace until I've had a notice stuck up in the post office. It had my name on the back of it. So be a good Hem, and put up a little bill, please. Reward—double the usual thing."

In the next few days, he visited some of the war hospitals around Edinburgh, but always returned at midday to play nurse. ("Breaking me in till't," was how his mother described these ministrations.) Then, finding her improving, he engaged the services of a neighbour woman to look after her, and set out for Eilean Aros.

But when he reached Oban and saw the familiar outline of the great hills of the Isle, he had not the heart to continue his journey. All was so different over there. That bitter business with Gurney obsessed him anew. What a world of miserable, tragic memories: Koechlin! And all that maimed lot out in Arc! And yet he would rather be back in his hospital than in Aros … Should he return at once, and so dodge this black dog of ennui? Yet when he was there, most likely he would be wishing himself in the Isle. Day by day he walked the Dunollie Road and looked across the Lynn of Lorn to the mists enfolding the Hill of the Two Winds and high Ben More—watched them clearing and coming again; searched the shore-line for the almost hidden opening of Loch Spelve, and marked the tiny blur that was Castle Duart; followed the cloud-shadows over the green slopes of Morvern and the grey Kyle below them. All so peaceful—so heavenly, that he felt benumbed by the contrast of the scene with the tense and hurried life across the Channel. He had "cafard" badly—was "fed up." Best get back. Marion was gone, and nothing mattered any more … Marion, yes; but why had she come in only at the tail of all his memories? Time counted for much in life, of course. But he could hardly have believed his thoughts of Marion would have blunted so readily ... Anyhow, he'd best be getting back.

He returned to Edinburgh to find his mother dying. "Cerebral embolism," said the doctor. "We wired you two days ago to Aros, but got no reply."

"Just my luck. Never got there. Never want to see it again."

"No? ... Thought you were fond of the place?"

"Not now, Doctor—not now," said MacLeod wearily.

One day more and his mother died. Four more, and he set out for Arc-en-Aulnoy.

XXII: Sister Mary

LE HAVRE three days later—a town still grey and spiritless. Between boat and train MacLeod called at the office of the Assistant Provost-Marshal once more. Greetings over with that suave officer, the surgeon said: "I've been worrying over Gurney. What really happened there? Can't you tell me anything?"

"Oh, yes—Gurney was the name, wasn't it? Sorry I wasn't able to tell you last visit. We have to be careful at the beginning of these affairs, you understand. Well, it was nothing serious, after all. And we had to let the little blighter go."

"But why? "asked MacLeod in amazement. "Well, he was a rather astute chap, and of some use to us—what is called an ' agent double' here. In the pay of both sides, you see. And drawing double pay, of course, little rat!"

"But wasn't he Boche?"

"God knows. Of course, you'll think it silly letting loose fellows like that; but we find it pays. We get odds and ends of information from them—give-aways that they don't notice themselves."

"But doesn't he admit he's working for the enemy?"

"Ah, no. He admits he's in their secret service, but claims it's only in order to work for us. And I've no doubt he tells Jerry he's in with us in order to work for them."

"Isn't that dangerous for us?"

The A.P.M. laughed. "Not much," he said. "There's quite a lot of his kind around. But they're too well watched to do much harm. They're a measly lot; but, as I say, we just pick their little brains, and take what we want when they're not looking. Oh, old Gurney's sort are really quite useful."

"My God! What a life."

"Yes—but chaps like that must have guts all the same, don't you think? Gurney runs a risk from both sides —not from one only—of being shot for a spy. And that means guts, doesn't it?"

"I suppose it does," said MacLeod reluctantly. "But what about friend Crossthwaite? I didn't see him on the steamer that night."

"No," said the A.P.M., suddenly grave: "Crossthwaite's was a different story. A brave man—but I'm afraid you won't ever see him again on any steamer, or anywhere."

MacLeod shivered. "As bad as that? "he said. "Gurney gave him away, I suppose?"

"No. Crossthwaite was a big man among the Boches; and we didn't need Gurney's help. And I doubt if we'd have got it if we'd asked. Odd chap, Gurney. All kinds of impossible loyalties sticking out the little beggar. Touchy too. Queer chap."

The surgeon rose to take his leave.

"Oh, but must you go?" said the A.P.M. "Really? Thought we might have time for a peg at Tortoni's?"

But MacLeod was too upset at the thought of Crossthwaite's death to stay longer, and explained that his train was «bout due. The bland officer once more expressed his infinite obligations to him on behalf of the Intelligence Staff. "Awfully good of you to take all that trouble about those fellows, y'know. And I'm so glad I've been able to reassure you about old Gurney."

They parted, and the surgeon hurried to the station ... Paris that evening. And next day Arc-en-Aulnoy.

He caught sight of the village as his motor descended the long road from Chaumont. There it lay in the cup of the valley—the little houses of grey stone that had a hint of rose-colour in it; the homely church spire, the mill bridge, the lavoirs by the river; the woods that enfolded the park and the big Louis Quatorze château where his work awaited him; and his heart warmed to the thought of it all. To-night he would be among his *poilus* again —steady fellows who didn't bother about the beastliness of war as he did, but got on with their job. None too eager to be healed, perhaps; but when their day of discharge from hospital, en permission, came, taking their fortune philosophically—happy in the thought of a few days at home before returning to the front. Yes, second nature to the French, this war, long looked-for. With MacLeod and his kin somewhat different.

And here at last was the familiar porch; and Henri, the old gardien, awaiting him, smiling welcome. Hem was there, too, and Street—how good to see them again! Hem cried: "All right about that watch, Médecin-Chef. I've got a notice up in the post office—most artistic." MacLeod thanked him, and turned to wave a hand to Mademoiselle Pinard, whose cherry-coloured skirt flashed down the corridor just then. Lord! how fine it was to be back!

At mess that night, he was bombarded with questions. How were the home-folks sticking it? Did they get potato and turnip in their bread just like us out here? Was the Channel any safer? And so on and on. And in turn he must ask about his cases. Was Aubré's stump well—healed? Had Quatrecóte's skull-flap done well? And Tournabien?—and Charmasson? So much was happening at home, abroad, and here; and someone knew this and someone knew that. Ah, but in the line up there, what was really happening? There were the official yellow telegraph forms in the post-office window each day, of course—faked stuff that nobody believed any more than they did the newspapers; for everything was mirage in this war. The Thing was too vast—beyond comprehension: no use speculating. Meanwhile here was their own bit of work—let them see to it. And so, after dinner, MacLeod made straight for his office to take a preliminary canter through official papers alone, since Henson had gone off to Chaumont for a "take-in."

He had scarcely begun, however, when the Directrice knocked and entered. "I've got such a lot to talk about that I couldn't speak of at table," she said; "but I won't bother you with it till to-morrow. All I want to say at present is that I have some good news for you. An old friend of yours came to us a week ago, Sister Mary Yarrow. She used to nurse for you in the Highlands, didn't she? She has been with our unit at Orange, and headquarters have sent her on here."

"Splendid!" he cried, his face flushing under the keen eyes of this grey-haired gentlewoman who was so careful of her flock. He was annoyed that he had coloured up, and that she had noted it. He knew now why she had come. Careful, oh, so careful. "Which ward is she in?" he asked.

"Salle Foch. But she's off duty to-night, so you won't see her till morning." She smiled at his too evident chagrin, showing an official tooth as she did so, and said good night.

"Oh, good night, and thanks for letting me know so soon," he said, closing the door on her. He came back to his work, but the spidery French writing faded out before his eyes; for already he was back in Eilean Aros, beside the tinker's tent on the shore of Moy; saw Mary Yarrow among the yellow whin, and heard her denounce a mad world.

A tap came to his door, and again the Directrice peeped in. "Oh, and there's another little matter you should hear of at once, perhaps. It has nothing to do with us, of course, but it has happened in our district, so we had better be on the alert, I think. You remember some German prisoners escaped from the British cages at Courbon about three months ago?"

MacLeod started guiltily, recalling the affair of Koechlin and his brother. Surely that business was safely past? And Koechlin had been discharged from hospital, well healed, some weeks before he himself had gone on leave? No leakage from Koechlin, surely? "Oh, yes, I remember," he said, assuming an air of indifference. "What's the trouble?"

"You know that the gendarmerie got one of them, but that the other never turned up?"

"Oh, yes."

"Well, old Gregoire, the charcoal-burner, found the body of the second man, buried in the Calvaire Wood, about a week ago."

"Buried?"

"Yes, in a regular grave—quite near one of his working-places. The gendarmerie have been busy. And the British prison-camp at Courbon have been mixed up in it too, of course."

"But surely they won't bother our little lot?"

"I really don't know. Our hospital is quite near the Calvaire, of course; and naturally the authorities have been making inquiries here."

"Here! ... What authorities?"

"Oh, the gendarmerie, and the British people from the prison-camp. And then there's an English officer in mufti—from headquarters, I believe; he called and saw Dr. Henson."

"Red tape?"

"Yes, just formalities, I think. But this officer is still here and still making inquiries. He's staying at the Lion d'Or; and so—in case he turned up to-night before you'd seen Dr. Henson—I thought it best to ' put you wise.'" She smiled, well pleased at having aired her bit of slang.

MacLeod thanked her. "But there's nothing in it," he said. "All the same, we're in a foreign country, so we'd better mind our p's and q's. No saying whose toes we may tread on, if we're not careful."

They said good night then; and he returned to his papers, but made little of them. Mary Yarrow and Koechlin kept popping up into his mind too frequently to allow of his doing any real work that night, and, worried and irritable, he retired long before his usual hour.

Next day he was early in Salle Foch; and there was Sister Mary, dark and tall, and the least bit gauche in her movements—just as of old. The eyes of the wounded *poilus* lightened as the two shook hands; and smiles passed from bed to bed as it was recognized that here were old friends meeting gladly after long parting. Sister Mary's glance rested for a moment on MacLeod's lame leg as he came forward with outstretched hand; and he remarked that her brief anxiety was replaced by reassurance as she noted how well he walked. But she was too frank to observe the etiquette of war as regards the wounded, and went straight to the subject of his injury. "Well, now," she said, "and you do bravely. I was afraid it might be worse."

He was glad to hear that least hint of the brogue in her tongue—so pleasant after the dipped English of the county people in his outfit there. And she was a pleb—somebody to range herself with oddities like Henson and himself against the patrician horde in the hospital—fine folk, but not exactly good mixers, and all a bit restrained by their sense of privilege. "And so you've left Orange?" he said.

"Yes. And a fine place it is. But so is this. And then, my friend, Miss Torrance, is here."

"Of course—I'd forgotten you knew her. Well, any news from Aros?"

"Plenty. But 'twill have to keep, there's so much of it. And we've work to do, haven't we?"

"Right. Let's get dressings over, and then we can have a good jaw."

They set about the ward-visit, and in an hour had finished. Then as they walked sedately and officially to the door, she gave him, first of all, some odds and ends of news about Moy and his family; then about the lads from the Isle, this one wounded, that one missing, and another killed. "Oh, I wish they'd stop it," she said very simply, as if speaking of two schoolboys fighting.

MacLeod devoured her with his eyes. Someone from home to talk to—what a wonder that was! Biit he had other ward-visits to do and must leave her now. So he proposed a walk in the early evening, when she went off duty—the old Roman road as far as Aubepierre —fine country. They could meet in the hall at five. She accepted gladly; and he was about to go, when she detained him. "Oh, but there's the queer thing I must tell you. Who do you think I saw here last week?"

"No idea."

"Wee Straw-Feet."

That staggered him. "Gurney?" he asked.

"I think that was the name. But I only once saw him in Aros, for he left soon after I came. The queer wee man with the ulster, that looked like a tramp, you'll mind?"

"Yes, that's Gurney. But whatever is he doing here? He's not a patient, is he?"

"No, no; he's staying at the Lion d'Or. And he's shaved now; but I'd know him anywhere. He's looking after the affairs of some poor dead man they found up in the woods hereabouts. And he's no end of a swell nowadays, is wee Straw-Feet. Fancy meeting him out here!"

"Yes," said MacLeod, so savagely that she bridled at his tone. "Just fancy. Well, see you at five o'clock." And he took leave of her rather brusquely.

XXIII: The wine of Aubepierre

AROUND Arc were great forests of oak and beech, hornbeam and larch, traversed by criss-cross paths making parallelograms of timber. The growth was dense, airless indeed on days of summer; only at wide intervals did the sky look through, where broad green rides ran for miles. But out of the valley great clearings for tillage broke into the close-set woods; and higher still, the hillsides rose timberless except for a lone clump of oak here and there. To the south was a plateau of wild moorland — the watershed between the valleys of the Aujon and the Aube: up there wide vistas of champaign might be seen, and little cool winds encountered. Over this lay the route to Aubepierre, whither MacLeod took Sister Mary that evening — an old Roman road, splendidly arrogant, as it thrust itself across the hills to some far-off goal of ancient days.

On one hand it crumbled down into yellow sandpits dotted with gorse; on the other it carved itself from the grey-green hillside, a sunburnt expanse only broken now and again by a group of pines — trees whose ancestors, it might be, had seen the first legions march westwards. For MacLeod the dark pines brought something of the air of Scotland to those heights, and despite the distance and his lameness, the old highway was a favourite walk of his. Another attraction was, of course, its link with Gibbon, whose men of war had been here. He could fancy the lithe sun-browned bodies of them, as they marched and marched through a hot noon or a winter's slush, their hawk's eyes ranging the valleys from that high vantage-ground for signs of barbarian attack ... Marched? ... Well, perhaps they didn't march, but rather loped swiftly onwards, as did the Chasseurs Alpins he had seen the other day in Arc, sidling along like the hillmen of Aros at a hare-drive on the Ben of the Two Winds ... Yes, the Alps must have taught the old Romans the swing of the mountaineer.

The reverberations from the Verdun forts came doubly clear up there, and the Roman road's embankments echoed the interminable rumble.

"Hear that?" said MacLeod, "the echo? You'd think the spirits of those old Romans were shouting back at the guns ... I wonder if it's defiance or exultation or what?"

Sister Mary did not answer, and he turned to find her looking away from Verdun to the peaceful valleys around Aubepierre: the rich fields spread out like a chequer-board, with here a spire and there a château-roof peeping out from embowering woods—a contrast indeed to the distant thunder of battle in the north.

"It's strange, isn't it," he went on—"all that peace down there, and yet the German guns so near?" She walked on in silence, and he followed, babbling again about old Rome. "Glory was the Roman watchword, y'know—not peace ... Now there's a passage in Gibbon ... Or is it in Caesar? ... By gum, it might even be in Napier's Peninsular stuff ... But, of course, Napier was really an old Roman, so it doesn't matter; and anyway it's jolly good ... How does it go?" He pondered a little, and then quoted: " 'None died more gloriously that night, though there was much glory, and many died.' ... Fine, isn't it, that sense of glory?"

"Glory be damned," said Sister Mary, turning on him with flushed cheeks.

"Of course, there's another side to it," he said confusedly.

"Och, I'm not blaming you. And it's all a muddle, as you say. But I'm remembering that lad with the bullet in his spine—Hiblot in Salle Foch." (He recalled the man—a half-man only now, paralysed from the waist down.) "And yet," she went on, "they're saying the Germans have no right to be using that gas of theirs. As if gas could chain a man to a bed of torment any worse than Hiblot's bullet." She strode off from him, herself warlike as any Amazon; and, crestfallen, he limped after. She soon turned, however, to say over her shoulder, "Not to mention the bullet in your own knee," for she had noted his slackening pace. "And me forgetting it, and it hurting you! We'll have to be turning back."

He protested they must really go on to Aubepierre— the quaintest of inns, the *patronne* a dear. And the draught-oxen!—she must really see them hauling timber —sleepy-eyed fellows, big as elephants and as strong. So they went on again; and the talk turned to Eilean Aros—to the household of Moy, and especially to its chief. Smiling, they recalled that it was he who was responsible in a way for their meeting out at Arc, and so for this jaunt to Aubepierre. But at last they came to discussing Gurney.

"Did ever I tell you of the only time I ever saw him in Aros, and him at the queer game—looking from a wee boat, through a barrel without ends, at the bottom of Loch Spelve?" she said.

"The skunk!" growled MacLeod. "And now he's here! Will we never be quit of him!"

"Who and what is he, at all?"

He told her what he knew of the man, but found himself uneasily avoiding all mention of Marion's part in the story; and by the time he had finished they had reached the inn at Aubepierre. At the door she summed up Gurney in simple, almost schoolgirl, fashion. "Just what I thought ... It's bad he is." And somehow the quiet statement made there in the rosy twilight sounded terrible as a sentence of doom. To be shut out from the world of Mary Yarrow! By the Lord! thought MacLeod, how hard women can be!

They sat down, hungry enough, to a plain supper of hare-ragout, confiture and a chunk of local cheese. Some wine there was also—a silky Graves; but of this Sister Mary only sipped a thimbleful, despite his protests that she did injustice to a rarity reserved by the *patronne* for himself and his friends. She, however, had problems to unravel which demanded all her wits, and therefore persistently declined. Already she was re-examining the history of Gurney.

"It's queer now," she said, "that wee Straw-Feet should be the man sent out on an inquiry into your district—so far away from Havre."

"Very queer. But of course, the little devil has wangled it."

"How could he? A bad lot like him would surely not have much pull with our people?"

"Oh, he's slim enough for anything, old Gurney. He wants to know every bit of the country, I'll bet. Why, even before I gave him away to the Provost-Marshal, he was suggesting he'd look me up at Arc. And I daresay he's been keeping his eye on Arc ever since."

"Spying's in his blood, you mean?"

"Yes, but there's more than that to it. Why should fie want to come within arm's reach of me again? I've given him away once already, haven't I?"

"Looks like he was a good hater, and wants to get back on you, Médecin-Chef."

"Yes, he was a good hater that night he bolted from Aros, years ago." And he told her of the scene at the water's edge on Loch Spelve. "Showed his teeth that night," he growled. "Like a ferret, he did."

"Well, you mind your step ... Maybe, however, it's just chance his being sent here."

"Nary a chance, Sister. I can figure it all out."

"More than I can."

"Don't you think that if another Sister got best on you, you'd be the least bit interested in her after-life?"

Sister Mary laughed uneasily. "Why, yes, I daresay I would."

"Aha! "He smiled, and tossed off a full goblet of wine, with all the airs of a knowing dog. "Well, Gurney wouldn't be much different, I'll bet! ... And I'll wager he knows there are plenty bickerings between French and English in mixed units like ours, and that the people at Marac have their knife in us; also that Captain Bee over there has a special scalpel for myself."

"Oh, come now, however could Gurney get to know all that?"

"By doing his usual job—picking other people's brains."

"Intelligence people's?"

"Why not? And by the same dodge he hears of this fuss about the dead man found in the Calvaire Wood: lets it get around that he knows this district, although he knows dam-all about it; pulls a wire or two, and grabs the job."

"You're marvellous, Médecin-Chef. You should be at the top of the Intelligence push, with a brain like yours."

"Grin away; but you'll see I'm right."

"Well, right or not about that bit, old Gurney's a bad 'un; and, if I were you, I'd give him johnny-up-the-orchard."

"What's that?"

"Chase him home. Wire the A.P.M. at Havre that he's after no good here, and spinning out his time, loafing."

"Blamed if I do," said MacLeod with flushed face, and quaffing another glass of Graves. "If Gurney wants a fight, he can have it. My wits against his any day."

"Then if it's wits that's in it, less of that wine, Médecin-Chef."

He dismissed the warning with a wave of his hand, and went on: "As for loafing—our Intelligence give these 'agents doubles' rather long rope, but keep an eye on them all the time. Give them old bones to worry, just to keep them out of mischief—away from Jerry ... See?" And he helped himself again to the wine of Aubepierre.

"I can see you're having too much wine," said Sister Mary, plump and plain.

"No, no. Just the right amount, my dear. There's no ' Drink to me only with thine eyes,' on this side of the table ... Lovely night, lovely wine, lovely woman ... Have a sip, yourself."

"Had heaps, thanks ... But about Gurney now. You weren't mixed up in any way with this dead man business at the Calvaire, were you?"

"Now, now, little girls mustn't ask questions of their good kind Médecin-Chef," said he, waggishly shaking his head, and again filling his glass.

She regarded his drink with disfavour, and rose. "Time we were getting back," she said.

"Wait a bit—wait a bit. Want to tell you something ... And that's this. I figure out this Calvaire show doesn't matter a curse to Gurney, as regards myself. No, 'tisn't that." And here he dropped his voice dramatically. "Fact is, there's a girl between Gurney and me."

Sister Mary resumed her seat at once. "Yes," she said, all sympathy. And on pretence of helping herself to wine, moved the bottle out of his reach.

"Or was, rather ... For she's dead," he continued, while his eyes grew moist and rolled sentimentally.

Sister Mary was silent, but a little colour rose to her temples.

"Gurney was fond of her ... So was I ... Marion ... Never forget her, never." He heaved a huge sigh.

"But he's quite an old man. Surely."

"Yes, but there it is, my dear—there it is ... That chap at Havre—the A.P.M., y'know—wanted to make out he might be her father, unbeknownst to her and all that, just like a good old melodrama ... But" — and here he thumped the table till the glasses rattled— "but I say no—no—no ... Too sweet a girl to have Gurney for father ... And then he's a Boche ... But no Boche about Marion ... As a matter of fact, the damned Boches killed her ... Sunk her hospital ship, blast 'em!"

"I see," said Sister Mary softly. "I'm sorry, Médecin-Chef."

"Nothing between us ... She wouldn't have me ... But I'll never forget Marion, y'know ... never forget her."

"Poor Marion!"

"Thank you, my dear." He was almost maudlin now, and made to kiss her hand.

She rose. "Oh, but how late," she said. "Time we were getting back. Ten's the hour for nurses, you remember. I can see Matron sitting up for me."

"Blow Matron," he said, and rose also, but somewhat heavily.

As they came out of doors the fresh evening airs brought him some way back to his senses. "Afraid I've been blithering a bit," he said.

"Och, it's all wee Straw-Feet's fault," she said cheerily. "And this Calvaire business must be a worry to you ... Well, I can see that the chief of a mixed hospital hasn't his troubles to seek. All kinds of queer jobs on your hands, I'm sure."

"So long's this Calvaire business doesn't get into the hands of those French johnnies at Marac, I don't mind," he said gloomily.

"And what have they to do with it? Who are they, anyway?"

"French Intelligence. And they've got their knife in us, as I told you—God knows why. Measly lot of neurasthenics!"

It was late twilight when they set out on the return journey. As they left the valley, they saw the great highway stretch ghostly white in the rays of a moon just rising; and to MacLeod, in that strange light, the old road seemed formidably long—its miles multiplied to leagues. The rest at the inn had stiffened his bad knee, too. Also it now came really home to him that he had been unwise in the matter of that rare Graves. And so, after half an hour's walk, he halted and suggested a short-cut he had just remembered—a footpath which cut off a curve of the great highway and saved a good mile: it should be close at hand. Sister Mary was the first to discover it; and they descended into a hollow to find themselves amid fields of high grass which obscured the route badly, shine the moon ever so bright. It was narrow too—so narrow that they must walk Indian file. Like most short-cuts it belied its name; and they had frequent halts to mark their course; but at last they noted with thankfulness that they were approaching the embankment of the Roman road on the farther side of the little valley.

"Land, ho! "cried MacLeod gaily, from a few paces ahead.

"Hush," said Sister Mary, "there's something queer on that slope in front."

They halted to regard a dark mass moving erratically through a film of thin mist on the brow of the acclivity. Now it appeared from behind a patch of gorse; now it was gone; anon it came into view ten or twenty yards to right or left of the bush whence it had at first emerged.

"Gurney? "she whispered, and clutched his arm.

"Nonsense!" he said; "you have Gurney on the brain. It's only a stray calf or foal or something." He had half an idea, however—remembering the affair of Koechlin—that it might be another escaped Boche from the Courbon camp; but he kept this thought to himself; he must reassure the girl, and, for that end, any yarn would do. Meanwhile he had only his whangie for weapon. Devilish awkward, this.

And now the thing, whatever it was, dived into the long grasses, and the ripple of these in the ghostly moonlight showed it coming straight towards them, and swiftly too —a beast of some kind, or a man crouching while he ran at incredible speed. It came on to the level now with a tumble and a roll, then halted suddenly. A savage head was tossed; white tusks showed and a slit-like angry eye; a grunt completed the picture, and MacLeod laughed aloud. "Wild-boar," he said. "He'll give no trouble ... Shoo!"He raised his swagger-cane. "Shoo!"

But the brute charged instantly, and at the same moment he felt himself swept aside by Mary Yarrow's powerful arm. He stumbled over his lame leg and fell. Looking up, he saw the girl swing her nurse's cloak from her shoulders, and display it at the length of her outstretched right arm. There came a swish in the long grasses, a drumming of hooves, and the cloak was gone.

He scrambled to his feet as she tottered towards him. "I'm a fool," she said. "Going to faint." MacLeod caught her as she fell; and, too good a doctor to hesitate, allowed her to subside gently to earth. He bent to take her pulse; found it recovering almost at once; and so seated himself beside her on a bit of outcropping rock. She was a strong healthy woman—shouldn't take long to come round. Over there a ruffle in the high grass marked the retreat of the beast. The cloak lay twenty yards away.

Sister Mary opened her eyes, sighed, and smiled wanly. "I suppose that pig knew I was Irish," she said ... "Support home industries, y'know ... They were always great on protection—these French."

"Quiet—quiet!" he growled. "And don't move, please."

She was silent for a few minutes. "Where's my cloak?" she asked. He departed and returned with it. "Much damage?" she said, still lying straight as an arrow.

"Two feet of a rip." He held the mantle up against the moon.

"Lord, what will Matron say! Here, let me out of this grass, or I'll be choked." He gave her a hand, and she rose. "Dear-a-dear," she said, examining the damage to her mantle, "pigs are pigs all the world over—no manners at all ... Whatever came over yon fellow?"

"I expect his mate had been shot some miles away; and then he just ran amok."

"The poor thing! ... But wasn't he a monster?"

"Yes; how big would you say?"

"As big's a house ... At least that's what I'll tell the girls at breakfast tomorrow." She sat down on the bit of rock. "Takes it out of you, fighting wild-pig," she said, smiling up at him with dancing eyes.

Very provocative she looked now in the moonlight, this Irish girl with her daring and jests and dark beauty ... And she had probably saved his life ... He felt strangely moved; and the wine in his head brought tears so readily to his eyes that he felt the least bit ashamed. All the same he wanted to sink at this girl's feet, lay his head in her lap and let her mother him a little. Adorable that, if only it could happen. But the next moment, as if to compensate against this sentimentalism, the wine that flushed his brain so handsomely a moment ago gave it a poisonous twist, and at once he was game for any escapade with a spice of devil in it. No tears now; for his eyes were hot, and his mouth dry. He turned on her, but only to see her face uplifted to the moon's pale austerity, a solemn regard in her eyes. And dulled though he was, it needed no telepathy to tell him that the beauty and mystery of the night had evoked in her the old awe, so close to worship. Yet he was still so little master of himself that he must break into that sanctuary. "A penny for your thoughts," he said.

She answered softly: "'Praise to the holiest in the height.'"

Uneasy, he turned away; he felt shut out of her world as much as Gurney was. But he would brazen it out—bring her back to earth again, by gad! Clearing his throat he asked casually: "By the by, wherever did you learn that dodge with the cloak?"

She sighed and awoke from her dream of beauty. "Oh, that," she said with a smile that raised the devil in him anew; "in the movies, of course—bull-fights and matadors and so on. And I didn't learn it extra well, either; for two feet of a rent in his cloak would get any wee bull-fighter the sack out of all Spain." She rose. "Well, we'd best be going on again if I'm to be in by ten ... Och, it's a great war, sure enough."

MacLeod laughed joyously at her nonchalance; while, as if by way of underlining her last words, the guns of Verdun suddenly gave louder voice. But though heavy iron doors were now slammed all over high heaven, MacLeod did not cease from his wild laughter—for the wine of Aubepierre is indeed a heady wine—and, still laughing, he took Sister Mary in his arms and kissed her.

She slapped his face, but he only cackled the louder; while she stood back, an angry scowl on her brow; then, recognizing the true source of his merriment, she smiled forgiveness. "Come on home now," she said; "for if that fellow with the tusks comes back, I'll waste no more of my cloak on the likes of you."

She walked off in front, and, still chuckling, Monsieur le Medécin-Chef de l'Hôpital Temporaire d'Arc-en-Aulnoy shouldered his swagger-cane and stumped unsteadily after.

XXIV: A fire is lit

NEXT day was "theatre-day," so operations kept MacLeod busy all morning; and he had only time to make a hurried visit to his wards just before lunch. When he went the round of Salle Foch—Sister Mary's ward—there was scarcely a minute for anything but official talk; yet as he reached the door he found opportunity to say: "Last night.—I'm sorry."

She smiled and held out a Cachet Faivre which she evidently had ready to hand.

"For my head?" he asked with a grin, relieved to find she took the affair so sensibly. "Bit of a scare, wasn't it? How do you feel yourself this morning?"

"Feel?" she said. "I feel that thankful I could be putting up one of those wee shrines you see at the side of the Aubepierre road ... Wasn't he big?"

"Big's a house," he assured her, and departed to his other wards.

A few minutes sufficed for what remained of a merely formal visit to the other salles, since Henson had already done all the major dressings. He must change quickly now if he was to be in time for lunch; so, kilting his surgical gown above knees, he ran swiftly upstairs and burst into his room, to find Henri—who acted as his batman—busy with cans of hot water beside the big sponge-bath. "A letter for M. le Major," said Henri, indicating the mantelpiece, where lay an envelope elaborately sealed with red wax.

He opened the packet, and found a tiny parcel of tissue paper with a visiting-card pinned to it. "Mr. Ludovic Gurney," he read; below the print was a scribble in pencil, "Lion d'Or." He fingered the package; but before he undid a single fold of the soft wrappings he had guessed their content, and his heart beat fast. Then slowly and carefully he unwound the tissue, and beheld what he had surmised so surely—the wrist-watch he had lost some months back, the glass in fragments behind the clay-encrusted screen of silvered wire, and only frayed portions of the leather straps remaining. The back casing, however, was clear of earth, for it had been polished to lay bare the name engraved there—his own; and raising his eyes to the mirror, he saw them filled with a puzzled foreboding ... He had trod on a toad in his path, yet here it was at the next turning ... By God, if Gurney gave him away about this, the Marac people would get busy; the hospital would come down to Class B; and he'd get the key of the street. Nice thing to go home in the middle of the old war, and be asked why you'd been sacked! ... And things would be magnified no end. The sensational newspapers would get hold of the story. "Secret burial of Dead German by British Doctor." If it got that length, the mud would stick to him all his life.

Yet it was strange that Gurney had parted with the watch—fairly clear evidence of his connection with the burial in the Calvaire. And the little devil would have witnesses, of course. What was his game? ... Playing the generous enemy in order to open a fresh attack? Was that it?

"All is ready, monsieur," said Henri, as he finished spreading the bath mat, and retired discreetly. But MacLeod hardly heard him—hardly, indeed, saw his own face now in the big mirror. For already, in fancy, he was back in the wood of the Calvaire, at the digging of a grave, while the crushed figure of Koechlin stood by his side. Yes, it must have been then it had fallen —a buckle doubtless giving way as he laboured at those heavy clods. How fantastic it had all been, that tragic episode. Fantastic, too, that chance had thrown this trinket at Gurney's feet. And now he had struck in revenge for the Havre give-away! ... Little fox— little fox! sitting so quietly in your room at the Lion d'Or, and waiting to strike again!

While he mused, the gong sounded suddenly—shattering, terrifying—and brought him back to the workaday world where people ate and drank and chattered about nothing. But he must keep a grip of himself, or he would go to pieces. So, locking the battered watch in his desk, he discarded his surgical suit, then bathed and got into uniform in double quick time. At table he showed a brave front, although inwardly perturbed; but somehow the mess sensed his interior gloom. They concluded, indeed, that he had been having a bad time at operations that morning, and immediately set about "cheering up old Mac." And so strenuous were their efforts to this end that he felt decidedly relieved when the meal finished. Then, excusing himself from the usual after-lunch visit to the café with Street and Henson, he made at once for the Lion d'Or and asked for Gurney.

The *patronne* was sorry; but the gentleman had gone to Marac and would not return till late. Marac!— the French Intelligence post—just as he had guessed! If Gurney got Bee mixed up in this business, then the fat would be in the fire. But it was no use guessing; he must just prepare for such a blaze as best he could. So he scribbled a hasty note to Gurney: "Come and see me to-night—any time"; and leaving it with the *patronne*, returned to hospital, secured a motor, and set out on a round of civilian patients in the neighbouring villages—work usually done by Henson, but claimed on this occasion by his chief, since therein lay distraction for an hour or two.

But those duties were done perfunctorily that afternoon, for his thoughts were elsewhere. Persistently his mind turned to the contrast of last night's folly with the tragedy so vividly recalled to-day by the recovery of that battered wrist-watch ... Mary Yarrow's roguish eyes and poor Koechlin's distracted gaze ... A mad world! Gurney and Marion! ... Yes, Marion was dead; and that kiss last night seemed now the basest treachery to her memory ... Aros; old Moy ... Oh, damn old Moy!—why had he sent that Irish witch to Arc? It all seemed some devilish conspiracy against his peace of mind ... Gurney, too! ... And now his thoughts were murderous towards the little man. In imagination he saw himself inveigling him into a visit to the grave in the Calvaire Wood, and then, on some pretext or other, farther into the depths of the forest. He had already buried one man there. Why not Straw-Feet also?

A nerve-racking day; and evening found him pacing the big bare chamber and awaiting his enemy. Why didn't he come—blast him! Should he telephone to the Lion d'Or from the office downstairs? No, that wouldn't do: he might let slip a tell-tale word or two; and he wouldn't put it past Straw-Feet to have someone listening-in. And so an hour passed. To and fro —to and fro. At last a tap came to the door, and he opened.

But it was only old Featherly, who hoped the Médecin-Chef was well. Thought he had looked worried at -lunch. Did he mind if he came in for a chat? ... MacLeod had him in at once. He knew what the old fellow wanted, and without more ado produced some eau-de-vie of great age—a gift from the Mother Superior of the convent at Giey, pour le Major écossais, because he had been kind to her little orphans when they were ill. And, not for the first time, the Honourable Osmund tasted and discussed the merits of the bottle labelled in the good Mother's fine script, "Prunes: 1899," as against those of "Prunelles: 1901." Yet, what with many reminiscences of Montana—including a lengthy digression on the salutary effects of work on The Land on the characters of certain "good old murderers" lent out by a neighbouring prison—it took the aged rancher many glasses, and till close on eleven o'clock, before he finally summed up in favour of "Prunelles: 1901." He departed, promising further yarns of reclaimed criminals, some other jolly evening. "Cheers you up, doesn't it, Médecin-Chef, when you see what The Land can do?"

"Yes, not to mention a much bigger thing—your own kindness of heart, Featherly."

"Oh, that!" said the rancher, wincing. "Nothing, my boy, nothing at all. It's The Land, you know, The Land"; and so departed.

Some ten minutes after he had gone, Henri knocked, and announced Monsieur Gurney; and the little man entered, the old-fashioned deer-stalker cap held in restless fingers. He clicked his heels and bowed, as Henri shut the outer of the two doors somewhat noisily. Gurney started at the sound, then discovering the double doors, skipped aside nervously as MacLeod passed him to close the second door. Noting his apprehension, MacLeod felt easier at once. "Won't you sit down?" he said; and the little man crept furtively to a chair. "Some eau-de-vie?" asked the surgeon.

Gurney thanked him and took the glass with a hand not too steady. He sipped in silence at "Prunelles: 1901," for a moment or two; and MacLeod also tasted, regarding him narrowly. "You got the packet I sent?" asked Gurney.

"Yes, it's mine all right," said MacLeod. He rose, and going to his desk, took out the watch. "What about it?"

"Nothing. I return it. That is all." His eyes had something of an appeal in them; and for the first time MacLeod saw that they were brown. Also they seemed to be asking a favour; a dog-like pleading was in them.

"What's the game?" said MacLeod harshly, hardening his heart. The dog-like eyes brimmed with tears and turned aside. And scarcely knowing what he did, MacLeod found to his astonishment that he had risen, and placed a compassionate hand on the little man's shoulder. But he came to himself instantly, and drew back as if retreating from some occult hypnotic power.

Gurney looked up reproachfully. "You still distrust me?" he said.

MacLeod paced across to the window uneasily. "Haven't I good cause?" he asked. Then turning of a sudden he tossed the watch at Gurney's feet. "There!" he said. "I'm taking no favours from you."

The little man rose wearily, as if broken in spirit.

"Stop," said MacLeod, crossing to him with energy, and pushing him back into his chair. "What the hell are you driving at?"

Gurney hung his head as the other gazed at him, angry and puzzled. And what was this? Damn it! the fellow was actually snivelling. No, he was shaking as in a rigor! The little man spoke. "I am cold," he said faintly. "An old friend—the ague."

MacLeod instantly flung aside the huge down covering of the bed, seized some blankets and wrapped the sick man in them. "Hold on," he said. "I'll light a fire, and get a hot drink." He set a match to the twigs under the well-seasoned logs on the hearth, and the fire blazed immediately. Then running downstairs to the nearest ward, he returned with a kettle of hot water, and made a tumblerful of toddy. Gurney sipped gratefully, and extended a trembling hand to the fire, now so well alight that—what with its blaze and the warmth of the summer night—MacLeod felt stifled. Even Gurney was already beginning to perspire and soon declared himself better. The surgeon, taking his pulse, found it slowing. "You're through with it," he said, rising from where he knelt by the side of the sick man. "A little more toddy, and you'll be as fit's a fiddle." He held the glass to his lips. "And now, what about opening a window?"

Gurney agreed and MacLeod limped across the room, threw the windows wide, and stood for a moment breathing deeply and looking out on the summer dark. What the deuce was he to do with this fellow? Gurney at any time was an undesirable—but a sick Gurney was doubly such. Should he have a car out and dump him in his lodging at the Lion d'Or—or put him in hospital? A little noise now caused him to turn, and he saw that Gurney had left his chair and was stooping over the hearth. MacLeod went to him at once. "Don't move, you fool!" he cried. But before he could reach him, Gurney had picked up the broken watch and dropped it into the central heat of the fire. Already the casing was molten, dislimning in the white-hot ashes, and only one little cogged wheel showed in red outline. The little man looked up with a smile of triumph. MacLeod looked on amazed. This gesture of destroying deadly evidence was clearly one asking for reconciliation—-but it had a touch of melodrama in it that hinted a ruse of some sort. Could it be that Gurney had tricked him by a mere simulation of illness into lighting the fire, so that he might the more effectively stage this affair? The surgeon's professional pride was touched. "Damn you for a fake," he said angrily. "There was no ague in that pulse of yours."

Gurney went calmly back to his chair and his blankets. "I wish it were indeed so," said he; "for it is bad while it lasts. But it passes quickly; and I shall soon be well again. I have been careless about my quinine of late."

Dubious, MacLeod glowered down at him. Even if the fellow had played a trick on him, he had taken some trouble about it. And he was evidently bent on being friendly; for there could be no doubt that the sole evidence about the complicity of the Médecin-Chef of Arc-en-Aulnoy in the affair of the Calvaire Wood was now destroyed. Gurney had indeed bested him in the game of magnanimity. A queer lot! What sort of chap was he in reality? A tiny glow of sympathy for the sick man, so grotesquely huddled in the bed-quilt there, made itself felt within him. A strange world, and all sorts of quaint people in it. And who was he to judge little Straw-Feet? "Some more 'Prunelles'?" he said, pouring out a glass.

Smiling, Gurney assented. In him, too, a little fire of friendliness was lit; the atmosphere of the room seemed to change in some subtle fashion. MacLeod proffered a cigarette, lighted it for him, took one himself; and they smoked in silence for a space. An odd pair, thought MacLeod. But why in all the world had Gurney done this? That wrist-watch might have made endless trouble for himself and the hospital: he might even have had to resign. Why had the fellow held his hand? ... At last a light dawned on him, and he broke silence suddenly. "Ah!" he cried, "there it is!—Marion?"

He turned a questioning eye on the little man, and saw that at the name, his whole aspect changed utterly. The face, so placid a moment ago, became contorted in a spasm of grief, and was instantly hid in the crook of an arm. Much moved, MacLeod rose and again crossed to the open window. Through the dark of the massed chestnut-trees by the river, a few lit windows showed brokenly. Verdun was strangely silent; the only sound that of a bell-frog crying chink-chink by the great park-wall. No, he couldn't look on at grief like that; it gripped too much. But a little murmur came from Gurney, and despite his dread of a scene, he came back to the sick man. What was he babbling? ... German! Yes, he was speaking German, at last! The truth would out! ... "What is it?" he asked, bending over him.

"Warum bin ich nicht gestorben von mutterleibe an," whispered Gurney in agony; and the surgeon knew enough of tongues to recognize the cry of Job in his dark hour: "Why died I not from the womb!"

The man was distracted beyond belief! This despised mercenary was capable of a depth of feeling he himself had never compassed. The discipline of his surgical training, he knew, had of necessity cut him off in some degree from the ordinary emotions of mankind; yet he had hoped never to be so blunted as some of his colleagues, such as Henson. But, listening to this crushed man's utterance, he felt anew his disability—felt himself restricted from an intensity of life he had never dreamed; and dumbly he resented it. Why! he had only to murmur a girl's name, and this poor creature was instantly peer with Job in spiritual suffering. Frustrate, he sat down, greatly humbled.

Gurney had now sobered, and turned clear eyes on him. "Pardon," he said.

"All right; all right! Have another peg."

The older man put up a protesting hand. "Yes, it is Marion. Do you not see why I have come? I must have news of her. You spoke in Havre of her death. That is certain, is it?" The words were almost wrung from him.

MacLeod moved uneasily. "Yes," he said; "it is certain."

Again they sat in silence for a time, and gazed at the fire's last embers. The little man seemed to have shrunken, and his grief-stricken countenance was pitiable; he appeared to age every minute now, and MacLeod had a wild fancy that he would shrivel and die—a mummy in those encasing blankets. He felt almost hysterical, and at last could contain himself no longer. "For God's sake, man," he said, "pull yourself together. We can't go on like this. What's wrong? Surely you've seen deaths enough, these last four years."

"Yes—many—many. And now it is only a young girl who dies; yet I become a broken man. You think that strange?"

MacLeod was silent, as if reproved.

"And," went on Gurney, "you think it strange, even when she was Marion?"

MacLeod steeled his heart, and lied: he would pluck out the heart of this man's secret. "Yes," he said doggedly. "I think it strange." And then to cover the lie: "She wasn't of your blood, surely."

Gurney shook his head, smiling a little bitterly, although his eyes glowed now with a secret pride. MacLeod saw the fire in them, and instantly understood. "Good God! "he said in a low voice. "A man of your years—in love with her?"

The strange little man bowed his head. "Yes," he said.

"But I don't understand," stammered the youth.

"Nor do I," said Gurney, very simply and with dignity. "But that was the way of it"; and he rose, discarding his many wraps, as if to go.

MacLeod was again humbled. There was nothing more to be said. Here were deeps he had never sounded. He recalled Gurney's mastery in music. Yes, only the art of Beethoven could shadow forth mysteries such as these; the solemn passages of the Seventh Symphony came back to him, with their profounds of tragic meaning.

But Gurney was moving to the door; and he hastened to take his arm, for his steps were uncertain. Strange that he should be escorting his one-time enemy with such solicitude! They went downstairs; and in the porch, the boars' heads, lit feebly by the rays of a single oil-lamp, seemed to grin down in irony on them— poor humans—bewildered by the whys and wherefores of life. No further word was now spoken; they went on to the park gates, and emerged in the moonlit village street. Past midnight now, and Verdun still silent. They turned a corner or two, and, a little way up the Chaumont road, beheld the gilt lion of Gurney's inn glisten in the moonbeams. Noting it, the little man paused, as if to say good night. But so frail did he look that MacLeod took his arm more firmly and continued his convoy. At the door of the Lion d'Or, the *patronne* met them in her night-wrap, a taper in her hand; and reproved them for the lateness of the hour. "Come another evening, when you're more fit," said the surgeon. Gurney only nodded, exhaustion in his every movement; and the *patronne*, seeing how things were, took his arm.

MacLeod turned homewards. Very peaceful and very fair the night, as the moon rode high above the little village—the same moon that shone on Eilean Aros even then. That passage from the Seventh Symphony still worked in his brain. White gable-ends and heavy shadows alternated in the irregular outlines of the little houses, until he approached the open Place where were the church and the Mairie and the château gates.

Somewhere in the oaks beyond the park a nightingale broke into song. It ceased after a dozen notes, and another answered in a different key. The first singer replied by a variation of the original theme; and MacLeod halted to hear ... Again the pause, again the music, and the pause again. He became impatient that the song should resume; for even the dark-blue heaven seemed to throb in sympathy with the melody so lately dissolved into the night. Here surely was the secret of this singer—those masterly pauses that by contrast of silence distil essential beauty from the notes just overpast, and evoke desire for renewal of the song. It was as if a spell held him rooted there; and he waited, breathless, until the rich notes poured forth once more —ceased—began anew—and ceased again.

And now it seemed the deeps of the sky would lose their loveliness did this song fail; the beauty of the shadowy woods must surely fade did it not return. Those simple notes were so small a thing; yet take them from out the symphony of night, and the earth lay as if dead —the trees turned to stone; let them but resume, and the violet sky, the choiring birds, and he—the rapt listener—were one in some divine harmony of the Master Harp-Player who

Harps without pause, building with song the world:

The bird was silent now; but a strange hum was in the air, and somewhere to the west a faint column, as of smoke, ascended the moonlit heaven. The hum grew louder every moment; lights appeared in the village windows, and from this one and that popped night-capped heads, almost Hogarthian in their quaintness. The hum had now a booming quality, as of a swarm of giant bees; and the cloudy column in the sky moved nearer. Presently a line of motor-cars appeared—an Army Service Corps on the move to the south; each car a replica of its grey neighbour, the interval of fifty yards between them exactly held; exact, too, the pitch of the note the machines gave voice to, a vast monotone. Over a hundred rolled past; and rising from the roadway the summer dust ascended— the pillar of cloud accompanying them. Silent at each steering-wheel sat a man in horizon-blue, looking neither to left or right, his eye on the auto before him. No sign of weapons was visible; but here surely was as dread a symbol of war as any show of bayonets. The precision of all, with its deadly intensity—this pressing forwards of stores and food for the combatants spoke clearly of the vastness of the conflict.

They passed; and the hum in the distance had already a faint resemblance to a musical note, as MacLeod halted outside the hospital porch to listen again for the nightingale. But no bird sang. There was only that distant booming as of a swarm of angry bees—gigantic, multitudinous, fell of purpose ... And throughout what ages must the Harp-Player agonize before he wove a note such as that into the song of the morning stars.

XXV: Race

NEXT morning the affair of Gurney was the first thing to occupy the waking moments of MacLeod; and as he donned his uniform, his mood towards the little man alternated between sympathy and distrust. That side of him which was Médecin-Chef of a French hospital dwelt on those few words of German which the little man had involuntarily uttered yesterday in a moment of distraction—words which discovered him at last as really Boche by birth, and, by all the rules of the game, an object for the heartiest hatred. But that other side, which concerned itself but little with the world of uniforms and bombardments, and dreamt so much of Marion and old days in Eilean Aros, found excuse for Gurney in many ways. Most likely wee Straw-Feet was at heart a neutral, no matter what his birthplace or upbringing—a creature, maybe, as denationalized as any Swiss—a cosmopolitan. Even if he were Boche, he was probably a communist—one of the Bebel and Liebknecht gang, perhaps. Anyway, the poor beggar was ill and ageing fast. Also there was his strange passion for the dead Marion. Quaint and tragic, all that. And, hang it! the duty of a doctor was plain enough: the man was sick, Boche or no Boche; he must look him up after breakfast, and see if that so-called ague had passed.

But at breakfast he got news which put all thoughts of Gurney out of his head. For Street and Hem had already been out to read the yellow war bulletins in the post office window, and brought back news of importance. It was the last day of May, 1918, and reports from the front between the Vesle and Marne were bad —very bad: the break-through of the Boches had not been held, and every day saw them smashing farther south and west. Despite the yellow bulletins, the truth must out: no matter for the assurance in the telegrams, so boldly displayed in the post office, that "le champ de bataille est couvert de cadavres allemands," the enemy armies were now close on Château-Thierry—in fact were already only ten miles east of that town—at Dormans. And anxious glances were cast by the Arc mess each morning at the big chart on the wall, where the succession of blue-pencilled curves had bellied more and more to the sou'-west for every day of the last five.

Apart from the general depression, MacLeod had his own particular worry. For his hospital was now rather hanging in the air, since the

Boche had got so well into his stride: the enemy, indeed, were a good two hundred miles nearer Blighty than himself and his staff. He communicated his thoughts to Leclercq, who sat beside him at mess.

"Yes," said the Frenchman, "one begins to feel a little isolate, if one is English. But for us French, it does not feel so bad. For if we evacuate, we can always go south where there is much France without any Boche in her ... But we shall soon have instruction what to do from Chaumont."

And, sure enough, by the post which arrived ten minutes later, there came a communication from the Service de Santé at Chaumont, asking MacLeod to prepare plans for a possible evacuation of his hospital. Fortunately the work had recently been easier: the wounded less in number—the wounds less serious; for the Verdun front had been quieter of late, since the Cambrai areas had become so active. MacLeod, therefore, set his staff to work at once: lists were soon completed, showing "stretcher" and "sitting" cases; and these were forthwith allocated to the various motor-ambulances; while nurses were also detailed. Dressings for the journey were prepared; but the victualling was only sketched in outline, since the Chaumont service had not yet indicated their objective.

Then Leclercq was consulted about emergencies. Suppose a battle suddenly swung their way before the evacuation of the hospital was complete—an unlikely happening, but one for which provision must be made —then who remained behind to look after the wounded?

"Of course, I stay," said MacLeod.

"Mais, non," grinned Leclercq, "that is to me, that duty."

"Why?"

"Because it is so in all the army of France. And your hôpital is attach to the army of Verdun, which is of France ... Yes, the youngest doctor always remain beind in a case like that."

"The devil you do! Ever done it?"

"But, yes."

"Where?"

"At the Col de Bonhomme, I have stay beind with the blessés."

"What happened?"

Leclercq smiled. "The battle came near our hôpital, and we evacuate—but not all ... Testevide, the older doctor, go off with most of the wounded. But I stay beind, with the two youngest orderlies, and the rest of wounded, because that is the order of the French Army."

"And then—?"

"Oh, ver' nice ... The battle move away a little, and then both sides shell the hôpital, because it is in between them. Ver' nice, thank you."

"Well—?"

"Then the Boche take the hôpital; and many of them come with the baionnette and look at me, and look at my wounded. But I have the white gown like an angel, and I look ver' sage; and they do nothing to us. Then all at once our soixante-quinze begin to fire, and the Boche go away ver' quick."

"Didn't try to make you prisoner?"

Leclercq's dark face flushed. "No, no," he said softly, "they could not make prisoner of me."

"Why not?"

The Frenchman tapped a breast-pocket in his tunic. "I always carry morphine for that ... If they take me, I swallow it."

Race ... There it was, that bitter hatred of the French for the German—so different from the British contempt and dislike. Indeed, it was clear that the French regarded the Boche as something subhuman. Only a week ago, MacLeod recalled, a young Chasseur Alpin officer had dropped in to lunch at the mess; and, someone having remarked the oddity of a tie-pin he wore, he had explained that the pin's head was a tooth extracted from a Boche whom he himself had killed. He had, it appeared, succoured a wounded German on the battle-field—given him a drink from his flask, and then passed on, only to be fired upon from behind by the man he had just aided. The Frenchman had returned, shot the Boche dead; and then in a frenzy of rage, picked up a pair of field-telephone pincers and secured this ghastly memento.

Old Featherly—aristocrat and idealist—protested; even rose from the table. Hang it all! it wasn't decent —it wasn't cricket—it wasn't done, y'know. But the young Chasseur Alpin had laughingly retorted that this was a serious war. *La morale* must be kept up; and the best way of doing that was to keep on hating *le sale Boche*. By way of illustration, he cited the case of his own general, who had recently appeared on parade mounted on a charger which wore a necklace of human ears—dead Germans' ears ... *Encore la morale*.

Yes, mused MacLeod, it was difficult for a Britisher to get the hang of a Frenchman's outlook on this matter. Up till yesterday, we had been an island race; to-day the aeroplane had wiped out insularity. But we had not as yet got accustomed to that change, so could not see ourselves just as much in the cockpit of Europe as our Allies. How, then, should we understand the Frenchman's abhorrence for the Boche—how sense the feelings of a nation that had sat for generations cheek by jowl with this ancient powerful enemy?

And no less did MacLeod sense a racial difference in spheres other than those of war. For, later on that same day, as they rested for a spell from their work at the evacuation lists, Leclercq pulled out a bulky typescript from a parcel of books on his desk. "I have a cousin who write a novel about the war," he said, "and he have take that incident of myself and my hôpital at the Col de Bonhomme, and made it into a bit of his story. It is trèsdrôle; and I shall lend you the pages, if you like ... It is ver' good."

MacLeod said he would be glad to see the tale; and Leclercq immediately tore several leaves apart from the script's fastenings. "Don't' bust it all to pieces," said MacLeod. "I'd like to read it as it stands."

"No, no, you would not like ... You are too - écossais ... too Puritan ... It is not all of the war, this roman."

"What the devil do you mean by ' too Puritan '?"

"Oh, la la! there are many women in this story—too many, mon Major. But no—there is one girl too few. For he have written six chapter, but have only put five —what you call seduction. One chapter wasted, not so? "He grinned mischievously.

"Race, again," snorted MacLeod. "Keep the damn thing. I don't want it."

"What did I tell you? Trop écossais," smiled Leclercq.

To change the subject, MacLeod asked him to visit Gurney after dinner, and look after his ague—if ague it were. "You ought to be a specialist in chronic malaria by this time," he said, "since you've had a bad dose of the Salonique variety. Take him up one of your quinine injections, in case he needs it."

"Yes, yes. I shall go. But why does that fellow sit so long in Arc? His affair about the dead man in the Calvaire is fini long ago. He is strange, that one."

"Yes, but he's sick as well as strange. And—in a way—he's a friend of mine."

Leclercq's eyebrows went up. "Frien'?" he repeated. "But he has something of Boche, that little man."

"Oh, everybody's Boche to you, if he isn't a Frenchman," said MacLeod, with asperity. "Anyway, please see him; and tell him I've a rush of work at present, but will look him up to-morrow."

"Ver' well. But he drink too much, that Gurney."

"Indeed?"

"But yes, it is truly so. I have seen him saoul more than once, when you were on leave, this last time."

MacLeod was startled, and recalled that night in Eilean Aros when he had found an unconscious Gurney on the Scarsdale shore, with an empty brandy-bottle by his side. A mad world! he told himself again; his mind on the story of Marion and this frustrate little man who had hobbled by his side through the moonlit streets of Arc only a few hours past—a story for which nothing but the passionate pleading of the nightingale from out the mystery of dark forests seemed adequate epilogue ... And now, this! ...

"Well," he said abruptly, "a man may be ill as well as drunk, I suppose?"

"Ver' true," said the Frenchman, rising to take his leave ... "Also, he may be Boche," he added darkly, and departed.

About ten that same night, Leclercq returned. "I am sorry," he said, "but I was right. Monsieur Gurney is ver' drunk again."

MacLeod hurried at once to the Lion d'Or, where the *patronne* at sight of him threw up despairing hands, and made many excuses. She had tried what she could with that monsieur; but he would not give her peace until she gave him much wine—too much, perhaps. But he was very noisy, and it was the only way with him. MacLeod sprang up the stair and, without knocking, entered Gurney's room.

It was a dishevelled and unshaven Straw-Feet whom he found, with one eye blackened, and a blood-stained cut on his cheek. Bleary-lidded and collar less, Gurney looked up at him guiltily. "Forgive me," he said, and swept a shaking hand to a corner of the room.

Only two candle stumps, set beside some papers on a table, lit the little chamber; but by their feeble glimmerings, MacLeod made out an assortment of empty wine bottles, some broken and all empty, lying in a waste-paper basket. "What's the meaning of this?" he asked harshly.

"Bad news," said Gurney tearfully, "—bad—bad." He pointed to a map of the battle-line spread on a table littered with the remnants of a meal. The candle stumps were set close to the chart, and MacLeod saw that fresh pencillings had been made on the familiar curves of the break-through between the Vesle and Marne. "Will they never stop?" whispered Gurney. ..."Are they mad? ... They got as far as the Ourcq yesterday ... This is the end ... Fini ... fini!"

MacLeod was amazed. Here was a new Gurney, lamenting the Allies' failure to withstand the German onset! Gurney, the suspect—the mercenary—the Boche spy—so crushed by the rout of the Allied armies that he needs must drown his sorrow in drink! "Tuts, man!—have sense— the game's not up as yet," he said, rallying him.

"They cannot—they cannot," whimpered the little man, clenching his fists, and turning off in despair. "They want Compiègne—they want Paris—they aré mad ... They cannot do it. I know—I, who tell you. They have not supports for all that. It is the end—the end. Fini—fini!"

Compiègne?—Paris? MacLeod's jaw hardened. He felt like strangling the little rat. He had misunderstood; and it was not the Allies' bad luck that Gurney bewailed, but the enemy's folly in overleaping himself! At last all the barriers were down: race would out; and Gurney stood confessed a Boche at heart, despite all his former airs of the cosmopolitan. And, by God! no ties of his with Marion would save him now.

Yet this blood-lust was but momentary, and was succeeded by a wave of exultation. Could they be true, after all, these maunderings of that old boozer? Yes, they could. Yes, the Boche had overleapt himself this time. That little swine was cute enough—he knew things. No supports ... My God! that was it! Fritz was done! ... He turned on his heel without a word, went quickly downstairs, and ran all the way to the château; then sent for Leclercq at once and 'gave him the good news ... The Boche was fini.

Leclercq, however, took the announcement philosophically. "Peut-être," he said.

"Good God, man! Can't you see? "But the Frenchman only regarded him gravely, and passed on to a matter nearer his thoughts. "What did I tell you? "he said. "That little man is Boche, of a certainty."

"Yes, yes; but the point is that he's right about the Vesle and Cambrai shows. They're done. Fritz is bust at last!"

"Peut-être. There is much fighting to be made. Also we must shoot this Gurney. He is a danger."

MacLeod fumed. These logical Frenchmen! No vision! The Boche really beaten; and all they could do was to fuss about shooting a miserable spy.

But Leclercq, unperturbed, lit a cigarette, and going to the open window, cocked an ear to listen to the faint rumble of the Verdun guns. The sight of him, slim and debonair in his horizon-blue uniform, calm and collected, and doubtless already busy in that quick Latin brain of his with plans for the destruction of Gurney, brought MacLeod out of his excited mood instantly. He laughed a trifle nervously and apologetically.

"Well, I suppose you're right," he said. "We must wait and not jump at conclusions; and, as you say, get on with business nearer home ... What about Gurney, then?"

"It is difficile. Is not Gurney, of a certainty, 'agent double '?"

"He is. The A.P.M. at Havre told me so."

"But officially he is of the British Intelligence, M. le Major?"

"The A.P.M. at Havre says he is."

"Then it is the British Intelligence who must deal with Gurney. But since you and all at the château are attach to the French Army, we cannot report direct to the British."

"Couldn't we report through the French Intelligence post at Marac? They could send over one of their Sûreté Générale fellows."

"No, no. You must remember le Capitan Bee at Marac has too many worries. He will say: 'This is not my affair—it is British '—and wash his hands of it."

"But look here, Leclercq—take it this way. This is a Provost-Marshal's job; and the Provost-Marshal controls the Military Police. The Military Police are therefore the competent military authority in a case like this."

"Yes, mais regardez, M. le Major—we are in the district of Chaumont in this matter of Military Police; and it is the Americans who control the district of Chaumont."

"Oh? To hell with the Americans!"

"It is difficile, mon Major."

"Couldn't we telegraph the A.P.M. at Le Havre and ask his advice? Why in thunder do they give chaps like Gurney so much rope! He comes out here and loses himself completely, so to speak; and they do dam-all about it."

"No use: I know these A.P.M., messieurs. Besides, they know all about this Gurney, even now, you may be sure, mon Major. They watch him well, of a certainty. It is their way."

"But that little swine is a Boche. He should be shot right off."

"Ver* true. But we must shoot him logically, mon Major."

"Hell!" said MacLeod, giving up in despair. "Have some 'Prunelles'?"

They sipped for a little without a word, sitting in a twilight dark. All was silence except for the throbbing of the distant bombardment away in the north; through the open window flowed a tide of warm air from the summer night. The sky was serene and moonlit; and against it rose the dark masses of the chestnut-trees, patterned by orange slits of light from the village windows—as on the evening just gone. Again there came the chink-chink of the bell-frog by the bridge on the Aujon. God, what a world! ... Gurney then—and Gurney now! ... Last night MacLeod could have walked on air, so elated had he been by the sweep of his emotions. Soft winds as from Eilean Aros itself—the very spirit of Marion, had invaded his bare chamber; and he had listened to a tale of passion whose profounds of sadness only the Elizabethans could have plumbed. Then he felt that life was greater than he knew. Now, with the sordid scene in that upper room of the Lion d'Or recalled, he saw himself as if foredoomed to hound this creature to a violent death; and a sickening sense of self-distrust possessed him. But he speedily reacted against this mood, and forced his mind into another groove. "Well," he said, charging glasses once more, "we're up a blind street in the matter of Gurney. Let's forget him."

"Si, si," said Leclercq.

"And whether Gurney's a Dago, a Swede or a Chink, he's right about the Hun. He's right, by God! Fritz has bitten off more than he can chew down Amiens way —and his numero's up, mon vieux!"

Leclercq sipped his eau-de-vie without any responsive enthusiasm, and regarded his chief with dark inscrutable eyes. "Peut-être," he said.

XXVI: Roundabout

ON the following day MacLeod could make no further move in the matter of denouncing Gurney to the military authorities, since he had an appointment in Chaumont. A French army surgeon there, Romain by name, had arranged to demonstrate to him some of the newer methods of localizing shrapnel by X-rays, when operating for their extraction. And extraction of missiles was always done in the French Army, whether the bits of metal were troublesome to the wounded or not; for the pensions authorities had their eyes on claims arising later on, if Pierre or Jean had still a bit of steel in his body. MacLeod found the work of Romain's radiographer quite wonderful, but was dubious as to its utility, and said so quite frankly. Many of the foreign bodies, he thought, might safely be left alone; for the adhesions due to the surgical interference—not to speak of the risks of the accompanying anaesthesia—seemed to outweigh any good done by operation. And pension claims were as likely to be made for painful operation scars as for shrapnel left undisturbed.

Romain countered these arguments, and long discussions followed about this case and that—so long indeed as to continue after dinner. And thus it was well after ten o'clock before MacLeod returned to Arc-en-Aulnoy. As he stepped from the auto he saw a light in his window, and entering his room, found Leclercq awaiting him. "Well? Fresh trouble, I suppose?" he said wearily.

"But yes—this Gurney once more. He have broken his leg—what you call a fracture of Pott's."

"Drunk again?"

"Si, si—diablement. He fall down a stair in the Lion d'Or; and le capitaine Henson send him to Salle Foch."

"The deuce!"

"Si, si ... Figure to yourself, M. le Major, that pig of a Boche—cet espion—in a salle full of our soldier."

"No end of a mess, that," growled MacLeod. "But if it's only a Pott's he's jolly well going back to the Lion d'Or. Let's have a look at him."

They went downstairs to Salle Foch, and found the ward in darkness save for a shaded lamp on a central table where two nurses sat at work, folding dressings. Snoring or gently breathing, the wounded lay for the most part asleep, although the faint throbbing of the Verdun guns strove to wake them to memories of the unceasing battle up there. One of the nurses rose silently and glided towards the surgeons; and, so dim was the place, that only by the tallness of her figure and the sway of it, did MacLeod make out that she was Sister Mary.

"Hullo," he said, "who asked you to do night duty?"

"Matron," she said. "But only temporary. She thought it best I should wait up and report to you, because I received the new case." She indicated a bed shut off by screens in a far corner of the ward, and added, "Nurse Martin's on the usual night duty, of course."

"Wise Matron," said MacLeod. "Let's see the patient."

They passed behind the screens and found an abject Gurney attempting to hide his bruised orbit and gashed cheek on the pillow. Sister Mary undid the elastic pressure at the ankle; and MacLeod, examining the injury, satisfied himself that it was only a minor fracture, as Leclercq had stated. "All right," he said to Sister, "put it up again"; and then asked Leclercq to find Henson.

The Frenchman went off with alacrity; while MacLeod and Sister Mary adjusted the bandages on Gurney's leg, and then, coming down the ward, passed into the corridor, where they could converse freely without disturbing the sleeping *poilus*.

"Och, poor wee Straw-Feet!" she said, "he's not very grand, is he now?"

"No. Has he tried talking to any of the men?"

"Aren't you the suspicious people here! Even Matron said she wouldn't put it past some of these strangers to break a leg if they could only get a story for the newspapers. She thinks he's some kind of a journalist."

"He used to be," said MacLeod, remembering old days in Aros. "But you haven't answered my question. Did he try to talk to any of the men?"

"Och, no, why should he do that, when he had me to talk to?"

MacLeod smiled. "Well, he'd get no change out of you, I'm sure."

"No, and he didn't try. Any time I came near him, he did nothing but hold my hand and weep over it, the poor wee creature. And him blethering about Eilean Aros and the fine days there long ago, that I was almost crying myself."

It was on the tip of his tongue to banter her—to say that he wished he also had been present to shed a few tears on that same hand; but there was a sound of footsteps on the stairs above, and Leclercq and Henson came down into the dimly lit corridor. It was clear even in the dusk of the place that a row was imminent between the new arrivals, for the American was ruffled. Angry glances were passing between him and Leclercq; and Sister Mary, discerning this, discreetly retired to her ward.

Henson asked at once if it was he or Leclercq who acted as deputy when the Médecin-Chef was absent from hospital.

"Why, you, of course," said MacLeod.

"Then, don't we take in civil cases if we have beds to spare?"

"Yes, if the cases are urgent."

"Well, if a man gets a simple fracture, and he's so boozed that he may make it compound—"

"Mais, voyez-vous," interjected Leclercq, "this man is Boche."

"In the name of Jim Hall," cried the American, "what about it! He may be Patagonian for all I care, but he's got a Pott's fracture. And a Pott's hurts like hell, even if you're boozed. I've had one, and I know."

"All right, old chap," said MacLeod, soothing him. "You did quite the correct thing. But, in the circumstances, I'd like this man moved back to the Lion d'Or right away."

"Certainly, sir. No objections to taking orders from you. I'll send stretcher-bearers toot-sweet." And with a venomous grin at Leclercq, he departed.

The others followed him slowly down the corridor. "Ver' humanitarian, this war," observed Leclercq sullenly.

"Oh, Henson doesn't know Gurney, of course, as you and I do, or he'd never have taken him in. But Gurney gets beyond a joke, my boy, with his drinking and what not. We must have the blighter shifted out of this district for good, or it will be hell and Tommy for all of us."

"But how to do it, mon Major, by regulation?"

"Oh, blast regulations! Get him out of this any way you like. I give you carte blanche."

"I shall consider," said Leclercq darkly.

"And you might see that an orderly sits up with him to-night. We can't send a nurse over there."

"No, no. We cannot send orderly for that. Gurney would make Boche talk to him. Myself, I will go for this one night."

"How lovely," chuckled MacLeod. "A humanitarian war, as you very justly remarked! No, mon vieux, you carry too much morphine in your pockets to make a good nurse. And Gurney's only to be shifted according to regulations, you remember."

Again the Frenchman gloomed darkly and was silent.

"I'll sit up with him myself," concluded MacLeod. "That's the only safe plan."

"Ah, you Scot of a Scot," said Leclercq, smiling now. "Too much conscience in your Scotland."

"Perhaps. But cut over to the Lion d'Or, and get Gurney's room ready, will you?"

Leclercq departed, while MacLeod turned back to Salle Foch to say that Gurney would be transferred at once. Sister Mary came out into the corridor with him as he concluded his directions.

"So Gurney remembered you? "he said.

"Yes. And it put years on me to think how long ago it is since I saw him in Eilean Aros. Isn't he fond of the Highlands, that wee man! Why ever can't you let him stay on here? I'd love to nurse him."

A change this surely, from her dubiety about Gurney, in the inn at Aubepierre. Curious how that little man broke down all suspicion, unless one steeled ^neself against his ingratiating ways. MacLeod thought, it best, therefore, to be frank with her. "He's really Boche," he said; and described the disclosures Gurney had unwittingly made the previous night. "When the wine is in, the truth will out," he concluded, parodying the old Latin tag.

The lamps in the corridor gave a feeble light; but it was enough for MacLeod to see plainly the dark eyes of Mary Yarrow as he spoke those last words—to see in them also a sudden intensity of regard give place to something strange and inscrutable. It was as if she had withdrawn behind some secret veil. A moment ago she had been all vivid and glowing, frank and free. But now—? What had he said to bring about a change so chilling? Already she was making to retire to the salle again. "Well, I'd best be giving Nurse a hand," she said. "Good night"; and so passed into the ward.

Leclercq and Henson's voices now sounded in the porch, and presently Leclercq came up with the orderlies and a stretcher for Gurney. MacLeod halted them and asked the Frenchman to wait for a little with the patient, once he had got him within the Lion d'Or. "I'll be over presently and relieve you," he said. "Want to get some things from my room, first of all."

In reality, however, he wanted nothing but to be alone for a little, for he felt shaken to the depths by what had just passed between himself and Mary Yarrow. "OEillade" was the French for that kind of thing—but how cheap a word for so intense an experience! Her dark eyes—the fire of them; and then the mists that so completely screened that profound regard of hers. The full energy of her will-power must have been at work there, to transform her so swiftly. From what danger had she shrunk? Something elemental and instinctive must have come into play when she had reacted with such intensity of purpose.

Entering his room, he crossed to the big mirror, and stared into the reflection of his own eyes as if he would read the meaning of the riddle there. And as he stared, there floated up from his subconscious a picture of the moonlit meadow beside the Roman road, and of two dark figures momentarily entangled—the girl repelling his clumsy caress ... "When the wine is in, the truth will out," he repeated ... True of Gurney, and true of himself ... Yes, the wine of Aubepierre had released the truth. It was humiliating to recognize that so trivial a means should lead to so great an end. But there it was—he loved her—-and yet that discovery had never come to light, but for a drunken escapade, with its commonplace accompaniment of a forced embrace ... But no, not commonplace: he now saw that kiss as of central significance. It linked up, indeed, with his first vision of her as she stood among the golden whin beside the tinkers' tent on the shores of Moy; for it was surely there that the truth first beckoned. But here was now no faint signalling—no half-god this whose feet were on the hill-tops, but Eros himself—joyous, yet terrible ... The witch ... the witch! By a single glance from eyes inscrutable, she had transformed that abasing memory of the Aubepierre road into a sudden glory. For it was she who had first divined the truth in that tense moment by the door of Salle Foch; himself, indeed, was only to make discovery at second-hand from her eyes' swift change ... What a roundabout way for love to come home to him! he thought; and his self-esteem glowed warmly at this subtlety of discernment.

Just then his eye fell on the volume of Gibbon he had meant to read by Gurney's bedside that night; at once habit asserted itself, and some imp within him whispered, "Wonder if Gibbon says anything about this sort of thing?"... Good heavens! Himself jeering at himself! ... In a trice all his cocksureness fell from him. A little ago he had been treading on air; now he was slack and oppressed as by a thunderous sky. Listlessly he picked up the book and moved uncertainly out of the room to keep his vigil over Gurney.

But as he came to the stair-foot he turned aside down the corridor leading to Salle Foch and Mary Yarrow. By all standards of reason such a move stood condemned; yet his mind was in a whirl, and, despite the imp of irony that played censor within him, the impetus of those bygone moments of elation carried him automatically onwards. He felt the unwisdom of it all, but he must see her to-night once more. He was fey, in fact, and the unseen powers of life below the threshold of consciousness led him automatically on. Here already was the door of the salle, and behind it—doom? He had entered the ward now, and a woman's figure had risen from beside the shaded lamp. He framed some idle excuse for his return after so recent a visit. "Is Dr. Henson here?" he asked, well knowing the American was most likely in his own room, reading up his cases.

"Hush!" whispered the nurse. "Not so loud, please"; and he gasped in relief to find it was only Nurse Martin who spoke. She came forward now and said that neither Dr. Henson nor Sister Mary was in the ward. Sister had gone off duty as soon as Mr. Gurney had been discharged.

He stammered an excuse and retreated. "Thank God!" he said inwardly. "I'd have made a mess of it." He made his way slowly through the sleeping village to the Lion d'Or, striving to command his thoughts, which were now up in a hunt of their own—away over hill and down dale—tallyhoing through morning mists, their fanfares welcoming sunbursts that were ever mirage. He halted at last, finding himself half a mile beyond the inn he sought; then turned, sighing, and made for it anew. He could not have believed it possible that this thing should have so shaken him by its alternating visions of splendour and misery. He did not even recall that his encounters with Marion, only a few years ago, had resulted in similar oppressions ... Marion indeed was forgotten.

A little stir of wind came in the roadside poplars, and with it the drumming of the Verdun guns became suddenly intensified. He started at the sound, then recognized it ... Good God! there was still a war toward! ... He had forgotten even that.

XXVII: At the Lion d'Or

HE hurried round to the Lion d'Or, relieved Leclercq of his charge, and found the little man quite sobered, but chagrined at the idea of MacLeod sitting up with him throughout the night.

"But it isn't done," he said. "It's not fitting ... A Médecin-Chef! ... Why not an orderly?"

"Because you might talk Boche, and get me into trouble for harbouring you."

Gurney's face fell; and bruised and gashed and with two days' stubble on it, this sullenness made it indeed villainous. He lay silent and straight for a space, obviously thinking hard; then, grunting angrily, attempted to ease the injured leg by a sidewise movement. But this pained, so he resumed his former position, and lay staring at the ceiling; while MacLeod looked grimly on, not unpleased to see a non-combatant taste a little of what the war-wounded were suffering.

"You lie still now, and thank your stars you haven't shrapnel in that leg," said the surgeon, composing himself at length in a couple of chairs, as he adjusted the feeble candle to his needs and took up his volume of Gibbon.

There was silence for some moments, and then Gurney spoke: "Of course I talked too much last night."

"You mean the drink in you talked too much?"

"Yes ... I felt as if I were recovering from an ether anaesthesia. You know what that's like. You simply can't stop babbling."

A happy memory took MacLeod. "Yes," he replied. "When the wine is in, the truth will out."

Ah! you little devil in the bed there, if you only knew the double entente in that! If you only knew what Sister Mary knew! ... And, come to think of it, wee Straw-Feet had helped make the roundabout road by which he had discovered what Mary Yarrow meant to him. But for Gurney's drunken gabble he would never have dreamt of misquoting that silly old saying to her. And she, in turn, would never have divined the truth so happily released by the wine of Aubepierre — would never have seen his clumsy attempt at an embrace as anything but a sign of befuddlement ... "There's a divinity—" and so on ... Yes, Gurney was undoubtedly a master-link in the chain of events which brought about that miracle. Boche or no Boche, he had been the veritable hand of Providence in this.

But the little man in the bed knew nothing of the daft dance in MacLeod's excited brain; he only eyed his attendant gloomily and said: "Oh, I don't forget. Although I had four bottles of that stuff, I can remember all right. It was the fresh break-through I was on, wasn't it?"

"Yes, you came out in your true colours last night, I'm afraid."

"Well, you know, I say all kinds of queer things when I get boozed. Dramatize myself, so to speak. And I see too many sides of this old war to be a good hater of any side. Sometimes I go *Poilu*, sometimes *Deutsch*, you see."

"No, I don't. Won't do, Gurney. Go to sleep."

"Ah, you don't understand. You're not *philosophe* enough."

"No, I'm not."

"You know what Goethe said when he defended his position as a non-combatant in the wars of his time?"

"No; and I don't care."

"Goethe said: 'How can I fight without hatred; and how can I hate without youth?'"

"Pretty slim, that."

"Pretty big."

"Too big for my little mind ... But, look here, Gurney, this *philosophe* stunt won't wash. You're a Boche all right, and there's no need to drag in poor old Goethe. He's dead, and so's Queen Anne. So shut up and go to ba-ba. Anyway, I'm reading a better man than Goethe." He fingered the pages of his book impatiently.

"Who's that?"

"Gibbon."

"My God!"

"Look here, if you don't keep quiet, I'll give you a hypo of morphia, right away."

There was a stillness then in the dimly lit room for about a quarter of an hour; for the little man fell asleep at last. But his splinted leg with its supporting sandbags required that he should lie on his back; and this in turn resulted in an occasional snore which irritated the student of Gibbon. An unusually loud stertor from the bed brought MacLeod to his feet, and, leaning over Gurney, he compressed that worthy's nostrils with forefinger and thumb. The snorer came half-awake, and turned on his side as if to escape this fresh discomfort; but the movement twisted the damaged limb, and he-awoke further; then lifted his arms in air, and cried: "Kamerad!"

"You've said it this time, old son," remarked the surgeon grimly.

From out his nightmare Gurney glared at him. "What did I say?" he asked.

"Nothing much. Only 'Kamerad,'" said MacLeod, readjusting the sandbags.

The little man relapsed again to his pillows and to silence; but after two or three minutes said: "Well, have it your own way ... In any case, it's all up with us ... We went too fast and too far."

"Who are 'we'?"

"Shall we say the enemy? The German armies on the new front, of course."

"I see."

"You know what Goethe said about speed?"

"I tell you I don't care what Goethe said about anything. He was a Boche; and you're another."

"True ... I was born in Cassel. Could I help that? ... A hundred miles farther west, and I might have been born Dutch."

"I wish you'd been born dumb. Do, please, go to sleep ... And don't snore."

Gurney, however, went on imperturbably: "But I want to explain how I made up for Cassel, by having Scotland for a godmother."

That took MacLeod's eyes off his book at once. "How's that?" he asked.

"I had a little commission business in Glasgow for some twenty years or so—shipping, and things like that. Didn't you notice my accent?"

"Your accent's like nothing on earth, except German."

Gurney's amour-propre was instantly wounded. "Should I be in your Intelligence, were my accent German?" he asked testily.

"Certainly, as long as they'd any use for you. But that won't be for much longer." His glance boded dark things.

Gurney smiled in defiance, and went on: "To come back to Scotland. My great-grandfather on my mother's side was a Scot, and bore your own name—MacLeod."

"Come off it!"

"Oh, but yes ... Your people didn't come from Sutherland, by any chance?"

"Suppose I'll turn out to be a Highland cousin before you've finished?"

"Stranger things have happened."

"Well, they don't happen this journey. My people came south from Skye."

"Then the cousinship is off. Mine came from Assynt ... Ever hear of the Thirty Years War? ... Time of Charles the First?" MacLeod nodded. "Well, a forebear of mine sailed over from Cromarty to Gluckstadt with MacKay's Regiment at that time— Murdo MacLeod by name. Fought against Wallenstein, if you please ... then settled down in Germany. And here I am."

"Won't wash, Gumey. Quite a nice yarn; but it won't go down."

"As you please; but it's true."

MacLeod eyed the little figure in the bed. "For one thing, you don't look the size," he said.

"No," admitted Gurney. "I expect they were big chaps in MacKay's Regiment."

"Yes, they had to be stout fellows to handle a pike in the old days."

"I had forgotten that," said Gurney. "Of course mercenaries had always to be big men."

"Mercenaries?" cried MacLeod, rising in wrath.

"Can you deny it? Yes: Scots as mercenaries ... Didn't they sell their swords or their pikes to the highest bidder?"

MacLeod stood speechless and scowled at the little man, who grinned in delight, and went on: "Yes, it's there that I take after my ancestor, Big Murdo. I'm not tall, and don't know the manage of a pike; but what little brains I have I sell to the highest bidder."

The surgeon raged inwardly. Ascribing his failings to a Scottish ancestry, damn him! Tach! it was time his blethers were stopped. "Your time for the dope has come," he said, and took out his hypodermic syringe once more.

"No, no," cried Gurney in alarm. "I have really no pain, unless I forget and move this cursed leg. And I feel I shall soon be asleep again. Also I am always sick after morphine."

"Oh, I won't give you an overdose."

"That hurts. I never dreamt of distrusting you."

"Thanks."

"But I'd really be grateful if you'd let me talk. I feel I've something of importance to say, if only I had someone to say it to."

"Well?"

"And then you're Highland—or at least of Highland stock, and will understand."

"Fire away then. But I suppose you won't be long?"

"It's this ... How shall I begin? ... Yes ... Look at the aeroplane of today—look at the automobile ... You didn't know Goethe had foretold them, did you?"

"See here, Gurney, I'm tired of Goethe. I thought your sermon was on the Highlands."

"It is; but this is how I get there."

"Well, hurry up with the bens and the glens, and leave old man Goethe alone. He makes me tired."

"I'm sorry, because I want to speak of him, first of all—but only for a little. He said one day—I think it was to Eckermann—that the great passion of the future would be for speed."

"By gum, then you don't take after the great passion of the future, Gurney. Get to business, please. What about it all?"

"Only that Goethe was right. But it isn't merely a passion, is it? It's a madness, widespread as the world to-day. These great engines tear through the sky and over the earth; and the sight of them infects men's minds ... Speed ... speed ... speed! And there are reactions from that in the whole of life. Look at this business of the Cambrai and Vesle break-throughs ... Too fast ... too far ... No supports ... Will you tell me that was not induced by the atmosphere of speed these stupid Junkers live in nowadays? Sheer madness!"

"Oh, give the Cambrai break-through a rest. And lie down, please." (For the little man in his excitement had risen on one elbow, his grotesque face flushed and angry.) "And as for madness among the Junkers, if you ask me they've been mad since August nineteen-fourteen."

"I'm not happy in my illustrations," murmured Gurney, sinking back with a sigh. "Let me take another. You know the story of your Thomas Huxley and the Dublin cab-driver, of course?"

"Can't say I do. But Dublin isn't the Highlands, is it?"

"Iin coming to them presently. ... Well, here is the story ... Your Huxley once lectured in Dublin, when I was young—more than thirty years ago; and, coming away from the lecture, he jumped into a cab, and said to the driver: ' Drive quickly.' Then after a time he found the cab wheeling into the open country. So he put his head out of the window, and asked the driver: 'Where are you going? ' And the driver replied—you know what droll fish those jarvies were, don't you?—the driver replied: ' Don't know, sir, but I'm driving quickly.' ... A symbol of the world to-day, MacLeod—yes, a symbol." He shook a solemn head.

"Symbol my foot," growled MacLeod. "You should have been a parson."

"And now that I've shown you that the world is mad, let me show you a way out. Yes, I know someone who could show us the way of escape."

"Yourself, no doubt."

"No, no," cried Gurney; and again he sat up, his eyes eagerly alight; "no, no—but Marion."

Talk of madness, thought MacLeod, the man himself was mad. But a little ago he had been jesting; yet here he was, returned already to his own most tragic memories. "Yes—Marion!" Gurney repeated in a whisper. "I think myself back to her and to the isle of the little glens ... to all her grace and fire and wisdom and quietude ... the very soul of the Gael. And I see clearly that only in her hands and in those of her race is there healing for a world so distracted ... When I think of her, MacLeod, it is as if she were my *daimon* —as if she herself spoke within me."

MacLeod laughed uneasily. "You'll be claiming the second-sight next," he said, attempting to hide how deeply these last words of Gurney's had moved him.

The little man smiled, and his voice changed to a livelier note as he retorted: "I might even have some claim to that, if all they say about my forbear, Red Murdo, is true. For he was namely as a seer through all the German wars of that time; although it was at Stralsund he was best inspired."

MacLeod rose and came forward eagerly to sit down on the bedside. "By Heaven, man!" he cried, "you'd wile the bird off the tree. Tell me of Murdo and Stral sund."

Gurney smiled again. "Here am I offering you the wisdom of Marion," he said, "but, like all your faithless generation, you seek a sign. Tuts! never mind those old wives' tales of second-sight; but turn to the true sight—the first sight—the kind your Shakespeare knew —' the soul of the wide world dreaming on things to come '—the insight that lies in the heart of your race —the instinct of the Gael for the fine and fit things in life."

MacLeod was touched, but strove again to conceal his emotion by *blague*. "Really," he repeated, "you should have been a parson," and so fell silent for a little. Then probing the thoughts aroused by Gurney's appeal, he went on: "But aren't you a bit off the mark? Doesn't the Gael dream moreof the past than of 'things to come'?"

"They're really the same for him, because he would have the best of the past carried on into the present, and so into the future. He holds past and present and future in a unity the people of the cities can never attain to. They haven't the time. It's speed ... speed ... speed with them. But the Gael has the wisdom of leisure"

"He has the leisure anyway, by gum. He jolly well sees to that!" sneered MacLeod.

"—He has the wisdom of leisure," went on Gurney, unheeding the interruption. "He really feels the flow of things we call time in a way we don't. Even his language shows that he senses that more finely than we do. Haven't you heard Charlie of Glenavoulin say: ' I will be going,' when you or I would say: 'I am going '? He feels instinctively—or at least the race he comes from feels—as their language shows—that' I am going ' means process; that ' I am striking' means nothing static, but continuous action—something that takes him on into the future. And so he says: ' I will be going,' or ' I will be striking.'"

"Charlie would be surprised to hear he was so great a scholar."

"He would indeed. For the last thing about Charlie is self-consciousness. Instinct, I tell you."

"I know—I know," said MacLeod wearily: "the simple life—that old story."

"No—the most complex life. You would not call the perfect balance of soul and body in Marion a simple thing. We should have to go back to the first Christian ages for anything so complete. The instinctive is not merely the simple, is it? Was all that came from the hills and the sea and the cleansing winds of Eilean Aros, and went to the making of Marion simple?" As he spoke a fierce clangour broke out in the night around Arc: the big guns in the far north. "Ah," said Gurney, "you hear! The great doors of iron close in the sky; and we are shut out from Tir-nan-Og ... and Marion."

"The simple life—the golden age!" murmured MacLeod.

"But the simple life people saw something. They were no fools. Yet they failed. But then they did not know Marion."

"No, nor Charlie of Glenavoulin—in his hut of wet sods, with its tin roof and its hens on the rafters. The cleansing winds of Aros have their work cut out to keep Charlie's house clean, I'm afraid."

"You're not *philosophe*, MacLeod, as I remarked already. You must judge a race by its best—not by its worst."

"I'll judge it by both," growled the surgeon. "And now, give it a bye, Gurney, and get to sleep, please. I'd much rather have your snores than your sermons, you know."

"Pearls before swine," muttered the little man, and lay back on his pillow.

"'You're drunk, Father William, the young man said,'" misquoted MacLeod. "Shut up now! I want to do a little Gibbon, if you don't mind."

"Talking of Gibbon," said the other, "do you know that Caesar—Julius, of course—fought at Maubeuge, once upon a time?"

"Oh, will you dry up; or must I really give you some dope?"

"—Fought against the Nervii," continued Gurney, despite the warning. "They were Celts, you know. And total abstainers. Fancy that!"

"Celts? The Nervii? More ancestors, I suppose. —I do wish you took after them in the matter of drink."

"Rheims, Soissons, Arras, Amiens, Berry-au-Bac— old Caesar was all over it in those days, fighting like billyoh. Funny, isn't it? And now we are at the same silly game."

"Cambrai too, I should think."

"Oh, go to hell!"

"All right. And you go to sleep. It's a bargain."

MacLeod returned to his book then; but after a little Gurney resumed his snoring, and further study of Roman history was impossible. So the Médecin-Chef of Arc-en-Aulnoy took out a pencil and began to draw idly on the fly-leaves of his Gibbon. From sketches of the slumbering Gurney he passed on to a gallery of the hospital staff, and finally specialized on pictures of Mary Yarrow. Morning light found him still at this last, and profile after profile he drew of Sister Mary; for the true artist is never satisfied.

XXVIII: The pine ridge

AT seven that morning MacLeod descended to the kitchen and interviewed the *patronne*, to whom he explained that her guest's injury was only slight, and in a week or so, with the aid of a single crutch, he would be able to travel to Paris, or wherever he wished to go. Meanwhile, how much would Madame take for the extra work of looking after him in the daytime? As for the nights, he himself would provide a male nurse. Forthwith Madame, smiling, handled some franc notes and undertook day-duty for a week, while MacLeod returned to the upper room to poke the sandbags into shape once more, and explain the new arrangement to the patient.

Gurney thanked him gruffly, adding, "And send me a barber, won't you?"

"I'll send every barber in the village," said MacLeod; "for that beard of yours is sprouting like Red Murdo's."

"Ah," said the little man, passing his hand over the white stubble on his chin, "even at my age Red Murdo's beard would still have been red, I'll wager. Another point in favour of the Gael."

And so they parted cheerfully enough, MacLeod returning to the château for a few hours of sleep, before resuming the day's routine. He appeared at lunch, and then got to work in his office at the driest of official papers he had seen for many a day—or at least so they appeared to him who had been back in Gaeldom and its dreams for half the night. Next he sent for Hemingway, whom he begged to take over night-duty with Gurney —in an unofficial capacity, of course—until things were straightened out. It would be only for one night; some of the others might oblige on other nights. Besides, they were slack at present, and Hem might get a snooze before breakfast. Hem agreed eagerly; this was a new adventure, no task at all, he assured his Médecin-Chef; a real change from the humdrum of the hospital as it was at present. "Funny old chap, Gurney," he said. "They say he's some kind of a Boche, really. But I don't believe it, y'know. He's too decent an old bird, although he does drink a little."

"Who says he's Boche?"

"Oh, well, y'know—perhaps it was Leclercq; but I just couldn't be certain, Médecin-Chef."

"Rot," said MacLeod. "Take it from me that old Gurney's more of a Scot than a Jerry."

Yet all the same MacLeod sought out Leclercq as soon as Hem had gone, and said: "We'd best have Gurney slipped back to Havre or thereabouts, in a day or two. All he needs is a stirrup of adhesive plaster and a crutch: it's only a Pott's, you see."

"But, M. le Major, you have given me carte blanche in the matter of reporting Gurney to the authorities. He is Boche—he is espion."

"Well, but who are the authorities? Even if we can locate them, there'll be no end of a row. And," he went on uneasily, "he isn't such a bad lot. Shouldn't go any further, if I were you."

Leclercq's dark eyes lit up. "Ver' well," he said; "I shall do nothing further"; and saluting, he turned on his heel, and went off humming, *Sous les Ponts de Paris*.

MacLeod looked after him, perturbed by his assured airs and the abruptness of his departure; but just then a post arrived, and he turned wearily again to official correspondence. This fresh batch of papers kept him busy well on into the evening, and so his visit to Gurney that night was somewhat hurried. He was tired, too; and he had little time for talk as he reapplied the elastic pressure, and installed Hem as attendant.

He retired early in order to make up for the loss of sleep the previous night; and dozed soundly until a little after five next morning, when he was awakened by a frenzied knocking at his door. Leaping from bed, he admitted a distraught Hem, who gasped: "Mr. Gurney's gone!"

"Dead!"

"No, no, sir. But the gendarmes came for him at five, with an ambulance, and took him away. And, as you know, my French isn't too good; and so all I could make out from them was, ' Ordre du Ministre de Guerre.' Yes, I'm sure it was 'du ' and not 'de '; but perhaps that's not important, although you never know, y'know. I do wish I knew more French. And then they had him in a stretcher, and bundled him off before you could say Jack Robinson. And the *patronne*'s in hysterics—and—and—oh, everything's all wrong! Isn't it too ghastly to rush the little chap off that way, and shoot him?"

"Shoot?"

"Yes, don't you know? They always come at five for that kind of thing hereabouts. That's how it was when they came for Bompard in Salle Kitchener, over a year ago—before your time—in Dr. Bowlitt's time, that was. And it's always gendarmes they send, not *poilus*."

"Whatever do you mean, Hem?"

"Well, it's all too dreadful. But cowardice before the enemy, and that kind of thing, y'know." Hem was almost girlish in his excitement; and there were tears in his eyes.

"I'd best hurry up to the Lion d'Or, and see what I can make out," said MacLeod, struggling into his uniform.

"But it's really no use, sir. They're gone. Two minutes, and they were off. It's not as if he was a *poilu*, y'know. These gendarmes know their job, too. Very polite. Put me aside quite gently, and asked me to have a chair. And poor little Gurney only half-awake when they laid him on the stretcher!"

MacLeod ran quickly up to the little inn. There he found the *patronne* and her domestics in hysterics, and could get nothing from them but weeping and declarations that the custom of the Lion d'Or was gone for ever, since they had harboured a *sale Boche* ... Yes, Gurney was gone. A far cry now for him to Eilean Aros.

Breakfast was a solemn meal that morning, not only on Gurney's account, but also because old memories of Bompard's sudden removal in like circumstances were revived. The Directrice confirmed Hemingway's tale. "Of course, Bompard being one of our wounded, Dr. Bowlitt was informed the night before he was taken away. The gendarmes would say nothing as to the reasons for it all; they only hinted at a court-martial; and there were a lot of formalities—papers to be signed and so on. But no one knew anything of it that night, except Dr. Bowlitt and myself. Poor Bompard didn't know till they wakened him at five. All the rest of the ward were asleep."

"And you never heard what came of him?" asked MacLeod.

"No; but the *poilus* said it meant one thing only." She lifted her hand in a gesture of despair, and rose to go.

After her departure the men smoked in silence for a little. Leclercq was the first to leave. "Oh, la-la!" he said airily. "C'est la guerre!" and went out.

Those few words seemed ominous to MacLeod. It was clear now that he had been too late in withdrawing Leclercq's carte blanche: the Frenchman had already pulled his wires, whatever they were; and Gurney's fate was sealed. And who could blame Leclercq, after all? War was war; and Gurney was only one in the mad hazard ... Dammit! why wasn't there more work to hand? The only real opiate for this kind of thing was work. He had a good mind to go digging with old Featherly in the kitchen-garden, and leave his ward visits to Henson for that morning. This was soon arranged; and presently he and Featherly shouldered spades and marched off to a patch of good earth near the Aujon's banks, where the ex-rancher proposed breaking ground preparatory to setting up hundreds of pea-poles and sowing billions of peas. "The Land, Doctor, the Land!"

MacLeod dug up the tough clods, overturning and breaking them with savage blows from his spade; and as he worked it dawned on him that he had sought this unwonted toil, less to escape brooding on Gurney, than to provide an excuse for his absence from Salle Foch that morning. Yes, he was funking meeting Sister Mary's questioning eyes. He had messed this business of Straw-Feet; and she would take the little man's end sorely to heart ... What a way that fellow had with women—could twist them round his little finger! First Marion, and then this girl. And Sister Mary would never forgive him if Gurney went to the post at Vincennes. He turned over an extra large bit of turf and smashed at it wildly.

"Steady on," cried Featherly, "or you'll blister your hands. Remember you're new to this game."

"Sorry," grunted MacLeod, abating his energy.

"Let me see," said the old fellow, coming over and inspecting the other's palms. "Oh, Lordy! you'd better chuck it, or you won't do any operating for a week to come."

The surgeon declined to stop, however, and by the lunch-hour his hands were badly rawed and useless for further digging. But he must get rid of his depression over Gurney: distraction of some kind he must have; a walk in the woods might help.

And so an hour after lunch found him on a deserted hill-road above the Aujon valley, making for a viewpoint known as the Pine Ridge, a favourite spot for nurses' picnics. But no such mild orgy, he felt sure, would disturb him that day; too dark a cloud had overcast the hospital staff from the events of the morning to allow of even so innocent a relaxation for some time to come. As he approached the hill-top he found his surmise correct: the place was deserted save for a few scraggy goats, nibbling peacefully on the grass-grown track.

The pines made a noble group as they overlooked the river valley. Below him the old highway curved downhill between a double line of poplars that leant across to one another in quaint attitudes, as if whispering secretly. But so steep was the descent on the farther side that a wide prospect was to be had over their massed tops— the rolling country which led to the foot-hills of the Vosges. Midmost of this landscape were well-wooded cliffs, flanking the Aujon for miles till they melted in the heat haze of the horizon; at intervals amid their dusk foliage rose-coloured gables, stout and ancient, appeared.

South and east ran the line of the valley, and away down there was Italy—the magic land. In olden days those walls, so faintly rose, had been hospices, monasteries, castles, great caravanserais—houses of call for wayfarers on the busy roads. He was already daydreaming, and far away from his everyday world of hospital and war and all that. It was not for nothing that his forebears had been shepherds and hunters— dwellers in the open, under wide skies. And so the free airs on the pine ridge wrought the old enchantment; for a little he forgot war and all its bitterness.

Through some such sultry afternoon in Old Spain had Quixote and Sancho fared. Half-hidden under the trees down there was haply a queer old inn, with Boniface busy at the wine-cellar yawning cave-like beyond the sunny courtyard; while, from the outer gallery, the dicing cavaliers shouted their pet tipple. And on the dusty roadway men-at-arms with morion and arquebus marched past, jostling pilgrim and pedlar aside. There, too, were fair ladies, finely horsed and with knights attendant; peasants gaily dressed for a *festa*; beggars tattered and limping; scholars and priests in grave argument; merchants in cavalcade discussing prices; a funeral with friars suppliant, mingling with a playactors' company who ranted a merry chorus at first, but soon joined with altered voices in chanting the misericordia; a poet withdrawn to a grassy bank, and noting with dreamy eyes all this pell-mell of life.

And then, although rose-coloured gables still peeped out of the boscage that stretched to the horizon's verge, the dream of the Middle Age vanished. For a faint rumour took the air in the distant north, then throbbed and thundered as could only thunder the hell of Verdun. Was the great fortress again in straits? There was something ominous in so sudden an outbreak after the day's silence up there. Vaux—Fleury—Douaumont—Damloup—which of her flanks was it that now cried out as if in agony? Janniard, the *amputé* in Salle Gallieni, could no doubt make a shrewd guess: he who had left Verdun so recently, his leg gangrenous to the knee. Or Bernard, the poor devil in Salle Albert, with Carrel tubes protruding from all over his back, might be able to localize whence that hammering came.

Bernard—Janniard? What would they have said, could they have seen their Médecin-Chef that day, struggling with a spade among clods till he rawed his hands—they who knew that any day fresh wounded might pour into Arc from Verdun? ... Verdun, where the surgeons, overwhelmed, worked night and day; while he played about with pea-poles! ... He felt indeed very helpless: the strain of waiting for work that never came was making him neurasthenic—that and this Gurney business. But the uproar in the northern sky now died as suddenly as it had arisen, and he sighed in relief. Whatever the alert, the danger had probably passed.

He descended now between the lines of quaint poplars; and just where they curved suddenly to the right, all thoughts of Verdun's spent surgeons were swept from his mind for there, advancing slowly uphill, her eyes on the ground, and all unaware of his presence, was Mary Yarrow. She was in outdoor uniform, and therefore off duty for the afternoon. Had the Gurney affair then weighed so heavily on her that she also had made holiday to counter her dismay?

She carried her Panama hat in her hand, for there was some shelter from the strong sun under a high bank at that part of the roadside. Listlessly she came on, while he halted; then, as she raised her eyes, she too came to a stand. And so they stood at gaze, only a hundred yards between them;

each as if in presence of an enemy whose next move had to be warily observed. But MacLeod now saluted, and limped forward; while she waved a languid hand, and, as if wearied by the heat of the day, turned aside to seat herself on the grass under the high bank's shade.

"Well," he said, as he came up, "you also wanted out of it, I suppose?"

"Yes; everybody's as if petrified down there." Her own face was impassive, mask-like. "But whatever have you done with your hand?"

He had forgotten the strip of dressing there. "Oh, nothing serious"; and he told her of his gardening exploits.

"That was foolish. You were trying to drive Straw-Feet out of your mind: was that it?"

"Something of that sort."

"I know. It's just the same with myself. It's all wrong, of course; and we should be glad to see the last of him. But it's hard nursing a man, and then—that."

He was silent; and she plucked the sun-dried herbage aimlessly for a little, then rose, saying: "Time to be going. I'm on duty at six."

They went up the hill slowly, an awkward silence between them, until they reached the Pine Ridge, and turned to look down on the wide champaign. Then, by way of breaking through the air of constraint surrounding them, he said: "The pines here—rather good, aren't they? Always suggest a bit of Scotland to me."

He had thought to divert her thoughts from what so surely occupied them; but he could scarcely have chosen a better means to channel them deeper still, for she said: "Yes"; and then added, "Mr. Gurney claimed some Scots blood."

"He did say something to me about that, not so long ago," said MacLeod uneasily.

"You didn't believe him?"

"Oh, but yes, I did," he answered with spirit, for he saw that she was now in a mood of irritation that would end by putting him in the wrong—make him out a monster without heart ... ("Damn women!" he thought. "When they have a grievance against the whole universe, they must fasten on some one poor devil and expend all their wrath on him!") He hastened to reassure her. "Of course, I believe him," he said. "Didn't he tell you about his ancestor, Red Murdo, and MacKay's Regiment, and the Thirty Years War, and all that—two hundred years ago?"

"No, nothing except that he had Scots blood in him. And then, when he heard I was Irish, he started wishing he had Irish blood as well!" She was faintly smiling now.

"The devil he did!"

"But something took me off just then, and that was all I got from him." Regret was in her voice; and it was all too clear that Straw-Feet had in some strange way cast over her the fascination he had exercised on Marion—perhaps indeed on all women. "I'm sorry I saw so little of him," she concluded.

MacLeod fumed inwardly. Hang the fellow! what a dance he led these girls ... He must, however, hide his resentment, and the easiest way for the moment was to continue the talk about Gurney. "Yes, he was really interesting," he said. "Daft about Scotland, in fact. Wanted to reform the whole world; and thought the Highlands alone held the secret of how to do it."

"Reform the world? Whatever did he mean?" She turned to walk on now, and MacLeod took place by her side.

"Well, he thought we needed a rest from big cities and industrialism and from rushing things generally."

"And wasn't he right?"

"But it's not so easy. Where should we be but for science and machinery and all that?"

"Maybe not at war, anyway. Maybe, indeed, wee Straw-Feet might be herding goats on the Pine Ridge there instead of " Her voice trailed off in a tremor, but its very notes were those of her indignant protest against the world's folly—notes he had first heard beside the tinker's tent at Moy. Years and years away that scene seemed now; yet she was here with him, as vivid and challenging as if time had not been.

Estrangement was nigh if he were not careful; at once he declared his sympathy with her and Gurney's point of view: he only wanted to see clearly all round, he said; and presently he was very fully recounting his discussion with the little man in the Lion d'Or. Insensibly also he depicted Gurney's standpoint in stronger colours than his own, and all unwittingly his desire to stand well with Sister Mary led him to distort the tale. At times she interrupted to get this or that bit of the argument clear—the meaning of some reference to Goethe—what place Marion had really held in Straw-Feet's life —how much did the little man make of environment in his view of a saner world—of the hills and the sea and such like? In the end MacLeod, confused by the bigness of the theme and by his cross-examination, found himself dubious of his own standpoint, and weakly admitted: "Queer, isn't it! Looking back, it seems Gurney saw more in the Gael than I did. I thought I had a good case, but now it's all different, somehow."

But by this the debater in the girl was keenly aroused; instinctively she was moved by a concession so generous, and at once swung round to the side of MacLeod. "Well now," she said, "what nonsense! Aren't you just making him out more of a Highlander than yourself?"

"But he really saw further than myself."

"He did, and he didn't. It was you that was seeing better than further; and that was just all round it."

"And seeing all round a thing's a Highland characteristic, you think?"

"I do. Haven't I lived in Eilean Aros? No, no, Straw-Feet was too much in the skies."

"While I kept to earth—to the merely practical?"

"No; but to the earth and the skies as well. Didn't I say you were seeing all round it? And how in a world like this could anyone see clearly by being practical and nothing more?" With such questions she bombarded him until he was bewildered; angry that he should not see how strong was his defence. In turn he became irritable; for no matter what line he took, she broke through and made it a thing of naught. If he attacked Gurney, she scouted his method of attack; if he saw reason in some of Gurney's pleadings she would have none of it. What could he say to a creature like that? He took refuge in silence.

"Whatever are you staring at?" she said.

"Oh, pardon! A look in your eyes that reminded me of something."

"Of what, I wonder?"

"Of the wine of Aubepierre," he said, suddenly bold.

"What nonsense!" She bridled a little, but her eyes turned away.

He felt the ground was dangerous here, so checked and veered to the discussion once more. "So you think after the war's over it might be worth while trying to reform this old world?"

His tone was jesting, but she took no heed of it.

"I don't," she said. "I think—once the war's over —each of us will have work enough reforming ourselves, let alone the world."

"Can't be long now—the end of the war, I mean. Gurney thought the Boche was finished by Cambrai and this new fight south of it; and he should know."

"Nobody knows anything about it, so what's the use of guessing?"

"Nonsense; a year will see the end of it. What happens to you, once it's all over?"

"Nobody knows anything, I tell you. So why should I bother about what's happening to me?"

"Well, I know what's happening to this child," he said with conviction. "I'm for right back to Eilean Aros."

She halted at once, and turned to look at him. "Oh?" was all that came from her lips, but her cheeks flushed faintly. Then without more ado she resumed her walk by his side.

"Don't you approve?" he asked. "Yes—but—"

"But what? Aren't you going back there?"

"I tell you I don't know anything—" she said sharply, and hastened her pace the least bit.

"Yes, you do," he cried, catching her hands, and swinging her round so that, quick-breathing and angry, she faced him. "Yes," he went on, peering into her face, "you did think of going back to Aros?"

"Please don't catechize me, Dr. MacLeod"; and she turned away.

But again he caught her hands and held her. "Why should my going there keep you from going?"

"Why, indeed?" she said, attempting defiance. But her voice failed pitifully, and her head bent low. All her defences were down; her whole body drooped away from him.

"Oh, devil take it!" he cried, "how you women will argue!" And clasping her in his arms, he kissed her roundly.

After a time they went on their way with a certain soberness, for they were nearing the village. "No wild boars, this journey," he whispered.

She laughed happily. "No; but there's worse. You'll have to see Matron about—this."

His face fell, but cleared again as he said: "Very well, but you must come with me and hold out your cloak."

"What a shame! Matron will be very glad."

"She likes us then?"

"I wouldn't go as far as that; but she likes one of us. And that's enough for two, you'll find; or I'll know the reason why. Step out now, and get it over."

Soon they came to where they looked down from the hillside on Arc-en-Aulnoy—its red roofs and spired church, on the Place and the river with its *lavoirs* and old mill-bridge. There was the great château, there the park with its lake and enfolding woods. In the clearing they could make out the sun-shelters where the wounded lay, and the white-clad nurses flitting around with meals or pinard or Carrel dressings—a busy scene, despite the recent lull of work in the operating theatre.

A lull? Yes, but listen. The guns of Verdun throbbed once more: the end was not yet. The two on the hill looked at each other as they hearkened, then descended to their task.

Book Three

Post War

XXIX: The return to Aros

SOME ten years later, on a day early in May, MacLeod was driving back to his home in Torness from an all-night case in Moy. His car was no longer the *Curlew*, but a four-seater tourer of quite modern type, and with gadgets innumerable. He had no birdy name for her, for she neither wailed nor sang—only gave forth a low hum as she sped onwards; so she was simply "the 'bus."

He glided up the little snap of a hill at Garmony and halted on the flat above to take in the beauty of the scene. Bailefraoich, or Heathertown, the place was named; but not a stone of the old clachan now showed above the heather and the gall; all silent those happy fields where children had run about the braes, and old wives knitted in the sun; far sundered their descendants in foreign lands. He shut off the engine and got out to gather primroses, which flourished more richly here than elsewhere in the Isle. So peaceful that scene, the only sound the calling of lambs and the answering bleat of ewes; the sky almost cloudless above Aros Sound that curved like a blue scimitar from the distant sands of Kilchoan to the cliffs of Innimore close at hand. Across the strait the white cots of Morvern dotted its seaward slope; a brown lugsail made slowly out from Drimnin, pointing north. Here were sun and wind and health-giving air, waves that clapped their hands in glee, hills of noble outline, great stretches of moor and wood and glen; and yet, but for that single sail on the Kyle and the dozen or so of cots on the Morvern hillside, he might to all appearance be a sole survivor in a land untenanted. He knew, indeed, that hidden away in the bays of the coastline, here and there, were little villages—Torness, Torlochan and the like; but taken as a whole the population was indeed small, and his practice bare enough. He wondered had he done wisely in returning to the old life here: his boy was growing up; there was schooling to think of. And this shut-in life for Mary, was it fair to her? As for himself, if he were not careful his knowledge of his craft would rust, so restricted was the experience to be had in the Isle. He must keep up the exchange of practices Robbins and he had made for some years back. It was good for them both: Robbins escaped from the smoke of Glasgow for a summer month, while he looked after Robbins' cases, and found time for some work at hospital. A great thing that study holiday in town;

although a month at it was hardly enough, was it? A shut-in life certainly, this in Eilean Aros.

Yet, in spite of all his brooding, the chiming of the waves far below—the happy airs of the place—had their way with him, and his mood of depression soon passed. Limper though he was, his body was strong; then he had ample leisure for Gibbon now and again. And, hang it all! he must really do some real reading of that old chap: he had been at him for Lord knows how many years now, and volume the ninth was still to finish; nine volumes out of twelve wasn't good enough; he must really buck up, and get on with that history. Anyhow, here was the fine country. (How his mother would have loved it, had she but lived to see it!) And life was good ... Heavens, what a day of sun and breeze!

Then—far cry though it was to the pine ridge above the Aujon—something in the Highland landscape recalled his mood when, years ago, he had looked out on that vista in the Haute Marne on a day as sunny as this. Yet the stillness here was unbroken by any drumming of great guns in fortresses war-beset; it was surely something other than the immediate scene which had brought back memories of the Aujon valley. Old associations, perhaps? But where did they come in? He must examine this. What was he about just now? ... He had come up a little ascent; looked out on a great vista of fine country; and presently he would descend through woods that clothed a hillside. So too had he done in France that day of happy encounter with Mary Yarrow which led in the end to their mating. Up a hill and down a hill, and Mary Yarrow coming towards him, while a wide prospect unrolled and the great sun shone. There was the link. So had it been in France, and so would it be here. For, once he had passed the wood on the slope of Leitir, he would see her approaching, as was her custom when he had to spend a night in Moy. He had wired that he would be home a little after five: she should be about the Forsa bridge by now. Donnacha would be with her; and, even so, two miles were enough for a child of six. Time he was in his car and hurrying. So starting up, he sped over the familiar road.

There was no sign of them on the flat beyond Leitir, where the road ran close to the bit of shore most favoured by Donnacha as a playground. Half a mile only now to the Forsa bridge; but he could make out no figure of wife or child there, only the dark arch in the shadow of its flanking willows. And now he feared some mishap at home, and accelerated; but he had barely crossed the humpbacked bridge, when he heard young Donnacha's shrill hail from behind. Drawing up, he turned in his seat and saw the rascal emerge from a blackberry bush, while presently Mary rose from the same ambuscade.

There were kisses; then he helped them aboard, and drove on. "Nice trick to play on a chap," he growled. "You made me anxious—not seeing you at the bridge."

"It was Donnacha's plan," said Mary placidly. "Did you get any sleep last night?"

"Four hours. It wasn't a bad case. Any messages?"

She smiled. "Only old Alasdair at Acharonich again. He wants you at once, of course."

He smiled in turn. "Catch me going over there without my tea, first of all. I know him."

"He telegraphed as usual for the family," she went on. "Said he was dying. And the whole six of them arrived by to-day's steamer."

"How long since his last illness—so-called?"

"Five months. When the snow was rather bad, you remember. You had to put chains on the wheels."

"Yes: January, that was."

"Dear-a-dear! The money those big men and women must have spent coming here from Glasgow, every few months, would build a church."

"Well, he won't die this turn either, I bet. Nothing but hypochondria."

"Those six passed our garden gate in a string, just like a procession of Assyrians in the British Museum. It's really becoming a kind of religious rite, this homecoming of the MacGilvrays every now and again—and the old man never dying."

"All the same, it's a fine thing. Not one of the six but thinks it's most likely a false alarm; but not one of them would let the old fellow down by staying away. Very Highland, that."

"Oh, I'm not blaming them; but can't you see the droll side of it?"

"Of course I do; but—"

"But we mustn't make fun of the Highlands?" Her dark eyes flashed mischievously. "The touchiness of you Scots!"

"All right, Ireland. Don't get ratty yourself; and please don't dump down Donnacha quite so hard. He was quite comfy on your knee."

"I'll dump down Donnacha's father, if he isn't careful," she said. "You won't see Acharonich tonight, if you're not good, my man."

Donnacha pricked up his ears at this second mention of Acharonich, and now intervened. "Father going to Acharonich?" he asked.

"Yes."

"Where the seals chase the salmon?"

"Yes."

"Father taking Donnacha to see seals?"

"Now you've done it," growled MacLeod under-breath to his wife. "That child should be asleep by eight; but if he's to go this run with me, it will be ten before he's abed. Whatever made you mention Acharonich? You know what a passion he has for seals."

"And a good thing he has. I believe he's going to be a great naturalist. He told me yesterday he was going out to get a lizard; and back he came with one in ten minutes' time. And this morning he wanted a snake; and off he went and got one right away."

"Good heavens, Mary! a snake?"

"Well, a blindworm, really."

"But you said a snake."

"And do you think that's all the care I have of him: that I haven't shown him the differ between a blindworm and an adder long before this?"

"Sorry, but you said a snake. And talking of what he's going to be, what about his schooling? Little chance for him here, I'm afraid."

"Time enough yet," said she, "to be considering all that. I'm for educating his lungs, first of all. He'll get good air in the Isle: better than the kind they have round city schools. And, to my thinking, he'll get the most part of what else he needs in the playground of the school here, and at our own fireside."

"Agreed. Passed unanimously. The most part is as you say, wise woman. I was thinking of the least part, perhaps; the kind of thing he has to earn his bread by."

Mary rocked with laughter. "Dear-a-dear!" she said, "but you do look far ahead. Give the child time to grow. And as for lessons and all that, isn't the schoolmaster here a good man for the early years. Didn't Angus MacLean go up to Edinburgh University, and take the medals in Mathematics and Botany right away?"

"Old woman with kettle," sang out Donnacha suddenly, and MacLeod slowed down at once. They were now entering Torness village, and passing along a line of croft-houses set close to the roadside. Midway in the string of cottages lived Widow MacAulay, an old woman with a passion for cleaning each household vessel as soon as used, and so spending a good part of the day crossing the road to and from the village pump, planted right opposite her dwelling. It was her stout slow-moving figure that had occasioned Donnacha's outcry, as she waddled right into the middle of the highway, fair game for a motor of any speed.

"That old lady will be the death of me yet," grumbled MacLeod. But they passed without mishap. "She's as slow's a walrus, and twice as heavy," he continued; "and if I—"

"Father take Donnacha to the seals to-night?" piped the youngster again.

"There, you see!" said Mary. "Who said the wrong word this time?"

"What did I say? I didn't say anything amiss."

"You said 'seal'; or if you didn't, you said 'walrus,' and that's worse. And now he's just got to go to Acharonich."

"Of course, put it all on father," grumbled MacLeod. "That chap, if you ask me, knows too much natural history for his age."

But his wife turned a deaf ear to him, and, leaning over Donnacha, whispered loudly enough for MacLeod to hear: "Yes, dear, father will take you to see the seals after tea. And mother will come to look after you both."

By now they were home, and as they drew up, the maid came out to help Donnacha disembark, and to announce a patient awaiting the doctor in the surgery. "It's a Mr. Rainbird," she said, smiling.

"Rainbird?" said MacLeod. "A strange name on so fine a day, eh, Flora?—Rainbird?" he repeated, stressing the first syllable.

"Och, yes," said Flora demurely, as she led the child away, "it is a good weather."

The doctor assisted his wife from the car, and then, making sure the girl was out of earshot, said eagerly: "Talking of Highlanders, did you hear that? Can you beat it for tact?" He repeated his question to the girl and her answer. "You see," he went on, "she agrees with what I say, but only with that part of it which makes no reflection on the visitor's odd name, and so avoids discourtesy to either ... Allow the Highlander to get out of a tight corner. Toujours la politesse!"

"Oh, come in and get your tea, and see this man. You know as much about the Highlands as a cow knows about a holiday. Aren't you only half-Highland yourself?—so what can you know of them?"

"But don't you observe how beautifully she got round me?"

"Nonsense! Any woman, let alone a Highland one, might see that she gave you the only possible answer."

"Still, there was a delicacy—"

"And haven't I that sometimes, even if I'm Irish?"

"Delicacy, yes; but not in argument, Mary. You just bludgeon me, y'know. Still there's always an effectual answer to the bludgeon." And he kissed her. "Finlay! On the main road! "But mercifully for her fears they were hidden from observation by the car on the one hand and the garden hedge on the other, or Torness village would have gossiped for months over such a tit-bit. Mary, with one swift glance as she disengaged herself, saw that this was so, sighed deeply in relief and ran indoors. MacLeod followed more slowly, and entered his surgery to find a fair stoutish youth, with an alert sun-tanned face, awaiting him. He was dressed in a tweed sports jacket and Oxford slacks, and carried his right arm in a sling of black silk.

"Afraid I've barged in on a busy day, Doctor," he said. "But I've hurt my arm, and want you to have a look at it."

"Let's see it then. Mr. Rainbird, isn't it?"

"Yes," said the youth as MacLeod helped him off with his coat. "I'm a painter of sorts, and was doing a little work round the Gribun rocks to-day. Footing's bad there, and I got a fall that landed me on this bit." He indicated the point of his elbow and its outer side.

MacLeod examined the arm, and assured him that nothing was broken; a bone had been bruised, and would be painful for some time; muscles ditto; rest for a week, and then let him see it again; no massage in the meantime. "Sorry your painting's hung up, and the weather so good."

"The weather, yes," said Rainbird, "quite too marvellous, isn't it?" And then, as the surgeon helped him on with his coat, he glanced round the well-lined bookshelves. "Quite a posh little place you have here."

MacLeod said it was nothing to write home about, but it served his turn, and asked where he was staying.

"Torlochan Hotel. My car's up at the inn."

"As far as that! Why not have tea here before starting?"

"I'd love to."

They went into the other room, and Mary gave young Rainbird tea which he declared "divine." He explained that he was up in Aros to paint rocks and waves and green things generally; he had a hunch on green at present, and the stone of the Gribun cliffs just about met the bill, since that green was not too obvious. "Not so scabrous as old Rawson's stuff, if you see what I mean." Green was wonderful anywhere, of course; and of late he had been trying for it in tissues—an olive curtain at a dress rehearsal, with the house-lights only a quarter on, and a face against it—an author's or a producer's—not a made-up face like an actor's, y'know—but one with a spot of pallor in it. Quite a good pattern could be got out of that. Only it was rather *vieux jeu*, wasn't it, nowadays? And so he thought he'd try rubbley things like the Gribun gabbro, if you followed him.

Neither MacLeod or Mary followed him easily; and when either expressed a liking for the work of some modern Scots painter who at times visited the Isle, he met their eulogies with an interjected, "Yes, but why—" which seemed to question the necessity for those artists' very existence; or by a languid, "But a bit dated, don't you think?" As he took his leave, Mary asked if he found his quarters comfortable in the hotel at Torlochan, and was assured that they weren't "quite too poisonous."

Sharp on his departure, they set about preparing for the run to Acharonich; and Donnacha, who had been a trifle despondent lest the arrival of Mr. Rainbird would interfere with his visit to the seals, roused into life once more. Soon all were packed in the car, and it moved slowly out through the village. As they neared the inn, they saw Rainbird enter his car and leave for Torlochan, steering quite skilfully with his left hand. Then they turned off at the cross-roads, and so lost sight of him as they sped on to the western seaboard of the Isle. Up along the ascending road they climbed to the high ground above Acharonich, whence they looked out to the white sands of Iona—twenty miles away as the sea-bird flies—and to the great sea-spaces between it and Staffa. A little chill was in the evening wind from off the sea, as the car ran down from the heights to the croft on the low ground; but they reached a sheltered place in the lee of some of old Alasdair's peat-stacks, and halted there, while MacLeod got off and entered the crofter's cottage.

He found the old man in bed; while seated around the fire, as solemn as a funeral, were his wife, three stalwart sons and three daughters almost as stalwart. With lugubrious countenance the old man detailed his symptoms. "I'm thinking it will be the wind round the heart, Doctor," he concluded.

MacLeod, having examined him and decided that it was only the old dyspepsia due to over-frequent indulgence in strong tea, agreed with this simple diagnosis, and immediately comforted the anxious family as well as the patient by declaring the affliction as not too serious. He happened, he explained, to have with him the very remedy for that condition, and producing a bottle of a simple alkaline mixture, induced the patient to partake of a dose forthwith. And very shortly thereafter old Alasdair declared himself a new man, and that the good Doctor had once more saved his life.

The situation was an awkward one for MacLeod; but he had encountered it often in this same house, and he met it with the necessary strategy. This meant the concealing of the essential triviality of the complaint, in order to justify Alasdair's urgent messages to his children; what time he allayed their fears, and conserved his own self-respect by disclaiming any miraculous powers in cases of the kind. And so, by an astute trimming of his sails, he at last withdrew from an embarrassing situation. "We can't blame these good folk," he said to his wife as he climbed into the car. "They're far from me, and naturally feel lonelier than they really are out here, with nothing between them and America but big waves. But he's all right again. Yet they will have it that I save his life every time I visit him. A nuisance, that!"

"Well," said Mary, as he started up the car, and they climbed uphill again on the homeward track, "speaking as a mere woman, and without any Highland delicacy —"

"Oh, shut up!"

"Well then, speaking as a person once a nurse, who got frequent rows from a Médecin-Chief who shall be nameless, I'd say: Take all the undeserved praise you get, for you'll need it to make up for all the undeserved blame that's handed out to you."

"Yes, quite so," said MacLeod imperturbably. "And talking about dressing-gowns, what about those seals, Donnacha?"

The boy clapped his hands in delight; while, very quickly now, they topped the height, descended the farther slope for half a mile, and drew up to disembark and scan the shore for their quarry. "There," said Donnacha, quiet and business-like, pointing to some slabs of rock on the sea-line where something moved obscurely. Leaving the road, he took cover among some whin bushes and advanced towards the beach as stealthily as a Sioux.

"What did I tell you?" said Mary triumphantly. "He's a born naturalist. There are three seals down there, and I never saw one till he spoke."

But MacLeod had noted by now an easier stalk, a big fellow with a brownish hide, who lay farther inland than the others, and at a spot where large boulders offered easier cover for approach. He whistled back the ardent Donnacha therefore; and all three, slanting quickly downhill through whin and bracken, made silently across a stretch of sea-tangle. But so slow and careful was their progress that fully a quarter of an hour had passed before they approached the great seal close enough to discover him asleep. His back was towards them, his side heaving, and to Donnacha's delight, he was snoring just like any human. After a little he heaved round on his other side, facing them with eyes still unopened, but yawning now as if in ennui of seal-life generally. They watched him for a little, and then, not having the heart to disturb a slumber so peaceful, crept silently off and up the hillside. Back to the roadway now and the car; and so home.

Flora met them at the garden gate, and again commandeered Donnacha, saying: "It's sleepy you are; and it's in bed you should be."

"Oh, but, Flora, wait till I tell you about the big seal that was snoring."

"Yes, but you'll wait till we get into the house; for I have a message for the Doctor."

"Another message? "said MacLeod wearily. "And myself as tired as Donnacha."

"Och, not a visit this time," said Flora. "It was just Mr. Rainbird that came back after you had gone away, because he had forgotten something. I was to tell the Doctor that there was a gentleman staying in the hotel at Torlochan, and that he had asked Mr. Rainbird to take the Doctor his kind regards."

"What name?"

Flora produced a scrap of paper from her apron pocket. "I made Mr. Rainbird write it down," she said.

MacLeod took the paper. "Gurney?" he said in a low voice.

"The wee leprachaun!" cried Mary joyfully, reading the scribble as if to make sure. "After ten years! The man has as many lives as a cat!"

"You're glad?"

"And why not? Aren't you glad yourself? There's worse than wee Straw-Feet in the world."

"I'm thinking of Donnacha."

"Of Donnacha?"

"Yes. And of the next war."

"Oh, put the car in and get to bed. You're worn out, and not yourself at all, standing there and talking of war. Get in with you now, and see if you'll not be real pleased to see wee Straw-Feet to-morrow."

"I wonder."

"Wonder away then," she said. "I'm going in to Donnacha. The next war! What nonsense, Finlay."

And she left him standing there, staring blankly into the far distance up the Kyle, where behind grey cloud-bars over Ben Shiant the sunset smouldered, angry and red.

XXX: The sanctuary

MACLEOD had to visit Moy next day, and also make some calls by the wayside. It promised to be a longish day, he assured his wife as they sat at breakfast; and just as they were finishing the meal, a telegram arrived that definitely made it still longer; for it asked him to go to Derarach, a call which added forty miles to the tour.

"That means the Glen More road; so you'll not have time to see Gurney," she said. "I'd hoped we might run up to Torlochan in the evening, and call on him."

"To tell the truth, I don't know that I want to see Gurney. Thought we were done with him. He's a stormy petrel. You know what followed his last visit to Aros."

"A lot of things: a murdering war for one, and I got married for another. But did Gurney make the war?"

"He helped to—blast him!"

"Oh, go on with you," she said, smiling. "It's ten years since you saw him; and aren't you just dying to hear how he saved his neck, over in France?"

"No, I'm not—really not. And if I did try to find out, I know what he'd say—' One passes, you know.' That's all I'd get from him. Anyhow, I've my work cut out for to-day."

"Couldn't you write a wee note asking him down to-morrow?"

"But how do I know what spare time I'll have tomorrow?"

"Oh, very well," said Mary, rising from the table, the least bit petulant.

"Leave it, please. I don't want to think about Gurney. He makes me sick. I believe I almost hate him."

"Oh, come now! Hate? Just a wee note for the sake of the poor girl he was so fond of."

"Marion," he said, and winced; then stood as if turned to stone.

She flushed at those signs of vivid remembrance; and he saw her dark eyes lighten for a second, as she turned abruptly and left him. Plainly she could be jealous, even of the dead. How should he explain that he had only been stung by his forgetfulness of Marion—that his sudden change of mood meant no agony of love frustrate by early death, no relighting of old fires? She would never have Gurney down to Torness after all this misunderstanding. Or, if she did, it would merely be by way of masking her real feelings in the matter of his old affair with Marion. Lord, how life was difficult! And how the past lived on! Meanwhile he would pack his surgical bag, and bring round the car. She would be all right when it came to the leave-taking for the day.

And fifteen minutes later it was almost so—but only almost. For Mary came out on the roadway, smiling, with a sleepy Donnacha, clad in his night-suit, to say "Happy journey" in bad Gaelic; while still smiling, she raised her cheek for MacLeod's salute: her cheek, but not her lips, he noted. And to his quick glance her eyelids looked the least bit reddened. "Damn Gurney," he said to himself as the car swung out on the first stage of his long round.

A fine morning: the sun's rays too level as yet to rid the air of sharpness; no wind from the salt Sound to slant the thin columns of faint-blue smoke from the roadside crofts, and yet the faint aroma from peat fires was subtly pervasive. Stillness everywhere, save for a distant cockcrow from Callachly and the purr of the car's engine as he drove slowly through the village, successfully evading encounter with various ducks and hens, a stray calf or two, and finally the Old Lady of the Pump. But once clear of the crofts he was free to go full pelt by shore and wood to his first house of call, at Allt-Criche, ten miles on his way.

He had a hundred miles to cover that day; and if mileage were all he had to think of the task was easy, and the time sufficient. The car, too, was running well, and the road-surface moderately good for a route described by the map-makers as "secondary"; four hours at most was all that was required for the mere motoring. But when seven halts had to be made, some of them involving leaving the 'bus on the high road, and travelling on foot over rough hill-tracks to a cottage a mile or more away on the moorland; when his cases were, as on that day, middling serious; when some little technical manoeuvre, like the tapping of a pleural effusion, was necessary, then the hours of the day seemed strangely short. Always was there some careful thinking to be done about this or that emergency, and a battery of questions from anxious relatives to be answered. Even in the intervals between cases, his mind was busy with problems arising from them; so that to the drain of physical energy involved by driving, and long tramps over rough ground, was added a slow ebb of mental power. He felt tired, indeed, by the time he had made his second-last call—that at Moy—and turned back to make the long detour to Dererach, late in the afternoon. It was after five when he crossed Ardura Hill and entered Glen More, on the farther side of which lay the house of his last patient that day.

All Glen More was lovely to him, but it was loveliest, he thought, in its first three miles, when entered from the Ardura end; for there hazel woods abounded, draping the banks of the Lussa River and the hill-slopes on either side with tender foliage in its early green. Beyond—to the west—the great peaks towered; while across the river the Glen of the High Corrie made fairyland, enticing the wayfarer to exploration of its wooded depths by its airs of withdrawal and mystery—so alluring were the shy graces of its pines and birches.

Just where the hazels thinned and the ground became more open, a stag bounded from the river's bank, crossed the road at breakneck speed, stretching nobly, and disappeared in the woodland clothing the base of lofty Sgurr Dearg. MacLeod immediately drew his car to the verge of the road, dismounted, and set out on foot on the highway. He knew whence that fellow had come —from Mainnir nam Fiadh—the Playground of the Deer—a place of sanctuary for the hunter's quarry at all seasons of the year, and he guessed that his hinds could not be far away. Nowhere else in all the Isle were finer heads than here; and despite the duty calling him to Dererach, he must have a look at them. In any case he knew his patient at Dererach from of old, a type of the same kind as Alasdair of Acharonich; so there was really no need for haste. He jogged on therefore; the ground on his right rose higher; then at a turn of the road, he came out from the screen of hazels; and there—magnificent—a group of stag and hinds stood at gaze amid a wild tumble of grey boulders and dark pines: haughty and scornful they were, eagerly questioning with great eyes; their every movement fearful, yet indignant at the trespasser so close to earth they knew inviolate. Soon, too, other companies of deer appeared on higher terraces of rock and pine, with as marked airs of mingled protest and curiosity as those near at hand.

He stood still and watched these wild graceful beings; while, almost as still, they regarded him steadily. Their very beauty was a mystery; a mystery too their instinct; and presently he found his lips silently shaping some words of his favourite scripture:

Canst thou mark when the hinds do calve?...
Their young ones are in good liking,
They grow up in the open field;
They go forth and return not again.

And now he recalled how Gurney had also a partiality for this old poem of Job. He had forgotten that side of him. Maybe it would be best to send him a note tomorrow, as Mary had suggested. But a sudden stir in the herd broke in on these thoughts, for one and then another of the group turned its head and looked, up the glen, its delicate nostrils wrinkling as it sniffed the light breeze from the west; and there was a restless moving to and fro, with a tendency to make farther up the hillside. MacLeod too turned to look westward, and presently saw a man's figure topping the rise of the road, half a mile off. As he came nearer, it was plain that he carried his arm in a sling: Rainbird, without a doubt.

The youth had also marked the deer, and now halted to scan them through a binocular. Soon it was clear from his movements that he had made out MacLeod's presence; for he slung the instrument to his side, waved a hand, and started on a slow trot forward that sent the deer farther up the slope.

"Hillo," he said, as he came up. "Great stuff, this wild life, Doctor. You also studying it?"

"Great," said MacLeod. "How's the arm?"

"Oh, not so dusty, thanks. Seen old Gurney around?"

"Gurney!" said the surgeon, in amaze to find the subject of his recent thoughts so near; "is he with you?"

"Rather! We're birdy and beasty people to-day. Left the car a mile or two back, and did a bit of the hill there. Then we separated, and we were to meet at this place where the deer most do congregate. He's potty on what he calls larachs—old ruined crofts, y'know; and wherever he sees a burn coming down the hill, up he goes looking for the good old stones. Funny old chap! So when I saw these beasties, I guessed I'd got the location he wanted me to strike." His glasses went up, and he regarded the deer. "Marvellous, aren't they?" he murmured. "Quite too divine! And so tame!"

"Tame? Not quite. But they know there's never any stalking done on this ground—probably hasn't been for centuries. And that knowledge is in the blood, so to speak. That's why they don't get scared. They call this place The Sanctuary."

"I see. Oh, I say, look at the green of those pines! But the stonework there isn't right. Don't like that rock stuff." He paused, considering; then went on: "I know," and, with some grimaces over his lame hand's uneasy functioning, jotted down a word or two in a note-book. "'Pines and Slagheap,'" he read out. "By gum, I'll give 'em it modern enough! That's a good meaty title, y'know. Just send the critics wonky. And wouldn't old Gurney throw a fit if he heard it!"

"Where is Gurney?"

"Up the last wee glen as ever was. Oh, but there he comes. And, I say, can't he stump it!"

The small figure of Gurney now appeared on the rise to the west; and, as he approached, MacLeod took to pacing nervously back and forth. He felt, indeed, that he was about to make a mess of a meeting so suddenly sprung upon him, and finally decided that the meeting should be brief; his excuse, the waiting patient at Dererach. But when the little man came up, a glow of pleasure on his face and his eyes dancing with eagerness, all MacLeod's stiffness thawed at the first hand-shake. Neither spoke for a little, for Rainbird's presence tied their tongues at the outset. But at last Gurney said: "Well, it is good to be back."

And MacLeod, fencing for position, answered awkwardly: "And how are the little glens to-day?"

"I say," said Rainbird quietly, "if you two long-lost brothers would only stop shouting, there will be some chance these beasts don't go off at a canter. Do shut up!" He was lying on a grassy slope, and had his binocular again in use. Gurney joined him there to borrow the glasses, and as he did so, MacLeod hung back, and so was able to observe the Straw-Feet of former days more closely.

There was really little change in him, except in externals. He was as alert as ever, although his hair was more marked with grey. (He must be close on sixty-five by now, MacLeod guessed.) A four-inch scar on his right cheek, well healed and evidently years old, was the chief distinction from the old Gurney; a minor matter was the contrast of his dress with that of former years in Aros; for he now wore a neat lounge suit of blue-grey Harris tweed, with a slouch hat of the same stuff, and the old shoes and straw packing were replaced by heavy brown brogues and rough grey hose. On the whole he looked prosperous. For some minutes there was silence as he observed the deer; then, as he handed the binocular back to Rainbird, he turned to MacLeod, saying: "It seems a shame to intrude longer."

"Hush!" said Rainbird, busy with the glasses in turn.

"Oh, they won't go far," said Gurney. "This is Mainnir nam Fiadh"—he gave the Gaelic name out like any native of the Isle—"The Sanctuary of the Deer, isn't it, Doctor?"

"Yes."

"Then we must respect the spirit as well as the letter of the name, Mr. Rainbird, and at least get out of sight of those fellows. They can scent us for miles, of course; but I'd feel easier under cover—away from the reproachful eyes of them. They must think us ill-mannered, I'm afraid. Let's go under the birches round the turn of the road. We'll be out of the sun there; and I want a smoke."

They walked east a little, and found a grassy bank in the birch-wood, where they were hidden from both sun and deer. "Sanctuary," said Gurney, lighting his cigarette, and extending himself, hands behind head and eyes closed, "a fine word. Sanctuary—reservation —enclave—for those lovely creatures ... A fine thing that."

"It pays, of course," said Rainbird. "Keeps up the stock."

"Oh, give the laird his due," said MacLeod. "There's also the sportsman's idea of fair play, isn't there? I mean, giving the brutes a sporting chance of a getaway."

"Romance?" said the young cynic. "Of course romance always pays—when you let a shooting."

"Sanctuary—enclave—reservation," murmured Gurney between puffs, "—keeping up the stock?—How about trying it out on men as well as deer, Mr. Rainbird?"

"Well, isn't it done in the States and in Canada with the Red Indian?" asked Rainbird.

"Yes, but hardly from the point of view of keeping up the stock," said the little man. "Rather from the idea of giving the poor beggars fair play. The alternative is one of those things that isn't done, you know."

"What's the alternative?"

"Allowing economic pressure to force the Red Indian into what is called civilized life. He is given a chance to live the life of his people—in a reservation."

"Oh, well, if you put it that way."

"Yes, that's what they do in America," said Gurney, sitting up of a sudden and tossing his cigarette aside, while he clasped his knees with hands whose knuckles whitened as they gripped. "But here we haven't as yet seen fit to grant an enclave to the Gael."

"What the hell are you talking about!" cried MacLeod, starting to his feet in anger.

"Yes," said Rainbird, "I agree with Dr. MacLeod. That's really a bit thick, y'know, Mr. Gurney. One can't tape out the Red Indian and the Highlander with the same bit o' string, can one?"

"I know nothing of the Red Indian," said Gurney, calmly and decisively. "And I don't measure one race against another with the same inch-tape. But surely I may be permitted to use the Red Indian as a simile for other races in a like impasse. And so I say that we're forced to the idea of a reservation—an enclave—-for the finest people in the world."

Rainbird winked knowingly at MacLeod, as who should say, "Leave him in my hands," and asked silkily: "And what exactly do you mean by the finest people in the world?"

"Oh, people like you and me, of course," said Gurney, turning a bland frozen smile on him, and an eye that gleamed invitingly to conflict.

MacLeod, angry and rebuffed by Gurney's refusal to take note of him in the fight, was instantly caught up into the cold fury of it by that keen glance. "Toe the line, Gurney," he said. "You're talking of the Gael, aren't you?"

"Yes, I am. I'm talking of the future of the Gael. And if the worst comes to the worst, we could always make an enclave—cut off the West Coast and the Isles, and keep the old life going there."

"Kind of a museum?" asked MacLeod.

"Kind of a sacred fire," said Gurney. "A peep-show for tourists all the same?"

"What else is it now? ... But no, nary a tourist in my enclave."

"How would you exclude them? Deer-fences?"

"No, by God! "said Gurney. "I'd have a smokescreen of poison-gas spread daily by aeroplanes. And if any tried to break through, I'd make a raft of their dead bodies and tow them back to Clyde!"

The opening of the skirmish had been mere sniping, but Gurney's last words were delivered like a stream of machine-gun fire whose energy was not to be gainsaid. It left MacLeod breathless: but nothing could daunt the thick-skinned Rainbird.

"Sound man," he said. "No use doing things by halves."

The youth's aplomb brought anti-climax; and neither Gurney nor MacLeod could refrain from smiling. The surgeon got to his feet, saying: "Well, I'm afraid I must attend to the immediate needs of the Gael, until you get your scheme through Parliament, Gurney. I've a sick man to see over at Dererach, and must be going." He offered to give them a lift in his car as far as their own machine. But they wanted another look at the deer, so he trudged back to his motor, and in a few minutes pulled up alongside the oddly assorted pair. By now he had overcome all his morning scruples about having Gurney down to Torness: wee Straw-Feet had again exercised his wonted fascination. "Look us up at any time you're over our way," he said, as he shook hands. "My wife will be glad to see you."

"Ah, yes," said Gurney, "I have pleasant memories of the lady in Salle Foch, and I wish you both all happiness."

MacLeod thanked him; and they looked into one another's eyes, each searching the other's thoughts. And the surgeon was sure the little man's were of Marion just then, for Gurney blinked and turned away as if he would hide some deep emotion.

Seeking to show his sympathy, MacLeod said awkwardly: "You know, I suppose, that the MacCormacks have left the inn, and gone north?"

"To Inverness; yes, I know," said Gurney briefly, while his face blanched, and the thin line of his lips narrowed. Clearly the old wound was still raw; but he composed his features and said with an effort at gaiety: "Tell your lady I make pretty bows to her and to the child, and say I hope to call later in the summer—at the end of August, perhaps. I go off to-morrow for three months to the Outer Isles—to Innis Fada for the most part."

"Yes," said Rainbird, shuddering, "to snoop around dying Gaels and frowsty old larachs and all that kind of punk. My God! To me that stuff always smells like a last year's bird's-nest!"

"It would," said MacLeod grimly, and drove on.

His case at Dererach took longer than he anticipated; and he was called in at not a few houses by the wayside after that, so that it was near nine before he got home.

"You're later than you allowed," said Mary, meeting him at the garden gate. "Was the car not behaving well?"

"No, no, car's doing splendidly. But old Colin at Dererach's real bad, and folks snapped me up on the way back—quite a lot of sickness round Gribun— minor things." Instinctively he avoided any immediate reference to Gurney as an additional cause of delay. His remembrance of the tiff that morning was still fresh; and any further talk about Gurney would be sure to recall Marion and the whole series of subtle antagonisms then aroused between Mary and himself at the mere mention of the dead girl's name. But later, at supper, he saw the unwisdom of silence on this point, and said: "Who do you think I met in Glenmore to-day?"

"Rainbird? Or not Gurney, surely?"

"Both." And in a single glance he saw she had divined why he had held back the news.

She in turn dissembled, and on the instant was outwardly gay. "Just fancy! Gurney back in Aros! And are his wee feet in straw again?"

"No: he's very tidy all over. Bond Street's his outfitter's address this time, I'll bet."

"Changed days ... And when's he coming down here?"

"Nothing fixed. Talks of going out to Innis Fada first of all. May come here in August."

"And how in all the world did he escape being shot out in France?"

"Oh, well, Rainbird was there; and we never got down to that. Anyway, it would have been rather a tender point, don't you think? We'll hear later, perhaps ... No, we talked of nothing but the Highlands and the Gael, and—" He hesitated.

"—And of the old life here ... I see," said Mary briefly. Their eyes met, and instantly both saw that their thoughts were again of Marion.

All the wildest unreason, this! thought MacLeod. But when were women reasonable—or men? ... Jealous imaginings haunting the past—what had they to do with the life of to-day! ... But there the thing was; and reason and logic seemed powerless in the face of a dream.

Mary rose from the table, her lips the least bit compressed, her step slow; and at sight of her changed air a sudden revulsion of feeling overcame MacLeod. He sprang to his feet. "Let's cut out this sob stuff, Mary," he said, his hand on her shoulder.

She turned to him. "Whatever do you mean, Finlay?"

"All these half-hints and half-thoughts about Marion. The girl's dead, and it's an old story, done and by with. By the way you go on, you'd think she was still up there, at the inn of Torness."

She smiled wanly. "It might be better for us both if she were," she said. "It's not easy fighting a ghost."

"Ghost be hanged!"

"Well, a memory then. For your brain's as busy as Gurney's with thoughts of that girl ... I see you brooding and brooding, time and again; and if it's not of her, what else is it? ... There are times, indeed, when I wish we were anywhere in the world but in Eilean Aros—where you knew her for so long, and where thoughts of her must come often enough, seeing this place and that place she was fond of."

"Tuts! it isn't as bad as all that, my dear. It's only that she was a fine lass, and her end so tragic ... Come now"; and he kissed her. "For me there's one memory that's above all else—and that's of yourself when first I saw you truly."

She smiled provokingly. "And where now was that, I wonder? ... In the meadows near Aubepierre?"

"No, no, you rascal!" he cried. "On the shores of Moy—among the yellow whin"; and he took her in his arms.

XXXI: Locum tenens

GURNEY, however, did not come to Aros in August, as promised. But in mid-September a card arrived, bearing the Lochboisdale postmark, and saying briefly: "Staying over the winter here. L. G."

"He's like a snipe in the gloaming, that wee man," said Mary, "—darting here, darting there. You never know where you'll find him."

And Straw-Feet lived up to this estimate, by again changing his plans, and turning up in Torness, long before the winter had passed. It was a raw afternoon in late February when he came up the sleet-covered path to MacLeod's house, and sheltered in the porch against an icy blast from the Kyle. Flora answered the bell, and was a trifle resentful when the little man asked in middling good Gaelic if the Doctor was at home; and after the manner of Highland servant-maids when dealing with amateurs in the ancient language, at once aired her best English. "He is indeed, yes," she said. "Will the gentleman come in?" and she showed him into the surgery, adding: "Just a wee meenit, please."

Presently the doctor appeared, but it was not MacLeod. The stranger, a man of MacLeod's own age, with a worn thin face surmounted by curly rust-coloured locks, at once noted the surprise on Gurney's countenance, and said: "I'm sorry; I see you expected Dr. MacLeod, but he is from home for some weeks, and I am acting in his absence."

Gurney explained that he was not a patient, but an old friend of Dr. MacLeod's. Might he ask —?

"Oh, Robbins is my name. The Doctor and I were old chums at college; so we see a good deal of one another, and sometimes change practices. Not usually, at this time of year, of course. But I've been a bit seedy of late, and he arranged to have me up for a rest. And it is a real rest, despite the sleet and the hail and the blasts —a real rest after nine months on end of slum-practice in Glasgow. Oh, Lord! what heavenly airs here, winter or no!"

"I expect MacLeod finds Glasgow fogs just as heavenly, for the moment. He'll be tramping the hospitals, of course; I know how keen he is on that kind of thing."

"Just what he's doing—or trying to, rather; for my practice is a busy one—although hardly a paying affair."

They talked on; and Gurney, regarding Robbins' spare figure, asked if he didn't find the long distances in Aros too much for him? Not in the least, Robbins said; he was an expert motorist, and had got to know the country rather well during previous visits—in summer, of course. And long journeys in the open were a fine change from crawling around in a car over greasy tramlines, in a congested city district. No, Mrs. MacLeod had not accompanied her husband; she and the boy had crossed to Ireland a week ago—to Monaghan, where her people did farming, he believed. Wouldn't Mr. Gurney come through and meet his wife, and have tea with them?

Gurney accepted; but he was afraid he must bolt immediately after tea, as he had arranged for the big steamer from the Outer Isles to call for him; he might even have to go before his first cup was finished. The motor from the inns was to pick him up as soon as the steamer's siren was heard, he explained to Mrs. Robbins.

That lady was a shy little woman, her hair greying early; but Gurney guessed from a quiet chuckle soon in evidence that she had humour and courage enough to bring her safely through the fight with the narrow ways of the household and her husband's poor health. She confided that at the earliest opportunity they meant to get a country practice—Highland for preference. She herself—they had no children—had completed half her medical course, and as soon as she had qualified, they would do wonders.

Gurney was enthusiastic at once: they were folk after his own heart, he assured them. No matter that the motive was the seeking of bodily health, they would soon discover that it meant finding health of mind as well. He would show them what he meant if Mrs. Robbins would be so good as to permit his use of the pianoforte for a little. And he played the air of *The Skye Fisher's Song*, profoundly moved, remembering his first hearing of it from Marion so long ago. Robbins and his wife were warm in their praise of music and player, and asked for more; so he played *Colin's Cattle, The Island Herdmaid*, and many others. When he ceased, Robbins said in his low clear voice: "I see what you mean"; while the shy woman at the fireside turned with a glow on her cheeks long absent, and thanked him with a glance that said she also understood.

"Yes," said Gurney, "there is the soul of a fine race in that music. And that race is dying, more's the pity. So be sure you come soon to the Highlands, Dr. Robbins, if you want to be in at the death. It will do you and me good, that tragedy, won't it? Purge us by pity and terror and all that, as we look on, eh? And never raise a hand to help? Oh, no; everything decently and in good taste! The end draws on so quietly, you would hardly believe me if I told you it was, nevertheless, a death by violence." His eyes were blazing now, although his voice was low; and he turned swiftly on the stool, and played the air of Patrick Mor MacCrimmon's *Lament for the Children*, transposing the wild pipe-music in masterly fashion. When he rose, he asked pardon. "It isn't easy, Mrs. Robbins, for us old fogeys to hide our feelings," he said. She protested her gratitude, however; and just then the steamer's siren boomed from the Kyle, and Gurney took his leave. But, by the by, he would be passing through Glasgow on his way south; so why shouldn't he look up Dr. MacLeod? Might he have his address? Robbins scribbled a line on a scrap of paper, as the horn of the motor from the inns now sounded from the road. Adieux were said once more, and the little man ran out into the dark and the rain.

The district in which MacLeod was deputizing for Robbins was a working-class one in the west of Glasgow. It lay on the flats close to the river; and February fogs were thicker there than on the rising ground to the north, known as The Hill, where Robbins had his home. A large part of The Hill was indeed an oasis in a desert of close-packed buildings; there were many gardens and trees around its villas, and in summer it was well-foliaged and thronged with song-birds. But in winter it was chiefly notable to MacLeod for its reserved old-world air. The district indeed was only tenanted by the successors of a past generation of middle-class folk who had bossed the shipyard workers living on the lower ground, at a time when Clyde-built shipping had enjoyed a boom for a long fifty years—an era that had just ended with the close of the war. Robbins' house was in a tenement block on the outskirts of this villadom; and as MacLeod left it each day to descend to the surgery in the slum area, his road at first led him along the crest of The Hill. Thence he could look out on a wide prospect if the day were clear—the Clyde valley and the distant Renfrewshire hills; the line of the river, marked by gigantic cranes, and a few funnels that showed over the tops of the poorer tenements huddling close to the docks. Between The Hill and this slum area was a buffer-state of buildings, housing a section of the workers who were comfortably off.

MacLeod recalled the contrast of the scene with that he had known from this same view-point in the years before the war. To-day the cranes were nearly all stationary, and few funnels moved up or down the river; the siren sounded seldom, and the noise of the riveters was an intermittent rumour only. But in the old days the terrific pressure of work could not be mistaken: the riveting went on with a rattle and a roar that was constant and overwhelming; the great cranes moved gingerly and surely with their huge burdens every hour of the day; the booming of the steamers' sirens was frequent; and, out of the clouds of steam and smoke, some new wonder of a ship moved every now and again, outward bound or inward. Yes, things had sadly changed.

But when he descended to the main thoroughfare, and noted the groups of unemployed standing idle at the mouths of mean side-streets and staring vacantly at the tides of busy passers-by in the high road, he was doubly appalled and depressed. Good hard workers these, if a bit too fond of their dram—men of fifty or thereabouts —platers, riveters, hole-borers, caulkers, riggers, ships' plumbers—he knew many of them as patients in previous exchanges with Robbins. And there they were—just the same as a year ago—with blank faces, hopeless, yet passionless— bewildered at a world that had dealt with them so scurvily.

Further down these side-streets was the younger generation at play— corner-boys of eighteen or twenty, many of whom had not worked a stroke since leaving school five years ago. And at the open windows of ground-floor houses were slatterns, each with the customary babe in her arms; while older children sprawled, untended, in gutters around close-mouths, or traversing these dark entries, reached puddled courts that led to primitive middens and back-land stairs. Children everywhere.

Depressing too the river-side itself, where the line of tall tenements was broken here and there by vestiges of an older era—decayed one-storey buildings of rubble and faded limewash, that housed old clothes shops, gaudy drinking bars, rag and scrap-iron stores, a greasy eating-house or two, a greengrocery with little of green about it—the region of the ultimate "down-and-outs": people who lived on the dole or parish allowance. Old or ill, or both, struggling on from day to day, heads hardly above water, they were so used to their desperate case that it had become second nature; the jest easier than the groan. Here also were swarms of children in the gutter, and slatterns at close or window. Before them ran the muddy street, wherein steam-lorries and tractors dragged heavy uncouth engineering "jobs"; while, across the way, the blank palisades or brick walls of the dockyards rose so close that not even a liner's funnel or masthead pennon could be seen—nothing, indeed, that would lend a bit of colour to the drab surroundings.

But despite the greyness of the scene, MacLeod had only to look east along this muddy highway; and, behold! framed in the pillars and bridge of the railway-crossing in the far distance, was a vista to entrance a painter—roofs rising irregularly, yet in series, to cluster round a noble spire; grey in grey—stone and shadow —like some mediaeval burg huddling for protection to the knees of its guardian château. And yet the reality was far other than the picture suggested. For the ragged line of gables was that of tenements only a grade less poverty-stricken than the slums he now passed along; and the spire that of the University.—Above, the great Seat of Learning; below—clinging to its skirts —the homes of the workless it was powerless to aid.

XXXII: Afterthoughts

ROBBINS had a surgery in a side-street off the slums; and here one Saturday night, after a hard two hours at consultations, MacLeod sat on in the hope of short-circuiting stragglers. For late-comers were frequent on Saturdays, and a trifle bibulous and quarrelsome; they demanded the instant return of the doctor, if he had gone home. The quickest way of getting rid of them being to accede to their demands, MacLeod had many recalls by telephone from the caretaker at the surgery, almost as soon as he had reached Robbins' house on The Hill. Better therefore not to be in too big a hurry on Saturdays. He would smoke a bit that evening, laze by the fire, and see what turned up in the next half-hour. It was a raw night, so he poked up the fire thoroughly: outside it was foggy, the streets miry, a thin rain drizzling down; from the main thoroughfare motor-horns and tram-bells sounded incessantly.

In the next tenement a pane of glass was smashed, high-pitched women's voices were heard in altercation, a police-call was blown; and an increasing hubbub succeeded as a crowd gathered. MacLeod followed it all in his fancy as he dozed by the fire: he could tell the various stages of these affairs by merely listening. There was a hush now—that meant the constables had arrived; and, shortly after, a noise of murmuring and of many moving feet indicated that an arrest had been made, and that the crowd was now scattering. But a few stragglers remained to discuss the case; among these a fresh quarrel soon developed, and went swiftly on to blows. Partisans of the rivals were loud in their comments; and MacLeod was soon aware that "Paddy" was having a worse time than "the wee yin." Finally it was evident that "the wee yin" had won; for the crowd now acclaimed him as "a fair wee marvel," and "handy wi' his mitts"; while the voice of "Paddy," as he was led off by his friends, was vociferous in declaring he could do things that he had not yet been able to accomplish. "I kin bate you—an' I kin bate yer brother—an' I kin bate yer brother-in-law," he shouted repeatedly, his voice declining in the distance.

Just then the surgery bell rang; and a murmur of many voices was heard as the caretaker opened the door. An argument followed as to how many friends of the patient were to be admitted; in the midst of it, the consulting-room door swung inwards, a tiny figure was propelled through it by the muscular guardian of the surgery, and the entry of a crowd of sympathizers prevented by a sudden closure of the door again.

The new-comer held a bloody handkerchief to his nose, and regarded the doctor beseechingly with a pair of familiar brown eyes.

"My God, Gurney!" cried MacLeod. "Whatever are you doing here?"

The little man mopped his nose carefully, and crossed to a mirror to regard its rather bloated proportions. "Scrapping," he said casually." Also looking for you. Got any cold water?"

The caretaker had at last coaxed the mob outside the premises, and in response to MacLeod's bell, now brought towels and basins of water both hot and cold; then hung around regarding Gurney admiringly, until MacLeod said: "All right, MacNab, you can get off now. I'll lock up. This is a friend of mine."

"Gled to hear it, sir," said MacNab. "He's a guid yin. It was juist 'hop an' go constant' for Paddy the nicht. He'll no' bother this corner again for a month o' Sundays, I'm thinking."

"That's good news," said the doctor. "Good night."

"'Nicht, sir," said MacNab; and so departed.

Gurney had seated himself by the fire, and was bathing his nose. The bleeding had ceased, but that organ was now of considerable size: he was indeed a grotesque Straw-Feet; yet dapper still—fashionable indeed— from the waisted overcoat he now rose to discard, to his brown linen spats and moose-skin shoes. "You are a beauty," said MacLeod: "almost as attractive as on that evening in the Lion d'Or. What happened tonight?"

"Navvy kicked a girl."

"I see. Didn't know you boxed."

"Only when there's need."

MacLeod regarded the little man with frank admiration. "You are a scrapper and no mistake," he said. "No wonder you got clear from the French in 'eighteen."

"But there was really no scrapping in that affair," said Gurney, squinting ruefully down his swollen nose, and dabbing it gingerly. "Just luck, and the use of one's wits."

"What happened?"

"Oh, we got as far as Troyes; and after that they couldn't find a stretcher carriage, so the medical super at Troyes put up my leg in plaster and gave me a crutch. Then all the trains got mixed up because of the Château-Thierry battle. So we lay around Troyes station till midnight, when we were sent on by Romilly. Shunted into the wrong siding there—quite a bad smash—people killed. After that my gendarmes collared an auto, and we went on by road; but they'd lost their heads over the collision—the burning train and all that. Then they lost the road to Paris. Then they lost me, poor devils!"

"Dammit, can't you be explicit! What came next?"

"Well, that derailing business had so upset their nerves that they drove right on for an hour without asking the way; they only halted when they got over the hill at Conde, and saw the Véry lights in the battle round Château-Thierry. Next they tried for the Paris road by La Ferte. Then they ran into a crowd of British convoying a big lot of German prisoners— really ran into them, mind you, for our lights were out. We knocked several of them senseless, in fact. Next there was a hell of a row with the British officers; and just to make things happier—all in the darkest of dark nights, mind you— some aircraft dropped a bomb or two on top of us. And then I lost my gendarmes."

"Killed?"

"No idea"; and again he sponged his nose, and squinted down it reflectively." Anyway, I didn't try to find them; just dropped my crutch, slipped among the Deutsch prisoners, and hobbled off with them at the word of command. Hardly any pain in the leg. Great thing plaster for a Pott's fracture!"

"Lucky devil. No trouble with the British?"

"Never a trouble. Quite the little gentlemen all the time ... You see, Pinson—the younger gendarme —was a bit of a joker; and when we boarded the train first of all—at Chaumont—he found a German *képi* in our compartment; and nothing would do, but that I must wear it. So he stuck it on my head. Very useful, that *képi*, in the mix-up ... Oh, yes, I passed for a Boche all right. And no questions asked till we got to the cage at Southampton, three weeks later. By that time I'd faked a story: regiment, number, papers; and even some letters from home."

"Southampton! Good Lord!"

"Yes, it was nice to see England again. And my seven months in the camp there were quite tolerable ... Then back to Cassel, of course."

"You did have luck."

"Well, didn't I need it, after the hole you put me in?" and he grinned.

MacLeod, grinning in turn, said: "Oh, fortune of war, you know"; and continued:" Now, what in all the earth were the British Intelligence doing about you all this time?"

"Just nothing: they thought I'd 'gone west'. I sent old Burton a Christmas card from Cassel—all angels and frosted glass and snow—soon's I'd got home, and offered my services to the British in the next war. He replied, 'Heard you were shot. Wish you had been.' Kind of him!"

"A queer crowd, your little lot! ... But, tell me, how did you find out I was here? Been to Aros?"

"Of course."

"How's Robbins?"

Gurney lit his pipe. "Looks ill," he said. "But he'll soon pick up, now he's free of this disease you call Glasgow." His voice had acquired a nasal note as the result of his injury; and he dabbed at his nose crossly, as if to free his speaking from this twang.

A noise of shouting again arose in the street outside the window, then the sound of running feet; but the hubbub soon abated in the distance. "What a nightmare, this place!" said Gurney. "Calibans pottering around in fog and grime and slush. Heavy faces of the damned, everyone.—Old Job knew them well in his time. How does it go?

> Men groan from out the city,
> And the soul of the wounded crieth out.

Wounded—yes, they're wounded all right; but they don't know it. And as for souls, they've lost them or they'd never abide such a life."

"Yes, it's bad," said MacLeod. "Yet, it's not all damnation, when you get to know them. But what I can't stick is their tenements. After my life in the open up yonder, I feel as if those great stacks of stone would fall and crush the life out of me some day. Going down a street here is like entering a canyon where the cliffs overhang."

"You're studying at the Infirmary, I hear. That should be a relief."

MacLeod's face lit up. "Yes, Tuesdays and Fridays: I get three hours twice a week there; and that's real good. The rest of the time—well, one must take it as it comes. Minor ailments mostly. And, as I say, they're not a bad lot at bottom, these slum folk. You mustn't be too hard on them, Father Gurney. They're not all kickers of little girls."

The little man smiled. "Agreed," he said. "Perhaps my face was paining me when I read the last lesson."

"No, not all bad," went on MacLeod. "And they haven't many chances of being good angels: the men unemployed; the women doing almost all the wage-earning. And that's little enough—bits of odd jobs as charwomen, you know. I mean, of course, the women over forty; for everyone under forty has an infant in her arms, or is obviously on the way to that. Too many kiddies."

"Much drinking?"

"No more than you used to do yourself ten years ago. 'A hunger and a burst,' they call it hereabouts."

"I've cut that out since—well, since this," said Gurney, and he touched the long scar on his cheek.

"Oh? I've been wondering about that slice. Noticed it in August. Where did you pick it up?"

"Labour riots in Barcelona," said Gurney curtly. "They want me badly there."

"But why?"

"Oh, leave it," said Gurney. "One civilization at a time; and it's Glasgow's turn at present. What about gambling here? That's always an index of how far they're down."

"Well, they do bet a bit; although none of them, most likely, has ever seen horse or jockey. The bookie is up every fifth close along here on pay-days—hides up a couple of stair-flights, and has a half-open door behind him as a place of retreat from the bobbies. Also half a dozen corner-boys as scouts. Must pay, the bookie business, to afford that number of watch-dogs."

"Stair's dark, of course?"

"Dark and dank."

"My God! And up yonder is Eilean Aros!"

"Yes, it's queer, isn't it?"

"Much illness?"

"Plenty. But it does get less. Public Health really makes some progress nowadays."

"Some! Don't tell me. They're only playing at it, so far. They don't get a chance, those Public Health chaps—don't get to the roots. I hear they even make artificial sunlight!"

"Yes, that's funny," said MacLeod. "Their smoke shuts out the sun; and, because of that, disease is bred. So they set up dispensaries where they make nice little artificial suns for their patients. *Alice in Wonderland*, you know." He smiled broadly.

"Please don't laugh," said Gurney. "The thing's too tragic. As I said, they haven't a chance. No Health Service has, while the man-in-the-street holds the purse-strings so tight. Also, these fellows are specialists; they're in a groove. They get to thinking that progress is something away from the primitive ... And it isn't. They concentrate and circumscribe, and think that's progress ... And it isn't. It's only a bit of progress. They have forgotten adaptability— pliability—what you will—elasticity is perhaps the word. Anyway, the primitives—the peasants, if you like—they've got it ... And Goethe had it: he was an all-round man if ever there was one. A great poet; yet he made some of the biggest generalizations in biology. Not a hodman of science, of course. Took care of his body: a great skater in his youth, you know. And when he died, that body could only be described as one of divine magnificence ... But your specialists! My God, is there anything worse than a muscle-bound bacteriologist!"

"Yes, yes, but what about ' Divide et impera '?"

"Well, what about it? Don't you lose range and width every time you specialize too deep and too long? It's a question of the golden mean, of course. But look at your parson, your lawyer: they're not human. Look at your"

"—secret-service man," interpolated MacLeod. Gurney grimaced as if in pain. "Don't," he said. "I've cut that out also."

"Sorry," said the other. "But isn't this loss of range—of width—only the cost of progress?"

"A cost that's too dear. And, as I say, it isn't real progress. Already you've lost the sun. And the sun's only the symbol of so much else you've lost—things of the mind and spirit. No, we need a clearer idea of what progress is, my boy. We must go forward to Eilean Aros."

"Back to peasant life?"

"With a difference. And I don't like the word 'back.' Also I'd make distinctions between peasant life and peasant life. I've seen many types that are fine; but I think the Gael the finest. In any case, any type of peasantry is surely better than this savagery of the slums."

"Oh, come now!"

"But I mean it! What else has your industrialism done, but plunged us back into savagery?"

"Machines to plough—are they savagery?"

"Machines to kill—what are they? Big Bertha and gas-bombs will end the next war in two hours. But it will take two years to bury your dead—if you do bury them. And your gas-bombs from the sky come from the same system that makes your slums—the system that shuts out the sun."

"The same system that makes the motor-ambulance. And a jolly good thing a motor-ambulance, if your child is down with an appendicitis and you're miles and miles from a hospital, with nobody near but a few hefty crofters singing the songs of the Hebrides."

"I know—I know—I know. All I say is that we mustn't go machine-mad. We don't want Big Bertha; and we don't want what that French chap said the Americans would soon have: machines to blow their noses and scratch their backs. No, no; we must go on to a simpler state of affairs. Forward to Eilean Aros."

"With the motor-ambulance flung in?"

"Certainly; and much else. Evolution spills nothing—not even the machine age. Nature didn't stop at the saurian, did she? And she won't stop at the robot. She makes mistakes, does Nature, as you must know from your biology. Else why does she go back and improve on her last job? She has afterthoughts, hasn't she?—kind of a trial and error business, eh? And she's sure to have an afterthought about this blasted mess, the great cities and all they stand for."

"I used to think that way," said MacLeod. "Not about afterthoughts of Nature and so on; but about the big cities. I-remember when I left this place to go to Aros, I climbed a hill to the south there—Cathkin, it's called—and came as near likening Glasgow to Gomorrah as anyone could. But what I find now is that when I'm in Aros I want back to Glasgow. And when I'm here I want back to Aros. It's all very puzzling. And, after all, the hospitals and science and all that are only possible in the great city."

"And what I say," said Gurney irritably, "is that you haven't tried them elsewhere. And your men of science that shut out the sun are a pack of fools. You want a new science, my boy, if that's all they can give you. And you're another fool, if you don't see what I'm driving at. I tell you Nature's going to make a better job of this one she has spoiled. But, of course, she'll take the good bits of the last stage along with her, and scrap the rest ... Damn this nose! It's beginning again!"

That swollen organ was certainly dripping red gouts once more. "Let's try a little science," said MacLeod. "Shall I pack it for you?"

Gurney became blasphemous on the instant. The beastly thing was so painfully swollen that he didn't dare let a hand come near it, he explained. There wouldn't be room for the tiniest pledgelet of cotton. He got up, examined his face in the glass, and groaned at the sight of it. "Falstaff's was nothing to this," he murmured; "but that old porker had something of a body to carry off the look of the thing, blast him! Look at it, MacLeod! Just look at it! Positively Socratic, the way it's spread out!"

"One of Nature's afterthoughts," suggested MacLeod unkindly, from the depths of his arm-chair. "There's no saying what old Nature's attempting with yourself by way of experiment."

Gurney gnashed his teeth at him, and .was silent for a little, what time he dabbed tenderly at a rosy tip that grew shinier with every sponging. But at last he sat down; then at MacLeod's suggestion stretched himself on a couch, and allowed the surgeon to apply some gauze soaked in lead lotion to the injured part. "You keep quiet now for a bit, and then we'll go home and have supper," said the surgeon, adjusting a pillow below the head of the little man. "By the by, about those afterthoughts—"

"Are you trying to gag me?" growled Gurney. "I'm not going to lie here, and be jibed at by you, young man."

"All right, Socrates. I was only going to say something in support of your afterthought idea. But if you don't want it, I don't mind."

Gurney lay silent for a bit, and then growled: "All right; let's have it."

"It was only this. I knew an architect once, and he told me that he could never get an idea down on paper quite right, until he'd got it down all wrong, first of all. Nicely drawn and measured too. A true child of Nature, it seems."

"Sure," said Gurney, in nasal notes that were almost American.

"But what I can't understand is why you're bothering about this industrial horror, if Nature's thinking hard all the time as to how she'll tidy it up—pretty-pretty. You're not giving her a hand, are you?"

"Sure," mumbled Gurney.

"But how can you give a hand, if you don't know an afterthought's coming until it's born? The thing will be there before you come on the scene, won't it?"

"Sure."

"Dammit, man, say something. I'm not going to dig the whole blamed scheme out of you."

The little man sat up of a sudden and cast the lead-lotioned clout in the fire, his Falstaffian nose again revealed. "You are a thickhead, MacLeod," he said bitterly. "Nature, of course, will help herself through people like you and me.

Nature is made better by no mean
But Nature makes that mean.

You know who said that?"
"Shakespeare."
"He didn't. He made Perdita say it. You don't know the first essentials of drama, my son. And Perdita was own sister to Marion, let me tell you."
"Surely not?"
"But surely yes. You didn't see that side of her. But it was there, God be thanked!"
"Well, never mind," said MacLeod uneasily; for he saw old memories stirring as Gurney blinked furtively and turned his head away. "I'm grateful you didn't quote the Man of Uz or your friend, the great Goethe. Only our own William, after all."

Gurney smiled, and recovered his composure. "The Man of Uz," he said reminiscently—" well, perhaps he also has something to say on the subject." He considered further, and then went on: "*Frage noch*"— but pulled up suddenly, saying: "Pardon, I had forgotten that Job spoke English as well as Luther's Deutsch. How does it go in your tongue? ...

 Ask now the beasts and they shall teach thee,
 And the fowls of the air and they shall tell thee—"

"You leave me guessing," said the other. "What have the fowls of the air to do with it?"

"Ask the wild duck what made him take to domesticity and the farmyard a long time ago. Nature is made better by means of the farmer. Or so at least the farmer thinks."

"Then the machine age is your wild duck? And you'll tame it? What a hope! When do we start?"

"As soon as we start thinking of our plight, and seek a way out. And that way is by discovering signs of Nature's afterthoughts. Then to work, my boy!— following her lead."

"As for instance? ... I mean, a sign of these afterthoughts?"

"Well, there's one that's staring you in the face, if you'll only open your eyes: the open-air movement among the young people of your own country and of many others. *Wander-vogel* they call them in Germany; hikers and trampers and campers-out, over here. You haven't seen much of that game as yet in Eilean Aros; but in summer-time it's going on all around the big cities."

"Yes: I've seen one or two in Aros. But all the open-air folk I've seen hereabouts have been motor-car owners."

"And, strangely enough, it was that automobile crowd that led to the trampers. The trampers saw the motor lot fleeing the city at week-ends, and learnt from them to get out, no matter how. I tell you that's a portent, MacLeod—an afterthought of Mother Nature. She's getting ready for a big change. These young folk with their rucksacks don't see as yet whither all this is tending. Just now it's only instinctive with them. All they feel is that it's good to get out and away from the city. They have an urge to it, that's all, as far as they're concerned. Can't you see it? All the big movements in history start in the same way—instinctively. Isn't that so?"

"Oh, I don't know about all. But I'm certain that Gibbon was wrong about that pearl fishery business in Britain. He says Caesar only came over to get a grip of those pearls. But really—when you come to think of it—old man Julius had an urge. He didn't know then that his crowd were going to give us law and order and civilization and so on. It was just instinct, as you say."

"Gibbon? Are you still mugging up that old romancer? Well, well! But leave him for the moment, and let's get this thing straight. As I say, these youngsters don't recognize what it is they foretell. They're all for the foot-pathway and a hey-nonny-no! They don't know that they're reacting against the very thing that gave us the war—the crowded city, with its mob hysteria; its nose at the grindstone of this speciality or that; its all-belly-and-brain way of life; its lack of leisure for wholesome meditation. And although they never bring the two things together in their minds, it just comes to this—they want the rucksack and not the gas-mask."

"And they'll want a jolly thick waterproof too, if they get as far as our little island."

Gurney frowned. "You're difficult, MacLeod," he said, sitting up aggrieved. "I wish you'd take me seriously.—Think of the life you and I have known in Eilean Aros—the life that made Marion what she was. Think of what might be made of the new generations if they lived, not at week-ends only, but always, in free air, clear sunlight and cleansing rains. And in sight of noble hills and great seas, how else should a people be but noble and great?"

"But the personal equation, my good man! Haven't I seen misery and uncleanliness enough among the Gael, even when his home was set among the finest scenery in all Albainn. Let me again remind you of Charlie of Glenavoulin—his miserliness, his scurvy skin, his matted beard, his hut floor covered with the hen-droppings he was too lazy to guard against."

"Of course, we can't force a man to be wise or happy; but we could at least give him the opportunity to be so."

"Yes—yes. But what I want you to see is that the personal equation goes further than even your given opportunity. Look at this. I don't know anywhere people who are braver and happier than a family in the worst slum hereabouts. Mercy Street it's called, God knows why! I must take you down to it some day; and there you'll meet folk that, for kindliness and cheerfulness and cleanliness, would be hard to beat. There are very few like the MacLachlans."

"Ah! a Highland stock!"

"Not for generations. They're Clydeside. And all the cleansing rain in the Hebrides won't wash the rickets out of their bones. Two of them are only three feet in height, because of deformed legs. And one of the two has been stone-blind for fifty years and more. No opportunities, I tell you, but what they have made for themselves. Every imaginable handicap—all these disabilities—and yet they're not unhappy."

"Even so, they would be happier in Eilean Aros."

"I'm not so sure. Anyhow, it's too late now for them to make a move. So the sooner Nature gets ahead with her afterthoughts the better. And you must catch your slum-dwellers young."

"We'll catch everybody," said Gurney, his eyes blazing," —everybody that's in the slums; and everybody that has helped to put them there—commercial men, parliament men, bankers, rentiers, parsons, schoolmasters, lawyers, bookies, publicans, doctors—every blighter that ever breathed soot in Glasgow, and said it was a fine day. But we'll forgive them all, if they'll only come up to the Highlands, and let us make men of them."

"But what about your enclave—your sanctuary for the Gael—the reservation, you know, that was to keep the crofter pure and undefiled?"

"There's room for both lots, my boy. You're no statesman. Get to work: that's the great thing."

"We'll get to supper, first of all," said MacLeod, rising and knocking out his pipe. "I'll 'phone for a taxi."

Soon they were seated in a car; and as it moved off, each stole a furtive glance at the other, for inevitably memories were now recalled of their last ride together: that to the office of the A.P.M. in Le Havre. But much water had flowed under the bridges since then; and it was a different MacLeod and a different Gurney that now touched shoulders as the taxi lurched heavily across the slum quarter's badly paved streets. Indeed, MacLeod saw that in some queer way they had crossed over to one another's positions at the time of the Havre incident. Then, Gurney had stood for Big Bertha and all the worst of the machine age, while himself had challenged that civilization. But to-day it was Gurney that challenged industrialism, while he made what he could of its defence. Each adored what he had burnt, and burnt what he had adored. Or almost that. What a whirligig life was. Where was there any sure standing-ground?

But they thawed after a little; resumed the discussion begun in the surgery; and, as they drove up to Robbins' house on The Hill, Gurney plunged once more into jeremiads against modern conditions in city life. "Town-planning! "he cried. "Can't they see that the towns are swallowing up the open, fast as they can build? Ever drive through the Black Country in Lancashire? One town shouldering up against its neighbour. You pass street-lamps at nights for hours on end, if you motor there. No, no, what we want is to plan the whole dam country, and stop this fool business of nibbling away at towns only."

Arrived at MacLeod's quarters, and at table there, Gurney did not cease his exposition of the new age he desired. The meal included a small platter of porridge and milk; and Straw-Feet at once took it as a text for simpler ways in dietaries. He recalled a tramp he had once made in the extreme west of Lewis. "Now, there's the primitive in all his strength. The croft, the cow, some sheep on the outfield. Fishing for the fisher who is crofter as well—who is miner as well; for he digs his fuel from the peat-moss. Farmer and shepherd and fisherman and miner. Builder also; for his cottage was made by his own hands. Carpenter too; for the furniture is of his making also. No specialism there: only the primitive's wonderful adaptability ... But it's about this good porridge I meant to speak ... I was in Bernera—that's an island in Loch Roag out yonder; and there I had the finest of all banquets in a wee croft-house that hadn't a bit of food in it when I knocked at the door. She was a MacRae, the old widow woman that answered my knocking, and had little English; yet I was able to make known my wants all the same; and she was able to make me understand that her people were from home, and that not a morsel of food would there be until they returned. Then, all at once, she saw a way out of the difficulty, and bade me enter. But I preferred a seat on the bench by the door; for the day was heavenly with sun, and there were faint breezes from off Loch Roag.

"And what does she do but run to her oatfield, pull some handfuls of ripe grain, and return with them, beckoning me indoors. Next she thrust the heads of the oats time and again into the heart of the peat-fire till they were well roasted, then shook them into a wooden bowl. A sheet of the whitest linen was laid on the floor; a quern brought out and placed in the middle of it; and down she sat and ground meal that scattered in flakes on the fair cloth she had set for them. Then out to the well for spring-water. Out again with a milking pail to the cow in the field close by. Then a pot on the fire. And there was I a few minutes later supping on gifts straight from the hand of God."

MacLeod got up as he finished, a glow on his cheeks. "Have some mercy on me, Gurney," he burst out. "You make me homesick for Eilean Aros. Man, I can smell the peat-reek, even as you talk."

575

But there was no stopping the little man. Several times that night his nose bled again. Several times MacLeod tried to silence him with an order to lie down, while he made another application of lead lotion to the swollen beak. But it was little use; for Gurney continued to testify faithfully against the iniquity of the great city until close on midnight. It was, indeed, only the ringing of the extension 'phone from the surgery in the slums that made anything like a real pause in the flow of his commination.

MacLeod came back from the 'phone much worried.

"Got to go down again," he said. "MacNab has had some trouble with a drunk, and made a mess of it. Sorry, but we'll have to say good night."

"But, my dear boy, I'll go down with you. We can talk as we go, can't we?"

"Let's go at once then; for we'll have to walk. Can't afford another taxi to-night."

The clock in the University tower boomed twelve as they emerged into the drizzle and fog. "We're for Mercy Street—the place I spoke of—where the MacLachlans live. But it isn't their house we go to. It's a chap's named Massey; and he's on Robbins' panel list. Stone-deaf with war-service with the guns. Also he's drunk most Saturdays, poor devil."

"A labourer?"

"Yes, when he can get a job ... My caretaker 'phones that Massey has called to say he thinks his daughter's dying. MacNab saw he was drunk, and tried to fob him off till morning. But the fellow got wild, and said he'd report me at the police station. So there's probably something really wrong."

They came downhill rapidly to the low ground where the slums lay, and threaded the mucky streets for a little. "Here we are," said MacLeod. "The big buildings's a model lodging-house, and round its corner is Mercy Street. Number seven we want." They entered the short street, and found the close. "Top flat," said the surgeon; and they ascended some badly lit stairs. At the first turn was a corner-boy and his girl, courting, even at that late hour. They went on to the third flight, and on the stair-head found a group of half-clad people gossiping. The doctor asked for Massey's house, and a door with broken panels rudely repaired with orange-box slats was shown him.

MacLeod knocked, but there was no response. He asked a dark Italianate youth in shirt-sleeves and hanging braces if the Masseys were at home. The man smiled. "Aye," he said; "but there's a row on there. Ye could hear Massey shoutin' for the last 'oor back."

The surgeon knocked again and again, but no answer came. "Any of you know if his daughter is ill?" he asked the group. "I am a doctor doing Dr. Robbins' work."

A blank silence fell on the cluster of busybodies, and they eyed one another with sly looks. MacLeod tried a thrust at the door with his shoulder, but it did not give. "Let's go down," he said to Gurney, and added when they were out of hearing of the group above: "Best have the police for this show."

A few minutes took them to the station, and MacLeod explained the matter to the sergeant on duty. A couple of plain-clothes officers were called from a back room at once—an elderly solemn-faced man of middle height, and a tall young man with all the marks of a recent recruit on him. As they set off for Mercy Street, the doctor explained the case to the older man. "Aye, aye," said that officer in a soft Highland voice, "the people here think of two things only—money and drink." Clearly he had nothing but contempt for Lowland scum.

Arrived again at the top landing of Number Seven, MacLeod found the group of Massey's neighbours still gossiping. To the policeman's inquiry if any of them had seen the Masseys since the doctor had left, several volunteered the news that they had heard movements in the house. The elder officer now hammered at the door and asked the occupants to open. There was no answer, and he briefly examined the two locks; then borrowed a large key from the next house, inserted it, turned it rapidly, what time the younger man placed his hand at the level of the lesser lock, and exerted all his strength against it. The door burst open to check against some obstruction in its lower half: Mrs. Massey, it appeared very soon, was sitting with her back to it, half-dazed with drink.

MacLeod and Gurney followed the policeman into the single apartment, a disordered kitchen, with a stump of candle shedding a dim light on its poor furnishings. Here was the deaf Massey—a middle-aged man, now somewhat sobered, but pacing to and fro with his head in his hands. There was no other occupant evidently. "Where's the girl?" MacLeod shouted in Massey's ear; but he made no sign of understanding. The woman was next interrogated, but only answered by a drunken leer.

The surgeon rushed to the bed, but it was empty. A dirty quilt lay evenly spread all over it: no sign of the patient there. He whipped off the covering, to find heaps of clothes disposed in a layer of equal surface, and close to the wall the body of a young woman of twenty. The bed had certainly been packed to hide her presence there. Dragging her to the edge of the bed, where the electric torches of the officers could aid him, he found her face purple, respiration gone, pulse gone, and eyeball insensitive to touch ... Suffocated? ... He threw off his coat. "Come on, Gurney," he said. "Loosen her things"; and immediately began artificial respiration. Gurney did as he was bid; and after several minutes of carefully timed movements, MacLeod stopped to listen for her returning breath. He was relieved to hear a faint sigh; there was now also a faint flicker of the pulse;

a few minutes more and an eyelid resisted his attempts to open it. She would do, after all. Her colour was better in a few minutes more; and shortly afterwards she attempted to turn on her side. But she was too fully doped with drink to expect much more from her; and the doctor turned to resume his coat and listen to the officers quizzing Massey and his wife.

The man was very incoherent; but at length it emerged that he accused his wife of making the girl drunk, in order to get hold of her week's wages. "Twenty-six shillings!" he cried. "And she'd go the length o' killin' her for that!" It looked as if the story were true, and that the same game had been played every Saturday for long enough. This Saturday, however, the mother had overdone the ration to her daughter; the girl had gone into a coma; and both parents had jumped to the conclusion that she was dying. Then when the father had returned without the doctor, fear had seized them lest the girl was really dead. They had striven, in a drunken frenzy, to hide the body, and in doing so had covered it so carefully that they had well-nigh suffocated her.

By this time Massey was almost quite sober, although his wife maundered on boozily. He could at last understand that he and his wife had been in danger of the hangman's rope, and that there must be no further drinking that night. MacLeod concluded that he could be trusted to look after his daughter until she recovered; and after examining her again, decided that she would be all right by morning, and that he could safely leave her. The officers agreed; and so the four men came out on to the landing to be again eyed eagerly by the crowd of neighbours, who were plainly disappointed that nothing so dramatic as an arrest had resulted.

But once out of that stuffy kitchen, and down in the cold airs of the city streets, the surgeon's mind misgave him. "I'd have done better to have sent that girl to the Infirmary," he said to the older officer.

"Och, they'd never take in a case of drink, Doctor," said the Highlander contemptuously.

"Well, I call it alcoholic poisoning," said MacLeod.

"Yes, yes, I see. Yes, yes, alcoholic poisoning ... Of coorse."

MacLeod halted. "No, I'll risk it," he said after a moment's thought. "I think she'll do. Might lose her job, if she went in there."

"What did I tell you, Doctor," said the officer as they parted. "Nothing but money and drink: that's all they think of down here." And squaring his righteous shoulders he disappeared into the depths of the police station's portals.

The two kept silence as they walked back to The Hill. The fog was now clearing, and when they reached the road that runs along the highest part of that eminence of villadom, MacLeod was able to behold the city stretching far to the south, a lacework of street lamps outlining it magically. How many Mercy Streets were down there? he meditated; and how many Massey families? Turning to put this query to Gurney, he found the little man abstracted, his eyes on the ground, his thoughts clearly elsewhere. "Well," said the surgeon, "what about the Masseys?"

Gurney started as if from slumber. "Man," he said, "but you startled me. I was trying hard to drive from my mind what I saw down there, and had just succeeded."

"As how?"

"By an old trick of mine: thinking of the bonniest scene I ever saw. Thinking back to Bernera in Loch Roag, and dreaming of that old crofter woman, out in her little bit of field, cutting the few handfuls of oats that were to make a meal for me that fine summer's day ... Loch Roag, and the sunlight and the breeze ... "

MacLeod seized his arm in a grip of iron and brought him to a standstill. "For Godsake," he cried, "will you hold your silly tongue, or you'll have me crazed! What's come over you to remind me of those things in a hell of a place like this?"

They had halted under a lamp, and Gurney looked up to see a white face and eyes that blazed as if threatening destruction. Then the grasp on his arm was relaxed, and MacLeod turned away, saying gently: "Sorry. But you mustn't talk that way, when I've just left Mercy Street."

"All right," said Gurney, trotting along by his side, while he chuckled and peered up into his face admiringly. "The true Gael," he said. "From repose to fierceness; then back again to repose ... Fine, man! ... By God, MacLeod, you'll be on my side yet."

XXXIII: The gathering

DURING the next week they saw something of each other in the evenings—but only in the evenings; for Gurney declined all appointments for the daytime, such as a lunch down town, or a morning visit to the Art Galleries. Thus they met at night in Robbins' house, or took a turn through odd quarters of the city; while Gurney renewed discussion on the abrupt gap between the life of the Highlands and that of the cities. All his old energy went into the argument; yet when out of doors his airs of furtiveness puzzled the surgeon: they seemed to proclaim some secret trouble, and in some strange way recalled his bearing on that midnight run in the old *Curlew*, many years ago, when he had so suddenly fled Eilean Aros. At times he would, so to speak, seek cover—suggesting a retiral to picture-house or restaurant. "Where we can talk quietly, without tiring that old leg of yours," was a favourite excuse.

On one such occasion, MacLeod had twitted him about his anxiety to get off the city streets, adding by way of guess: "You're no longer in Barcelona, you know."

Gurney had darted a swift glance at him, put up a hand to his scarred cheek, and, smiling wryly, said: "Well, yes; that affair did happen at night."

Still teasing, MacLeod continued: "Then why not take your constitutionals in the daylight?"

But Gurney only shrugged shoulders in non-committal fashion, and fell to silence.

It was this hidden worry that was active, no doubt, when, one night as they walked along Sauchiehall Street, the little man proposed a sudden end to their strolling. There had been heavy rain earlier; the streets washed clean, the air no less—a contrast to the choking fogs of a week ago. In the windows of shops now closed, brilliant lights still shone, and would shine far on into the night—a new way of advertising that was little to Gurney's peace of mind, it appeared; for, although the violet dark of the fine winter evening hung over the city, a crystal clearness was in the air of the lavishly lit main thoroughfares. Gurney looked round uneasily; then found escape at sight of a tall man in Highland garb striding past him. The Highlander carried an oblong box of black wood; and the little man fixed his eye on this. "See!" he said excitedly to the surgeon. "A piper! And he's making for St. Andrew's Halls, I'll wager. That means a gathering to-night. We must see that." He wheeled at once, MacLeod with him, and they followed in the wake of the lad with the feathered Balmoral.

"A gathering?" asked the surgeon.

"What else? This is the season for gatherings. Reunions they call them. Natives of this place and that. Uist and Barra—Lewis—Jura—Lorn, it may be. Anyway, it's not Eilean Aros, for that was a month ago."

"Ah," said MacLeod wearily; "an endless address by the chief or some other bigwig; a boring concert; and then a dance—an assembly they call it, don't they?"

They came to where, under the glass-roofed shelter in front of the huge building, groups of big men and sturdy, well-favoured women stood in quiet talk, awaiting friends before entering. A word or two of Gaelic overheard by Gurney was enough for decision that his guess was right: his brown eyes lit up, and he nodded triumphantly to MacLeod; then bored eagerly into the crowd around the ticket-box in the entrance hall, leaving his companion to follow as best he could. A few minutes later he emerged from the crush, waving two slips of paper, and dashed for the stair that led to the balcony, while he signalled MacLeod to follow. So anxious was the little man to secure seats that he had vanished out of sight before his friend reached the turn of the stair. Yet it was just there that MacLeod wanted him most, for, looking down on the throng in the entrance hall, he suddenly recognized among the many upturned faces one that he knew ... Surely that was Rainbird! He craned forward to call Gurney, and confirm his find. But the little man was still out of sight; and when he again turned his eyes on the hall below, the face he had taken for that of Rainbird had disappeared.

At the entrance to the balcony, he found Gurney awaiting him impatiently, and growling: "Room for two in the centre row. What kept you? Leg all right?"

"Leg's fine. But I thought I saw young Rainbird down there. Then I lost him."

"Rainbird!" said Gurney, with a startled look. "Are you sure?"

"No ... Come to think of it, he hadn't Rainbird's girth. No, of course, it couldn't be Rainbird."

Gurney looked relieved on the instant. "Well," said he, "let's have a look at the Gael en *masse*"; and he conducted him to the seats he had marked out.

The great hall was almost full; but away in the distance the platform was as yet untenanted. Behind it was the big many-columned organ, where sat an organist, blasting forth a staccato version of Highland airs with such immense energy that one looked to see the silken shades around the huge roof-lights toss in that tempest of sound. But the lamps' draperies hung immobile; and the mighty peals of the organ could not drown the buzz of talk from the assembled multitude. Expectancy was in the air; and the people looked to this side and that for friends long unseen. Oblivious of the blaring and roaring from the immense pipes or the radiance from the giant lanterns, they gossiped on without thought of the imprisoning walls or the countless other boxes of stone lining the miles of streets surrounding their meeting-place. They were not, indeed, in that place at all just then; for talking—talking—talking, eagerly and purposefully, to friends in front, at back, or at their sides, they saw all variously in their mind's eye—a familiar line of hills rising from the sea, a grey loch's rocky shore, a clachan where two rivers met among the birch and hazel, or the smoke of a lonely croft rising from a moorland's vastness. They were, indeed, back again in the good days of childhood: and Donald and Farquhar, Ishbel and Flora, were no longer the big men and sturdy women who had entered here a little ago, but wee folk, tramping barelegged to school by peat-moss and heathery brae; herding kye; or gathering early blaeberries high on the ben. Or, it might be, they saw themselves as lads and lassies of larger growth, busy at the spreading of hay, the cutting and turning of peat, or—merriest of all—at a gillie dance in the old schoolhouse in their native glen.

Fine the great organ, ramping and roaring; lovely the great lights, silken-clad; and stately the walls, fit for a palace to welcome great heroes. But more clearly sensed than things so immediate were visions of wee kirks whose walls were only rough stone, lit by dim oil-lamps; where the only music was that of voices—not too well attuned—singing the line in good Gaelic ... Three thousand of them here, considered MacLeod, and yet in spirit, how far away!

He whispered his thoughts to Gurney, who snapped: "And why only in spirit? If they had guts at all, they might be back there in the flesh as well? ... Oh, the Gael, the Gael! he'll break my heart!"

MacLeod, fearful their neighbours might hear, abruptly changed the subject. "Where's the programme?" he asked. "Are they Lewis, do you think?"

"Dropped it on the stair ... Never mind: these shows are all the same ... There! the organ's finished, thank God! ... And here come the pipers."

Yes, a wail had arisen from below the platform; then a march was struck up, and on came the pipers, their plaids proudly streaming. They strutted once around the stage; and then, dividing to either side, halted and continued their shrill music. Next, the platform party filed on, carefully arranged as to precedence, mitigated by the desirability of having as many Highland costumes in the front row as possible, without offending notabilities who were kiltless. And, on the whole, officialdom had done its task well, for the front row held only one man in Sassenach evening dress—a notable contrast to the others in striking tartans, neat doublets, and lace frills. But the variety in sporrans was what drew the eye most readily—immense in black and white goat-hair; tiny and business-like in pigskin or otter or grey seal—with tassels and without. For the fat fellows each sporran was a misfit, and some of the huge goat-haired purses trailed ludicrously—the perspiring wearer as much a sacrifice to fashion as any Sassenach in a silk hat.

But the audience was not critical, and cheered loudly as a functionary in a dark kilt-suit denoted the chairman of the evening by leading him to the midmost chair in front. This man, slightly built and middle-aged, tall and with a military bearing, was in full Highland dress for evening wear, correct in every detail as per tailor's catalogue: green doublet with silver buttons, a reddish tartan kilt that set off, his slim figure well, and diced hose of red and white masking thin shanks. "Leader of the mannequins," growled Gurney.

The pipers, who had by this time passed on to a strathspey and reel, ranted to the end of their piece and departed. They were replaced by a Gaelic choir: a dozen woman and as many men, accompanied by a conductor in a rather old-fashioned evening dress of Lowland type. This leader grouped his singers carefully, and then, with a sudden uplift of his hand, launched them into a song in praise of their native hills. The Gaelic was Greek to MacLeod at that distance, but the air was of great beauty—a beauty wellnigh destroyed by the antics of the conductor. For sometimes he punched with his fist, as if threatening the singers; sometimes nodded his head as vigorously as a Punch-and-Judy puppet; and finally bent his knees in a succession of quick movements that emulated those of a jumping-jack toy. The choir filed off, however, to thunderous applause.

The official in the dark kilt-suit (the president of the association, most likely) now rose, and in conventional journalese conveyed to the chairman how much they were honoured by his presence there that evening. They had had many chairmen, but never before—and so on and so on. He would briefly recount the services of their illustrious chief to his country, and—not least —his services to that part of the country in which they themselves were specially interested—their own homeland. A list of military appointments followed, mingled with the names of many conflicts in the Great War at which their hero had been present. This concluded, he went on to say that their chairman was the father of his flock in their own countryside. It was true that he was not always so frequently there as he or they could wish; for business interests kept him much in London. But as long as they found him ready to lend a willing ear to such of his tenantry as—as—as—desired to approach him regarding their tenancies and—and—other matters, they certainly could have no cause to do anything but bless the day that made him their feudal superior ... Louder cheers than ever; and the dark-kilted one resumed his seat.

The chairman now rose in all his slim elegance. Another thunderous round of applause. He spoke clearly and unaffectedly of the beauty of their native land; told a fishing story of a local worthy, that sent his audience into peals of laughter; switched over to a glowing description of Hebridean sunsets; and passed on to an equally glowing account of the virtues of the peasantry who were his people. Many of their ancestors, he said, had gone out into the great world, and made names for themselves that would be cherished gratefully by, not only this country, but by the Empire. And talking of the Empire—here followed an indication of the laird's politics at some length, with numerous puzzling references to the laws of political economy; and it was evident that the speaker was a man who would not readily let slip any opportunity of forwarding the interests of his own political party. But his hearers became somewhat restless as he waxed more fervent in the cause of Empire; and the astute chairman, sensing antagonism, at once turned back to the bens and glens, telling his hearers that their duty was plain—namely, to continue the great work done by their forefathers in sending out from their native glens a constant stream of magnificent specimens of manhood to—er—er—enrich the world for—for—for that world's betterment ... Applause like the roar of many waters as he sat down.

Gurney had curled himself into a knot of disapproval that was by this time manifest to all in his vicinity, and as the speaker finished, grunted: "But what about their staying on at home—to enrich their native glens for the world's betterment?"

Inadvertently he had spoken in a louder voice than he was aware of; and angry cries of "Hush!" and "Order!" came from the crowded benches all around.

Gurney glared back at the strong men and fine women behind him. "Helots," he muttered; and, taking a used-up envelope from his pocket, he began a rapid sketch in pencil. In a moment or two he grinned as if satisfied with his work, and handed the paper to MacLeod. The drawing was in line only, but marvellously graphic. A series of miniature trouser presses was shown, with screws and double flats complete, but all radiating from a central point like the ribs of a fan. "What's the game?" whispered MacLeod.

"Prize for a best-dressed Highlander. A kilt-press. Each pleat with its own little screws." He chuckled, and cries of "Hush!" again arose from the benches near at hand.

Further trouble was, however, now averted by the announcement of a well-known Gaelic singer's name; and a fine lad in a quiet Highland kit came easily and naturally on to the stage to sing *The Island Herdmaid* in the old tongue. He gave it delicately, clearly, enchantingly; then withdrew in boyish confusion to great acclaim; but reappeared instantly, sang again with the same art and modesty; and was once more vigorously applauded.

A Lowland woman-singer next came on, and attempted *Deirdre's Farewell to Albainn*; but her rendering missed every beauty of that tragic melody—a song that only a Gael can sing. Yet, despite all her blunders, the simple lovely air from the old Celtic world of thousands of years ago wrought its accustomed miracle, and moved the great gathering profoundly.

Next came a violinist, a lady from London town, whose conception of fitting music for a Gaelic festival was to play selections of Scottish airs—mingled Highland and Lowland—wherein a jig succeeded a slow air, and a slow air a jig. The tramping of thousands of feet accompanied the jigs, while a bored silence awaited the end of each slow movement. "We're enjoying ourselves fine now," said Gurney with a horrible mimicry of the Highland accent as the player retired.

Ah! but who is this? A girl in white, massive-limbed and comely, moved with the grace of a deer to the platform's edge, and began *Faill-ill-o*. True Highland, this lass; and at the close of her song even Gurney applauded warmly.

"It's there—it's there after all, you see," he whispered excitedly to MacLeod. "Wasn't she fine! ... Man, if we could but get her like back to their own hills, what could we not do to put life into the dead bones of all the world ... Give the countryside first place, and set the cities to minister to it: not the other way about, as we have it now. If we keep on as we're doing with this industrial business, I tell you, we'll all go to pieces. Hurrah, here she's back. Isn't she a wonder!—stepping out like a thoroughbred!"

The tall girl in white now sang *My Kindly Lass*, and sang it so finely, the audience would hardly let her go. But, no, she was not to sing again till after the interval; good money had been paid for other singers, and they must be heard. So on came a clumsy fellow in badly fitting evening clothes—stiff as a wooden figure from a child's Noah's Ark—and sang *The Road to the Isles* without the least hint of understanding: the typical English baritone without whom no gathering was complete. *Father O'Flynn* came next, sung still worse. Then the interval was announced; and Gurney and MacLeod rose to go.

In the entrance hall, however, they hung about before departing, to note the crowd there discussing the concert and looking about for friends. MacLeod saw that a change had come over the spirit of the assembly. The first enthusiasm of reunion with the companions of childhood and youth had already flown; remembrances of early days on shore and hill were no longer heard. All the talk now was of the present and of the city. Was

Alasdair "getting on well"? And was Ewan busy in the bank? Chrissie was "getting on" in her new place, of course. She was nursemaid in a very rich family, wasn't she? Yes, indeed, and Duncan was in the Clyde Trust since August last, and was "getting on" fine ... MacLeod communicated his discovery to Gurney. Why this great change in these good folk? Those girls with cheeks of apple-red colloguing with the lads whose healthy out-of-doors airs witnessed them true Highland—they too were at this talk of "getting on"!

"Oh, can't you see? "muttered Gurney. "The damned mannequins on the platform have hypnotized them into believing they're supermen, because they've reached the height of a seat up there and a kilt-suit at fifty guineas. And the audience know how they got there, of course. By "getting on" in the big cities of the south—making money and climbing socially. Not a man or woman in the area but wants to be on such a platform some fine day, apparelled like Solomon or the laird. And to gain that eminence they'd sell their souls to this blasted industrialism—to the soot-merchants, my boy—to the men who stole the sun—the men who stole the sun."

"Yes, yes," said MacLeod hurriedly, for the little man was gesticulating, and had attracted attention once more. "But hadn't we better be going?" And he edged him out of the hall and towards Sauchiehall Street.

Gurney, however, was not to be silenced by this manoeuvre of MacLeod's. In the hall or out of it he would testify to his utter rejection of what he had seen there. "Talk of the cleansing winds being powerless with Charlie of Glenavoulin!" he cried. "Charlie was only physically unclean; but half these people are spiritually unsound. Fancy that fellow telling them to clear out of their native isle, so as to make the rest of the world a better place! And remember how they cheered him, the sycophants!"

"But I thought the Gael was your trump card for regenerating the world?"

"He is still, but not when he's denationalized like that lot," fumed Gurney. "The city has done for them, I tell you."

"Tuts! Why exaggerate? There are fine folk in plenty, in there."

"Isn't it what I say? I only claim part of them as rotten. Talk about exaggeration!"

"Hush! Not so loud. Here's Sauchiehall." In the glare of lights in this open highway, Gurney became furtive again, and suggested right away that he had better get a tramcar going citywards and "home," as he called it; although where "home" was, MacLeod never discovered. They halted opposite a window full of arty draperies and brilliantly lit, and awaited a car for Gurney only, since MacLeod had to go in the opposite direction. "Well, a most instructive evening," commented the little man, "—most instructive." He paused for MacLeod's reply, with a view to a renewed tirade against civilization.

But the surgeon was staring at a figure of a man in an overcoat close buttoned to its upturned collar, who had swung hurriedly past. "By the Lord, there's Rainbird again," he cried. "And I'll swear he saw me. Just got the corner of his eye ... Wonder he didn't recognize us? "And he set to running after the figure in the close-buttoned wrap. But Rainbird—if Rainbird it was—at that moment leapt from the pavement aboard an omnibus, which stopped momentarily to pick him up and then went off at surprising speed.

When he returned he found Gurney had retreated to a dark entry, close to the shop-window where he had left him. The little man was staring straight in front with eyes that did not seem to recognize his friend. "Funny thing that," said MacLeod. "I'm sure the beggar saw us." Gurney made no reply, only continued his blank stare; but his hand went up to the long scar on his cheek. A tram going citywards drew up close to where they stood. "Here's your car," said MacLeod.

The little man roused to look at it, and shook his head. "No," he said, "I don't think I want it just yet. And you go home, lad."

"Nonsense! I'll see you off first of all."

"Please, MacLeod. You don't understand. It's safer that way."

"What's up? Isn't Rainbird straight? Can't I help?"

"Cut off like a good boy now. I'm all right."

"Why not come home, and bed at my place?"

Gurney smiled, and to renewed pleadings shook his

head obdurately. "I'm waiting here till you go," he said. "It's best that way. There's the rain on again. Do go. I'll be all right. See you later— perhaps." The last word was in a tone of defeat; and again MacLeod pressed him to let him play host for a single night. But Straw-Feet was obdurate; and at length MacLeod wished him good night, crossed the street and boarded a west-bound car.

As he ascended the tram's stair he looked back. Gurney—a forlorn little figure—still huddled in the dark entry, and looked out with stony eyes at a street becoming emptier of passers-by every moment now, as the rain increased to a sudden downpour, and squalls sent it scudding in sheets.

XXXIV: Spring cleaning

GURNEY did not again turn up during the fortnight of MacLeod's further stay in Glasgow, at the end of which the surgeon returned to Aros. There he found a new Robbins—robust, sun-tanned, and more confident than ever that he must at once discover a practice in the Highlands if he was to preserve sanity of body and mind: a sentiment echoed by his wife with more firmness than MacLeod expected from so retiring a little lady. "Mr. Gurney settled it for us," she concluded, as they awaited the steamer on the morning of their departure. "He thinks the future of the world depends on the Gael."

"*Peut-être*," said MacLeod, recalling Leclercq and old days of discussion in France. "Yes, it's a great war."

"A war?"

"Between town and country, I mean ... I can't be as cocksure as Gurney about the Gael; but Gurney's worth listening to. And I expect he's right about the big cities having to change; they're rotten with money or the want of it. But you can't wait till the cities mend their evil ways, Robbins. Clear out, and get your health back: that's the great thing."

"You bet," said Robbins.

"As for me," went on MacLeod, "what I want is that the Highlands should change, if I'm to stay on in them. Too few people, too long distances—"

"Too much rain," interjected Mrs. Robbins.

"No, no," cried MacLeod fervently; "it's rain and water—God's own water!—that make us the stupendously fine race we are. After an experience of the villages of France, I blush no more for Eilean Aros or Inveraray. Whatever changes, leave us our climate."

"Talk about Gurney being cocksure!" said Robbins. "But there's the steamer, and we must be off. Goodbye, old man ... Where's my oilskin, Janey?" ...

A few days after the departure of Robbins, Mary and Donnacha arrived from Monaghan; and the MacLeod household settled down to its usual routine, "if routine could adequately describe a household ruled by Mary and Donnacha: a *menage*," MacLeod declared at breakfast on the morning following their home-coming, which must henceforth find a new way of life; for its central idea, he protested, seemed to be the seeking out of devices wherewith to disturb the peace of anyone wanting to do a bit of study.

"Pass the marmalade, please," said Mary in dangerously quiet tones, and then continued: "Meaning yourself and Edward Gibbon, I suppose?"

"I do," said he. "May I have the marmalade again?"

"The dear' knows then," said she, "you've been longer at the reading of that *Decline and Fall* than the man took to write it, and you're only half-through with it."

He started uneasily. "How do you know how long he took?"

"I looked up father's cyclopaedia at home, and it says eighteen years. And by all you've told me, you've been twenty at it; and you'll be twenty more, if you ever finish."

"Twenty?—Well, of course, there was a war on, once upon a time, wasn't there? Not very conducive to study, the war."

"Not for your kind of study. Old books."

"What else should I study? "

"Life, my boyo. And give the books a rest. Wasn't there a bigger war than any Gibbon ever heard tell of going on all around you out there? And studying wasn't needed for that; it just soaked into you, didn't it? Men and women—the whole pell-mell clean broke, and tearing their hearts open for you to see! And after all that, you'd go on reading Gibbon, would you?"

"But don't you see that's different? We must study the past, because the same problems as the ancients had turn up in the life of to-day. We read about the past to discover what we are to expect in the present."

"And that's just where your toes turn in, my great historian! All you can expect in this life is the unexpected. Wasn't the war full of it? Isn't this wee village full of it? Man alive! open your eyes, and go out into the road there, and you'll see finer things than any book can tell you of."

"But that's different."

"Isn't that what I'm saying? The one thing's life; and the other's only second-hand stuff."

"I know—I know ... Pass the marmalade, please."

"You don't know ... And the marmalade's close beside you ... Even Donnacha could tell you things you don't know; for he has eyes in his head. Haven't you, Donnacha?"

"Yes," said Donnacha, "two." And he rimmed his empty egg-shell, desperately seeking further nourishment.

"Well then, tell father about the funny wee men we saw on the two piers yesterday."

The boy straddled shyly across his chair as if to aid his memory, and said: "White whiskers and brown leggings on two wee quins."

"Twins," corrected Mary, laughing; "and both of them seventy. I never knew before that the Gillie Breac was a twin ... We thought we saw him over in Morvern, on the pier there. He didn't come aboard the steamer; and yet when we crossed all those miles of water, there he was, waiting us, when the boat drew in to Aros Pier—the Gillie Breac again, as large as life. I declare the sight of him fair put the heart across in me. It looked like witchcraft, or something just as queer ... So, when we landed I went up to him and told how I'd seen him over in Morvern, half an hour before. 'Och!' said he,' that's Seumas, my twin brother.' ... ' You're very like,' I said; whiskers and leggings and all.' ... ' Deed, yes,' said he; ' and isn't that the great trouble! We're so like that sometimes I don't know myself whether I'm here or over in Morvern.'"

"What on earth did he mean by that?"

Mary rose, sighing, and handed him his volume of history. "He meant that there was no fun in Gibbon. There's your great book! Come on, Donnacha, and let's get up the hill. This is no place for human beings. And be you thankful, son, they didn't call you Edward Gibbon MacLeod at your christening." These last words were timed to allow of her reaching the door along with Donnacha and so escape a threatened heave of the history-book after them. She returned in a moment, however, to peep in and say: "And talking of the study of history, let me give you fair warning that it's now well on into March; and to-morrow there's going to be the grandest spring cleaning here you ever saw."

"No fear of me seeing it," said he. "I'll arrange a long round of visits, to-morrow, to the ends of all the earth."

He was as good as his word; and, next day being fine, he wired a brother-practitioner in Morvern, arranged to do a consultation promised some days before, and crossed in old Campbell's lug-sail.

Returning in the afternoon, he noted the strong sun and the fine north wind as propitious for the spring cleaning. He landed on the shore below his house, and so had to approach that dwelling from the back, where signs of the fray were plainly evident. Carpets hung on lines on the moorland behind the kitchen garden; and the paths in that enclosure were encumbered by chairs overspread by this article and that of his wardrobe, his uniform among them; while, strewn on the washing-green, were several trunks and kit-bags— mementoes of old days of war—gaping wide to be aired.

He smiled; for there was little dust in Eilean Aros, yet had this ritual of the spring to be annually observed. From what magic of the past had the custom descended, he wondered—-what mystery of the old Druids had been at its beginning? Some purging of family altars, perhaps. In any case a superstition as notable as the avoidance of May for weddings, or the taboo against green for the dress of a bride. He stumbled over a footstool; then, finding the back door so piled with impedimenta as to forbid an easy entrance, he skirted the gable to reach the front door. He walked on grass here, and his footsteps were unheard by Mary in the sitting-room, where she lay on a couch, her face buried in her crossed arms.

MacLeod caught sight of her thus as he glanced in at a side-window in passing. He stood stock-still on the instant. It was not only her grief that held him there; for on the table close by her lay a little brown-paper parcel untied, and alongside it the white gloves he had bought for Marion in Havre so many years ago. Near them was a visiting-card with a few words scribbled on its obverse—he could not read them from that distance, and he had no need to; he remembered too well— *For Marion. With love. F. M.* How clearly he recalled asking the saleswoman to enclose that card, since he had then hoped to post the parcel some day soon. And all those years that little parcel had lain in some old trunk, to be at last so untimeously discovered.

His first impulse was to enter and comfort her; but even as it came to him, his feet turned away from the house and sought the shore. Here was that old obsession of Mary's returned; and he had thought it quite dispelled by their reconciliation after the crisis of a year ago, when the return to Aros of that stormy petrel, Gurney, had so upset them both. No Gurney this time; only a pair of old-fashioned gloves, bought in a moment of war ennui in Le Havre, donkey's years away. Stowed in some old baggage with other mementoes of the war—medals, diaries, case-books and photos, there they had lain, awaiting chance discovery. And now, this! ... If only he had remembered—

Mary must, however, be brought to her senses about the business. She was needlessly hypersensitive over a bit of sentimentalism that belonged only to the past ... But here he halted, for he saw that he was over-stating the case for himself ... Marion's image did haunt him even in the present: his old association with the girl and Gurney had been too close to let the memory of either be easily effaced. And then there had been his callow love affair with the girl—the kind of encounter that leaves its mark, not from any depth in it, but because youth is youth ... But what could there be in all that to stir jealousy in Mary's heart—to make her think herself only a second best? Fantastic, in one so practical and homespun! Unfair to him and to herself! If she persisted in this folly, she'd make shipwreck of the whole' outfit!

He strode on angrily over the springy turf, and away from the house; had soon, indeed, spurred himself into a temper for a battle royal, but, almost as soon, saw the folly of this ... After all, she might be taking things more sensibly by now—might be making light of the whole business, once she had considered it fairly ... And those gloves must really have been a bit of a shock to the poor girl. Challenging things, gloves—gages thrown down, damn them! ... Oh, but give her time, and she'd come all right in the end.

He sauntered, therefore, along the shore for a full half-hour, then turned back to the main road; and, coming down it as far as the motor-shed, he entered there and started up the car's engine. Mary would hear, and know that he was back from Morvern. Fair warning. The rest was on the knees of the gods.

He spent some ten minutes making various adjustments to the machinery, then walked back to the house. Mary met him at the open door, smiling sunnily. "You're back too soon," she said. "We're not half done."

He rose to the challenge. (Things might not be so bad, after all. Sensible Mary.) "Let me give you a hand," he said. "Anything heavy want shifting?" He came into the sitting-room, and glanced casually around ... (The gloves, thank God! were gone from the table.)

"Off with your coat, then, and come through to the back," she said. "There are tons of stuff we want indoors at once." And she went to the stair-foot and called: "Flora, please send Donnacha down to give father a hand."

There was an instant scramble of feet on the stair; Donnacha appeared; and all repaired to the encumbered garden at the back, where they had a strenuous afternoon, Donnacha doing wonders in directing the layout and transfer of furniture, from pickaback on father. "The best spring cleaning we've ever had," said Mary. "Where would I have been this day, but for you two strong men!" MacLeod had never seen her more gay and light-hearted.

But he awoke that night beside her, and heard her stifled sobs. "What is't, my dear? "he asked, his arms around her.

She kept silence for a time, despite his pleading; but at length whispered: "It's only that I'm thinking of Donnacha."

"And what then?"

"I'm thinking we're hardly wise to be keeping him on in this quiet place, and he growing up so quickly."

"But I thought your mind was set on keeping him here because he'd have health and good schooling in Aros for years to come."

"I know. But now I'm just crying to think what a fool I've been. And I hadn't the courage to tell you I'd found out I was wrong, for I knew you were liking the place so well yourself."

"And don't you too like it well?"

"'Deed, yes. But there's Donnacha."

-" Maybe you're right. But go to sleep now."

"You'll think of it, Finlay?"

"Sure. I've thought of it often. But let's think further of it in the morning. Go bye-bye now. You're overtired with all that heavy work to-day."

She seemed reassured; but it was long before she fell asleep. And it was longer still for MacLeod himself: far into the night he lay awake, thinking—thinking ... Poor lass! she loved Eilean Aros well; but she would tear it out of her heart, if so be she might thereby put Marion further from his thoughts.

Towards morning he dozed a little, and when he awoke saw his way clearly; for he had found by then three good reasons for leaving Eilean Aros. First: This daft obsession of Mary's bade fair to play hell with all of them, if it continued. It seemed cowardly to give in to her; but in this matter he must cut his coat according to the measure of his cloth. Second: For Donnacha's sake, later on, they must be nearer secondary schools and a University. But this need not mean life in the crowded city, nor the lack of fresh air and the homely fireside such as Eilean Aros already provided. There were surely such things as country practices within twenty miles of towns with schools and colleges in them. Third: As to himself, he would benefit by access to post-graduate work, if such a change were made. At present, he feared he would, before long, rust in his studies, in the restricted medical practice afforded by Aros ... Yes, Mary's, Donnacha's and his own good demanded an immediate move to fresh fields.

At breakfast he found Mary's efforts to appear lively too weak to pass muster. With her, it was clear, a reaction had set in to the emotional stress of yesterday; and indeed he felt in himself a similar fatigue. There were thus long spells of silence at the meal; even young Donnacha sensed something amiss, and strove in his childish way to mend matters by broaching innumerable subjects of interest, chiefly drawn from the animal world.

As they rose, MacLeod remarked that, as the morning was wet and stormy, and he had a slack day—only a few visits close at hand—his most profitable task would be the overhauling of the car's engine. Mary agreed and added, that now the spring cleaning was over, she had chosen her day's portion in a general tidying of the rooms, with some rearranging of pictures and rugs and so on. She must, however, have a stiff walk in the evening, storm or no storm.

MacLeod snapped at this hint of a *rapprochement*. "Right," he said. "A good stretch will do us both good."

It was a dusky twilight when they emerged, clad in oilskins and sou'westers, to find a pelting rain and a good strong breeze from the north in their faces as they took the road through the village. At the point where the Draolinn road turned off, MacLeod halted, and felt in his breast-pocket. "I've a letter I must post to-night," he said. "Let's get it over now. I may forget it on the way back."

They reached the little cottage with the enamelled-plated post-box in its wall. A dim yellow light fell from the tiny window beside it, and MacLeod held the letter close to the pane so that Mary might read the superscription. She saw that it was addressed to the Highlands and Islands Medical Service Board.

"You post it," said he.

"But why?"

"It's my resignation. Best make it a joint affair."

"But—Finlay—!" She turned away.

He waited.

"I can't," she answered at last, her head still averted.

"Nonsense!" he said; and he approached the letterbox.

Her hand grasped his instantly, and she took the letter from him, passing it below the oilskin coat to a pocket in her tweed jacket. "No," she said. "Let's get on with the walk."

He turned with her at once. They passed through the last group of crofts in silence, and came out on the Glenaros road where it ran close to the shore. It waa darkening quickly now; the rain battered on their oilskins, and with heads bent to the gale they marched on. In Glenaros woods the trees swayed, roaring; and torrents drummed and boomed over scarred cliff-faces. Seaward could be dimly made out the Sgiath Vore—a skerry where breakers pulsed white and thunderous. Spindrift sped down the Sound in great sheets, and all the voices of storm called aloud from the dark waters there—mutterings that rose to shrieks in an instant and subsided to mutterings again, and gabblings that threatened till they were drowned in cries as of sharp agony.

At a turn of the road where the full force of the blast brought them to a standstill, Mary caught MacLeod's left hand with her right. Instantly he came in front as if to shield her; but, laughing, she pushed him off, and staggered on by his side, her hand still clasping his. Thus they tramped on to Aros Bridge, and standing midmost of its arch, peered down at the swift race of the river swirling bank to brae. Dark was now come fully; and the hurricane sweeping down Glenaros was no whit less wild than that on the Sound. Out there, a mile off, the two winds must meet and set to fighting; one could hear them at it even now—hammer and tongs, in Berserk fury. So Mary thought, and shouted her imaginings in Finlay's ear. He heard never a word, but nodded his head vigorously; and, thinking she proposed a return, took her arm.

She had, however, no thought of so early a retreat, and so broke free. She must have her fill of it. On the summit of the arch she stood, her arms uplifted, fronting the gale as if welcoming its buffets. MacLeod, uncomprehending this ecstasy, and fearjng her too close to the low rampart, seized her waist, and, the wind aiding, ran her down the homeward side of the bridge until they reached the river's bank. Here she sank on a boulder, laughing at his error. All he could do was to snigger foolishly to keep her company, the while he tried to shout an explanation of his dread. But the halloos of the wind and the crash of breakers beat down all his puny attempts to get above them. And so, with laughter neither heard, communicated only by their heaving sides as they leant against each other and were blasted—half-staggering, half-trotting— along the shore-road home, they came at last to shelter in the lee of old Campbell's cottage, and halted there, close together against the gable-end's lichened wall.

A lock of Mary's dark hair, wet and wind-blown from beneath her sou'wester, flicked against MacLeod's brow. He tugged it mischievously. She smoothed it back, but tossed her head high in laughter the next moment to find it still rebellious. "Let it rip," he whispered, and turning up his sou'wester's brim he laid his cheek against hers ...

Next day was clear and sunny, with a hint of frost in it; and the Sound, calm after storm, had a guileless air, as if it knew nothing at all of the uproar last night. Subtly this change in the outer world may have helped to work a change also in the moods of Finlay and Mary. In any case, the morning found them both on guard, more than a little self-conscious, and with some obscure barrier between. Their thoughts, each saw, went back beyond the night of tempest to the earlier passages of yesterday. And yesterday was indeed a jig-saw puzzle for MacLeod. Some bits were still a-wanting before it could be fitted into shape with the rest of life; and he felt that the least haphazard move might discover the emergence of a picture distorted and forbidding. Then suddenly the riddle's severed elements fell into place one after another, as simply, as inevitably, when Mary spoke a few words and he answered her. And for the life of him he could not say whether or not the picture that resulted was one to his liking.

Mary came into the surgery in the early forenoon, as he dressed a cut finger of Donnacha's; she laid last night's unposted letter on the table. "We forgot this on the way back," she said, reddening a trifle.

"Can't you post it yourself when you're up at MacPhedran's?" he asked, with a grin at her confusion.

"Do your own foul work," she retorted, smiling.

"It's not really mine: it's Donnacha's," he replied, as he knotted the last twist of bandage, and handed the letter to the boy. "Here, laddie, run up to the post with this, and see what it'll bring you."

"A present?" asked the youngster eagerly.

MacLeod's face became grave. "Yes, a present," he said, "—a big one"; and he turned his back, pretending to arrange his dressings.

The boy glanced questioningly at both: something was amiss, he saw. But thoughts of the present soon came uppermost in his mind; instantly he shot from the doorway with the letter in his hand. And Mary, with brimming eyes, crossed to the window to watch him pelting towards the turn that took him into the Draolinn road where was the little enamelled post-box.

XXXV: Cause célèbre

AN answer came in a few days' time from the Medical Service Board. They regretted MacLeod's decision to resign, suggested he might care to reconsider it, and asked if any recent difficulties had arisen in the practice: if so, would he kindly make the Board acquainted with these, and possibly the Board could help to have them removed. He showed the letter to Mary, and having read it she handed it back without comment.

"Well?" he asked.

"Well?" she queried in return.

"Oh, leave it," he said irritably, tossing the note aside and taking up the rest of his correspondence. She departed from the room in silence.

Again for several days the old sense of strain returned between them. Then—the letter still unanswered—they drifted, little by little, back to the easy acceptance of each other which had prevailed before the day of the white gloves discovery.

It was about a fortnight after that day, on an afternoon towards the end of March, when MacLeod was hurriedly called to Carsaig—some thirty miles off, in the sou'west of the Isle. The case there was one of some difficulty, so that it was nightfall before he set out on his return journey; the moon only in her first quarter and with many clouds that almost hid her thin sickle; the air moist but with a certain rawness that hinted a return of the frost which had ended only two days ago.

The dark was a matter of little account to so old a traveller on the island roads as the surgeon; but this return of a frost that had so recently gripped the countryside for a whole week and frozen many a mountain tarn virgin of ice in the memory of the Aros folk, was a matter of some concern to anyone who knew the Gribun route which MacLeod must now essay on the way home. For there, on a two-miles' stretch, the road edged warily between the sea and cliffs five hundred feet high—cliffs whose rock was brittle and gave readily after frost succeeded by a thaw, and still more readily when new ice had formed to wedge the rifted stone wider still. Time and again in past winters he had prised huge boulders off his path at that point with fence-stakes or the like, before he could get fairway for his car. And now, as he ascended Glen Seilisdeir, all his thoughts were on what awaited him at Gribun. At the Beallach, just where the road began to descend to the shore, the stone was good and seldom broke, and he was almost tempted to halt there as was his custom, and look out for the faint ray from the lighthouse on Skerryvore, thirty miles away, and only to be seen from the height of the pass. But to-night no halting to peer for that faint flicker so solitary in the waste of waters; no shutting down of his engine so that he might listen to the roar of hill-cataracts or the crying of winds in the high gullies far inland: but cautiously, yet without delay, all his lamps showing, he swung down the narrow path carved out of the cliff-face. Two sheep-gates to open, and then the Gribun crofts were alongside—Gribun where once had stood the House of the Couple: that tragic abode, for one sole night, of Iain and Rona—their wedding-eve—when a great block of stone from the precipice had crashed down and buried both.

And now, by the wayside on either hand, mass after mass arose dimly, each as big as a church—wrenched by ice from the heights above in bygone ages, and scattered on the grass and scrub at the cliff-foot—like an archipelago come ashore. But the headland shouldered closer now; and here in olden days the giant debris must have thundered straight into the sea, across what was now the highway. Round Creag Vore the worst would be past, for beyond that cliff the high bastions swept inland and the road should be clear. But at this point he had not yet reached the Creag, and the purr of his engine echoed loudly from the great rampart only a few yards off, on his right; while on his left, so close was the sea that the salt spray tossed over his near-side lamp. Yes, once round this bit, and then the open road for home! And on the instant he braked at the apparition of a great rock wedged in torn earth and straight in his path.

He dismounted and examined the block. There was plainly no passage for a car even in daylight: the thing looked a ton in weight. Nothing for it but to turn on his tracks and get home by the Glenmore detour. Sickening that! for he was now only twelve miles from home, and by the Glenmore route he was sixty. Bad luck when a fellow was so tired! He stamped cold feet and grinned sardonically at the plowtering waves—at the sea-birds calling plaintively on him to take away his great lights and leave them to their accustomed dark. Then a speck of light caught his eye, a mile—or was it half a mile?—along the homeward way. He watched it, but it did not move. What could it be? Yes—tinkers at the cave near Derryguaig! Two or three of those stout fellows with a good caber, and they might lever that beastly rock into the sea.

He set off at once, found his distance nearer than he had guessed; and, sure enough, it was a tinkers' camp: MacAllisters for a wager, to judge by the red beards of them, as they lay snug by a fire under the shelter of two tilted rocks. Old Duncan raised a tousled head (who else but the MacAllisters could it have been!) and gave the cadger's salute by asking the time.

"Late enough for a man held up by a rock-fall at the Creag," said MacLeod. "Stir your stumps, Duncan, and bring a pole, will you?"

"God! if it isn't the Doctor," cried Old Duncan, rising stiffly. "And is the cliff down again? Well, well!" and he gave some hasty commands in Gaelic to two lads who still lay prone. From the low-hooped tent near by, a woman's head protruded—red-haired also—and some children's voices were heard. The lads went off at once up the hillside towards a planting to seek stout wood for levers, while Old Duncan turned to regard a scraggy horse tied to an uptilted cart. "If I had a rope now that would stand a bit of a strain, we could be yoking Seoras there to the pulling of that big stone. But man, man! such a time as we've been having with rotten ropes and broken halters! Nothing but poverty, Doctor! Nothing but poverty, you'll understand! Aye, aye; the willing hand, but nothing but poverty! ... But sit you down and warm yourself till the lads come back with a caber for that dirty bit of rock ... Aye, aye! ... And God knows what possessed the men that made that road and them putting it where they did, with the whole world coming down on you after the least bit of frost."

MacLeod lay down on some heaped bracken stalks, and as he did so, saw farther into the low cave. In the depths of it someone stirred, then sat up, rubbing sleepy eyes: while Old Duncan, beholding the doctor's inquiring regard, broke in with: "Och, just a friend on a kind of a holiday with us, so to speak. But we'll not be troubling him. No, no, the lads and myself will be shifting that big stone all by ourselves. Easy it should be with strong lads like them." Then, addressing the figure in the shadows: "Lie you down and rest, sir. It's just the Doctor, and him stuck by a fall of rock. No occasion to worry, sir—no occasion at all."

But the man in the depths of the little cave left his lair and crawled forward on hands and knees over the bracken-covered floor, into the firelight. "Good evening, Doctor," he said, pausing quadruped-like. Grinning out of a mask of stubbly white hair was the face of Gurney. He wore a dilapidated hat of Donegal tweed, and when he stood up there was revealed a ragged ulster, which, but for its lighter tint, might have passed for the tattered coat he wore at the time of MacLeod's first encounter with him on the *Cateran* long years ago. All that was lacking was the straw peeping from eyelets in the worn shoes.

"Yes," said the surgeon dryly, "I thought you'd turn up. But why the masquerade?"

Gurney took no heed of the question, and—unperceived by Old Duncan—closed an eye in a sly wink, while he said casually: "And so the cliff's down again! Anybody with you?" As he spoke he edged away from the fire, and taking the elbow of MacLeod he led him down to the beach and out of earshot of the tinker. "Seen friend Rainbird on your travels today?"

MacLeod started. "No," he said. "Never heard he was here again. What's all this mystery about Rainbird, anyway?"

"Oh, a Government bloodhound, of course. And he wants me badly. That's all."

It was dark down there beside the tangle and the restless sea; but MacLeod was sure that could he but see the little man's brown eyes just then he would behold them burning with hate, so tense that voice.

"I don't understand—"

The other gripped his shoulder. "They're working the 'undesirable alien' stunt," he whispered fiercely. "If they get me, it's good-bye to Eilean Aros for ever." His tense hand communicated that his whole body shook with suppressed emotion.

"The devil! Why didn't you come to us?"

"Safer for me not to. Safer for you also. I've been with Old Duncan for a week, tramping the roads—pigging in caves and thickets. Rainbird won't tumble to that for long enough; and meanwhile I get fine dreams of the old days here."

"But I don't make it out. What has Rainbird—? Oh, what's the use of gassing! Can't I help?"

"No, no. You mustn't be mixed up in this."

"But it's maybe not so bad as you think. Hell! I can't get the hang of you and Rainbird. Look here, Gurney, I'll risk anything to see you clear."

"Don't tempt me. Man alive! it's hard to think they can shut me out from Eilean Aros!"

"Don't you see a way clear to dodge them?"

"Don't ask me," said Gurney, turning aside as if to return to the camp-fire.

But MacLeod hauled him back on the instant. "By God, I know what you want—a crossing to Croggan like the last, eh? That's it, isn't it?" Gurney was silent, and the other went on: "Yes, the *Princess* comes in for cattle to-night for the Oban weekly sales! We can do it! I'll run you back through Glenmore!" He was already forcing Gurney away from the cave and towards the blocked car's headlights, half a mile away.

The little man, the least bit dazed at this sudden prospect of escape, resisted for a moment, then let himself be led along the shore-road. "But Old Duncan—" he said aimlessly, looking back at the glow in the cave-mouth.

"Damn Old Duncan! And anyway, it would take a dozen tinkers to shift that rock this side doomsday. Come on!"

Ten minutes later they had clambered into the car; and, starting the engine, MacLeod swung her carefully round and rushed back on the track he had come. Behind them arose some faint halloos from the tinker encampment; then all sight and sound of Old Duncan and his clan were lost as they rounded Creag Vore. MacLeod prayed fervently no fresh fall of rock would now intervene between him and the Beallach, where the danger-zone terminated; but his fears vanished as they gained the heights above Glen Seilisdeir, and knew themselves safe from further risk of a blocked road. Coasting down the glen, they were able to converse freely. "Well, don't you think I'd best have the whole story now?" said the surgeon.

"Oh, it's all old war stuff. Ever since then the Yard have had people like me marked down, right back from those days in Le Havre. Not a man of my lot there can cross the Channel now, without the most damnable dodging. Faked passports have to be very good since the war, you know. And for a man like myself, just starving for a sight of Aros and its little glens. Oh, what's the good of talking ... You understand?"

"Yes, yes. I understand," said MacLeod, remembering Marion.

Gurney slouched silent for a little in his corner; and the car stole silently down the hillside terraces to the lower levels. A white gable came into the arc of the headlights and flashed past. "Kilfinichen Church," said MacLeod. "We'll make Croggan in good time. And—look!—there's a spike of the moon just through that cloud, and what's that down below there—above' Loch Scridain? Mist, my boy, mist! We're in luck. Mist on the sea to-night—and so the *Princess* won't be too early at Croggan Pier, my hero! Oh, yes, we'll make it."

The road past Derarach was difficult, and here the talk was interrupted as the surgeon felt his way by a twisty sea-marge, where the least error might bring to an end all hopes of a successful escape for Gurney. Past Ardvergnish now, and round Loch Beg, and on to the cross-roads at the mouth of the Great Glen. No wayfarers were on these wild roads at this late hour; and there now came a waste of hills and moorland for the next fifteen miles, with only two little cots in all that distance. The night hid the great hills on either hand, but the echo of the throbbing engine witnessed their nearness; and while they saw nothing but the ribbon of road in the lamp-glare, yet both men knew the countryside too intimately not to sense something of the awe that ever fell upon the traveller in Glenmore even on the sunniest of days. Those great fields of hills, with the cleft where lay the road stealing among them, held the old wonder of the early world, when man ventured forth into such a wild with his life in his hand. It looked as if anything might happen in such a scene; the stage appeared set for some tragedy in accord with the frowning, brooding spirit of the place. No legends, indeed—although the Great Glen had many—could add to the airs of dark enchantment of a region where Macbeth might fitly have communed with the dark sisters. But no Macbeth was here, thought MacLeod; only wee Straw-Feet, mourning his lost Marion and reaping the aftermath of war—tragic enough in his own queer way.

"And so you had a real hunch to get back to Aros?" he asked.

"Yes—for years, as you know; but I didn't get a chance till three years after the Armistice—the summer of 'twenty-one. I got across then; but they bagged me at Victoria. That was the beginning of the ' undesirable alien' business, and I was deported."

"They had all your record, I suppose?"

"Yes. Also that devil, the A.P.M. at Le Havre — fellow with the soft voice, you remember—was a witness. I was ' agent double '—a bad man. So back to Cassel ... But I got through again in 'twenty-five, and had four good months in Aros—spring and summer— although you never heard of me. Then back again."

"Back where? ... Look out now for jolts. Road's devilish at this bit, and we begin to climb. Getting near Cruach Choireadail ... Back where? I was saying."

"Continent—various. And I tried every year after that, but couldn't get safe stuff in the way of faked passports till last year."

"Then Rainbird spotted you at Torlochan?"

"Not quite. They hadn't begun to look for me in Scotland; and Rainbird wouldn't have heard of me then. No; he was really on holiday that journey: his painting stunt quite genuine—not a blind. But of course a C.I.D. man is always on the look-out for business even when holidaying, and I think he was the least bit interested in me professionally before we parted."

"But why on earth did you stick to Gurney for a name when you were on the run?"

"Just devilment. Doing the unexpected thing sometimes pays, you see. Then when this damned *cause célèbre* started in Paris a year ago, and they couldn't find me, descriptions of Mr. Gurney were circulated, and Rainbird doubtless remembered me."

"*Cause célèbre*? Whatever was that?"

"Ah! I'd forgotten. Didn't tell you that bit. Sure to mug it up somewhere. My head's not what it used to be. Getting old. Yes, a nine days' wonder in Paris. All over that Alsatian fellow you buried in the Calvaire Wood."

The car swerved, and MacLeod drew up in amazement. "Koechlin's brother!" he cried.

"Yes, that was the name—Koechlin. Alsatian. Belonged to Colmar."

"But what on earth had Koechlin to do with you?"

"Kind of a *House That Jack Built*. 'This is the man all tattered and torn, That kissed the maiden all forlorn, That milked the cow with the crumpled horn,' and so on. When the war was over Koechlin went back to Colmar and made money in some business or other. Having made money, he looked around for a good use for it. And the first thing he must do, it appears, was to try clearing his brother's memory from the stain of having fought on the wrong side. He would have him acknowledged as a good

Frenchman; his remains disinterred from the Calvaire grave, and given a patriot's burial in Colmar. Money talks, you see ... But hadn't we better be going on?"

"Time enough. I can't drive while this is on my mind. My God! The happy war!" He shut off the engine. "What came next?"

"The thing was taken to Paris. There were interpellations in the Chambre des Députés; almost a Government crisis, in fact. Koechlin's money continued to talk. They went on unravelling the matter of his brother's death, and got as far as the Courbon prison-camp— which was a British affair, of course. Inquiries next at the British War Office, where it was found that an investigation had been made at the time of the discovery of the escaped prisoner's body in the Calvaire, in nineteen-eighteen. Who made the inquiry? An agent of the British Intelligence at Le Havre: a certain Mr. Ludovic Gurney. Would the British Government kindly have Mr. Gurney's evidence taken on commission? The British Government regretted this could not be done, as Mr. Gurney was no longer in their employ: in fact, Mr. Gurney was a German, a native of Cassel it was understood, and what was known as an ' agent double ' at the period referred to. That, or something like it, is probably what went on."

"Heavens! How those French persist ... And poor old Koechlin! Just like him!"

"And so, when I read all this in the French journals, I thought it time to leave Germany. The honour of La France was at stake, it appeared. Koechlin was demanding burial in the soil of France for his brother who had fought against France. No, no, that must not be ... And then the other side cried out that the poor man had been under duress—had been forced to serve with the Boche. Koechlin must indeed ask for a funeral with military honours ... And so they went at it, hammer and tongs. Oh, yes, *cause célèbre—oui, oui — l'affaire Koechlin*. Indeed, it was time for me to leave Cassel. And so, as it was not good that Cassel should know I had been ' agent double,' I went south—to Barcelona. Then I had trouble there, and all the time I was longing for Aros. By chance I got a Spanish passport. Then Aros, and Rainbird on holiday. And so The House That Jack Built."

"And now Rainbird's in the isle again?"

"Sure. I saw him in Moy three days ago, although he did not see me. Too business-like for painting this time; and another man with him. I'll bet he just wasn't too sure of me that wet night in Sauchiehall Street after the Gathering, or he'd have lifted me right off."

"And what would have happened?"

"Deported to Cassel. And the German Government would be advised I was arriving. Oh, splendid publicity for Ludovic! More noise about the *cause célèbre*. And good-bye to Eilean Aros for me."

"Not if I know it," said MacLeod, starting his engine and resuming the journey into the depths of Glenmore. "You'll get round them again, old chap; for we'll catch that old cattle-boat this night as ever was. But keep quiet, for I'm going to speed her up a bit."

They had now to climb the stiffest part of the Glen road, but soon they were over the summit, then down to Ishriff, and through the woods by the banks of Lussa; over Ardura Hill and along the good surface of the stretch to Kinlochspelvie. Fog here on the Loch— denser, too, than it had been on Loch Scridain; and Gurney doubted if the *Princess* would reach Croggan that night in such a mist.

The remaining four miles along the southern shore of Loch Spelvie were soon covered, and the proximity of Croggan Pier was presently made known by the lowing of cattle awaiting shipment in the *Princess*. The car slowed down a little way from the pier, near a penned field where the routing and roaring of cattle indicated that some beast—a nervous stirk, maybe—had invaded a herd not his own. Dogs barked excitedly, and some hefty fellows appeared out of the mist, brandishing sticks as they leapt into the enclosure to risk life or limb if they might but save their stock from hurt. MacLeod waited till the alarm was over, then called one of the herds and asked when the steamer was expected.

"Och, she might be in any minute now, Doctor," said the man, peering inquisitively into the dark where Gurney sat. "But then again she might be hours, with the mist coming and going like this. We can only be waiting. The telegram said she left the Oban at half-past ten." More excited barking of his dogs, and he again disappeared up the hill.

Croggan Pier was a point of arrival and departure for cattle and goods only, serving a rather deserted countryside. A few poor cots passed for "the village," and there was no inn. So the doctor now opened a bag and produced the emergency rations he made a point of carrying on journeys as long as that to Carsaig—some sandwiches and a Thermos containing tea, also a brandy flask. Both men were hungry, cold and damp, and more than ready for the meal. That over, Gurney said he was sleepy, and snuggled down in a corner of the car. "Do you mind if I doze a bit?" he asked.

"Right. But I must get out and make sure that shark Rainbird isn't around."

"Kismet," said Gurney. "I'm bone tired; and if he's there, he can have me."

"Not if I know it, old son," said MacLeod as he locked the door of the car; and, turning up his heavy coat's collar and thrusting hands deep in pockets, he made off to the pier, where he chatted with this farmer and that—countryside friends, and patients of his from time to time. Discussion of market prices, gossip about local worthies, and stories of close shaves the *Princess* had experienced in former nights of mist, when collisions with trawlers or groundings on the coast had been averted just in time by her skilled captain—these were the staple of the talk as MacLeod passed from group to group and made sure that no stranger was present who might have a professional interest in Straw-Feet. This settled, he left word with the pier-master that he would be taking a nap in his motor, and wished to be called immediately the steamer arrived.

Returning to the car, he found the little man dozing deep under a couple of rugs; so, securing a wrap for himself, he lay down in the opposite corner and was soon asleep.

It was a raw dawn when he awoke, and the mist had cleared sufficiently for him to see the pier still steamer-less. But this thinning of the fog was only temporary; soon a bank of vapour streamed in between the headlands and shut out everything in a grey haze. Gurney was still asleep, but had evidently been recently awake, for his rugs had now been discarded and laid on the seat beside him. Upon them were neatly arranged some slips of alder-wood, a few pieces of bent tin, and several brass screws and butterfly-nuts of tiny proportions. An open clasp-knife lay on the floor among some shavings; this MacLeod took up and shut for safety, and at the click of its closure the little man roused and smiled.

"No news of the steamer yet—and it's now near six," said the doctor. "We've been here a good seven hours. I'm afraid it's a wash-out, Gurney. What's this you've been making?"

Gurney drew a small contraption of wood and tin from the pocket of his ragged ulster. "Bit of this," he said. "Old Duncan had some nuts and screws lying around in his cave—God knows why—so I bagged them, and started a model." He opened the toy fan-wise, and MacLeod recalled the hasty sketch he had made at the St. Andrew's Halls Gathering. "Kilt-press for a best-dressed Highlander," said Gurney solemnly; then picked up the odds and ends from the rug and stuffed all back into his pocket.

"You're bitter, aren't you?" said MacLeod.

"No more than there's need for. Isn't it bitter for me to leave Eilean Aros to the mercy of that clan?"

"What clan?"

Gurney's face went livid behind the mask of white stubble. "The clan of the best-dressed Highlander," he said. "Damned mannequins!"

"I know," said MacLeod wearily. "They have the whip hand. And who's to save the Highlands from them?"

"The clan of the true Gael. Man alive! I've more of the race in me from that one blood-drop of Red Murdo who came over to Gluckstadt, than all those tartan and lace merchants we saw on that platform." He looked out of the window as he spoke, and the hillside across the loch showed through the mist at that moment. "Look," he said," there's Gualachaolish. Have you ever tramped the drove track there, to the west of Carn Ban?"

"Often."

"And what did you see? Larach after larach—the stones of a hundred dwellings in ruins since the great clearances, when men were less than sheep. And what better are you to-day, in reality, for all your Gatherings and all your talk? You're still exiles, and your land more than ever a wilderness."

"I know—I know," said MacLeod, shifting uneasily and flushing.

"You don't know. Or if you do, it's only on the surface. God! if you Gaels would only get it deep down into your hearts, what could you not do with a race like yours!"

"Aren't you a bit extravagant about the Gael?"

"No more than Keats was about the Greeks. 'The eye brings with it what it sees,' as your *bête noire*, Goethe, said. If you can't estimate your own worth, get out to the Central Plain of Europe and hear what the world thinks of you."

"Thank you, I've seen enough of the Central Plain of Europe. One war at a time, please. But about Keats now. He was a poet, of course—"

"And it's only your poets—the men who hear the overtones of life—your dreamers—that will give you back Gaeldom."

"Diviners of Nature's afterthoughts?" asked MacLeod, with the least hint of a sneer.

Gurney checked at this sign of irritation. "There," he said, "don't let's quarrel. We have only a little time together now. I may never set foot in Eilean Aros again. And I'm old and weary. But don't despise those afterthoughts."

MacLeod softened. "And why despise our own thoughts, old chap? Haven't we brains?"

"Despise neither. But our own thinking is too feeble if used alone. There is that other thinking your Wordsworth knew—

A motion and a spirit, that impels
All thinking things, all objects of all thought,
And rolls through all things.

You must join forces with that great tide. But only your poets and prophets can tell you of its flow. Easier to go with the tide than against it. Easier to let old Mother Nature help you."

Devilment seized MacLeod at the preachiness of the little man. "And aren't you a bit of a prophet yourself?" he said; but could have bitten out his tongue when he saw Gurney turn away his head in disappointment.

There was silence for a little; then MacLeod stirred, saying, "I'd best cut down to the pier and see if there's no word of her. We're risking things, sitting here on an open road."

He got out and tramped off into the mist. In the fields the cattle crowded close together in their pens, chilled, and fearful of their strange quarters; a stray dog or two slunk despondently past. At the pier a couple of tired herd-laddies leant sleepily on a rail, and through a window in the store-room, he saw half-a-dozen farmer folk stretched on sacks in uneasy slumber. For a little he talked to the herds about the chances of the Princess getting across that morning, then left them hurriedly as from out the mist which hid his car came the sound of a throbbing engine ... Somebody monkeying with his old 'bus? ... He ran back through the grey vapours, encumbered not a little by his heavy overcoat.

No, there was his car as he had left it. Yet still an engine throbbed. Another car was concealed in the mist beyond. Yes, there it was—the Daimler from the Hotel at Torlochan? Damn! He guessed the truth now, and limping—almost breathless—came near enough to touch a rear mudguard of the Daimler just as it shot off on the road to Kinlochspelvie. From its window a fair-haired youth poked out his head and looked back at him, business-like and stolid—Rainbird.

For some moments MacLeod stood rooted to the spot in despair, gazing into those curtains of mist whence the engine throbs came fainter and fainter; then turned slowly back to his own car and wrenched open the door. Empty! This was the end, then! ... Some little hard things were under his feet—several of the little brass screws for the kilt-press. Good-oh! Wee Straw-Feet hadn't gone without a struggle!

But despite all attempts to call up imaginations of a way out, it was a very half-hearted and bitter MacLeod that cranked up the engine and climbed into the driving-perch. "*Cause célèbre!*" he muttered, as he started on the homeward track. "Oh, yes—*très célèbre!*"

XXXVI: Mary

AS he rounded Loch Spelvie a little breeze sprang up and the sun broke through. Patches of azure sky now showed; the mist rose and trailed along the hillsides; while the loch's surface, fretted with little waves, was at last revealed. At Seanavaile he was seven miles from Croggan by road, but—such was the circuit he had made—the pier there was only a little over a mile from him, right opposite, across the water; and he could distinguish, albeit still through a haze, that no steamer had yet reached it.

It was at Seanavaile that the road left the shore and turned inland among the birch and hazel that clothed the slopes of Ardura Hill—the way twisty, and its many curves hidden by boscage as the ascent grew steeper, so that careful steering and many changes of gear were needed. And then—the irony of it!—over the still air of loch and wood and hill came the long wail of a siren, betokening the approach of the *Princess*. A bare thirty minutes earlier, and Gurney had been safe. The thought came like a thunderclap, just as he reached an abrupt rise on the road, combined with a sharper curve. Another blast sounded from that siren beyond the headlands, and to MacLeod's ear there was in it the very essence of all bitterness and regret: so much so, indeed, that for the moment he was distracted from the task in hand, fumbled both steering-wheel and levers, and the next instant found himself flung among withered moss and bracken beyond the nearside wheels of his car now plunged deep in the soft red earth of the roadside ditch.

He got up, unhurt but dazed, saw the car was too securely bogged to be recovered without several helpers and many planks, and so set off uphill to tramp a mile to the sheep-farmer's on the further slope. After a time sufficient odd workers were collected from the fields around, and then a full hour was spent in digging and in manoeuvring stones and timber before the car was set once more upon the highway, while half-an-hour extra was taken over replacing damaged linch-pins and such oddments. But at last he was off, disgruntled and weary; asking himself, between curses, what had become of Gurney by now.

Ardura safely crossed, the road was safe for the rush homewards; and he put the car all out through Lochdon and Torosay at a good forty to the hour. The sun was now stronger, as was also the breeze from the nor'west, so that the mist lay no longer on Aros Sound. Fairer than ever, that fine stretch of water: what a heartbreak it must have been to Gurney, as he came that way this morning, to think he might be looking on it for the last time. Yonder was the steamer, already well out from Torlochan. Possibly Gurney was even now on board her, shipped from that port; but more likely they would take him by way of Torness. If MacLeod hurried he might even yet see him. But perhaps they might be delayed—waiting for papers, warrants, and that kind of thing. In any case he could do Torness in twenty minutes now: he must have a shot at seeing old Straw-Feet again.

He scorched on, only slowing down at the crofts of Torness, on the look-out for the old Lady of the Pump. But fortunately she made no appearance, and soon he had halted before his own door.

Mary came running down the gravel path, and from her first words he learnt that she knew all. "Oh, poor wee Straw-Feet!" she cried, her face flushed with excitement.

"Where is he?"

"At the inns."

"What's happening? Are they taking him by this steamer?"

"He doesn't know. And Rainbird would say nothing. Only referred me to his chief—a big wolf of a man, who begged to be excused discussing the case."

"And Gurney? How is he?"

"Quite at ease. He sent for me early—at seven; and we talked."

"What about?"

"What else but the Highlands was there to talk about? And what could be done to bring their own people back to them from the great cities and let them be their own selves again. Then I had to come back to get Donnacha off for his morning jaunt to the pier. And when I left, Straw-Feet was playing old Gaelic airs so finely—*The Island Herdmaid* and the like."

"The sitting-room piano that used to be MacCormack's?"

"Yes."

"Ah!" said MacLeod, remembering old days. "Let's go up to him."

They walked towards the inns, and as they turned the smiddy corner a closed motor from the inn door moved off on the road to the pier. The village constable sat beside the driver.

"There they go," cried MacLeod. "They're for the morning boat."

Panting, they ran back to their house and hastily entered the car. MacLeod fingered the starter, and she fired instantly; but the clutch was erratic. Something was wrong—a bit of damage received at the crash on Ardura had lain hidden until now. He tried over and over again to get the machine to function, but without result; then dismounted and helped Mary from her seat. "No time to get this fixed," he said briefly. "Let's run for it."

They started trotting for the pier, a full mile away, MacLeod limping badly, for the long motor-journey had stiffened his bad knee. And at half the distance Mary had to halt, panting. "Go on by yourself, Finlay," she said. "You must see him. I'll come on soon's I get my breath."

He pulled up. "Bad luck," he said. "Sure you don't mind?"

"Go on, man. It may be your last sight of him." And, exhausted, she sat down by a dykeside.

MacLeod set back his elbows and loped off. But at the turn of the road he saw he was too late. Only four hundred yards were between him and the pierhead; but already the *Clanranald* had cast off her hawsers. Yet he did not stop, and soon his feet were thudding on the boards of the pier. The steamer had backed away and was now turning inwards a little towards the land again as she set out on her way down the Sound: her course should take her within fifty yards of the pier. On she came, and already he had spotted the village policeman; and beside him—yes—there was Gurney, the old hat of dirty tweed low on his brow, his hands deep in the pockets of the ragged ulster. And there was Rainbird, as nonchalant as ever; and beside him a tall fellow, elderly and with a military bearing, presumably Rainbird's chief.

He holloaed and waved his handkerchief. The constable saw him and nudged his charge; and Gurney, looking up, rose to his feet and waved a hand in return. Then, thrusting his other hand deep into the old ulster, he produced something which he held aloft. Even at that distance MacLeod recognized the little model of that old jest, the kilt-press, as Straw-Feet expanded it fan-wise.

"The little devil!" muttered MacLeod. And just then the constable tugged at Gurney's elbow in the interests of official decorum; and, still juggling with the contraption, the little man resumed his seat.

"Father, father," said a voice at MacLeod's side; and he turned to find Donnacha accompanied by Flora. The boy had made his usual morning visit to the pier, and his father had passed without observing him in his excitement. "You can run, father," acknowledged Donnacha handsomely.

"Yes, when there's need, laddie," said MacLeod, taking him up in his arms. "Let's see you wave to Mr. Gurney yonder."

The child waved exultantly; and possibly his shrill cry of "Good-bye!" reached Gurney's ears. In any case, at that moment the little man tossed the plaything in his hand overboard, and turned to hide his face in the crook of his arm.

The steamer's white wake broadened now as she sped on. Further and further she drew off, making for Ardtornish on the Morvern shore. MacLeod was still straining for a last look at his friend when Mary reached his side. "He's gone then," he said, taking her arm as if for comfort. "God! but it's hard ... Come, Donnacha."

The boy grasped his hand, and the three went back slowly on the homeward way, while Donnacha asked questions of his father about seagulls and oyster-catchers and terns and cormorants. To-day was a birdy day, he declared, and shouted on Flora for confirmation. But Flora was far behind, having snatched the chance of a word or two in the old tongue with a shepherd lad from Oolava, her own countryside; and Donnacha elected to wait for her.

Arrived at home, MacLeod and Mary went out to the strip of moorland behind, whence could still be seen a faint speck denoting the steamer far down the broad Kyle. Fair the green shores there, and noble the hills that towered above them: Straw-Feet would revel in the sight of the sunshine playing on the thin waterfalls backblown to the cliff-top of gaunt Innimore on a day of breeze like this. And, clear of all mist as was now the sharp air, how kingly would Cruachan appear to his eager eyes. "God! what a day for a man that loved the Highlands, and him leaving them!" said MacLeod.

"Yes," said Mary; "he'd talk of nothing this morning but the Highlands."

"I know."

"I don't rightly understand all he wished to be doing for them. But if he could have stayed he'd have found a way, the wee leprachaun!"

MacLeod was silent.

"It's hard it's always the people who love this land the best that must be leaving it."

He made no answer.

"Is there no one at all that could be doing what wee Straw-Feet wanted, Finlay?"

He still kept silence, his eyes set on the spot where the steamer's smoke had but vanished.

"Man alive, can't you speak?"

He turned and smiled at her, never a word on his lips. But his eyes were alight.

Mary caught fire from them, and a shining radiance was in her face. "Then it's staying we are," she said—"Marion or no Marion ... And God forgive you, Finlay MacLeod, for dragging that out o' me."

Critical comment on John Brandané's plays
JOHN BRANDANE'S PLAYS

LENNOX ROBINSON in *The Observer*: "I am certain that in John Brandane Scotland has got a very fine dramatist—perhaps a very great dramatist. The Glen is Mine, I am told, succeeds wherever it is played in Scotland, and I can well believe it. In The Lifting Mr. Brandane has made a play ot great poignancy and beauty."

Daily Telegraph: "In Mr. Brandane the National Theatre Society of Glasgow has found a dramatist worthy to lead the cause ... He has insight, humour, and a lively sense of dramatic conflict."

Education Outlook: "Mr. Brandane has a pretty humour, and in The Treasure Ship, a comedy in four acts, we get plenty of it. The characters are skilfully drawn and the dialogue is smart and witty, with a true Scottish flavour ... There is a delicacy and grace in the handling of the theme. The volume contains two other plays, both of considerable merit."

Aberdeen Press and Journal: "The one-act Rory Aforesaid displays the John Brandane of The Glen is Mine at his wittiest. Based on a very old French farce, the play loses nothing by its ancestry, and is sheer and perfect comedy."

www.ingramcontent.com/pod-product-compliance
Lightning Source LLC
Chambersburg PA
CBHW050157240426
43671CB00013B/2157